SIGHT READING SUCCESS
PIANO GRADE 4

MALCOLM RILEY & PAUL TERRY

RHINEGOLD
EDUCATION

WWW.RHINEGOLDEDUCATION.CO.UK

FOR STUDENTS

Sight reading is an important and enjoyable musical skill. The more you practise the better you will get, and working carefully through this book will help you.

Use the CD included with this book to hear how the pieces should sound. Listen to the music carefully to check your playing. Most of the written instructions are also spoken for you on the CD. The tracks can be downloaded onto an MP3 player if you find that easier to use next to the piano.

From the beginning of the book to piece 19 you should listen to the recording of each piece *first* to hear how it should sound (except when you are asked to do otherwise). Then play the music on the piano, copying what you have heard. From piece 20 onwards, make sure that you play first and then listen to check that you were correct. Up to piece 41 there are spoken reminders about important things to notice in the music, but after that you are on your own!

Tick the box when you have finished each section or piece, so that you know which ones you have tried – it's not sight reading if you keep playing the same pieces!

If you find any of the examples on the CD are too fast when you are starting out, there are software programs available on the internet that can slow down the speed of music on any CD played on a computer. One that is free to download is: **Speedshifter** (available from www.abrsm.org/en/students/speedshifter).

FOR TEACHERS

This book follows the sight reading requirements for the Grade 4 piano exam of the Associated Board of the Royal Schools of Music (as revised in 2009). It is also suitable for all piano students who wish to improve their sight reading skills.

A unique feature of the books in this series is the inclusion of a specially-recorded CD which students can use at home for additional guidance, and to check the accuracy of their own playing. Encourage your students to use it as a tool to evaluate their own playing and learn from their mistakes, as well as a support for when you are not there to help.

Sight Reading Success progressively introduces each of the elements in sight reading, along with many useful tips and exercises to improve fluency. Each book builds on the skills taught in the previous volumes, so it is recommended that your students work through Grades 1, 2 and 3 before starting on this book.

The second part of the book includes exam-standard pieces to play in lessons or at home. Take a few minutes in every lesson to check progress and help with any difficulties, and encourage regular sight reading so that students have confidence when going into their exam.

Tick boxes are provided for students to record their progress through the book.

USING A METRONOME

A **metronome** is a device that will click a regular pulse at any speed you wish to help you keep in time when practising. There are several on the internet and the one at www.metronomeonline.com is free and easy to use. The numbers around the dial indicate the speed in beats (or pulses) per minute: the higher the number, the faster the speed.

FINGERING

 1 In Grades 1 and 2 you learned to use the printed fingerings to get your hands into position at the start of a piece. For Grade 3 you sometimes needed to extend a finger to reach particular notes, or to change the position of your whole hand to fit over a different set of notes.

These extensions and position changes are more common in Grade 4 and you will be expected to work out more of the fingering for yourself. Start with this short tune for your right hand.

First spot the four black notes needed – there is one in each bar. Next look at the fingering and notice that:

- At the beginning of bar 2 your second finger has to cross over your thumb for the F♯
- Although no further fingering is given, your little finger will need to extend upwards for the E♭ in bar 3
- In bar 4 you'll need to play the B♭ with your third finger, otherwise you will run out of fingers before you get to the last note of the piece.

 2 The next short piece is for both hands, although the right-hand part is easy. Only the first note in each hand has a printed fingering, so you will need to work out the rest of the fingering for yourself.

Notice that the first note of every bar in the left hand is C, which you are told to play with your fifth finger at the start of the piece. However, the notes that follow the C get higher in each new bar. Get ready to extend your left thumb more as you play through the piece. This may be easier if you use your second finger rather than your third for each of the quavers from the second bar onwards.

There is a new sign in this piece. The short line under the first note in the left hand of each bar is called a **tenuto** mark (meaning 'held'). It tells you to emphasise the note by holding it for its full length and giving it a little extra weight.

The direction at the start, 'Tempo di tango', refers to a South American dance called the tango. Its most famous feature is the rhythm played by the left hand in every bar of this piece. It doesn't need to be fast, but aim for a clear contrast in the left hand between the *tenuto* note at the start of each bar and the *staccato* crotchets on beats 3 and 4.

Listen to the left-hand part on the recording, and then try playing just this part before adding the right hand.

3

In the following piece there are a number of places where you have to play two notes together in the same hand. When fingering is given for this the upper number applies to the upper note and the lower number to the lower note.

Look through the music and notice that the left hand changes position in bar 3. There is a rest before this to give you time to make the change. But beware! There is also a large leap for your right hand in this bar, from low D (played with the thumb) to high D (for which your fifth finger would be an obvious choice). This is immediately followed by an extension to reach F♯ (probably with your second finger) at the end of the bar. Now try playing this piece.

Andante

 4

Study the fingering in this piece and be ready to play four notes together in the last bar. The music should sound majestic and can be played quite slowly.

Maestoso

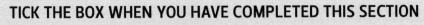

You do not *have* to follow the printed fingering in the exam, but if your own choice of fingering leads to hesitations or awkward gaps in your playing you are likely to lose marks.

TICK THE BOX WHEN YOU HAVE COMPLETED THIS SECTION ☐

$\frac{6}{8}$ TIME

 5 Grade 4 sight reading can have any of the time signatures used in earlier grades ($\frac{2}{4}$, $\frac{3}{4}$, $\frac{4}{4}$ or $\frac{3}{8}$), or it may be in $\frac{6}{8}$ time. The top figure of the time signature tells you how many beats to count in each bar, and the bottom figure tells you which type of note forms the beat. So, in $\frac{6}{8}$ time you count 6 quavers (eighth-notes) in each bar, providing that the music is not fast.

 6 As you can see in the next example, the quavers in $\frac{6}{8}$ time are written in groups of three. The first note of each group should be slightly emphasised, to create two main beats in each bar. Listen to the music before playing this piece for yourself.

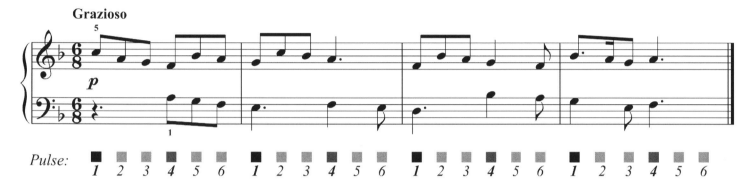

 7 If the music is fast, counting in quavers is too much of a rush. In this case, count just two beats per bar, each of which is a dotted crotchet in length. Listen to how the next piece is counted on the recording and join in by clapping in time with the spoken pulse (there will be a two-bar count-in before the music starts).

Now try playing this on the piano. Even if you play it a little slower than the recording try to give the impression of two dotted-crotchet beats per bar, rather than six quaver beats. Remember to read ahead as you play so that you can avoid a gap when you jump to the second set of staves in the piece.

8

When a piece is in $\frac{6}{8}$ time, remember to look at the speed before you decide whether to count six quavers a bar, or two dotted crotchets.

In this next piece notice the tied notes and A♯s in bar 2. Another A♯ is needed just before the end, but all of the other As in the music are A♮s. After listening to it, try playing the piece yourself.

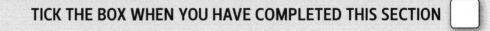

There are more pieces in $\frac{6}{8}$ time for you to play in the rest of this book.

TICK THE BOX WHEN YOU HAVE COMPLETED THIS SECTION ☐

STARTING ON AN UPBEAT

 10 The first beat of a bar is called the **downbeat** and should sound a little more strongly than the other beats. In Grades 1 to 3, sight reading pieces start on a downbeat, but from Grade 4 onwards you may have a piece that begins on an **upbeat**. This is where one or more notes come before the first barline.

There are two things to remember about upbeat starts:
- you need to work out on which beat of your count-in you should start playing
- upbeat notes should be played less strongly than the downbeat that follows them.

 11 This tune is in $\frac{4}{4}$ time and begins with a crotchet (or quarter-note) upbeat. Listen to the recording and then play it for yourself on the piano: you should begin playing on the last beat of your count-in.

Pulse:
1   2   3   4   1   2   3   4

 12 When a piece begins with an upbeat, the last bar of the music is often shortened by the length of the upbeat. So, in piece 10, the last bar contains only three beats as there was an upbeat of one beat – if you add these together you have the four beats that you would expect in $\frac{4}{4}$ time.

The next tune is in $\frac{3}{4}$ time. It too has a crotchet upbeat (made up of two quavers), so begin playing on the last beat of your count-in. After listening, play this piece on the piano.

Pulse:
1   2   3   1   2   3

 **13** This tune in $\frac{2}{4}$ time has a quaver (or eighth-note) upbeat, which means that it starts just *after* the last beat of your count-in. You may find this easier if you insert 'and' between the counts, as you'll hear on the recording. Listen first, and then try it out on the piano for yourself.

Pulse:
1 and 2 and 1 and 2 and

 **14** The next tune is in $\frac{6}{8}$ time. As it is marked 'slowly', you can count six quavers in each bar. The opening upbeat should therefore be played on the last quaver of your count-in. Listen to the recording first and then play the piece, counting carefully at the start.

Pulse:
1 2 3 4 5 6 1 2 3 4 5 6

15 This is a fast piece in $\frac{6}{8}$ time, so it is best counted in two dotted crotchets per bar. It starts with an up-beat of three quavers, or one dotted-crotchet beat. You should therefore start playing on the last beat of your count-in. Listen to the recording first, to hear how to count this.

Pulse:
1   2   *1*   *2*

TICK THE BOX WHEN YOU HAVE COMPLETED THIS SECTION

TEMPO MARKINGS

 16 There are a few more foreign language terms for tempo and mood that are useful to know for Grade 4. This list includes terms that were introduced in previous grades. You can hear how to pronounce these words by listening to track 16.

Lento	very slow
Adagio	slow
Andante	fairly slow
Andantino	slightly faster than *andante*
Moderato	moderate speed
Allegretto	fairly fast
Allegro	fast
Vivace	lively or quick
Alla marcia	in the style of a march
Cantabile	in a singing style
Espressivo (or espress.)	expressively
Giocoso	merrily
Grandioso	grandly
Grazioso	gracefully
Leggiero	lightly or delicately
Maestoso	majestically
Mesto	sadly
Poco	a little (e.g. *poco allegro* – a little fast)
Ritmico	rhythmically
Scherzando	playfully or jokingly
Semplice	simply
Tempo di minuetto	at the speed of a minuet (steady 3 time)
Tempo di tango	at the speed of a tango (see section 2)
Valse lente	slow waltz (slow 3 time)

The descriptive words in the second part of this list are sometimes combined with the tempo directions in the first part. For example, *Adagio espressivo* means 'slow and expressively' while *Allegro ritmico* means 'fast and rhythmically'.

17 New expression marks you may find in Grade 4 sight reading pieces are **tenuto** marks and **pauses**. Tenuto marks were explained earlier: look back at section 2 to remind yourself. You will need to play them in piece 19.

You may also see a pause sign (𝄐) above the staves in some pieces. If the pause is printed above the last note of the music, it simply means that you should hold the final note for longer than its normal length. For example, if the last note is a quaver with a pause, you might decide to make it last at least as long as a crotchet.

If a pause comes in the middle of a piece, you must briefly stop counting while you linger on the note with the pause. Afterwards, immediately start counting again at the original speed. Listen carefully to the counting in the next piece and then play it for yourself on the piano.

18 Notice that you need to change to the thumb in the right-hand part of bar 2, even though it starts in the same way as bar 1. The left-hand fingering in the first two bars also needs care. Play lightly, and don't forget the pause at the end.

TICK THE BOX WHEN YOU HAVE COMPLETED THIS SECTION ☐

KEYS AND KEY SIGNATURES

 Grade 4 sight reading uses the same key signatures as Grade 3 sight reading.

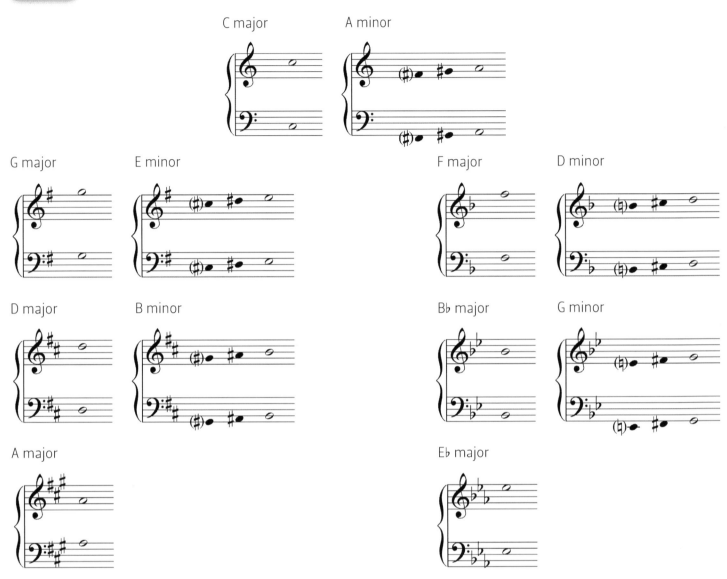

Although there are no new key signatures to learn, there are often more accidentals in Grade 4 sight reading. They are often used to add colour to the music, or to create a brief visit to a new key. Remember that an accidental applies to the note after the accidental sign and to any note of the same pitch that comes later in the same bar. So, in the next piece, the right-hand note marked by an arrow is B♭ because the flat sign at the start of this bar stays in effect until the end of the bar.

From here until the end of the book, try sight-reading each piece at the piano *before* listening to the recording in order to check your playing. Have another go at playing the piece if your first attempt did not seem very accurate.

Allegretto

🎵 **20** This piece is marked to be played slowly, so count six steady quaver beats per bar. The first half should be quiet, but the dynamics increase in the second line of music.

Adagio

TICK THE BOX WHEN YOU HAVE COMPLETED THIS SECTION ☐

ON YOUR OWN

 Now you need plenty of practice in playing new pieces! The more you can do, the easier sight reading will become.

Work through the rest of this book, and use the recordings to check your playing. If you hear differences, try to work out why. Tick the box when you have played each piece, so that you keep trying new ones.

Things to check before starting a piece of sight reading:
- The time signature – are you going to count in twos, threes or fours?
- The tempo – how fast should you count? Remember to count yourself in for two whole bars.
- The key signature – are there any black notes to remember?
- Are there any accidentals, and do any of them affect later notes in the same bar?
- The fingering given for the start, and any changes of fingering during the piece.
- The dynamics – where should you play loudly and where softly?
- Any legato, staccato, accent and tenuto markings.
- Are there any patterns in the music that will make it easier to read,
  and are there any leaps or rests that may be tricky?

Things to help you practise:
- Try playing slowly at first if that helps, and build up to a faster speed later:
  a regular pulse is more important than the speed at which you play.
- Try getting the notes and rhythm right first, and then play it again adding in changes of dynamics
  and details such as legato, staccato and accents.
- Try not to look at your fingers as you play, but keep your eyes fixed on the music.
  Get used to feeling your way around the keyboard without looking at it.
  Look ahead in the music to spot what is coming up.

Things to remember in the exam:
- The examiner will give you half a minute to look at the piece before asking you to play it.
  Use this time to try out the music – don't be afraid to do this, the examiner won't be listening!
  Play the opening and the ending, and perhaps any tricky bars.
  The examiner will tell you when to finish the try out and start playing for real.
- If you keep to a regular pulse at the marked speed and get most of the notes right,
  you will pass your sight reading!
- You will be heading for a top mark for sight reading if you also play fluently and bring out the
  expressive details of the music.
- Keep concentrating until you have given the last note its full length.
- **Try not to hesitate, even if you make a mistake.**
  Hesitations and stops are the most common reasons for a disappointing mark in sight reading.

Good luck with your Grade 4 sight reading!

SLIMETIME

STEVEN PUCHALSKI

with contributions by
BRIAN J. EDWARDS
TAVIS RIKER
STEVE SHAPIRO

A Critical Vision Book
First published in 1996
by Headpress

Headpress, PO Box 160
Stockport, Cheshire
SK1 4ET, Great Britain
Fax: +44 (0)161 796 1935

Compilation, editing and layout by David Kerekes and David Slater

Front cover: Promotional artwork for **The Nights of Terror**.
Back cover: Promotional artwork for **Ilsa Meets Bruce Lee In The Devil's Triangle**, announced but never made.

British Library Cataloguing in Publication Data

Puchalski, Steven
Slimetime : a guide to sleazy, mindless, movie entertainment
1.Motion Pictures 2.Motion pictures - Reviews
I.Title
791.4'375

ISBN 0952328852

Publishers Note

This book contains choice material from each of the 27 issues of **Slimetime**, the debut number of which was dated October 1986 (opening with a review of **Godzilla 1985**), and the last, June '89 (closing with **Vengeance: The Demon**).

Changes have been made to the original reviews for inclusion in this book. Notably, placing the films under a more common UK release title in preference to their US title (i.e. **Shivers** as opposed to **They Came From Within**; **Christmas Evil** as opposed to **You Better Watch Out**).

For the most part, the movies are in alphabetical order. But **Slimetime** wasn't simply an A–Z reviews 'zine and, seeing as two movies or more would often be assessed back-to-back, or several films by a specific director overhauled together, readers seeking specific titles ought to check out the index.

The three genre essays which close this book, covering Biker, Blaxploitation and Drug movies, first appeared in **Shock Xpress** magazine. They have been revised and updated for inclusion here.

Finally, a thank you to Roy Tynan for helping to bridge the Transatlantic gap in the closing stages of this project.

contents

introduction

Before entering this world of B-movies and video dementia, let me explain that this is clearly not a comprehensive guide to the exhaustive genre. Forerunners like Michael Weldon have toiled long and hard, and have still only shattered the crust, and this is far from the final word on the subject. But hopefully, this book will clue you into a number of grungy cinematic delights, while giving you a taste of what it's like to be young, stupid and full of enthusiasm for some of the most bizarre, unheralded niches of movie making. And afterward, if you have a taste for even more obscure fare, you can check out my more recent mag, Shock Cinema (how's that for a subtle plug, eh?), which can be acquired for $5US an issue. For further info, feel free to write to: Steven Puchalski, PO Box 518, Peter Stuyvesant Station, New York, NY 10009, USA.

Next, I need to thank several people who were instrumental in Slimetime's original success, including John McDaid, who helped jump start my creative engine; Julie Cohen, who was there throughout my obsessions; my good friends and collaborators, Tavis Riker, Brian J. Edwards and Steve Shapiro, who accompanied me on the happy path of cinematic derangement; Hungry Charley's, which fuelled my writing with quantities of flat beer 'n' cheddar fries; all of my long-time supporters and subscribers; and last but not least, Rick Sullivan, the grand inquisitor of The Gore Gazette, who first made me realise there were other poor bastards out there with a love for this type of trash (and who could make some quick beer money by writing about it). Leaping to the present, my unmeasurable thanks to David Kerekes and Headpress for approaching me on this endeavour, and most importantly, to Anna, my new bride, who continues to feed my passions, both on paper and off.

For uninitiated readers, this book is essentially a compilation of my first film 'zine, a sickly-green newsletter appropriately entitled Slimetime, which was published from October 1986 to June 1989, and focused on any movie that didn't fit into the established mainstream. And although on a simple level, this book is just a collection of irreverent reviews, it is more importantly, a gonzo glimpse into a time when the drive-ins thrived, New York City's illustrious 42nd Street was littered with triple-bill grindhouses, and sitting in your living room, watching a video could never overshadow the pure joy of seeing Fred Williamson kick Whitey's ass on a big screen.

Sadly, nowadays all that is gone. The drive-ins I used to haunt during my college years have been turned into squeaky-clean mini-malls, the cool mom 'n' pop video stores have been buried by corporate-owned chains, and The Deuce – once renowned for its unsurpassed array of porno booths, convulsing junkies and gorgeous old theatres stinking of Lysol, vomit and the long-spoiled popcorn – has been gutted, with the promise that Disney's deep pockets will scrape the once-beloved 42nd Street clean, and transform it into just another generic tourist trap.

How did I first get involved with this cinematic netherworld, you ask? Let's set the Way-Back Machine to the early '80s, when, after years of programming my college film series (which entailed spending long hours sitting in the dark with close friends and even closer six-packs), I got the itch to write about some of my film favourites. Because at the time, few people seemed aware of the True Classics, like Beyond the Valley of the Dolls, Head, A Bucket of Blood, and hundreds of others.

My frequent trips to the seamier edge of New York City only fuelled my love for these no-budget gems, and it was sometime around 4 o'clock in the morning, in the summer of '86, that I found myself standing on a rooftop just off Times Square, with several friends. And after a lively discussion about our latest grindhouse excursion, I arrived at the (then) half-baked idea of creating a newsletter which catered to the type of celluloid schlock that I wanted to read about – but without falling prey to the humourless adoration that most 'zines were guilty of.

At the time, I was broke, drunk and working a dead end job (not unlike most of my readers) in a middle-class cesspool named Syracuse. The fourth largest city in New York State, it's the type of place where the sky has a perpetual blue-grey tint from the massive factories on the North side of town, where the weather ranges from rain (six months of the year) to waist-deep snow (the other six months), where Budweiser is considered a pretentious beer, and where, after a while, everybody seems to go a little nuts.

Most important, since I had access to an unsupervised copy machine at my workplace (like most other novice 'zine editors) I gladly allowed my employer to pay for my hobby, and the following three years worth of writing and film-going rests in between these covers. After 27 issues of Slimetime, I finally called it (and soon afterward, Syracuse) quits and packed my bags for New York City, where I've managed to stay (relatively) sane amidst the perpetual chaos.

But enough of myself. Let's put this introduction to bed and move onto what you're here for. The movies... My only wish is that after digging through this book, you might get motivated to actually check out a few of these wondrous, rot-gut gems for yourself. Because the way I look at it, if I can even convert one person to the sleazy joys of a '60s biker movie, my job is done.

Enjoy.

Steve Puchalski

reviews

200 MOTELS

FRANK ZAPPA/ TONY PALMER 1971. Frank Zappa was the engineer on this A-train to psychedelic incoherency, and he somehow got MGM to lay out $667,000 for this self-reflexive mental onslaught. With Frank directing the 'characterisations' and team-mate Tony Palmer taking on the 'visuals', Zappa clues us in from the very beginning: "Touring can make you crazy," he announces. "That's what **200 Motels** is all about." Starring The Mothers of Invention as themselves, with Theodore Bikel as the omnipresent commentator and Ringo Starr as Larry the Dwarf (who dresses exactly like FZ and is first seen lowered from the ceiling on wires, with Aladdin's Lamp in his hands). It's all set on one soundstage, with the cast roaming from one set to another, and its own artificiality is The Joke. In addition, there's tripped out concert footage, speed-drenched film editing and solarised photography 'til you see God (or get cataract)... Yes, we're in the nightmarish realm of free-form filmmaking, but in this instance there's even less of a structured storyline than **Head** had. Basically, it's just a series of skits, loosely tied around Zappa and his band – the results are sometimes surrealistic, often pretentious and on a *couple* of occasions, truly funny. (Frank's **Magical Mystery Tour**?) Nowhere near successful in its goals, but there are enough moments of solid strangeness to keep any '60s throwback fascinated... The visual high point involves their visit to the quaint town of Centerville, where the eye-throbbing video-

generated effects kick in. (No illicit drugs on *this* set. Nope. None whatsoever, officer.) And the animated sequence about Schmertz Golden Rot Gut Beer is pure, non-stop dementia. Even if you've been dozing off through the first half, set your alarm for this killer sequence! Mark Volman and Howard Kaylan are hilarious as live-action first cousins of The Furry Freak Brothers, and even Keith Moon frolics about (and OD's) in a nun's habit. There's plenty of bugfuck acidhead FX at the end, and this project reeks with un-commerciality (such as by having characters bellow "I'm so commercial I could die!"), but a little of this nonsense goes a long way. The bottom line is that Zappa made a good attempt, but it just doesn't hold together 'til the end. This flick is probably best enjoyed while solidly entrenched in Owsley-Land (isn't that the new addition to Disneyworld?), but even if you're not Flying a Giant Bird, it's still a colourful (albeit overlong) dose of experimental cinema.

33 ¹/₃ REVOLUTIONS PER MONKEE

4/14/69. All MonkeeHEADs unite! Recently unearthed, this very *special* special features the Postfab Four during their primo 'anarchic phase', and that makes for 60 minutes of mutant fun! Hammond wrestler Brian Auger (?) and Auschwitz pop star Julie Driscoll (?) lead off the hour with some 'Biblical' rock 'n' roll, delivered on the psychedelic forklift. Soon the Monks are 'transported' to our **Laugh-In** styled stage, and brainwashed into their proper identities as Monkees #1 though #4. But wait! This hour is brought to you by Aerowax™, for a "shine as hard as nails". Now the Monks are "wind-up men", here for your plastic amusement. They are promptly aced to make way for Darwin's conceptual dancers, showing the origins of man. You don't *get* this on **21 Jump Street**. Later we journey into 'solo segment' Hell, as our Monks explore their innermost fantasies (No! Please!). Micky tortures us with a soulful duet on 'I'm a Believer', and Peter fails miserably in his George Harrison set. Mike does a hilarious duet with, uh, himself, offering 'Hey, Mr. TV Man, Where Do You Make Your Moral Stand?'. Davy defames musical comedy (hard to do, I know) with his insipid fairy-tale 'fantasy'. Next, it's the sterilised rock 'n' roll number, with all four Monks stumbling their way through a 'classic rock' medley (with greased hair, Davy looks like Eddie Munster) featuring Fats Domino, Little Richard and 'The Killer' (Jerry Lee turns in a blistering set) hustling their bad selves for a quick buck. The Ciara Ward Singers give us a gospel 'Dem Bones' (with chroma keyed skeletons, no less), and you know 'Listen to the Band' can't be far behind. You get a free-for-all psych-jam, with bad chroma keys, percussion jams, groovy camerawork, and The Buddy Miles Express. Heavenly. So tune out, turn off, and drop dead with The Postfabs. It's a stone gas, baby. [TR]

THE ABOMINABLE DR. PHIBES

ROBERT FUEST 1971. Here's a Late Show fave with Vincent Price hamming it up as the title madman, the pasty-faced (and revenge-minded) Dr. Anton Phibes. But unlike later day psychopaths who butcher anyone who stumbles along, Phibes spends his evenings systematically dispatching a coterie of surgeons, whose professional ineptitude caused the death of his wife and his own facial disfigurement. He sets about killing off the docs by adapting the Ten Curses of the Pharaohs to his murderous goals – such as being bitten to death by bats, watching the blood pumped out of their own body, stripped of their flesh by locusts, plus other yummy demises. The police are baffled (they're also kinda stupid), so most of England's medical profession are cold meat before they've tracked down Phibes... Along with the methodical series of grim (yet witty) killings, the film's occasional dips into solid goofiness vividly stand out – like when Vincent tickles the ivories of his pipe organ while accompanied by his mechanical band, The Clockwork Wizards; or when he shares a glass of champagne with his beautiful and icy assistant, Vulnavia (Virginia North), and has to pour the drink down a hole in the back of his neck. Price speaks only a handful of lines, but his menacing presence sustains the tone, in tandem with the film's visual flair and clever script. You can't take any of this stylised story seriously, but Robert (**Last Days of Man on Earth**) Fuest's elegant direction and the beautifully designed sets and costumes help create a tight, severely twisted package. And how can you *not* love a horror film that ends with the strains of 'Over the Rainbow'?

THE ABOMINABLE SNOWMAN OF THE HIMALAYAS

VAL GUEST 1957. Since **Harry and the Hendersons** is raking in the bucks by turning Bigfoot into a big, stoopid puppy, I decided to check out this '50s feature and see how Bigfoot's kissin' cousin, the Yeti, was treated. Well surprise surprise! This is a fairly interesting, occasionally intense little item. Written by Nigel Kneale (who also created the excellent **Quatermass** series), Peter Cushing stars as a scientist and Forrest Tucker is his mucho-macho mountaineering guide. Together they head into the Himalayas in search of the mysterious Yeti – the legendary Abominable Snowman that's been trudging about the peaks for the last umpteenth years... Climbing sheer slopes and dealing with certain death at every turn, solid characterisations emerge and the first half becomes less a horror film than a battle of wills – while Dr. Cushing simply wants to verify the existence of the creature and study it, Forrest and his bloodthirsty crew are there for The Hunt (and the potential profit), loaded down with bear traps, steel nets and ammo galore. Of course, *after* they kill one of them, the mountaineers realise that it wasn't the only Yeti on the mountain top. And considering they're 10 feet tall and weigh in at 650 pounds, the climbers have a reason to be a little worried. Oops!... Some overly dramatic subplots – such as

Cushing's wife trying to convince him to abandon the expedition, and a Buddhist village complete with an all-knowing, all-seeing, all-stereotypical High Lama – are unnecessary padding, but the remainder of the film is solid entertainment. Cushing is fine as always, and Forrest Tucker, in his pre-**F-Troop** days, proves to be a great character actor (and a lot better than he was in **Cosmic Monsters**). This isn't your usual B-movie, either – don't expect snarling snowmen molesting beautiful women (like the inane ad leads you to believe). It turns out that these creatures don't have a savage bone in their bodies (they aren't stupid beasts, either), and the flick is all the more effective because you only see glimpses of the Yeti, until the end. Most of the credit should go to Val Guest for his suspenseful direction, and to Kneale for his remarkably intelligent script. Exploitation fans might be disappointed that it isn't schlockier going, but that's tough shit...

THE ADVENTURES OF MARK TWAIN

WILL VINTON 1986. Last summer, a grimy little distribution house, Clubhouse Pictures, decided to make a few quick bucks off of unsuspecting kids, by releasing a line-up of the worst commercial swill since The Care Bears took a candy-coated shit on the grade-school set. There was **Go-Bots The Movie**, a Heathcliff monstrosity, and they even had the nerve to re-issue the 20-year-old **Hey There, It's Yogi Bear!** as a new feature... One of these films was **The Adventures of Mark Twain**. The ads were obnoxiously childish, it only played weekend matinees, and the ads barely mentioned that this was the first Claymation feature by award-winner Will Vinton (**Closed Mondays**, **The Great Cognito**, etc). And there was absolutely *no way* to know that this is also one of the most spectacular animated films in years... The beginning is deceptively slow, filled with the usual kiddie fodder – Tom Sawyer, Huck Finn and Becky Thatcher hitch a ride on a combo-riverboat/balloon/spaceship which is captained by none-other-than Samuel Clemens – His destination: Haley's Comet! And while this trio of brats are onboard, they encounter several of Twain's famed creations, including the Jumping Frog of Calaveras County. (It's ho-hum so far, but the surprisingly supple clay animation is enough to keep you going through the first half hour.) At midpoint, though, just when you fear terminal mediocrity has set in, the more adult side of Vinton turns up – as if he realised he'd appeased the juvenile audience and could now get onto *real* business... There's a meeting with a malevolent Satan; a modern retelling of Adam and Eve; discussions of death, mortality and the dark side of human nature; plus the true reason for Twain's journey to the comet. James Whitmore contributes the voice of Twain, and if the film occasionally falters story-wise, this is still a *major* accomplishment for its endlessly-imaginative technique. Definitely, a film that deserves more attention than it received from the limp wankers at Clubhouse Pix.

THE ALIEN DEAD (1979)
BIOHAZARD (1984)
ARMED RESPONSE (1986)
CYCLONE (1987)

Fred Olen Ray started off his career doing makeup work and quickly graduated to directing his own film projects. Anyone outside of hardcore horror/genre addicts might say 'Fred Olen Who?', but this guy's quickly becoming one of the most prolific independent directors in fandom, by pumping out his films to drive-ins and video stores across the country. Well, I have to admit that until this month I'd never seen a Fred Olen Ray film – so I decided to pull on my cinematic hipboots and wade into his film career. Four features in a row. Six straight hours... Burp!... For **The Alien Dead** (US: **It Fell from the Sky**) (1979), Fred directed, co-scripted and cranked out a basic creature feature – a few crude gore effects that are more laughable than shocking, a 'gosh, haven't I seen that before' storyline, and if it was filmed in black and white you'd have trouble distinguishing it from any other early '60s cheapie. Buster Crabbe (looking old, but still surprisingly agile) gets top billing as the sceptical Sheriff Kowalski, even though he only appears for 10 minutes and has three pages of creaky dialogue... Set in a nebulous backwoods area of Florida, it seems that the local country folk are disappearing mysteriously into the swamp. There's rumours that 'some rotten monster' is to blame, but when a nosy newspaperman decides to investigate, he discovers it's only a horde of blueskinned, bony-faced zombie-vampires who like to rise out of the watery depths to search for fresh blood and to kidnap young ladies. Sure enough, one of those gawd-danged Radioactive Meteorites from Outer Space is to blame, though they never get around to explaining HOW or WHY it's changing the population into bogeymen and bogeywomen – and the movie eventually turns into a third-rate **Night of the Living Dead**. There's plenty of hick-homicides to keep you watching (even though the whole production is staggeringly dim-witted), and one big plus is that the flick is never boring. The best part about the film, in fact, are the supporting characters, who make the cast of **Green Acres** look like Mensa candidates (most of them with 'nudge-nudge, wink-wink' names like Corman, Griffith, Paisley, and Krelboin) – there's old, backwoods loonies who ramble on about Eddie Von Richthoven, giant possums and germ warfare, and the best is a dead-from-the-neck-up deputy who casually informs a husband of his wife's murder with "she's deader than Mother's Day at an orphanage... Her face looked like a plate of corned beef & cabbage." No question **The Alien Dead** is a mediocre cheapie, but it's also eminently watchable for schlock fanatics – the perfect type of fodder for a rainy Saturday afternoon... Onto **Biohazard** (1984). With a step-up in budget from the practically barren **Alien Dead**, Fred Olen Ray directed, produced and wrote this throwback to the old-fashioned science-run-amok flick. It's not a bad idea, but the film is so derivative at times that you can't help but shake your head and grimace. There's bits of **Scanners**, slices of **Buckaroo Banzai**, huge hunks of **Alien**, as well as basic similarities to every monster-on-the-prowl movie ever made... It all begins at a top secret research lab in the middle of the desert, where a bunch of half-baked scientists are breaking into alternate dimensions. Of course, the Army interferes and accidentally releases a pint-sized Creepy Critter from Dimension ?, which looks like a cross between an upright lizard and a rabid Billy Barty. "I have a feeling it's terribly afraid of *us*," pleads the scientists, but the government wants it D.O.A. A.S.A.P., and their alien-hunt eventually leads to face-gashings, de-caps, torn apart victims oozing mouthful of foamy phlegm, and funny puppet-creatures that'll leap at your Adam's apple. Fred Olen Ray improves on his technical side and stays with his strong suits – a long line of eccentric supporting characters who keep getting sliced up, and a standard B-movie plot that integrates enough R-rated silliness to keep '80s audiences happy. The cast features bleach-blond Angelique Pettyjohn and the world's funniest push-up bra, and Aldo Ray 'stars' as General Randolph (with a whopping five minutes of screen time). Let me add that *everyone* in the cast deserves to spend the next 10 years working summer stock versions of **Annie**. They all suck. There's no suspense to speak of and the phoney baloney dialogue is as stiff as Aldo's shorts, but the funky finale really takes the flick over the top, as F.O.R. hits all three Rules of Drive-In Filmmaking: Load it with action. Pour on the blood. And keep a sense of humour nearby at all times... The end credits alone run about seven minutes, with countless out-takes of the cast flubbing their lines, along with a kickass version of 'Rockabilly Rumble' by Johnny Legend and the Skullcaps! I'll admit that **Biohazard** ain't no classic, but in the few moments when Fred rips loose, he approaches the same type of genre-homage goofi-

ness that Joe Dante pulled off in his pre-sellout days of **Piranha**... What's next from F.O.R.? **Armed Response** (1986), which gives him a multi-million buck budget and national distribution. Unfortunately, even through he's cracked through The Big Time with this crimeland revenge-drama, the script and characters are still mired in the one-dimensional wastelands. Standard stuff, but it's somewhat redeemed by a good cast of capable schlock-movie pros who were previously beyond Fred's budget limitations. Lee Van Cleef and David Carradine star as a father/son team – Cleef is an ex-cop who's seen it all (yawn) and Carradine is his seemingly non-violent offspring, complete with pretty wife and vomitably-cute kid. But when one of the family is offed during a run-in with Japanese mobsters (lead by Mako) over the possession of a dumb li'l jade statue, Cleef and Carradine dig their automatic weapons out of mothballs and head into Chinatown for a showdown. Laurene Landon and Dick Miller turn up quickly as a pair of high-priced, short-tempered thieves – Miller in an orange leisure suit and Landon armed with a .45 revolver and a 36½ bustline. Even Michael Berryman joins in the fun, as a Yakuza hitman who wears a Smile button. There's macho men and women, kidnappings, double-crosses, acupuncture torture, and more insidious oriental stereotypes than you can shake a Bamboo shoot at. Oh hell, why not toss in some Vietnam flashbacks for good measure? When you've got this many clichés, what's a few more? In addition, this is one of those movies where the people are always doing stupid things to keep the plot lurching along. Don't you want to stick a scriptwriter's head into a septic tank when they have their characters doing things like getting into their car without noticing that there's someone in the back seat, or turning their back on their enemy after a fight (especially when *everyone* knows the bag guy ain't dead yet)... F.O.R. gets high marks for his polished direction which, when combined with crisp photography (especially during the finale night-time shoot-'em-up) is some of his best work, nevertheless, the film as a whole is so routinely impersonal that it comes off as a forgettable director-for-hire project... Lastly, there's **Cyclone** (1987), which turns out to be Fred's most consistently entertaining film so far. Fred lends a comic book feel to the action and, as in **Armed Response**, he uses a full array of identifiable character-actors to help add an extra dimension to his supporting roles... First off, I should warn you *not* to get turned off by the fact that Heather Thomas stars in the flick. Yes, it sent a chill down my spine to think that **The Fall Guy**'s tousled-blond airhead is starring in her first film, but luckily, Fred knows how to best use her – put Heather in tight-fitting costumes and keep the script moving so fast that she doesn't have time to leave a bad taste to your mouth. She won't be playing Lady Macbeth in the foreseeable future, but as a motorcycle-riding gal who's on the run for most of the movie, she's not as atrocious as you'd first think. Jeffrey Combs, hot off his Stuart Gordon double bill, co-stars as Heather's brainy boyfriend, an inventor who has just perfected a high-tech, radar-invisible, nitrous-oxide-propelled super-cycle with the firepower of a small battleship. And sure enough, everyone is after this one-of-a-kind dingus, and eventually Ms. Thomas has to hightail it to safety... There's deceptions, espionage, oriental industrial spies (yes, *more* slanty-eyed stereotypes), bumbling detectives, and a pair of punk assassins – all of it tossed together as if the movie was a Shake 'n' Bake product. F.O.R.'s playful style comes through this time around, despite a few lapses in order to appeal to a wider (and stupider) audience (i.e. check out those, **Miami Vice**-style pop tunes). He's learning how to keep his action brisk, while he's keeping some of America's best genre actors out of the soup kitchens. Martin Landau looks like he's got a bad hangover throughout, as the head villain (he was probably still sick to his stomach from co-starring in **Harlem Globetrotters on Gilligan's Island**); Martine Beswick (**Dr. Jekyll and Sister Hyde**) and Robert

Quarry (**Count Yorga, Vampire**) play a pair of shifty gov't agents (Quarry seems to have a case of the infamous Raymond Burr Bloating Syndrome); and would you believe that ex-Bowery Boy Huntz Hall is *still* around, as a leering ol' cycle shop owner, whose eyes bug out at the sight of Ms. Thomas. As for Heather, her fans will enjoy the fact that she wears virtually sprayed-on stretchpants throughout, and the intelligent viewers who hate her guts will savour the scene where she's given electroshock. Doing her best *not* to look like a fashion model she instead comes off like a G-rated version of Barbara Crampton (**Re-Animator**). The flick is barely R-rated, so don't expect graphic violence or steamy sex. The action is mostly on the level of car chases and motorcycle stunts, and the whole enterprise could have been an average TV-pilot – sort of a distaff version of **The Fugitive** crossed with **Knight Rider**.

THE ALLIGATOR PEOPLE

ROY DEL RUTH 1959. Originally stuck on the bottom-half of a double bill with **Return of the Fly**, this is a fast-paced, empty-headed, but thoroughly entertaining studio cheapie, with a cast of contract players including Bruce Bennett, Lon Chaney Jr., and B-movie scream-queen Beverly Garland (**It Conquered the World**, **Not of this Earth**). It all starts when Bev's new hubby (**Rocky Jones, Space Ranger** star, Richard Crane) takes a powder while they're on their honeymoon, stepping off a train and disappearing without a word. But when she tries to trace his whereabouts, she ends up at Bayou Landing, Louisiana – a swampy little town where gators scurry about the streets, the residents are mighty unfriendly, and large crates of Cobalt 60 sit suspiciously on train platforms. Plus, Lon stumbles around with a three-day growth of beard, a stomach full of cheap hooch, a laughably-fake hook for a hand, and an atrocious Southern accent. While Bev makes a class-A nuisance out of herself, searching for answers, Garland's beau stumbles out of the wilderness with a face like a burnt waffle. It seems that the old scientist down the road (doesn't *every* small town have one?) is experimenting with human subjects, as well as the local wildlife (hence the film's self-explanatory title). By injecting injured people with a chemical from the pituitary of alligators, they end up with spectacular regenerative powers, but it has one 'small' drawback – it also turns them into leathery luggage-heads with laryngitis... The cast is uniformly barren of dignity (even Garland looks like she was getting tired of her type-casting), but the Has-Been Ham-It-Up Award goes to Lon Jr., as the whiskey-soaked gator-hater, who gets to rant, rave, drool, punch out Bev, and spout pages of idiotic dialogue such as "Dirty, stinkin', slimy gators!" It's the performance of a lunch-time, and worthy of the case of ripple he probably received for the week's work... Packed with silly action, overwrought hysterics, and at the end, a numbingly-dumb gator-man costume... Another black and white favourite from the 1950's! Pure dreck.

THE AMAZING MR. BICKFORD

BRUCE BICKFORD 1987. This hour-long video has some of the most severely brain-damaged animation I've sat through since tripping across the grim featurette **One Night on the Town** (and that's high praise, indeed). Imagine a demented Will Vinton on peyote, and the result is Bruce Bickford... His animation wizardry first gained attention in Frank Zappa's 'Baby Snakes', but this collection really showcases his weirdness – from early, nasty shorts to later, even *nastier* bits of nightmarish surrealism. Everything in Bickford's warped world is alive, most of it's unfriendly, and there's no narrative to speak of – just a barrage of brutal (often beautiful) images, with whole armies of humanoids stabbing each other, getting ripped apart by machine guns, or just decomposing before our own eyes. On a purely technical level, his work is remarkably complex, yet with a raw, home-made look. On a psychological level, it's just plain fucked up. The camera never stops to give us a

moment to breath, and it's all so overloaded with disturbing images your brain can't possibly assimilate it in one sitting. The only (small) drawback is having to deal with Zappa's discordant soundtrack... And just when you thought you were safe, the video climaxes with several long stream of consciousness sequences, with figures melting and growing and melting and reforming and melting and turning inside out and–AARRGHGGGHH! I'm freaking out! Where's the Thorazine?!... In other words, the ending's a pisser, and Bruce Bickford is the Owsley of clay animation. Not exactly 'entertainment', but hypnotic as hell.

AMAZON WOMEN ON THE MOON

JOE DANTE / CARL GOTTLIEB / PETER HORTON / JOHN LANDIS / ROBERT WEISS 1987. During that smoky haze known (affectionately) as the late '70s, we all remember guffawing (really?) at those hit-and-miss send-ups of TV and movies. Do names like **Groove Tube**, **Tunnelvision**, and **Kentucky Fried Movie** bell a ring (ring)? Well, then scoot down to the Cineplux and catch **Amazon Women on the Moon**, brought to you by Messrs. Dante, Landis, Bartel, etc. The stuff is still hit-and-miss, and the same pattern prevails (the short spoofs are funnier than the more elaborate sketches), but the technical accuracy is hilariously improved (they even duplicate the film splices in the bad movies!). You'll thrill to the 'In Search of...' parody called 'Bullshit? or not?', which attempts to prove that Jack the Ripper was *actually* the Loch Ness Monster (and stages a 'bullshit re-enactment' to prove it). One of my favourites was 'Video Pirates', a swashbuckling saga of seafaring video mavens who attack a ship for its booty of VHS and Beta. Short but great. Most of the sketches (many by J. 'make it BIGGER!' Landis) are tres hokey, but when Russ Meyer shows up as a deviant vid rental clerk who rents a 'personalised' tape to an unwitting youth, you know *some* fun is to be had. And for those who (like me) stick around for the credits, they tacked on a brilliant parody by 'D-Cup' Dante based on those paranoid 'sex madness' films of the '30s. Oh yeah, the El Cheapo sci-fi parody of the title is pretty funny too. (Sybil Danning plays one of these tall Amazonian drinks of water. Urgh!) So if you're ready for a chunky dose of Cinemoronics, **AWOTM** is a reliable chucklefest (guffaw). [TR]

ANDY WARHOL'S BAD

JED JOHNSON 1977. The ads made this festering feature look like a cheap porno film, and although it was rated X in 1977, I'm not really sure why. It's uniformly immoral, but when did that attitude deserve an adults-only scarlet-letter? Beyond that, there's a little gore, some down-played sex, but most of all, a bunch of deviant fucks in search of cheap thrills. Let me add that this is a surprisingly good film – a clever combination of slick-sick violence and underground weirdness... Ageing baby-doll Carroll Baker stars as Mrs. Aiken, a strong-willed housewife who runs an electrolysis salon in her Queens dining room, and in between hairy customers, she co-ordinates an all-woman crime ring – an employment agency that specialises in extortion, murder, movie theatre arson, crushing guys' legs, and other nasty goings-on. Yes, her employees are a jolly bunch of social deviants, and the flick comes off like a low-key John Waters story with naturalistic acting. Shrill-queen Susan Tyrell is *great* (and supremely annoying) as Baker's dowdy, baby-toting daughter-in-law. Perry King, in his pre-**Riptide** days of self-respect, is a hunk punk who carries around photos of his victims, like some kind of blood-caked visual portfolio. Best of all is the aforementioned Carroll Baker, who's a scream as the primacting matron who one minute doesn't appreciate 'toilet talk' in her house, and the next, is sending her crazy dames out to beat up an old man and stab his dog... Sure, the film is populated with characters so grating that you want to beat them over the head with an axe handle, but that's half the fun, and this movie wins top marks for cruel humour, lowlife characterisations, and a wonderfully sicko script by Pat Hackett and George Abagnalo (i.e. the theatre owner is on the local news, discussing the deadly fire: "Thank goodness we were showing a lousy movie, or more people would have died.')... Is it technically a comedy? Absolutely!! Even the few vestiges of humanity (King refuses to kill an autistic child) are steeped in strangeness. Mundane reality and matter-of-fact violence merge into gross-out high-points, such as a mother tossing her bawling baby out of a high-rise apartment window, spattering the sidewalk (and startled passers-by)... Jed Johnson takes the director's chair after Paul Morrissey's long-term run with the Warhol factory (the X-rated **Frankenstein** and **Dracula**, plus **Flesh** and **Trash**), and come to think of it, **Bad** would make a great co-feature with Morrissey's recent dirtball-excursion into NYC's Alphabet, **Mixed Blood**. Co-starring Stefania Cassini and Cyrinda Fox, and with music by the late Mike Bloomfield, this potential cult-movie is highly recommended for the sick arthouse crowd. **Bad** is definitely a grim geek show. Four stars!

ANDY WARHOL'S TRASH

PAUL MORRISSEY 1970. Warhol may have his name in the title, but this gritty little underground flick was more the brainchild of Paul Morrissey, who took on the directing, scripting and photography. It's a product of deranged love, which still packs a rancid right-cross, even after almost two decades. From the first close-ups of the lead actor's blemished ass, you know you're in for Dirtbag Cinema at its grubbiest. Joe Dallesandro stars as an 18-year-old, long-haired stud who can't get it up any longer – not even when his gal goes down on him for a blow job. To put matters simply, Joe's too fucked up from heroin to even care about sex. He has that continual junkie nod and tends to pass out in the middle of conversations. And you can find him sitting on street corners, going through withdrawal, or shooting up (in loving close-up) when he's lucky enough to score some skag... It's a rambling, voyeuristic look at his life on the Lower East Side of New York City, with his roommate Holly Woodlawn, who picks through garbage for a living and furnishes their apartment from the local trash cans. Shot with an almost documentary feel, this pathetic pair sit around, arguing about drugs, rubbish, welfare, and their life together. But several sleazy incidents give it the semblance of a storyline: Joe runs across an acidhead hippie chick, who invites him back to her pad while continually whining "I neeeeed some acid!" Holly invites a high school doper over to her place, to sell him drugs and get into his teenaged B.V.D.'s (oh, did I mention that Holly is a female impersonator?) – finally sticking a needle into his ass and ripping him up on heroin... Joe breaks into a rich couple's apartment and ends up turning on the trendy wife, but after Joe shoots up, the couple have no idea what to do with this deadwood drug fiend... And the high point is Joe and Holly's appointment with the Welfare Man, who's afraid to touch anything in their apartment without wiping it down first... Some of the characters are so annoying that their shrill voices eat into your brain like a family of earwigs, but I'm sure that's exactly the effect Morrissey was after. It's a harsh ride through lowlife geekland, and any viewer hoping for cheap thrills will be sorely disappointed. SEE Joe screw Holly's ultra-pregnant sister! WATCH Holly masturbate with a beer bottle! WALLOW in this flick's brilliant scuzziness! There's loads of male and female nudity, but there's no turn-on value to it – the whole effect is like sitting in a roomful of methadone patients for two hours. But for some weird, unexplainable reason, I loved it! And unlike John Waters' flicks, which are high-laff freakshow, the characters in **Trash** will have you both cringing and giggling, from their ring of twisted reality... Joe D. went onto other roles with Morrissey, in the X-rated **Frankenstein** and **Dracula** duet, only to disappear from movie screens (he was recently seen in Coppola's **The Cotton Club** in the small role of Lucky Luciano). Morrissey is still churning out the movies, with 1985's **Mixed Blood** being his urban-scum masterpiece.

ANGEL OF VENGEANCE

ABEL FERRERA 1980 (US: Ms. 45). This is without a doubt the best vigilante/urban revenge film to hit the theatres in a long time. We've had our fill of righteous do-gooders slaughtering street scum, but we've never met up with anyone as perversely whacked-out as Zoe Tamerlis is in **Angel of Vengeance**. Most of these films follow the tried-and-true formula established by **Death Wish** – the main character (or their family) is assaulted, so they take up a gun and spend the rest of the movie sending bullet-riddled assailants to the County Morgue. But director Abel Ferrera (**Bad Lieutenant**) turns this basic premise on its ear by adding some flashy camerawork, a few weird twists, and a portrait of madness to rival Polanski's **Repulsion**; coming up with an exploitation-film-deluxe... The first 10 minutes is one of the most brutal and stylish intros in a long time. Thana, a mute young woman, is walking home from her job in NYC's garment district when she is suddenly pulled into an alleyway, robbed, beaten, and raped by a masked sicko (Ferrera, in a touching cameo appearance). Bruised and bloody, Thana thinks her nightmare is over when she arrives at the apparent safety of his apartment, but instead, she comes face-to-face with a different burglar, who proceeds to rape her again. This time, she fights back and ends up wasting her assailant – but instead of calling the police, she proceeds to chop him up into little pieces and stocks her fridge (the chunks are slowly distributed around Manhattan, placed in tourist's cars, or fed to her neighbour's dog). Grabbing the dead man's .45, she hits the streets looking for revenge, plugging away at any man who gets in her way; and when she runs out of potential muggers, she dresses up as a prostitute and lures in new victims. Soon, any male who approaches her (including her boss) is a deviant in her glazed-over eyes – and all hell erupts at the company Halloween party when she arrives as a pistol-packin' *nun*... From this film alone, you know director Ferrera had a hot career in front of him (or at least a dangerously-diseased one), even though his other early works, **Driller Killer** (an unwatchable mess about a guy who goes crazy from the punk band in the next door apartment, and kills people with power tools) and **Fear City** (a high-gloss detective yarn set on Times Square, about dead strippers) show nowhere near the promise. He even went on to direct some first-season **Miami Vice**. But equal credit goes to Ms. Tamerlis, giving it her all in a made-to-order role for a sleaze-queen – she gets to kill, maim, go nuts, take off her clothes, and never utter one line of dialogue (and thank goodness, too! To see how mediocre she can-be when she opens her mouth, take a look at Larry Cohen's **Special Effects**). This is a true exploitation film – nasty, immoral and vicious – but with enough unique style to surprise even the most jaded action-addict.

ANGELS' WILD WOMEN

AL ADAMSON 1972 (AKA: ROUGH RIDERS). Al Adamson is without question one of the most notorious cut-rate directors of the '60s/'70s. A true cinematic hack, Al could churn out the sawbuck-budgeted swill at will, with a legacy that includes **Cinderella 2000**, **Blood of Ghastly Horror**, **Blazing Stewardesses**, to name a few. If there was a cheap monster costume collecting dust or a new fad that could be exploited, Al was there with a camera; and he jumped on the late-'60s motorcycle gang bandwagon with this tasteless tale featuring his regular troupe of non-actors: Ross Hagen, Kent Taylor, Vicki Volante, and his silver-lipsticked Mrs., Regina Carrol. Every moment of the film is stiff, unbelievable, hokey, or technically lame, but its saving grace is that Adamson piles one violent incident after another, at the expense of all logic. On a purely sleazy level, it rivals Al's other infamous cyclefest, **Satan's Sadists**... The story is a melange of half-assed storylines, but at the forefront are the title characters — a gang of avenging bimbos in easy-open halter tops, with a leader (Regina) who brandishes a bullwhip and pummels any male to within an inch of their worthless life. They even go so far as to rape a muscular farmhand just for kicks. Don't take this for some feminist diatribe though — it's solid grime! And while all of their men are off at a cycle competition (guzzling half a brewery in the process, and dribbling the other half down their shirts), the ladies (in a great, bizarro plot twist) wind up at Spahn's Movie Ranch and meet King, a tasteless Manson clone who runs a commune for lost bimbos-turned-love slaves. But it isn't until King drugs one of the ladies, rapes her, and then has a cheesy li'l human sacrifice that they realise he may not be *that* nice a guy. Then the shit hits the fan... This ultra-dumb flick is as purely exploitative as they come, but it's good to see some *strong* female stereotypes for once (then again, I'm always a sucker for a woman with a whip).

THE ANGRY RED PLANET

IB MELCHIOR 1959. What if Irwin Allen and Aaron Spelling collaborated on a so-called 'science fiction' movie in the '50s? Well, I believe it would look something like this... In this epic (pfaw!) tale

of the First Manned Mission to Mars, four astronauts, three guys and a woman, are sent to the Red Planet (see title) to see if it's worth sending a First Manned Mission to Mars with three guys and a woman. Clothed in cheapjack space-suits, ordinary shotguns at the ready, they encounter some of the silliest alien critters that a '50s SF-monster movie could offer... All the monster scenes are filmed with a red filter. In fact, *every* scene with our heroes checking out the alien landscape is red, which is really painful during close-ups of Nora Hayden, who is not only a goddamn fucking airhead, but when that light hits that heavily-made-up face (her lips and eyebrows look like they're literally drawn on with a thick black marker) she is reeeally hideous. (Like, she could've played the title creature in Terence Fisher's **The Gorgon**, know what I mean? Yech!) As for her male co-stars... There's a stereotypical Man of Science, complete with goatee, a weapon-happy twit who is constantly fondling his zap gun as if it were a giant prick, and a macho, always-in-control captain who could've passed for a Cone-head if his forehead had been any higher. Geeks, all. And my goodness, isn't everybody *casual*, considering this is the First Manned Mission to Mars and all; Jesus, I expect them all to start *yawning*. "Well," says the weapons man, fondling his zap gun, "shall we go out and claim this planet for Brooklyn?" One would think they were taking a taxi to a cocktail party or something... But fuck these people. Let's get to the Meat of the Movie: THE MONSTERS!! (One has to think about what's *important*, yes?) There's a big people-sucking plant, the almost-kinda-sorta-nearly-famous bat-rat-spider-crab-creature-thing, and my personal favourite: a huge, shapeless thingy with rolling eyes and a sort of claw-like appendage that pops out of its 'mouth', that pursues our ze-roes, er, I mean heroes to their rocketship. There's also a multi-eyed alien who offers the one survivor and the people of Earth a message (well, more of a *threat*, actually) at the end. One of the most intelligent, well-written masterpieces of American science fiction cinema ever made. (Just kidding, haw haw!!) [BJE]

APOCALYPSE POOH

T. GRAHAM 1987. This video made my day! Every so often an idea comes along that's so preposterously silly it must've been born after guzzling down about 19 pitchers of cheap sangria. And in this case, the genius behind this ballsy 10-minute laff riot, T. Graham, actually made good on the concept — unlike most folks who'd have passed out in a pool of their own vomit the moment they got home... I didn't know what to expect from the title, but after the first wise-assed sequence (the jungle footage intro from **Apocalypse Now**, with Winnie the Pooh theme music taking the place of The Doors), I was completely hooked! Just don't let Disney's shysters get wind of it, or else Graham's dick will be nailed to the wall, because from then on the tape ingeniously intercuts clips from Pooh cartoons with **Apocalypse** dialogue. Pooh is pulled by a runaway kite to 'Satisfaction'; Tigger appears during the 'Fuckin' tiger!' sequence; and best is Piglet as Dennis Hopper's mindblown photojournalist. Most of the humour is dead-on perfect, and some of the lip-synching is so precise that I still laugh my ass off every time I watch it (I'm up to my 8th time). Graham's even included an FBI copyright warning up front, to garnish the gag!... But wait! There's even *more* tagged onto the tape! A trailer for **Blue Peanuts**, with Snoopy doing Hopper's dialogue from **Blue Velvet**; the animated Archies singing The Sex Pistols' 'God Save the Queen'; and a wonderfully moronic coming attraction for **Phil's Parents' House**, with dorky Phil giving you a straight-faced tour of his folks' suburban cesspool ("This is our hot water heater," he monotones)... Wow! I hope T. Graham continues to churn this stuff out, because he packs more laughs into 10 minutes than most filmmakers give us in two full hours. Funnier than Kirk Cameron getting a lobotomy!

THE ASTRO-ZOMBIES

TED V. MIKELS 1967 (AKA: SPACE VAMPIRES). Fans of 'So-Bad-It's Terrific?' Cinema know that a film can be badly acted, atrociously photographed, clumsily directed, illogically scripted, and pathetically cheap – but there's an internal rhythm of Pure Awfulness that can make it a classic (such as the works of Al Adamson or Ray Dennis Steckler). Unfortunately, auteur Ted V. Mikels rarely reached beyond his own bland cinematic ineptitude. His films are mildly amusing for their extreme lousiness, but down deep you realise this guy is just your average hack with a camera. Best known for fetid films like **The Corpse Grinders** and **Blood Orgy of the She-Devils** (he certainly has a flair for titles though, eh?), for this early hodgepodge he sat down with Wayne Rogers, uncorked a vat of wine and hacked out a script combining mad doctors, zombie killers, innocent babes, and enemy agents. And with *all* this going for him, Ted *still* couldn't get it right!... A series of unsolved mutilation murders are giving the cops a headache, but they have a suspicion that the deranged Dr. DeMarco and his suburban experiments in Thought Wave Transmission Through Radio Frequencies are to blame. Indeed, DeMarco (John Carradine) and his one-eyed, matted-haired, perpetually-stooped lab assistant Francho are in the basement at that very moment, piecing together their first 'Astro Man'. They take a fresh corpse, do a complete blood switcheroo, shine some lights on 'em, and then perform a synthetic heart transplant – thus creating a nearly indestructible, skull-faced servant with a huge photocell embedded in its forehead. Meanwhile, in a much more tedious section of the screenplay, Tura Satana co-stars as a femme fatale foreign agent who's intent on stealing DeMarco's discovery. This only leads to loads of secret agent stupidity (most of it *really* talky), with Tura doing her finest Natasha imitation. The most fun (and lemme warn you, it ain't much) is had whenever the film cuts back to Carradine and Company, because the crazed ol' doc is always good for a chuckle, what with his fish-tanked brains, beakers full of dry ice, bikinied babes strapped to lab tables, and verbal hooey. And do you want to know the action-packed heights this film scales? In order to kill the Astro Zombie, Carradine simply throws a lever and it falls over dead. Oooh! Terrifying!... As you can surmise, this movie is deadly DULL, and it's never so creatively stupid to elicit the amount of laughs you're hoping for. Static camerawork; underlit scenes; all the 'scientific' apparatus looks like it was scav-

enged from junkyard scrap, kitchen utensils and photographic equipment; and even Carradine looks bored. Ms. Satana is always fun to watch, but at least Russ Meyer (in **Faster Pussycat! Kill! Kill!**) gave her something substantial to do on-screen – here she just bats her two-ounce eyelashes, lounges seductively on couches and shows off her gams. Co-starring Joan Patrick as the fiery-haired Janine (who's used as bimbo bait for the creature)... Pure idiot fodder. Nothing more.

ATRAGON

INOSHIRO HONDA 1964 (AKA: KAITAI GUNKEN). Welcome to another Toho Studios production by monster-movie-maker extraordinaire, Inoshiro Honda; but this time he steps away from Godzilla's city-stomping antics and supplies us with a colourful action-fantasy incorporating government agents, an undersea kingdom, an amazing Super-Sub, and one quick appearance by a giant rubber creature (so as not to disappoint his slobbering monster-mavens)... The dastardly Mu Empire, which sunk into the ocean 10,000 years ago, threatens to take over the entire world by causing massive earthquakes. But if you think the landlubbers are going to sit still and allow some arrogant pack of toga-draped bozos to take over *their* planet, then you must've been watching too many Ozu films recently, because a small entourage immediately leaps on a boat and heads into the Pacific to thwart the Mu's plans. But first they track down a AWOL Jap general, who has spent the last 20 years on a remote island, designing the ultimate weapon – a giant, drill-nosed flying submarine christened Atragon. The set-up for all this is somewhat slow-paced, with a full hour of standard spy school dramatics, including traitors, enemy agents, honourable soldiers, and even a sappy family reunion between a long separated father and daughter. But things quickly pick up when Manda, a giant prehistoric snake (who happens to be the Mu's god) and the futuristic battle-mobile Atragon take centre stage, and we eventually get to witness the complete obliteration of Mu Acres. Atragon bores through walls like a pro, plus there's great earthquake miniatures, fiery explosions, heat beams, freeze ray-guns, and plenty of obvious strings holding up Mr. Snake. The submarine special effects are just as entertaining as anything **Voyage to the Bottom of the Sea** ever threw together, and the last half-hour is a four-star joy for any Toho-addict. That's when the filmmakers decide to drop any pretence of characterisation or plot subtlety, and get down to the non-stop destruction. Yeah!... Although **Atragon** misses being a Classic due to its plodding first-half, later that year the same production team (scriptwriter Shinichi Sekizawa, cinematographer Hajime Koizumi and FX-wizard Eiji Tsuburaya) would re-team with Honda for their masterwork, **Godzilla vs. the Thing**. And Manda (who, despite the rumours, is *not* a distant cousin of Ollie, from **The Kukla, Fran and Ollie Show**) would eventually get a chance to decimate London in **Destroy all Monsters**.

ATTACK OF THE 50 FT WOMAN

NATHAN HERTZ 1958. Allison Hayes, whose slimy husband's adulterous activities have turned her into an alcoholic near-mental case, is wandering around the desert one day when she sees a big transparent globe floating earthward from the sky. Out of the globe comes a bald space giant. Mr. Giant doesn't say much, but he's just oozing with radiation. Ms. Hayes runs screaming back to town, where nobody believes her hysterical babbling, least of all her shitbucket husband. Infected with the giant's radiation, she grows to a height of 50-feet. Having outgrown her bed in which she's been wallowing in self-pity, she rips the roof from her house and walks the streets of the town in her underthings crying, "Ha-a-arry! I want my husband! HA-A-ARRY!!" The acting, dialogue and so-called 'special effects' are so unbelievably awful that instant guffaws and slapping of the forehead are almost inevitable. Allied Artists are to be blamed for this one. [BJE]

ATTACK OF THE PUPPET PEOPLE

BERT I. GORDON 1957. 'Attack,' my ass... John Agar and friends are reduced to a height of six inches by a lonely old doll-maker and his shrinking machine. He dresses them up as dollies and keeps them on a table for company, amongst a big prop telephone, pencils, etc. Finally, John and co-star June Kenney manage to escape into the Big Outside, where they encounter a 'giant' alley cat, a 'huge' dog, and almost get crushed under the wheels of 'gigantic' cars. A tip of the hat (and a kick in the ass) goes to producer-director Bert I. Gordon (**The Magic Sword, War of the Colossal Beast**) for this exercise in extreme silliness. [BJE]

BAD TIMING: A SENSUAL OBSESSION

NICOLAS ROEG 1980. Beginning with Tom Waits' melancholy 'Invitation to the Blues', this proves to be one of the most unrelenting films ever about the 'joy' of love. Dark, depressing and unforgettably grim, in addition to being one of my favourites. Nicolas Roeg's psycho-sexual study stars soon-to-be-wife Teresa Russell in her first (not to mention only) great performance, and following his penchant for hiring musicians for lead roles (Mick Jagger in **Performance**, David Bowie in **The Man Who Fell to Earth**) Roeg cast Art Garfunkel as a womanising, absolutely hateful louse. At the core of the film is a steamy love affair set in Vienna, but Nic fragments the drama into a narrative puzzle bathed in vague symbols (Gustav Klimt paintings) and kinky trapping (trampoline-bouncing strippers). And Roeg really knows how to juxtapose his images for visceral impact – the nastiest being his segue from orgasm to operating table seizure!... The story opens on a cheery note with Milena (Ms. Russell) rushed to the E.R. for a possibly fatal drug overdose, and we flashback to the beginnings of her torrid romance with windbag psychoanalyst Garfunkel. But while their wanton encounters melt the screen (the most painful looking takes place on her apartment stairs), Milena begins pouring down the liquor and gets progressively more self-destructive. It's no wonder, since Garfunkel is such a humourless dork – squeezing the emotions out of every action and turning every feeling into pseudo-intellectual babble. The story is wrought with sexual longing and loss, and it's a chilling portrait of emotional manipulation posing as love, with a man using a woman and then tossing her aside like a spent rubber. As for the sadistic shock ending, featuring one of the most repellent suicides in film history – well, let's just say this definitely is *not* a good 'date' film. Some melodramatic dialogues slow down the obsessive spiral, as do various subplots, including Teresa's previous marriage to Denholm Elliott and the investigation by Viennese flatfoot Harvey Keitel (in an unusually restrained performance and with a clipped accent covering his NYC snarl) as to the truth behind Russell's pill-popping condition. Was Teresa insane? Or did Art have a hand in her suicide?... The acting is solid, with Garfunkel utterly believable (and unlikeable) as the sick dickhead. And Russell (whose stint as a southern miss in **Track 29** belonged in a Peoria road company of **A Streetcar Named Desire**) is alternately sexy, slutty and sympathetic – pulling off several of the screen's finest screaming fits and loony bouts. Though a little obtuse at times (what Roeg film isn't?), the final effect is difficult to shake off. A sleazy arthouse masterwork!

BASKET CASE

FRANK HENENLOTTER 1982. This is the perfect example of a low-budget horror flick that transcends its limitations to become an all-time classic. Director Frank Henenlotter combines loads of graphic gore and lots of 42nd Street humour with an original story that (thankfully) strays from the simple-minded psycho-on-the-loose genre. And surprisingly enough, it even has sympathetic characters and a touch of human tragedy amidst all the blood-soaked close-ups... Duane (Kevin Van Hentenryck), a suburban-looking hick, comes to NYC with a pocketful of cash and a locked wicker basket – and whatever's inside has a powerful appetite, holds telepathic conversations with its owner, and seems to be particularly adept at tearing off faces (yipes!). These aren't random slaughterings though, because we quickly learn that the thing in the basket is Duane's deformed ex-Siamese twin brother – a razor-toothed lump of flesh named Belial. Originally attached to Duane's right side, but surgically separated when they were children, they're presently searching for the hack-happy doctors who tried to kill Belial when they chopped the two apart (luckily, Duane rescued his twisted bro from his hefty bagged-and-left-out-for-the-trashmen fate). Since Belial is surprisingly strong for his size, it isn't long before he's ripping at the Docs' guts, chewing on their heads and messin' up the carpets with *all* that blood! Meanwhile, Duane is starting to go off the deep end because he can't get any peace from his brother's telepathic brow-beating and he can't even get laid without *really* nasty consequences... Great locations are used throughout, including the dumpy Hotel Broslin with its liver-damaged clientele and a grindhouse men's room complete with kung fu flick background grunts. Though crude at times (whadaya want on a $160,000 budget?), the sound design is lively (especially during the surgery scenes); the special effects (including some stop-action animation) are impressive; the bloodshed is imaginatively grisly and prolific (the flashback to their father's fate is hilariously left to the imagination); and overall, this is a top-notch cheapie – it sure doesn't look like a first commercial feature. Easily one of the top 10 horror films of the '80s... Warning: The version I've seen (several times) is unrated, but I've heard that a cut-down R-rated print once circulated to justifiable audience irritation (in other words, they were pretty fuckin' pissed off)...

BASKET CASE 2

FRANK HENENLOTTER 1990. Even though director Frank Henenlotter doesn't think much of his original **Basket Case** ('82), I still consider it (as well as his second feature, **Brain Damage**) one of the best low budget horror romps in years. Miles better than this long-awaited sequel, which prefers to go for the funny bone, while avoiding the vomit bag (of course, the almighty R-rating might've precipitated this change). This flick picks up immediately where the first left oft with Duane and his mutant lump of an ex-Siamese twin brother Belial falling to the street from their window at the sumptuous Hotel Broslin. Escaping from their hospital room, they find their way to the Staten Island home of Granny Ruth (Annie Ross), who conveniently runs a Commune for Freaks. While there, Ruth lends Belial an understanding ear ("I understand your pain. But ripping the faces off people might not be in your best interest," she advises him, straight-faced), in addition to carting around his wicker basket so he can leap on the *really* nasty Normals. And double romance is in the stars, because soon Duane falls for Ruth's granddaughter, while Belial finds his own true love in the form of Eve, a similarly malformed resident... The first film found its heart and humanity by concentrating on Duane and Belial's plight, so it's strange that this time around Duane comes off like an unappealing stiff, and even Belial is sorta bland. Luckily, the supporting freaks are great fun, and nearly steal the show. Henenlotter must've spent most of his (comparatively) large budget concocting their LSD-influenced latex look, and this bizarro bunch is both sympathetic and (heh, heh, heh) prone to violence when provoked. Only when they go on the war path (about halfway through) does the movie really get rolling. There are a couple of creepy attacks, and Henenlotter's nicely diseased sense of humour comes in handy for a love scene between Belial and Eve – with these two horny blobs groping each other's gnarled flesh, before going at it like two Cane Toads in heat... Sure, Henenlotter's directorial finesse is progressing and his film stock is less grainy, but the script is jokey to the point of annoyance sometimes. It's never subtle, rarely scary, and I sorely miss the original's Time Square ambience. Kevin Van Hentenryck returns as Duane, looking long in the tooth, low in the IQ, and in desperate need of some remedial acting lessons. Don't quit that day job at White Castle yet, Kevin!... Though I was admittedly a little disappointed, when taking the film on its own merits, it's still more original and demented than much of the garbage getting distributed nowadays.

THE BEES

ALFREDO ZACHARIAS 1978. Alfredo Zacharias (**Demonoid**) directed, wrote and produced this bee-movie to cash in on the then-upcoming Irwin Allen disaster, **The Swarm**. Well, we all know how good Irwin's production turned out to be (I think Vincent Canby called it 'a warm glass of phlegm posing as a motion picture...'), and though this film isn't much better, at least it didn't cost 12 million bucks. The *only* reason I managed to sit all the way through **The Bees** was because of its cast – a trio of big-league drive-in perennials *together* in one pic, and what a technically incompetent mess they're stuck in! Angel Tompkins (**The Naked Cage**, **The Teacher**) is a newly-widowed insect handler who walks around Manhattan with a travel bag full of bees; John Saxon is her smart-as-a-whip, yet boring-as-a-brick co-worker/lover; and John Carradine is Uncle Ziggy, a scientist with an atrocious German accent that's chock full of bent-English such as: "Yha! Zee bees ahh somevhere!' And they're all involved with an American genetics corporation which is experimenting with South American killer bees! The scientists want to breed them for a more docile nature, as well as increased honey production, but the now-standard evil-businessmen-in-search-of-a-quick-buck secretly import the deadly strain to the US. Soon, there are huge black swarms of these little critters buzzing about, scaring the wits out of everyone, and for 20 minutes we get endless extras running around with fake bees pasted to their faces. There's a few nice shots of the swarms hovering over US cities, but most of the time it looks like they simply superimposed the same image of swirling oatmeal over each attack scene. Meanwhile, our American stars sit in their lab, mumbling about synthetic pheromones that'll confuse the swarms, and Carradine communicating with the creatures via computer. The ending comes straight out of left field, when super-intelligent mutant bees appear and start giving orders ("You want us to conduct peace negotiations with BUGS?"). Except for the indiscriminate panic sections, this flick is pale and interminable, with lotsa stock footage, dozing dialogue and direction that makes most sitcoms look trail-blazing. Plus, it's getting a bit pathetic watching five-zillion-year-old John Carradine chew the carpeting in this type of creature feature (Saxon, at least, deserves this type of cinematic fate). **The Bees** is your basic crummy movie, pure and simple.

THE BELLY OF AN ARCHITECT

PETER GREENAWAY 1987. Finally a worthy successor to **Captive** in the 'pretentious arty crap' sweepstakes: Peter Greenaway's brilliantly annoying **The Belly of an Architect**. Brian Dennehy (in a riveting performance) plays Stourley Kracklite (!), an American architect who goes to Rome to stage an exhibition/tribute to Boullee, a French architect of the 1700's. Almost from his arrival in Rome, his stomach begins to plague him and in his overworked, obsessed frame of mind, he imagines that his young wife (Chloe Webb) is poisoning him. He wanders the ancient ruins, runs into a guy who likes to chop off the noses of statues and collect them (a sequel, 'The Nose of an Idiot'?), takes up postcard correspondence with his long-dead idol, and basically loses all control. Greenaway's fondness for our anxieties (and our anatomies) suggest a more cerebral Cronenberg. But unlike the vernacular that **Slimetime** readers might enjoy as metaphors for this (leeches, parasites, Sybil Danning), Greenaway uses a super-literate (read obscure) framework. And speaking of framework, Greenaway (**ZOO**, **The Draughtsman's Contract**) is fast becoming a visual master of settings and compositions. So for fans of Roman architecture, Xerox overkill, artistic obsessions, and postcards to dead people, **The Belly of an Architect** is a great film you'll probably never get to see. Great music by Kim (Kraftwerk) Mertens. [TR]

THE BEST OF GUMBY

1987. For the 30th birthday of every kid's putty-pals, Gumby and Pokey, f.h.e Video has released a collection of **The Best of Gumby**, hosted by Gumby's creator, Art Clokey... If you have never seen any of the '60s Gumby featurettes, or if all you know about the character is the bendable toys and the Eddie Murphy routines on **Saturday Night Live**, then you're in for a real treat, because these shorts are as funny (and weird) as they were 20 years ago. Seven of his adventures are packed into this 45 minute excursion of clay animation, starring little green Gumby and his orange horse, Pokey. Just like a normal youngster, he lives in a nice suburban house with his Playdoh mom and dad; but unlike the interminable goody-goodiness of old kids' shows like **Davey and Goliath**, these two characters are always off on some outrageously half-assed adventure that'll end up with them chased by robots, shot at by western desperadoes, or becoming a snack for a dinosaur... my favourites on the tape include: 'In the Dough', where G & P attempt the art of baking. But when a talking hunk of dough lures them *into* the oven they discover another world of living cakes, pies and pastries – all of which want to *eat* Gumby and Pokey!... 'The Witty Witch', where the duo are caught by a cackling witch in a helicopter and imprisoned in her dungeon, awaiting a 'horrible' fate. The supporting cast includes an ape-like creature with a devil head... And in 'The Small Planets', they run away from home and take a rocket ride into deep space, searching for a quiet asteroid to live on. Unfortunately, all the li'l planets are already inhabited by other kids who've run away, and they all want to be left *alone*!... The animation is quite good for its era, and Clokey allows his imagination to run amok. Fans of **Pee Wee's Playhouse** will especially go nuts over this loopy collection. It's loads of nostalgic fun.

BEYOND THE VALLEY OF THE DOLLS

RUSS MEYER 1970. From the auteur who created **Mudhoney**, **Vixen** and **Faster Pussycat! Kill! Kill!**, it's the self-proclaimed 'not a sequel to **Valley of the Dolls**'. Not only is it Russ Meyer's big-budget masterwork, but it has the proud distinction of joining **Psych-Out**, **The Trip** and **Head** as one of the great cinematic legacies of The Acid Years (and if you didn't already realise, I've got a soft spot in my heart – and head – for this trippy little genre). And would you believe that this drug-caked, sex-engorged camp classic was spawned from the pen of Roger Ebert? Sure, the guy's a blustery

THE FIRST OF THE SHOCK ROCK!

See how
three switched-on girls
in a hard rock group
break into
the Hollywood scene...
and crawl to the top!

Beyond the Valley of the Dolls

The **Sorcerers' Apprentice** providing the mood. Every type of sexual coupling is on display (male/female, female/female, male/'Superwoman') and the no-holds-barred finale is made up of equal parts gruesome death, medical miracles and howlers like "You will drink the black sperm of my vengeance!" Wow! Heavy! Meyer aficionados will recognise regulars Charles Napier, Erica Gavin and John LaZar, and we're even treated to a syrupy moral tacked on the end for us to chortle through... After kicking 20th Century-Fox in their collective asses with this flick and his (mediocre) follow-up, Irving Wallace's **The Seven Minutes**, Meyer returned to the ever-sleazier realm of indie-filmmaking. But as far as I'm concerned, **BVD** is his crowning achievement. I love it

THE BIG BIRD CAGE

JACK HILL 1972. The sequel to the ultra-money-making **The Big Doll House**, this Jack Hill Filipino project is another in a long line of 'nubile-American-women-trapped-in-a-barbaric-foreign-prison' flicks that pummelled the grindhouses in the early '70s... Anitra Ford (star of **Invasion of the Bee Girls** and ex-prop-bimbo for **The Price is Right**) plays a sex-crazed Caucasian cutie who's been rounding her heels with the Heads of State. But after she's kidnapped by Pam Grier and her gang of unwashed political revolutionaries during a night-club shoot-out, Anitra is unjustly implicated in the killing and lands in the local lady's hoose-gow – a bamboo hell in the middle of the jungle, where the women are forced to work the fields (what the heck *do* they grow in the Philippine jungle? We never find out.) and take abuse from Third World wardens. If they rebel, they get a one-way ticket to The Bird Cage, which is filled with shrieking crazy women. Of course, after watching an hour's worth of torture, humiliation and one-take filmmaking, Ms. Grier finally gets around to organising a full-scale prison breakout for the Sorta-Big Finale – blowin' up the barracks, machine-gunning the matrons, and they even take time out to rape one of the comic-relief gay-male guards ("No! Not like *this*!" he lisps as they straddle his blubbery girth)... If you're looking for grim punishment or *hardcore* degradation you won't find it here, though. It has the usual assortment of cat fights, mud wrestling and gang bangs, but it also takes almost *half an hour* until the first mass shower (as this genre goes, that's a long time for a group soaping). Luckily, the cast's tongue-in-chequebook style helps add to the Laugh Factor – Pam G. and cohort Sid Haig (a regular in most Jack Hill films: **Spider Baby**, **Blood Bath**, **Coffy**, etc.) write the whole project off as quick rent money, and Ms. Ford is perfectly typecast as a bitchy brat princess... Compared to recent high-grime flesh pageants like **Escape from Hell** this movie's pretty mild, but it's still worth several solid laffs.

BIG TIME

CHRIS BLUM 1988. Tom Waits has been churning out songs of love, blood and liquor for years, and he's finally committed his musical persona to film, after acting assignments in **Ironweed**, **Down by Law**, **Rumble Fish**, et cetera. But how to describe this guy to a novice? He's part poet, part performer, part prankster; mixing the absurdist sensibilities of David Byrne and the appearance of Ed Norton through Charles Bukowski's bar bill. Then give him the singing voice of an ill-tuned blender. This self-proclaimed 'Un Operachi Romantico' won't win Tom any new fans, but those familiar with his raspy growl and stale cigarette smoke ambience will enjoy this tour through the whiskey-glazed recesses of his mind. Structured more like a theatre piece than your typical concert, he takes his stage show and mixes it with dreamy interludes and a surreal set featuring a bed and bathtub. With the grin of a satisfied snake, he hunches over his mike with dark glasses shimmering, belting out his songs which run the gamut from caustic rants to heart wrenching ballads. He tinkles the ivories like a

blimpoid nowadays, but I've gotta semi-admire anyone who can write a line like "This is my happening, and it's freaking me out!" There's hope for the big dork yet!... Originally X-rated (though a fairly soft-R by today's standards), **BVD** is a psychedelic soap opera with no cliché left untouched or undefiled. There's dope, acid, front-seat fondling, gyrating hipsters, and loud music – all in the first five minutes, and the entire hallucinatory enterprise is so tightly edited and fiercely photographed that it'll make your head spin on its spinal column... Meet The Kelly Affair, an all-girl (and hilariously BAD) rock 'n' roll band who are playing senior proms until they hit LA with fame, fortune and fornication on the horizon. Dolly Read stars as the wide-eyed lead-singer, Kelly, along with her two band-mates (Cynthia Myers and Marcia McBroom) and her groovy boyfriend/manager (David Gurian). Before you can say 'contact high', they're all invited to Ronnie 'Z-Man' Barzell's pad for a party with The Strawberry Alarm Clock singing 'Incense and Peppermints' live in his living room. There they'll encounter no-scrupled Hollywood gigolo, Lance Rock; shirtless heavyweight boxing champ, Randy Black; and city-wide nympho and porno-priestess, Ashley St. Ives ("You're a groovy boy. I'd like to strap you on sometime."), played by the ever-overflowing Edy Williams... Changing their name to The Carrie Nations (and under the tutorage of Z-Man), these musical misses storm the pop charts with their album 'Look On Up From The Bottom', and from there it's a non-stop barrage of sweaty couples, mediocre music and endless parties; all punctuated by ladles of tacky, overstated melodrama (there's even a slow-motion run through the woods during a romantic interlude). Luckily, not one iota of this nonsense was taken seriously by anyone on board, and that's a MAJOR reason why this flick is still so effective as an ultra-tacky mind-blower. Kelly (and all her once-innocent comrades) are tested by the decadence of California – they switch bedroom partners, screw over The Establishment, deal with surprise pregnancies and suicide attempts, and it all culminates at a bizarro costume party at Z-Man's. Everyone smokes reefer and downs peyote, with coloured lights and Dukas' deranged lounge lizard, and the harsh red and blue lights give it all a barroom glow. And I particularly loved the larger-than-life facial contortions as he wails such favourites as 'Hang on Saint Christopher', 'Innocent When You Dream', 'Clap Hands', and a sizeable portion of 'Frank's Wild Years'. One major annoyance is its arty over-editing, which keeps cutting away to other characters (Waits playing a janitor, usher, ticket seller...) in the *middle* of songs. Sure, the technique helps link

together the numbers, but it's damned irritating too. At least director Chris Blum avoids the pandering audience-adulation shots... Accompanied by Michael Blair (percussion), Ralph Carney (saxes), Greg Cohen (bass), Marc Ribot (guitars), and Willy Schwarz (accordion), Waits is truly taking the seedy night-club into the '90s. And what a great double bill this would make with Laurie Anderson's equally amazing **Home of the Brave**.

BIG TOP PEE WEE

RANDAL KLEISER 1988. Man, I've been waiting for this movie all year. When I saw the trailer I never stopped laughing. So when this Pee Wee fanatic paid his five-fuckin'-fifty and settled into his seat, you can bet he was stoned and ready for a trip through Pee Wee's twisted mind. But what he got was a bland, grey-tinged film full of tired jokes and romantic scenes. No weirdness-induced land of craziness for Pee Wee to play in, just a dull grey world where everyone is nasty. Seems now Pee Wee thinks he's some kinda lover with minute-long kisses and tender dialogue. But Pee Wee! Look in the mirror! You're a grown man in a small suit speaking through your nose. No real girl would even look at your picture in a magazine. And what the hell are you doin' with a talkin' pig?! Pee Wee can not be a real life character! And who chose Randal (**Blue Lagoon**) Kleiser for a director? Go back to working with people who are as insane as you are! Don't think you're a Valentino in size 3 pants. Your devoted fans aren't interested! I don't think I laughed once at your self indulgent orgy of tired jokes and cute animals. I want my Pee Wee back! [SS]

BILLY THE KID VS. DRACULA

WILLIAM BEAUDINE 1966. Let's share a moment of silence for John Carradine, who died on November 27, 1988 at the age of 82. In his long career he appeared in some truly great films, as well as some classic clinkers. So in typical **Slimetime** fashion, what movie do we choose to review from his illustrious past? One of his BIGGEST pieces of shit!... What a stinker of a high concept! But unlike a lot of the trash Carradine appeared in during his last quarter century of acting, this flick is so deadly dull that it's painful to endure... When the fake rubber bat jiggles across the Western sky, it means that everyone's favourite vampire, Dracula, is riding the range in the 1800's. Carradine stars as the legendary Count – leaving his teeth marks as a goateed gentleman travelling by stagecoach across the Old West. And of all the pretty misses available, Drac has to lust after Betty, who just happens to be Billy the Kid's main squeeze. In the name of dramatic License, Billy is por-

trayed as a whitebread goodnik – a reformed man who's left behind his thieving, cold blooded, widow-and-orphan-killin' ways due to the love of a good woman. Carradine poses as Betty's uncle in order to infiltrate her homestead while setting up his own abode in an abandoned cave... While the horror aspects of the plot are halfway enjoyable, you'll cringe and quickly OD on all the western shenanigans. There's superstitious immigrants wielding wolfsbane, the crusty old country physician, black-hatted sidewinders, and ultra-annoying hick stereotypes. At least John C. snarls and hams it up in grand style (he was probably just happy to have a role with more than a dozen lines). Co-star Chuck Courtney is a particularly anaemic Billy, and it might've been more fun if they had kept him as a slimeball, with both title characters vying for the Head Shitheel Award. But instead it's all predictable hokum. The 'epic' confrontation between 'em at the end (a whopping 15 seconds) woke me up just in time to groan through the thoroughly revolting happy ending. And isn't it strange that sunlight doesn't seem to affect vampires in this version? Oh well, I guess it's just nit-picking to point out that they have Dracula roaming the countryside at high noon. Directed by William Beaudine (**Jesse James Meets Frankenstein's Daughter**), it's packed with all the excitement of watching mould grow. Yet another video to chuck into the fireplace.

BLACK ANGELS

LAURENCE MERRICK 1970. This flick doesn't fuck around. It's a blaxplobiker, drive-in mutation with opening moments that had me gasping for air. It doesn't maintain that speed-freak pace, but it's still relatively nasty, anti-social and unintentionally hilarious. The plot involves two competing cycle gangs (one white, one black) and their run-ins with each other *and* The Pigs. The surprise is that the term Black Angels refers to the COPS and not the Biker Brothers, and the police are more evil and devious than any chopper-head in the entire movie... Director Laurence Merrick cranks up the proceedings with lots of senseless violence, with everyone slugging, slapping, knifing, or pissing on each other – even members of their own gang. The movie flies promptly into high gear when a revenge-crazed member of the all-black gang (The Choppers) announces "Whitey's gonna pay *plenty* before I'm through!", and zooms off to take on Chainer (Des Roberts), the leader of The Serpents. One high-speed chase through town later, the plot settles down to focus on The Serpents and their hassles with the local brass-balled lawmen, who are continually trying to pit the gangs against each other. The cops back stab and lie to get their way, and unsurprisingly, the bikers are the coolest characters in the whole film. They party a bit, booze it up, scare a few nuns, and have their usual stand-offs with The Choppers, but under all that worn leather they're just your typical fun-loving dirtballs with a code of honour... And though I was kinda disappointed when the black bikers and their hate-honky clichés virtually disappeared in the second half, there was still plenty to keep any bad film fiend in raptures: laughably choreographed fights, plywood sets, straight-off-the-street actors, blouseless females, and inspirational dialogue like "You filthy, no-good, egg-sucking, finger-lickin', snot-pickin', scuzzy-faced rat!" And I haven't even mentioned the music yet! Yow! The soundtrack is so grating and '60s-pretentious that any self-respecting music lover will be slashing at their wrists with a broken beer bottle. I only wish the violence had been a little more graphic and hard-edged... The unexpected ending takes a few notes from **Easy Rider**'s downbeat finale, and after a great kick-ass Rumble Deluxe during the last five minutes, all the bikers end up killing each other while the police sit back and watch the slaughter. Extremely cynical, though a little too preachy... Overall, an OK trip for biker-completists.

BLACK CAESAR

LARRY COHEN 1973. At long last! A video release for this Time Square classic – and for a grindhouse novice, it's one of the best initiations into the Blaxploitation field. Director Larry Cohen originally wrote it as a starring vehicle for Sammy Davis Jr. (!), but with Fred

'The Hammer' Williamson in the title role, the urban bucks started rolling into American-International's coffers. It's also one of the few blaxploiters that started off on the right foot, by hiring a good director/scriptwriter, instead of casting first and filling in the hackneyed story later on. Cohen pushes all the right buttons for the first hour and gives us your basic 1930's Warner Brothers' gangster flick (**Little Caesar**, **Public Enemy**), updated and transferred to the streets of Harlem... It's the tale of Tommy Gibbs, who we first encounter as a street-smart young shoeshine boy who's taken under the Mafia's wing after aiding in a hit. Years pass, and he quickly integrates the Mob and follows the motto, "It's a jungle out there, and it takes a jungle bunny to run it" – working his way up through the all-white syndicate by paying off the cops, pocketing politicians, and eventually kickin' the white bosses out on their butts and taking over their turf. But while he's slaughtering off his competition with automatic weapons, he's also screwing the Brothers and Sisters. In other words, his thirst for power and money has changed him into a 'white Negro' asshole... There's plenty of clichéd melodrama in Tommy's rise to infamy (his girlfriend is unfaithful, his mama dies, and his homeboy becomes a gospel-spouting reverend), with more unnecessary subplots crammed into the storyline than any 94 minute movie could possibly accommodate. But once Gibbs is on top, everyone wants the sucker crushed into the pavement, and it's all a set-up for The Big Fall, when Williamson finally loses his cool and Cohen cuts loose with a four-star dizzying climax. The last 20 minutes are a *knockout*, with The Hammer running from assassins and staggering through midtown Manhattan with a hole blown in his stomach. His final confrontation with the corrupt police Captain wins the Audience Approval Award of 1973, when Gibbs bashes away at the racist scumbag with his old shoeshine box, and ends up shoe-polishing the Pig's face and forcing him to sing 'Mammy' at gun point. Wow, I'd LOVE to have heard the 42nd Street crowd during that scene!... This is Williamson's best role (though that isn't saying much if you've ever suffered through one of his Jesse Crowder series) and he plays a self-centred bastard quite effectively. Fully aware of his screen presence, Fred struts his stuff like he could hit out-of-the-park homers with his dick. The rest of the cast (Julius Harris, D'Urville Martin, and Gloria Hendry, who also pulled time in **Slaughter's Big Rip Off**, **Black Belt Jones** and **Savage Sisters**) remain firmly in One-Dimensional-Land , but Art Lund pegs the Vile Meter as the city's Top Cop. Let's not forget the soulful sounds of James Brown's soundtrack either... And if all *this* weren't enough, wait until we get around to its absolutely off-the-fuckin'-wall sequel, **Hell up in Harlem** (when Cohen *really* got to screw around)...

BLACK SHAMPOO

GREYDON CLARK 1976. I *still* can't believe I sat through something called **Black Shampoo**... And it's about as awful as you'd expect... Every white, rich floozy in town wants an appointment at Mr. Jonathan's Hair Salon. As played by John Daniels, he's a tall, black stud with his shirt unbuttoned to his waist, and a John Thomas that's always available for house calls. Whether he's being fondled by teenage nymphets, or getting the ol' squat-thrust from their boozed-up Mom, he always keeps his cool. But when local gangsters move in on his new receptionist, disrupt his hair styling business, and beat up his gay assistants, Jonathan says "enough is enough" and single-handedly takes on The Mob... The ads make it look action-packed, but mostly, this flick is a string of heavy-R sex scenes for the inner-city Crack crowd. Except for a bit of off-screen torture (one of the gays gets a heated curling iron crammed up his ass), and the finale, where Jonathan eventually shoves a pool cue through the Mob kingpin (ouch!), the whole production is yawningly tame. You *might* enjoy it if you're a fan of crappy, black soap operas, but everyone else will grimace through this whole seedy enterprise, with its tacky solarisation segues, hilarious mid-'70s leisure suits, and ass-wrenchingly awful soundtrack. *Nobody* escapes unscathed in this no-budget chunk o' shit – the gays are all limp-wristed whiners; the women are all whores; and Daniels has all the charisma of a colostomy bag. It was 'directed' by Greydon Clark, who went on to subject the public to **Satan's Cheerleaders**, **Without Warning** and **Joysticks**.

THE BLACK SIX

MATT CIMBER 1974. ...Or 'The Brothers Go South and Shove a Size-12 Combat Boot Up Whitey's Butt'. How many different sleazy genres can you squeeze together into one inept film? How about a blaxploitation/biker flick set in redneck territory? Next, make sure no one in the cast can pass a basic high school literacy class, much less an acting class. Sounds promising? Well, the first half hour will have you in Badfilm Heaven, but from there it's all downhill... It all starts when a white girl and her black boyfriend (uh oh, this sounds like trouble already!) are kicking field goals and completing passes (wink wink) out on a deserted football field late one evening. In roars the woman's brother, along with his gang of cycle-driving racists, and they immediately chain whip the poor, unarmed dude to death. Who's gonna get revenge? Enter the Black Six, played by a half dozen N.F.L. stars grabbing extra income during the off-season in order to pay for their steroid shots. None of them can act worth shit, but they certainly cut a lively path through Cracker-Town. This six-pack of black, army vet muscle aren't velour villains though. In fact, they're the nicest, friendliest, most loveable guys in North America. When we first meet 'em they're even helping out an elderly widowed farmwoman by loading bales of hay for her. And while eating dinner they keep their elbows off the table, use napkins (probably the biggest acting challenge for these guys) and call people 'ma'am' and 'sir'. Straddling their choppers, these Brothers tool from town to town, avoiding the hassles of the big city. Oh sure, these guys occasionally lose their tempers – when they can't get served at a rathole roadside greasy spoon, they toss the counter out the front window and literally tear the roof off the place – but they're just so gosh-darned likeable while they're destroying property that you *gotta* love 'em (or so the scriptwriters hoped). The only thing that gets them more riled than honky racists are honky murderers, so when Bubba (Gene Washington) learns of his younger brother's untimely death (remember that chain whipping at the beginning?), the audience is prepared for some SOLID ass-battering. Too bad it never really comes! The intro primes us for non-stop, home-bred, knuckle-sandwich justice, but once Bubba and his pals return to his home town the storyline blankets the fun with predictable family drama, soul searching and preachy polemics. Even when you think the action's *finally* going to commence, such as when both sides come face to face in a tavern (and I got myself psyched

SIX TIMES TOUGHER THAN 'SHAFT'! SIX TIMES ROUGHER THAN 'SUPERFLY'!
See the 6 biggest, baddest and best waste 150 motorcycle dudes!

up for a grand-scale barroom brawl, chock full of random, senseless violence), the entire scene just shrivels up and disappears... Blaxploit-fanatics can at least keep themselves amused by admiring the funky wardrobes – it looks like The Six grabbed their threads at the Jim Brown Thrift Shop. There's a surprisingly low Violence Factor, but the finale rumble is admittedly a doozy, with 10 minutes of skull-bashing and ball-busting when an army of ofay bikers take on The Six. There's great mayhem (at long last), loads of pasty-headed corpses, fiery explosions, and even a fat gang leader in a Viking helmet, named Thor... Pretty tedious going for a while, but with sporadic moments of inspired lousiness. What else would you expect from director Matt Cimber (aka Matteo Ottaviano), who later tried to make Pia Zadora into the new cinematic sex-kitten with his incest-and-open-blouse slop-opera **Butterfly**?

BLADES

THOMAS RONDINELLA 1988. Troma trashola! And I initially thought, just what the world needs – another comedy/horror flick which doesn't deliver on either end. But surprise (!), this one isn't half bad. The set-up is sorta clumsy, but once the plot gets rolling, you realise it actually has a fair share of clever moments. A spoof on **Jaws**, this movie moves the locale from the beach to a ritzy golf course, and gives us a killer lawnmower as the title terror... Sliced 'n' diced bodies are mysteriously turning up in the rough or buried in sand traps at a local country club, but the peckerhead management covers up the deaths to avoid bad publicity. And if the viewer couldn't figure it out from the predatory lawn-level camera angles and the sound of slicing grass, the culprit is a pissed-off industrial-sized mower with a mind of its own. All this nonsense is played refreshingly straight, without any campy winking-at-the-camera, and some of the scene-for-scene **Jaws** parodies are perfect (i.e. when a veritable army of gun-totin' rednecks take to the links to flush out the killer, or slicing open a captured mower to check out the mulch bag for body parts). The characters are strictly cardboard and most are played with all the verve and gusto of a haemorrhoid commercial. Exceptions are Robert North as the alcoholic golf pro, and chrome-domed Jeremy Whelan, who's hilarious as the Quint-like handyman with a past grudge against the lawnmower. Way overlong (it might've been better as a half-hour featurette), but nicely executed by director/editor Thomas Rondinella (who also sliced together Troma's **Girl School Screamers**). There's only a bit of graphic violence, but it makes up for it with absurd charm (which is more than I expected from a Troma turd). Don't trip over yourself renting it, but you could do a *lot* worse – like paying $6 to see **Ghost Dad**.

BLOOD BATH

MARIO BAVA 1972 (US: TWITCH OF THE DEATH NERVE; AKA BAY OF BLOOD). This little item is **The Jazz Singer** of blood-caked drive-in fare – though certainly not a perfect film, it helped set a dubious precedent for hundreds of horror films to come. It was one of the earliest Slice 'n' Dice Flicks, where you spend the entire running time counting down, as a bunch of brainless, unlikeable characters are systematically chopped up into fertiliser by an unseen psycho. Not much plot. Not much characterisation. Just a cast of pea-brained victims tossed together at an isolated bay (although it could have been a summer camp or a high school, for all it mattered). Mario Bava (who gave us '60s classics such as **Black Sabbath**, **Planet of the Vampires** and **Dr. Goldfoot and the Girl Bombs**), he tries his best to ladle on some suspense along with the graphic bloodshed. The end result is a bit obvious and occasionally tedious, but it's not too bad when you compare it to the tripe that some recent filmmakers pass off as horror films. It all starts happily enough, as an old, wheel chair-bound matron is brutally strangled, complete with choking noises and a tongue rolled out of her mouth for the 'bloated corpse' effect. Then we're introduced to our cast of potential corpses – a group of blithering idiots, posing as teenagers; a blond bimbette named Helga, who has more bust than brains; a dippy entomologist who talks to his bug collection; and a shifty-eyed caretaker who virtually has the word 'guilty' mounted to his forehead with a nail gun. The body count is rather low, compared to today's high-power kill-a-thons (such as Lucio Fulci's pasta-land productions), but for the early '70s, this was pretty radical stuff. Decomposing corpses pop up from the sea, bloodshot eyes peer from holes in the walls, and when the murders actually occur, their Gruesome Quotient is rather high (i.e. when a gal is hacked in the neck by a sickle, not only do you see the sliced flesh in loving close-up, but the open wound gets to bubble for a moment). Bava gives us the now-standard meat-cleaver-to-the-face, and he even uses the ol' two-naked-lovers-impaled-by-a-spear that was recycled in **Friday the 13th**. Unfortunately, the hardcore moments are often interspersed with solid snooze. Besides the grim sequences, there's lots of hideous early-'70s mod fashions to laugh at, a constant stream of phoney baloney chills while the surviving couple tries to figure out who the killer is, and piss-poor acting from Claudine Auger and the entire graduating class of the Cardboard-Is-Us School of Hysterics. But on the positive side, the out-of-the-blue ending is certainly strange enough to take you off guard... Though it may have lost some of its impact in the passing years, **Blood Bath** is still a good little exercise in carnage.

BLOOD DINER

JACKIE KONG 1987. Lightning Pictures vies with Troma and Empire for the award of Top Trash Distributor of the year. First they give us the wonderfully-deranged **Street Trash**, and they follow with this full-scale, gore-drenched monstrosity. In fact, **Blood Diner** could have been THE cheap-shit splatter film of '87, except for the small problem that the entire thing sucks! First off, they got Jackie Kong to direct, and since their last film was the utterly-unredeeming **Night Patrol** (with Linda Blair and The Unknown Comic), it doesn't really inspire confidence in the project, does it? The film has the look, the plot, and the level of no-holds-barred gore of any good Herschell Gordon Lewis film, but the script's manner of mindless humour undermines it all. The storyline is basically a hokey retread (or rip-off) of Lewis' **Blood Feast**, except that H.G.'s talent of blatantly taking lowlife gore to its unnatural limits is subverted by a continual **Gong Show**-type of snideness. It has some great gross-out ideas and (happily) nobody restrained themselves to secure an R-rating, but if you thought Troma liked to pander to the lowest level of audience stupidity, wait until you see this obnoxious side-show!... It begins when two little boys, Georgie and Mikey Namtut, see their crazy Uncle Anwar killed by the cops, and 20 years later they grow up to be yuppie grave robbers (played badly by Rick Burks and Carl Crew). They dig up their Uncle's corpse, rip out his brain, stuff it in a glass jar, and it speaks to them with an atrocious Jewish accent – and it's 'comic' dialogue is so fucking lame it's like listening to a Henny Youngman triple album. They run a health-food diner during the day, but by night they try to resurrect Sheetar, the Queen of their deviant blood cult, by sewing together pieces of their 'immoral' vegetarian victims. And while you're at it, can you guess what the 'secret ingredient' in their tuna surprise and fish fingers is?... There's virgins to sacrifice, a Lumerican Blood Buffet to concoct, a wrestling scene that coulda been out of a 'Santo Gold' commercial, a climax at a punk night-club, plus nudity, gore, zombies, cannibalism, loud music, decaps, and blood-caked meat cleavers. Whew! The only things this flick lacks is wit and intelligence, the two most essential ingredients. Director Kong has publicly compared this film to Monty Python Meets **Night of the Living Dead**, but Jackie's just spouting out of their PR-hole with that pre-

tentious fuckin' statement. Even though the fake brains and internal organs are prolific, the characters are still ultra-annoying, the direction is strictly geek-level (no surprise since Kong's career-long producer has been softcore porno peddler, Bill Osco), and the whole thing has the cheesy feel of a made-for-video feature (which is low-praise indeed). No matter how much I loved the movie's reprehensible excessiveness, I absolutely loathed its desperately unfunny dipshit-humour. If all you care about is the Blood 'n' Guts Quotient though, you can't do much better than **Blood Diner**, but personally, this fucker simply grated on my nerves... Honestly, why spend almost one-million-dollars on a H.G. Lewis 'homage' when you could just give Lewis the money and let him make his own damned movie?

BLOOD HOOK

JAMES MALLON 1986. Troma barfs up another one! Though not as thoroughly wretched as their **Fat Guy Goes Nutzoid!!** or **Igor and the Lunatics**, it's still a chunk of true drivel. But what else would you expect from Kaufman and Herz, who'd stick their names on any celluloid bowel movement they could wring a quick buck from? Unlike most of their pathetic product, at least this entry has a couple moments humorous enough to keep you from shoving the video tape down the garbage disposal. That's about as close to a compliment as I can get... It's Idiot Teen Time again, with a carload of japs and jocks heading out to the lake for some fishing fun in the sun. And I can't decide which group is stupider: The rural townies are so backward they make the supporting cast of **Deliverance** look like Rhodes scholars (including a Vietnam vet who refers to himself as "a time bomb ready to go off"), and the tourists are represented by a loathsome pack of suburban shitboxes who compare their campsite to **On Golden Pond** with Peter Fonda (it's a joke, get it?). There's even a big 'Muskie Madness' fishing contest to add a heaping of suspense! Gosh, I wonder who'll win?! I bet you won't give a damn either! But murder brings the flick to life, when the assorted half-wits and dumbshits begin disappearing. Some kind of mysterious predator is fishing for PEOPLE – hooking a foot-long tackle into their stomach, or around their neck, and reeling them into the depths of the lake. It's a slim plot, all in all, but the ending is crudely amusing, when we learn who (or what) is responsible, and we're treated to ground chuck corpses, bloated carcasses, and a first-hand glimpse at the evil effects of rock music. Don't expect high doses of gore though – there's some relatively tame flesh-rending when the hooks take hold (plus a bit of PG-level nookie), but not much else. You know all the generic characters by heart (such as the pathetic 'hero', who saves the day in a fly-casting dual), and there's no suspense in seeing any of them snuff it. Actually, it's sort of a relief to see 'em disappear. Directed by James Mallon, there's more fun in watching a bug-zapper on a summer night. It's another monument to money-sucking mediocrity from Troma.

BLOOD OF GHASTLY HORROR

AL ADAMSON 1971. Al Adamson pix are always a howl (**Brain of Blood, Horror of the Blood Monsters**). He has no pretensions that he's creating Low Art, or even Slick Sleaze. He inherently knows his product is one-week-only drive-in trash, and he had a monopoly on 'em long before Troma stole the spotlight. This is one of Al's most infamous piecemeal productions. It looks as if each of his actors filmed their scenes at different times, the script was revised every two hours and most of the production crew was on Thorazine. Surprisingly enough, the real story behind this mess is even stranger to swallow! Here's a quick lesson from Shoe-String Filmmaking 101: One of Adamson's first movies was a standard police/crooks melodrama helmed under the title **Echo of Terror** and released in 1965 as **Psycho-a-Go-Go!**. A year later it reap-

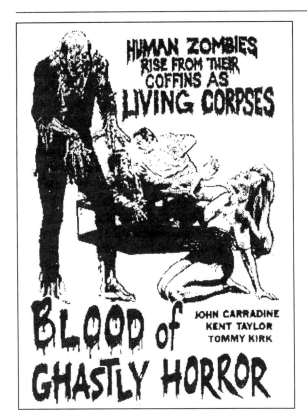

HUMAN ZOMBIES RISE FROM THEIR COFFINS AS LIVING CORPSES

BLOOD of GHASTLY HORROR

JOHN CARRADINE
KENT TAYLOR
TOMMY KIRK

peared with some John Carradine mad doc footage as **The Fiend with the Electronic Brain**. Then four years later Adamson-regulars Kent Taylor and Regina Carrol added some sequences and it made the rounds as the 'all-new' **Blood of Ghastly Horror**. After that, it's been known to pop up on the late-late-show as **The Man with the Synthetic Brain**. Geesh! Talk about recycling! Was it worth all the effort? Well, I'm sure Adamson lined his pockets with some extra greenbacks suckled from unsuspecting horror fans, but as for us paying customers, the result is pure mental anguish... Within the first 10 minutes there's a monster attack, some heist footage, dopey narrators commenting on the non-action, and if you're already confused, then join the club. None of it really makes much sense, but the script-tailors baste it together and pray that everyone at the drive-ins will be too busy trying for Third Base to notice the 'slight' inconsistencies. It seems that one of the guys from the jewel robbery at the beginning was the son of Kent Taylor, and he was turned into a crazed criminal by Dr. Carradine's experimentation. John C. plays Dr. Vanard, a brilliant brain specialist who manufactures fake brains, and ends up stuffing one of his whacko designs into a shell-shocked Vietnam vet (Kent's son), thereby turning him into a homicidal moiderer. The grief-crazed Kent Taylor, meanwhile, concocts a potion that turns people into killer zombies – beginning with his pet geek, Acro, and culminating in a plan to do the same to Vanard's makeup-laden daughter, Regina Carrol (the real-life Ms. Adamson). Regina struts about with her ample charms and meagre talents (did she ever appear in a film that wasn't directed by her hubby?); and remember Tommy Kirk, the cute teen heart throb from Disney's **Old Yeller** and **The Shaggy Dog**? By the mid-'60s he looked like he was vying for the lead role in 'Lost Weekend, Part 2'. The tedious crooks' storyline is the dominant factor toward the end, with the head meanie chasing a mother and daughter (who unknowingly have the loot stuffed in the kid's doll) through the tundra. GOT ALL THAT, FOLKS?!... You've got to have an incredibly high *bullshit* tolerance to survive this stinker, believe me. Oh, it's funny as a one-shotter, but you won't

want to add this flick to your video collection (except maybe for use as an ashtray). No thrills, no blood. not one iota of 'Ghastly Horror', and it's even a bigger disaster on the technical side! Bad sound, flat photography and plywood sets that harken back to the grand ol' days of **Space Cadet**. I'll be lenient on the cast though – they were probably too sedated to even realise what film they were making. Oh yeah, it's also brought to us in the astounding new process of CHILL-O-RAMA! – just don't ask me what it means.

BLOODSUCKING FREAKS

JOEL M. REED 1978. *The* unofficial winner of the nastiest, gross-out, what-the-fuck-are-they-doing-to-that-woman movie. Also known as **The Incredible Torture Show** (a more accurate title, too), this vile, disgusting little classic from the diseased brainpan of 'auteur/sleazebucket' Joel Reed is the ultimate this-is-so-sick-it's-hilarious gore/porno film... Visit Dr. Sardu's House of the Macabre (we pronounce it mack-a-bree), an off-off-Broadway theatre that specialises in good old fashion Grand Guignol entertainment; like chaining a woman down, cutting off her fingers and plucking out her eyes. For 80 minutes you get to wallow in pain and stupidity, as the scriptwriter(?) pads out a Svengali-like plot with a shitload of obviously-faked, but nevertheless grisly punishment. Shot in grainy 16mm, it all looks like it was filmed in an unheated basement – but it's also one of the few schlock films in recent memory to actually give the viewer *more* perversity than their ads promise (whether we want it or not, that is). Yes, for a nominal rental cost, you get to see (1) naked, cannibalistic women behind bars, (2) a **New York Times** drama critic kicked to death by a Lincoln Centre Ballerina, and (3) a woman's teeth pulled out by a sadistic dentist, so that she can't bite off his dick during a blow job – and then a power drill is used to bore into her skull, followed by the insertion of a straw and a demonstration of the lost art of brain-sucking. And amidst all this foolishness, Dr. Sardu and his half-pint assistant seem to have a swell time, overacting and playing the whole thing for ghoulish laughs; the other actors are painfully inept (graduates of the George Lazenby School of Drama); and all the women look like they were pulled from 42nd Street strip joints with the promise of a free meal. So, if you haven't gotten the message yet, **Bloodsucking Freaks** is a repellent, sicko-drama (just take a look at the ad campaign for it, which the **New York Times** had the infinite good taste to run); it has absolutely no redeeming values whatsoever; it's sadistic, morally reprehensible, and Jerry Falwell would take a dump the size of Rhode Island in his trousers if he was forced to watch it – but it's definitely an item not to be missed by any deviant moviegoer.

THE BLUE EYES OF THE BROKEN DOLL

CARLOS AURED 1973 (US: HOUSE OF PSYCHOTIC WOMEN; AKA: LOS OJOS AZULES DE LA MUÑECA ROTA). Let's hear it for Paul Naschy, who starred in all those amazing Spanish monster movies, such as **Dracula's Great Love**, **Vengeance of the Mummy** and **Frankenstein's Bloody Terror**. Unfortunately, he also spent his free weekends stuck in mediocre crap like this so-called 'shocker'. Directed by Carlos Aured, this film certainly is a letdown. First off, don't believe the vid-box from Super Video (HA!), with a bare-chested guy getting tortured by a pair of dominatrixes, because IT NEVER HAPPENS! Instead, this turns out to be less a gory horror/sex romp than a mock-Hitchcock murder mystery... It starts out mildly enough (and continues that way throughout), with Paul N. hitchhiking his way across the countryside. He's an unemployed drifter, and wouldn't you know it, he promptly runs across the local Mansion of Nutso Broads. Three sorta-beautiful sisters live there – one is confined to a wheelchair, another has a metal hand and the third acts like a red-headed Spanish Fly addict. The first half is Solid Snoozeland, but when blue-eyed, blond-haired young girls from the village start popping up dead and mutilated (their eyes are torn out), the pace begins to pick up. Is Naschy the killer? Or is one of the sisters to blame? And if so, which one? Don't expect a logical conclusion though, because the killer comes outta left field, and so *you* won't have to endure this brainsucker, allow me to give away the 'surprise' ending – a psychiatrist has been hypnotising the paralysed sister, and under his power she walks around and chops up young girls, in an effort to avenge the death of the Doc's own blue-haired, blond-eyed (or is that the other way around?) daughter... What did they do, make this shit up as they went along? It's a murky, slipshod mess... The gore consists of a few quick shots of unsocketed eyeballs being carried around and a tiny bit of blood splattering. The only reason to keep watching is if you're a Paul Naschy groupie, because he really gets to strut his stuff in this Euro-entry – he stabs a guy during a fight, runs from the cops, gets his foot stuck in a bear trap, and Paul even gets to show off his girth during a couple of routine sex scenes. Truly, he's Spain's answer to Cameron Mitchell... Except for him, this flick is humourless and unexceptional in every department. A muddled yawn-a-thon.

BLUE SUNSHINE

JEFF LEIBERMAN 1978. Here's a creepy little film that barely got distributed. Director Jeff Leiberman (the guiding light behind miniclassics **Squirm** and **Just Before Dawn**) rips loose with a twisted concept incorporating drug paranoia, suburban killing sprees, ex-hippies, unsettling violence, and the fear of baldness... The local death count takes a drastic leap when a number of seemingly ordinary folks start losing their hair by the handful, and with it, their sanity – going off the deep end and filling the vacancies at the morgue. All the murderers have two things in common, though – they all went to Stanford University in the late '60s and they all tried a form of LSD called Blue Sunshine. Yes, our old friend chromosome damage is to blame, 10 years after the fact, turning all these now-upstanding members of the community into hairless homicidal maniacs (sort of a psychotronic rethinking of **The Big Chill**). This premise soon leads to family-butchering, tossing a woman in a blazing fireplace, baby-sitters chasing cute little children with big sharp kitchen knives, and a panic in a tacky discotheque. Happily, the film never turns into a preachy diatribe about the consequences of drug use. Leiberman simply acknowledges that plenty of college kids have tried acid, and he builds a solid horror story around that fact. (Ever hear the one about the hippie baby-sitter who was so stoned she put the baby in the oven, thinking it was dinner?)... Zalman King stars as Zipkin, the innocent-man-wrongfully-implicated-in-the-crimes, as well as the *only* person who understands the connection between the killings. Amidst the relatively unspectacular supporting cast, two stand-outs include Robert Walden (the weaselly li'l shit from **Lou Grant**) as a shaky surgeon, and Mark Goddard (after his stint on **Lost in Space** he's apparently been 'Lost in the Unemployment Line') as a Congressional candidate – and Maj. Donald West is actually pretty convincing as a slippery-dirtbag-politician (isn't that term a little redundant?)... The low budget is evident throughout (it's sort of sad when they stage a political rally and can only find two dozen extras to sit in the audience) and the direction alternates between the effectively quirky and the crude. In the hands of a more stylishly grotesque director (like Cronenberg) or a more full-tilt sleazier one (such as Larry Cohen) this could have been a cult classic. Instead, it's only on the fringe of the bizarro pack, but that's an admirable accomplishment all the same. **Blue Sunshine** packs quite a bit of unnerving fun.

BLUE VELVET (1986)
PEGGY SUE GOT MARRIED (1986)

You can add Coppola's name to the list of yuppie sellout brown-nosers, and keep David Lynch's name high on the list of cinematic originals continuing to offer untainted, unconservative films to those with the brain power to appreciate them. **Blue Velvet** is everything the Reagan generation doesn't want to see – America as a twisted, rotting cesspool glazed over with media-induced happiness. **Peggy Sue got Married** is a mindless, corporate version of Capraesque concepts, badly directed (check the opening high-school sequence for details), overflowing with Spielberg-level sentimental crap, offering a sexist and pandering solution to a halfway interesting (somewhere down there, before all the shitheaps rewrote it) idea. I'm sure that Ron and Nancy ordered a screening of this garbage to cool down after watching **Top Gun** for the eighteenth time. A friend suggested that Coppola's recent family tragedy might have had a part in creating this swill. OK, so maybe 'Apocalypse Now II' might have been a little hard to get through, but this is simply sellout material. I'd love to lock Kathleen Turner in a dark room with Dennis Hopper's Frank from **Blue Velvet**, with Dean Stockwell singing that strange song with the portable lamp. I think it'd be only a matter of minutes before she'd start screaming and pulling her eyes out of their sockets. (Makeup by Savini, of course...) [TR]

THE BONE CRUSHING KID

HSIA CHENG HUNG 1979. Ocean Shores Video has released a slew of obscure Chinese martial art films, including such oddities as **Two Crippled Masters**, **Of Cooks and Kung Fu**, and **Eunuch of the Imperial Palace**... The titles and synopses on the boxes are in both English and Chinese (including such enlightening descriptions as 'Bloody Fight!' or 'Exciting Story!'), and I grabbed this tape because it looked particularly fun-filled *and* asinine. And it certainly didn't disappoint me, I'm glad to report. So, if you're dying to watch a bunch of orientals mercilessly beating the crap out of each other, you're going to bust a gut on this Rhapsody In Chopsocky. It's a comedy kung fu chuckle-fest with a Jackie Chan-style combination of fighting, gymnastics and klutzy slapstick – the martial arts answer to The Three Stooges. The plot is fairly shaky, but as in most good drive-in films, the action is *so* relentless, numbing and totally unbelievable that the lame storyline takes a back seat... Shou-fu, a bumbling tea-server, secretly loves the Emperor's daughter, but since he's nothing but a lowly servant his chances at romance are nil. Being a good-hearted guy, Shou-Fu one day saves an old man from jail by spending the money he'd saved for martial arts school – and guess what? The old guy turns out to be a first class teacher of kung fu, and he happily agrees to humiliate and torment Shou for most of the running time. Ultimately, Shou learns the deadly Seven Hands Style of kung fu and takes on every pompous warrior in the Province, chopping and kicking the bejesus out of the pointy-headed stock villains. There aren't any credits, so I don't know who the star is, but he does a fine job looking like a boob and 'accidentally' stumbling his way through opponents. He dresses up in weird costumes (including a dotty old woman), incapacitating dozens of evil slants, and although the movie's relatively bloodless, at the end Shou *does* get to crush a few bones. Definitely not for anyone interested in logic, characterisation, or serious-minded kung foolery, but it's great fun for the unpretentious hordes who want to watch 90 minutes of unbridled human destruction. It also has the *worst* stock music soundtrack I've ever had to sit through (they even have the nerve to toss in the Pink Panther theme), plus an imbecilic assortment of fake-sounding SLAPS, STOMPS and BOINGS to accompany the fighting.

THE BRAIN

EDWARD HUNT 1988. WOW! This Canadian-lensed monster-fest doesn't fool around! It's fast paced, wildly excessive, silly as all heck, and it even crams some low-rent Cronenbergian concepts into its plot. And after picking my way through one too many lame new releases, this came as a happy surprise – a film that successfully combines the gross-out weirdness of '80s exploitation with the sheer, unpretentious fun of '50s drive-in fare... Director Edward Hunt hooks your attention from the first minutes, when we meet a teenaged girl with a 'slight' problem. Whenever she's alone in her bedroom, her teddy bear begins crying blood, giant claws burst from her TV's picture tube, and the killer tentacle she fends off with a pair of scissors turns out to be her mother. (Oops! Sorry about stabbing you in the gut mom.) It's a hot, loopy intro, and the story doesn't let-up either, because this death is only one in a series of grisly, 'seemingly unrelated' suicides and murders taking place around town. Luckily, Dr. Blake, the renowned psychologist and host of the popular (or should I say *too* popular?) TV show 'Independent Thinking', is working diligently on the case. Played by the ever-sinister David Gale (who's gotten his head reattached since **Re-Animator**), the viewer has the distinct feeling that this doc is a whacko – maybe because he keeps a throbbing mutant brain as a pet. But when the film's 'brilliant but misunderstood' high school hero (played by Tom Breznahan, who's never as annoying as he has every right to be) is forced into therapy at Blake's high-tech institute of drooling loonies, he starts experiencing uncontrollable hallucinations. You see, this size 15 triple-E brain in the Doc's fish tank gives off hypnotic waves when it's not busy digesting white mice (or the occasional whole human) for brunch, and this nutty grey matter just keeps eating and growing until it looks like a six-foot-wide, rabid Madball from Hell. The entire town quickly falls under its murderous mind manipulation, and soon they've got a middle class massacre on their hands, with Tom and his pretty girlfriend (Cyndy Preston) on the run from the glassy-eyed population... Essentially, this is your basic 'teens discover a monster and no one believes 'em until it's TOO LATE' plotline and it's all utterly preposterous, but who really cares when a flick is so downright enjoyable on a pseudo-trash level? It knows exactly when to go for the stylish shot, unexpected twist, creepy moment, or schlocky blood bath. So put your brainpan on auto-pilot, grab a cold one and be prepared to give three cheers for this wonderfully dopey creature feature!

BRAIN DAMAGE

FRANK HENENLOTTER 1987. Director Frank Henenlotter is back on the screen after five years, and if this follow-up to **Basket Case** isn't in the same instant-classic league, it's still a solid laff-a-minute sleazefest. The best flick of its kind since **Street Trash** (and that's high praise indeed)... The non-human star of this show is Aylmer (basically pronounced Elmer) the Parasite, an ugly li'l foot-long, worm-like critter with a face only an acid-addled Tex Avery could've created. One day he (or should I say It?) escapes from his bathtub home in his elderly keepers' apartment and takes up residence next door with average-guy Brian (Rick Herbst). What's so special about Aylmer? He's an immortal creature who's been around for centuries, and he enjoys latching onto the back of your neck and injecting a blue fluid into your brain. It's a hallucinatory chemical that keeps you so happy and sedated that you don't mind as Aylmer burrows its way under your skin. Poor Brian initially doesn't know what to think when he finds himself in Altered States-ville, but soon Bri and his talking (that's right, it fucking TALKS, courtesy of horror host Zacherley) sidekick are pals, with Aylmer showing him the good life of tripped-out bar-hopping. Even an auto graveyard's beauty is enough to go spazoid over. And whenever blissed-out Brian needs a helping hand (or a mouthful

of razor-sharp teeth), Aylmer lunges at an assailant's forehead and grabs a quick brain-snack for himself (burp!)... At times it gets a little heavy-handed with the (hopefully) unintentional anti-drug allegory, like when Brian's friends begin worrying about his mental state. But then Henenlotter hits us with the ultra-bizarre; Combining the pale, harsh grimness of a cold turkey withdrawal, with the inherent sicko humour of having Aylmer serenading Brian with the cutesy 'Elmer's Theme' while the guy is going through convulsions. And how could any sleaze-junkie *not* laugh their ass off when in the middle of an Italian restaurant, Brian's meatballs suddenly turn into little throbbing brains? Several of the hallucinations are amazing – high-calibre brain expansion on an independent budget! The special effects are imaginative, Jim Muro provides some fine Steadicam work, and the performances are so uniformly mediocre that Aylmer receives top acting honours... It doesn't cut the same emotional gut-response that the relationship between the brothers in **Basket Case** did (speaking of **BC**, fans of that flick will get a cheap guffaw at the in-joke), but this film is technically in the stratosphere compared to Frank H.'s first effort, while remaining just as demented. Maybe a bit too esoteric to be a big hit, but it should cultivate a nice cult status in years to come. It's miles better than the usual trash on the market, with more gruesome bloodshed and vile death than most videophiles are ready for. Of course it's plainly obvious that the film was hacked in order to obtain an R-rating (though considering how quickly it flew through theatres, an unrated release probably would've *helped*). The big question is, why didn't they restore it for the video release? Maybe if we *all* write Paramount Home Video and tell them we'd like to see the now-infamous blow-job parasite-murder sequence, they'll reconsider and – Er, then again, maybe not... Even edited, this movie comes off as one of the year's sleazy best.

THE BRAIN FROM PLANET AROUS

NATHAN JURAN 1958. King of the psychotronic cheapies, John Agar (**Curse of the Swamp Creature, Zontar, The Thing from Venus**) stars in this b/w B-movie that's tons of fun! It's a true classic! 70 minutes of crisp science-fiction goofiness that can't be beat (well, **2001** is a *bit* better, I guess). **Arous** doesn't waste a moment in getting to the guts of the story (or wasting any of their film stock)... Geiger counters suddenly go off the dial, and nuclear experts determine it's coming from deserted Mystery Mountain. So, Scientist Steve (John A.) and his assistant take an afternoon spin to check it out, and find a newly-blasted cavern with enough radioactivity to hard-boil their brainpans. They're also greeted by a giant, floating, luminescent alien brain named Gor, from the planet Arous (it's pretty damned ridiculous looking, too). With its big ol' mind set on world domination, the power-hungry creature incapacitates Agar and possesses his body, and when he comes off the mountain, all sorts of chaos breaks loose: the normally gentle Agar suddenly tries to rip off his girlfriend's blouse, his dog attacks him as if he were a stranger, and his eyeballs glaze over and emit deadly energy more powerful than the A-bomb (that's a dead give-away as far as I'm concerned). This is one of Agar's best roles, and he perfectly captures the hokey flavour and manic mood of the film – going thru convulsions, conversing with The Space-Brain, or light-heartedly burning human beings to a cinder. While possessed, he's hilariously egomaniacal – facing down-Generals with his plans to rule the world and blowing up airplanes full of innocent people with his radioactive peepers. A schlocky conclusion puts an end to the fun, though, when another brain named Vol appears to save the day by inhabiting John's doggie and informing the earthlings on how to kill Gor... What finally destroys this All-Powerful World Dominator? Well, Agar simply chops it up with a handy fire axe. Now wasn't that easy?... **Arous** has a good concept, which it executes *very* enjoyably, some neat photography, and efficient direction by Nathan Juran, who previously helmed such classics as **The Deadly Mantis**, **20 Million Miles to Earth** and **Hellcats of the Navy** (with Ronald McReagan and his soon-to-be-withered spouse, Nancy Davis). **Arous** is one of his best. It's top-notch Sat. afternoon entertainment!

BRAIN OF BLOOD

AL ADAMSON 1971. After demolishing every imaginable schlock genre – space operas, biker gangs, monster movies – what does shitmeister Al Adamson come up with next, with the aid of co-producer Samuel Sherman? A return to the Mad Doctor flicks of the late '60s! And the result belongs in the same echelon as his other So-Bad-They're-Hilarious epics, which he churned out from 1970-1972 (**Dracula vs. Frankenstein**, **Satan's Sadists** and **Horror of the Blood Monsters**). Unfortunately, his career seemed to run out of steam after this stream of howlers, and Al settled comfortably into straight-forward mid-'70s mediocrities such as **Stud Brown** and **Nurse Sherri**. Adequate enough drive-in fare, but they seemed to lack that one-of-a-kind Adamson Trademark, where everything he touches turns into unintentional laughs. But onto the matter at hand... Our film begins with the news that Amir, the powerful ruler of Kaleed (it's somewhere near India, since they flash a postcard snapshot of a Taj Mahal-like temple on the screen), is dying. So he's wrapped in aluminium foil (no joke) and shipped to Dr. Kent Taylor, an unorthodox surgeon who's sorta-perfected a messy technique for brain transplants. The Doctor operates (literally) out of his home, and for his blood supply, he keeps a couple of teenage girls manacled in the basement, where they can be tapped every so often by the Doc's dwarf assistant, Angelo Rossitto. But when the Doc can't find a suitable body to transplant Amir's brain into, he ends up shovelling it into the skull of Gor, his seven-foot-tall bald servant, whose face was burnt off with battery acid. This wasn't too bright an idea though, because when Amir wakes up and sees his new, lumpy-featured body, he's pissed off, to say the least. He pummels the Doc, and eventually, Gor (not only with Amir's brain, but his voice too – I guess the Doc also transplants vocal chords) and his old girlfriend hit the trail and start ripping up citizens... There's all sorts of plot unravellings: One of the dungeon debs escapes and crawls around the musty cellar, Amir's followers get suspicious of the Doc's medical hanky-panky, and power-

hungry Dr. Kent searches for Gor with a sonic disrupter that looks more like a vacuum cleaner attachment... All the Adamson touches are on display – airheaded actors, busty babes and dumb dialogue, not to mention a nice, cynical ending. They could have used a bit less restraint with the fake blood though, and the GP-rating is strictly due to a couple moments of goopy brain surgery close-ups. (Why don't you stick your fat fingers into the incision a few *more* times, Doc?) For all you Adamson-ophiles out there (I think they can be counted on one hand), the film features a veritable rogues' gallery of his supporting players, including Grant Williams, Vicki Volante, Zandor Vorkov, and last but certainly least, Mrs. Al herself, Regina Carrol as Amir's mistress... All of this is absolutely mindless if you're in the mood for a Real Movie, but it's recommended unequivocally if you want to laugh *at*, and not *with* a flick. It's mind-bogglingly inept, and doofy as hell! Needless to say, I liked it a *lot*.

THE BRAIN THAT WOULDN'T DIE

JOSEPH GREEN 1959. Brain movies. I love 'em! **The Brain from Planet Arous**. **Brain of Blood**. **The Brain Eaters**. And of course, there's this crisp little chucklefest. It's dim-witted, sleazy and (unlike lots of '50s passion pitters) true to the silliness of its ad campaign!... You can tell right off the bat that Dr. Bill Courtner (Herb Evers) is a brilliant (but unorthodox) physician, because whenever patients die on the operating table, he takes charge and happily digs into their brains with both hands. He's also got that fanatical Colin Clive gleam in his eyes, so I bet you he's also the thief who's been snatching the leftover limbs from the hospital morgue (since everything's allowable in the name of science). This flick doesn't just sit on its clichés though, and in the first few minutes, while Bill is driving with his beautiful fiancee, Jan, his car misses a turn and crashes. Of course, this doofus walks away from the accident in one piece, while his bride-to-be is decapitated. Ever the considerate, caring leading man, the Doc grabs Jan's head and runs to his secret laboratory. Stuff a few tubes of solution into her brainpan, connect up a couple D-cells, and voila (!) from the neck up she's back to normal (though understandably perturbed at the whole experience). It's an unforgettably hilarious image, watching this bandage-swaddled head jabbering away on a lab table (hmmm, an antecedent of **Re-Animator**?). Meanwhile, the Doc is searching the strip clubs and beauty pageants for an appropriate body to transplant her head onto (while giving '50s audiences a cheap chance to ogle some dames in swimsuits). And just in case the story isn't goofy enough for your tastebuds yet, the bodiless Jan begins having telepathic conversations with the Doc's closet creation – an eight-foot-tall killer Conehead from Hell... Herb Evers is downright scuzzballish, Virginia Leith hams it up as the title body part, and Leslie Daniel is actually good as Kurt, the obedient assistant. Dramatically OK (for this type of drivel) and silly as all heck, with wall-to-wall overwrought dialogue as an added bonus. But boy, are there a *load* of loose ends left dangling. What did they do, run outta film stock at the very end? Nevertheless, this movie is lotsa old fashioned fun for schlockaholics.

BRIDE OF THE MONSTER

EDWARD D. WOOD JR 1955. You know you're in trouble when a commercially purchased tape (from 'video classics') is recorded at Long Play but considering this was written, produced and directed by the two dollar wonder (namely Edward D. Wood Jr.) i'm not surprised at all this wonderful feature stars a surprisingly coherent Bela Lugosi as the very foreign Dr. Vernoff and a very large but badly dressed Tor Johnson as his mute muscle-monster simply named Lobo it seems Bela has come here from an unnamed country after being expelled when he told his government that he could make an entire race of muscle-bound mute fools who all look exactly like Tor (hmmm, good idea!) now he lives on Lake

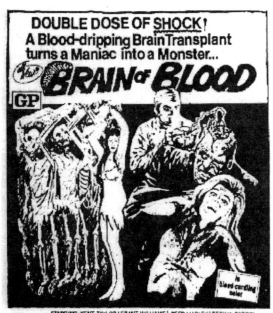

DOUBLE DOSE OF SHOCK!
A Blood-dripping Brain Transplant turns a Maniac into a Monster...
BRAIN OF BLOOD
GP

STARRING KENT TAYLOR / GRANT WILLIAMS / REED HADLEY / REGINA CARROL

Marsh (where there's always a storm brewing) where Tor kidnaps unsuspecting strangers so Bela can strap them to a table, put a salad bowl on their head and shine a light in their face apparently this process will leave the lucky victim "as big as a giant, with the strength of 20 men... or... like the others... dead" (thus releasing them from the film) if that's not all, he also has a pet killer octopus which he keeps.... well.... i can't quite figure it out, but it's either in a holding tank in his lab or at the lake in the backyard anyway, since the big breasted cub reporter heroine is engaged to the clean cut young cub homicide detective, of course both are concerned about these mysterious disappearances, which are being credited to the Lake Marsh Monster ("monster... monster... ah!" says the police chief) so the reporter heroine goes out to Bela's house to investigate (alone, of course) meanwhile, Bela's being visited by Dr. Strowski who, apparently, is an ambassador from Bela's 'country' with news that Bela was right after all and now he can come home well, this pisses Bela off so much, he throws Strowski into the octopus tank, forcing Strowski to wrap the rubber arms around himself and die (though from what i could tell he certainly couldn't have drowned, since there's no water in the tank) meanwhile, Tor kidnaps the big breasted heroine and sends her to Bela to be hypnotised so she can respond to silly hand gestures (expertly executed by Lugosi) finally, he dresses her in a wedding gown, straps her to a table, puts a salad bowl on her head and is about to shine a light on her face when the hero bursts in and gets chained to a wall not only that, but Tor has fallen for the heroine's big breasts, so when Bela is about to shine the light in her face a second time, Tor knocks him out (you getting all this?) lets the girl go, straps Bela to the table, puts a salad bowl on his head, and shines a light in his face leaving Bela with platform shoes, bad makeup and a sinister expression Tor goes nuts and torches the place while Bela walks around chased by police until the hero throws a boulder at him, knocking him into the octopus pond meanwhile, the lab goes up in nuclear fission (did I mention the experiment was atomic?) So... didja get all that? this muddle was surprisingly entertaining, thanks to Ed's considerable talents his trademark dialogue ("The ground is alive with crawling things... crawling death!"), his now famous special effects techniques, some of which are still used today (y'know... platform shoes for monster height, wax scars, using stage lights on a boom stand to symbolise a cosmic device, intercutting 'octopus in his habitat shots' with shots of a rubber octopus in a puddle... stuff like that) and his tradition of only using the finest actors (even Bela remembers most of his lines) i watched this real early Sunday morning and it set up the perfect day not too long, not too engaging and not too intelligent (and i didn't sleep through it either). [SS]

BRING ME THE HEAD OF ALFREDO GARCIA

SAM PECKINPAH 1974. After the success of **The Wild Bunch** and **Straw Dogs**, Sam Peckinpah conned MGM into backing this project. Unlike his earlier films, Sam had complete control *and* final cut, and what emerged is this uncompromising Sleazeball Epic, with a brass-balled cast headed by Warren Oates. This South-of-the-Border adventure begins when a pregnant young girl is tortured until she admits the father of her illegitimate child is the local Lothario, Alfredo Garcia. The family patriarch puts a million dollar bounty on Alfie's head (they don't want him alive, they don't want his corpse, they just want the severed head as proof. Nice guys, eh?) and every money-hungry lowlife killer is quickly on his trail across dirt-poor Mexico. Speaking of lowlifes, we first meet our 'hero', Benny (Warren O.), plinking the ivories at a touristy piano bar, when two American hitmen size him up for information on their prey. Soon Benny buys his own machete and heads for Garcia – the joke being that the guy is already dead – all Benny has to do is dig him up and take a little off the top. Crossing the backroads in a battered red convertible with his main squeeze (Isela Vega) by his side, the first half of the movie is the set-up for the weirdness and violence to come – a weather-beaten love story that climaxes at Garcia's fresh grave. The last 45 minutes is a dark and brooding mindroaster, with Oates nearly going mad from revenge and greed, after pulling himself from a premature grave. HE begins rambling to himself, or just talking to The Head, which he lugs around in a bloody cheesecloth sack – flies buzzing hotly around the rotted flesh. The whole ending is so pervasively nihilistic that it's almost funny, even though it oozes with double crosses and death. And Sam P. pulls off a finale that's disturbing, nasty, and yes, even poetic. Wow! If I had a hat, I'd tip it to him... Warren Oates is amazing as the ever-sunglassed Benny, and next to James Woods, he's the finest tough-talking, no nonsense, lying son of a bitch in recent memory. Between this film, Monte Hellman's **Two Lane Blacktop** and Thomas McGuane's **92 in the Shade**, Oates should have been a major star, but instead he just kept staring in drive-in drivel (**Drum**) or playing second banana (**Stripes**). Too bad! The eclectic supporting cast includes Gig Young and Robert Webber as the pair of US shooters – men so tough they'll elbow-bash a whore in the face just for touching 'em. Peckin-pal Kris Kristofferson pops up as a 'friendly' biker who roughs up Oates. "You are definitely on my shit list," says Warren, before ventilating Kris' gut. And as in most Peckinpah films, the female characters are abused throughout, though Isela Vega manages to maintain a modicum of sympathy (when she isn't being treated like a slab of meat)... It's a film as rancid and blood-caked as the title head (in addition to being easier to stuff into your VCR). Peckinpah's best! Period. Accept no substitutions.

BROTHERHOOD OF DEATH

BILL BERRY 1976. This relative latecomer from the '70s blaxploitation craze delivers the 42nd St. goods, and it even sports a *bit* more depth than usual. Under all its piss poor acting and technical sloppiness, there lurks an effective actioner which peripherally tackles a few racial issues (imagine **Mississippi Burning** if Fred Williamson had starred). Yes, it's Deep South Dipshit time again, with a small band of blacks pitted against every backwoods cracker in Dixie. The story begins in the late '60s, during the days of L.B.J. and Vietnam – where we meet a trio of black foot soldiers (led by Roy Jefferson as Raymond). During their combat against the VC they get a taste of 'sick-assed' warfare, plus expertise with booby traps, night fighting and commando chicanery. Yet despite their wartime success, when these heroes return home they discover *nothing* has changed. Every white pinhead in town is still a dirt ignorant redneck and a jacket laden with military medals

crackles across the sky, the grass over the grave flops open, and a bare-chested oriental extra leaps out of the hole, ready for kung fu combat... Unfortunately, after the laughter dies down, you realise there's a film attached to this opening scene – in fact, it's a film that has absolutely *nothing* to do with Bruce Lee *or* this prologue. And worst of all, this schlocky-chopsocky is *BORING!*... Our dime-store hero, Bruce *Lea*, is a kung fu instructor who sets out to avenge a fellow instructor's suspicious demise. Subplots appear mysteriously and disappear without a trace, and a lot of time is spent on a pointless love interest with some scantily-clad anglo-chick. There's a few horribly-edited fight scenes at the very end (but they all cut off just as it starts getting violent), the good guy wins, the bad guys lose, and the white bitch gets a ricochet bullet through the heart. (Oh, did I just give away the ending? Now you have no reason to rent this shitty film... No need to thank me.) Badly directed, badly photographed, *horribly* dubbed (when was the last time you heard Asian actors trying to do Southern drawls?), and as dull as watching the cable Weather Channel for 90 minutes... R-rated, but I have no idea why. The celluloid equivalent of rabies shots, avoid it at *all* costs. (Directed by Umberto Lenzi under the alias Doo Yong Lee.)

A BUCKET OF BLOOD

ROGER CORMAN 1959. This film begins with the line "I will talk to you of Art." Well, this *is* one of my all-time favourite films, but let's not go overboard. This five-day wonder has been overshadowed in recent years by another Roger Corman/Charles B. Griffith comedy/horror collaboration, **Little Shop of Horrors**, but this movie is the darker side of the duo. It's a quickly-shot, low-budget satire about creativity, acceptance, love, and murder! There aren't as many cheap jokes as there are in **LSOH** and its unsettlingly downbeat tone makes it a harder sell, but I think the end result is one of Corman's best. Plus it gives Dick Miller the role of his career. (Yeah, I know he's the current darling of B-movie fans, but he's actually GOOD in this film)... Miller takes top billing as Walter Paisley, a downtrodden busboy at the local beatnik-filled coffee-house, The Yellow Door. While the temperamental artistes read their poetry and argue about life ("...to the uncreative, you might as well be in your grave. Or in the Army."), poor Walter has to clean up their empty cups and endure their ridicule. When he's alone in his apartment, shy Walter pulls out the modelling clay and tries to emulate his idols, but it's no use – the guy's a talentless bumbler extraordinaire, squeezing his lump of clay into even lumpier shapes while ordering it to "Be a nose!" But one day, just by luck, a neighbour's cat gets stuck inside a wall of his apartment and

doesn't mean shit to 'em. The violence starts when a pack of beer-bloated bigots rape a black girl, but instead of the usual homeboy retaliation (i.e. kicking whitey in the butt till his asshole comes out the other end), Raymond decides to fight back from *within* the system – registering the black citizens of the county to vote, in hopes of getting their own political candidates into the local offices. Soon he's got busloads lined up outside the registration centre and Mr. White Trash starts getting worried about losing their meal ticket, so they call in the friendly neighbourhood Ku Klux Klan to stop these obstreperous coloured folks. And it quickly leads to one burnt Baptist church, one bullet-riddled Brother, an assassinated 'nigger lover' sheriff, and a virtual take-over of town. Luckily, Raymond and his Nam pals have that jungle warfare experience to fall back on, and you'll be cheering as the white-sheeted worm-bags drop like flies during a southern fried fire fight! Yeah!... Considering its solid storyline, I only wish the actual filmmaking had been tighter. The actors (many of them off-season gridironers) are uniformly atrocious, the dialogue is banal and the characters go largely unexplored. At least they utilise their rural locations well. The violence and blood-thirstiness are downplayed, but then again, I'll gladly take a substantial story over fake plasma any day. Directed by Bill Berry, this is a blunt crowd pleaser that goes for the gut without skimping over the brainpan. Besides, in an era when a former Klansman/white supremacist/dickwad like David Duke can still get elected to public office, *any* film where the KKK gets their collected heads battered into pulpy matter is A-OK in *my* book. Right on!

BRUCE LEE FIGHTS BACK
FROM THE GRAVE

DOO YONG LEE 1978. First things first. This movie wins the award for Best First 15 Seconds of Any Film This Decade! It opens in an ordinary graveyard, except that there's a cardboard tombstone stuck in the middle of it, with the words BRUCE LEE, 1940-1973 stencilled on it in big red, block letters. Suddenly, a bolt of lightning

Walter accidentally stabs and kills the feline while trying to chop it out. Never one to waste a golden opportunity, Walter covers the carcass (complete with the knife still in its side) with clay, titles it 'Dead Cat' and gets his 'artwork' exhibited at the coffee-house. The owner is unimpressed ("Yeah, you're a real artist. Now go in back and scrub out those garbage cans."), but the cretin critics start raving about this new-found genius. And while the females are flocking to him ("Take me away to some cool blue place, and gas me," offers one chick), Walter is solely obsessed with winning the woman of his dreams, Carla (Barboura Morris). With his instant fame, Walter's ego takes on superhuman proportions, and he acquires a black beret, cigarette holder, paisley cravat, and a crazed notion that he really *is* a talented sculptor. His long-time fantasy becomes twisted reality, and when his adoring public demands more works of art from him, Walter ends up using human subjects next. To the film's considerable credit, even when he's going off the deep end and killing for his Art, sympathy is etched into Miller's role. He's an innocent in a world of pretensions, and on the route to fit in, he takes the fork in the road labelled 'Murder' (pretty deep, eh?) – An Everyman who destroys himself in order to obtain the woman he desires. But this black-and-whiter isn't all gloom and depression. One highlight is seeing Bert Convy (as an undercover narc) getting a griddle in the skull and becoming Walter's latest masterpiece 'Murdered Man'. Plus there's constant hilarity at the expense of the Beat Generation – jokes about organic food, bad folk music and hip cat dialogue that'll make you choke on your espresso. Best of all, Julian Burton is a standout as the reigning King of Cool, Maxwell H. Brock. His poetry is the grooviest: "Life is an obscure hobo bumming a ride on the omnibus of Art... Burn gas buggies and whip your sour cream of circumstance and hope... Creation is. All else is not. What is not creative is graham crackers. Let it all crumble to feed the creative." Far out!... Got the point yet? **Bucket** is an often brilliant mix of horror-schlockola, beat comedy and touching character study. Four stars!

BUCKTOWN

ARTHUR MARKS 1975. Welcome to Redneckville, USA, where an innocent black man can get his skull drop-kicked down the block anytime the white population feels like it. But with a blaxplosive cast like Fred Williamson, Pam Grier, Thalmus Rasulala, and even Carl Weathers (who gets to upside a few whiteys with a baseball bat), you *know* things are gonna change... Williamson stars as Duke, who pulls into town with his leather threads to attend his brother's funeral. Cynical Ms. Grier is the town's top-heavy tootsie (as well as Duke's brother's old squeeze), and she simply considers Fred "another jive-ass city spook". But Freddy decides to stick around and search for his bro's killer – reopening the Club Alabama, butting knuckles with the honky goon squad, and grabbing a quick gorilla-in-the-washing-machine with Pam... He's a fighter. He's a lover. He's a one-note actor, but Williamson is the perfect action star. Even in a film this silly, he manages to keep a straight face while he's beating everyone to a pulp. Eventually he calls on his old friends, and a posse of Mean Inner-City Homeboys heads to the rescue, whose main joy in life is cracking open some serious white skin. But after this imported muscle kills off the opposition, they turn out to be just as greedy a bunch of swine as the crackers were, by continuing the same type of penny-ante extortion, terrorism and murder. What's Fred gonna do? That's a silly question – he's going to light up another foot-long cheroot and kick some black ass! And dig this ending: Freddy breaks into a local armoury and 'borrows' a fucking tank! Just watching The Hammer driving a tank through the sheriff's office is worth the price of admission alone, not to mention the long, excessively brutal (just the way I like 'em) punch-out that caps it all off... It's an obvious, by-the-numbers blaxploiter, but the great cast helps pull it

off. It's too bad though, that after powerhousing the screen in **Foxy Brown** and **Coffy**, Pam has to play second-fiddle to Williamson's macho-shit routine. This film also has the most offensive line-up of stereotypes (both black and white) I've seen in some time. And what a string of racial insults we get to endure! Blandly directed by Arthur Marks (**Friday Foster**), it's adequate ghettoplex entertainment. Nothing special though.

BUMMER!

WILLIAM ALLEN CASTLEMAN 1973. What's it like to be a rock 'n' roll groupie? Well, if this phoney baloney tale is any indication, it's like being trapped in a dim-witted, boring movie... It has some good, schlocky credentials to back it up, but to no avail. Producer David F. Friedman broke new ground in gore with H.G. Lewis in the '60s, with **Blood Feast**, **2000 Maniacs** and **Color Me Blood Red** – and by 1970 he had teamed up with William Allen Castleman for classic sexploit-shit like **Trader Hornee** and **Thar She Blows**. But Friedman and Castleman farted out a real window-rattler with **Bummer!** (with Castleman picking up overtime as the so-called 'director'), an outlandish attempt to leech onto the Rock 'n' Roll Bandwagon without knowing a thing about music... The Group is the name of an (inexplicably) popular California band, who 'trip around' and have 'groovy' times on the road. They even have a trio of groupies to keep 'em amused – there's a pretty, rich blond, Barbara (Connie Strickland), and two aspiring actresses in search of kicks, Dolly and Janyce. Looking for bad melodrama? Well, you can stop searching. Everyone within camera-range is chock full of clichéd hang-ups. The drummer, Gary, doesn't have the nerve to tell the rest of the band that he's in love with Barbara (a real faux pas, since it disrupts the band/groupie caste system). Duke (Kipp Wittman), the lead singer, is still sweet on his ex-wife, but learns to care for Dolly because down-deep she's such a nice wholesome kid who sucks dick. Worst of all, the fat ass bassist, Butts (Dennis Burkley) is the obvious, drunken shithead of the bunch – ordering the groupies to "strip, bitch", before forcing them into a lesbian shower scene while he blubbers incoherently and plays with himself on the toilet seat. The first half goes nowhere slowly, with unlikeable characters and rambling narrative. The second half gets a little grimmer (but no better) when Butts rapes a girl after a show

You Don't Have to Assault a Groupie... You Just Have to Ask..!

BUMMER!

A FAR OUT TRIP THRU A HARD ROCK TUNNEL

and they lose their gig. So the vanful of unemployed musicians head to the mountains for some R&R, inviting the gals along for woodland whoopee. Poor lardo Butts doesn't have a groupie to abuse though, so he gets drunker and ornery-er, until he turns into the Psycho Fat Boy of the Forest. And as the title promises, the ending is a severe bummer of bloodshed, bathos and blunt ragging on their moral turpitude... I'm not sure who this flick was supposed to appeal to: It's too restrained (despite sporadic nudity) for the sexploitation crowd. It's not pathetically hilarious enough to become a modern **Reefer Madness**-style camp relic. And it's simply too grating to be enjoyed by anyone – there's even a tacky musical-montage with all the couples kissin' and huggin' and strippin', while some sappy love song bleats in the background. It's the pits. One vomit scene does not a schlock film make.

C.C. AND COMPANY

SEYMOUR ROBBIE 1970. Sooner or later, we had to get to this howler. It's one of the most wrongheaded biker movies ever created! How could it possibly be worse than **The Mini-Skirt Mob**, **Pink Angels** or Brad Grinter's **Devil Rider**, you might wonder? First, how about casting Joe Namath and Ann-Margret in the leads? Whose idiotic idea was this? And why didn't they hire Pat Boone too, while they were at it, just to completely fuck up the movie? The worst part is that the producers had enough cash to finance a relatively vile li'l spitkicker, but instead spent their budget trying to make Joe Namath into an action hero (which is next to impossible since 'Broadway Joe' looks about as tough and menacing as the Pilsbury Doughboy). Namath pokes his dorky face and gratingly dumbshit persona into the role of C.C., a member of the grime-crusted chopper gang The Heads, whose constituents have names like Pig, Crow, Lizard, and Zit Zit. Internal tensions erupt when Joe and his pals find fashionable Ann-Margret and her broken down limo in the middle of the desert. When fellow riders Sid Haig and Greg Mullavey try to rape her, Good Ol' Joe saves her photogenic ass (for himself), and even takes up dirt bike racing in order to impress her. Of course, The Heads' leader, Moon (the gloriously vile William Smith), gets P.O.'ed at C.C.'s all-too-respectable behaviour, so he whips Namath into Geek Dip. And instead of revelling in rumbles, drug-drenched orgies and morally unacceptable bloodshed (*all* the necessary elements of a good bikerama), all we get is Joe's intellectual dissatisfaction with his fightin' and whorin' companions. In camera-bug Ms. Margret he's found a more expensive filet of fish, so he ditches his gang for the weekend, and journeys with A-M to – are you ready for this nonsense? – the 'Fabulous Flamingo Hotel' in Las Vegas, where the two dance, discuss the possibilities in life and roll on the carpet (discreetly naked). Then, during a 'happily-in-love' montage, Ann gets to sing! NO! *Fast Forward!* Phew, the things I have to endure in the name of film criticism... It's hard not to grimace every time Namath steps onto the screen. And I don't even want to mention Wayne Cochran, who makes a night-club appearance looking like an albino Gucci Tonto. By the end, when Joe and A-M ride off together into the night, you'll be so sick of this crap that you'll want to shove a fork into director Seymour ('Never let him near a camera again') Robbie's eye. At least the always despicable William Smith salivates with a vengeance and keeps a glimmer of disgustion glowing throughout, as does most of the good (if wasted) supporting cast. The writer (Ann's hubby, Roger Smith) must've studied up on cycle films before spewing out the script, because all the elements are present, but they've been so homogenised for the mass market that the movie never strikes *any* of the right chords. And would you believe that some critics were suckered in by this Hollywood bastardisation of a perfectly sleazy li'l sub-genre? Arthur Knight of the **Saturday Review** called it 'The **Ben Hur** of motorcycle pictures' (obviously someone dosed his Fresca during the screening).

CAFÉ FLESH

RINSE DREAM 1982. Most hardcore porno films are solid shit created for only two reasons: To get the viewer horny and to make the producers rich. Sure, some people might think there's some 'artistic value' to it all, but they're just kidding themselves as they flog their bishop... Of course, **Café Flesh** turns out to be the prime exception to everything I've just said. It's the best hardcore-X flick I've ever seen. In fact, it's more imaginative and thoughtfully conceived than many of the other movies in this book. Why? Probably because the filmmakers didn't *want* to make a porno film in the first place, and hoped that all the 'wet shots' would get dropped before it got to the public. The result is part science fiction, part performance art, and part fleshfest. Sure, it might've been even more effective without all the triple-X bits, but unlike similarly-rated rotgut, at least this time around there's a slim purpose for their inclusion... Set in the near future, when love is meaningless and sex is all, we're years after the Nuclear Kiss has left 99% of the population unable to have sex without retching. These Sex Negatives torture themselves with memories of the past by attending Café Flesh, a post-nuke night-club where Sex Positives perform for the audience's continual frustration. And these on-stage set pieces include some fabulously twisted fantasies (i.e. a housewife is raped by a milkman in a rat costume, while a trio of bibbed 'babies' pound their high chairs with bones). We also get the full, quite effective range of skin and genitals and groping and tonguing (but on the other hand, how many tines do you want to see a guy come on a woman's stomach?); and while most X-flicks look mechanical in the dipstick department, in this case, it's *supposed* to look choreographed; Director Rinse Dream (love that pseudonym!) keeps the gymnastics highly stylised and intentionally humorous, plus the film's technical edge is impeccable – great sets, creepy music, and stark neon-soaked cinematography by F.X. Pope... There are actually characters too! With dialogue! Plus (got those nitro-glycerine tablets ready?) semi-competent acting! Our host, Max Melodramatic (Andrew Nichols, doing a tremendous takeoff on **Cabaret**'s M.C.) ridicules the audience in-between Elvis and Brando imitations; Angel is a wide-eyed virgin from Wyoming on her first trip to the city; Nick and Lana (Pia Snow aka future Scream Queen Michelle Bauer) are a tenuous couple – he's a Negative, she's a closet Positive, and they're both desperately trying to cling to their corroding relationship; and then there's Johnny Rico, the King of the Dongs and the type of guy who's so cool he doesn't take off his sunglasses, even while eating out... The most unusual aspect though, is how blatantly abusive the whole endeavour is to the Raincoat Crowd which normally checks out X-flicks. Whenever there's a graphic scene, the editor cuts to the leering crowd (who all look like candidates for **Satyricon 2000**) and we realise *we're* just like these poor slobs in the Café audience. Filled with acidic dialogue, this is a vision of despair which could be easily interpreted as a metaphor for AIDS. Geesh, can you believe it? A cool, thought-provoking porno film, and perfect fare for a cult audience (which unfortunately, it never found).

CAGE

LANG ELLIOTT 1989. What do you look for in lowrent cinematic slop? How about 90-minutes of non-stop, gratuitous violence, with beefcake dimwits beating the bejesus out of each other? This flick promises all this and more, but doesn't deliver a fraction of the silliness found in other mano-a-mano romps like **Bloodsport**. Most annoyingly, the filmmakers ignore every opportunity for sleaziness, almost as if they were ashamed of it. Don't they realise the *only* reason to watch a movie this moronic is to see low-browed steroid cases pummelled unmercilessly. Is that too much to ask for? I guess so... It begins on an original note (just joking) with a Vietnam flashback. Lou Ferrigno stars as Billy, who's shot in the skull during the first minutes – the slug miraculously missing all that solid bone, lodging in his teeny-weeny brainpan, and giving him an IQ equal to most lunch boxes. Reb Brown (**Yor, The Hunter from the Future**... Will he ever live that flick down?) co-stars as Billy's loyal Army buddy. And though director Lang Elliott tries for heart-warming sentiment (barf), the sight of Big Lou reading Dr. Seuss is just too tacky to watch straight-faced. Besides, the Vietnam buddy routine was old hat a decade ago – now its got a half foot of mould growin' on it... The action picks up (barely) when two gangsters trick Billy into fighting for them in an illegal Steel Cage, Bare Knuckle, To-The-Death Tournament run by the oriental mob (headed by James Shigeta). These 'human cockfights' could've been a grabber, and indeed, Lou gets the shit pounded out of him for a couple short brawls, but the action keeps grinding to a halt whenever the cast (for some incomprehensible reason) decides to talk! Did I forget to mention that the film is also so racially offensive it makes **The Deer Hunter** look like a love poem to the Third World?... You get the picture. This is barely competent swill. Ouch!

THE CALIFORNIA REICH

WALTER F. PARKES / KEITH F. CRITCHLOW 1975. Which is the most repellent film in this entire book? You've found it! Not for gore, or sex, or general sleaze though – this film is a true, undiluted glimpse of American-bred hatred and intolerance that'll give you chills. For this hour-long documentary, directors Walter F. Parkes and Keith F. Critchlow somehow got their cameras inside the California contingent of the National Socialist White People's Party (fuckin' Nazis, to you and me) and gives us a look at this sick pack of fuckheads, on their own turf. Best of all, the film avoids easy knee-jerk shots by approaching The Movement dead seriously, and interviewing its subjects intelligently. It's all the scarier for trying to understand what brews their bullshit, instead of simply condemning it. There's no narration, and it doesn't need it, because the subjects dig their own hole eloquently enough. And though it's nauseating to watch these dirtbags wax their philosophy about an idyllic all-white America, it's also fascinating, in the same ghoulish way an auto fatality is... The film profiles a diverse handful of 'believers', most of whom are just mindless losers who're too stupid to solve their own problems, so they blame 'em on the Jews and Blacks. And though many fit into the Jesse Helms-style, chromosome-damaged redneck stereotype, others look like normal, suburban guys – self-proclaimed "decent, law-abiding white folk" who preach white supremacy and fear by warning women about getting "raped by gibbering He-Niggers". The leader of the San Francisco unit has a 20-year history of reform schools, jail and electroshock treatment, and though he tries to come off sympathetic and persecuted, he's just a paranoid pea brain. We also get to watch a family teaching their kids to 'Heil', while the li'l tykes brag about wanting to be policemen when they grow up so they can "kill niggers". Meanwhile, a housewife shows us how to make a Swastika symbol cake, and hubby shows off his automatic weapon collection. There's also an Army sergeant who openly solicits for The Party on base; a birthday party for Adolf Hitler; and wait until you see their idea of Christmas! There are Swastikas on the tree ornaments, Santa's got a Nazi armband, and you'd be laughing if it weren't all true... The filmmaking technique is klunky, but it never blunts the compelling subject matter. This is powerful, stomach-knotting reality, and the overall effect is like picking up a piece of food and finding maggots underneath.

CANE TOADS

MARK LEWIS 1988. From Australia comes a hour-long documentary which manages to find a wealth of humour in that continent's disastrous infestation of Cane Toads. The result is one of the weirdest true tales ever put to film... You see, in 1935, some Aussie 'geniuses' imported 102 innocent li'l Cane Toads (bufo marinus) from Hawaii to save the local sugar cane crop from grubs. The grubs quickly disappeared, but half a century later, with a reproduction rate of 60,000 eggs annually from each female, the Cane Toads have virtually taken over North Queensland. They're everywhere, and nothing seems to halt 'em! Director Mark Lewis mixes a Toad's Eye View of their lifestyle (eating habits, mating habits, et cetera) along with human interviews from a broad spectrum of obsessive Toad-o-philes, including toad lovers (who keep them as lumpy house pets), toad haters (who purposely swerve back and forth across the highway in order to squish them) and even toad junkies (who smoke toad secretions in order to "see consciousness through the eyes of the toad"). And one of my favourite images is the toadskin book given to Prince Charles and Diana as a wedding present. Packed with information and belly laughs, we observe human attempts to build a town monument to the creature; listen to local folk songs (such as 'The Cane Toad Blues'); and even get a taste of toad necrophilia, when a male mounts a *very* tire-flattened member of the opposite sex, rotting in the centre of the road, and takes up residence on top of her for six full hours... Like **Roger and Me**, much of the humour is at the expense of the film's dim-witted humans, and without a doubt this is the **Spinal Tap** of ecological disaster documentaries. Just as hilarious, but in this case all too true. A favourite!

CANNIBAL APOCALYPSE

ANTHONY DAWSON 1982 (US: INVASION OF THE FLESH HUNTERS; AKA: CANNIBALS IN THE STREETS). Now that Vietnam sagas are hot shit again, let's move onto a blood-caked, horror-filled, Nam-a-rama from director Anthony Dawson (Antonio Margheriti). And if you couldn't guess, this is another Italian gut-cruncher cannibal-fest, and a mediocre one at that, but it *does* have an interesting concept (sorta like, 'What if George Romero directed **Coming Home**?'). John Saxon, who's slowly vying for the title King of the Z-Movie, with credits like **Nightmare on Elm St.**, **Blood Beach**, and **Battle Beyond the Stars**, stars in another gung-ho non-part, as he takes on the armies of the undead while fending off the overweight neighbourhood nymphet... In the Vietnam-based prologue, a bunch of American soldiers, led by John S., end up Mi Lai-ing a village of miniature Ho Chi Min's. There they discover a pair of MIA's who, unbeknownst to their rescuers, have contracted a rabies-like disease which makes them crave the taste of flesh – *human* flesh, that is! Suddenly, 10 years later, a crazy vet (named Charles Bukowski, nudge, nudge) goes on a rampage, beats up a motorcycle gang, and chomps down on a woman's throat for a quick between-meals snack... Can he be stopped? (Maybe)... Are there more vets like him? (You betcha!)... Is John S. *himself* infected? (Let's hope so)... And what happens to the people they bite? (As per the Official Zombie Guidebook, the victims turn into flesh-eaters, too – biting out tongues and smashing the skulls of every extra within arm's-length)... Unlike Romero's hordes, though, these guys could pass for normal, except that they take an occasional nibble out of their neighbour. The movie's slow going for a while, but it picks up during a chase through the sewers, with rats crawling up the vets' legs, cops with flame-throwers in their path, and lots of stinky water to wade in. Plus, there's a short, but grim finale and a so-called 'surprise' ending to cap it off. But even though **Cannibal Apocalypse** has its fair share of dumb action and Saxon's one-dimensional presence, the whole package is fairly routine – the gore is relatively tame for an '80s Meat-Ripper (it was edited for American release) and the dubbing (*horrible* Italian actors with *terrible* American voice-overs) is particularly pathetic this time around... Oh well, I guess I've just come to expect more brain-cringing sickness from the Italian gore industry. In fact, the trailer at the end of the video, for **Night of the Zombies**, has *five times* the violence packed into its *two minutes*. Maybe I'll rent that one next time.

CANNIBAL HOOKERS

DONALD FARMER 1987. This raunchfest has all the trademarks of a quick 'n' dirty video feature: from the bleached out colour and home-shot fuzziness, to the tinny sound and all-amateur cast. But writer/director Donald Farmer certainly knows how to pour on the Karo Syrup and keep the vilest viewer amused. There's absolutely no time wasted here; the first five minutes we're greeted with a heart-warming sequence in which a kill crazy prostitute lures a man to a hotel room, steps on his face with her boots, shows off her flat chest, and then chops the john up with an axe. Then Lobo (a manservant who makes Tor Johnson look like Miss Manners) disposes of the cadaver while showcasing his stream of bloody spittle... Meanwhile, on the 'nice' side of the tracks, Amy Waddell and Annette Munro star as two annoying sorority pledges who discover cheap(ly-produced) thrills when the bleached-bitch leader of Gamma Zeta Beta (politely nicknamed 'The Pig Fucking Sorority') gives them a seedy initiation prank – to pose as hookers and pick up a trick on Hollywood Boulevard. So, bedecked in leather slut-ware, the tawdry teens take to the streets and eventually end up at a very unorthodox whorehouse, populated by a makeshift family of the title tarts, who begin by knocking off the co-eds' geeky boyfriends. Some dazzling plot, eh? Personally, I think these filmmakers were less interested in a solid script than they were in having nubile actresses in sleazy lingerie lick raw entrails for the camera. There's more skin than scares on display, with a femme supporting cast that's willing to squeeze into the trashiest fashions or strip at the drop of a sawbuck. Painfully chintzy, but not much worse than most other sex 'n' gore flicks that make it to home video with the aid of a lurid (and often completely fabricated) cover. And I've got to give Farmer credit for getting it made and in the marketplace, unlike so many people who talk 'til you're sick with no results whatsoever on the shelves... Outside of some obvious exploitation-film references, good location footage of California night life and a special appearance by Eric Caidin in his Hollywood Book and Poster Company milieu, this is your basic home-brewed blood bath. A no-budget sleaze-pageant that wallows in depravity and panders to vidiots who sit home every night whacking their bishop (and to these fringe filmmakers, that last line might just be a compliment).

CAPTIVE

PAUL MAYERSBERG 1987. Long-time Nicolas (God) Roeg collaborator Paul Mayersberg directs his first foray into the world of erotic surreality, kind of Patty Hearst meets Owsley in the pages of **The Face**. Irina Brook plays a hopelessly well-off gal who is sheltered by her dad, played by a hopelessly well-paid Oliver Reed. She is then kidnapped by several fashion models, earnestly trying to act. They wear cute baggy sweaters and say things like "Don't be ridic!" When Patty asks if they want money, they reply "we *are* money". They hang her upside down until she decides to join in and wear baggy sweaters too. Now, believe it or not I *liked* this movie. Not many directors have the guts to be pretentious and obscure, and Mayersberg does both with ease. Of course the acting is on a par with a Benetton commercial (the sweater influence), but the set-ups are imaginative, the score by Michael Brook is great, and booze-addled Oliver makes a solid effort to stand upright. A friend suggested to me that liking bad arty movies is really the same as liking cheap sleaze movies. Well, it's time for a regular column on PRETENTIOUS ARTY CRAP, and **Captive** is a worthy entry in the field. [TR]

THEY IMPRISONED HER BODY, BUT FREED HER MIND.

"MOVIES LIKE 'CAPTIVE' ARE AS RARE AS PEACOCK'S TEETH." —Vincent Canby, New York Times

OLIVER REED   IRINA BROOK
CAPTIVE

CARNIVAL OF SOULS

HERK HARVEY 1962. After walking away from a car accident in which she was the only survivor, a young woman begins hearing strange voices and seeing spooky white-faced persons who appear wherever she goes. This constant lack of privacy starts getting to her head, especially since she can see and hear these eerie ghost-like figures and no one else can. Don't be fooled by the almost non-existent budget and a cast of no-names; this is actually a nice little work of quiet horror, an effective, genuinely creepy little film that may leave one feeling slightly uncomfortable afterwards. If you're looking for projectile puke and quivering guts, this ain't gonna be your cup of tea, but it deserves mention, at least, for the fact that you don't necessarily need a zillion bucks and a pack of drooling, cash-hungry investors to put on a good horror show. By all means, check it out. [BJE]

CATCH US IF YOU CAN

JOHN BOORMAN 1965 (AKA: HAVING A WILD WEEKEND). John Boorman certainly is an eclectic director, and his scattershot career has given him a reputation as visionary as Kubrick, yet as half-baked as Ed Wood Jr. From commercial successes like **The Emerald Forest** and **Excalibur**, to the fantastically muddled **Zardoz** and the wondrously crafted, conceptually dense and absolutely asinine **Exorcist II: The Heretic**... But Boorman's first excursion into commercial filmmaking was this frantic musical comedy, featuring a wacky young-rock band on a romp through mod London. Obviously, the studio thought they were getting a quick knock-off of **A Hard Day's Night**, but instead of the charismatic Beatles, poor Boorman was stuck with the dreary likes of The Dave Clark Five! So he went a different route, by lacing the tale with cynicism as well as a groovy, pop style. From the opening sequence on, Boorman blows away Richard Lester in terms of editing, camerawork and composition, plus it sports a much darker edge. Too bad it never really connects with the funny bone. And it might've been helpful if The Dave Clark Five had more than one memorable song to their credit ('Catch Us If You Can'), since this *does* claim to be a musical... The kick-ass beginning has 'The Boys' waking up to another typical day. After a bouncy tour of their abode (complete with removable staircases, trampolines, and a steam organ alarm clock), the interchangeable quintet slip into some hip attire and head off to their jobs as professional 'stunt boys' with severe cases of Saint Vitus Dance. Barbara Ferris co-stars as the desirable 'Meat For Go!' girl, whose youthful smile livens up London adverts for beef, and who joins lead singer Steve (Dave Clark) on a virtual travelogue of the city. Sometimes the satirical episodes are razor-sharp (with takeoffs of snooty ad-men and upper-crust wife swappers), and at others it's deadening (you'll want to hit the fridge and the loo when the romantic horseback riding begins). The script by Peter Nichols is scattershot, but luckily, Boorman has style flowing from every orifice – effortlessly shifting into high gear for a groovy party (with guests literally swinging from the ceiling); or suddenly exposing the true **Withnail**-esque underbelly of the hipsters' movement, with an unheated community of penniless longhairs asking for pot or 'horse'. Boorman's lens lingers on fascinating details, and its darker tone puts the film close to the **O Lucky Man** school of caustic cinema. It even has a statement on The Five's own commercialisation (shades of **Head**!)... This is a good, uneven, under-seen film. Not much solid plot and chock full of tiny faults, but very cool in its vision.

CHAINED FOR LIFE

HARRY L. FRASER 1950. This 'tragic story' from the '50s poses the unique question: what happens when one Siamese twin sister is accused of murder, and the other is obviously innocent? The tale would be odd enough if two separate actresses in one Jean Hill-sized dress were to star, but these anything-for-a-quick-buck producers hired *real* Siamese twins, Violet and Daisy Hilton, to star as The Hamilton Sisters. Then director Harry L. Fraser missed his opportunity for a so-tacky-it's-terrific classic by opting for a workman-like pot-boiler. First you'll wanna laugh. Then you'll wince. And before long you'll be as bored as I, because even though this flick is a solid contribution to Exploit Physical Handicaps Cinema, it's never as continually odd as **Terror of Tiny Town** or as ball-bustingly diseased as **The Crippled Masters**... For this somnambulistic back-stage drama, the brunette-and-blond Siamese sisters play famous singing stars who are suckered into a marriage scam by a slimy con man – with one sis marrying gigolo Andre (Mario Laval). Complications ensue (as they always do) when blond twin Dorothy actually falls for the fast-talking, immoral Romeo, while Andre's beautiful assistant/paramour Renee gets jealous. And these C-level soap-operatics lead to generous helpings of murder, courtroom shenanigans, sappy sympathy-wringing, and even a kindly blind minister who gives the sisters the faith to go on (instead of having a Doc hack 'em apart)... Though only 65 minutes long, it's padded with excruciating tunes sung by the tone-deaf twins and seedy burlesque acts who've had their mediocrity immortalised on celluloid. And you *know* you're in trouble when the most memorable section of a movie is an accordion solo. Recommended for the terminally curious only.

CHAINED HEAT (1983)
SAVAGE STREETS (1984)

Every good schlock-o-phile knows Linda Blair all too well, right? Well, I'd like to take the time to officially nominate her as Worst Drive-In Actress of the '80s. Period. Sure, lots of other contenders come to mind for that dubious title, but after re-watching Linda's two 'big' hits in one sitting, I'm positive that no other performer in recent memory has the complete and utter lack of acting ability and emotional diversity... After her initial success in the early '70s at vomiting bile in **The Exorcist** and being turned into a shower-room-popsicle in the TV movie **Born Innocent**, Linda's career went straight into the crapper. In 1979, she starred in her first genuine shit-movie, Mark L. Lester's **Roller Boogie**, which unsuccessfully tried to mould her into the Annette Funicello of the disco era, by stuffing the now-chunky Miss Blair into a silver lamé swimsuit. Ugh! It was a worthless piece of crap, unless you get turned on by roller skating heifers... Well, after trying the Jamie Lee Curtis route with the utterly-predictable **Hell Night** in 1981, Linda signed up for the lead in a two-bit exploitation project called **Chained Heat** – and little did she realise it was to become one of the forerunners in the '80s resurgence of slammer-slut flicks. Even though Linda *hated* the final product for its unredeeming sleaziness, this is nevertheless the film that helped put her career back in the black. It's not even a very *good* Broads-in-Bondage movie (it doesn't hold a candle next to director Paul Nicholas' follow-up, **The Naked Cage**), but it certainly comes across with the rancid goods. The supporting cast alone is a roll call of grindhouse faves: John Vernon, Sybil Danning, Tamera Dobson, Henry Silva, Edy Williams, and Louisa Moritz – the entire Executive Branch of Scenery Chewers Inc.! But what these bozos lack in talent, they make up for in nasty tempers and the willingness to spit up their dignity in the face of a hefty paycheque. So get ready for face-slashings, razor-attacks, chain-whippings, nightstick-beatings, and of course, the obligatory shower scene (once again proving that female prisoners are the cleanest persons in the whole wide world). And thankfully, director Nicholas had chubbette Blair keep her clothes on most of the time – a good idea since Linda was *solidly* entrenched in the Ultra-Babyfat Zone... Story-wise, our maximum security heroine stars as Carol, the 'new fish' in the cell-block – a first-time offender who quickly discovers that the guards are crooked, the cons are murderous and the warden is an ol' scumbag lecher. The rest is your standard black cons vs. white cons battle, complete with a drug war and concluding prison riot. Sybil plays the reigning Queen of the Dykes, leading a pack of hardened inmates who never take the time to button their blouses properly; John Vernon is the coke-snorting warden, who enjoys nude Jacuzzis with his prisoners, which he videotapes ("Don't call me Warden! Call me Fellini!" he bellows); and Stella Stevens is the head guard, who rents out her sexier wards to a local pimp. All of the co-stars look like they were having a ball, but Miss Blair is so wooden and passive that I swear she must've been stuffing valiums down her throat like they were chocolate bars. What does it take to put some energy into her performance? Electroshock treatments?... Overall, **Chained Heat** is strictly by-the-numbers trash, but what it may lack in originality and hardcore violence, it certainly makes up for in its sincere sleazeball intentions. There's enough scenes of women beating the piss out of each other to satisfy any drive-in smuthead, plus, if you get bored with the story you can pass the time counting how often the boom microphone can be seen... A year later, Linda struck back with **Savage Streets**, a run-of-the-mill revenge piece directed by Danny Steinmann (who would later bless theatre screens with **Friday the 13th: A New Beginning**). This time around, the not-at-all versatile Miss Blair plays a cool street-chick, who's first seen struttin' down the boulevard with her entourage of painted up slutmeat – and for almost a half-minute you sorta believe Linda's portrayal of a vacuous, 23-year-old high school bimbo. But complications arise when a carload of leathered thugs nearly runs down Blair's deaf-and-dumb sister and sets the creaky gears of the storyline in motion. It's gang war time, folks, and one gratuitously protracted gang-rape later, Linda and her cohorts hit the streets in search of blood, with Linda equipping herself with bear traps, a crossbow and a black leather jump-suit that makes her the tops in Vigilante Chic. Since the villains are such vile, perverted, stock characters (not to mention how atrocious their acting is), we'd like to see them all die slowly *and* painfully. We're ready for some *solid* suffering and veins-in-my-teeth vengeance, like at the end of **Last House on the Left**, but director Steinmann shies away from any extreme, graphic violence (shucks!), so that when a guy falls into an awaiting bear trap, we only *hear* the gurgling noises he makes... basically, this film shrivels up at the moment of truth, and even Blair turns out to be half-wimpy – what she needs is a lesson from Robbie Lee in **Switchblade Sisters**. Plus, there's plenty of stupid high-school hi-jinx padding out the running time, such as fighting with the local rich-bitch princess, pulling pranks on the teachers and even getting expelled from school. You get the feeling this movie doesn't know whether it wants to be **Death Wish** or **Rock 'n' Roll High School**. The supporting cast includes (once again) John Vernon, who tags along in a tiny role as the h.s. principal and grabs second billing for his marquee value (?) alone; and Linnea Quigley smiles blithely, wears a cute ponytail, and has her cherry repeatedly popped, as Linda's wide-eyed, innocent li'l sister, Heather. Once again, Linda is in wide-screen format, and Steinmann keeps her in baggy clothes or shoots her from the chest-up most of the time, so the entire audience doesn't shout 'Whoa! She's put on a ton!' in unison. Complete with painful 'music' by John Farnham, **Savage Streets** is your basic, slick, pre-packaged filler that just doesn't cut it for the serious action freaks. There are some fun touches along the way, but Miss Blair is particularly pathetic (especially when she tries to play a tough cookie). After sitting through both of these pooped-out programmers, I think you'll agree Linda Blair is so naturally one-dimensional that she's the ultimate drive-in personality... And if you can believe it, since this duo first appeared she's churned out even worse sewage, like **Savage Island** (the castrated US version of **Escape**), Jackie Kong's putrid **Night Patrol** and the Yugoslavian-made **Red Heat** with Sylvia Kristel. In 1987, she did **Nightforce** with Cam Mitchell and Richard Lynch – a lame jungle-rescue in which Linda gets to show off a trimmed-down figure. But since she's paired with scene-stealing Claudia Udy (who tends to take long showers, and spends most of the film stripped naked and locked in a bamboo cage), Blair still comes off with as much sex appeal as a slab of meatloaf... All of her roles are virtually interchangeable, and though I doubt Linda will ever make a really *good* film again, I'll still keep tabs on her bumpy career. She's a schlock magnet! Where garbage goes, she follows.

CHERRY 2000

STEVE DE JARNATT 1986. Melanie Griffith is a mega-buck hotshot nowadays, after **Working Girl**, **Something Wild** and various Tinsel-town turds. So let's take a peek at a past project she'd rather sweep under the carpet, that collected cobwebs in Orion's cold storage for two years before getting released to video. The first problem might be with the title, which makes the flick sound sus-piciously like a porno/sci-fi combo (sort of like Al Adamson's **Cin-derella 2000**). The second problem is that the entire film reeks of recycling! It's a dumb disaster that clunkily mixes **Westworld** with **Mad Max**, and is only made *barely* watchable by Griffith's appear-ance. Not as bad as utterly wrongheaded mindpus like **Solarba-bies**, but it's close... Pamela Gidley co-stars as Cherry 2000, the near-future's computerised, domestic sex toy. But when her yuppie 'hubby', Sam (David Andrews), gets frisky and tries to schtupp her

on the wet kitchen floor, she shorts out – so this card carrying member of Dickheads-Are-Us has to head into the desert to pick up a new model 2000. First he has to link up with Ms. Griffith, as a buckskin-wardrobed tracker with an orange Mustang and hair to match. The wilderness is filled with your standard population of grubby, violent marauders, and after a while it gets *worse* than idiotic, such as when Melanie and David stop in mid-escape in order to make out on the hood of her car. Will Sam find another robot to practice squat-thrusts on? Will Melanie teach Sam the true meaning of love? How many good supporting cast members (Ben Johnson, Brion Jarnes, Tim Thomerson) will be laid out by Michael Almereyda's lame script? And when a movie is *this* mediocre, do we even care?!... Male lead David Andrews has all the charisma of a sewer grating, and it doesn't help that his character is such a whiny shitbox. Melanie's flat role doesn't fare much better, but she tries her best to look sexy while firing off heavy artillery... All the more depressing since you can see so much cash wasted on this low-intelligence outing. This movie doesn't even cut it as exploita-tion material – it's strictly PG-13 all the way.

CHRISTMAS EVIL

LEWIS JACKSON 1980 (US: YOU BETTER WATCH OUT; AKA: TERROR IN TOY-LAND). Over the last few years, horror films have come under fire for their so-called potential to warp impressionable minds. The most infamous public outcry came years back during the release of **Silent Night, Deadly Night**, the routine kill-a-thon that had rabid parents and alarmist media-watchdogs picketing throughout the Yuletide season. But the most extraordinary variation on the psy-cho Santa theme is this low-budget gem, because it truly takes the Spirit of Christmas to the cleaners. With an unproven star and writer/director at the helm, the best that was expected was a competent, high concept schlockfest. Instead, director Lewis Jack-son pulls off a wonderfully unrelenting horror blend of **Miracle on 34th Street** and **Taxi Driver**, featuring a four-star performance by character actor Brandon Maggart. And where previous Xmas exer-cises in evil simply used the season as a selling gimmick, this flick tries to sympathetically explore the roots of madness, while showing how the holiday itself can further fuck up one's mind... As a small child, li'l Harry saw Santa Claus in flagrante delicto with his Mom, and Maggart (a pudgy-faced cross between Pee Wee Her-man and Norman Bates) is the grown-up result of the trauma. The guy's an abnormal psychologist's wet dream! He's completely obsessed with Santa Claus and the Christmas season, and though some of his activities don't seem *too* weird (keeping up Xmas decorations all year round), his voyeurism problem is a little ex-treme. You see, with a handy pair of binoculars, Harry watches all the neighbourhood kids in their bedrooms, while keeping tabs on who's naughty and nice in a bound, gold-trimmed volume. Most of the year Harry leads a normal (if lonely) life, heading an assembly line that makes Jolly Dream Toys. But this year, as December 25th approaches, he lugs out a sewing machine and begins crafting his own Santa suit. He doesn't plan on emulating the fat ol' geezer who ladles out the good cheer, though. His is a Santa who passes judgement on non-believers, and isn't afraid to dole out severe punishment. While the first half of the movie details Harry's grow-ing dementia, the second takes us along on his Christmas Eve excursion, posing as Kris Kringle. In one genuinely heart-warming sequence, Harry steals toys from his money-hungry employers and gives them all to a children's hospital; then in the following scene the tone twists 180 degrees when he takes a hatchet to a pack of hum-buggers. And unlike horror films that revel in cheap one-liners, this movie has the viewer chuckling from the absurd juxta-position of images and ideas. How could *you* not laugh when the police pull in a line-up of assorted Santas for ID-ing? Or when angry adults form a vigilante party to stop Harry, their own children protect poor 'Santa' from harm. But the most daring twist comes at the end, when the filmmakers boldly slice away the veil of realism and leave us wondering whether the final image is simply a delusion in Harry's sick mind, or an actual mad miracle... Despite obvious budgetary restrictions and a touch of amateurism behind the camera, director Jackson manages a complex glimpse of a confused loner who's pushed around by society, and who embraces the Santa mythos to empty his anger on those who deserve it. Maggart never resorts to cheap histrionics either – he keeps Harry's derangement more internalised, and in the long run, more effective. It's remarkably fine-tuned work for a film of this seemingly-grimy nature, and his performance is in a league with other classic horror whackos, such as Tom Basham's kid show host in **The Psychopath** and Terry O'Quinn in **The Stepfather**. Of course, all this brilliance is utterly wasted on audiences wanting nothing but splatter. The violence is quickly dispatched and any gore is minimal, but any viewer who gives the tale half a chance will discover a world of creepiness and despair... Though packaged with various lurid titles emphasising the body count, **Christmas Evil** is above all an original work. An under-seen, under-rated classic in off-centre lunacy that should darken any holiday festivities. Ho ho ho.

CIAO! MANHATTAN

JOHN PALMER / DAVID WEISMAN 1972. Edie Sedgwick was a top model and actress for a couple of years in the mid-'60s, part of Andy Warhol's cadre of non-stars – basically just famous for being on the right drugs at the right time in front of the right media. She is also the subject of this very interesting sort-of-autobiographical film about the defeat of decadence and malaise of people who obtain everything and retain nothing. Edie died three months after filming this little gem – called Susan in this film, though it looks like directors John Palmer and David Weissman just turned the camera on her and allowed her brain dead babble to etch itself into the celluloid. Edie's a west coast heiress who lives in a tent in a dried up

pool (can you say symbolism?), narcissistically surrounded by giant blow-ups of herself. Home after three years in a mental hospital, Edie runs her mouth incessantly about her past and takes off her clothes at every opportunity to expose her newly siliconed breasts ("She's sorta proud of them," explains Jeffrey, the male maid)... Around her story are hung a bevy of interesting characters. Our narrator is Butch, a simple but wise young kid from Texas who picks up Edie at the side of the road, naked and stumbling, and brings her home to her rich distracted Mom ("I don't have time to build a flying saucer... I have to go to work!") who's too busy building a pie-

shop empire to pay any attention to her daughter outside of sending her to the 'fabulous' Doctor Braun (Roger Vadim), who just fucks Edie and then gives her shock treatments. There's also the wisecracking manservant, Jeffrey, who's eager to leave this insane family and sees in Butch a chance to do so. Palmer and Weissman tell Sedgwick's sad tale through a series of flashbacks (actually footage from a 1967 Chuck Wein film starring Edie, Viva and Paul America, that was abandoned because of suicide attempts and overdoses) – We meet drug dealer Paul America, Edie's only true love, who begins her descent into brain death with speed and cocaine. We meet the elusive Mr. Verdecchio, a Mercedes-clad 'big wig' who watches all the goings-on of the world through television monitors., sending his electronix whiz and part-time drummer Tom (who bears a striking resemblance to Jesus Christ, get it?) to do his bidding. We meet Dr. Robert, fixing up his heroines with shots of vitamins and methedrine ("Robert's shots are better than cocaine!"). Things get really weird when they all meet at the opening of Dr. Robert's new health spa (the guests include Allen Ginsberg and Peter Orlovsky, naked and chanting), leading up to a telling conversation between Tom and Paul in jail, where they exchange keys, crosses and tears in a surprisingly touching moment. If all of this seems a bit scattered, it is – but Palmer and Weissman manage to turn this borderline muddle into the best film to come out of the Warhol era, taking what must have been a mish-mash of incoherent black & white fashion footage and incessant drug-damaged rambling, and turning them into a coherent criticism of the War Hole maxim. The old footage is expertly cut and redubbed, turning an unfinished hip spy thriller into inspired rhetoric concerning the helplessness of God. Palmer and Weissman never preach, merely allowing the pathetic-ness of Edie herself to make their statement about what *un*fame can do. Filled with symbolism from head to toe, Palmer and Weissman have created an **El Topo** for the 'now generation' – a coherent, interesting indictment of a personality that feeds upon itself. [SS]

CLASS OF 1999

MARK L. LESTER 1990. It's **Suburbia** meets **The Terminator** in Mark L. Lester's futuristic follow-up to his own sleaze pageant from a decade ago, **Class of 1984**. One half of the film is non-stop action; the other half is wedged tightly with a wonderful cast of celluloid has-beens and wannabees. What more could you ask for? (How about a less-than-$6 ticket price?) Though it loses all grip on reality, who really needs reality anyway? It's fast-paced, science fiction sludge with a great set-up and enough craziness to keep it consistently watchable... In the near future, the Department of Defence is called in to control the nation's deteriorating school system with a brilliant new plan of employing robot teachers in the classroom. These 'Tactical Education Units' look as real as their flesh and blood counterparts – but that isn't difficult when the humans are as pasty as Stacy Keach, who plays the unhinged official behind the machines. Phoning his role in from Venus, Stacy sports albino contact lenses, a grey pony tail, and a blow habit that keeps him stuck in this type of junk... The principal of Kennedy High School (Malcolm McDowell, who doesn't even *try* to act anymore) certainly has his share of discipline problems. Not many schools have a handgun checkpoint at the front door, storm troopers patrolling the hallways between classes, or a surrounding community that makes Alphabet City look like Park Avenue. So bring on the Battle Droids! There's Pam Grier (who's always a welcome sight) as the chem. teacher; musclehead Patrick Kilpatrick running the gym; and John P. Ryan (**It's Alive!**) as the over-zealous history prof., who hilariously uses corporal punishment on disobedient punks. At first, this half-baked scheme seems viable – that is, until the robots start killing the leather-encrusted kids. And after wasting 9/10's of the cast, the finale has the robo-instructors going after our hero (a reformed gang leader) and his sweetie (the principal's rebellious daughter)... Director Lester has churned out some great drive-in classics (in addition to **Class of 1984**, there's **Truck Stop Women** and **Stunts**), and though this one's energetically filmed, it never breaks free of its formula constraints. It's pretty cool mindsewage, and nothing more. (You mean you thought there might be some subtle, underlying social commentary to all this? Nahhh!) Co-starring Joshua Miller, the half-pint psychopath from **River's Edge**, as a 'Edge'-snorting teen.

COCKSUCKER BLUES

ROBERT FRANK 1972. Banned and withheld for years (either by The Glimmer Twins or Her Satanic Majesties Request), this heartwarming document of the Rolling Stones' '72 assault on Main Street USA is finally black marketing its way to the VCR's of hardcore rock fans. Thrill! To Keef on the nod in locker rooms across America! See! Nude groupies cavort on the DC-9 while the Stones beat out a tribal riddim! Watch! The Stones prove that you *can* always get what you want, and if you try sometimes, you might make it to the stage! Smokin' renditions of 'Midnight Rambler', 'Brown Sugar' and 'Satisfaction' are sandwiched in amidst the debauching. Grin! In hilarity as Warhol, Cavett and Capote make the scene backstage! Wonder who is in control here as the camera pans to the soundman, obviously on Planet X, tapping the shotgun mic (uh, test?). Edge of your seat suspense as Mick almost trips leading Stevie Wonder to a mic to sing 'Uptight'! Snore! As Keef indulges in Bonzo/Moonie style 'TV off the balcony' artistic expression! What an interesting double bill with **Ladies and Gentlemen...**, the sanitised docu they released of the same tour. Needless to say, *this* film captures the Monkey Men doing more of what they do best, and that's *illegal*! So **C.S. Blues** is 90 minutes of grainy, dilated viewing, good for an evening of ripping your joint and letting it bleed. Cheers, mates! [TR]

COFFY (1973)
SHEBA BABY (1975)

Pam Grier, the undisputed queen of the blaxploiters returns with this pair of flicks dredged from American-International's warehouse... **Coffy** was the brain child of director/writer Jack Hill, one of my personal Drive-In Hall of Famers after hits like **Switchblade Sisters**, **Spider Baby** and **The Big Bird Cage**. Hill always knew how to kick off a flick, and this one is no exception. "This is the end of your rotten life, you motherfuckin' dope pusher," Grier snarls, before blowing a dealer's head *clean-off* at close range with a double-barrelled shotgun! It's a four-star start for an actioner that ranks alongside **Black Caesar** and **Three the Hard Way** as my fave grindhouse classics... Pam stars as E.R. Nurse Coffin, and she's a woman with a problem. Her little sister went catatonic at the end of a heroin needle and now 'Coffy' is on the loose, looking for retribution. And if it's gotta be caked with fresh blood, so be it! By day she's helping out at the Juvenile Drug Detox Clinic, and by night she's luring junkies into the boudoir by loosening her lingerie and promptly snuffing 'em out. Her biggest hassles come when the Las Vegas mob try to take over the black drug market. First they baseball bat her cop/boyfriend's skull into Brain Damage Land ("He may be able to go to the bathroom by himself someday," diagnoses the cheery physician) and then the mobsters take a pit-stop to maul Ms. Grier's size triple-A lungwarts. So Coffy infiltrates the syndicate and finds herself stuck between the warring faction of homeboy King George the pimp vs. outsider Arturo Vitroni... It's a simple enough plotline, but Hill knows how to pace the action, and he mixes the melodrama with the kick-ass violence in just the right proportions. Hill's hand is on the pulse of the sleaze-aholics, and he never skimps on the female flesh or nasty notions. This was Grier's first full-scale star vehicle too, and she emerges as a verita-

ble walking oestrogen dispenser. She even gets to shed a tear and act up a small storm, before blowing the gonads clean off the lead shithead. Allan Arbus co-stars as the stereotyped Italian mob boss, with '70s drive-in perennial Sid Haig (remember Dragos from **Jason of Star Command**?) as his chrome-dome henchman. And talk about cinematic excessiveness! Whenever two women get into a cat-fight, both of them get their blouses torn off; when someone's hit by a car, another car has to run over the corpse a moment later; and when a Brother is being dragged by a car, it has to climax in a 60 m.p.h. race down a city street with the body bouncing off curbs. Ouch! This is true blue Grimace Cinema, and I loved every moment of it!... A little more imaginatively brutal than usual and a *lot* more streetwise, **Coffy** is solid junk food for the mind. Check it out!... For the second half of our Pam Grier double-header, we jump two years later for **Sheba Baby**. Director William Girdler left his horror roots (**Three on a Meathook**, **Asylum of Satan**) to lens this blaxploiter, and it unfortunately pales next to the full-blown scuzziness of **Coffy**. The action's lame, the sex is bland, and it's all PG-level pabulum. Though well-crafted, it's thoroughly uninspired, once again proving how important the right people behind the camera are. This time Grier is a more standard celluloid heroine, Sheba Shayne, a private detective whose father is getting pushed around by some Louisville black mobsters who want to take over his business and loan. But when Sheba hits town, it becomes evident that she won't take shit from no jive ass syndicate dickheads (especially after they almost blow her up with some ignition-triggered dynamite). Sheba starts spitting back, and most of the script is predictable tit for tat: She breaks up a big drug deal, they shoot up her Daddy's store with automatic weapons, etc. Worst of all, Pam looks bored most of the time, since the plot keeps her hair up, her clothes on and her methods of revenge disappointingly low-key. Even when Pam hauls out the heavy armaments, and heads a chase through a carnival with a (not-so) funhouse, the results are only so-so. A couple demeaning stereotypes (including a felt-hatted falsetto loan shark who sounds like he stepped out of **Hollywood Shuffle**) keep the unintentional laughs flowing, but the big problem is with the title character. Sheba is just a little *too* Goody-Two-Shoes. She's squeaky clean and almost strives to be a female James Bond (though quality wise, maybe more like Matt Helm). By this time, the studio was trying too hard to find a cross over hit for Pam, by stuffing her into a formula storyline complete with a sappy romance to slow down the show. And when she tries to emote at her injured pop's bedside, you realise why Ms. Grier never played Shakespeare in the Park. It's not entertaining enough to keep you cheering for the characters, and not crude enough to keep your attention from wandering to what's in your refrigerator to snack on... Maybe Girdler was just too whitebread for this type of assignment (though he also directed the black **Exorcist** rip-off, **Abby**) – he seemed a lot more comfortable with clean-cut dorks like Christopher George and Richard Jaeckel (in trash like **Grizzly**) before his untimely death. Overall, what we have here is typical inner city mindrot that cops out by not allowing Pam Grier to do what she does best: Kick ass!

COMBAT SHOCK

BUDDY GIOVINAZZO 1984 (RELEASED 1986). Director/writer Buddy Giovinazzo originally filmed this indie effort as **American Nightmare**, and I can't imagine any big-time producer sitting though, much less distributing, this grim, repellent tale. Luckily, Lloyd Kaufman and Michael Herz, the quick-to-make-a-buck sleaze-merchants from Troma Pix grabbed it up, changed the title, and tossed it onto the skid row circuit. Now it's out on video, and although the box makes it look like any other war-veteran-revenge flick, don't let it fool you. Without a doubt, this is the ugliest, nastiest little movie I've seen in a long time. And I loved it!... Imagine **The Deer Hunter** if John Waters had directed, and you get some idea of the magnitude of this grim gem. Ricky Giovinazzo stars as a scuzzball Vietnam vet who lives an urban cesspool of utter squalor, with his whiny, overbearing wife and mutant baby. He lives in filth and dirt – he has no job and no money for food – he's beaten up by street thugs and accosted by junkie buddies – and he spends his days staggering the streets and waiting in unemployment lines. Just to add to his misery he's also plagued by graphic Nam flashbacks, complete with ripped-apart colleagues and POW camp maggot torture. There isn't much plot beyond that; mainly this is just a sick slice of life, resembling a dirtball version of **Taxi Driver**... The film starts slow, but gets weird *very* quickly, culminating in one of the most spectacularly rancid scenes I've had the pleasure to view – incorporating his family, a handgun, an oven, *lots* of fake blood, and a quart of spoiled milk. Made on a next-to-nothing budget amidst authentic Staten Island poverty-row settings, this film looks like a labour of twisted love. I mean, what other feature motion picture in recent memory would have us watch a desperate junkie without a hypo ripping a hole in his arm with a coat-hanger and manually stuffing the heroin in? And even if the technical side lags a bit, Director Buddy G. and his crew create some cheap-but-very-effective work – his camerawork and editing are tight, many of the scenes have a nice, hallucinatory feel, and the constantly-rasping child (shades of **Eraserhead**) looks like a diseased Muppet Baby. The acting is predictably amateurish, but Veronica Stork stands out as the shrewish wife with a voice as pleasant as gargling with a

mouthful of broken glass. And Ricky G. is so perfect in the lead that you tend to forget he's only acting (at least I *hope* he's acting) – with long, stringy hair, grubby clothes, and burnt-out stare, he's the perfect cut-rate urban psychotic; and when he announces "Today's one of those days where anything that can go wrong, does," you *know* you're in for a long, nasty ride. Chock full of gut-level intensity, this sordid vision of American life is a brilliant exercise in schlock excess. Gruesome as fuck, and even kind of funny (if you have a severely bent sense of humour). Not to be missed!

COMIC BOOK CONFIDENTIAL

RON MANN 1989. Contrary to popular opinion, comic books were never just for kids. For proof, here's a compact but fascinating documentary of comic art from fringe-culture filmmaker Ron Mann (**Poetry in Motion**), which profiles 22 of the most influential artists and writers who've worked in the field. Of course, it's impossible to cram the entire varied history of comics into one 90 minute film, but Mann covers most of the bases – from superheroes and horror, to undergrounds and independents – culled from over 60 hours of interviews. Though a little thin on new info for die-hard fans, it's a fine overview of comics' evolution from the '30s to the present, showing how they've mutated from 10¢ funny books to $19.95 graphic novels, in addition to becoming a medium for some of the finest, funniest artists of our century... In the beginning comics were simple children's fun, but when heroes like Superman took off into the stratosphere, a profitable industry was born. And while illustrators like Will Eisner (with his shadowy **Spirit**) and Jack Kirby began asserting their personal style, the boundaries of good taste were pushed by E.C. ('An Entertaining Comic') when they began spewing out wonderfully gory titles like **Tales from the Crypt**, which focused on death, murder, mutilation, adultery, perversion, and all the other great American values. One of the best bits of the film has William Gaines discussing E.C.'s tongue-in-cheek High Concept brainstorms (i.e. 'guy murders his wife and eats her, to destroy the evidence'). The film glides from **Mad Magazine** (whose first issues were – and still are – the funniest damned thing on the planet) to pompous Stan Lee and his band of angst-ridden superheroes, and pays tribute to the late '60s underground movement, which erupted like a stoned Vesuvius with **Mr. Natural**, **Fritz the Cat**, **The Fabulous Furry Freak Brothers**, and auto-biographical stories tinged with psychedelic brilliance. Robert Crumb and Gilbert Shelton are both hilarious with their recollections of a breakthrough era that gave artists the freedom to break any taboo (and in one instance, get sued by Disney for having Mickey and Minnie screwing each other). The documentary wraps up with a sizeable showcase of '80s illustrators and comics' long overdue validation as a True Art Form. While the mass-market companies still grind out the same flaccid fantasy, these artists are tackling politics, growing up, and survival in this absurd, occasionally nightmarish world; Bill Griffith dresses up as Zippy the Pinhead and sings his theme song; Lynda Barry recalls the day Home Economics covered both sewing machines and tampons; Sheri Flenniken takes on capital punishment by having Trots and Bonnie presiding over a wading pool electrocution; and the ever-personable Harvey Pekar gripes into the camera. Also featured are Charles Burns ('Big Baby'), Art Spiegelman ('Maus'), and Frank Miller ('The Dark Knight'). But aside from the chronological compression, the most fascinating (and infuriating) moments are when Mann touches upon the '50s alarmist groups who accused the comics industry of corrupting their snotty-nosed kids and turning them into a "mass of jangled nerves" (included is old propaganda footage of a li'l boy reading a comic and then stabbing a tree). Their allegations led all the way to Senate hearings and the development of the restrictive Comics Code (aka a pack of censoring shitheels), plus a string of spinelessly goofy titles such as **Young Brides**, **Cowboy**

Love and Nature Boy... It's great to observe the artists behind the artwork, and an interesting idea was in having the illustrators reading the dialogue as the camera focuses on their panels. But Mann could've dropped the cheesy limited animation montages (which reminded me of the old Marvel cut-out cartoons), since the close-ups of the art and the hilarious covers are perfect on their own. Nit-picking aside, this is a loving tribute to a long-neglected field. Chock full of fond memories for comic collectors, and one of a kind.

CONFESSIONS OF AN OPIUM EATER

ALBERT ZUGSMITH 1962 (AKA: SOULS FOR SALE). Don't believe for a moment that this is based on Thomas DeQuincey's classic **Confessions of an English Opium Eater**. This film may have a similar title, but it's rooted firmly in the cheapjack world of Albert Zugsmith, the exploitation king who bounced Mamie Van Doren to fame with **Sex Kittens Go to College**, **High School Confidential** and **The Beat Generation**... Vincent Price plays *Gilbert* DeQuincey, an ever-curious boob who stumbles into a turn-of-the-century Tong War and has a full-scale, opium-glazed adventure in slave-girl Chinatown. It's a tale where life is cheap and so are the sets, with a very confused Vince wandering through San Francisco's oriental underworld. It seems that the insidious Ling Tang is the Big Tong in town, and those wacky Chinamen are busy selling gals at auction again! But not if semi-heroic Price has his way – going up against assassins hanging upside-down in windows, battles in secret passageways under the city and The Death of 1,000 Cuts! Sorta like 'Indiana DeQuincey and the Temple of Dope'... Every out-of-work oriental extra in Hollywood who could fake broken English musta been hired for this stereotype-fest, and Vincent's primary job is to keep running from them. But just when you think it's gotten about as ludicrous as you could expect, wait until Vincent hits his first opium den and tokes up! Buckle yourself into your seat for an incredibly silly slo-mo rooftop chase, complete with tacky hallucinations of snakes and skulls! Wow!... Vincent eventually chills out and breaks up an auction where the black-market babes are suspended in Bamboo cages, and these women are so cheap they'd dance the hootchy-kootch for half a bowl of rice and an autographed picture of Sidney Toler. The last we see of ol' Gilbert DeQ. is him getting sucked down a sewer. SERIOUS WEIRDSHIT! I bet I can guess what these filmmakers were smokin' during the shoot... And what fuckin' inscrutable narration we're treated to! "The path of righteousness lies around us, for the eye that will see and the foot that will follow." Someone's been cribbing from the fortune cookies again, methinks! Not one of Zuggy's best, but it's certainly his strangest

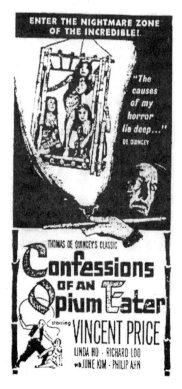

– **Opium Eater** is so tackily exotic and off-the-wall idiotic, that it's a MUST SEE for the Laudanum crowd! An expose so scandalous that you'll shit a brick from laughing so hard!

COONSKIN

RALPH BAKSHI 1975 (AKA: STREETFIGHT). This is Ralph Bakshi's third feature, after **Fritz the Cat** and **Heavy Traffic** (and before selling out with commercial dung like **Lord of the Rings** and **American Pop**), and as far as I'm concerned, it's his rancid masterpiece! Although the film is bookended with live-action sequences that fall somewhat flat, the animated sections contain some of the finest, *nastiest* images ever put to film. Period... During its initial release, **Coonskin** became one of the most controversial films of the year – Bakshi was branded a racist by frothing black organisations (such as CORE) and pickets formed in front of the theatres. Buckling to pressure, the soft-bellied swine at Paramount (aka Gulf+Western) dropped the film like it had leprosy and after a time Bryanston Pictures (the people who brought us **The Devil's Rain**, god help us) picked up the distribution rights and the movie seeped into limbo after a couple weeks of mediocre grosses. But now, **Coonskin** is back for all of us to judge for ourselves, and although it's true that *every* black in the film is portrayed as either a junkie, whore, pimp, psycho, or greedmonger, it's also true that *no* racial or social group gets off unscathed by Bakshi. Black and white, male and female, gays, Italians, and bigots – **Coonskin** takes them all on with a razor edge that rips deep at the flesh. By transposing Uncle Remus' simple tales (Br'er Rabbit, Br'er Bear, Br'er Fox, and The Tar Baby) to a modern, urban American setting, Bakshi paints a blood-caked call for social rebellion – it's no wonder that the film's original (and much more suitable) title was **Coonskin No More**... Scatman Crothers and Philip (Michael) Thomas star in the live-action segments as two escaped convicts waiting for their getaway car (driven by Barry White and Charles Gordone). And while they sweat it out, Scatman tells Thomas the story of Brother Rabbit, Brother Bear and Preacher Fox's (animated) adventures in Harlem, and their encounters with every style of White-backed corruption and repression imaginable. There's Miss America, a beautiful red, white and blue whore who beats up Brothers with her brass knuckles; Black Jesus, who dances naked in his pulpit while collecting money to 'kill whitey'; plus heroin dealers, corrupt cops, and a grotesque Mob Boss that makes Don Corleone look like Captain Kangaroo. There are beatings, shootings, knifings, a decapitation by a ceiling fan, and more unrelenting, unflinching violence than any live-action movie could possibly get away with. People are riddled with bullets every three minutes, and the searing highlight is when they put LSD in a local Pig's drink, and we're treated to a hallucination sequence that'll rip the spine outta your backside. Blood *pours* across the screen. The live-action is sometimes awkwardly integrated, but you have to admire Bakshi's vision of taking the animated film to a new level, and for 45 minutes, this flick is the most brutal chunk of celluloid you'll find. It's strong stuff, with a powerful message... While you're at it, try to locate a copy of Bakshi's **Mighty Mouse** cartoons. About two-thirds of the episodes were shit, but the other third has some of the weirdest humour to hit cartoon-TV since **Rocky and Bullwinkle**.

CRAWLSPACE

DAVID SCHMOELLER 1986. First off, you know something is fishy when a movie is released nation-wide in October, only to turn up at your local video store four weeks later. And when Charles Band's name is in the credits (the producer who brought the world such lasting works of art as **Laserblast** and **Troll**) you have the suspicion it *could* be a hunk of steaming faeces. But then you notice Klaus Kinski's name above the title, and you realise that there is a slim chance the film could be worth the time. From *real* movies, like

Aguirre, Wrath of God and Fitzcarraldo, to crap like Death Smiles on a Murderer, Schizoid and Venom, Kinski seems to latch onto any script that has a cashier's check attached – but like another one of my favourite actors, Dennis Hopper, it seems as if Kinski can do no wrong when it comes to crappy classics. He's always interesting to watch and there's always the gut feeling that in real life he's as depraved and psychotic (if not more so) as the character he's portraying. He just looks like the type of guy who'd run a rusty machete through your skull because you asked for an autograph. (Hey, does *anybody* out there have access to his controversial autobiography, I'm So Wild About Your Strawberry Mouth?)... But, returning to the film in question, Crawlspace is a slight, but not half-bad, psychological thriller. Klaus plays a landlord who rents out apartments to young women (yeah, *I'd* rent a room from a guy like Kinski... Sure...) and then spies on them through a series of crawlspaces that criss-cross the building. Of course, the moment they sign the lease, they're dead meat, because Klaus is the type of fun-loving guy who plays sadistic mind games with each victim; enjoys Russian Roulette after each murder; terrifies his tenants with large, pet rats; and keeps an emaciated woman caged in his attic, along with all his Nazi paraphernalia. The first half drags, while setting up the slim plot (they throw in the obligatory 'pretty-but-incredibly-stupid-non-actress-looking-scared-scenes' every few minutes), but when Kinski goes completely bonkers the film really pulls together, as he goes after the only reasonably-intelligent young lady in the film. Though it's R-rated, there's a minimum of the splatter we've come to expect in this type of quick-buck production, but a hefty dose of suspense at the end (a Klaus-trophobic chase through the rodent-infested crawlspaces) makes it a generally worthwhile, if not particularly original, addition to any schlock-viewing list.

THE CRAZIES

GEORGE A. ROMERO 1973. This early effort from George Romero originally appeared in 1973 to disastrous reviews and limited distribution (it pops up on late-nite cable every so often, sliced to ribbons). A paranoid horror/action film, it might disappoint the gut-cruncher audience who've come to expect gallons of bodily fluids and internal organs flying into the camera lens; but anyone else should enjoy watching Romero on the loose with a shitload of squibs and automatic weapons galore... The whole thing begins in Evans City, a calm, little town on the out-skirts of Pittsburgh (where else?). But one evening, without any warning or explanation, the Army appears, equipped with white de-con suits, establishing martial law and quarantining the population. It seems that a nearby plane crash has unleashed a bacteriological weapon on the neighbouring town – a virus which drives people insane. We've already witnessed a father going completely nuts in front of his terrified little kids – killing his wife (off-screen) and setting his house ablaze – but this is nothing compared to the anarchy that erupts when this little bug (code name Trixie) gets into the water supply. While the typically-callous government officials argue about whether to destroy the town with a nuclear blast, the Army has its hands full, rounding up hundreds of potential madmen (and women). The soldiers invade houses in the middle at the night, dragging everyone to the local high school, where we get to watch hundreds of extras sputtering and drooling, while they're packed in the hallways like sardines. But unlike the slow, easily-repelled zombies in Night of the Living Dead, these are crazed townfolks who fight back with pitchforks and shotguns (including a sweet li'l old lady who has a nasty way with a knitting needle). The script (by Romero) is pretty routine, but there's lots of odd, nihilistic twists, including a repressive-father/innocent-daughter combo who end up in bed together when the virus hits 'em. There's the now-traditional company of stock characters – the Army commander

who has second thoughts about the whole enterprise, the 'I-told-you-so' scientists, etc. – and to its disadvantage, the film is saddled with two completely unlikeable bozos in the lead roles. But unlike most low-rent sleaze-shows, which would take the easy route, painting the Army in black and white terms (either heroic victims or macho jerks), Romero portrays them as manipulated pawns, fighting a war they can not win on a foe's home turf (gosh, sounds suspiciously like another 'police action' that the Army was going through at that time, eh?). Though it's not on par with the Dead trilogy, Martin or Knightriders, this is fast-paced violent entertainment. And as an additional bonus, we get a hilariously pretentious song over the end credits, 'Heaven Help Us' by (urp!) Carole Bayer Sager and Melissa Manchester.

THE CREATION OF THE HUMANOIDS

WESLEY E. BARRY 1962. Reputed to be one of the late Andy Warhol's favourite films; I'm not sure if that rumour is true, but if you like good, cheapo SF movies, this may become one of *your* favourites, too. It's a bit like watching Blade Runner with a $1.98 budget... While a bunch of garbled, foreign voices shout at each other, we are treated to an atomic blast light-show as the credits run. And years later, the Earth is still a mess, recovering from their 48-hour World War III, in which 92% of the population was blown off the map. But amidst all the destruction and death, mankind can still generate its own breed of asshole – this time in the form of a Gestapo-style organisation called The Body of the Order of Flesh and Blood. They're a racist bunch of shitheads, led by a super-egotist named Cragus, who spend their copious free time harassing 'clickers' – pale, humanoid robots who comprise a growing proportion of the work force. Unbeknownst to the humans, the robots have a secret temple in which they are transforming their own kind into human lookalikes, complete with emotions and implanted memories. In fact, even though they still have cogs, gears and green blood (from their copper-tubing), these robots are actually *better* than real humans – more perfect and virtually immortal – but they've also inherited the very-human instinct of killing ("Mankind is a state of mind," comments one humanoid). With the aid of a crazy old scientist, they're given synthetic thalamus units which evolve them into higher be-

ings, and when The Order uncovers this secret plot involving these "soulless, godless, imitations of man", the first thought out of their pea-brains is "Exterminate them!" ('They're spoiling us with atrophy," one of the readers proclaims). Add to that a series of shocking secrets – that Cragus' sister is in *rapport* with a 'clicker', and Cragus himself might have fallen for an evolved humanoid... There isn't much action, but the surprisingly literate screenplay has plenty of fun plot twists and there's wonderful dialogues about human vs. robot superiority, the evolution of machines, and robotic religion. Dudley Manlove (from **Plan 9**) co-stars as one of the bald, black-eyed humanoids, but unfortunately, the rest of the cast is so wooden that you don't know whether they're brilliant actors impersonating idiots, or if they're really *that* untalented (I'll take bets on choice number two) – but the other aspects of the film are so damned interesting that you can overlook its casting inadequacies and financial limitations.

CREATURE FROM BLACK LAKE

JOY HOUCK JR. 1976. Some horror movies are so unique in their subject matter and so genuinely frightening that they leave after-images in your brain forever. This isn't one of them... Two biologists travel from Chicago to Louisiana to investigate rumours of a Bigfoot-type creature that's been stomping around the woods for years, screaming its head off and occasionally killing and eating the locals. Actually, it only kills three people during the course of the movie... The beginning is a little misleading. Jack Elam and friend are rowing their boat around the lake while the credits roll. Suddenly a hairy hand reaches out of the water and pulls Jack's friend down into the slime. Hey, I thought, they don't waste any time here. Unfortunately the rest of the film consists mainly of the two biologists walking around questioning the locals... This is really dull stuff. The dialogue isn't even so-bad-it's-funny; it's just *lame*... We *finally* get to see the 'monster' when he shows up during the last half hour (an actor in a phoney monkey suit), maims one of the biologists (off-camera) and pushes their van over. The film ends with the two 'heroes' in teary-eyed joy because they're both still alive and vowing to find the creature again. Oh boy. This thing didn't end soon enough for me. It doesn't even deserve to be called a 'monster movie'. Joy Houck Jr. is to be blamed for this yawnfest. GET HIM!!! [BJE]

THE CREEPING TERROR

ART J. NELSON 1964. Okay, how 'bout this: A monstrous, man-eating *Killer Carpet From Outer Space*!! Well, actually, it's about as monstrous as a Twinkie... and it doesn't really eat, it just kinda, well, flops onto its victims... but, hey, it *does* come from *Outerrr Spaaace*! Uhh... okay, so this isn't exactly **Alien**. Let's discuss this unbelievable exercise in Cinema Pathetique... A spaceship lands in Lake Tahoe (ah ha ha! Ha!). Out crawls a hulking, sneaker-footed (sneakers? Why those couldn't possibly be the feet of the poor guys sweating like pigs under that ri-fucking-diculously lousy monster 'costume', could it?) alien critter that plunges its mouth down onto its victims, making suspiciously (hilariously) human-sounding gobbling sounds as its dinner pretends to be in great distress. It wanders through the woods, screaming (some guy going EEEAARREEEAAAH) while crummy background music is being played on a piano offstage (dunt-dunt-DEENT-dunt-doont-doont-dunt-dunt)... It attacks a bunch of schmucks sitting around listening to some asshole playing bullshit on his geetar ("I triiied to forget her, and I reallyyy did tryyy..."), wanders into a gymnasium where a bunch of teenyboppers are having a dance and swallowing them all one by one, etc... It's said that director Art Nelson literally lost the entire soundtrack; I guess that would account for the fact that the whole thing is narrated, from the 'plot' down to the actors' dialogue... Really, you've got to see this goddamn thing for yourself

to understand why I say that despite the fact that most viewers seem to consider Ed Wood Jr.'s **Plan 9 from Outer Space** to be the Worst Movie Ever Made, *this* tragically·stupid little item gets *my* vote for that category... Heck, it won the Golden Turkey Award... okay, so that doesn't count for shit, either... [BJE]

CRIMES OF THE FUTURE (1970)
STEREO (1969)

There are only a handful of filmmakers who are so uniformly intriguing that I'd be willing to sit through *anything* they churn out. David Cronenberg is one of them. Well, before class acts like **Dead Ringers**, before even his first feature **Shivers** (still the best mutant, slug-like aphrodisiac parasite movie ever made), David C. directed, wrote, photographed, and edited these two hour-long student films. Most folks will need super-human patience to endure 'em, but completists will be eager to try anyhow. First we have **Crimes of the Future**, which covers all of Cronenberg's now-familiar territory and proves the guy already had his act down pat, in incorporating high-tech institutes, physiological disorders, deranged docs, plus a sterile *mise en scène* that always maintains maximum disorientation. And to be honest, this would be the perfect parody of a Cronenberger if he hadn't made the thing himself. The plot (if you can call it that) follows a dour young physician (Ronald Mlodzik) as he roams various hospital grounds and narrates our tissue-paper-thin tale. He begins at the House of Skin, which is studying the effects of Rouge's Malady (named after a mad dermatologist, one symptom is Rouge's Foam oozing from your ears). Later he visits the neighbouring Institute of Neo-Venereal Disease, with a patient (once the head doctor) who has mutated, regenerative organs. And in what other movie could you come across the Oceanic Podiatry Group, or the concept of Artificially Induced Puberty? In the debit department: There's no sync sound, no effects, and no life to *any* of the proceedings. For this type of youthful endeavour it's ingeniously crafted and overloaded with witty (though unfleshed) concepts; but it's also so cold that you quickly lose interest. Luckily, in later projects, Cronenberg learned how to skim the surface of his personal obsessions in order to isolate the choicest (and most coherent) bits, while adding a touch of humanity to it all... Looking for something even more obtuse, clinical and unfathomable? Here's deviant Dave's very first film, the b/w **Stereo**. Filmed like a corporate research film, a scholarly voice-over (sorta) explains the goings on, much of it sounding like scraps later used to better effect in **Scanners**. It charts a group of experimental subjects who've had surgery on their brains to make them telepathic, and now, after three months of testing, the cameras are brought in to record the results. The movie then examines *all* the different aspects of their telepathy – the good, the bad and the boring. The subjects are paired into mentally attuned teams, and though Cronenberg name drops exotic topics like necrophilia, homosexuality, telepathic communes, and how one pair had their larynxes removed in order to up their psychic ante, he doesn't actually show anything, except lots of bored young amateur actors giving each other furtive glances (to suggest they're reading minds). Fascinating at first, it quickly gets silly and pretentious, while overdosing our brainpans with nine-syllable psychobabble and ignoring any dramatic possibilities. Admittedly well-constructed, and with a grainy mock-*cinéma vérité* look, but without much of a point except as an exercise in catatonia. Maybe Cronenberg achieved exactly what he was after – two techno-oriented, pseudo-scientific shorts – but his stimulating ideas are sabotaged by the stultifying pace.

CRIMEWAVE

SAM RAIMI 1986. OK, here's an obscure one for you. Also known as the **XYZ Murders** and **Broken Hearts and Noses**, this is an incredibly stylish film from the writers/directors of **The Evil Dead** and **Blood Simple**. This time, they try their hand at a dark, slapstick comedy involving murder, jealousy, hysteria, and pest exterminators. Like the best of Frank Tashlin's features, the entire film has an unreal, backlot look, and you can see that these guys were trying to create the equivalent of a live-action Warner Brothers cartoon. (For example, they re-work the old Wile E. Coyote gag – having a guy miraculously surviving a dozen-story fall onto concrete only to be run over by a truck when he stands up.) There's a bunch of great set-pieces and some really original filmmaking, but the only problem is that the whole damned thing ISN'T FUNNY! The script is dreadful, most of the actors are inept, and after a while even the energetic technique wears thin – it all begins to feel like a precocious film major's wet dream... Just for the record, the plot concerns an annoying Jerry Lewis-clone and how his romantic misadventures lead him into implication of a murder; Louise Lasser 'stars', but she's only in it for half an hour; and the only fun comes from Paul Smith (Beast Rabban from **Dune** and Bluto from **Popeye**) playing a growling ogre of a psychopath with a weasely partner who electrocutes victims with a portable generator... I can't say it's a good film (it took me three tries before I could sit all the way through it), but it is a really screwy failure. For the curious only.

THE CRIPPLED MASTERS

1982. 'That evil villain – Dr. Latex Scar!' If Shakespeare did a lot of Thorazine and worked at Wendy's for six months, he'd write **Crippled Masters**. Without a doubt the most sensitive, understated, lushly evocative kung-fu movie starring two amputees I've ever seen. You're hardly out of the credits when arms are hacked off, courtesy the aforementioned Dr. Latex. The poor guy grovels around for a while, then he gets beat *again* after taking refuge in a coffin maker's shop. Finally leaving the village (good move, bud) he hides out on a farm until he's discovered (farmer: "Are you a man or a ghost?" Mr. No Arms: "Would a ghost be eating pig swill?"). He starts over, working as a farmhand (sorry). Back in psycho village, one of the thugs falls out of favour with Dr. Latex, and gets the royal acid treatment, turning his legs into burnt matchsticks (such a heart-warming family film). Mr. No Legs somehow ends up at the same farm, and Mr. No Arms exacts a little revenge. But soon the OLD MASTER appears, with a stand-up idea (sorry). 'Let's train you guys to do a whole bunch of fight scenes where we stop the camera every five seconds!' 'WOW! OK we'll do it!' And so we're off on a non-stop barrage of strange fights, many in Iambic Pentameter: What an epic. Even better than **Soul Brothers of Kung-Fu**. [TR]

THE CURSE OF BIGFOOT

DON FIELDS 1972. Okay, you wanna talk bad movies? Here's one: A bunch of high school students (a little older than today's high schoolers) are snooping around an ancient Indian burial ground looking for the Missing Link (well, uh, isn't that the first place *you'd* look?) and what do they find but – Bigfoot's Tomb! And now that they've disturbed the Big B's resting place, the mighty Bigfoot (all five feet of him) goes on a 'rampage' of 'destruction'. Bad. Awful. Terrible. El Stinko. Starring Absolutely Nobody and featuring no special effects to speak of. As for the Bigfoot costume, you're sure to find something more convincing 'round Halloween time when all those crummy kiddie costumes with the one-piece suit and the face-mask with the wrap around string start showing up in K-Mart. Get drunk, no, fuck that, *get wasted* before you watch this one, and if you get so trashed that you can't remember it the next day, so much the better for you. At least you had a great time laughing at *everyone involved* with this pieceashit the night before. [BJE]

CUT AND RUN

RUGGERO DEODATO 1986. After catching the first 10 minutes of this South American Blow-Buster, I actually thought it might turn out to be a good film. In the first scene, Michael Berryman, the wild-eyed bald geek from **The Hills Have Eyes**, leaps out of the swamp with a pack of **Emerald Forest** rejects, attacking a make-shift drug co-op with machetes and blowguns, turning the lot of 'em into green card gator bait. Poison darts through the neck! Machetes whacked into the head! Death galore! Yeah!! Unfortunately, after that solidly bloodthirsty opening, the movie sinks into a conventional yawn-yarn with has-been American actors trudging through Amazon locations. It seems that drug-dealers have been getting slice-and-diced, so a feisty female TV reporter flies down to the jungles of South America to break the story – and we get this ditzy blond stumbling toward Sudden Death with her camera crew in tow. There's also an idiot subplot about a missing American kid who's being held hostage, but when the kid turns out to be professional nobody Willie Aames (teen-idol shithead from **Eight is Enough**), it becomes apparent that anyone with a modicum of good taste *wants* to see the talentless bozo hung by his nuts from the nearest palm tree. But before you reach for the No-Doz, the proceedings finally pickup during the last 15 minutes and we get sleazeshow mondo-meanie Richard Lynch (**Demon**, **Deathsport**) as a Jonestown fanatic, sputtering and raving in his best madman tradition about 'purifying mankind' by killing every coke smuggler this side of the Rio Grande... Director Ruggero Deodato, who normally churns out pasta-land chunk-blowers such as **Cannibal Holocaust** tones down the gore for the mass-market, and despite the occasional murder the film remains fairly tedious. A couple great sections, but the overall results are mediocre but watchable if you're a fan of jungle carnage. Oh yeah, Karen Black also makes a mercifully short appearance, but I'm sure no one really gives a shit...

CUTTING CLASS

ROSPO PALLENBERG 1989. Rospo Pallenberg has co-scripted some of John Boorman's finest films, such as **The Emerald Forest** and **Excalibur**; and though the move into a director's chair isn't always an easy one (take for example Paul Mayersberg, who's tops when collaborating with Nicolas Roeg, but on his own shat out the somnambulistic **Nightfall**), Rospo has hatched a satisfying li'l suburban deathfest that initially invites comparisons with **Heathers**. But it's nowhere near as sardonic in its mix of high school kitsch and killing sprees, and relies too heavily on a connect-the-dots storyline... Welcome to Small Town USA, with Donovan Leitch as Brian, a glassy-eyed teen weirdo who's spent time in a mental institution and has a crush on Paula (Jill Schoelen), a straight-A cutie. And to complete the triangle, her beer-brained boyfriend (Brad Pitt) is jealous of the psycho's affections. The plot livens up when the bodies start amassing – the art teacher is baked in his own kiln, and I particularly enjoyed the grim Xerox machine murder, where the victim's face is crushed on the glass while the copier spits out death mask portraits. Who's responsible for the body count? The script by Steve Slavkin knows how to twist expectations, and since the entire cast is off-kilter, *everyone's* a potential suspect, such as the shell-shocked janitor ("I'm the custodian of your destiny!") or even the jailbait-lech principal, Mr. Dante (Roddy McDowall). Most of the kids are portrayed as vapid vacuumheads, but credit goes to Leitch, who has an effective Emilio Estevez/**Repo Man** look as the ostracised shock treatment candidate; and Schoelen (**The Stepfather**), who's turning into a likeable young actress – a C-level Winona Ryder, despite having to play a peppy cheerleader-type. Wasted (once again) is Martin Mull, who plays Jill's dopey father and spends the film crawling through the woods with an arrow in his gut... Pallenberg's voyeuristic camerawork is good for some creepy sequences and a nasty Shop Course finale (then again, I'm a sucker for Brad Pitt's head getting squeezed in a vice), but I sorely missed the mysticism and general weirdness of Rospo's own scripts. Competent swill, but it's no real surprise the film never got a full theatrical release.

DAMNATION ALLEY

JACK SMIGHT 1977. Roger Zelazny's novel is great. The movie ain't. George Peppard, before he finally started earning an income on **The A-Team**, and Jan-Michael Vincent of **Air-wolf** unfame are among a handful of survivors of a major nuclear nastiness riding to, of all places, Albany, New York in a futuristic, heavily-armed van. On the way they have to get past some hungry giant scorpions, killer cockroaches and an occasional shifting of the earth's surface. Special effects buffs will yawn to death. Fans of Zelazny's work will spit at the screen. Directed by Jack Smight. Thanx a fucking lot, Jack, you artless tool. [BJE]

DARKTOWN STRUTTERS

WILLIAM WITNEY 1974 (AKA: GET DOWN AND BOOGIE). Gather 'round, blaxploitation addicts, for the weirdest damned urban saga you'll ever witness! A comedy/musical/motorcycle miasma with absolutely no redeeming value whatsoever, except that it's *so* utterly outrageous it reaches a level of incomprehensibility only true 42nd Street mavens will appreciate. I swear, you won't believe this flick!... A female gang of motorcyclists tool into Watts one afternoon, led by Trina Parks as Syreena; and after getting hassled by the Ghetto Alert police (imagine the Keystone Kops as racists with pump shotguns) they head to the rib joint Hog Heaven, which advertises 'free watermelon with every bucket'... Right about now (only five minutes into the flick), I started to realise this wasn't some run-of-the-mill Inner City idiocy. Sure enough, it's an ultra-stereotyped, absolutely brain-damaged comedy aimed at black audiences, but created by a pack of (obviously drug-addled) white guys. Scripted by George Armitage (who also penned the Quisinart hippiefest **Gas-s-s-s**) and directed by William Witney (who made about a billion B-westerns back in the '30s and '40s), but the biggest hand (preferably to the solar plexus) goes to the set design by Jack Fisk, which combines Willy Wonka with Ken Russell. The result isn't always big on laughs, but the package is so consistently demented that it had *me* slack-jawed (which made it easier to pour down the beer)... The virtually invisible narrative has Trina searching for her lost mom, Cinderella, who ran the local abortion clinic. But who *needs* a coherent story when you've got – a cocaine dealer in a white cowboy suit, pedalling a 'Pot-sicle' cart; a karate choppin' Brother who breaks through doors (even at his own house), because turning the knob isn't dramatic enough; cycle-straddling KKK'ers with crosses strapped to their cissy bars; a Grand wizard in red leather hip boots and taffeta underwear beneath his sheet; and a supporting cast that breaks into song and dance at the drop of a felt fedora (even in the middle of a prison break, when a cageful of glitterised cell mates begin doo-woppin'). But the *best* comes when we get to the sinister Cross Foundation (run by a Colonel Sanders lookalike), with Cross crawling about in a satin cape and pig ears, slapping two slabs of ribs together when he gets sexually aroused, and keeping kidnapped blacks caged in the cellar for use in cloning experiments. (*Now* do you believe how screwed up this movie is?)... I'm not even gonna try to criticise aspects like acting, believability, continuity, etc. – because such 'subtleties' play no part in a dumb-assed film like this one. I just want to know where they dredged up all those wild, cornea-singeing threads – fashions that would've given Liberace wet dreams... The only 'star' is Roger Mosley, who flushes away all his pride as Mellow, a Superstud-type who ends up sucking his thumb when Trina dumps on him. Plus, it even has Dick Miller as one of the Pigs. What more could any fan of funky filmic flotsam wish for?

THE DEAD COME HOME

J. RIFFEL 1988. On the surface, this Upstate NY-lensed no-budgeter might sound like any other corpsefest, featuring a cast of college-age cretins getting systematically slaughtered. IT IS... An assortment of guys and gals (all of them relatively unlikeable) buy up a creepy old mansion with plans to renovate it, and in the process smash a tombstone in the front yard. Big mistake, you peabrains! Suddenly, all the doors and windows seal behind them, and the trapped buttheads begin dying at the hands of a wrinkly old woman wielding a pair of scissors. A cranky crone (actually a guy sporting two pounds of cheap latex) isn't the most imposing figure, of course, but the stakes are raised when her Swiss-cheesed victims begin returning from the dead to lure in fresh meat from the group. Don't expect any big special effects – just lotsa blood caked little ones, like severed limbs, gushing wounds, and sharp implements lodged painfully into flesh and bone. Little lapses abound though – For example, how about an explanation for *how* the dead are able to 'come home'. Oops! I guess writer/director J. Riffel let that one slip by him. And if you're looking for scares, forget it! The flick's fairly watchable on a simple 'I wonder how the next bozo will get butchered?' level; but it's only nil in the Originality Department, with the audience always five minutes ahead of the script. The acting is routine, though the cast seemed to enjoy their transitions from Braindead to Undead, after which they had a reason to ham it up... Efficient dreck, but bound to get lost in the shuffle.

DEAD OF NIGHT

BOB CLARK 1972 (US: DEATHDREAM). This is a surprisingly good fright flick from Bob Clark, the swine who lowered IQ's across the country with the **Porky's** series and the Sly Stallone ego-drenched nose-pincher, **Rhinestone**. It's also one of the few films from the early '70s to even acknowledge the Vietnam War in its plot, and it proudly wears its social conscience within the confine of a schlock horror movie... John Marley and Lynn Carlin star as an average father and mother who get an announcement that their son, Andy, has been killed in Vietnam. Stubborn-headed mom won't allow herself to believe the bad news, and strangely enough, the next day Andy arrives at their front door, safe and sound in his Army uniform. Oops! Looks like the government screwed up again! Sure, Andy's a little quieter than normal and he tends to stare into space a bit more, but he's probably just been traumatised by his combat experiences. Right? Or do you think that just *maybe* Andy's mom 'willed' him back from the grave and now he's one of... (portentous pause)... THE WALKING DEAD?! Well, anyone who's seen any variation on 'The Monkey's Paw' knows that something's fishy, and even though Marley senses *something's* wrong, his wife is so overjoyed that her son isn't gook-bait that she ignores little oddities, like when Andy strangles the cute family dog in front of a bunch of children. Andy also tends to go out for secret midnight strolls, in search of transfusions of fresh blood to help slow down the rotting process. Eventually Dad crawls into a bottle, Mom turns into a blithering idiot, and Andy begins decomposing in front of his old girlfriend while at the drive-in (for your information, they're watching a double bill of 'Death in Space' and 'The Spacenauts')... Despite the film's obvious no-budget, some inherent creepiness prevails, and there's a brooding undertone that echoes the Vietnam vets' own post-war experiences. Don't think that this is some heavy-handed allegory though. **Dead of Night** is your basic, effective chiller. There's a few quick deaths ('Squish' goes Mr. Extra under the wheels of Andy's car), a grim ending in the cemetery and some good makeup (ripped-up necks, rotted skin) by a young Tom Savini. Soft-spoken Richard Backus co-stars as the Nam Zombie, and scripter Alan Ormsby (**Deranged, Cat People**) purposely keeps Andy as a morally-ambiguous character – sure, he's murdering people for their plasma, but he never asked to come back from the dead, did he?... Overall, this is down-and-out ghoulish fun from the folks who later gave us (gulp) **Children Shouldn't Play With Dead Things**.

THE DEADLY SPAWN

DOUGLAS MCKEOWN 1982 (AKA: RETURN OF THE ALIENS – THE DEADLY SPAWN). This may initially look and sound like drive-in dreck in the **Critters** mould, but it just happens to be a wonderfully blood-drenched schlocker. It may start out a little slow and routine, but by the end you'll be amazed at what the filmmakers were able to accomplish on a budget that most major productions would spend on coffee for their crew... The story begins with a straight forward alien invasion intro, during which two teenagers stumble upon a newly-fallen meteorite, and within moments they're reduced to kielbasa by an ever-growing horde of tadpole-like flesh chompers. Since they transport up drain pipes, soon the entire neighbourhood is getting chewed into cud. And do you wanna talk about a mouthful o' teeth? Look no further! These little guys are an ortho-dontist's nightmare! Soon afterward, we encounter the Mama Alien, who measures in at seven feet tall, has three 'heads' and leads a school of babies who feed off of human flesh like piranha on Speed, in some marvellously disgusting special FX side-shows (which usually involve a victim's face getting pulled to pieces). These carnivorous little creatures have only three things on their minds – eating, growing and multiplying in soggy basements, and I laughed my ass off when they decide to invade a blue haired women's luncheon... There's also a few human characters worth mentioning (though they're never as much fun as the monsters, of course), such as the young kid who's obsessed with **Famous Monsters** mag and movie makeup, and his older brother, who's a whiz in astronomy. Even though they're stock characters, they come off a *bit* more intelligent and resourceful than usual... The blunt, but effective direction by Douglas McKeown keeps the in-herent silliness subdued, and though the set-up is nothing special, the pay-off is a waist-deep display of death and dismemberment. For a low-budget flick, it comes across with some wildly suspense-ful set pieces, and the ending is a seemingly-endless battle for survival, complete with cheesy decaps, chest burstings and face rendings. Starring Charles George Hildebrandt and Tom DeFranco, this is a heartily recommended little exercise in alien toothiness. It's loads of crude fun!... But be forewarned: A sequel is in the works, but since it's headed by a different director, I'd hold my breath on it being even remotely as good as the original.

DEATH SMILES ON A MURDERER

ARISTIDE MASSACCESI 1973 (AKA: LA MORTE A SORRIDE ALL 'ASSASSINO). In general, I've learned that US horror films prefer to fit within a proven formula. On the other hand, the European ones often seem to follow no formula whatsoever, and work on an original 'whatever happens, happens' logic that's all its own. It might not make for much coherency, but at least there's less chance of it putting you to sleep. Here's a case in point. I first caught this muddle years ago at around 2 a.m. on the Late Show. It was sliced to ribbons for commercial TV, and seemed absolutely unfathom-able (of course, it could've been the case of beer I'd drunk a half hour earlier). Not surprisingly, the uncut, Italian language version sans subtitles makes as much sense, in addition to having all the (extremely) fake gore intact. Mr. Aguirre himself, Klaus Kinski, nomi-nally stars as a veins-poppin'-out-of-his-forehead Doctor and Ewa Aulin (who earlier starred in the wonderfully wrongheaded **Candy**) is his guinea pig patient. For a while Klaus experiments in his lab, looking appropriately deranged amongst his Pyrex, while mixing up a handy serum that brings corpses back to life. But the majority of the film is a convoluted cross between a Mario Bava supernatural killfest and one of those European period-piece dramas that only

Cinemax seems to dredge up (the classy types, where the women don't have stretch marks). There's a large cast of aristocratic family bozos, loads of atmosphere, unexplained visions, and a smattering of violence (like when a maid gets shotgunned in the face) – all basted together by director Aristide Massaccesi. The ending's REALLY stupid (meaning I enjoyed it), when poor Ewa gets boarded up in a basement alcove, only to reappear as a revenge-motivated ghoul. Flip-flopping from her doe-eyed, blond self to a decompos-ing skullface, she scares the linguini outta the entire family – es-pecially when she flirts her way into a gent's bed, and then turns off the charm when her face rots off. And sicko cat lovers will applaud the killer kitty, which rips a guy's face to shreds. Not a moment of this hokum is scary, but my biggest regret is that Kinski doesn't do more than scowl through his handful of scenes, before getting garrotted halfway through it (shucks!)... A little slow but endearingly confused, this film is like watching four different mov-ies that'd been edited together by a chimpanzee.

DEATH TRAP

TOBE HOOPER 1976 (AKA: EATEN ALIVE). After the initial promise of **Texas Chain Saw Massacre**, Tobe Hooper certainly has been chucking out the big-budget stinkeroos, eh? **Poltergeist** was his running leap into the Hollywood dungheap, via Steven 'My shit don't stink, but my films do' Spielberg. **Lifeforce** was entertaining enough in its own messy way; and **Invaders from Mars** looked great, but why remake the movie in the first place? And **Texas Chainsaw 2** was Tobe's personal snot-rag to the movie-going public – wasting not only Dennis Hopper, but proving once again that Gobble and Blowus at Cannon Films can screw up even the simplest concept... But onto **Eaten Alive**, his first feature after gaining cult notoriety and before blowing his talent on this string of gun-for-hire projects. It begins when an ex-prostitute, who can't

cut it in the Boner Biz, runs across the dilapidated Starlight Hotel, which is managed by scraggly Neville Brand. Sure enough, it turns out he's one of those maniacal religious zealots, and after pitchforking her into a holy mess, he tosses her carcass to his pet crocodile... Basic plot: Hotel guests come, annoy Neville, and end up in the backyard swamp as Living Luggage Lunch... Neville cackles away and is nicely convincing as the bayou bloodsplatterer, and what his co-stars take away from in realistic suspense, they make for in over-the-top campiness: Carolyn Jones looks fat and pale as the tough whorehouse madam, William Finley (**Phantom of the Paradise**) is *really* funny as a spastic father, Robert Englund is the local redneck shit-for-brains, and Marilyn Burns (who obviously didn't learn her lesson after **Chain Saw**) returns as the shrieking damsel in distress.... Hooper was obviously trying to recreate the grimness-level of his first film, but instead of *severe* dementia, he only achieves an EC-Comics-style Flee-For-Your-Life feature. No big scares on board, but it's fun watching Neville menace a cute li'l girl with his bloody scythe and his croc even gets to chew up the kid's adorable puppy (Heh heh heh). Too bad the gator effects are unbelievable, the plasma-spillage is tame (i.e., when Mr. Reptile chomps down on a head, you don't see it burst into seven pounds of ground round), and it's all derivative as hell. At least Tobe keeps the story moving, and it's never too boring.

DEATH WARMED UP

DAVID BLYTH 1984. Here's a New Zealand raunch-a-rama that runs on the schlock principle 'Why stop at a simple stabbing to the gut, when a couple dozen will do?' Director David Blyth brings a stylish look and frenzied pitch to this tale of medical monstrosities, but though it obviously *wants* to be the NZ answer to **Re-Animator**, it's never as dramatically involving or wickedly deviant as the Stuart Gordon gut-buster. Nevertheless, it's crammed with huge dollops of gore, nudity, disgusting effects, and a hit-and-miss anything-for-a-gross-chuckle attitude... For years, the mad Dr. Archer Howell (you can tell he's 'mad' because he spouts gospel like "WE are the new messiahs!") has been working on a way to extend life. The results have been mixed. With a hypodermic the size of a lawn dart, he injects his living (and thoroughly unwilling) subjects and turns them into glassy-eyed zombie-assassins, and at his island psychiatric hospital the Doc's been perfecting his Trans-Cranial Surgery techniques (aka taking a Black and Decker power drill with a ½-inch bit to a patient's skull). Enter two fun-loving young couples who come to the Doc's isle for a sun-and-sex day trip. Just by sheer coincidence, one of the four is a survivor of Howell's past experimentation – a run-in that left him in the loony bin for several years after pump-shot-gunning his parents. Immediately, the carload of kids encounters the Doc's twisted entourage of mutantheads with their pea-brains set for mayhem. They're grey! They're ugly! Their skulls visibly throb! And if they get a little *too* excited, their whole danged head explodes in a tsunami of pus! And the film hasn't even gotten up to full steam yet! There's motorcycle maniacs, impalings, guttings, immolations, loving close-ups of the daffy Doc poking his fat fingers into mushy brains, and the lengthy finale features a carnage soaked breakout of the mental misfits. It's Invasion of the Runny-Faced Geeks From Down Under!... The film is nicely photographed by James Bartle, with claustrophobic underground W.W.II tunnels and hospital corridors adding some chills when the ooze gets predictable. Gary Day is fun as the ego-crazed Dr. Howell; David Letch gets the Sleazebucket Award as spider, the snivelling, rodentile henchman; and the leads (Michael Hurst and Margaret Umbers) aren't nearly an annoying as they had every right to be. This flick is nothing unforgettably spectacular, but it's consistently repugnant and it makes a good six-pack companion.

DEATHSPORT

HENRY SUSO / ALLAN ARKUSH 1978. New World and Roger Corman tried to repeat their wallet-padding with this similarly titled follow-up to **Death Race 2000**. Besides re-snagging David Carradine for the lead, they signed up perennial baddy Richard Lynch and **Playboy** pictorial/action queen Claudia Jennings. What they managed to *forget* was to invest a little cash, write a decent script and (most important) interject a dab of humour into the proceedings. Freshman directors Henry Suso and Allan Arkush (pre-**Rock 'n' Roll High School**) exhibit no talent whatsoever for hardcore exploitation throughout this futuristic actioner, which is packed to the brim with cut-rate silliness, but played absolutely straight and stiff as an ironing board... Set 1,000 years after the great Neutron War, the planet is a wilderness inhabited by nomadic Range Guides, as well as militaristic holdovers from the past who ride on Death Machines (aka cheap Japanese motorcycles), capture subversives (aka a bunch of tired stuntmen) and drag them back to Helix City (aka a very unconvincing matte painting) to appease the wild-eyed demands of the high mucky-muck, Lord Zirpola, who's been diagnosed by the royal physician as having brain rot due to radiation. Meanwhile, David Carradine is the unshaven Range Guide, Kaz Oshay, decked out in a white loin cloth and cape; and the more visually appealing Deneer (Claudia J.) is his partner in grime. In between Zen platitudes and stilted line readings they spend the film on the run from Ankar Moor (Lynch), a legendary traitor to the Guides. The long awaited Deathsport is nothing but your basic arena combat, pitting motorbikes against plastic sword carrying prisoners. And wait until you get a load of the oft-mentioned Cannibal Mutants, who turn out

to be rag-swaddled grunting extras with painted ping pong ball eyes... It sounds as if they culled concepts from a dozen more-successful SF flicks, put 'em through a meat grinder and came up with this celluloid goulash. Even Carradine and Jennings have problems buying this shit and bringing any spirit of fun to their limp roles (though Lynch sputters and slings spittle quite nicely as the ego-mad villain). Their utter seriousness in the midst of this Z-grade muddle is enough to drive you crazy after a while, and even though the script keeps things moving, there's no real rhyme or reason to any of it. The filmmakers couldn't even get the bloodshed quota right, and all we get are dull, repetitive Hand Blaster zappings. As for the horrible spacey music – would you believe Jerry Garcia helped out on the guitar work? At least someone had the good sense to fully exploit Ms. Jenning's figure – she runs about in a skimpy costume for most of the flick (but then again, so does Carradine. Ugh!) and whenever she's being tortured she's naturally in the buff... Passable Saturday morning crapola, but pretty disappointing too.

DEMENTIA

JOHN PARKER 1955 (AKA: DAUGHTER OF HORROR). Long on style and short on subtlety, this eye-popping portrait of insanity has found a cult rep in recent years due to its experimental tone. There's no dialogue (although some reviews say Ed McMahon narrates it, the 16mm print I caught was without Ed's plastered pipes, and probably all the better for it), just incessant soundtrack wailing by Marnie Nixon and a wonderfully grating jazz score by George Antheil. The photography has a nice shadowy feel and several eerie images linger, yet it's still sorta dull at 60 minutes. Sure, the filmmaking is more innovative than most '50s junk, but slow pretentious boredom is a big drawback too... It begins like a distaff version of **Eraserhead**, with mental mess Adrienne Barrett (as the ill-titled' 'Gamin') sitting in her sparse, dingy one-room flat – becoming increasingly frantic as her reality and fantasy collide. Nothing much happens, but it all *looks* great, and director/writer John Parker soaks it in stylistic indulgence and loads on the meaningful symbols... Deciding to roam the city after dark, a midget newspaper vendor (Angelo Rossitto) sells her an edition with the banner headline 'Mysterious Stabbing'. Undaunted, she ends up at the swanky night-spot Club Pronto, on the arm of Bruno VeSota (who really stretches his dramatic range by thesping a playboy bon vivant). The best comes when Adrienne's taken on a tour of her psyche by a tall man with a black stocking pulled over his head. Led to her parents' tombstones, she has a vision of her alcoholic, slob father stretched on a bed in the middle of the misty graveyard; plus her slutty mom lounging on a sofa, stuffing chocolates into her face. And when Adrienne stabs her dad, we wonder if it's a re-enactment of the past, or just a dark subconscious desire. Either way, it's knocked her completely off the edge. She goes chasing after a tacky paste necklace, is hit on by greasy musicians, filets VeSota and tosses him from a window like a 300 pound sack of rutabagas, and spends an interminable amount of time running from the cops... At least this isn't your ordinary psycho-fest. It's refreshing to see a feminine take on the situation, and the film works best as a paranoid nightmare with moments of sickly funny violence (like when Adrienne unloads an unwanted severed hand onto a very confused flower seller). And without question, the scariest moment is watching bloated Bruno eating a chicken dinner in close-up. Laughably overwrought and very different, not to mention barely distributed in its day due to censorship problems.

DEMON

LARRY COHEN 1976 (AKA: GOD TOLD ME TO). As far as I'm concerned, Larry Cohen is one of America's most imaginative genre directors. With efforts like **Black Caesar, It's Alive, Q**, and **The Stuff** to his credit, he's proven that even when his final product isn't completely successful, his vision is a decidedly warped one. Unfortunately, his recent work has virtually leapfrogged theatrical distribution, and has gone straight to video. His two later projects, **Island of the Alive** and **Return to Salem's Lot** (both with Michael Moriarty) did just that. It's too bad, since Cohen's films are masterworks of intelligence compared to the mindrot that's being passed off on home video nowadays. Most recent horror films are satisfied to simply shove a handful of warm intestines into the camera, and most of the public will eat it up without any misgivings. But there are a *few* filmmakers out there (Romero and Cronenberg first come to mind) who have managed to combine original, sophisticated stories *and* gratuitous shock value into audience pleasers. Well, Cohen could fit into this elite sub-group, except that (1) his technical skill has yet to catch up with his artistic visions, and (2) his films have never caught on with the public. Sure, **Cinefantastique** or **Fangoria** may run an article on Cohen, but when you go to see one of his films, you feel like Chuck Heston in **The Omega Man**... Well, to get onto the matter at hand, **Demon** is a case in point. An

intriguing idea, a cast of solid A-Minus actors, plenty of violence, and a complexity not often found in an American fright film. Of course, it didn't make Dime One, even if it is one of Cohen's best films. It begins when a series of seemingly ordinary citizens inexplicably begin to go nuts – a sniper atop a skyscraper picks off pedestrians, a father slaughters his entire family, and a policeman (played by a dead-serious Andy Kaufman) goes bonkers at the St. Patrick's Day parade and unloads his service revolver into the crowd. Each killer is disturbingly calm, collected and completely without remorse, and just before they croak, detective Tony LoBianco asks them the same question, "Why did you do it?" Their answer is identical – "God told me to." The film then traces LoBianco's search for the truth behind the murders, and it leads him through a serpentine trail of seemingly unbelievable tales: Artificial insemination, virgin births, UFO encounters, religious riots, and his own personal relationship to these crimes – all filtered through the mythos of the Catholic Church. Best of all, I'm sure any die-hard Christian would shit a brick at Cohen's Biblical reinterpretations, as well as his ideas about the origins of God and His use of terrorism and fear in keeping mankind disciplined. The end is a little fragmented and half-baked (and since the sound is pretty garbled, you'll be glad to see it on v-tape, so you can rewind and catch all the dialogue), but this is still a remarkably creepy little feature... Amidst some wonderful directorial touches, such as a knife attack on a flight of stairs and a great sequence in a black pool hall, Cohen pulls together some effective NYC locations and an eccentric supporting cast. Sandy Dennis looks like she's in a trance as LoBianco's wife, Sylvia Sydney turns on the tear-duct pathos as a nursing home resident, Deborah Raffin is Tony's decorative girlfriend, and sleaze-show scene-stealer Richard Lynch (**Invasion USA, Cut and Run**) is barely discernible as the final piece in the puzzle. On the negative side, the effects are a bit cheesy, the tone is too heavy-handed at times, and that booming soundtrack *has* to go; but if you give yourself over to Cohen's premise and allow him to shoot away with his buckshot spray of ideas, you'll be in for a unique treat.

THE DEMON LOVER

DONALD G. JACKSON / JERRY YOUNKINS 1976 (AKA: DEVIL MASTER). Several years ago in New York City, I caught a documentary featurette entitled **Demon Lover Diary**, by Joel DeMott, which follows the caustic adventures of cameraman Jeff Kriendes when he's hired by two Michigan factory workers-turned-independent movie moguls to shoot a 14-day flick called **The Demon Lover**. It's a wonderfully scathing look at the inept real-life horrors of schlock moviemaking (with the pair literally chased out of the state and fearing for their lives), capturing a savage view of the bottom-of-the-barrel film biz. Unfortunately, *that* great film isn't available on video yet. Instead all we have is the flaky feature that resulted. And boy, is it a dirt-cheap chunk of crud! A film where the in-jokes are more important than the plot, and the guy in the cardboard demon mask is the most subtle cast member. Perpetrated by people who think they can make extra points by naming characters after comic/horror celebs like Frazetta, Kirby, Ackerman, et cetera; it's also a technical fiasco, with the camera rocking back and forth so much during conversations you'll need Dramamine. The only truly frightening aspect of the movie is its graphic glimpse of '70s Geekdom, since the cast seems to be comprised of every dorky Fan-type they could lure on screen with a tray of hors d'oeuvres. Co-director Jerry Younkins stars as Lavall Blessing, a pudgy Satanist with hair down to his elbows, who rants to his college-age coven about his awesome supernatural powers (which most of 'em scoff off as being 'metaphysical bullshit'). To deal with these sceptics, Lavall tosses a naked woman (luckily he had one on hand) into his pentagram, conjures up a shadowy creature to do his bidding, and one by one the unbelievers are dispatched to that great Non-Acting Troupe in the sky. Younkins is unintentional ridiculous (there's nothing more embarrassing than a fat twerp who thinks he's a macho stud), and the tale never moves beyond middling mind rot – while a detective checks out leads, Lavall flexes his flab and the demon (with red light bulb eyes) weeds out the cast. "Death is a really heavy thing," says one supporting bullethead upon hearing of a friend's murder, and the film might've been a tad more effective if the clueless cast didn't have so much trouble reading the cue cards. Gunnar Hansen keeps a straight face in a small role as Professor Peckinpah (groan), an expert in occult mumbo-jumbo, and there's loads of ugly local colour to pad the running time to barely feature length. But what the movie really needed was to lighten up and laugh at itself a bit. At least the last 10 minutes is a joy, because the entire dumpy cast of unknowns gets to *kill each other* when they're possessed by Lavall. We get a crossbow to the groin, axes into the back, self-mutilation, and buckets of fake blood. Think of the dry cleaning bill! It probably rivalled the entire budget! Years later, co-director Donald Jackson went onto better things – the absurd mess **Rollerblade** and the surprisingly likeable **Hell Comes to Frogtown** – but I have a feeling he'd prefer to keep this jumble off his re-sumé.

DEMONS

LAMBERTO BAVA 1986. A theatre audience made up of total strangers is forced to get to know each other as they band together in an effort to keep from getting torn to pieces. It seems that the grisly violence in the new horror film they've been watching is happening, scene-for-scene, within the theatre. This causes some audience members to die horribly as they turn into demon-possessed monsters with pus-spouting sores, or get their throats bitten out by said demon-possessed monsters. Nobody can get out of the theatre, because some supernatural force won't let the doors open. Darn. That means we're treated to one of the most enjoyable demonic-possession movies since **The Exorcist**. This Italian-produced production also offers an important message: People who are possessed by demons should not fly helicopters. [BJE]

DEMONS 2

LAMBERTO BAVA 1987. First off, I have to admit that I was never a rabid fan of Lamberto Bava's original **Demons**. Sure, it was a fast-paced gut-muncher, but the script weaknesses kept it from the supremely twisted realm of instant classics, like **Street Trash**. Well, the sequel is another step down, and I can understand why it never received the widescale release the first did. Besides jettisoning all semblance of logic, it's also been trimmed (both theatrically *and* on video) to an R-rating. And as we all know, an Italo-zombie flick without guts is similar to the concept of non-alcoholic beer. What's the fuckin' point?!... The first **Demons** had flesh-renders coming off of a movie screen and attacking the audience, and it ended with the demons rampaging throughout the city. This entry in the pasta-land Chunkblower Sweepstakes takes place in an apartment building full of badly-dubbed, unlikeable *GQ*-clones, and it intercuts a TV show they're all watching, about a quartet of tiny-brained teens who for kicks break into the 'Forbidden Zone' – the walled-in area of the town where the original zombies have been quarantined. And if you remember the first well enough, you'll experience lukewarm deja vu at all this nonsense; cuz soon a full-fledged demon erupts from the TV screen (*a la* **Videodrome**'s elastic cathode-ray tube) and the whole building is under siege by grazing ghouls. Of course, all the doors and escape routes are electrically operated, so when the power goes off, the residents are all trapped, like chopped liver at a bar mitzvah. Soon these whiny, yuppie-types are turning into blood-thirsty, drooling monsters, and the big problem with the flick is that I considered the change an

improvement.... Lotsa slime, ooze, rotted teeth, and well-deserved death help pick up the pace in the last half hour, but compared to the original, this one moves like an Eric Rohmer film. Plot lines appear and disappear without resolution, the script has holes large enough to cram Raymond Burr through, and Bava shoves every conceivable idea (good or bad) into the fray. On the good side, there's a demon doggie who's hilariously repulsive, and on the bad, we get a **Gremlins**/**Ghoulies** creature who instead belongs in a Punch and Judy show. A *lot* of potential grimness was lost in the pursuit of a safe R-rating, and all the exorcised bits are obvious – just as someone's going to lose an internal organ, the scene is clipped... Overall, **Demons 2** is nothing special, but even a semi-effective Italo-idiocy is worth checking out eventually.

DESTROY ALL MONSTERS

INOSHIRO HONDA 1968. This is one of my favourites, right up there with **Infra-Man**. For sheer, mindless entertainment, they don't come much better... In the year 1999, all the giant creatures of the earth are herded together on Ogaswara Island (known fondly as Monsterland), and they're kept in line with force-fields and nox-ious-gas buoys. That means that within a couple square miles we've got the combined forces of Godzilla, Mothra, Rodan, and Minyah (Godzilla's obnoxious little kid) – plus their whole scruffy entourage, including Manda (a giant prehistoric snake), Spigas (a giant spider), Baragon and Anguiras (a couple giant dinosaur-types), and plenty of other giant goobers. But when all the imprisonment devices suddenly shut down, the whole danged world becomes a potential playground for the city crushers – Rodan hovers over downtown Moscow (no matter what the ads claim), Mothra crawls toward Peking, Baragon pops up beside the Arch de Triumphe, and best of all, Godzilla lays waste to New York City, wading through the Hudson and sending river front property values plummeting with his atomic-age bad breath. And ultimately, they all converge on Tokyo (those lucky people!) in one of the most incredible barrages of Toho pyrotechnics I've ever seen. Missiles! Rockets! Flames! ROARR! Grrrr! AIIEEEE!!... Now, take a guess who's to blame for all this? Oral Roberts? Oliver North? Nope, it's just a bunch of nasty alien invaders from the planet Kilaak (looking remarkably like oriental women in silver-lamé body suits), who are secretly radio-controlling the escaped creatures and commanding them to use the major cities of the world as a punching-bag. But after a few flying saucer battles on the moon, the earth-folks manage to regain control of The Monster Pack (hip hooray!) and the Kilaaks retaliate by releasing their secret weapon, everyone's favourite three-headed scene-stealer, Ghidrah! By the end, the movie turns into a battle-royale, with *all* The Big Guys taking their turns at giving Ghidrah his just desserts (Godzilla, in

particular, seems to take great pleasure in using Ghidrah's heads as a door-mat)... Director Inoshiro Honda cranks up the film with non-stop excitement, and when the monsters aren't stomping the shit out of a metropolis, they're beating each other to a rubbery pulp – and when the monsters aren't taking centre stage, the human characters are shooting and killing each other – so there's destruction at *every* level and in *every* direction. It's more whole-sale demolition than any single brain can handle in one sitting. I love it!

THE DEVIL

CHANG JEN CHIEH 19??. Craig Ledbetter from **European Trash Cinema** prompted me to pick up this nasty li'l item, and I can say without hesitation that it's the finest worm-vomiting movie I've ever seen!! Holy cow, talk about an oriental freakshow! This obscure import contains moments that'll have any hardcore splatter 'n' slime fa-natic on the floor in a fugue state... Directed by the always popular Chang Jen Chieh, I can't really think of much good to say about this Chinese crock – the photography's fuzzy, the editing is sloppy, and the storyline is fractured to the point of incoherence, but when they decide to pour on the gore, this turns into the Hong Kong equiva-lent of **Bloodsucking Freaks**. There's running sores, boils, vermin of every genus, and most of all *all SNAKES GALORE!!* Big ones. Little ones. They musta trucked 'em in by the cartload! The fun begins when a woman's head is smashed in with a B.F.R. (Big Fuckin' Rock) during the title credits, and moments later (and without any explanation) an old woman slices open a guy's stomach and starts pulling out fistfuls of bugs and slop, while the guy slowly spits up a pailful of live worms. Soon there's all manner of green and red slime oozing from torn flesh, while worms crawl in and out of people's mouths. Sounds great, eh, Slimetimers?... Unfortunately, this gruelling pace isn't sustained, and American video-viewers get dropped into the horribly-dubbed shreds of a love story between a playboy shitheap named Mr. Koo and a beautiful airhead named Miss Chang (first name Shirley). Plus, an annoying brat named Ding Dong is always underfoot with his grating li'l voice... *Suddenly* (everything in this film happens *suddenly*, because the guy who butchered together this US print must've been downing sterno with both hands), a ghostly vision of a witch woman with an acid-scarred face is floating outside Mr. Koo's room, apparently looking for retribution for a past wrong, and just to make sure the audi-ence stays awake, every so often a supporting character becomes 'possessed' with spasms, seizures and snake-mouth. Most of the time, **The Devil** is a laughable soap opera, with Miss Chang learn-ing that her new hubby is a complete and utterly detestable cad, but every so often it hits you over the skull with a scene that'd blow the eyeballs out of an MPAA-censor's sockets. The end is a complete rinky-dink blood bath, when the Bad Guy chops off his own hand with a butcher knife, spits up a stomachful of creeping crawlers straight *into* the camera lens, and proceeds to rip himself to pieces while every type of disgusting critter pours forth from every available orifice. A full minute-and-a-half of this shit. Solid after-dinner entertainment... Check it out, if only to see how truly brain-diseased the seemingly-quiet people of China can be if they really try.

DEVIL GIRL FROM MARS

DAVID MACDONALD 1954. Imagine out-of-this-world idiocy! Your dreams come startlingly TO LIFE with **Devil Girl from Mars**. You thought Americans and Czechs had a lock on bargain basement sci-fi? Wrong! Those Brits can sure deliver big laughs on tiny budgets. A mysterious (sure) flying saucer lands in the Scottish Moors, and the residents at the nearby inn are, uh, interested. An American reporter and a cranky old scientist *just happen* to be in the neighbourhood investigating a plane crash that stock footage

provided at the start of the film. When the ship lands, it puts a plot-enhancing force field around the inn, keeping all those bad actors on the lounge set for our amusement. When the alien emerges, our creature of the title ends up being Naya, a sassy feminist in a Grace Jones leather outfit who packs a mean ray gun. Also, with a device that looks like three swizzle sticks, she can summon her destructo-robot, a frigidaire with a police siren for a head and Muppet felt for arms. Wowee! Decision making abounds as the 'pathetic earth creatures' try to avoid becoming 'seeds to fertilise the Martian race'. Where's Gerrit Graham when you need him? Whenever the devil lady goes away, there's plenty of time for romantic interludes, as our intrepid reporter finds true love with the 'lady from the city'. And these folks can put away the booze, too. But then the old innkeeper checks in with the choice line – "well, while we're still alive, might as well have some tea." We have to thank those wacky wankers at Monocle Pictures for delivering a classic entry in the 'wobbly saucer' genre. By the way, I wouldn't want to spoil the ending. Such inanities should be savoured like fine Pink Champale, served in a Gumby mug. Cheers! [TR]

DIE, MONSTER, DIE!

DANIEL HALLER 1965. If you're an H.P. Lovecraft fan, you might want to take a dump on producers James H. Nicholson and Samuel Z. Arkoff after sitting through this loose (no, change that to *miserable*) adaptation of 'The Colour Out of Space'; but taken on its own minimal merits, this is a silly bit of nonsense from the pre-gore days of schlock cinema. And what monster-movie fanatic could pass up the once-in-a-lifetime (thank god) pairing of Nick Adams and Boris Karloff?!... Nick stars as an American tourist who journeys to Arkham, England in a search for the infamous Witley Estate. All the local residents are terrified of the place, and if their warnings weren't enough, there's plenty of 'subtle' hints that Nicky should turn tail, head home and pull the blankets over his head: Dead,

the ULTIMATE in DIABOLISM
.....can you stand PURE TERROR?

BORIS KARLOFF
NICK ADAMS
SUZAN FARMER

Die Monster Die!

.COLORSCOPE

blackened vegetation litters the path to the mansion; large, locked gates deter trespassers; and shrouded figures peer at him thru the unnatural fog. Once he makes it into the mansion, things don't get any better, either. Creepy Karloff rolls about, as the wheelchair-bound patriarch, Natum Witley. The servants are passing out at the dinner table. And there's a mysterious, glowing Whatzit down in the cellar (all English manors have 'em, right?). None of this phases Noodleheaded Nick though – he just keeps diddling with Boris' pretty daughter, because he's too stupid (or horny) to suspect anything is wrong, The first hour is slow going, with only Karloff keeping us from catatonia, but once the characters begin mutating into spotty-faced killers it picks up a bit of steam. If you couldn't already guess, the thing in the basement is a meteorite, and its green radiation is slowly softening the family's combined brainpan while transforming them into dime-store monstrosities. And for the final showdown/chase-thru-the-house, Boris becomes a bald stand-in covered with glow-in-the-dark paint. Directed by Daniel Haller, who later monkeyed around with HPL's **The Dunwich Horror** (which could've been a classic, if only Peter Fonda hadn't departed from the lead at the last moment), there's a few twisted images which remind you it was once a Lovecraft tale. But the majority of it is consistently laughable trash. Boris gives the proceedings an air of dignity, but Nick Adams (**Frankenstein Conquers the World**, **Monster Zero**, **Mission Mars**) has all the charisma of a cold bologna sandwich on Wonder Bread.

DIMENSION 5

FRANKLIN ANDREON 1966. I've finally found a worthy entry in the **Slimetime** 'schlock Saturday afternoon sci-fi misfire' category. This super-boring talkfest gives one a glimpse at how Ed Wood might have directed **You Only Live Twice**. Or maybe a **Star Trek** episode titled 'City on the Edge of Burbank'. Jeffrey Hunter (who would go on to obscurity in many Italo-Spanish co-productions) stars as a Lithium-addled Bond clone who spends most of his time going 30 seconds into the future with his K-Mart time travel belt. That's when he's not *talking* on the 'vid-phone' to another Equity 'boss type' about finding the hideout of supervillain Big Buddha (!), who turns out to be Oddjob in a wheelchair. Add the music by 'Score Productions', and you've got to be kidding me. Old Jeff has a female sidekick (played by TV vet France Nuyen) and they run

around the backlot a little. When they're not *talking*. They run into Oddjob's musclemen, named Stoneface, Squeaky, and Genghis (sure). They are forced (hopefully at gun point) to say lines like "Hey, there's more cooking here than chop suey!" Yes, it's the URANIUM 240! Concealed in rice containers! After a couple of phoned in fight scenes, the actors collect their paycheques and go home, while the editors find some more stock footage of planes landing to pad out this... this... Wait, I should mention that **Dimension 5** was written by Arthur C. Pierce, who went on to greater fame with **2001**. Quite a... just a second... I'm getting this note from one of my assistants.. Oh, that was Arthur C. *Clarke*! Well, I'll bet he's happy he didn't write **Dimension 5**. [TR]

DOLEMITE

D'URVILLE MARTIN 1974. At long last, a diseased video distributor (Xenon Video Inc.) has had the guts to resurrect the career of Rudy Ray Moore – unquestionably the *worst* blaxploitation star of all time! And between this flick and its sequel, **The Human Tornado**, we have two of the most sledge-hammer-stereotyped, anti-intelligence epics of all time! THE most pathetic kung fu comedy/actioners in the history of 42nd Street cinema, they're all but unwatchable for anyone except the seriously demented (which unfortunately for our braincells, includes most of us here at **Slimetime**). Each film is nothing but a 90-minute ego-massager for urban-night-club 'comic' Rudy Ray Moore, who looks into a mirror and sees a cross between Richard Pryor and Fred Williamson – but in truth he's just a sorry lard ass with a wincible wardrobe. The Benny Hill of the grindhouse set!... Rudy stars as Dolemite, a street-smart pimp who's arrested on trumped-up drug charges. But when his young nephew is killed in a narcotics-related drive-by shooting, Dolemite squeezes outta his cell and agrees to work undercover for the Feds in order to bring the town's drug czar to justice. Hitting the streets with his entourage of adoring, karate-chopping poon-tang, he antagonises his competition by forcibly buying back his old night-club, pipelining a slew of women (who inexplicably spread their legs whenever this fatshit snaps his fingers) and abusing every corrupt, racist white asshole in Actors Equity. And when he isn't dealing with his ever-adoring public, he's verbally blasting his enemies with his intolerable, rappin'/rhymin' dialogue! This superstud even has his own skimpily-dressed Dolemite

Dancers!... It's a true Boom Mike Watcher's Delight, and Rudy's such a puffy-eyed mess throughout that I wouldn't doubt it if you told me he was popping PCP like it was Pez candies. Be fore-warned though, all this nonsense is pretty slow moving until the last 10 minutes, when everyone gets to partake in a kick-butt free-for-all, with Rudy Ray looking less like a martial arts expert than a guy with a painful rectal itch. Directed and co-starring D'Urville Martin, who's been in enough good blaxploiters (such as **Black Caesar**) to know better... My professional advice: Check out **The Human Tornado** first. The follow-up is loads more fun simply because it's *so* fuckin' incompetent (trust me, there *is* logic at work here). If you enjoy that one, you can then complete the Rudy Ray Experience, including his in-concert performance video, **Rude** (once again proving that any piece of tripe can get marketed nowadays)... Rudy Ray Moore. He's big! He's bad! He's FAT! And he needs a flatbed truck in order to lug his ego around with him!

THE DOLL SQUAD

TED V. MIKELS 1973. The infamous Ted V. Mikels **(The Corpse Grinders, The Astro-Zombies)** is at it again with another low-budget churn-'em-out, so he can keep himself and his seven live-in mistresses out of hock. I was hoping for some type of gutter-level babes and bloodshed classic, but instead, **The Doll Squad** turns out to be a tediously inane actioner that barely reaches TV movie level... When an evil, foreign extortionist blows up a manned-rocket at Cape Kennedy, the US government (boo! hiss!... Oh, wait a minute. You mean they're the *good* guys in this movie? Don't make me laff!) sends out that super-secret band of furious femmes, The Doll Squad (tah dah!). Led by head-bimbo, Sabrina, this band of bimbettes fights for justice, truth and the freedom to look like talentless models. And like all good CIA agents, they shoot first and ask questions later, torturing prisoners into submission until they discover the ringleader of the terrorists (played by Michael Ansara)... You thought **Charlie's Angels** was bad with three high-fashion floosies? This film's got *three times* as many (in fact, Mikels tried to sue **Charlie's Angels** for stealing his idea. I don't think he made a cent) – but unlike **CA**'s, these gals keep getting bumped off one-by-one throughout the picture. The last half hour has them roaming about in bikinis and skin-tight action-wear,

infiltrating Ansara's fortress and learning of his Master Plan to infect the world's water supply with Bubonic Plague! But do we actually get to see entire cities dropping like flies? Nope. The actors sure talk up a storm, but the excitement is nil. The 'Big Finale' has a few limp explosions and lotsa gunplay, but the PG-rated blood-shed is minimal (i.e. when a woman is shot in the face, you only see the blood spurt from the back of the head). There really isn't much to recommend about this film – there's some wimpy hand-to-hand combat and third rate James bond weaponry (flame-throwing cigarette lighters, lipstick radios, mace-spraying rings), but at its 100 minute running time, it seems *twice* as long (blame the film editor, who was – take a guess – Ted V. Mikels). As for the cast, can you say dull, mindless and not even particularly good-looking? Francine York comes off the best as Sabrina, but isn't there something seriously wrong with a film that manages to make Tura Satana (star of Russ Meyer's **Faster Pussycat! Kill! Kill!**) look mundane? This is pretty dull stuff... The *only* thing I enjoyed were the split-second psychedelic/kaleidoscopic segues between each scene. Dig it!

DOLLS

STUART GORDON 1987. Stuart Gordon, between directing **Re-Animator** and **From Beyond**, tried something a bit subtler and his kick-in-the-ass reward from Empire Prod. was almost no theatrical distribution whatsoever. Sure, it's better than 90% of their pathetic pix, but if it's a tough sell, Empire would rather dump it into the video wasteland and not worry about it... Like Gordon's other flicks, **Dolls** has some fine, violent sequences with plenty of nasty humour (such as when a girl's teddy bear comes to life and mauls her parents), but this movie is definitely *not* for pin-headed gore-mongers. Instead of inspiring to gross-out the audience, Gordon is tinkering with childhood fantasies and fears, mixed with a dab of old-fashioned ghoulishness... A little girl and her parents (a block-headed father and an evil stepmother) are travelling through the English Middle-of-Nowhere when their car breaks down. Oddly enough (OK, so it really isn't odd at all. So sue me.), they find a creepy mansion and a friendly (albeit slightly crazy) old couple who invites them in. It turns out the Seniors are toy-makers, and their home is a veritable museum for dolls. Toss in a few more stranded characters (including a couple of ultra-annoying Madonna-clones) and you get the feeling Gordon is trying for an **Old Dark House**-style of dark-and-stormy-night filmmaking. It's certainly not a complete success, but the pace picks up when one of the female dumbshits maliciously tosses a doll on the floor. From then on, you know she's dead slutmeat! You see, these cute li'l toys are alive and they can be quite bloodthirsty (especially if they think you're an asshole) – taking chunks out of your flesh, stabbing repeatedly at you with tiny knives or simply ripping your eyeballs out of their sockets. The dolls' animation is effective, and when they *really* start attacking, it's fairly silly (but undeniably fun) may-hem. The mood is shattered, but it all had me laughing out loud at these rabid Barbies and Kens... Guy Rolfe and Hilary Mason are OK as the oldsters, and surprisingly enough, the sweet little girl (Carrie Lorraine) didn't annoy me as much as I thought she would. All the other characters made me gnash my teeth until my gums bled... Despite the fact that everything is telegraphed *far* in advance, this is a modest, sorta-effective addition to Gordon's short filmography. Try to catch it if it's a CHEAP rental.

DOPE-MANIA

1987. Wow! Only Rhino Video could get away with lashing to-gether clips from all those ridiculous anti-drug propaganda movies from the '30s through the late '60s, and end up with this hokey, hilarious masterpiece! So get your mind-warping substances ready, kids, because for 60 minutes we get to wade knee-deep in marijuana-crazed youths – smoking, killing and eventually leaping out of windows to their death simply because they've taken a quick puff of the dreaded reefer! As any red-blooded, government-hypnotised American knows, dope leads directly to mainlining heroin and gargling Drano, until the future leaders of Our Country are turned into marijuana addicts – "floating out of the world of reality, toward a midnight of eventual regret and despair." And we get to revel in brutal crimes, weird pot parties, evil drug peddlers, and more all-out, full-blown campiness than you can shake a joint at. My favourite sections include: **Chinese Justice**, a gritty newsreel showing the execution of a bunch of oriental drug-addicts, who are one-by-one shot in the back of the head; **Use Your Eyes**, an offensive, '60s how-to guide for policemen, showing them how to find and arrest those dope-smokers while they're in the privacy of their own home; and **One-Way Ticket To Hell**, in which a nice girl joins a motorcycle gang, smokes a reefer, and two months later she's a snivelling junkie, pouring down six bottles of Seconal and ending up in a sanatorium (gosh, I hate it when that happens). At the end, they tack on chapter one of **The Weed of Death**, a *silent* western serial with dialogue cards such as 'There's too much marijuana smoking on this ranch, and it has to stop!'... And audiences actually fell for this type of horseshit? It's scary to think that people were *that* stupid, but on the other hand, they're still churning out propaganda like **The Drug Knot** and **Tough Love** in order to help extend the dope-a-phobic paranoia of right-wing shitheaps... This is a video you'll want to watch over and over, until your brain gets soft and mushy. Even if you thought **Reefer Madness** and its off-shoots were a bit slow-paced, **Dope-Mania** takes care of that problem by hacking out all the tedious crap and giving us only the heart of the goofiness. I only wish the tape had been longer.

DR. DUCK'S SECRET SECRET, ALL-PURPOSE SAUCE

Michael Nesmith (the John Lennon of The Monkees), spent his time on this comedy/music collage instead of touring with The Tired Trio in recent years. In structure, it's similar to his Grammy-award winning **Elephant Parts** (in fact, most of it is made up of clips from his short-lived, low-rated **Television Parts**), but in creative content, it's more like a bad cable-access show. His musical guests include Jimmy Buffett, Jim Stafford and Rosanne Cash, a trio of the most obnoxious no-talent scuzzballs the so-called entertainment industry could mass-produce. A good five minutes of hilarity crammed into a 90 minute run time. Ouch!...

DR. GOLDFOOT AND THE BIKINI MACHINE

NORMAN TAUROG 1965. Nothing in Vincent Price's long career of horror could've possibly prepared him for the SHEER TERROR of starring on-screen with one of the most FRIGHT-INDUCING performers of all time: Frankie Avalon! American-International decided to attempt an off-shoot of their waning Beach Party series, by tossing teen heartburn, er, heart*throb* Avalon outta his swimming trunks and into a dim-witted secret agent setting. The result tries so hard to be 'wacky' that it makes the Matt Helm series look like Tom Clancy... Frankie stars as Craig Gamble (aka Agent 00¼), a bumbling operative for Secret Intelligence (ha!) Command, who unwittingly discovers that gorgeous, indestructible, man-hungry robots are being rolled off an assembly line by the nefarious Dr. Goldfoot (Price, in gold Aladdin slippers), for a plan to have 'em marry the world's richest playboys (including co-star Dwayne 'Dull as a Doormat' Hickman). Some plot, eh? But with a title like this, what did you expect, Paddy Chayefsky? Will the helmet-haired Frankie (who's also fallen for one of the luscious automatons) save society from certain seduction? Nobody cares! Because even a

trenchcoat can't cloak the fact Avalon has all the natural charisma of dry toast. At least we're lucky the guy doesn't get to sing! Of course, Vincent is always fun to watch (with or without his dignity) – whether he's demonstrating his latest invention (a disintegrating lipstick), or surrounded by a bevy of gold-bikinied casting couchettes who take the opportunity to Watusi whenever the generic surf 'n' barf soundtrack kicks in. Price is egomaniacal, money-hungry, pompous, and altogether nasty as heck – and it's a pleasure to watch the Master of Menace at work, with his dungeon full of booby-traps, flashing computer banks, and clumsy assistant named Igor. Director Norman Taurog visually puns his way along, thanks to previous experience with live-action cartoon characters such as Jerry Lewis (**The Caddy**) and Elvis Presley (**Blue Hawaii**). There are also clay-animated title credits courtesy of Gumby-creator Art Clokey, Looney Tune sound effects, and several winks to other AIP products (such as cameos by Eric Von Zipper and The Pendulum)... Admittedly energetic, hopelessly hokey, and so damned nostalgic it makes the bile rise. It was followed by Mario Bava's **Dr. Goldfoot and the Girl Bombs** (with Fabian, no less!).

DR. HECKYL AND MR. HYPE

CHARLES B. GRIFFITH 1980. I pulled this one out of my own private video vault – something I recorded off Elvira's Movie Macabre about four years ago and never watched, and it was sorta cool seeing all those old commercials from Cleveland. This Golam-Globulus production stars Oliver Reed in a take-off of the ol' Jekyll/Hyde thing. O'Reed is a very *very* ugly podiatrist with very big feet in a medical centre of loonybirds (I think this is *supposed* to be a comedy). There's a Dr. Hoo who specialises in a new process called Acu-Tickling, constantly brandishing a pair of feathers, and the consistently obese Dr. Hinkle (Mel Welles) who's currently concocted a new potion that turns fat ladies thin in a matter of minutes. Dr. Heckyl follows this girl to the bus stop every day to leer and smile with his disfigured teeth, and when the girl shows up at his office (her name is Coral Collen) he tries to pick her up ("my heart is in your feet"). Of course she screams her head off, so he decides to kill himself with an overdose of Dr. Fatso's potion ("Two drops can kill a horse"), and the potion turns him – you guessed it – 'beautiful' (or as beautiful as an overweight O'Reed can be). The one catch is, he tends to get real angry at anyone who doesn't think so, so he kills them (surprise). He tries to run down women with his car (great pick-up artist), picks up a whore named Liza Round (the film is full of 'great' jokes like this), kills his downstairs neighbour by sticking her foot in a light socket, and throws all the bodies in a dumpster ('Flynn's Bins'). By the end things get really silly as O'Reed keeps switching identities. Coral finds love in the ugly but good hearted Dr. Heckyl while Mr. Hype just wants to screw her and kill her. Dr. Hoo drinks the potion and turns into his secretary (?). Finally Heckyl/Hype is shot in bed with Coral and dies saying "Now we're dead, and I'm still a virgin". Great ending, eh? Not great cinema or even good comedy, but not as bad as you would think. REAL BAD humour and O'Reed's performance keep it together. Directed by Charles B. Griffith (the writer of **The Wild Angels** and **A Bucket of Blood**) and with cameos by Dick Miller as a garbageman ("garbage is my life") and Jackie Coogan as the annoyed Police Chief Fleacollar. [SS]

DR. PHIBES RISES AGAIN

ROBERT FUEST 1972. "What man could conceive of such a bizarre way to kill?" "A man called Phibes. Dr. Anton Phibes."... I've never seen the first **Dr. Phibes** movie, so the recap at the beginning was helpful. ("There have been many tales of the abominable Dr. Phibes. All of them unfortunately true!") It's been three years since the good doctor's wife was killed and the Doc himself disfigured (in a take-off of **The Phantom of the Opera**). Phibes and his wife have been in suspended animation until the 'moon reaches alignment with the rest of the universe', letting him roam again. The indomitable Vincent Price reprises his role as Anton Phibes, champion of elaborate murders, who keeps his face on throughout (in a great Edgar Bergen imitation, Vince doesn't move his mouth through this whole movie!), this time caught in a race after the 'secret of eternal life' which will bring his beloved back to life. Also after this secret is Dr. Biederbecker (Robert Quarry), a 100+ year old middle-ager whose continuance is necessitated by The River of Life! In his search, Phibes kills very imaginatively — by scorpions, by spikes through the head, by crushing a man into a 3'x5' box ("I don't know about his body, but I suppose we should give his head a decent burial."), and by sandblasting a man's face off! I'd just like to know where Phibes finds things like giant wind machines and sandblasters in the middle of the desert. It's all strictly PG, but the scenery chewing gestures by Price and his 'goddess of mime', Vulnavia (Valli Kemp) are worth the price of admission. Good 'Saturday afternoon with nothing else to do' viewing. [SS]

DRIVE-IN MADNESS

TIM FERRANTE 1987. Exploitation fanatics should get a solid kick out of this video tribute to the lost days of drive-in movies. Director/producer/writer Tim Ferrante mixes wonderfully idiotic trailers and interviews into a 90 minute grab bag that highlights some of the absolute *worst* clinkers ever to reach the screen. An ode to Trash Cinema. With (somewhat hokey) narration by James **Return of the Living Dead** Karen leading us by the nose, we're treated to coming attractions for no-star epics such as **Don't Open the Window**, **Blood Bath**, **Macabro**, **Nurse Sherri**, **Girls For Rent**, **Blazing Stewardesses**, and (*my* favourite) **Blood of Ghastly Horror**. There's a conversation with Forrest J. Ackerman, who tells us about his experiences on the set of **Dracula vs. Frankenstein**. Schlock kingpin Samuel M. Sherman gives us some backyard info on Independent-International Pictures. The ever-more-vacuous Linnea Quigley makes an appearance for the hairy-palmed T&A crowd. Bobbie Bresee comes up with some half-baked comments, including how bringing back the drive-ins would 'clean up the drug problem' — this earth-shaking declaration from an actress who played a killer bug-woman in **Evil Spawn**. Most recognisable are George Romero and Tom Savini, who ramble away for a few minutes, with Romero hitting the video's intellectual high ground with some observations on today's disposable culture. The entire package is a little uneven and I doubt any film scholars will be quoting from it in their dissertations, but for a fun overview on the decline of the American drive-in and the upsurge of videomania, it hits all the bases: A little information, lots of self-proclaimed expert testimony and plenty of cheap laughs. The only adverse criticism is in the video's continually lame interruption by a pair of actors portraying a typical couple from the '50s. But for the majority of the programme, you can happily switch off your brain and bask in the ever-grainy world of Cinemanure.

EAT AND RUN

CHRISTOPHER HART 1987. This is definitely the pay-cable oddity of the month. It's a *terrible* fucking movie, but it has one of the goofiest ideas I've sat through in some time. In a nutshell, R.L. Ryan (the lardo from **Toxic Avenger** and **Street Trash**) stars as a bald, 500-pound space humanoid who waddles around the city eating Italians... Now you might ask yourself, with a plot like *that* how could it be a loser? At the very least it should provide some dumbass laughs, right? WRONG, because instead of focusing on Ryan's cannibalistic alien, culprit — er — director Christopher Hart spends most of the time following Ron 'No-Personality-Whatsoever' Silver around as a cop who's investigating the recent upsurge in missing persons. He's the type of genuinely unfunny comic character that you'd like to see shoved headfirst into a vat of pigshit. But I guess the director thought Silver was a laugh riot, cuz this goofhead stinks up the screen for most of the 84 *long* minutes... Meanwhile, all *we* want is more footage of R.L. Ryan chewing up citizens (you never actually see him ingest anyone, unfortunately) and spitting out their shirt buttons. Ryan doesn't say a word as (get this) Murray Creature, but he's the only good thing in sight, especially when he's dressed up in his size-68 Boy Scout outfit, or licking his chops after a fresh meal. The rest of the film *sucks*, of course. It's slow, pathetic, and laced with so much lame, inept humour that I'm surprised Troma didn't have their logo encrusted on the credits... I assume they were trying to make a 'cult' movie, but they left out all the essentials... No gore. No sex. No humour. No fucking way!

EEGAH!

NICHOLAS MERRIWETHER 1963. Just when you think you've seen every type of teen exploitation flick imaginable, here's another brilliant new concept: What if an eight-foot-tall prehistoric caveman named Eegah (complete with club and animal skin) made his way to civilisation? Well, this could have been a great film, but in the hands of director/producer Arch Hall Sr. (using the pseudonym Nicholas Merriwether) it turns into a minor motion picture with enough idiocy to keep you watching, even if you aren't exactly enjoying yourself... It starts off when a teenybopper (Marilyn Manning) catches a sighting of the creature and spreads the word. Of course, most of the townsfolk don't believe one bit of her story, so Marilyn, her dad (played by Arch Hall Sr., under yet another pseudonym, William Watters), and her greasy heartthrob (Arch Hall Jr.) head into the desert in their dune buggy to search for the swinging Cro-Magnon. You want action?!

You want excitement?! Well, there ain't a speck of it here! Only loads of pathetic laughter at watching Richard Kiel (once again typecast as The Big Whatzit) in a K-Mart wig and beard, gurgling incoherent Cavemanese ("Urgh. Lubba bluh." — Actually, it kinda reminded me of Stallone's dialogue in **Rambo**). Eventually, Marilyn and her dad are kidnapped, and we learn that Eegah isn't such a bad guy after all — he's just a misunderstood lug who wants nothing more than a few friends to liven up his Lifestyle of the Ugly and Unintelligible... See Eegah shave for the first time! See Eegah bring Marilyn flowers! See Eegah rip Marilyn's blouse when his hormones kick into third gear! And would you believe that *all* this action is stretched into 92 minutes of screen time? There was more plot in any half-hour episode of **It's About Time**. During the last 10 minutes our heroes escape and Eegah cries 96 tears for his lost love, before heading toward the town. He wants his woman back (!) and he smashes down prop doors and smells his way to Marilyn's house – finally running amok at a teen pool party. Even the ending is pretty lame, but since it's the most exciting part of this fiasco, I won't bitch too much... On the performing side, Arch Hall Jr. sings up an off-key storm, proving once again that any guy off the street can become a movie star if his father's directing the picture. And wait until you hear the songs he 'treats' us to – my fucking god! He makes Barry 'Shitstick' Manilow look like Bob Dylan! Just be prepared to leave the room the moment Arch Jr. picks up his guitar and exercises his tonsils... Not the Badfilm classic I was hoping for, but **Eegah!** is temporarily amusing if you're in the mood to have your intelligence insulted and your brain softened.

EL TOPO

ALEJANDRO JODOROWSKY 1971. Alejandro 'Chuckles' Jodorowsky's Zen Western epic demanded I light the made-in-Taiwan-Buddha-incense-burner and smoke the leopard-skin-pipe-from-hell before trying this symbolism-till-your-brain-explodes-no-sync-sound fest. This film is so full of stuff it made my head hurt, but it's a good type of pain. Y'know, the dull sort of throb you get when you keep pressing on an infected tooth till it hurts. Or the kind of pain you get in your crotch after masturbating yourself through 12 hours of porn films. Yeah, that's more like this film – a pretentious, overblown, over-embellished piece of enlightened celluloid nonsense that I ended up liking a hell of a lot. Obviously written and directed by a madman in size 20 shoes, Dr. Jodorowsky wore all the (black) hats in this one – producer, writer, director, and composer. And if that's not enough, he also stars as our Master Gunfighter named El Topo (The Mole), embarking on a two hour surrealistic journey toward absolute Zen enlightenment only to be blinded by the knowledge he seeks ("like the mole who tunnels through the ground searching for the sun"). We find our anti-visionary hero and his always naked son as they stumble upon a massacred village complete with a river of blood, and he goes off to avenge the evil deed. First he finds a group of bandito scumbags who like to suck on women's shoes and fuck images of naked women that they draw in the sand (I guess that's what they did before blow-up dolls). Then he stumbles upon the fortress of the Colonel, an illusion of a dictator who must be dressed and toupeed by his woman slave so he can preside over more bandito-scumbags who like to waltz with shackled monks and then ride them like donkeys while they blow their noses in pages of the bible. Soon Mr. Topo is leaving his now-robed son with the monks and rides off with the woman slave who requests that he kill four master gunfighters who reside in the desert (*now* things begin to get weird). Master #1 is a blind, gaunt, Jesus-like figure who lives in a small-walled fortress guarded by a man with no legs strapped to a man with no arms (wait'll you see these guys climb a ladder); Master #2 lives with his family dressed in heavy Russian military garb whose father is a babbling idiot and whose mother chirps like a bird; Master #3 lives in a pen of dead bunnies; and Master #4 sort of reminds me of a cross between Terry Gilliam in **Monty Python and the Holy Grail** and The Master in **Kung Fu**. Having obtained enlightenment from these masters he is ready to join up with a group

of deformed weirdoes who live in a hole in the ground and are trying to join a town of sadistic assholes (sort of like NYC) who like to rape young black boys so they can string them up. After a public-humiliation-fuck-a-midget sequence he has another son, just after he finds his first son... Well, reading this back it sure sounds like a mess on paper, but on film after about an hour it starts making a sort of hallucinogenic sense. Filled with wonderfully pretentious images and dynastic Japanese statements, this is definitely an entertaining, mindbending, image-rich hunk o' film (it was one of John Lennon's favourites, no surprise), with a great soundtrack of droning annoyances and fantastically executed images designed to explore the beauty of disgust. Rumour has it 'Dr. J' filmed this entirely in sequence, sort of making it up as he went along. Don't expect any on-screen haemorrhaging, just gallons and gallons of psychedelic Zen Vomit from the mind of a crazed Chilean. Definitely recommended. [SS]

ELVIRA, MISTRESS OF THE DARK

JAMES SIGNORELLI 1988. Elvira's a rock 'n' harpy – she's a skintight porchlight – a slimy slithering succubus – a one woman Sodom and Gomorrah – a walking hormone – a size E breast in a size C bra – why, she could drown me in her spit – serve me dinner on a sabre tooth plate – she's got a leopard skin interior and a chain steering wheel – she's a slap in the face of the Morality Club – she's a tit joke a minute – she's a poodle's pink mohawk – a prepubescent's best friend – she can do things with pasties a normal man can only dream of – she's a tarred and feathered movie hostess – she's a knockout in black panties – she's a tattooed monster of sexual innuendoes and has a sneer even Elvis is jealous of – Her movie? Well, it has something to do with an inheritance which brings her to the ultra-conservative Falwell Massachusetts, nose-to-nose in a morality struggle with Chastity Pariah and a mortality struggle with her Uncle Vinny over a book of spells. And then there's the kindly townspeople who want to burn the Big E (and her breasts) alive. The more plot the movie attempts, the less it succeeds, but for cheesy jokes, you don't get any dumber than "Sorry I'm late, but so's my aunt". [SS]

END OF THE ROAD

ARAM AVAKIAN 1970. "This may sound somewhat theatrical, but would you mind telling me where I can go for $58.75?" Jake Horner is at his 'end of the road'. Unable to handle the demands of daily life and suffering a major identity crisis, he lapses into catatonia. On a train platform, he is found by 'Doctor D' (James Earl Jones) and is spirited off to 'The Farm', a Fellini-esque rehab centre in the country, for special care. Aram Avakian's film of John Barth's complex novel is an undiscovered gem from an all-too-brief period (late '60s-early '70s) when artistic (read 'difficult') films boasted fine casts and studio production values. Some of the more abstract psychedelic sequences in **End** might seem dated to a '90s 'yuppie scum' audience. However, most of the film has an 'in-your-face' style (courtesy fine camerawork by Gordon Willis) that truly evokes modernised writings of Barth, Tom Robbins and Thomas Pynchon, an elusive connection that hasn't succeeded often on screen. After 20 years, the film's off-centre mixture of black humour, caustic wit, and profound disillusion still hits the spot. Starring a pre-detox Stacy Keach. [TR]

ENDURANCE

1985. This concept must've been mindroastingly fun at some point, but *not* in its final incarnation. Not after the schmucks at New Star Video got their tampering li'l hands on it... Imported from Japan, **Endurance** is a real-life game show that took the Land of the Rising Sun by storm. And it's the most apologetically sadistic and mean-spirited competition you'll ever witness. Two teams of

adult male idiots are forced to endure the most asinine (and sometimes painful) stunts imaginable while their wise-ass hosts crack jokes. The contestants are dragged for a mile on their asses across gravel and logs; licked by unfriendly lizards; bitten on the face by catfish; forced to swallow whole sheep's brains and baby bottles full of Tabasco sauce; made to suffer through below zero weather in their underwear; drink beer and then see which ones can hold their bladder the longest; hung upside down with hot coals on their feet, while magnifying glasses are used to roast their nipples; and (in one of my favourite scenes) the quite-willing contestants are tied down on a cross, after which rats are placed on their bare chests and little children beat them with rocks. Why do they go through all this public embarrassment and physical agony? Is it for the prizes? (Probably not, since all they win is a lousy six-day trip to the US.) Do they see themselves as modern-day samurai? Or is it all due to the fact (as a friend of mine once stated during a moment of drug-induced awareness) 'These guys were hit by The Bomb! They're all mutants!'... If there's a portion of their body that can be abused, it'll end up pummelled. If there's a wild animal that can paw, claw or salivate on them, they'll allow it. And if it can be ingested (usually raw, cold and whole), they'll eat it. It's a complete fuckin' freakshow, and I'd love to get a gander at the sake bill for the writers who come up with these torturous stunts. I never really laughed out loud at any of this nonsense, but there's a Weirdness Level at work that makes the whole thing compelling (though a 90 minute dose of it is a little much)... Now, the warning: All this is perfectly acceptable (albeit sick) entertainment. But there's always some 'creative' goon behind a desk who wants to 'improve' upon a good idea. So instead of simply translating the damned show and leaving twisted enough alone, New Star decided to add 'comical' narration (as in, NOT FUNNY FOR ONE DAMNED MINUTE!). This never-ending barrage of lousy jokes and lame accents dilute the on-screen sadism, and though this type of dickheaded over-dubbing might make the show more appealing to dim-witted viewers who want to chuckle at stupid foreigners, it's just another example of pandering to the lowest possible IQ level. (Of course, you could always turn the sound off, but then you'd miss the contestants' screams of pain). **Endurance** is a curious little item, and luckily it's inherently strange enough to withstand its US distribution dipshits.

EVEN DWARVES STARTED SMALL

WERNER HERZOG 1970 (ORIGINAL TITLE: AUCH ZWERGE HABEN KLEIN ANGEFANGEN – more closely translated as 'Even Dwarves Have to Start Somewhere'). Director Werner Herzog is primarily known as the temperamental genius behind **Fitzcarraldo** and **Aguirre, Wrath of God**, but if you thought these epics in indulgence and jungle insanity were off the deep end, here's one of his very first features. Would you believe one of his early, *really* weird films? Featuring a wailing soundtrack, exotic setting, stark surreal images, and a cast comprised exclusively of dwarves. But despite being a truly twisted work, it's not a great film by any means. It's overlong and repetitive, yet unforgettable for its gruelling effect on the nervous system and number of ill laughs it evokes... Our setting is a stony, isolated compound called The Institution, which doubles as a minimum security prison for a small group of dwarves. But the moment their captors leave for a day, the inmates tear down the phone lines and go on a rampage of destruction: Riding motorcycles, cackling gleefully, breaking dishes, burning flowers, and wrecking everything that represents Authority to 'em. The only administrator on duty is one equally-tiny 'instructor' who barricades himself in his office while the others heave live chickens through his windows. Running amok, this 8-pack of half-pint maniacs eventually take their muzzled frustration out on each other, tormenting a pair of blind dwarves who eerily go about their daily routine in the midst

of the chaos; indulging in sexual games on the oversized furniture, with beds so huge they need a start to get on them; and even to senseless killing of their farm animals. Sounds demeaning to the actors? Nope, cause it's even crueller on the viewer, who feels mentally assaulted by this powerful, but unnerving portrait of revolution. By the end you'll feel like you've gone insane too, especially listening to the smallest of the inmates, Hombre, who has the most hideously infectious chortle. I couldn't stop laughing at the endearing li'l homunculus. Herzog utilises his usual (over)long takes to stultifying effect, but several hilarious sequences (such as a bug collection with the insects dressed in li'l bride and groom clothes, and a beetle with a tiny top hat) keep you from OD-ing on the comically curdled destruction and unceasing Germanic gibbering of the cast. And just in case you wondered, it's never explained *why* everyone in the cast is under four-foot-tall, they simply are. Is it all some kind of monstrous metaphor? Or just an excuse to have a gang of demented dwarves crucify a monkey? Probably a little of both, knowing Herzog's fucked up mentality. Without a doubt, this is a film only a madman like Herzog could (or would want to) make... Included in the cast is a one-legged chicken.

EVIL BRAIN FROM OUTER SPACE

TERVO ISHII / AKIRA MITSUWA / KOREYOSHI AKASAKA 1956. Nowadays, only the most die-hard fans of Japanese junk movies remembers Starman (also known as Super Giant), the superhero who blazed a cheesy path across oriental TV screens during the late '50s. In the '60s, a crafty US distributor bought the rights to a bunch of episodes and stitched them together into four feature length flicks (the other titles include **Invader from Space**, **Atomic Rulers of the World** and **Attack from Space**), and even today they hold up as wonderfully silly, SF nonsense filled with unpretentious stupidity. The Rising Sun's equivalent to **Space Patrol** from Shintoho Co., featuring creaky kung fu and papier-mâché production design... Dig this hokey plot! Balazar, the evil ruler of the Planet Zumar, may be dead, but his brilliant brain lives on in a preservation unit (which looks suspiciously like a piece of cheap luggage). And like all intergalactic slimeballs, Balazar wants to subjugate the universe, beginning with that grubby li'l planet named Earth! The High Council of the Mophead Galaxy (a bunch of tin-foil robots and baggy starfish-men sitting at a dining room table) meets on the Emerald Planet (a sloppily painted backdrop), and for some dumb reason decides to save our planet by sending resident superlug Starman to the Earth's aid. Disguised as a human (he wears a business suit over his costume), Starman and his ever-present pot belly go after the cerebral suitcase, which a bumbling bad guy loses in the river. And it triggers a series of events that include the involvement of a one-legged thug, a couple obnoxious brats, and several unforgettably chintzy atomic ape mutants. But my best advice is to ignore the puddle-deep plot and simply enjoy the action! Monster Mavens will be in orbit, because the idiotic fisticuffs and inept gymnastics never cease, with extras in tights and ski masks leaping about, baring their wiggly fangs and flailing their limbs like someone put sterno in their haemorrhoid cream. Luckily Starman's always on the scene to pummel 'em into smegma... Hard to believe, but the stilted dialogue is even *worse* than normal – "This is no real doctor. This is a Zumerian mutant," the narrator dryly informs us; and a police dispatcher gives the A.P.B., "You are to procede to the area and seek a monster." With Ken Utsui, Junko Ikeuchi and the ever-popular Shoji Kakayama; I haven't seen this stuff since I was 10 years old, and it holds up as *really* dopey fun. The perfect antidote for a Saturday morning hangover.

EVIL DEAD 2

SAM RAIMI 1987. Sam Raimi's long-awaited sequel to his 1983 **Evil Dead** is sleaze-ball entertainment at its best and most outrageous.

With a three-million dollar budget and a step up from 16 to 35mm, Raimi and colleagues take the same over-the-top sicko-comedy route that Tobe Hooper tried in the disappointing **Texas Chainsaw Massacre 2**; but this film succeeds where the other failed because Raimi's playful style ingratiates himself to the viewer, instead of playing down to them. This director knows his audience's expectations, and he gives us what we want and *more!*.... After a short re-cap of Part One (strangely enough, instead of re-using old footage, they decided to re-film a slightly-different version of Part One), we pick up the instant the first left off, back at the old-demon-infested-cabin-in-the-middle-of-the-secluded-woods. The Book of the Dead may have been destroyed, but the nearby hills are alive with the sound of ancient, soul-thirsting terror. Bruce Campbell, the lone survivor, is still kickin' after being swatted around by Unseen Forces, and there is a new bunch of strangers on the scene – a young woman looking for her disappeared parents (her dad is the Professor who helped unleash these naughty ol' spirits), her yuppie boyfriend, a redneck vet, and his wife. No need to tell you the plot, especially if you're familiar with Part One, because it's pretty much identical this time around. The five characters spend 85 minutes getting chased, beaten, sprayed with gallons of red or green goop, and one woman gets an unexpected 'snack' when a popped eyeball flies into her mouth. The group never leaves the possessed property until the end, and you sometimes wish the makers attempted something a little more innovative in the plot department. Luckily, the gory set-pieces are more elaborate than the previous outing, since Raimi had the cash this time around to properly visualise his wilder concepts. The Demon Shemps are more extensive than ever, with lots of stop-action to give it a Harryhausen-on-Acid look... And once again, it's fun to watch dorky Bruce Campbell get the shit knocked out of him – he's thrown down staircases, bashed in the head, dropped into mud holes, covered in slime and blood, and he gets to chop off his own infected hand with a chain saw. He chases his dismembered hand around the cabin; his dead girlfriend's loose head puts the bite on him, literally; when he looks into a mirror and sighs "I'm fine", his reflection replies with "We just chopped up our girlfriend with a chain saw. Does that sound fine to *you?*"; and by the end he's transformed into a Terminator-style monster-killer... Unlike the first **Evil Dead**, which slowly built-up until you were pummelled out of your chair during the final blood bath, Part Two starts off at top speed and tries to maintain it until the end. And with Raimi's wild directorial style, it almost completely succeeds, like an EC Comic popping to life, complete with impressive 'Demon's-Eye' views. Less a horror film than a gross comedy (the gore is so relentless that most of the audience ended up laughing through the bloody bombardment), overall, it gets A+ for style, wit and carnage, but only B- for overall concept-originality. Nevertheless, it's *still* the trashiest fun I've had at the movies this year.

EVIL SPAWN

KENNETH J. HALL 1988. I got suckered into this video quickie after catching its fast-paced (and thoroughly disgusting) trailer. Though there isn't one original moment in this cheapjack retread of **The Wasp Woman/The Leech Woman** concept, writer/director Kenneth J. Hall pumps up the gore and skin quotient to satisfy '80s audiences who've been suckled on video sleaze. Bobbie Bresee (star of **Mausoleum** and **Ghoulies**, but best known for her famed cameo as Smeg's mom in **Surf Nazis Must Die**) stars in this two-bit monsterama, alongside John Carradine (who gets one minute of screen time as Dr. Zeitman, a skin doctor) and Forry Ackerman (a whopping three second cameo as a pool cleaner)... In the prologue, we learn firsthand that alien microbes from the planet Venus (we're talkin' BIG microbes, with sharp teeth and several eyes) escape from a laboratory and start chewing up people's necks while turn-

ing their victims into murderous, drooling zombies with the dry heaves... Meanwhile, in Tinseltown, famed model and movie starlet Lynn Roman (Bobbie B.) is beginning to fret that she's over the hill. She must be in her mid-thirties, and already her career is on the skids and her supply of studs has withered up and blown away. More than anything in the world, she wants to win the title role in the upcoming mega-buck production of 'Savage Goddess', even though she's 10 years too old for the part. As if by fate, a woman (Carradine's creepy assistant, played by Donna Shock) shows up at Lynn's doorstep with a highly-suspect Fountain of Youth serum. One syringeful in her veins works wonders, despite a few unexpected drawbacks – such as she turns into a toothy, eight-foot bug every so often. Turns out, the Doc's assistant is a crazy lesbian who's in love with Ms. Bresee, and she has cheesecake photos of her idol plastering her apartment walls. But enough of this sexual confusion, because Bobbie is addicted to the serum now, and whenever she loses her temper she mutates into a grade-D insectoid with long pincers and razored teeth. A cheap, but fun creature suit to boot... There's a fair amount of gratuitous gore throughout – including arms ripped from their sockets, Bobbie vomiting into the camera, and some quick torso-piercing. But mainly, this ego-massager is just an excuse to have Bresee primp on-camera and take long, hot showers. Yet it still doesn't hide the fact that she can't even read her cue cards with any subtlety. Her terrible acting perfectly matches her pathetic, stilted dialogue... Overall, it's mindless, '50s-style fun, ladled with enough gore and stupidity to keep schlock fans awake. 75 minutes of Deja Vu Cinema... 'Twas Vanity killed the bimbo.

THE EXECUTIONER

DUKE MITCHELL 1982. This dime-store crime flick evokes **The Godfather** in its advertising. Are they kidding? Coppola's film spent more money on Brando's bedtime snack than this movie had for its entire budget. But financial liabilities aside, director/producer/star Duke Mitchell spawned the most unintentionally hilarious tale of Mafia mayhem ever made! From the opening assassination, featuring the urinal electrocution of a cripple, you know you're in for some truly brain-damaged schlock. In fact, over a dozen murders occur in the first five minutes, as two hot-headed hitmen shoot everyone they encounter (except for one little black child, so I guess we're supposed to realise they aren't *all* bad). A four-star intro, and it only gets better, folks! It's one of the worst, most technically inept, yet consistently incredible pieces of celluloid dreck I've sat through in months! A crapola classic!... Under the pseudonym of Dominic Miceli, Duke Mitchell headlines as Mimi, a syndicate newcomer who moves to LA from Sicily with a full wardrobe of leisure suits, navel-cut shirts and cheap jewellery; and soon pulls together a small army of 'guts, brains and balls' to take over the town. Before you can boil a pot of linguini, the Mob bosses of America are shittin' their drawers when Mimi begins returning pieces of kidnapped Dons by Registered Mail. And following his bloodthirsty motto "You're in, or you're in the way", Mimi and his trusty goomba Jolly (Vic Caesar) nonchalantly pump shotgun at all the competing pimps and bookmakers in rapid fire succession. As the years pass (the only way you can tell is because there's more talcum powder in everyone's hair), other business endeavours include entering the porno film biz (an excuse for a few skin shots) and tackling Superspook (Jimmy Williams), the town's #1 pimp, who they crucify on Easter morning. It's a nasty, silly, totally immoral yarn, chock full of unflinchingly gratuitous rub-outs, such as when Mimi gets a tad paranoid so he casually slaughters *everyone* in the supporting cast – hanging one lucky ex-pal by a meat hook through his eyeball! Or setting off a time bomb at a funeral and blowing up the mourners. This film has more corpses than any other film since **The Day After**. And since they didn't have the spare cash to pad the story out or hire anyone with a lick of acting background, Mitchell had to rely on the important things: Non-stop violence, extortion, bloodshed, and a breakneck pace – except for the hilariously earnest monologues where Mimi bellyaches about the pain the Sicilian people have suffered through. My heart's bleedin' (as is most of the cast). So if you can ignore its occasionally racist remark or hateful attitude toward women (simply warm hunks of disposable meat), you'll fall in love with the olive oil-soaked ode to organised crime. And if anyone knows where to obtain a copy of the gut-bustingly incongruous soundtrack by (who else?) Dominic Miceli, do the world a favour and keep your trap shut.

EXTREME PREJUDICE

WALTER HILL 1987. After a few years of paying the rent with such bogus 'Non-concept' fare as **Brewster's Millions** and **Crossroads**, Walter Hill has bounced back with his best actioner since **Southern Comfort**. High-tech weaponry and jawlocked line delivery abound as Nick Nolte (looking good, but that neck belongs on a tight end) and Rip Torn barrel through the Southwest as Texas Rangers on a drug hunt. Powers Boothe is outstanding as Nick's old buddy, who is now the kingpin of a Mexican drug empire. The ill-fated 'love triangle' with Maria Conchita, oh, the one with the big moraccas, is the 'stupid' part of the film, but fairly painless as Hill is not one for heavy exposition. The subplot with the covert military operation (script by John 'shitheap' Milius) is fairly nifty, and gives veteran scenery munchers like Michael (**Scanners**) Ironside and Clancy (**Buckaroo Banzai**) Brown ample time to grimace accordingly. The final big blow-out at Boothe's Mexican fortress is mind-blowing nastiness; no doubt Sam P. would be grinning ear to ear as the mercenaries go head-to-head with Boothe's private army, with some heads *not* making it to the finish (sorry, I didn't mean to insinuate decaps, but action fans should be rejoicing by this time anyway). Nice to see an action film with *balls* making the rounds instead of shoebox wimp-outs starring certain tool-oriented Australian dirt farmers. Hill holds his own. [TR]

EYE OF THE TIGER

RICHARD SARAFIAN 1986. Yeah, I realise this flick has been playing pay-cable for a while, but late one night in a fit of boredom, I gave this low-grade actioner a shot. Wow! Unlike other recent Gary 'Head Like an Engine Block' Busey blow-payments such as **Bulletproof** (which should've been retitled 'Eighty-proof'), this is a neat little B-movie. Although utterly predictable, this ruralised **Death Wish** is kick-ass fun... Gary stars as Buck, an ex-con/family-man/Nam-vet (what a combo of clichés!) who returns to his dim-witted home town and finds that a gang of vicious bikers (but a particularly safety conscience gang too, since they all wear crash helmets) are running wild. Led by a chrome-domed William Smith, the redneck pocket-sized sheriff won't do diddle to halt the bikers' rape, murder and drug-running spree, so Busey decides to try out the one-man vigilante biz armed with a double-barrelled shotgun. Unfortunately, this only leads to a dead wife, a comatose kid and a house with several drive-through entrances. This gang is so ultra-despicable they even dig up his wife's coffin after the funeral and leave it on Busey's front lawn! Revenge kicks in when Gary calls on his Miami-based ex-cell mate (who studied at the Al Pacino/**Scarface** Dramatics Academy) for aid in the form of an armoured pick-up truck with mortars. So you want to see scummy vermin put through serious pain?! Say no more. There's non-stop explosions, decaps with razor wire, high-speed lassoings, and even a stick of TNT showed up a badguy's asshole! It's all hokum, but director Richard Sarafian (**Vanishing Point**) proves he can crank out manipulative manure at its finest. Yaphet Kotto essays the usual 'Minority Buddy Of The Star' role, no-necked **Slimetime**-fave

William Smith looks constipated throughout, and Busey basically plays himself – in other words, a good-ol'-boy lunkhead. And why did they call it **Eye of the Tiger?** Because the only song they could afford was a repeat of the **Rocky III** theme by that 'one-hit-and-it's-back-to-the-day-job-D'Agostinos' band, Survivor. Just turn the volume down whenever the music begins to swell... A fast-paced, old-fashioned 'take the law into your own hands' flick.

THE FALLS

PETER GREENAWAY 1980. After far too many years of having his films underappreciated (**A Zed and Two Noughts**), or never even distributed in the states (**Drowning By Numbers**), Brit filmmaker Peter Greenaway hit paydirt with **The Cook, The Thief, His Wife, and Her Lover**... But let's set the Wayback Machine for his first foray into feature films, which is not only his most difficult to categorise, but also the hardest for any average moviegoer to sit through. The kicker: It's nearly 3½ hours long! 200 minutes of talking heads and obtuse comedy!... It takes the form of a methodically-structured mock-documentary that analyses the V.U.E. (Violent Unknown Event) – an apocalyptic (and never completely explained) ecological upheaval that has affected 19 million people and has something to do with ornithology. **The Falls** presents us with 92 short biographies of people changed by the V.U.E. – but only those with surnames beginning with F-A-L-L, from Orchard Falla and Antopody Fallbatts, to Anthior Fallwaste. Some victims speak their own languages (which only adds to the confusion, since no two languages are alike and the syntax tends to change at a moment's notice), others are said to have grown feathers, one woman keeps trying to teach her dog to fly (in one instance, by pushing it out of an airplane), and one gent has fallen in love with a rather perplexed turkey. Immortality is one advantage, though the V.U.E. may also add or subtract from their height or leave their placentas with eggshells... Greenaway stitches together the interviews, along with weird vistas, monologues by so-called 'experts', music by Michael Nyman, handheld newsreel footage, moments of cheap humour, and exaggerated artiness which eventually makes it a satire of its own pseudo-intellectual pretensions. Imagine Monty Python as directed by Jean-Luc Godard... I should warn you, some sections are dry as dirt, parts are utterly tedious and without apparent purpose, and we never actually see any of the physiological mutations (shucks!). But I, for one, fell into its quirky rhythms. The overall effect is like stepping into a whole new universe. A frustrating challenge at times, but a worthy one for intrepid filmgoers.

FASTER PUSSYCAT! KILL! KILL!

RUSS MEYER 1965. "Lades and gentlemen, welcome to violence," the narrator immediately promises, and since Russ Meyer is behind the camera, you know that bold statement isn't just a load of hype. Meyer has always been the King of '60s Adult Breastploitation – providing society's slobbering hordes with the slickest, finest dirt to grace grindhouses. Look at his legacy: **Motor Psycho, Mudhoney, Vixen**. And this one is no exception. It's a thinking man's raunch from the good ol' days. Though barely PG, it still packs a wallop with its totally amoral thrills, pneumatic cuties in search of kicks and hilariously scurvy portrait of the underbelly of American outback society... Meet Varla, Rosie and Billie, a trio of curvaceous go-go dancers poured into skin-tight teasewear, each with her own high-test convertible. Whether it's playing 'chicken' in the desert, catfighting amongst each other or swimming the backstroke, these are hard women with fast cars, cold hearts, no scruples, and a low tolerance for wimpy men. Tura Satana (and her all-black wardrobe) stars as Varla, their heavily mascara-ed ringleader – an exotic hellcat who redefines the term 'man-eater'. Long-term Meyer vet Haji plays second fiddle, with an accent that would put Herve Villechaize to shame. And Lori Williams, the blond of the bunch,

keeps a radio on at all times so she can boogaloo in her sexy white hot pants... Their adventure begins when they interrupt the light-hearted plans of a happy-go-lucky young couple. First they completely wreck the guy's evening by killing him, then they kidnap his petite, bikinied girlfriend and take her along for the unwilling ride of her life. The first 25 minutes is *classic* sleaze! A trash epic! It settles down a bit for the second half, by introducing a storyline (heaven forbid!), when the quartet of chicks stop off at the homestead of a nasty, crippled and *rich* old man. The desert drama kicks in when they decide to bilk the ol' degenerate outta his hidden fortune, but first they have to deal with the guy's muscle-bound son, who's nicknamed The Vegetable for his prowess at glassy-eyed stares and monosyllabic dialogue. Meanwhile, Stuart Lancaster nearly steals the show as the tongue-wagging patriarch who can't keep his eyes (or mitts) off the lasses... There's passion, greed, fear, a 'fuck society, I'm having a good time' attitude, and melodrama that goes up to '11', with one incredible plot twist after another. See Tura snap a guy's spine like it was a bread stick! Watch the women chase a wheelchair-bound senior citizen with their car! See The Vegetable take on a roaring hot rod with his bare hands! It's one of the best Badgirl films of all time, with Tura karate chopping her way through her greatest role (then again, that's not saying much if you consider her other flicks were Ted V. Mikels' **The Astro-Zombies** and **The Doll Squad**). Women-in-Trouble addicts weaned on '70s and '80s epics like **Caged Heat** and **The Naked Cage** might balk at the relative tameness of it all, but if they can't appreciate The Great Masters, it's *their* loss. Rapid-fire editing, crisp black and white photography, non-stop excitement, and Meyer pulled it all off for under $50,000! Plus, you haven't lived until you've heard The Bostweeds sing the theme song ('Pussycat, she's livin' reckless/Pussycat, she's ridin' high/If you think you can tame her/Well, just you try'). A true masterpiece!

THE FASTEST GUITAR ALIVE

MICHAEL MOORE 1968. This MGM, colour-saturated musical/western would've been virtually unwatchable if Elvis Presley had essayed the lead, as the producer had first hoped. But instead they settled for (are you ready?) Roy Orbison! As a cowboy? Talk about a cast-

ing crock o' shit! As our gunslinging hero, Roy has all the charisma of Don Knotts and he should've sued whoever convinced him to change his image — for this flick he's minus his dark glasses and black duds, and sports a Wayne Newtonesque hairdo while warbling some of the limpest songs in memory (no-hits such as 'Good Time Party', 'Pistolero', et cetera). Oh sure, Roy's voice is as smooth as ever, but most of the time I couldn't hear him because I was laughing too hard at the gaucho outfit they stuffed him into, or the square dance choreography... Roy stars as Johnny, a pudgy-faced western wimp with a multi-octave singing range and a specially-equipped guitar that doubles as a rifle. "I can kill you with this," Roy says, brandishing his acoustic armament, "*and* play your funeral march at the same time." At first glance, Roy is simply tiding across the ol' West with a wagon full of singing cuties called The Chestnut Sisters. But in actuality, he's a Confederate spy intent on stealing a shipment of Union gold, while romancing the ladies with his tired tunes. But do you wanna know how dumb this film really is? Halfway through, when the South loses the Civil War, this dink decides to *return* the fortune in gold because keeping it would make him a common crook. I'm sure we'd *all* make that choice, wouldn't we?... The plot would fit comfortably into a half-hour TV episode (too bad the film's 87 minutes long), and this G-rated nonsense isn't even campy enough to keep you awake. Mostly, I felt sad for poor Roy, who looks rightfully nervous during the dramatic scenes. He must've had a bad month at the race track to have to sign onto this celluloid turd. Co-starring Sammy Jackson and a tribe of Indians played by make-upped soup kitchen candidates who saw too much **F-Troop**.

FAT GUY GOES NUTZOID!!

JOHN GOLDEN 1983. Lloyd Kaufman and Michael Herz strike again with this stinkwad of a film, which Troma scraped off the Men's Room floor and decided to distribute. It's as bad as you can imagine. Maybe worse. John Golden directed and let's hope somebody blinds him with hot pokers before he gets the chance to pick up another movie camera... Tibor Feldman stars as Roger, a scuzzy ex-con who can't take the 9-to-5 working world, so he grabs his geeky pal, Hugo, who's a counsellor at a summer camp for retarded adults, and they hit the road. Little do they realise, a non-verbal tub o' lard with a scruffy mohawk (Peter Linari) has hidden in the back of Hugo and Rog's truck. Imagine Lenny from **Of Mice and Men** as interpreted by King Kong Bundy, and you've pretty well summed up the depth of Linari's performance... Most of this snoozer chronicles their cross-country adventures with this idiot (whom they nickname 'The Mooka') in tow: Vomiting in fancy eateries, going spastic at a punk club, spilling food, and breaking up a wedding ceremony. This flick's idea of Pinteresque wit is to have this pathetic retarded man fart uncontrollably. Hey, I'm the first guy to laugh at Bad Taste, but not when it's so depressingly inane (not to mention tame). It's like being trapped in a stalled elevator full of Lyndon LaRouche impersonators — ALL the characters are utterly intolerable... and the ending is just a hunk of sentimental clap-trap, when Roger helps The Mooka escape from a hospital psycho ward, since down deep the Fat Guy is just a slow-witted ball of fun. Gimme a fuckin' break!... The storyline has more holes in it than Jimmy Hoffa, and it's a total embarrassment, both technically and conceptually. If Troma paid more than a case of Thunderbird for it, then they were ripped off. Worse than **Surf Nazis Must Die!** Worse than your grandparents' home movies! Better than **The Love Boat** (but then again, so's rectal cancer). No violence, gore, sex, foul language, or cheap laffs, and worst of all, it'd probably get a G-rating, except for the fact you see a guy's naked butt for 10 seconds... Oh, fuck it — I don't even want to talk about this thing any more. Next!

FIEND WITHOUT A FACE

ARTHUR CRABTREE 1958. Originally released on the lower half of a double bill with Karloff's **The Haunted Strangler**, this is a seemingly common black-and-whiter that suddenly *explodes* during the last 20 minutes into full-blown monster-mania! Even though a large part of it slogs along, there's no way I can't recommend a film whose finale takes off into the stratosphere of schlock, with one of the best creature-concepts around... A mysterious death outside an American army base is only the start of the unexplainable circumstances. It seems that there's an atomic plant nearby that's generating the base's energy ("Take some more rods out. We need more power!") and there's plenty of early hints that the radiation is to blame. You see, something small and *very* deadly has been chowing down on the supporting cast – grabbing their neck from behind and crunching down *real loud* on it – and since the monsters are invisible, the filmmakers take their sweet time in showing them off to us. They're undeniably nasty little critters though, sucking out their victim's *entire* brain and spinal chord from two tiny holes they bore in the back of the neck... But just as the film starts getting interesting, the middle section suddenly begins to plod along with a bunch of uneventful subplots – the townsfolk lead a posse, a crazy ol' professor salivates, and our army hero (Marshall Thompson) investigates. It turns out that a thought-materialisation machine is to blame – a nutty device that gives form to thought and has created (with the aid of all that pesky radiation) a 'mental vampire' that has to drain human beings of their brains in order to survive. And during the last reel we finally get to glimpse these 'fiends' and it's definitely worth the wait. They're oversized, antennaed brains that flop about, with a tail-like spinal chord that twists around their victims' necks in a strangle hold. By the end, there's dozens of these things hanging from trees, scaring the cast, and jumping at anything that might have a brain inside its skull. They're creepy li'l shits, without a doubt... Luckily, they splatter when you shoot 'em or take an axe to them, and my favourite part of the film is the solid four minutes when the army schmoes gun down an onslaught of creatures that keep flying into their windows. It's all exceptionally gory, especially for the '50s, with some effective stop-action animation (not to mention loads of slime and ooze)... Arthur Crabtree competently directs, along with wonderfully sinister music by Buxton Orr, and even if the first hour is pretty mundane, you've gotta love that last brain-slaughter! The ending alone makes **Fiend** *an instant classic* from the '50s.

THE FINAL COMEDOWN

OSCAR WILLIAMS 1972 (AKA: BLAST). Financed in part by The American Film Institute, this is an angry fuckin' film! Lost in the shuffle of blaxploitation no-brainers, this cinematic call for action may not be subtle, but it sure is powerful as hell. It's right up there with **Sweet Sweetback's Baadasssss Song**... A young pre-egoed Billy Dee Williams stars as hot-headed revolutionary Johnny Johnson, who keeps Angela Davis and Huey Newton pix on his wall, a semi-automatic beside his bed, and begins the film at the breaking point, ready to waste some whiteys ("If you lived in my skin for one day, you'd blow your fucking brains out," he tells his white hippie girlfriend). Starting with a brilliant, explosively-edited opening, the entire film takes place during a day-long police siege on Johnny's HQ. In the melee, Johnny is shot in the gut and experiences flashbacks which explain the roots of his rage, and the evolution of his thirst for violent change. From being turned away from jobs by bigoted white bosses and watching neighbourhood kids bitten by rats in the night, to seeing friends freaking out from the white mans' drugs and getting hassled by the fuzz at the slightest provocation (like driving a car), this flick wears its rage in six-foot-tall, blood red letters, and persuasively argues how the Black Man has been systematically reduced to the Dead Man by society. In the meantime, back on the backfield, a veritable army of heavily-armed Pigs are leaving a body-strewn path through the ghetto – murdering every minority who passes through their crosshairs during their search for Johnny. And the finale is a full scale, downbeat urban blood bath. Sure, the over-dramatic love story softens the tone a bit, and first-time director Oscar Williams has a few awkward moments; but the stakes are kept high and most of the film is absolutely riveting. Too bad Williams never went onto better things, instead opting for Filipino kung fu fodder like **Hot Potato**. Co-starring D'urville Martin, Raymond St. Jacques, and R.G. Armstrong as a bigoted blockhead; this film has kick-ass violence and a social conscience to boot! Four stars!

FIRE MAIDENS
FROM OUTER SPACE (1955)
TEENAGERS FROM OUTER SPACE (1959)

Are you ready for a pair of cheesy black-and-white '50s sci-fiers? You know the type. Plastic spaceships, simple-minded stories, and actors who can barely read their Jim Beam label, much less a script. Well, here are two classic examples for your files (of widely varying quality)... **Fire Maidens** is a true tarnished oldie. So bad, it's – well, almost interminable. For the first 20 minutes you'll be

reaching for the java to stay awake, as you watch a US/Great Britain space rocket with a quintet of astrobores charting a course for the 13th moon of Jupiter. But what a surprise when they land and discover the planet looks more like Iowa, and luckily the place has a breathable atmosphere because these courageous dorks are too stupid to remember their helmets. Of course, the fun *really* starts (30 tedious minutes into it) when they meet their first Fire Maiden – a mute cutie in a mini-toga left over from a nearby Hercules pic. These guys quickly follow her trail (while maintaining all the grace of The Bowery Boys) to a palatial cavern. Turns out this female society is the remnants of Atlantis (conveniently titled New Atlantis), and they plan on sousing up the astronauts and using them for breeding purposes, because the only male on their world is a white-haired ol' codger who's their Dad. Of course, these Dumbshits From Space object to the idea of becoming sex toys for this pack of skimpily-attired bimbettes (if not, there wouldn't be much of a plot – but on second thought, there *still* isn't). But first let's take a few moments to revel in their 'delicately' choreographed Fire Maiden Stomp, staged to a muzak rendition of 'Stranger in Paradise'. *No one* will be able to keep a straight face during this sudden en masse Eruption of Dance, which kinda reminded me of Twyla Tharp in need of Preparation H... This is a true backyard production, utilising a couple leftover sword 'n' sandal sets, a nearby woods, one natty monster suit, some casting couch contestants as the Maidens, and a conspicuous lack of braincells. All this is good for a couple Badfilm laughs, but there aren't nearly enough to recommend it. Typical '50s dreck, best watched (or even better, *not* watched) at four in the morning... Next up is **Teenagers from Outer Space**. The hokey title and ad slick lured me in – and surprise! – its less-than-low-budget laughs quickly won me over. And all the credit has to go to Tom Graeff, the director/producer/writer/photographer/editor/special effects coordinator. Who is this guy, the Orson Welles of crap? Truly, a man of many titles, but few talents. Unlike **Fire Maidens** though, this flick is fast-paced, consistently loopy fun!... After a drill-like spacecraft winds its way into a deserted field, alien humanoids (wearing Air Force flight helmets and gas masks) crawl out and show off their incontestable power by ray-blasting a pesky dog into a heap of bones. They're invaders from a planet whose population consists of militaristic, emotionally null lemmings, and their philosophy is: 'Oh, don't mind us. We just want to use the earth as a breeding ground for Gargans, our primary food supply. Soon herds of giant crustaceans will roam the prairies and everyone on your planet will be dead. Oops!' But one independent-minded alien teen, Derek (David Love, aka – you guessed it! – Tom Graeff!), revolts against his meatheaded elders. And once Derek hits 'civilisation', he learns all about quirky mankind by stumbling upon a small town, a room for rent and a brunette dish named Betty (Dawn Anderson). Before long, he's attending pool parties with debutantes, unaware that the evil assassin Thor is on his trail, zapping these puny mortals into instant medical skeletons. Will the earth be saved from invasion by this extraterrestrial teen with the interplanetary pompadour? Or will he be too busy swapping saliva in the tall grass with Betty? Sounds silly? Sure, but while most flicks of this ilk are tedious, this one just keeps barrelling along. By the midpoint there's a dozen flesh-stripped citizens and a shoot-out at the police station, so who cares if it's presented with all the subtlety of a Rudy Ray Moore adaptation of **Othello**? It's lively as heck, and the ending is *sooo* dramatic I nearly spit up my beer! Just wait until you see the showdown with the giant Gargan (represented by a lobster shadow superimposed over the picture). Oooh! Talk about startling realism! Talk about pulse-pounding drama! Talk about a dime-store laff-riot! And acting honours have to go to Bryan Grant as the kill-crazed Thor, whose technique amounts to grunting "I'll get you!"... It's all wonderfully tacky! Yeah!

FIRST MAN INTO SPACE

ROBERT DAY 1959. Here's a b/w SF/horror B-movie that's more cheap thrills than hard science. Though there's a few space flight special effects thrown in in the beginning, **First Man** is most successful as a schlocky monster-on-the-loose time (and braincell) killer... A cocky astronaut is shot into space ('The Highest Man in the World', the newspaper headlines boast), but when his craft runs into a cloud of space dust and explodes, he's transformed by those pesky cosmic rays into a one-eyed meatloaf-man. He's a crusted-over zombie in search of blood, be it from the local blood bank or fresh from the open wound, and he roams the countryside searching for sustenance (gosh, there were so many aliens/monsters/mutations lumbering through the woods in the '50s, that I'm surprised more of 'em didn't bump into each other). How do the authorities know the spaceman's to blame? Because all the victims have meteorite dust in their wounds, of course... Watch the cops pull the blood beast over for speeding! See the creature stumble into lots of inexpensive props! Get hammered over the head by the standard moral question: Should they try to save his life, or should they send out the Marines and blast him to bits? Personally, this astro-idiot was such an annoying shithead before the accident that I'd vote for the ol' Villagers-and-Torches routine. But instead, the filmmakers opt to make him a tragic, heroic figure – just another victim of man's unending quest for knowledge (yawn), which means a boring, needlessly 'deep' finale... The first half hour is pretty slow-paced, too, setting up the uniformly unlikeable characters, but once the reign of terror begins it quickly slips into full-tilt lunacy. The creature is appropriately repulsive, and this film has some of the most outrageous foreign accents ever emitted by a supporting cast. It's all very silly, of course (or couldn't you guess?), but it's also a nifty bit of '50s nonsense.

FLESH FEAST

BRAD F. GRINTER 1970. This dumb li'l low-budgeter is slow going, but don't press that STOP button, because by the end you'll be slack-jawed at its straight-faced stupidity. Veronica Lake tried to resurrect her faded career by not only starring in this Miami-lensed mess, but also by producing it in tandem with hack-director Brad F. Grinter (one of the two vermin responsible for the only Christian, anti-drug, gore flick in recent memory, **Blood Freak**)... Dr. Elaine Frederick (Veronica L.) is a brilliant scientist, with a laboratory in her basement and a screw loose in her noggin. Using larvae and a bank of flashing, coloured lights, she's working on the biggest threat to the American way of life since Julio Iglesias, and as long as the script sticks to Lake's experiments we're in schlocky (albeit slow-paced) heaven. She steals bodies from the hospital, slices 'em apart with a hacksaw and hangs their carved chunks from handy meat hooks. A leg here. A torso there. She's also got a full-scale maggot farm, where she grows flesh-eating mutant larvae which are used in (are you sitting down?) Fountain of Youth treatments. Add a few *more* inept ingredients, such as dead secret agents littering a path to her door, a bevy of nubile nurses in her guest rooms, and a bunch of atrociously-accented dullards representing nebulous Foreign Powers. It turns out that some shifty South Americans are subsidising the Doc's research, and they keep referring to how Ms. Lake will aid Their Leader, who's going to start a revolution in their country as soon as he loses a few excess years. And if you couldn't guess, The Leader turns out to be the wrinkly Nazi himself, Adolf Hitler. The best moment is when Lake gets revenge by strapping 'Dolf down to her surgery table and tossing handfuls of hungry maggots at Der Führer's face. That alone deserves a round of applause... Not much to recommend though. There's no gore. No sex. No talent in front of, or behind the camera. Just a vast wasteland of cinematic brainlessness and a couple unexpected laughs. Firmly entrenched in the Sub-Al Adam-

son School of Slime, I'm just happy it only lasted 72 minutes.

THE FLY

DAVID CRONENBERG 1986. I've seen this one twice so far and both times I nearly cried at the end. No, really! This may be the single most *sympathetic* monster movie made in years. One might be slightly surprised to realise this after seeing photos of the title creature in the pages of **Fangoria** magazine. David Cronenberg's remake of the classic '50s version of **The Fly** is alternately heart-breaking and disgusting. There are some very nasty special effects here. (Squeamish types, take note.) Jeff Goldblum, who plays the scientist whose experiments in matter teleportation backfire with serious consequences, (resulting in his genetic code being merged with that of a common housefly) is very convincing and *damn good* at what he does here, and all power and good karma to him and his career in the future. See it, dammit! (But don't talk all the way through it, like all the assholes at the Westcott did – SP.) [BJE]

FORBIDDEN ZONE

RICHARD ELFMAN 1980. Now that Danny 'Oingo Boingo' Elfman has churned out a batch of mainstream music scores (**Beetlejuice**, **Batman**), let's take a gander at this, his *brother's* first directorial effort – an instant cult item that blew into New York City for a few midnight shows back in 1982 and then disappeared into the woodwork when the flick didn't click with the Village set. Person-ally, I don't pretend to understand much of it either, but I *love* it anyhow! The overall effect is like watching a live action, drug-soaked Max Fleischer/Betty Boop short; with characters suddenly breaking into song and dance, blatantly two-dimensional sets, over-sized props, cartoony black-and-white photography, plus moments of pixilation and cell animation (by John Muto). Of course, the Mystic Knights of the Oingo Boingo provide the wild score and when Satan (played by Danny Elfman) breaks into a hellish varia-tion of 'Minnie the Moocher', I truly expected Koko and Bimbo to step into the frame at any moment... The large cast of severely brain-softened campers includes Herve Villechaize as King Fausto

of the 6th Dimension, Susan Tyrell as Queen Doris, plus Viva, Joe Spinell and the ever-babbling Kipper Kids. The plot (if you dare to call it that) begins when the Hercules Family moves into a new house which happens to contain a passage into the 6th Dimen-sional Forbidden Zone, and when daughter Frenchy decides to peak into the gateway, she finds herself poured into the anything-can-happen netherworld. The half-pint King wants Frenchy for his personal concubine and though she isn't adverse to the idea, the rest of her oddball clan decides to rescue her nevertheless. There's a topless Princess (Gisele Lindley) heading the torture chamber, human chandeliers, dancing frog/men, hideously stereotyped pimps (in black-face), and wait until you see Herve and Tyrell making out on the dining room table! I've seen less disturbing images in snuff films! But the BIG question is, will Squeezit the Chicken Boy find the courage to save them all?!... The film tends to lose momentum every so often, but it always snaps back with another demented turn. Meanwhile, the audience just sits there in shock at its indescribable strangeness. I'm tellin' you, this flick is *so* excessive that for once Susan Tyrell *doesn't* seem to be overacting; and obviously some sort of previous acquaintance with dangerous hallucinogens is necessary to fully appreciate this item. The result is one of the most outrageously unhinged movies I've seen in some time. Completely warped in its perspectives and inaccessible to all but the hardcore weird.

FORCED ENTRY

NORM ORSCHNORSCHKI 1988. Distributed by Subversive Propaganda Inc. ('For over 200 years, giving the people what they want – whether they like it or not'), this hilarious 45-minute video from first-time director Norm Orschnorschki comes complete with liner notes and a press release, and it plays at being an ultra-right-wing public service film, while simultaneously putting a rusty stake through this type of fundamentalist drivel. A spot-on take-off filled with tongue *through* cheek humour!... Focusing on the red, white and blue community of Lynchburg, Virginia, the Neighbourhood Vigilante Committee presents a shocking look at urban crime, drug-addled deviates and moral decay. With the Holy Smolderin' Cross on the Mount Church providing the spiritual salvation and the Confederate flag flappin' overhead, these vigilantes vow to rid the landscape of all 'dope-crazed punks'. Meanwhile, our omniscient host, Justice Jim 'Stonewall' Jackson warns us of the depravity which will overrun the nation if vigilantism isn't adopted. And just to prove his point, we're shown a crime dramatisation, as seen through the victim's eyes (the wonders of VICTI-VISION). One min-ute an innocent young girl is skipping merrily down her street, and the next she's stuffed into a passing car by a quartet of masked thugs. There's the ringleader Uncle Chuckles, Bozo the wheel man, Sluggo the cold-blooded killer, and Mr. B the sex maniac – and they typify the 3 D's: Degenerates, Dope and the Devil! First they shoot her up (and we get some groovy psychedelics) and then they take a cattle prod to her in a graveyard. And who's to blame, according to 'Stonewall'? Hedonists! Communists! Rock 'n' Rollers! Secular Humanists! (What, no aliens from Venus?)... Norm O. beauti-fully utilises his low-budget ($7,000) for full effect and the sharp satire is usually on-target, with Norm turning these 'message movies' inside out by emphasising their arrogance and hate-mongering. So close to the truth it's *scary*! Gene Scott couldn't have done any better (but *he* would've been dead serious)!... My only gripe: The William Castle-inspired SHOCK-O-RAMA effect is truly annoying! Whenever an atrocity is about to occur, a 95db buzzer cuts through your skull like a circular saw. Ouch! Neverthe-less, send Norm some cash now, so he can continue spewing out politically-correct films!

FOXTRAP

FRED WILLIAMSON 1986. Fred 'The Hammer' Williamson grabs the director's chair again, along with starring, producing and coming up with the story for this dose of Italo-idiocy... So, are you ready for hard-hitting action? Are you interested in non-stop thrills? Are you prepared to be BORED OUT OF YOUR SKULL by a pedestrian PI flick? Yep, this is one of Big Fred's worst – a throwback to the **Shaft** rip-offs that plagued the urban grindhouses in the '70s... Freddy's pushin' the half-century mark, and every time he tries to emote it looks more like he needs some Pepto-Bismol, but he's still trying to be a low-rent James Bond... After getting beaten up by a trio of strangers, professional bodyguard Thomas Fox (F.W.) is hired by a slimeball millionaire (Chris Connelly) to go to Europe and find a missing heiress. A solid enough start, but once Freddy hits the south of France, the film takes a nose-dive into dreamland. See Fred walk the streets of Cannes! See Fred walk the streets of Rome! See Fred pad his crappy film with local colour! There's a couple fist-fights along the way, but mostly we get to watch Williamson wearing down his shoe leather (yawn-city). And with his mothballed white suit and a 10" cheroot jammed twixt his teeth, Fred puts the smooth moves on every two-bit European actress, "You must be *some* man," blond tramps moan before they throw him on the bed (they all end up dead, though, so F.W. can have a quick mourning scene to show off his legendary acting talent), and every 15 minutes the film erupts (actually, it's more of a quick belch) into an action scene that lasts a whopping 25 seconds or four punches – whichever comes first. Fred even gets help from a comic-relief fudge-packer who knows kung fu!... Oh yeah, I almost forgot about that danged missing heiress. It turns out she's being 'kept' by a greaseball gangster, which leads to a few creaky plot twists, telegraphed double-crosses and some MacGuffin about porno videos of local politicians. But what we want is some serious ACTION! Luckily, during the last half-hour the death count soars as the remaining budget is spent on squibs. *Everybody* ends up dead! Good guys! Bad guys! Mobsters! Whores! Allies! Everybody *except* Williamson, of course, who promises a sequel in the near future, called **The Fox and the Cobra** (cringe)... **Foxtrap** is best seen in a 42nd Streeter with a gang of friends, where you can spend the dull sections rousting junkies and beating off the cockroaches.

FRANKENSTEIN CONQUERS THE WORLD

INOSHIRO HONDA 1966. Director Inoshiro Honda and FX man Eiji Tsuburaya (those neat guys who brought us **Godzilla, King of the Monsters, Mothra, Rodan,** etc.) teamed up again for this story of a young boy who, after eating the radioactive heart of the Frankenstein Monster (which was shipped to Japan by the Nazis during W.W.II) grows into an enormous (but basically good-natured, unless frightened or attacked) semi-human beast. When corpses of farm animals begin popping up, villages are found smashed into bits, and people are being eaten, it's easy to guess who gets the blame. But when Baragon, a giant reptile with floppy ears who spits lightning (not to be confused with Barugon, the monster fought by Gamera in **War of the Monsters** [aka **Gamera vs. Barugon**] which was made by a different studio) finally shows himself, Frankenstein (as he's called) turns out to be the hero as he and Baragon are pitted against each other in a monster-wrestling match to the death. Mr. Stein doesn't actually, uh, 'conquer the world,' but he does snarl and grit his teeth a lot. The special effects aren't quite up to par with some of the Godzilla films, but it's fun anyway... The late Nick Adams is the American scientist. Heck, check it out. (Incidentally, Frankenstein fought a giant octopus in one scene; in fact, this was originally going to be released as **Frankenstein vs. the Giant Devil-Fish**, but that footage wound up on some mysterious cutting-room floor before American monster fans got to see it. What the fuck!) [BJE]

FRANKENSTEIN MEETS THE SPACE MONSTER

ROBERT GAFFNEY 1965. What do *you* enjoy in a film? Bad actors? Stilted dialogue? Stock footage galore? Yes, that and more can be found in this damaged, Z-grade classic from the early '60s.

'I think it needs re-writing.' –DC

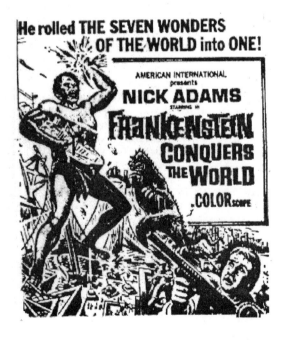

'I think it needs writing, period.' –SP

At first glance, astronaut Frank Saunders seems like an ordinary bad actor, but pull back his Velcro scalp and you find transistor tubes and a tangle of wires, because he's actually a robot who's to be sent on the first mission to Mars. But when his face is blasted away by a mysterious heat ray, he goes on a rampage (thus, he's referred to as Frankenstein, for some cockamamie reason), stopping convertibles and terrorising innocent beachniks. And if that isn't enough plot for you, there's an alien invasion taking place on the local beach, led by a bald, snivelling alien with Mr. Spock ears. What do they want from Earth? Female breeding stock, of course! Can the android with a face like a raw meatloaf save the world? Or will the aliens continue kidnapping bikini-clad gals? Oh yeah, in case you were wondering: Mull, the terrifying $1.98 space monster (an Extra in a furry suit and fright mask) makes a quick five minute appearance, so that the title wouldn't be a complete fabrication. There's lots of groovy (not to mention lousy) rock 'n' roll music, including hits from The Poets and The Distant Cousins, and the whole thing is padded out to an immense 80 minutes with grainy file footage of cars driving down the street, soldiers marching, and space shots. Plenty of nice black and white palm trees, too! Filmed in Puerto Rico, it's truly bad. I loved it.

FREE GRASS

BILL BRAME 1969 (AKA: SCREAM FREE!). I predict Russ Tamblyn and Richard Beymer will be the next two counterculture burn-outs to have major career resurgence. They've both recently spent time chewing the scenery at **Twin Peaks**, but their careers were on the skids in the late '60s. Everything looked golden after they both co-starred in **West Side Story**, but eight years later, they were re-united in this psychedelia-tinged poverty-row ozoner from director Bill Brame (**The Cycle Savages**). And these bottom-of-the-barrel hippie flicks just happen to be one of my favourite schlock genres, with their dated duds, trippy trappings and groovy lingo... Tamblyn stars as a manipulative drug-dealer – wearing a floppy hat to hide his electroshock perm and permanently-dilated pupils; Beymer is a friendly hipster who falls into the seamy world of drug running; and Lana Wood is 'Snow White', a cubehead chick in a microskirt, who falls for the beaded Beymer. During the not-very-action-packed story, Beymer and Lana fall in love, discuss how super drugs are, and take in some acid atmospherics with the local flower children. Oh yeah, Beymer also practices his 'peace and love' philosophy by pummelling a cop. Since he's on the run from The Man anyhow, Beymer takes Tamblyn up on his offer for one last border run, so he can make enough cash to retire to Dayton, Ohio (?). But Beymer freaks out when a couple Feds are shot during the deal, and Tamblyn chills him down by spiking his drink with LSD. So fasten your cerebellum belts, kids! It's Bad Trip Time! Whoaaa! And don't you love it when a film is packed with hallucination sequences obviously conceived by people who've never dosed in their lives, much less had an original idea? The movie has its brutal edge (including a rape, execution-style killings, an immolation, et cetera), but the ending is solid silliness, with Beymer and Tamblyn whacked off their brainstems and experiencing lots of downer **Trip**-rip-off light shows. The reason for the title? At the end, Beymer gives away all the illegit booty – 100 kilos of free grass – to every slobbering stoner in town... Most of the cast plays it straight, except for Tamblyn, who seems to be the only one in on the unintentional joke. Or maybe he has just fucked up on the set? And clean-cut music industry annoyance Casey Kasem co-stars as the most laughable dope dealer imaginable. Despite some tedious stretches, it's recommended for anyone into counterculture nostalgia, or members of the Russ Tamblyn Fan Club.

FRIDAY THE 13th PART VI: JASON LIVES

TOM MCLAUGHLIN 1986. First of all, I'm *not* a big fan of this particular series of films. I thought the first few were crude examples of Gross-Out Cinema, but with a major distributor's backing. They tried to walk a tightrope by giving horror fans their fair share of gore, while not offending the general public – the result was a boring, assembly-line product. (The exception was Part 4, which I thought was fairly nasty and fast-paced.) But onto Part 6. In this episode, Tommy, the kid who 'killed' Jason Voorhees in Part 4, is grown up, but still haunted by memories of the hockey-masked mass-murderer. Joined by a spooked friend (Ron Palillo, who looks like he's been on welfare – or heroin – since **Welcome Back Kotter** was cancelled), they dig up Jason's grave (good idea, eh?) and find a maggot-riddled corpse. But suddenly, here comes a stray bolt of lightning, which just *happens* to strike the open grave, and Jason pulls a Frankenstein-style recovery, complete with super-human strength. He grabs his old mask (which Tommy *happens* to have brought to the cemetery), kills Horshack, and stumbles onto a bunch of yuppie teens who, by *utter* coincidence, reopen the infamous Crystal Lake Campgrounds that same weekend. Toss in a wino gravedigger, an asshole sheriff, and a busload of brat campers, and you've got a typical cast of victims... There's no attempt at characterisation – just throw the people on the screen, give them a few pages a stock dialogue, and let Jason knock 'em off. The killings *do* pile up (16), but all of them are uniformly routine and mechanical, and the film usually wimps out at the moment of True Glopiness in order to safely maintain its sacred R-rating. There's a fist through the torso, a steel spike in the gut, four crushed heads, two face-bashings, a double-decap with a machete, a broken end of a bottle to the throat, four knife stabbings, and a nasty spinal snapping. Does Jason die at the end? Well, he's filled with bullets, stabbed in the heart, and a motorboat propeller rips away most of his throat, but since he's the Wile E. Coyote of mad slashers ('he takes a whackin', but keeps on hackin'...'), you know he'll be around for the umpteenth sequel... Basically, this is slick, empty-headed entertainment, with no suspense, thrills, or imagination. But the filmmakers keep the production moving at top speed, and they throw in some flat in-jokes to show us that even *they* don't take these films seriously anymore. After a while it becomes so predictable and *so* outlandishly cartoonish, it resembles some kind of demented Saturday morning cartoon show, as designed by Charlie Manson. Painless and brainless., with ol' Alice Cooper dusted off for the rock soundtrack.

FROM BEYOND

STUART GORDON 1986. This is another Lovecraftian tale of gross-out excess from the ghoulish hands of Stuart Gordon. But unlike Gordon's first instant-classic, **The Re-Animator**, which transcended its B-movie origins with a hefty dose of weird humour and an over-the-threshold gore level, his follow-up simply revels in the ooze and slime of the '50s/'60s drive-in movie. While his previous flick twisted the age-old conventions into a gnarled masterpiece, **From Beyond** enjoys following the basic by-laws of the genre – take one mad scientist, a few unsuspecting victims, a goopy monster to chew' em up and spit 'em out, and toss 'em into an old mansion... This all leads to the ultimate question, is **From Beyond** any good?... It's *very* entertaining on an ultra-schlock-level, though it falls short of **Re-Animator**'s originality. One big problem is the rating – Gordon was compelled by Empire Prix, er, Pix to cut the film in order to receive an R-rating. Subsequently, a good deal of gore was shedded to appease the butt-heads at the MPAA (as we all know, the entire civilised world would crash and burn if they allowed too much hokey-monster-violence to find its way into an R-rated film). And since this movie depends *completely* on the repulsive special effects, a lot of its impact was obviously lost in the cutting. Jeffrey Combs and Barbara Crampton (both from **Re-Animator**) join forces with Ken Foree (the heroic black dude from **Dawn of the Dead**) to tell the tale of Dr. Pretorius and his Resonator, a device that allows you to observe the creatures which inhabit other dimensions. Unfortunately, when you are able to see *them*, they are able to see *you* – so after Pretorius' head is twisted off by a mysterious force, we get our trio of strangers heading to Pretorius' mansion of unnatural terrors. It seems that the 'vibrations' given off by the Resonator not only open up a dimensional rift, but they enlarge the pineal gland of the brain, unleashing the baser human instincts. So before you know it, Jeffrey is running around with a worm-like gland poking out of his forehead, sucking on unwilling eyesockets; Dr. Pretorius emerges from his dimensional-nap as a half-man, half-monster, holy terror; Barb removes her glasses, lets down her blond hair, strips to her undies, and becomes a leather-lingeried sexpot ready to wriggle onto any warm form; and Ken Foree gets the dubious task of reciting all the dumbshit dialogue, such as "What the hell is *that*?" and "Let's get outta here." The special effects range anywhere from good to amateurish, but compared to any other Empire Production, they're mind-blowing. And unlike the old-fashioned monster-movie where the violence was implied (due to censorship restrictions) and the monsters looked all too much like a guy in a cheap fright mask (due to budget restrictions), Gordon pulls us into an arena of effects overload, cramming each frame with as many slimy, bizarre creatures and as much queasy bloodshed as he could conjure up... Overall, it's pretty silly stuff – but the direction is flashy and fast-paced; the actors are competent in their purely 2-D roles; and horror hounds should love its non-stop parade of mutating monstrosities. But die-hard fans of Lovecraft's original work won't be thrilled with this 'adaptation' since it's about as close to the source material as **Die, Monster, Die!** was. It ain't art, but I enjoyed it... Just for your information, Stuart Gordon's **Dolls**, which he filmed *before* **From Beyond**, is still collecting dust after a mediocre run in the Midwest. Oh well...

THE G.I. EXECUTIONER

JOEL M. REED 1971 (AKA: WIT'S END; AKA: DRAGON LADY). When a flick has been sitting on a shelf for 13 years and then Troma decides to release it, watch out! Nevertheless, I had a scrap of hope for this item since director Joel M. Reed (**Bloodsucking Freaks**) was at the helm – but don't look for any skull drilling or castration-sandwiches this time around. It's strictly B-movie spy time!... A kidnapped nuclear scientist from Red China is being held in Singapore by Lim Tax Singh, the head of the Triad Tong; so the government recruits night-club deadbeat Dave Dearborn (played by the eminently lacklustre Tom Keana) to take on the case since Lim is an old foe of Dave's. Loads of scenic beauty doesn't compensate for a sluggish plot and tedious technique, but then again it's all too typical for Troma and fully expected from anal-auteur Reed. In between bed-hopping, Dave hits the local night-spots in search of the crime bosses, picks fights in a whore house, and gets involved with secret agents, hippie panhandlers and his old girlfriend, Foon Mai Lee (the obviously *not* Asian Victoria Racimo). And it all gives a new meaning to the word tedium! A least there's a *few* dumb thrills in the last reel, with everyone shooting, chasing, torturing, shanghai-ing, or screwing everyone else. But it's all too little too late, because this film is so snooze-inducing that by then I'd almost forgotten the *reason* all these creeps were chasing each other across the orient. It takes equal doses of discrete humping, macho malarkey, always willing women, and ever brainless bone-heads – and wraps 'em all up in a threadbare blanket of clichés. In the acting department, Tom Keana is a walking slab of Spam. It's rare to see a film star so utterly devoid of any charisma whatso-

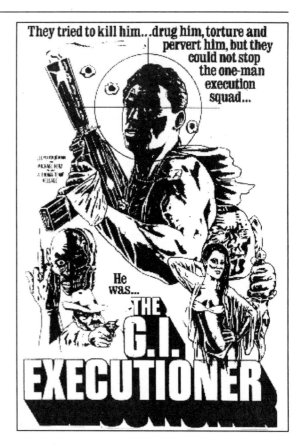

ever, and when he attempts to emote it's like watching Raymond Burr try to do the Limbo. At least the distaff side of the cast is fun and photogenic. Angelique Pettyjohn shakes her abundant cleavage as a ditzy stripper, and Janet Wood plays Dave's blond nubile 'niece', who keeps his bed warm for him. Despite some good local colour (i.e. constant interruption by $20 whores and groovy floral shirts), this is completely unremarkable crap. Avoid it!

GALAXY OF TERROR

B.D. CLARK 1981 (AKA: MINDWARP – AN INFINITY OF TERROR; AKA: PLANET OF HORRORS). Let's get the essentials out of the way at the top. Yes, this *is* the SF flick where the female crewmember is stripped naked and raped by a horny 20-foot-long space larvae. Besides this 'classic' sequence, there's few reasons to check out this well-mounted, but utterly lame production. If you're an **Alien** rip-off completist, you might want to laff at the oh-so-similar-I'm-surprised-they-didn't-sue set decoration, photography and monsters (not that **Alien** didn't borrow its own share of ideas from flicks like **It! The Terror from Beyond Space** and **Planet of the Vampires**). On occasion, producer Roger Corman's warped, any-thing-for-a-jolt personality oozes to provide some punch, and there's an easily-recognised cast of victims on board (Edward Albert, Erin Moran, Ray Walston, Robert Englund) – so this 80 minuter passes by *sorta* painlessly (not unlike a kidney stone the size of a Chicken McNugget)... Sometime in the near future, a rescue ship is sent to the distant planet of Morganthis, a murky wasteland where a bunch of visiting humans have been shredded into strip steaks by some unknown THING. The rescue team is a cross-section of every warmed-over stereotype imaginable, and for the first half hour you get this nagging suspicion that the actors are taking all this nonsense dead serious. But when they all take a jaunt out to explore a very organic-looking alien pyramid, the creatures start popping out of the woodwork – and none of the actors can escape schlock overdose. The monsters are big. They're mean. They've got loads of tentacles. And they like to pop-top crewmen's skulls. Soon everyone's on the run and – oh *hell*, I don't have to tell you how this type of drivel progresses; but it includes worms, vomit, pureed corpses, and semi-disgusting creatures in all shapes and sizes. The filmmakers should've jettisoned the romantic sideline between Erin ('I was once a star') Moran and Edward ('I was always a nobody') Albert, and they *really* could've used less metaphysical horse-shit as an excuse for a conclusion. It's one of those infamous non-endings, where the credits suddenly roll, everyone in the audience says 'What do you mean, it's over? What the fuck?', and they end up chucking their empty beer cans at the screen... The entire cast sleepwalks through the film, but once again I have to single out Erin Moran, who plays the empathic interest of the group. She's so pathetic you'll almost wish they'd hired someone more talented – like Linda Blair. But don't dismay, because Erin's awarded one of the gristliest demises, when an alien squeezes her guts out (and you'll want to view this scene over and over, I bet, just to see Joannie Cunningham's pudgy face reduced to a substance resembling strawberry jam). All in all, 'Galaxy of Tedium' is your average 3 a.m. time killer that could've been a bit bloodier and a *lot* less dim-witted. Expect a small shovelful of grubbiness and not much else... An interesting credit buried at the end: Production designer, James Cameron. I bet this movie isn't on his resumé any longer.

GAME OF DEATH

ROBERT CLOUSE 1979. Pathetic Film of the Month Award goes to this high-gloss, no-dignity production that pisses on the grave of Bruce Lee, then rubs their audiences' faces in the soggy soil. You see, Golden Harvest Pix had a couple fight sequences (a whopping 15 minutes worth of material) from the movie Bruce Lee was working on when he died. So, in order to cash in, they built an entire kung fu film around these short scenes and had the nerve to advertise that it 'stars' Lee... Next they hired a woefully unsuccessful Bruce Lee lookalike to pad out the rest of this fiasco, in addition to weaving in unrelated scenes from Lee's other films (**Chinese Connection**, **Return of the Dragon**). This leads to some 'slight' continuity problems (such as mismatched sets, costumes, lighting, etc.), but the biggest laughs come when they superimpose a *still* of Lee's face over The Double's. As for the plot – syndicate mobsters want international kung fu film star 'Billy Lo' under contract, but when Lo sez 'no', they ship out a hitman to take revenge. Too bad the guy couldn't aim, because it would have shortened this plywood production. Instead, Billy gets shot in the face and survives (with a bit of plastic surgery, of course), and while the world is told that he's dead, Billy starts bouncing around Hong Kong in disguise (a scraggly beard), searching for his so-called assassins. And after sitting through the first 80 minutes of this celluloid enema, the actual Bruce Lee *finally* snaps a few spines in the new footage, taking on Kareem Abdul-Jabbar in a David and Goliath match-up that's a hoot-and-a-half... But overall, this is a scummy, laughable cash-in on Lee's name, with director Robert Clouse (who helmed first-class kung fu fests **Enter the Dragon** and **The Big Brawl**) trying valiantly to relive old successes... Overweight Hugh O'Brian pathetically dukes it out with The Double, while booze-brothers Dean Jagger and Gig Young ham it up on the DT Express, and Colleen Camp appears as Billy's rock-singer girlfriend (she gets to warble the theme song, 'Will This Be the Song I'll Be Singing Tomorrow?'). As a martial arts movie, **Game of Death** *sucks*, but as a ludicrously inept mess it succeeds on all counts. Sort of a **Plan 9** for kung fu cretins. Yuck-o!

GAMERA VS. GUIRON

NORIYAKI YUASA 1969 (AKA: ATTACK OF THE MONSTERS). Any fan of Japanese monsteramas *must* be familiar with Gamera, Daiei Studios' giant, flying, fire-breathing turtle. Here we have his fifth appearance, as well as one of the most childish (and funny) entries in the series... An unoccupied flying saucer lands on Earth and arouses the curiosity of two young boys (one Japanese, one American) who step inside to check it out. The saucer takes off and minutes later the kids find themselves zooming through space. Out of nowhere pops Gamera, who flies along beside the ship and joins the little brats in a *race*. (Simply a-*may*-zing how Gamera can *breathe* in the vacuum of outer space!) Gamera's size and incessant screaming don't bother the kids in the least. "Gamera's *always* been the children's friend!" one of the whelps says... The saucer lands on a distant planet and the kids meet the ship's owners: two female aliens (oriental ones, of course) in tight-fitting space suits... The aliens have a 'watchdog': Guiron, a four-legged beastie with throwing discs on the sides of its knife-shaped head. Gyaos, the laser-spitting dinosaurian fought by Gamera in **Gamera vs. Gyaos** (aka **Return of the Giant Monsters**) is also living on the planet. When he threatens the aliens' fortress, they unleash Guiron and Gyaos gets a foot chopped off, causing him to hop around on one foot, flapping his wings in pain. (Quite a 'watchdog' *indeed*. Why not go all out and get a giant Pitbull with jets? Hee hee! Sorry, couldn't resist that one.) "Why do you have such monsters anyway?" the Japanese kid asks. "You're so advanced and all!" The kids soon discover their hosts have something *real mean* up their sleeves: they want to munch out on their *brains*! ("We'll gobble their brains raw!") Understandably, the kids freak. ("Let us go! We're not good to eat!") Gamera arrives in the nick of time, but before he can rescue the kids, he's gotta get past *Guiron*. Fight, fight! Guiron lets loose with his throwing discs and his sharp head, cutting up Gamera *real good* and spilling Our Hero's green blood onto the ground. *Will* Gamera defeat this evil monster? *Will* the treacherous aliens get their lunch? Can you stop snickering? You will believe a turtle can fly. (Sorry again.) 'Way to go, Gamera!! [BJE]

GAMERA, SUPERMONSTER

NORIYAKI YUASA 1980. Made up mostly of some of the best monster-wrestling scenes from previous Gamera movies, this is the blazing saga of a boy's pet turtle that one day, just for the heck of it, turns into the giant, flying, fire-breathing monster-smasher Gamera. Gamera does somersaults and screams a lot as he battles Baragon, a mean-spirited reptile that shoots a freezing spray from its tongue and flashes a radioactive rainbow from its back in clips from **War of the Monsters**; Gyaos, a flying fox-like dinosaurian in clips from **Gamera vs. Gyaos**; Viras, a tentacled alien from **Destroy All Planets**; Jiger from **Gamera vs. Monster X**; and Guiron, a knife-shaped monster that shoots deadly serrated disks from the sides of its head, from **Gamera vs. Guiron**. Also tossed in for some silly reason are clips of bizarre spacecraft from the animated cartoon features **Galaxy Express 999** and **Space Cruiser Yamoto**. And whenever one of Gamera's combatants first appears, his name is flashed on the screen... in Japanese. This one will leave you cheering, snickering and laughing out loud all at the same time. [BJE]

GANJASAURUS REX

URSI REYNOLDS 1987. No matter how viciously I may attack any other film, *here* is the absolute dregs – a petty-ante home-made production from Rhino Video. The idea behind this alleged 'comedy' (a monster-movie made by and for potheads) might have sounded mildly amusing while the creators were doing bong hits in their living room one night, but the final product hits Maximum Painfulness within the five minute mark. It's the story of a bunch of dope-addled weed-brains in Southern California, who have developed grapefruit-sized Cannabis Sequoia seeds – genetically mutated marijuana that'll grow a plant the size of a redwood. And a half-hour into the story (and with no rational explanation of where it came from), out pops the title creature, a giant dinosaur with an appetite for reefer. In addition to the peacefully dim-witted hippies, there's also a dino-obsessed professor, his (sorta) beautiful daughter, a nerdy assistant, and a team of government scum-sucking Gestapoids who want to eliminate all the marijuana in the country... Obviously filmed in the actors' own homes, it makes Cheech and Chong's low-grade antics look like Molière in comparison. There isn't a laugh, not a chuckle, not a smile in the entire grainy flick. And how many jokes about dirty laundry, vegetarians, and short-term memory loss can a human being stomach in one sitting? Not enough to make it through this malodorous mess. In addition, the special effects are the absolute *worst* I've ever sat through, outside of super-8 home movies. During the Ganjasaurus Rex sequences, a big papier-mâché head is used for close-ups and hideous blue-screen for the long shots... Will the gov't nuke Rex? Will the dopers get busted? Will the film EVER END? Who cares, because at 100 minutes, this waste of good videotape is so padded out and tedious that I'll make bets *no one* will be able to sit through it without a healthy dose of Fast Forwarding. Directed by Ursi Reynolds and written by the entire cast, I couldn't believe it took 10 people (and probably that many bottles of Thunderbird) to churn this crap out... I'm usually a sucker for giant-monster movies, but after suffering through this shitter, I just felt like a sucker, period. Tame and toothless, avoid it like an Osmonds Reunion.

GATOR BAIT

FERD AND BEVERLY SEBASTIAN 1974. Claudia Jennings is one of the true high priestesses of the '70s exploitation movie. After a stint as **Playboy**'s Playmate of the Year, she racked up an impressive list of genre classics, such as **Unholy Rollers**, **Truck Stop Women**, and **Deathsport**. Jennings had the perfect combination for a hearty drive-in audience – she was pretty, she was tough, she wouldn't take any shit, and she'd unbutton her blouse at the drop of a paycheque. And although **Gator Bait** is one of her less impressive efforts, it's still an adequate li'l bayou tale of redneck revenge... Desiree Tibidoe is a backwoods Cajun wildcat who travels the swamps, poaches gators, and minds her own business. But since she's played by the photogenic Ms. Jennings, whose outfits tend to run on the skimpy side, she also has to fend off all the horny locals, who'll risk their hides for a taste of coonass 'hospitality'. The townsfolk consist of the biggest collection of half-witted white trash to grace a movie screen in some time, but Desiree knows how to handle herself, as in the case of one peckerhead who tried to rape her several years earlier and ended up with his balls sliced off. But the shit *really* hits the fan when Desiree is blamed for murdering a local boy (she's innocent, of course) and soon the sheriff and a posse of drawlin', droolin' kinfolks head into the swamp to settle the score. But with the help of her younger brother and sister, Desiree chews 'em up and spits 'em out (even if her bayou accent tends to wander off at times)... Despite it all, the set-up is pretty standard and the payoff is a bit disappointing, but good location scenery and a scuzzball cast of characters help speed along the proceedings. Anyone looking for huge dollops of nudity and violence will shrug off this exercise in feminine vengeance, though – especially if they're used to the grim charge of classics like **I Spit on Your Grave**. Claudia gets to show lots of cleavage while playing her usual ultra-tough, no-nonsense woman and she uses a pump rifle like a pro, but the film itself never goes as far overboard as you'd expect it to... Personally, I was disappointed by the lack of sleaziness, but that's not to say it's a bad film. Co-starring Bill Thurman (**Creature from Black Lake**), with

Janet Baldwin as Desiree's cute-as-a-button, wide-eyed li'l sister (who gets a shotgun blast to the crotch). **Gator Bait** is another entry from the 'auteur' team of Ferd and Beverly Sebastian (that's right, the guy's name is actually 'Ferd'), who between them not only produced, directed and wrote the thing, but also scored the music and handled the cinematography. The only smart choice they made was to hire Claudia Jennings. If not for her presence, this film would have sunk without a trace, like all the other Sebastian non-epics, such as **Flash and Firecat** with Dub Taylor, and **The Hitchhikers** with Misty Rowe. What a cinematic legacy, eh?

GHIDRAH, THE THREE-HEADED MONSTER

INOSHIRO HONDA 1965. Four giant monsters with a difference of opinion are the stars of this colourful instalment of Toho's Godzilla series. A princess of an unnamed country is the victim of an assassination attempt by gangsters when a bomb explodes in her plane, blowing it to pieces in the air. Shortly afterwards, she mysteriously reappears in Japan, claiming to be a Martian and predicting disaster. Everyone thinks she's nutso but she makes headlines anyway, which draws the attention of the bad guys, who go to Japan to make several hilarious attempts to dispose of her. Meanwhile, Rodan the giant pterodactyl flies out of a sinkhole and zooms over Japan at supersonic speed, Godzilla suddenly appears in the Pacific, blowing ships out of the water with his fiery radioactive breath... and up in the mountains, a recently-fallen 'meteorite' explodes and gives 'birth' to Ghidrah, a winged, armless, three-headed space dragon. Like Godzilla, Ghidrah is a fire-breather, and his only purpose for existence seems to be to cause as much death and destruction as possible... Godzilla decides to visit Japan and meets up with Rodan, and the two take an immediate dislike

to each other, and the Monster Wrestling matches we monsterholics enjoy so much begin. Fortunately, the Aelinas, the tiny twin fairies from Infant Island, happen to be in Japan to make an appearance on a variety show, where they sing a song of praise to their god, Mothra. ("Why do you weep, God of Happiness?" they sing.) They are persuaded by the panicky Japanese to convince Mothra to come to Japan to help stop the monster invasion. The original Mothra is dead, having been beaten to death by Godzilla in the previous film, **Godzilla vs. the Thing**, but her giant caterpillar offspring is still alive, and he swims from his island paradise to Japan. (Actually, there were two of them in **Godzilla vs. the Thing**. What happened to the other one, I wonder?) Eventually, the duelling Godzilla and Rodan cross paths with Ghidrah, and all hell breaks loose until Mothra slithers onto the scene and engages in conversation with the three giant malcontents in monster talk, which is translated for us by the Aelinas ("Oh, Godzilla! Such language!"). Mothra tries to convince Godzilla and Rodan to team up with him to destroy Ghidrah for the sake of the Earth's very existence. At first, they refuse, much preferring to kick each others' butts and smash cities. But then, they have a change of heart, marking Godzilla's historic (?) transformation from a villainous menace to a Hero. And while the monsters are fighting it out, the gangsters are shooting it up with the cops, so we have two separate battles going at once... I must have seen **Ghidrah** at least 20 times. I fucking *love this movie*! Great special effects, cool miniatures, fun soundtrack and hilarious dubbed dialogue make this a must for any Slimetimer's video collection. Loads of laughs and lots of fun. So see **Ghidrah** and watch the monsters kick the shit out of each other. Brought to you by Japan's master monster-makers, director Inoshiro Honda and FX man Eiji Tsuburaya. Yaaaay! [BJE]

THE GIANT LEECHES

BERNARD L. KOWALSKI 1959 (AKA: ATTACK OF THE GIANT LEECHES). A swamp-land programmer from American-International, executive producer Roger Corman and director Bernard Kowalski (**Sssssss**). It's nothing beyond your standard '50s monsterola – it's fast, cheap, and it has more rural dirtbag characters than a trio of Erskine Caldwell novels. Plus, it's a whopping 62 minutes long, so how can you go wrong?... SomeTHING is killing off the locals, every time they wander off into the boggy wilderness. Maybe it's those man-sized sucker-creatures that we glimpsed in the pre-credit sequence? Well, whatever the heck is responsible, the cameraman seems more interested in focusing on sexy Yvette Vickers as Liz-Baby, the tramp of the bayou, who's married to that 'fat pig' (as Yvette unaffectionately refers to him), Bruno VeSota. Ms. Vickers, who also co-starred in **Attack of the 50 Ft Woman**, sluts about in her sprayed-on skirts and hip-cut robes, playing her usual B-movie heel-rounder. But Bruno finally gets fed up with his cuckold role, and loaded down with a double-barrelled shotgun, he chases Yvette and her ultra-shitpot boyfriend into the swamps. What follows is love, lust and loads of water-logged stuntmen in flabby rubber leech suits – bobbing about the backwoods, slurping up the human blood, and trying not to let their zippers show on-camera. And these cut-rate creatures store their victims in an air-filled underground cave, just in case they need a quick midnight snack. Of course, no one back in town believes VeSota when he says that Monsters killed his spouse, but our brick-jawed, granite-headed hero, Ken Clarke (yawn!), grabs a load of dynamite and some handy scuba gear, and heads off to play Mr. Muy Macho... There's the usual dumb-ass hypothesis of the critters' origin (Is the atomic radiation from Cape Canaveral to blame?), and most of the dialogue is so frighteningly BAD that you actually believe the supporting casts' relatives must have been laying pipe with their first cousins for the past several generations. (Speaking of inter-family copulation, did you know that Pat Robertson's parents were first cousins? Hmmm... That might explain a *lot*.) Frogmen eventually spear 'em. Is it 'THE END'? *I* certainly hope so... Silly stuff.

THE GIANT SPIDER INVASION

BILL REBANE 1975. 'The scream you hear may be your own!' –from the ads... A meteor crashes to Earth near a small hick town, resulting in a so-called 'black hole' to another dimension being opened by the resulting crater (what bullshit) and releasing a hungry horde of alien spiders upon the world. It's panic time as hundreds of tarantulas and one or two arachnids the size of Volkswagens turn the peacefully dull dinksville into a bloody battleground of gut-crunching spiders and irate citizens. The fact that the giant spiders are the size of Volkswagens is easily explained: what the filmmakers did, literally, is to dress up a Volkswagen as a spider, complete with puppet legs that move up and down, up and down, as it crawls (or rather, drives) down the street. Alan Hale, Jr. (couldn't get a decent job after **Gilligan's Island**, eh, Al?) plays the sheriff and recites one dumb line after another, as does everyone else in the cast, thanks to an incredibly inept screenplay, which isn't helped at all by Bill 'Nobody' Rebane's directing. There is, at least, lots and lots of particularly nasty-looking blood, and snickers aplenty (if not outright guffaws) at the shamelessly phoney spider-monsters and the Town of Dimwits. One of the funniest giant-bug-on-the-loose movies ever made. [BJE]

GIGANTIS, THE FIRE MONSTER

MATOYASHI ODO 1955 (AKA: GODZILLA RAIDS AGAIN). Despite the misleading title, this is actually the sequel to **Godzilla, King of the Monsters**, though distributed by a different US studio which decided (for some dumb-assed reason) to change the creature's name from Godzilla to Gigantis during the dubbing. Swell idea, buttheads! Fans of the Big Green Guy won't want to miss it though, because this flick is from the good ol' days when Godzilla was a lean, mean, rampaging juggernaut who decimated cities and depleted populations – instead of the scaly teddy bear he soon became in later entries, like **Son of Godzilla**... When a disabled plane lands on barren Iwato Island, the pilots are faced with two battling prehistoric beasts: Spiny-backed Anguiras and Godzilla (though technically, it must be Godzilla's twin, since the original died from the Oxygen Destroyer). Mankind's messy radiation has once again resurrected these hibernating behemoths, and they're both pretty pissed off about it and decide to boogie on down to Osaka for some exercise. STOMP! CRASH! ROAARRRR! Here they come! 40 stories tall, spittin' atomic fire, and when Godzilla and Anguiras get rockin', watch out you puny humans! It's four-star destruction time, with some incredible, high-speed, rubber monster mayhem! The creature suits (Wait a minute! You mean those are costumes?) are unusually seamless, and there are some truly spectacular effects by the always excessive Eiji Tsuburaya, including a pagoda toppling and subway cave-in. A trickle of romance and a prison break provide the pint-sized drama, but happily to report, the homo sapien subplots never get in the way of the simple fact that GIANT MONSTERS ARE ATTACKING THE CITY!! For the most part, the film takes itself seriously (a fact that might dismay Godzilla fans who only like to laugh at the campiness), the dubbing isn't too inept (in

other words, no one has a Brooklyn accent), and Godzilla even gets some sympathy at the end, when he's overpowered by mankind's weapons. A round of applause to director Matoyashi Odo; and a poke in the eye to the dolt who re-edited it for US consumption, Hugo Grimaldi. Required viewing for any monster buff!

GIRL SCHOOL SCREAMERS

JOHN P. FINNEGAN 1985. Rule #1: If you're gonna give your film a knockout title like this one, the least you can do is make the finished product live up to the name. But since this is yet another Troma Team teaser, I guess you have to take what little you can get. It's unpretentious trash – a little slow (OK, a *lot* slow) with a depressingly low sleaze content... It all begins at the Trinity School for Girls, your average, run-of-the-mill Catholic college where the perky misses are forced to wear matching mini-skirts. As a special project, seven of the young ladies (plus one wrinkly nun) are packed off to the nearby Welles Mansion to inventory the palatial estate before it's put on the auction block. Little do they realise, there's a wormy-faced ghost residing in the attic of the house, traipsing about in a wedding dress and sending nosy li'l kids into catatonic shock. Add a few naughty nighties and illicit smokables to the concoction, and there's enough ingredients to keep any bimbo-watcher smiling. Unfortunately, the filmmakers never live up to the inherent potential of the material. The ghost disappears for most of the movie, there's no gratuitous nudity, and the violence is kept respectably restrained. At least the filmmakers would have an excuse if they'd invested some energy in a script – but instead they pass off the same old lame story we've seen a dozen times before. One of the college gals, Jackie (Mollie O'Mara), finds the secret diary of Jennifer Welles – a girl who died mysteriously, 40 years ago in the mansion. And if you can stomach the coincidence

(*I couldn't*), it turns out Jackie looks *exactly* like the deceased. Pretty startling plot twist, eh? (No.) Amidst sorry seances and dull dialogue, we're flooded with cheap flashbacks to years hence – with pretty Jennifer and her rich (and slightly disfigured) Uncle Tyler hanging around the house, and how Jennifer spurned her uncle after he announces his incestuous longings for her. By now I was going into melodrama overdose. There isn't a corpse in sight for the first hour, but the last 20 minutes pick up when the homicidal spirit *finally* shows up for some surprisingly bloodless killings. One gal gets a meat cleaver to the face, while another quickly gets meathooked and hung up to dry. None of the killings are very original or suspenseful, but at least they're more exciting than watching the characters talk you into a state of narcolepsy. But just as the film gets rolling, satanic Uncle Tyler shows up and promptly gets his eyes poked out by the vengeful spirit of Jennifer. The End... Directed by John P. Finnegan ('Not *THE* John P. Finnegan!'), this flick is too tame for the discriminating drive-in set, yet it's probably more fun than flossing your teeth with razor wire.

GLEN OR GLENDA

EDWARD D. WOOD JR. 1953 (AKA: I LED TWO LIVES). This is essential viewing for all schlock scholars, for as any fan of crapola readily acknowledges, Ed Wood Jr. was the grand master of low-budget tripe. His films were indescribably cheap and unbelievably inept, but they've weathered the test of time for several reasons that no other moviemaker has been able to duplicate since – his scripts were crammed with howlingly outrageous dialogue, his stable of actors were all well-versed in scenery-digesting, and best of all, Wood was seriously demented in both his life and his work, and that twisted enthusiasm oozes through every sprocket hole of his films. **Plan 9 from Outer Space** is his most accessible work, because of its overdose of cheap laughs, but **Glen or Glenda** gets my vote for weirdest hodgepodge of cine-moronics. A self-proclaimed portrait of 'stark realism', poor frail Bela Lugosi hosts this mock-documentary nonsense from a worn easy chair. Playing with dry ice. Bugging out his eyes. Reciting pretentiously incomprehensible dialogue such as: "Bevare! Bevare! Bevare the big green dragon that sits on your doorstep. He eats little boys. Puppy dog tails and big fat snails." A monologue fit for a Hungarian junkie, eh?... For this 'serious' (HA!) study of transvestites, Wood pulled out all the stops, mixing bad melodrama with stock footage galore – cattle stampedes, factory scenes, lightning storms, African rituals, and it always returns to Boozehound Bela and his incoherent mutterings... A suicide leads to a police investigator asking a psychiatrist about sex changes and fetishes, and thereby hangs our flaccid tales. Meet Glen (played by Wood himself, under the pseudonym Daniel Davis), a seemingly ordinary Joe. Dating a normal gal. Living an average lifestyle. But when he's alone, he pulls out the angora sweaters and goes out on lingerie shopping sprees. "Give this man satin undies, a dress, a skirt... And he's the happiest individual in the world." The film argues that heartless society should be more sympathetic to his plight, but by now Glen is dressing up in high heels and slinky skirts for walks down Main Street. And soon Glen begins hallucinating, with a horned devil popping up from behind his sofa – leading him into a life of earrings and evening gowns! And when he admits his problem to his fiancee, Barbara (Dolores Fuller), the result is Drama! Pain! Loud groans from the audience! "Love is the only answer," says the all-knowing psychiatrist, and all ends well... The second segment (yes, there's *more*!) is about Alan, who does housework as a child, and therefore grows up feeling he should be a woman. But when doctors discover he's a 'pseudo-hermaphrodite', Alan spends the next two years in a foreign hospital getting hormone shots and a sex change; and Wood doesn't forget to give us a slice-by-slice report of the procedure. Soon, Alan is Ann, and another happy human being walks the streets of

America... I'm so choked up I can't go on! The acting, the direction, the script – they're ALL so dreadful. This is either the most radically imaginative film of the '50s, or utter garbage. YOU DECIDE!

GODZILLA'S REVENGE

INOSHIRO HONDA 1969. This was certainly an inferior Inoshiro Honda effort compared to his previous Godzilla epic, **Destroy All Monsters**. A young Japanese boy is constantly hassled by a bully and his gang, and his feelings of helplessness and weakness cause him to have dreams that he visits Monster Island and watches Godzilla kick the shit out of the island's other titular inhabitants. He meets Godzilla's kid Minyah, who not only shrinks himself down to the boy's size, but becomes his pal and talks to him. ("Hi! Come on over! I won't hurtcha!") It seems that Minyah is also prey to the bullying of the other monsters on the island, especially an electric, cat-faced creature named Gaborah (The same name as the bully who bugs our young hero. What a koinky-dink!). The scenes with Gaborah are about the only original monster-battle footage in the entire film. Eiji Tsuburaya, the man responsible for the bee-yootiful special effects in such Toho classics as **Godzilla vs. the Thing** and **Ghidrah, The Three-Headed Monster**, up and died while they were making the movie; so what we've got here is a bunch of clips from other Godzilla flicks, and more stock footage than we deserve. The opening credits are superimposed over scenes of monsters attacking cities from **Destroy All Monsters**, accompanied by hilarious rock 'n' roll theme music... And Godzilla battles Ebirah the giant lobster, Aspiga the giant spider, Govy the monster bird, and a bevy of jets in scenes from **Son of Godzilla** and **Godzilla vs. the Sea Monster**... When I was 12 years old, I *loved* **Godzilla's Revenge**. Now, years later, I get twitchy watching that goddamn little kid hiding behind bushes, watching the monsters fight, saying things like, "Guy! That's boss!" every time Godzilla pummels a monster senseless. In fact, this film is so annoyingly 'cute' that sometimes it makes my nuts contract into my stomach. Even watching it stoned doesn't help (unless you turn the sound off and put on some hard-drivin' music during the monster fights). However, we must remind ourselves that this particular entry in the Godzilla series was, after all, made for the kiddies, who made up most of the audience of every Godzilla movie *I've* ever gone to see (the exception being **Godzilla 1985**). And the violence level is a little high for a kids' film made during the '60s. In any case, *caveat emptor*, Godzilla fans. [BJE]

GODZILLA 1985

KOHJI HASHIMOTO 1985. **Godzilla 1985** is *not* a re-make of **Godzilla, King of the Monsters**, despite the media's attempts to make decent monster-loving folks like you and me believe otherwise. Raymond Burr does, however, reprise his role in the original as reporter Steve Martin, the American journalist who happens to be in Tokyo at the time of Godzilla's first attack. Once again, American scenes have been added to the Japanese version, and once again, the American scenes suck. But you'll have a good laugh watching Raymond 'Has-Been' Burr standing around doing basically, er, nothing, and the general campiness of the whole film does come off quite nicely. A 15-foot robot with moving eyes, jaws and arms was used in the film, though Christ knows why; they rarely use the damn thing and instead stick mainly to shots of an actor in a dinosaur suit. But what a suit it is, kids. Certainly beats the duck costume used in **Howard: A New Breed of Hero**. There are some great destruction scenes and a lot of beautiful photography, and just enough intentional humour to keep the occasional seriousness from seeming too pretentious. By all means, pick up a couple of six-packs and/or some marijuana and have fun watching Godzilla do the Monster Stomp on mankind. Personally, I'll take an 80-ton fire-breathing dinosaur over Rambo any day. [BJE]

GODZILLA ON MONSTER ISLAND

JUN FUKUDA 1971 (AKA: GODZILLA VS. GIGAN). The Big Green Guy once again waddles his way across the orient in another Toho epic. Well, maybe 'epic' is too grand a term – how about 'coma-fest'? And director Jun Fukuda continually emphasises the kiddie aspects in an attempt to turn Godzilla into a 400 foot, fire-breathing Care Bear... An out-of-work cartoonist (who comes up with dinkheaded ideas like 'Momagon, monster of too-strict mothers') is the human-sized star of this silliness, which is set around a World Children's Amusement Park featuring a Godzilla Tower and a Monster Museum. The first major flaw is allowing the homo sapien storyline to absorb most of the running time, with some type of spy guy rubbish slowing down the pace and leading us quickly toward our fridge's refreshments... Some evil six-foot cockroaches (posing as corporate bigwigs – which isn't too big a stretch) are hatching a plan in which giant monsters invade the human race, and the only people who can stop 'em are a courageous cutie and her comedy-relief hippie assistant. And it all adds up to – instant BOREDOM! Matinee audiences across the globe must have been ransacking theatres during this drivel! Hey, I can enjoy a slow, stupid, uninvolving plot as mush as the next idiot sometimes, but *this* is ridiculous!... But meanwhile, on the legendary Monster Island (and it's about fuckin' time they mentioned it!), the inhabitants are *TALKING* to each other! That's right, adventurous schlockophiles, they actually *talk* this time, though the dialogue won't be putting David Mamet out of a job ("Hey, Anguiras!" "Whaddaya want?" "Somethin' funny's goin' on. You better check!"). And if you can pick yourself up off the floor after this moronic display, you'll find out it only gets dumber!... Several of the creatures are heading (via assorted stock footage) to the mainland, and as expected, all hell breaks loose. Tiny toy tanks are no match for these sweaty stuntmen! Li'l rockets can't penetrate their plastic suits! Laser beams only make 'em laugh (probably because the beams look like they were scratched directly onto the film stock)! And soon a quartet of city stompers – Godzilla, Ghidrah, Anguiras, and a new addition Gigan, a one-eyed whatzit with hooks for hands and a buzzsaw in his chest – all begin beating the crap out of each other. The alien bugs plan on having Ghidrah and Gigan destroy Tokyo (oh, *that's* a fresh idea!), but not if good guy Godzilla and his knee-crawling pal Anguiras can do the two-step on their faces first. Any good Toho fan can predict the result: Razed skyscrapers. Flames. Showdowns. And Godzilla even gets to demolish his life-size amusement park mock-up... Thank goodness for this last minute dose of destruction (most of it shot in half-light, so you can't see their zippers)! But still, the overall result is pretty limp. At least Inoshiro Honda had a talent for keeping the bordering dramatics halfway interesting, while bringing a visual flair to the proceedings. Fukuda's only visible aptitude is in slapping a camera down in front of a bunch of monsters and letting 'em bash the shit out of each others' polystyrene hides. The human story is deadening, the battle footage is sparse and bland, and even the monster suits seem to need a good dry-cleaning. In other words, *not* one of Godzilla's best. It's fine for a few ludicrous laughs (if only to hear our title behemoth verbalise), but in between those couple chuckles, it's a long, dry haul.

GODZILLA VS. MEGALON

JUN FUKUDA 1973 (US RELEASE 1976). First off, the ads for this film showed Godzilla and Megalon standing on top of the World Trade Centre in NYC, with helicopters and jets circling them... Now, let me put it subtly, THIS *NEVER HAPPENS* IN THE DAMNED MOVIE! But I like the ad, nevertheless... Now onto our movie...Yes, those idiotic humans are at it again with their atomic testing, blasting a hole in the earth and unleashing a shitload of trouble in the form of the Seatopians, an advanced underwater race that runs around in togas and cheap junk jewellery. It turns out that one-third of Sea-topia has already been destroyed by the landlubber's nuclear tomfoolery, so these guys have a reason to be a little pissed off. But when the Seatopians unleash Megalon (he's a flying, giant, bug-eyed beetle with power drills for hands and a big, rubbery star growing out of his forehead), a bunch of Japanese scientists unleash *their* secret weapon, a robot named Jet Jaguar. On the human side of the cast, there's the obnoxious little kid who always pops up in these films; the stupid adults who stand around 'oohing' and 'aah-ing' with their thumbs up their asses, during the monster attacks: and a bunch of *dubbed* American actors as the Seatopians, who look like a Skid Row touring company of **A Funny Thing Happened on the Way to the Forum**. Ultraman, er, I mean Jet Jaguar flies to Monster island and convinces Godzilla to join in kicking some insect butt, and it's about time, too, because Godzilla's *barely* in the first half hour — a bad move since nobody watches a Godzilla movie to study the narrative structure or the scintillating dialogue. They wanna see The Big Green Guy stomping on cities or doing The Rubber-Suit War Dance on top of another monster's cranium. And when the monsters finally take centre stage, watch out, because we get a half-hour of non-stop action and miniature-crushing. Even Gigan pops up (a large, metallic, bird-thing with a buzzsaw on his chest) for the rumble, and in one of my favourite scenes, Godzilla gets gashed in the shoulder and *squirts* about a quart of blood (that's a monster-size quart, too!). The stuntmen in the monster suits look like they're having a great time, too, clobbering the crap out of each other (at one point, Jet J. literally *snaps* one of Gigan's arms over his kneecap), and the final fight lasts such a long time that you tend to forgive the uneventful first half. Plus, there's a great, hokey, 'Jet Jaguar' theme song *in Japanese*!... As Godzilla movies go, this one is *really fun*. It's not as good as the original, or **Godzilla 1985**; it doesn't have as much non-stop destruction as **Destroy All Monsters**, but it's miles better than **Godzilla on Monster Island** or **Godzilla's Revenge**. It Certainly doesn't have the best Godzilla costume, but with such a silly movie surrounding him, does it *really* matter if he looks a little rubbery? I'd give it three Rising Suns out of a possible five.

GODZILLA VS. THE BIONIC MONSTER

JUN FUKUDA 1974 (AKA: GODZILLA VS. THE COSMIC MONSTER; GODZILLA VS. MECHAGODZILLA). When Godzilla suddenly goes berserk after years of defending Earth against other giant monsters and being an all round swell guy, the Japanese must prepare for yet another monster invasion. And when a *second* Godzilla appears and challenges the first one to a brawl amidst a background of exploding buildings, it's time to sit back with a cold beer in one hand and a joint in the other and sigh, 'Aahh, *this* is what I need.' For monster movie freaks like myself who have to have their Godzilla fix now and then, **Godzilla vs. the Bionic Monster** is a colourful shitload of fun... Godzilla #1 turns out to be a giant robot in disguise. The robot is a powerful weapon belonging to a bunch of power-happy aliens (shades of **The Mysterians**) whose green simian leader smokes cigars and brags "Godzilla — your powers are *no* match for *MechaGodzilla*!"... It's kind of an unfair fight, cuz Godzilla has both Anguiras, a spiny-backed reptile, and new monster King Seesar, who looks like a sort of mutant Pekinese, on his side. Poor MechaGodzilla is stuck with a bunch of green-skinned apes who think they're David Carradine in **Kung Fu**... One of the most violent (and gory, except in TV prints) entries in the series, we advise you to check this one out. [B|E]

GODZILLA VS. THE SMOG MONSTER

YOSHIMITSU BANNO 1971. I bet you think this is just another dose of Rubber Monster Mayhem from the Orient. Well for their 11th Godzilla feature, Toho tried to make it socially relevant by tacking

SEE THE MIGHTY GODZILLA IN A FIGHT TO THE DEATH WITH HIS BIONIC DOUBLE!

ALL NEW! NEVER SEEN BEFORE!

CINEMA SHARES

GODZILLA VS. BIONIC MONSTER

on an ecological message. The result: A first-class aisle-roller, featuring everyone's favourite fire-breathing dinosaur battling a 500-foot tall lump of sentient sewage! And how can anyone without a tin ear *not* gag at the theme song 'Save the Earth' ('Too many fumes in our oxygen/All the smog now is choking you and me/Good lord, where is it gonna end?'). The only thing that could've made it worse is if William Shatner had warbled it... As unchecked pollution ravages our planet, a giant, lumpy, red-eyed mineral monster named Hedora (in Japanese it means 'pollution', and in every other language it translates into 'cheapjack costume') lurks offshore, spewing deadly filth out of its blowholes during its search for food. In between toking on factory smokestacks to gain strength (Yeah, I *know*. It looks just like Hedora's smoking a bong), Hedora flies over the city, farts sulphuric acid on the population and drips goo all over the countryside. While Hedora changes its shape every 10 minutes, a cute li'l tyke (in fact, so damned cute you want to shove his fat face in a Quisinart) leads the search for answers and predicts Godzilla will soon arrive to save the day (he probably read the title). Sure enough, in stomps The Big G., just in time to get buried in a tidal wave of runny Hedora shit (they say it's 'sludge' pouring from Hedora's lower regions, but I'm just telling you what it *looks* like). The last 20 minutes has them beating the piss out of each other, with Godzilla finally punching his oozy opponent in the eye (Ker-splurt!). And after stomping him flatter than a keg of Piels, he rips out Smoggie's guts and tosses 'em across Japan. Godzilla even *flies* at the end, using his atomic bad breath! What drama! What pathos! What a dopey piece of crapola! Chintzy, vapid and so unbelievably bad it's almost loveable! It's the type of movie you watch while continually shaking your head, thinking 'I can't believe people actually *made* this!' (especially the sudden tour of a groovy psychedelic night-club where teens boogie to anti-pollution songs; or those moralistic mini-cartoons crammed between scenes). It's all aimed at a 9-year-old mentality, which is still a couple notches higher than most John Candy movies, and just so you don't leave the theatre without indigestion,

that rancid theme song pops up again at the end as the rug-rats bid sayonara to their overgrown radioactive saviour. Check it out and prepare to be bowled over by sheer, undiluted cinemoronics.

GODZILLA VS. THE THING

INOSHIRO HONDA 1964 (AKA: GODZILLA VS. MOTHRA). I first saw this one on 'Monster Movie Matinee' on a Saturday afternoon in 1972, and I've been a die-hard Japanese Monster Movie freak ever since. **Godzilla vs. the Thing** is not only one of the best of the Godzilla monsteramas, but it's also a *great* introduction to this particular brand of creature feature. Hell, you've got your great special effects, you've got your funny dubbed dialogue, some shit-kickin' monster fights, and a weird soundtrack by Ikiru Ifukuki; not to mention one of the best Godzilla costumes of the whole series. (In fact, the actor *inside* the suit should have his name in the fucking credits, cuz he's *terrific*. [Haruo Nakajima, who played Godzilla in 11 out the first 12 movies – SP]) But onto the story... A hurricane washes a gigantic egg onto the shores of Japan. A corporation calling itself 'Happy Enterprises' buys the egg from the village of fishermen who found the sucker and build a metal and glass incubator around it, planning to put it on public display (and charge admission, of course). "This monster egg; Is there a good chance it will *explode*, do you think?" asks one clever dink... The Aelinas, a pair of tiny telepathic twins (whom we met previously in **Mothra** and later in **Ghidrah, The Three-Headed Monster** and **Godzilla vs. the Sea Monster**) informs a reporter, his photographer and a scientist that the egg was washed away from their island by the hurricane and that it belongs to their 'god', Mothra (an enormous moth, of course). The Aelinas and their new friends go to Happy Enterprises and try to convince the money-men to return the egg, but it seems they're more afraid of losing profits than they are of the prospect of a newly-born monster thrashing the countryside. ("I *bought* this egg, it belongs to a *company* now, hahahaha!") See, the egg is

about ready to hatch, and in the baby beastie's search for food, well – you know. ("It wouldn't *want* to cause any trouble, but...") But real trouble is yet to come: Godzilla, everybody's favourite fire-breathing dinosaur, has erupted from the earth and is doing the Monster Stomp all over the place, melting tanks with his fiery breath, stumbling into buildings and scaring the shit out of the fleeing populace... This is not the heroic, two-fisted Godzilla who defends earth against giant aliens in later films; This is the *meeean* Godzilla, bent on smashing anything to do with mankind... Our three human heroes and the Aelinas take a trip to Mothra's island hoping to convince the natives to get Mothra to go to Japan and fight Godzilla. The natives aren't too keen on this idea because (a) Mothra's egg hasn't been returned, and (b) their island was used for atomic tests after W.W.II, which turned the place into a poison factory. "Why should we help you after what you've done?" the visitors are told. "May your land be ruined like ours!" There's another problem, too: Mothra's pretty old, see, and isn't too far from death. But the Aelinas break into song, everybody's moved, and Mothra flies off to fight Godzilla, and to save her unborn offspring. Meanwhile, Godzilla's still on the loose, and by now the American and Japanese armies have combined forces in an effort to electrocute him in an electrified net. (In later films, however, we see Godzilla gain *strength* from electricity.) Mothra swoops onto the scene just as Godzilla is glaring malevolently down at her egg, ready to smash it into little pieces. She dives out of nowhere and bats him liberally about the head with her enormous wings, drags him around by his tail with her mandibles, sprays him with poisonous pollen, etc. But Godzilla beats the living shit out of her anyway and collapses, singed and beaten, beside her egg – which hatches, revealing two slimy, bright red caterpillars, whose first order of business is to go after Godzilla... Yes, director Inoshiro Honda and FX whiz Eiji Tsuburaya have done it again, and this is one of their best collaborations. If you're a Godzilla fan, or just dig

monster movies in general, and if you own a VCR but still *haven't seen* this one... well, what the hell are you doing?! Get off your ass and go rent this sucker! [BJE]

GODZILLA, KING OF THE MONSTERS

INOSHIRO HONDA 1956. Here's the one that spawned the whole bizarro menagerie of mutated behemoths from the East. Director Inoshiro Honda and SFX man Eiji Tsuburaya put their heads together (clank!) and came up with this, the *single best* (Period) of the '50s city-smashing dinosaurs. For Americans, shitheap Terry Morse was called up from his septic tank to direct some footage with Raymond 'Bloat' Burr as American reporter Steve Martin (no relation to a certain famous comedian, who shall remain nameless). Burr is visiting Tokyo to see his friend Dr. Serizawa during a series of mysterious ship-disasters off the coast of Japan. The cause of this phenomena is, of course, Godzilla, who lumbers out of the sea and, with his fiery, radioactive breath and skull-shattering roar, blows Tokyo away like a sneeze will blow away a line of coke. Serizawa has invented a secret weapon that might be of use in disposing of the 400 ft-tall monster, but he's afraid it might fall into the wrong hands. "Well," says his fiancee's boyfriend (Sssh! Don't tell Serizawa!), "You have your fear, which might become reality... and you have Godzilla – which is reality." This film is interspersed with badly-edited shots of Burr standing around looking serious, and his useless narration pollutes every other scene, but we do get to see Godzilla push a building down on top of him, ha ha! The voice-dubbing is the pits (can you count how many times the word 'phenomenon' is mispronounced?) but that's not surprising, this, after all, being the first Japanese monster movie to be released in the States. Sure, Godzilla is a guy in a suit in most scenes, (other scenes using puppets) but the grainy, moody black and white photography often makes the Big G. look quite realistic for a non-animated '50s giant monster... I tell you, if that bloodless buttfucker Ted Turner turns **Godzilla** into one of his 'colorised' bastardisations, which are made *solely* to appeal to the tastes of shit-fucking headless idiots who simply cannot watch a movie unless it's in colour, I'll shit in a shoe box and mail it to him, postage due... My favourite line, unfortunately, comes out of the mouth of Raymond Burr: "If he saw a monster," he says, "he's had too much sake." [BJE]

THE GORE GORE GIRLS

HERSCHELL GORDON LEWIS 1972. Eyeballs plucked out with a fork! Faces burnt to a crisp with an iron! Heads deep-fried in boiling oil! Heck, it sure sounds like prime slime material to me!... This is Herschell Gordon Lewis' last gore flick (as well as one of his most notorious), and surprisingly enough, the ads for this one don't exaggerate in the least! This is one grim fucker! University Union Cinemas showed a trailer for this film (on loan from **Gore Gazette**'s Rick Sullivan) at the last All-Night Drive-In Sleaze-Film Festival, and it nearly cleared the theatre with its absolutely-unconvincing, but nevertheless-rancid, *non-stop* display of violence, torture and mutilation. Plus, it also has a special appearance by Henny Youngman (he's right at home playing a sleazy club owner). HGL tosses in plenty of gratuitous nudity (stripper's dancing, women fondling themselves, etc.) to appease the grindhouse audiences, and every 15 minutes we get a *long*, grisly death scene which makes shit like the **Friday the 13th** series look like the wimpy-assed middle-class time-killers that they are. When the bloodshed arrives it's nastier than you'd ever expect – at one point the murderer takes a meat cleaver to a woman's head, chopping and hacking (in close-up) until there's nothing but a pile of red, lumpy pulp. Another victim is beaten on the butt with a hefty meat tenderiser until her derriere looks like a slab of freshly-chopped sirloin. And in one of the most outrageous scenes, the killer snips off a woman's nipples with a pair of scissors and fills two cocktail glasses with the 'fluid' that streams out – one gives white milk, the other chocolate... The plot (Oh, there's a plot? Will wonders never cease?) involves a greasy, egotistical detective and a pretty (but annoying) female reporter who run about town investigating the murder of a go-go girl; and of course, they keep tripping over more freshly torn-apart corpses as the story progresses. Who's responsible for the crimes? Could it be the local psycho Vietnam vet, who crushes melons with painted-on faces in order to bring back the good ol' days of the war? Or possibly the band of self-righteous women's-libbers, who protest strip joints by beating up the clientele? I'm not telling whodunit, but in the asinine finale, the killer jumps out a window just in time to have their head run over by a passing car (Oops! Squirt!). And if you're familiar with Lewis' style, you know there's plenty of grim humour tossed in to liven up the non-bloodshed-segments – one woman is whacked in the head while blowing bubble gum and the bubble fills with blood; there's always the *same* lame pack of camera-happy reporters spastically clicking away at the scene of every crime; and the final credit actually reads 'We announce with pride, this movie is over!'... Without a doubt, this is one of Lewis' finest. If you've got a strong stomach, you'll get a couple good shudders, lotsa giggles and plenty of complaints from visiting friends. It's a crude, sicko delight!

GORGO

EUGENE LORIE 1961. 'Mother love, monster style' –TV Guide... A small island off of Ireland is wiped off the face of the earth. No one knows how or why, it just isn't *there* anymore. (*We* get to see its destruction though.) An expedition is sent to the area to find some answers, and what do they find but a gigantic prehistoric reptile with wild eyes and nasty, sharp, pointy teeth! At first, everyone is stunned and terrified. Then visions of megabucks dance in their heads, and they drug the beast and whisk him off to Battersea Park, amidst a great deal of fanfare. Imprisoned and helpless in a huge arena, poor Gorgo stands around screaming piteously to himself as audiences, in the safety of their seats surrounding the monster, seem to find him hilarious in his captivity, and they laugh and laugh at him and seem to have all the intelligence and cool of a Dome-ful of S.U. sports-fan assholes. Then, *Mama Gorgo* appears, and Everything Goes To Hell. Yes, it seems that the captured dinosaurian is only a *baby*, and as big as it is, in full standing height it doesn't even reach its mom's knee! Mom is *pissed off.* She wants her kidnapped offspring and she wants it now. The army's efforts to blast the monster out of England's coastal waters prove totally useless and she's off to London, destroying *everything*

as she goes. Panic grips the city and everyone runs screaming through the streets as the city is torn apart around them in a gorgeous special-effects show. People commit suicide by leaping from windows in droves rather than be killed by Ms. Monster... In this colourful British production heavily influenced by Toho's monster series, we are treated to Great Shot after Great Shot of beautifully photographed chaos and destruction that will make any giant-monster fan pound his fists on his knees in delight and want to see it a few more times. Obviously, we loved it. Check it out, goddamit! [BJE]

GOTHIC

KEN RUSSELL 1987. "Will we never get out of this madhouse?" one of the characters screams, and *you* might think the same thing if you're in search of an evening of straight-forward entertainment and you stumble into this movie... Director Ken Russell, after a stint in the US with **Altered States** and **Crimes of Passion**, spazs out with another of his cinematic 'biographies', this time focusing on future-novelist Mary Shelley and poet Percy Bysshe Shelley during a visit to Lord Byron's palatial estate in the early 1800's. And as expected, Russell treats us to a dazzling (and virtually incoherent) look at a weekend of spooky storytelling, laudanum-induced hallucinations and sexual escapades – though compared to some other Russell excursions (**Lisztomania** first comes to mind) this movie is practically lucid. So, if you're interested in learning more about these literary figures, I'd suggest you read a book on them instead, because Russell certainly takes liberties in presenting his subjects and he very nearly beats you over the head with his correlations between their nightmarish visions and their future

works... But viewed as your basic, pretentious horror film, Russell runs through a hit-and-miss selection of disturbing imagery. He bats about a .500, which isn't bad, but it's not great either. Written by Stephen Volk, the characters *literally* conjure up their personal demons and expose their obsessive drives, and we get everything from your typical leeches and bugs, to your less run-of-the-mill breasts-with-eyes and a knight with an armour-plated phallus. Natasha Richardson, Julian Sands and Gabriel Byrne are all fine in the leads, but since this is the type of film where EVERYTHING is a cipher, I never became involved emotionally with any of the characters – they always stayed pawns in Russell's directorial game of pop psychoanalysis. The beautiful sets and photography only add to the mood-soaked proceedings, and there's a few vividly rendered hallucinations, but if you're looking for *solid* twistedness, don't expect anything nearly as flamboyant (or disgusting) as **The Devils**. Instead, this feature falls somewhere into the grey area along with **Mahler** and **Savage Messiah** – films that will piss off a lot of viewers because they are alternately disturbing, tedious, hypnotic, and overwrought. But *I* wouldn't miss them for the world.

GRAVE OF THE VAMPIRE

JOHN HAYES 1972. William Smith, one of the Exploitation Cinema's greatest resources (from '70s gems like **Invasion of the Bee Girls** and **Angels Die Hard**, to more recent mindrot like **Maniac Cop** and **Eye of the Tiger**), takes the lead in this low-budget vampire film, which happens to be one of the more originally plotted, unjustly ignored bloodsucker bashes of the '70s. Unfortunately the production *looks* so amateurish it had audiences thinking they had stumbled into just another no-brain ozoner. But the shocks are surprisingly vivid, as is its unique Family Feud subtext. I first saw it on the Late Show when I was a teenager, and the intro instantly seared itself onto my brain... The story begins in the '50s, with two young lovers enjoying a night-time tryst in (where else?) the cemetery, when a nearby coffin opens and a fanged figure emerges from his grave. But instead of killing both victims, the ghoul feasts from the boy's jugular and then pulls the girl into an open grave and brutally rapes her. It's an unforgettable, nightmarish intro; and nine months later, a male child is born to the rape victim. The infant might be a tad grey at first sight, but he acts healthy. And even if it seems odd that the tyke has a fondness for fresh blood over mother's milk, his slightly-deranged mom takes it in her stride and simply fills his baby bottles straight from her own vein. It's pretty fucking grim, if you ask me... Most of the film is set in the present though, with the now-adult half-vampire son (Smith) on the revenge-soaked trail of his 'father' – tracking Dad to a college campus where he teaches night courses on the occult and feeds off of nubile co-eds. Smith enrols in one of his father's classes and eventually goes head to head with his evil papa. The film is great when it concentrates on the cat-and-mouse conflict, but the last half hour is a mess, with one too many nitwit twists, a sudden lapse of logic and an insipid love story souring the mix. At least the surprisingly brutal showdown in the last minutes will keep anyone from nodding off... With a bit more polish (and maybe a more bankable star) this film could've been a mass-market classic. As it stands though, the supporting cast is cliché-ridden, the direction is routine, the drama wavers drastically – *BUT* the script by John Hayes and David Chase explores such engaging territory that the tale stands out, despite all its glaring faults. It's also aided immeasurably by the two leads. Smith is a solid presence (and articulates his dialogue as well as Sly Stallone) and Michael Pataki (**Dracula's Dog**) pours on the slimy charm as the literal lady-killer. A powerful, but unfocused chiller.

THE GREAT ROCK 'N' ROLL SWINDLE

JULIEN TEMPLE 1980. The Monkees made only one film – **Head**. Well, here's the other side of the coin, as provided by The Sex Pistols; a film that is diametrically opposed in terms of musical style, yet the end result is roughly the same. Each production gives us a fun-house reflection of their era, while taking the time to skewer the media, the record business and their own commercialism... **Head** accomplished its goal by swaddling itself in psychedelic trappings and in-jokes, and **The Great Rock 'n' Roll Swindle** does it with an appropriately razored edge and a 'fuck-off' attitude to itself... It's actually kinda scary if you compare The Monkees and The Sex Pistols on a purely business level – each group was manufactured from a High Concept, both were products before they were a band, and eventually they were crammed through the meat grinder of Big Business. They padded their pockets, got sick of the whole damn scam, and separated... The Monkees proved the marketing poten-tial of TV on the youth audience, by saturating the airwaves with their faces, their voices and any other type of garbage they could mass synthesise. The Sex Pistols took a more devious approach – instead of blatantly appealing to the mass market, their Svengali-esque agent, Malcolm McLaren, wanted to create something new and subversive, and then proceeded to sell it by way of anti-publicity that was composed equally of controversy and spittle. In a nutshell, **Swindle** is a history of The Sex Pistols – but instead of simply documenting the band's rise, director Julien Temple (**Absolute Beginners**) takes us on a jury-built examination of their fame from the inside out. He lashes together footage from The Sex Pistols' shows (everything from their first audition to their last concert in San Francisco), pin-headed critical opinions of their music ("I think most of these groups would be improved by sud-den death"); scraps of a fictional storyline; animated episodes of The Pistols on tour through the shitboxes of America; miscellane-ous bits from Russ Meyer's aborted feature, **Who Killed Bambi?** (obviously the Martin Bormann jokes were his); and (mostly) the business philosophy of Malcolm McLaren, who makes his first appearance in a head-to-toe leather body suit. It's no wonder Johnny Rotten tried to stop this film's release, since the group itself comes off as nothing more than a pack of 'unlovable spiky-tops'... Our first lesson is 'How to Manufacture Your Band', and we're subsequently shown how to screw over the record companies and make loads of money by bouncing from label to label; how to manipulate the media and the public; how to package Anarchy and make it sell to pretentious youth; how to cultivate generation gaps to help sell your product; and most of all, how a group who no one could hear on the radio, buy records for, or get tickets to, could become England's No. 1 Public Enemy. And intermingled with their steel-toed stomps to fame and fortune, Temple also pours on the flashy, excessive nuttiness: You get the 1780 Gordon Riots, with villagers hanging and burning mannequins of The Sex Pistols; a transvestite dwarf and McLaren (in a 'Cash For Chaos' T-shirt) dancing to '(You Need) Hands'; and an old man in under-pants being beaten with a guitar by a dominatrix, while Tweety Pie sings 'I Tawt I Taw a Putty Cat'... Yes, this film is a first-degree, multi-layered mess, but it's also one of the most brilliantly cynical and hilarious films on the modern music scene ever made. Lots of die-hard Sex Pistols fans might not agree with this film's ideology, but you can't ignore this flick's ice-pick honesty (even if it does play by its own sneaky rules). Repeated viewings are advised...

THE GREEN SLIME

KINJI FUKASAKU 1969. What a title! What a theme song! What a movie! It's a cheapjack piece of shit! Not only is it one of *the* most laughable Japanese productions to ever cross the Pacific, it's also got the worst special effects I've ever seen outside of **Space Patrol**. It looks like most of the spaceships should be piloted by Gumby!

Director Kinji Fukasaku (**Message from Space**) took some American greenbacks, added some English speaking two-bit actors (including Richard Jaeckel, who follows in the pride-gulping tradition of Nick Adams and Russ Tamblyn), and spat out this thoroughly abysmal, unforgettably hilarious feature. And I'll bet you a sawbuck that the bigwigs at MGM felt like horses' asses when they got a gander at what their money had wrought... Set in the near future, the space station Gamma 3 (Can you count the wires holding it up? 1, 2, 3...) is the location for this dim-witted and painfully protracted gut-buster. When a team of explorers land on an uncharted asteroid, they unknowingly bring back a glob of the green title goop. But unlike most slime that just sits on the floor and lowers the prop-erty values, this alien variety tends to slither about and grow into six-foot-tall, one-eyed, tentacle-flapping, stuntman-encased crea-tures who feed on energy. In addition to reproducing faster than Catholics, they electrocute anyone within tentacle's length, and soon there's dozens of them flailing about and zapping the crew. As long as the gloriously silly Green Slime are attacking, the film is top-notch, stooopid fun. Unfortunately, it's not all just monsters and mayhem – there's a tediously macho conflict betwixt the two male leads (Jaeckel and Robert Horton) over the ship's Italian sex-pot, Luciana Paluzzi. All this unnecessary emotional baggage only slows down the pace (in addition to giving audiences an oppor-tunity to run to the bathroom), and let's face it, the only reason we're sitting through this thing is for the outrageous Slime Battles. And when they finally arrive, they're worth the wait! Ray guns from Buster Crabbe serials can't stop 'em! The pathetic acting level doesn't halt 'em! Even the so-called script doesn't help, since the human characters seem to have the combined intelligence of a grilled cheese sandwich... Everyone's so stalwart! Everyone's so serious! Everyone's so downright LOUSY! How could *any* self-respecting actor keep a straight face during this hunk of muck? Along with the Lego miniatures, there's some frighteningly garish sets and costumes that scream late-'60s indulgence, and it all helps to make **The Green Slime** one of the most visually asinine movies ever made! It's a *classic* in simple-mindedness and a must-see for monster-movie addicts – in addition to being eminently enjoyable after downing half a bottle of Finlandia. It's a numbing experience! (See it for yourself, and come up with your *own* list of derogatory adjectives for it!)

GRETA, THE TORTURER

JESS FRANCO 1979 (AKA: WANDA, THE WICKED WARDEN; AKA: ILSA, THE WICKED WARDEN). Jess Franco, the skagbag who cluttered grind-houses with cut-rate junk like **Castle of Fu Manchu** and **Venus in Furs**, had just finished his notorious **Barbed Wire Dolls** and de-cided to double his investment by using the same sets and much of the same cast in another perversion-and-debasement-to-women flick. But for this one he pried Dyanne Thorne and her 42-inch lungwarts away from her **Ilsa** series and gave her the bitch-warden title role. And nowadays, this celluloid haemorrhoid is on display from Cinepix Video, with a title change to cash in on the **Ilsa** notoriety... Welcome to the Las Palamas Clinic, which was established to treat sexually deviant women, such as nymphoma-niacs, lesbians and prostitutes – but everyone's favourite debaser, Dyanne Thorne, runs the jungle-based hospital like it was a Nazi concentration camp. There's flesh-brandings, gang bangings, whippings, shit-caked asshole licking, injections of acid up an inmate's cunt, and in a prolonged scene Dyanne uses a woman's bare chest as a pincushion (and then grinds them in even deeper by laying on top of her)... And if that wasn't enough for any fetish freak, the movie starts right off with showtime at Greta's Camp of Torture (complete with crotch-level camerawork), while Dyanne unloads her torso into a Mister Bubble tub. Unlike most women-in-cages flicks where the prison wardrobe consists of hot pants or mini-skirts, **Greta** does them one better by skipping the underwear department completely and by just giving the gals a shirt that hangs down to their butt... So much for the essentials – lots of nudity, loads of sick violence (though you never see any *graphic* bloodshed until the end), plus plenty of physical torture for the inmates and mental torture for the audience who's watching this rancid raunchfest. And would you believe they even find time to stick in a story (!): A righteous doctor wants to expose the truth behind the Clinic's torture, shock treatment and general naughti-ness, so he gets an innocent young woman to pose as an inmate and infiltrate the system. From there on, it's the now-standard structure – innocent gal behind bars, unsympathetic warden, fat sadistic guards, and a cross-section of ill-tempered prisoners who like to pick fights (in this case, nude wrestling matches in the shower) with the cell block's fresh meat. There's also the solitary male guard who films the assorted atrocities and sells them as Snuff films, and a REALLY SICKENING finale that'll have you squirming in your chair, when Dyanne is torn apart and eaten (in brutal close-up) by her crazed inmates... Amazingly enough, I've heard rumours that this particular video version was *heavily edited*, and if that's true, I'd have to see the uncut version for myself to believe it, because this sucker is bad enough as it is. Jess Franco couldn't direct one of his own bowel movements, much less a motion picture, and he unwisely jettisons the inherent campiness of the old **Ilsa** films (i.e. that wacky exploding diaphragm) in order to plow straight into the depths of cruelty and depravity. It's all so flatly filmed though, that most of the time it's like watching a lousy porno film without the porn. As for the cast, I get a headache just thinking about their level of incompetence, and even Ms. Thorne is looking long in the tooth. She must be pushin' 40 years old, and I think her and Sybil Danning should team up for a prison film set in the State Home for Sagging Screen Bimbos... I can't say I'll be watching this one again soon (or ever), but if you're *desperate* for an overdose of grade-Z sleaze, **Greta** is definitely the way to go...

GRIZZLY

WILLIAM GIRDLER 1976 (AKA: KILLER GRIZZLY). '18 feet of gut-crunching, man-eating terror!' screamed the ads. This is one of those churn-'em-out nature-goes-whacko movies that were made in the '70s to cash in on the success of **Jaws**. This time, the killer kritter is a towering, mean-spirited grizzly bear. Christopher George is a ma-cho forest ranger who can't convince his boss to close the camp-grounds when the hungry beast starts ripping campers to pieces and gobbling them down, leaving just enough bloody slop to gross out people who happen to stumble across what's left of the bod-ies. Mr. Bear likes to play with his dinner before he eats it, ripping off one girl's arm and slashing her face to ribbons (WHACK-RIP-WHACK-RIP), crushing a little kid to its chest and tearing him apart while his screaming mom watches, then killing her too, etc... Rich-ard Jaeckel is an expert on grizzlies who is called in to help track the beast down. Ordinary shotguns are, of course, useless; so, as an incredibly clever finish, our heroes use a *bazooka* to blow our hairy friend away... The killings are, at least, pretty nasty, and there's lots and lots of fake-looking blood... inspired by **Jaws**? Can you say, *Rip-off?* [BJE]

GROTESQUE

JOE TORNATORE 1987. This snoozer had all the makings of a rancid li'l romp. There's a cast headed by Linda Blair, Tab Hunter and Donna Wilkes (**Angel**); a plot revolving around psycho punkers; and a lumpy-faced monster who looks like a first cousin to The Slime People. I couldn't imagine anyone being able to screw it up, but then again, I never guessed at how lethargic and limp Joe Torna-tore's direction could get. He misses every opportunity at becoming even moderately savage, and the result is never believable, rarely gory and only humorous at the very end. In other words, this flick is *so* bad, it makes Linda Blair look good!... Ms. Blair and her pal Donna head up to the mountains to visit Linda's dad, a jolly ol' codger who's a Hollywood special effects/makeup man. So right off the bat we have an elderly couple, a pair of young bimbettes and a secluded cabin – not forgetting a van load of evil-tempered, foul-mouthed, spiky-headed punks. Their wild-eyed leader is Scratch (Brad Wilson) – a snarling, salivating social deviant who's supposed to be the Ultimate Nasty, but instead comes off only as a low IQ-ed annoyance left over from **Surf Nazis Must Die**. Sure, the guy's well-coifed, but he's strictly from the slobber-and-sneer school of over-emoting... After ladling on the foreboding dialogue and idiotic fake scares (you see, Dad keeps dressing up in his latex designs and scaring folks), I was almost relieved when the villains pop up and begin killing off the characters. Plus, there's the mind-straining mystery of who (or what) is Patrick, the unseen family member they keep hidden in the secret room?... 'I hate everyone in this movie and I hope they all die,' I kept wishing, and the Badfilm Fairy must've heard my pleas, because almost everyone is snuffed out by the midway point – leaving Linda trudging through the snow in her P.J.'s while the two remaining punkoids chase after her. Tab Hunter (remember him?) finally *straggles* in during the last 25 minutes to look concerned, grab his paycheque and play Mr. Revenge in the final reel. And though the ending is stooopid, at least it wasn't as big a waste of film stock as the first hour-plus. A teeth-grindingly bad, unnecessarily tame, 80-minute turd. That about sums it up.

THE GRUESOME TWOSOME

HERSCHELL GORDON LEWIS 1967. As any sleaze-buff already knows, H.G. Lewis was one of the first directors to pour out the gore to movie audiences, and his ground-breaking **Blood Feast** is the **Birth of a Nation** of splatter movies (and like **Birth of a Nation**, it's almost impossible to sit through nowadays because it's so badly-dated)... **The Gruesome Twosome** is one of his more obscure 'epics', and it's worth your time for the weird prologue alone, with two talking mannequin heads discussing hair styles and murder for several minutes (pad out that running time, Herschell!), until, in typical HGL fashion, one of them gets a knife through the head, with blood pouring out... But onto the plot, eh? A young woman rents a room from a couple who run a wig shop, which advertises '100% human hair' (Uh oh! Sounds like trouble already!). The landlady's a run-of-the-mill, grey-haired, grandmotherly-type, but there's also Rodney, her brain-damaged psycho-son, who spends his afternoons attacking new boarders. And sure enough, before you can say, 'security deposit', Rodney is hacking away at the new tenant, slowly peeling back her bloody scalp as his equally mania-cal mom chuckles gleefully. But she's not the first gal to disappear from the local college, so one flaky female, Cathy, decides to be-come a bubble-headed Nancy Drew and investigate the murders... Like any HGL exercise, this is basically a lot of extraneous footage, intercut with some *graphic* gore (like a liver being ripped from a girl's stomach cavity, and of course, fondled for the camera). The film is padded with non-stop irrelevant stupidity – let's count all the unnecessary footage: (1) Follow the school janitor home from work. (2) Watch a supporting actress take a PG-rated shower, for no apparent reason. (3) Film close-ups of a guy's mouth, chewing on potato chips. And (4) don't forget to throw in some giggly co-eds, go-go dancing in nighties... All the college girls are pretty brainless, constantly discussing how wonderful wigs are, and even the star, Cathy, seems like a mushhead most of the time. Conse-quently, the murderous mom and son turn out to be the most entertaining characters. Sure, they're dangerous psychopaths, but how could you *not* like a mother who'd give her son an electric carving knife for a present, which he promptly uses to rip open the throat of their next potential tenant? Oh, yeah, there's an 'action-packed' finale with Rodney chasing Cathy with a machete, but luckily (and in loving close-up) she stabs a hatpin into his eye... On the minus side, the production values stink, and Cathy, the most obnoxious character in the film, *doesn't* get hacked to bits. But on the plus side, the janitor has an outrageous Swedish accent, the deranged twosome are so sick they're hilarious, and there's a shitload of blood and gore and internal organs packed into its couple gore scenes. I enjoyed it.

GUIDE TO SAFE SEX

1987. Wanton emotions! Back-seat dating! The hideous results of young love! Yes, you guessed it! The companion piece to Rhino Video's **Dope-Mania**, this 'artificial insemination by Johnny Legend' is more nonsense from the past – this time with one important social message: Cheap sex leads to countless numbers of blind, deformed, or hopelessly insane young men and women. Another hour-long package from those geniuses at Rhino, packed with '40s/'50s nonsense about irresponsible teens on the road to disas-ter when they don't listen to their folks about staying out late... It's all here! How young women are seduced by sailors on leave! How *not* to grope your first date! How the only response to syphilis is quitting school, leaving town, and becoming a hermit! And if you have sex before marriage you WILL CATCH VD! It moves from the inherent silliness of **Dating Do's and Don'ts**, where Woody won-ders how to ask a girl to the Hi-Teen Carnival; to the historical curiosity of **Ship of Shame**, a Navy VD film about a bunch of shore leave swabbies searching for loose women; and the severe weird-ness of **Tomorrow's Children**, a 1932-propaganda-piece about forced sterilisation, where operations are handed out like they were parking tickets. A few mediocre silent nudie-shorts inter-sperse the action, giving the viewer a chance to go to the bath-room and grab a fresh beer without having to pause the tape... A little repetitive, and not nearly as much fun as **Dope-Mania**, but it still gets a solid recommendation. Where else can you see this type of crap.

HALLUCINATION GENERATION

EDWARD A. MANN 1966. Run for your lives!! The drug fiends are coming!! Someone shovelled the dust off of this laughable relic, and oooh what a stinker it is, kids. Directed and written by Edward Mann, this is the type of flick in which Drugs make you run down the street, screaming at the top of your lungs (and come to think of it, paying *admission* to see this movie would probably elicit the same response). Don't go into it expecting hippie clichés or kitschy kicks (such as in **The Trip** or **Psych-Out**) – it's pure b/w Euro-dreck set in trendy Barcelona and blandly narrated by Bill Williams (Danny Stone), an innocent who's quickly indoctrinated into the drug-drenched night life of bohemian beatniks. There's heroin, opium, morphine, epinephrine, bennies, airplane glue, ether, and best of all, LSD cocktails! "This contains a glimpse of eternity," Eric The Pusher (George Montgomery) beckons to Bill while spacing out on acid to Eternal Concepts, such as comparing the universe to a lemon jaw breaker. Bill soon falls for a doe-eyed German girl ("She wasn't a great dancer, but she turned me on") and before we know it, the two are man and wife, and it's Domestic Soap Opera Time (Zzzzzz). Bill becomes a disillusioned writer (is there any *other* kind in this type of bad drama?) while his wife tries her best to support his quickly escalating temper and bar tab... And all this time, the viewers are asking themselves 'Where the *hell* are the

hallucinogenics?' But don't fret. Eric eventually doses Bill and we get a few minutes of long-overdue Pharmaceutical Phun – colourised flashes, gyrating clock mechanisms, myriad reflections, white mice scampering, and a gun in his hand turns into a bat (Special credit should go to 'Abstract LSD effects by Paul Radkan and Fima Noveck'). Meanwhile, the local Beats turn out en masse to groove on his crazy visions. He's Flying a Giant Bird. Crossing over on The Train. Swimming the High Seas. But as every good propagandist knows, just one taste of LSD leads directly to permanent addiction and terminal overacting... Except for this trippy interlude, the plot crawls along and for a while it even turns into a heist caper, with a zonked-out Billy following Svengali-Eric's orders. (Trying to pull off a robbery while you're on acid? Good idea!) Montgomery is pretty fun, playing the cool cat connection, but the majority of this movie is leaden (in addition to being moralistically straight-arrow). Grainy photography, flat direction, amateurish acting – hey, this is the type of boring flick that could give illegal psychedelic drugs a bad name! Fun for the tolerant acid completist though.

THE HAND

OLIVER STONE 1981. Before director Oliver Stone began churning out Oscar machines like **Platoon** and **Wall Street**, he wrote and directed this oddball horror gem concerning a prominent cartoonist (played by Michael 'if it's Oscar night, I must be on the set of **Jaws: The Revenge**' Caine) and his descent into insanity following a tragic car wreck where his drawing hand gets sheared off. At first, his publisher tries to continue his comic strip using a new artist (Charles **Roger Rabbit** Fleischer), but the new guy's spaced-out plotlines piss M.C. off. So Mike decides to take a teaching job at a rural college. Ever since the accident, though, Mike's been having, uh, *funny* dreams. His severed hand is still creepin' around, and that sucker still has quite a grip. Mike's wife (Andrea Marcovicci) is losing touch with him, opting to touch a tofu-yoga wimp who runs a consciousness something-or-other. Mike beds down with a sultry student (Annie McEnroe) who likes to suck on the fingers of his prosthetic hand. Ooh. A fellow professor at Oakie U. warns Mike about these 'blackouts' he's been having. Of course, Mike's 'magic hand' is soon doing some real damage, and Stone keeps the connections quite enigmatic, *and* the ambience distinctly off-the-wall. When the wife and kid pay Mike a visit at his secluded cabin, it turns into 'Kramer vs. The Hand'. Caine's performance is very good, certainly among his best, and the supporting cast is equally fine. Sure, a few silly moments (not that bitchin' accident scene, though) and a finale in a mental hospital that truly redefines the word 'What?', but Stone definitely builds some nice atmospheric scares, and his script ideas were liberally ripped off by **Nightmare On Elm St.** and its like. Recently picked up for home vid, **The Hand** is worth a look. (Oh yeah, Carlos Rambaldi did the gripping special effects.) [TR]

HARDCOVER

TIBOR TAKACS 1989 (US: I, MADMAN). Director Tibor Takacs' first feature was the surprise money-raker **The Gate**, which featured a few cute effects, but little in the brainpan department. This, his second effort, was barely released. Though not much better, it at least showcases sexy Jenny Wright (**Near Dark**) who stars as Virginia, a young woman who likes to spend her evenings reading cheap horror novels and scaring the bejesus out of herself. Her latest double dose of trashy tales are by author/part-time alchemist Malcolm Brand: 'Much of Madness, More of Sin', about a psycho in a black cape and beret who conducts horrifying experiments (i.e. mating a jackal with a human), and 'I, Madman', featuring a similar looking whacko who slices off his own face for the woman he loves. Maybe Virginia's active imagination has gone too far this time though, because soon she's seeing this fictional sicko waiting at

bus stops. And after her friends start turning up mutilated, the Madman begins crashing her dreams with pieces of the victims grafted onto his deformed visage. Yes, it's basically another 'where does reality end and fantasy begin?' terror tale – slicker than average, but with a deadwood supporting cast. Even pretty Jenny is a bit too ditzy to be *really* sympathetic (then there's the fact she keeps lightin' up those cigs. Ugh!). At least the killer doesn't crack bad jokes, unlike other publicity-bloated disfigured dream murderers; and he's a fairly gruesome ghoul, with chunks of dead flesh basted together into a face. Chock full of deviant ideas (i.e. the Madman wants to scalpel out Virginia's heart and wear it as a necklace), it's still a patchwork production, not unlike the villain's puss. Funniest scene: Ms. Wright's visit to a sleazy book publisher with fare like 'Moby's Dick' and 'East of Edith' The ultimate verdict: Starts good, gets stupid. Oh well.

THE HARLEM GLOBETROTTERS ON GILLIGAN'S ISLAND

1981. AARRRGGHHHHH! I've still got the emotional scar tissue from watching this wretched disaster! How bad is it, you ask? Imagine the *worst* possibility, and then *triple* it! What a chunk of shit!... Though the entire bunch of castaways was rescued in one of their two previous TV movies, the Howells have turned the island into a hotel complex and all of the aged sitcomers have returned as co-owners. They still live in those idiotic bamboo huts, sleep in hammocks and fall over each other like nitwits – but now there's **Love Boat**-style bikinied tourists roaming about, so that Skipper can ogle them, like some kind of pot-bellied pervert. Almost all the old cast members who couldn't get work for the last 20 years are back, and gosh, it's pathetic watching these no-talent buffoons run about the backlot. (Bob Denver looks worst for wear, with greying hair and skin to match.) Tina Louise is the only one with the dignity to turn down the paycheque (of course, she was also pushing 50 at the time), and although Jim Backus gets third billing, he only turns up during the last three minutes... Meanwhile, somewhere over the Pacific, The Harlem Globetrotters are in their private plane when Coach Scatman Crothers informs them of an electrical malfunction. Landing in the ocean, they're menaced by the shark in **Jaws** (they throw basketballs at it and it goes away) borrowed from the Universal Backlot Tour, and wind up on Gilligan's Island, practising b-ball with coconuts... Martin Landau and Barbara Bain then appear as a pair of villains (along with their orange robot, George) who want to take over the island because of its supply of Supremium, a new form of energy with which they can rule the world (oddly enough, it looks just like a plastic rock with a 100 watt bulb inside). Even those who forgave Landau & Bain for **Space 1999** won't be so kind-hearted to the pair this time around... After a few lame attempts on the castaways' lives (none of the them successful, unfortunately), it all comes down to a basketball game for the possession of the entire island (complete with network sportscasters) between The Globetrotters and The New Invincibles, a team of radio-controlled, bucket-headed robots led by Landau. Add to that the typically horrible laff-track and you get a movie that's so insultingly inane that you can't believe your eyes – it makes that original series look like Beckett. Chewing on broken glass is more fun.

THE HAUNTED PALACE

ROGER CORMAN 1963. Though it's credits read 'Edgar Allan Poe's **The Haunted Palace**', this is actually based on the novel **The Case of Charles Dexter Ward** by Mr. Sunshine himself, H.P. Lovecraft. What did Poe contribute? The title, which is taken from a poem of his (talk about 'creative publicity'). Director Roger Corman takes the reigns for his usual dose of cheap thrills and atmospheric skulduggery, complete with a truckload of dry ice, cobweby sets, and another ghoulish turn by hickory-smoked Vincent Price... It begins long ago in Arkham Massachusetts, with the evil-to-the-bone Joseph Curwan (Price) co-ordinating a maiden's sacrifice to an unseen Monster of the Pit (one with serious gastritis too, from the sound of it). When the townsfolk take torch to him, Vincent curses them all, and a century later (my, how time flies in these quaint New England villages) we meet Curwan's much more friendly great-great-grandson Charles Dexter Ward, once again played by Price. He arrives to collect his inheritance and finds the *same* pack of B-actors playing the town's descendants, all still collecting splinters at the local tavern, The Burning Man. And since the generations-old Curwan curse has led to a series of mutant births in town – eyeless, mouthless monsters kept hidden from the light of day – the villagers are still sorta pissed off. Stubbornly ignoring the warnings about the creepy palace, Price checks it out for himself and instantly discovers his startling resemblance to his crispy kin, not to mention a lardy Lon Chaney Jr. as the caretaker. Before Price can escape with his subtlety intact, Curwan's everlasting spirit tries to usurp his body, giving Vince a chance to masticate the masonry during schizoid battles for control of his own mind. And though you'd think killing off his neighbours and resurrecting his dead mistress would provide Curwan with enough hobbies, he still finds time to scurry down to his dungeon/torture chamber and mate human damsels with those nutty Elder Gods (in particular, the four-armed green one in the pit)... The film does a semi-decent job adapting the Lovecraftian angles. Corman didn't have the resources to capture H.P.'s dark prose in visual terms, but at least he kept to the basic premise, so fans of the Mythos wouldn't get too pissed off. Of course, Rog makes the mistake of showing too much of the monster, instead of letting imagination rule... Not as heavily stylised as the best of the Poe series, but still a moderate success. Saturday matinee fun, co-starring Bruno VeSota as a barkeep and a web-fingered Elisha Cook.

HEAD

BOB RAFELSON 1968. Let us discuss The Monkees. When Peter, Michael, Davey and Micky first plowed their way onto network TV, no one considered them anything but a bunch of money-grubbing Beatle-clone dirtbags, posing as musicians. And nowadays, after their 9000-city Take-the-Money-and-Run Comeback Tour, the Monkees (sans Michael, who didn't need the cash) are again earning their old reputation as no-talent bozos riding the coattails of the '60s resurgence. But if you catch their old series, you realise that these four young hipsters were pretty adequate comedians, and if they weren't the greatest musicians, at least they had a lot of fun dispelling the rumours that they couldn't even play their own instruments. Their TV show was important for another reason – in an era where **Petticoat Junction** and **Here's Lucy** purported to portray the typical American youngster, this show was DIFFERENT, with sensibilities forged by current teenage ideals and which parodied the mindless junk that saturated the airwaves. (In fact, Timothy Leary called their series "A mystic-magic show. A jolly Buddha laugh at hypocrisy")... But enough of history, because we're on the verge of discussing their first (and only) feature film, **Head**, which is not only one of *THE* penultimate films of the late '60s, but it's also one of my top five favourite motion pictures of all time... In real life, The Monkees were getting fed up with their pop-idol status, and they decided to take the Big Step – from their Emmy Award-winning series to the rigors of the feature film – and they came up with a giant fart into the face of their own commercialisation; a free-form, full-circle vision of the Monkeemania phenomenon. Written by Jack Nicholson after spending several heavily 'medicated' days locked in a secluded hotel room in Ojai, California (with the four stars providing idea inspiration), Jack's final script utilises the typical 'wacky-rock-band-and-their-adventures' format

and promptly takes off down a dozen different avenues at one time. Within a sharp satire of American media, **Head** analyses The Monkees' manufactured image and their television-moulded personalities, while racking up high marks on the Surreal Meter. Beginning with Micky's suicide attempt off a bridge, the film follows the Cathode-Ray quartet through a 'typical' day – dealing with rabid fans, dandruff commercials, Coke machines, giant roaches, fake arrows, drippy ice cream cones, and they even find time for a bit of music ('Porpoise Song', 'Circle Sky', etc). A cohesive plot synopsis, you ask? Nonsense, because director Bob Rafelson (**Five Easy Pieces**, **Black Widow**) instead gives us a fragmented, dream-like structure that slices up reality like a loaf of Wonder Bread, juxtaposing one situation upon another until the entire film turns into an acid-soaked hurly-burly of off-centre comedy. There's singing, dancing, homages to old films, clips from old films, celebrity walk-ons (including the likes of Frank Zappa, Annette Funicello, Victor Mature, and Vito Scotti), self-satire, *lots* of druggy in-jokes, and constant unrelenting strangeness... Despite all this, the public stayed away in droves. The Monkee teenyboppers (whom the film tended to ridicule) couldn't understand the flick, the psychedelic crowd (to whom the film was directed) wouldn't *dare* be caught at a (shudder) Monkees movie, and *everyone* was undeniable confused by the ad campaign (designed by a McLuhan-influenced assoc. professor of communications at Fordham) which had no mention of The Monkees, and instead consisted of a long close-up of John Brockman's head (who?). Or maybe it was a sign of the times, considering that Richard Nixon had been elected president of the United States only one day before the film's world premiere. A coincidence, or what? And what the hell does the title mean, you might wonder? Just check out the front leader of any feature film. HEAD. Well, I saw this film for the first time about 15 years ago. Since then I've sat through **Head** half a dozen times on the screen and another dozen times on video, and as far as I'm concerned, it's The Monkees' own **2001** – their **Yellow Submarine** – their **Godzilla vs. the Thing**. Not just a good film, not just a weird film, this is one of the most cleverly-conceived masterworks of the LSD era. And would you believe me if I also said it was one of the few most cerebral *and* hallucinogenic movies ever made? All on a G-rating? Well, you'll just have to check it out for yourself, won't you?... "You say we're manufactured, to that we all agree/So make your choice and we'll rejoice in never being free/Hey hey, we are The Monkees, we've said it all before/The money's in, we've made of tin/We're here to give you more" –The Monkees' 'War Chant'.

HEATHERS

MICHAEL LEHMANN 1989. From the first lilting bars of 'Que Sera Sera' to the blood-soaked finale, I was hooked by this demented teen-suicide comedy which even has the normally-staid mainstream critics drooling over their Raisinets. The Heathers are a trio of teen super-bitches (all conveniently named Heather) who lead the social pack at their high school. Winona Ryder stars as Veronica, a new half-hearted addition to the snobby clique who gets annoyed at the Heathers' malicious pranks and initially relieves her pent up aggressions by scribbling wildly in her sketchbook between classes (oh, by the way, I *loved* the monocle). But when she links up with pistol-packin' psycho-delinquent J.D. (Christian Slater, doing a savage Jack Nicholson impersonation), something in Veronica's pretty little head snaps and under J.D.'s tutelage they start to take revenge on the school shitheels. Of course, one thing leads to another and soon the pair are feeding a cupful of toxic cleanser to Heather #1, which initiates a nose dive through her glass coffee table. Lest you forget, this is a hilarious comedy (and it's not just *my* twisted sense of humour – normal people in the audience were laughing too), and one highlight is the Mineral Water legacy which awaits a pair of dick-brained jocks... This on-target satire takes pot shots at the teen scene with a bazooka, while razoring away at the wrongheaded roots of peer popularity. Unfortunately, the flick goes ultra-soft and mushy for the wrap-up, but most of the time it's a pure joy for viewers who still dream of slipping a pipe bomb under the Homecoming float. Slater gives the funniest, most immoral performance so far this year as the suburban Charlie Starkweather, and Ms. Ryder is so wickedly endearing (not to mention drop dead gorgeous) that you can almost forgive her for appearing in pig slop like **1969**. This is no Molly Ringworm pubescent-teen-angst fest – it's a high school film with TEETH and loads of grim humour. It's also one of the year's best surprises.

HELL'S ANGELS FOREVER

RICHARD CHASE / KEVIN KEATING / LEON GAST 1983. 'We exist. We are the warrior in you, and our message is dangerous to the existing order... They branded us as outlaws. We know, as you, only outlaws can be free.' –The prologue... No, this isn't a fictional cycle-drama like **The Wild Angels**. It's the Hell's Angels' own story, told their own way – A fascinating documentary glimpse into their world. It never digs too deep (probably because the filmmakers didn't want their faces dislocated), but for biker flick completists, it's a must see! Starting with a quick introduction about how the organisation grew from displaced W.W.II vets weaned on excitement, to Hollister California's notorious 4000 cycle invasion in the '50s; the movie then intercuts hand-held footage ranging from 1973 to 1983 (with three different directors taking turns: Richard Chase, Kevin Keating and Leon Gast). The rambling result is alternately engrossing and tedious, and though the myth-making is a little heavy-handed at times, I bought into it... We get to sit in on their parties and meetings, and there's even an Angels wedding and funeral service. And be prepared to watch endless shots of them toolin' down the highway, one hundred strong, on their Harleys.

We also get to learn about their leaders: Sonny Barger, their Oakland chapter chief (who was railroaded on petty drug charges and spent four years in Folsom) and Sandy Alexander, the head of the NYC faction (located on beautiful East 3rd Street. You can't miss it). Sure, they're rowdy and aggressive, but they are proud of what they stand for and envision themselves several notches above the other two-bit cycle clubs. They're a virtual family, with a code of honour, and they go outta their way (on-camera) to portray themselves as patriotic Nice Guys who'll occasionally lose their temper if somebody else eggs 'em on. But there's also enough peripheral beatings, stabbing and on-display armaments to get the *real* point across. Don't fuck with the Angels! It's too bad their women get the short end of the story – they end up looking like little more than pliable slaves. But the film takes a turn to the paranoid when it gets to the 1979 government raid on Hell's Angels headquarters. We get a gander at where our tax dollars go – into half-baked projects like B.E.T. (Biker Enforcement Team), whose mission was to break up the Angels, no matter what laws they had to bend in the process. Utilising covert infiltration (since 1965), the case ended in court with 14 months of racketeering charges. The end result: Acquittal... Also included are quick concert appearances by Angels' pals Willie Nelson, Bo Diddley and an emaciated Jerry Garcia... Are they criminals? Are they fascists? Are the racists? These questions arise from time to time, but don't expect any solid answers, because this film sees them as they perceive themselves – as fun-lovin', beer-guzzlin', adult-sized versions of Dennis the Menace (with a little bit of The Lone Ranger tossed in for good measure). "Shoot us, or get used to us," they challenge the world. That's their attitude. This is their movie.

HELL'S BELLES

MAURY DEXTER 1969. American International churned out a veritable avalanche of low-rent biker flicks throughout the '60s, and though the later productions had almost interchangeable plots and charac-

ters, this one is a slightly better entry. Director Maury Dexter (**The Mini-Skirt Mob, Maryjane**) gives the film all the innovation of a TV movie, but a capable cast and good cycle stuntwork add some flash to the generic tale... Lantern-jawed cowboy, Dan Holt (Jeremy Slate, also of **Hells Angels '69**) sure loves his new chopper, which he won in a desert endurance race, but unfortunately so does bikerama-veteran Adam Roarke (**Hells Angels on Wheels, The Savage Seven**) as tough-talking gang leader, Tampa. Roarke and his small band of dusty cycle-jerks promptly take off with Slate's prized possession, and when Jeremy tries to steal his bike back, all he ends up with is a two-by-four to the gut. But Tampa isn't a complete bastard, because in trade for the cycle he gives Slate one of his highway hussies – Jocelyn Lane, a steamy (though constantly whining) brunette in a tight, black leather mini-skirt. After some lame squabbling, Jeremy and Jocelyn unwillingly team up and head out – Jeremy is obsessed with getting his dumb ol' chopper back, and Jocelyn comes along so she doesn't get stranded in the middle of nowhere. And though the pair bicker constantly, you just *know* that the Machoshit Good Ol' Boy and the Feisty Cynical Sexpot are eventually gonna fall for each other. Ain't that sweet? Whenever the duo opens their mouths for a moment of soap opera introspection (Jeremy wants to own a ranch someday, and Jocelyn admits she joined the bikers so she could have a 'family'), you want to stuff a crusty sweat sock down their throats, but the script keeps 'em on the move as much as possible... Meanwhile, the gang is ahead of them on the road, creating chaos and becoming a public relations nightmare – they torch a gas station, bust up a grocery store and generally become local pains in the bum. Finally, Jeremy gets the gang into the middle of the Arizona desert, and he slowly picks them off with the aid of conveniently loose boulders, annoyed rattlesnakes and his survivalist savvy... Usually, I don't enjoy the cycle pix where the bikers are the flat-out stock villains (I prefer the brooding anti-heroes, such as in **The Wild Angels**), but this is a rare exception. There's a smattering of bloodless demises, chain-whippings and chopper-faceoffs, but instead of solid scumminess, the filmmakers opted for the standardised good guy/bad guy posturing. As for the cast, Slate comes off as a no-charisma Charles Napier-clone, but leggy Ms. Lane keeps the hormone-level high in her tight-knit wardrobe and Roarke is fine as always as the fuckstick leader. Plus Angelique Pettyjohn (the green-haired **Star Trek** space bimbo from 'The Gamesters of Triskilion') bounces about as Roarke's current cycle slut... Lightweight and unnecessarily moralistic at times, but it's still surprisingly entertaining, with enough dumb action to keep you brainlessly amused.

HELL COMES TO FROGTOWN

R.J. KIZER / DONALD G. JACKSON 1988. Despite its great title and ad campaign, this direct-to-video science fictioner had three initial strikes against it. (1) It's yet another **Mad Max**-esque, post-apocalyptic adventure. (2) It was directed by R.J. Kizer (who fucked around with the Japanese version of **Godzilla 1985** by re-editing it and adding the Raymond 'All You Can Eat' Burr footage) and Donald G. Jackson (**Rollerblade**). (3) It stars wrestling shit-wit Rowdy Roddy Piper... On this info alone, I expected the absolute worst. Cringe-city. But surprise, as dime-store actioners go, this one isn't half bad. Only about 40% bad. The beginning sets up some nice satirical swipes at the entire genre, but it doesn't keep it up for long. Set 10 years after the bombs fell, Roddy Piper stars as Sam Hellman (aka Sam Hell), a lone wolf scavenger who happens to be one of the few sexually potent males on the planet. Perennial warrior-queen Sandahl Bergman slaps on a pair of prop eyeglasses and co-stars as a scientist at Medtech – an all-female corporation set up to continue population growth – and she hires Hell to go out into the Barren Wasteland and impregnate as many

women as possible. Together, Roddy and Sandahl zoom into the desert on their spermatozoan mission: To head into the aptly-named Frogtown, rescue a pack of fertile woman who've been kidnapped by Commander Toady, and eventually have Mr. Stud knock 'em up. The two stars butt heads for a while, but eventually they infiltrate the off-limits, mutant city, where the frog-headed citizens barter and trade for women and weapons. ('OK! Hold it! Do you mean that the scriptwriter actually wants us to believe that in 10 years, atomic radiation turned all the frogs into upright, intelligent, humanoid-types who speak English?' Why? Don't you buy it!) And sure enough, it ends with a limp desert chase between a whopping *two cars* (I guess they ran outta budget before they ran outta screenplay), with all the plot 'surprises' well-telegraphed... The very beginning has a fair share of tongue-in-cheek humour (such as a chastity belt labelled 'Property of Provisional Gov't' and equipped with explosive bolts. Ouch), but after a while the excessive hamminess wears thin (though I was sorta hoping for at least *one* frog legs joke). As the film's Semen Saviour, Piper is the US equivalent of Paul Naschy – a big, dumb lug who's supposed to be a woman-magnet (believable as heck, eh?). Ms. Bergman's career continues to fade, while staying stripped to her undies for much of the running time. Familiar faces (at least to Slimetimers) William Smith and Rory Calhoun also turn up as, respectively, an arrogant border cop and a desert-rat pal of Roddy's. The effects are relatively unimpressive – mostly burnt-out industrial sets and one particularly effective frog mask – and it's all bloodless and surprisingly tame. Predictable rubbish, all in all, but it could've been a *lot* worse (for example, Hulk Hogan could have stared).

THE HELLCATS

ROBERT F. SHATZER 1968. Once again, it's motorcycle-mania, but this time with a feminine edge! Though a fun drive-in flick is lurking somewhere, director Robert F. Shatzer (**Bigfoot**) couldn't find it if it leapt up and bit him on the dick. Instead he opts to keep the proceedings tame and moralistic, though it distinguishes itself by being one of the few films to refer to grass as 'Mary Jane' without meaning it as a joke... A co-ed cycle club named The Hellcats makes extra cash by running drugs across the border for a mob kingpin named Mr. Adrian, but the heroes of the movie aren't nearly as much fun. Dee Duffy stars as Linda, a Sandra Dee-clone whose fiancé is offed by Adrian's hitman, so she teams up with her beau's Army Sarge brother, Monte (Ross Hagen), to track down his killer. Going undercover as fellow bikers, the two locate the Hellcats' favourite gin joint, The Moonfire Inn, where they talk tough, kick butt and join the pack of potheads (with sexy Sharyn Kinzie as sicle-queen Sheila). From then on, the film is loaded with long, seemingly-unscripted sequences: The chopper crew abuses a peaceful artist and his model, baby-sits the pack's perpetual acid-head, chain brawls with a rival gang (which ends when Monte lectures them on the need for 'peace'), and motors down to Mexico to pick up drugs from a pair of Latino losers and their junkie moll. Soon Sheila is falling for Monte's 'Then Came Bonehead' mannerisms, but this flick is so wimpy that the moment the two start making out, they cover up with a convenient blanket. By the

end, the Hellcats realise what a shitheel Adrian is, turn goody-goody and rumble en masse against him. Ho hum. At least the phlegmmakers let the bikers ride away scot free... Hagen is a 180 pound meatloaf in black leather, and though Ms. Duffy is blond and built, she's also a continual whiner, so who cares? The rest of the acting would make a great public service message for illiteracy, considering how badly the gangsters stumble over their lines. The whole thing is barren of thrills and utterly mediocre, with grating music sung by Davy Jones & the Dolphins and Somebody's Chyldren. Yuck! What a sack of rubbish!

HELLRAISER

CLIVE BARKER 1987. Successful King University grad Clive (**Books of Blood**) Barker enters the ring as a horror/gore director with this unspectacular but diverting opus, adapted from his own story 'The Hellbound Heart'. Shades of **Blue Velvet** and **Nightmare on Elm Street III** abound as a newly married couple move into a creepy new home. Hubby Andy Robinson (the psycho from **Dirty Harry**) is all smiles, but his new wife can't forget her illicit fling with a malevolent drifter, complete with Roeg-influenced sex-montage sequence. Hubby rips his hand moving a bed (!) upstairs, and brings his spurting hand up to the attic, where his wife is lost in thought. The blood drips on the floor (real *loud*), bringing out a half-formed slimer from... *beyond*! This weird creature turns out to be none other than wifey's old flame. But at this point the guy is having a hard time keeping his *face* on, so he hits up the lady for help. This becomes kind of Dorian Gray in reverse, with the sultry wife bringing unsuspecting pickups home, only to be bludgeoned and sucked dry so that Mr. Face can pick up the pieces. Meanwhile, there is this puzzle box. Mr. Face holds onto it for dear life, and no wonder. If tampered with, it brings these S/M **Space 1999** rejects out of the walls. These 'Cenobites' from Dimension 5 (just kidding) like to torture and maim earth folk in search of cheap thrills. Soon hubby's teenage daughter enters the action, opens the puzzle box (by accident, of course) and enters a bloody hallucination from... *beyond*! This is all silly stuff, but Barker is a surprisingly good director his first time out, helped by a good FX team and competent actors. The gore/slime quotient is high, with an up-to-date 'kinkiness' no doubt inspired by Lynch, et al. Kudos to New World for *not* cutting out all the grimness (well, we'll wait until it opens national...). [TR]

HERCULES IN THE HAUNTED WORLD

MARIO BAVA 1964. It's flex those pecs time, folks! These Italian Hercules flicks were churned out on a virtual assembly line back in the '60s. Steve Reeves was the first to mop up as the badly-dubbed son of Zeus, and the formula was soon chiselled into stone: Find an interchangeable steroid star, some colourful locations and babes in togas. But this particular edition to the series is one of the most enjoyable, since it also adds to the brew the ever stylish Mario Bava (**Black Sunday**) as director/cinematographer and Christopher Lee as the villainous Lycos, who has taken over the kingdom while Hercules was on vacation. Reg Park (who's muscles may be maximus, but who's acting talent is minimus) takes the lead, wearing a K-Mart page boy wig and swaggering through the plaster sets. For this el cheapo episode, beautiful Queen Dianara is placed under a spell and The Oracle (a mystical broad in a party mask) convinces our beefcake bozo that the only way to save her is to journey to the Kingdom of the Damned. That's right, it's 'Hercules Goes to Hell' or 'A Funny Thing Happened on the Way to Hades'! So instead of the usual 'toss a few expendable extras around for 90 minutes', Herc tackles a fantasy realm full of atmospheric sets and moody lighting. With gigolo pal Thesius at his side, and unfunny comic relief from a tagalong dweeb, Hercules enters the Netherworld and encounters non-stop campiness! He juggles

some foam rubber boulders, evades the evil (but endearingly dumb) Rock Men, side-steps the naked damsels (with their tresses conveniently covering any naughty bits – remember, this is 1964), discovers plants that bleed, and continually avoids a hot foot (next time he should wear something heavier than sandals). Sure, the solemn romantic dialogue will have you giving raspberries at the screen, but the conclusion has top-notch, tongue-in-cheek thrills, with Lee trying to drink Dianara's blood (deja vu from his Hammer flicks) while an army of flying, cobwebbed zombies crawl out of their caskets to thwart Hercules. Wow! I only wish they hadn't dubbed Lee's velvet voice with some coarse US actor's... Originally double billed with **Castle of Blood**, this is a wonderfully silly costumer. Admittedly there are some slow moments (such as whenever anyone's talking), but Bava js a master of his craft and knows how to wring thrills and style from the most generic production values. Snooty moviegoers that've been weaned on I.L.M. megaeffects might toss this li'l flick aside, but I consider it nostalgic Greek goofiness and satisfying Saturday afternoon entertainment.

HI, MOM!

BRIAN DE PALMA 1970. Does anybody remember all those socially-and-politically conscious underground comedies from two decades ago (like **Putney Swope**)? No? Well, a young director named Brian DePalma churned out his fair share of 'em. After limited success with obscurities such as **Murder a la Mod**, **Woton's Wake**, **Dionysus in '69** and **The Wedding Party**, DePalma struck paydirt with his comedy **Greetings**, which co-starred an unknown actor named Robert DeNiro. And in this follow-up (originally called **Son of Greetings**), DeNiro continues his character of John Rubin, disturbed Vietnam veteran and future insurrectionist... This isn't an easy-going counterculture flick, like **Beyond the Valley of the Dolls** or **The Trip**. Instead of the obvious topics (sex, drugs and rock 'n' roll), **Hi, Mom!** takes on voyeurism, pornography, guerrilla theatre and urban guerrillas. It's NYC shoe-string filmmaking at its most uncompromising, and though it's essentially a comedy, the portions that stick in your mind the longest are the darkest bits... DeNiro begins his urban excursion by renting a 'typical' Manhattan apartment from slumlord Charles Durning, complete with dilapidated furniture and a combination kitchen table/bathtub. He decides to take his penchant for peeping-tomism into the profit area by secretly filming his high-rise neighbours and selling their amorous adventures to porno-king Allen Garfield. And along the way he decides to seduce one lonely young lass from across the street and make it the backbone of his movie. Though it all sounds relatively sordid, DePalma plays it for light-hearted laughs, while mixing his cheapshot jokes with some disturbingly on-target social comedy, the caustic centrepiece of which is the 'Be Black, Baby' sequences – 16mm, black and white segments posing as a documentary for N.I.T. (National Intellectual Television), about what it is to be Black. The high point is an avant-garde theatrical experience in which a highbrow white audience is forced to wear black face while the performers (in white face) proceed to feed them grits, steal their purses, beat them senseless, and sexually abuse them. Believe it or not, it's the cruellest, yet most scathingly brilliant skit I'm seen in a long time. Gloves-off humour with plenty of point-blank pot-shots at sedate, middle-class liberals. It culminates with DeNiro becoming Mr. Urban Revolutionary, and learning that he must infiltrate the system from within in order to destroy it... This entire film is probably too inaccessible for typical, present-day audiences (you know – morons), but many of the film's commentaries still hold true. DePalma experiments with gimmicky techniques (fast-motion, split-screen) which would pop up in his later works, but this is essentially low-budget Angry Young Filmmaking. And though the flat-out comedy is pretty obvious, DeNiro plays it to the hilt and always keeps a hint of psychosis to the role. Too bad the music is so lame (friends of yours, Bri?). Overall, **Hi, Mom!** is an interesting curio that takes on near-legendary status due to its 'Be Black' brainpan-melter. Unforgettable.

HIDE AND SHRIEK

JOHN HOUGH 1988 (US: AMERICAN GOTHIC). This Canadian-lensed psycho-parade starts out relatively tame. A bunch of kids fly out for a weekend of beerin' and ballin', but they're forced to land their plane for repairs on a secluded stretch of country real estate. It's a typical beginning for a slasher pic – a forest, some randy campers, no way to radio for help, a quickly approaching sunset, and loads of ominous noises from the bushes. I was almost ready to throw in the towel and go to bed early instead of sitting through another by-the-number dead-teen clone. But director John Hough (**The Legend of Hell House**, plus a lot of shitty films like **The Incubus**) has more on his mind than a body count. There's a genuinely creepy imagination at work here too, particularly when the teens run across a quaint old farmhouse owned by the plumped-out pair, Yvonne DeCarlo and Rod Steiger, playing your not-so-average, religiously-entrenched country folk. Best of all, their backwoods trio of offspring, Fanny, Woody and Teddy (Janet Wright, Michael J. Pollard and William Hootkins) are full-grown adults who act as if they're 12-years-old and enjoy playing murderous 'games' with their new friends. Once the killings begin, it's like The Waltons in **Texas Chain Saw Massacre**! I especially enjoyed the death of the Bitch Princess, who's strangled with a jump rope – and there's a mummified baby that'll have expectant mothers fleeing for the exits. Low on bloodshed, but high on the Sickometer, plus there's a smidgen more character development than we've come to expect – Hough goes for a decidedly non-hack approach in the first half before slicing straight into the jugular for the wrap-up, with the last 15 minutes taking unexpected turns into solid dementia... Pollard and his siblings are great, running about in cowboy and injun outfits with cap guns blazing – and Steiger only occasionally spits up the scenery, which is a record for this hard-to-believe Oscar winner. This film also proves that you don't need bad puns and in-jokes to create an effective humour-laced shocker. As a whole, **Hide and Shriek** isn't as epic in scope or emotional depth as classics like **Spider Baby**, but it's still a nice treat for audiences bored with run-of-the-mill dreck.

HIGH SCHOOL CONFIDENTIAL

JACK ARNOLD 1958. Personally, this is one of my favourite '50s juvenile delinquent films. Thanks goes to producer Albert Zugsmith for concocting the hokiest, campiest treat of the teen rebel era, with some of the oldest (and stupidest) high school kids in history. When it first opened it was called a controversial exposé on the conditions of 'today's high schools', but nowadays, we all realise that this movie's pure crapola... It's the usual story, with all the swinging chicks, dads, dolls, and cats of Anytown High School dealing with the Evils that infect Our Youngsters. There's a bunch of misunderstood kids and irresponsible parents, plus some short 'educational' lectures on 'maryjane' and 'reefers', cuz every local 'wheathead' is 'blasting a joint' or 'torching some weed'... Sure, it's laughable anti-drug propaganda, but the film's real fun comes from its 'all-star' cast – Russ Tamblyn stars as the new kid in town, who has an eye on the presidency of the local gang, The Wheelers-and-Dealers ("That's the way the bongo bingles," he explains); Mamie Van Doren is his platinum blond, liquored up, sexpot aunt (?); Jackie Coogan has a pre-Uncle Fester role as a jazz musician; Michael Landon is a square-jawed, soft-headed football jock; and Jerry Lee Lewis pops up for a quick theme song from the back of a moving pick-up truck. Tamblyn blows on the scene and promptly tries to seduce a prim teacher, has a hot rod chase with the fuzz, and listens to bad beatnik poetry at the nearby coffee-house ("Tomorrow we can cough blood on the moon, soon/Tomorrow is dragsville, cats."). Of course, you can rest assured that justice prevails in the end, with a hilariously preachy finale which tries to

convince you that marijuana immediately leads to heroin addiction and social leprosy... A true schlock classic, and along with **Rock 'n' Roll High School** and **The Nutty Professor**, it's the most fun you'll ever have in school.

HILLBILLYS IN A HAUNTED HOUSE

JEAN YARBROUGH 1967. From the director of **The Devil Bat**, **She Wolf of London** and **Here Come the Co-Eds** (pretty staggering credentials, eh?) comes a flick that's so amazingly dumb it'll have you in Crappy Film Heaven. This (sorta) sequel to **Las Vegas Hillbillys** once again focuses on three dinkheaded country-western musicians on the road to low-budget laffs. Ferlin Husky, Joi Lansing and Don Bowman star, respectively, as Woody Wetherby, Boots Malone and Jeepers – singing at the drop of a hat as they head to Nashville in a steer-horned white Cadillac. Well, before you know it they've decided to spend the night at a haunted house, complete with cobwebs and skeletons left over over from a Munsters garage sale. So far it's like a zillion other ghostly B-movies (except that guest stars just *happen* to pass by, equipped with musical instruments, so they can add to the cacophony), but the flick takes off when we learn that the old mansion is just a front for a basementful of foreign spies led by Madame Wong. And she's aided by the entire Horror Contingent of Ageing Actor Inc. – John Carradine, Lon Chaney Jr., Basil Rathbone, and Anatole the fleabag gorilla. Their plan is to steal formulas from the nearby atomic missile plant, and it's no wonder if security is so lax that all you need is a white lab coat in order to convince the janitor to let you into the room labelled 'TOP SECRET'. Enter some US agents from M.O.T.H.E.R., who only add to the confusion by suspecting that our trio of hick heroes are the *real* spies. "What proof do you have that you're entertainers?", the gov't agent asks Ferlin. Not much, if this movie's any

indication – but it's all so overplayed and mindless that I rather enjoyed their South-of-the-Mason-Dixon silliness... Carradine, Chaney and Rathbone are all fun to watch, even if they aren't given much to do besides bicker amongst themselves. At least they look like they had a good time slumming together. And Joi Lansing wins the Heaving Breasts Award of 1967, though after a while I wanted to heave the rest of this talentless bleach blond down an elevator shaft. Her fantasy/musical sequence, during which she sings (and I use the term loosely) about Gowns, will make you want to puke on her shoes... I should also warn you that this movie has more shitty music than you can possibly tolerate in one sitting, and the last 15 minutes is nothing but a Nashville jamboree hootenanny retch-fest. Trust me – unless you're a music masochist, just shut off the movie the moment the stars drive away from the mansion... Despite the ear-drum pain, **Hillbillys** is a dopey li'l time killer, and fine Saturday afternoon fun for fans of Cinemapathetique.

HOLLYWOOD BOULEVARD

JOE DANTE / ALLAN ARKUSH 1976. First, a little background on this All-Time Classic: Roger Corman laid out $60,000 to a pair of recent film school graduates, giving them free reign of the New World film clip inventory and a 10-day shooting schedule with a cast of Corman-regulars... The young directors were Joe Dante (**Gremlins**) and Allan Arkush (who went on to make two of my favourites, **Rock 'n' Roll High School** and **Get Crazy**, before he got stuck doing shit like **St. Elsewhere**), and although their first effort didn't make a cent, I consider it one of Corman's best investments, because it's *the* injoke movie of all time... Candice Rialson (hot off of **Candy Stripe Nurses** and **Summer School Teachers**) stars as Candy Wednesday, a hick chick looking for a job as an actress in Hollywood. Unfortunately, every agent in town is after some casting-couch-favours first, until she runs across Walter Paisley (everyone's fave B-actor, Dick Miller), who gets her a flow of grimy roles with Miracle Pictures (their slogan: 'If it's a good picture, it's a Miracle!'). What Candy doesn't know, until it's *too late*, is that the actresses at Miracle are being killed off, one-by-one... But let's ignore the entire storyline – because the *real* point of the film is to lampoon the life of Hollywood's 3rd rate moviemakers, while paying an oddball tribute to them. It's a movie that satirises drive-in movies, while becoming the ultimate example of one. The humour is hit-and-miss for a while – some of the sections are just plain dumb, but a lot of it is truly inspired. Classic episodes include: the impromptu massacre of 200 Asian soldiers on the set of 'Machete Maidens of Mara-Tau'; the drive-in premiere of Candy's first film (it's third on a triple bill), where she's nearly raped by the projectionist; the making of 'Atomic War Brides', which combines a plea for world peace with alien-mutant car chases; plus, they sew together stock footage from a half-dozen Corman sleazeshows, such as **Death Race 2000**, **The Big Doll House** and **The Terror**, for maximum cost-cutting... There are cheap jokes galore, lots of low-rent in-humour, and a cast that seems to be having as much fun (if not more) than the audience. Included are a trio of cult favourites: Mary Woronov as the egotistical bitch-starlet, Mary McQueen; Paul Bartel as the perfectionist director, Erich Von Leppe; and Dick Miller, who reprises his starring role from the 1959 masterwork, **A Bucket of Blood**. Plus, Forry Ackerman and Robby the Robot make cameo appearances, and a very sickly Godzilla has a couple quick waddle-ons... I can't imagine how *any* self-respecting drive-in fanatic wouldn't enjoy this hilarious mess. It's one of the best intentionally-funny Bad Films of all time.

HOLLYWOOD CHAINSAW HOOKERS

FRED OLEN RAY 1988. Fred Olen Ray must be main-lining No-Doz in order to keep up his recent directorial pace. He just keeps churning out the no-budgeters, and his new releases include **Deep Space** (an alien-rampager), **Star Slammer** (interplanetary women-in-prison) and this empty-headed little tale, starring Gunnar 'Leatherface' Hansen and Linnea 'Vacuumhead' Quigley. Personally, I'd recommend picking up the video just to laugh at the trailer for **Evil Spawn** that's tacked on the beginning; but that notwithstanding, **HCH** is fair fun for the undiscriminating sleaze-fiend. It isn't even close to being a good film – there's too much lame humour, the story is wafer-thin and the bloodshed is disappointing – but how can any self-respecting slimeball resist a film about prostitutes brandishing Black and Deckers?... The LAPD has arrested a whore who dismembered one of her johns with a chain saw. She's a bleach-blond spacecase, but while the cops are trying to squeeze some info out of their culprit, there's a whole pack of 'slice-happy sluts' killing off their clients. Meanwhile, a private eye shitpot named Chandler (who hands us dopey narration like, "being a dick is a 24-hour-a-day job") is searching for a young runaway (Linnea Q.), and finds her stripping at a lowlife ho' bar. What Chandler discovers all too late, is that she's a disciple of a secret religion, and the film (finally) gets amusing once we learn all the whores are followers of a theology where the chain saw is worshipped as "the cosmic link by which all things are united". Big, bearded Gunnar is the cult's Egyptian priest/leader, and they have a temple downtown in an abandoned warehouse... Fred doesn't skimp on the nudity, but there's no real gore or on-screen dissections. Instead you just see the naked prostitutes brandishing their saws while getting spattered with blood and chunky bits. Linnea shimmies topless at the club, runs about in mini-skirts and leads the Virgin Dance of the Double Chain Saws – continuing her career as the Cocktease Queen of Trashola, with the camera lingering on her like a fly on horse shit so no one notices she can't act worth beans. Gunnar is pretty funny (even if he isn't given much to do), and unlike the smirkers in the cast, at least he has the good sense to play the comic elements with a straight face... There's a glimmer of a great gory comedy buried somewhere amongst the cheapjack muck, but it's quickly lost amidst all the pandering mindlessness. Despite an amusing little chain saw duel at the end, between the two lead femmes, it's all fairly inept and nonsensical. But then again, what did you expect?... And the sequel – **Student Chainsaw Nurses**? Hey, Fred. You're kidding, right?... Fred?

THE HOLLYWOOD STRANGLER MEETS THE SKIDROW SLASHER

WOLFGANG SCHMIDT 1979. The director of this relatively standard meat-market killfest is listed as Wolfgang Schmidt, but all my sources tell me that the man actually responsible for this grainy mess is none other than Ray Dennis Steckler. Unfortunately, this recent effort exhibits very little of the gutter genius he perpetuated in **Incredibly Strange Creatures...** and **Rat Pfink a Boo Boo**. Unlike most of his productions, Steckler opts to stay strictly behind the camera on this one, and with damn good reason – the only major male role is such an utter scumbucket that only a piss-poor no-talent mock-thespian would have the nerve to take the part. Luckily, Pierre Agostino happened along, and he soaks up the whopping 75 minute running time as a horny photographer who roams Hollywood Boulevard in search of teasing tarts who are willing to strip for a private photo session. Of course, once he has them alone and they shed their clothes, he crushes their windpipe while his continual, monotonous voice-over bores a ragged hole into the viewer's brains: "Just another piece of garbage... Die, garbage, die... I snapped her neck pretty good... heh heh..." Pierre, as you can see, plays the first half of the title, and just to prove that the scriptwriter wasn't a misogynist, we get Carolyn Brandt (Ms. Steckler; who's no longer the leggy starlet she was in her hubby's mid-'60s movies) playing the second half of the title – as a Plain Jane cashier who spends her lonely evenings slicing up the local wino population

with her trusty switch-blade... There's plenty of bared flesh and no one skimps on the fake blood, as we've treated to one murder after another. Good grief, there are *seven* in the first half-hour alone! And of course, these two social misfits have to eventually meet, and The Strangler falls head over heels for The Slasher (auhhh, ain't that sweet?). And what gal wouldn't go for a seedy-looking twerp who roams the red light district and bugs out his eyes at the very thought of a female? Well, to make a tedious story short, the final death count is Pierre-9, Ms. Brandt-5, and there's a finale to rival **Romeo and Juliet** in unintentional laffs... Steckler/Schmidt makes good use of the grimy alleyways of skidrow Hollywood, and since virtually the entire film is narrated by The Strangler, I'll assume they didn't even have the cash for sync-sound. Voyeuristic and repetitive, I have to admit it didn't keep me from laughing out loud when Pierre smothers a blond bimbo who's wearing nothing but a KISS beach towel... NOT one of the great lost classics of all time. Even the gore is sub-standard.

THE HOLY MOUNTAIN

ALEJANDRO JODOROWSKY 1973. Alejandro Jodorowsky is without a doubt one of the great mystical freaks of modern cinema. And if you thought his first midnight movie mind-blower, **El Topo**, was the ultimate in drug-drenched filmmaking, you are sorely mistaken. He saved all his *really* off-the-wall ideas for this follow-up, which unfortunately never reached the same strata of cult success – probably because Jodorowsky doesn't attempt to appease the viewer one iota. Sure, there's a wisp of a story for us to cling to (if you need that type of assurance), but meanwhile every vague, ultra-pretentious Symbol on the face of the earth is hammered home for the two hours, and by the end you feel as if every brain cell has been wrung dry and refilled with Mescal. Even if you can't score any acid, the introduction will make you feel as if you've been dosed, as it barrages the audience with disturbing (often twistedly humorous) images and shatters any preconception of things to come. We're witness to flowers blooming from stigmata; crucified, skinned rabbits carried by gas-masked storm troopers; birds flying from gaping bullet wounds; an old man taking out his eyeball and giving it to a passing child; 10 prostitutes and a chimp going to church in see-thru blouses (just the whores, not the monkey); plus my favourite, The Great Toad and Chameleon Circus, featuring a flotilla of frogs wearing tiny conquistador outfits. Had enough yet? Not me! This shit goes on for over half an hour! And by then you'll either be hypnotised by its genius, or want to hide under your blankets 'til it goes away. And if you can keep track of all the Christ references, you win a lifetime supply of Communion wafers. It's a solid nightmare of hallucinogenic proportions, and would you believe Jodorowsky was totally straight when he filmed it? (At least that's what he told the press.) Even after the semilinear story kicks in, it remains as wonderfully outrageous and incoherent... Christ steals a ride on a large hook dangled from the top of an immense tower, and inside meets the White Master (named for the colour of his hair, clothes, fingernails, platform boots, et cetera). But when Christ attempts to battle The Master, his naked black slavewomen pull a small octopus from an incision in Christ's neck, and then give Jesus a bath (complete with close-ups of the Messiah's ass), while a hippo sits in the tub beside him. "You are excrement," The Master informs Jesus as the Indian music wails incessantly in the background; and working together the pair gathers a pack of thieves, each representing a different ill of society. There's Venus, a cosmetic industry Romeo who animates corpses with electrical devices (so a dead bishop can give himself his own last rites); Mars, a woman who produces hydrogen bombs and anti-matter rays; Jupiter, a wealthy 'artist' who produces his work on an assembly line; Saturn, who works in tandem with the government to brainwash children into hating other races; Uranus, a financial advisor to the President, who orders the mass execution of four million people in order to save the economy; Neptune, the chief of police, who castrates prisoners with a pair of scissors and saves their testicles in jars; and lastly, Pluto, an architect who devises low-cost housing which just happens to look like coffins. The Master's grand scheme: To raid the Holy Mountain and rob its wise men of their secrets. But first, they must gain wisdom, which entails sitting around a pop art fireplace, burning their money and shaving their heads... As you can see for yourself, Deep Significant Meaning oozes from every single frame, and even though you can see The Messages coming from a mile away, it's all so strikingly visualised that I was suckered in by it – in particular the ending, which is so ballsy you can't help but laugh. And I'm sure much of it was spontaneous since Jodorowsky filmed it all in sequence. There's some pretty perverse shit taking place on-screen, plus scads of nudity, violence, general repulsion, and brilliantly deranged dialogue ("His feet stink like a rotten dog," one thief gripes, while washing Christ's legs. "He has beautiful hair," replies The Master). Even though sections often fall flat or tumble into utter unintelligibility, I can't fault a film so steeped in bold, unapologetic originality, especially compared to the pabulum that's been gracing theatres lately. It's on par with **Eraserhead**, and that's high praise from me indeed.

HORRIBLE HORROR

1986. Don't look for this critter at your local video vault, because the only way to latch onto it is to purchase the tape at your local K-Mart (yep, you heard me right). But at $9.87 it's the bargain of the month, because this programme is crammed with almost two hours of the dumbest coming attractions and film clips from the '50s, all hosted by our favourite puffed-up booze-hound, Zacherley!... The framework for this excursion into drive-in heaven is that Zacherley's being evicted from his castle (the usual papier-mâché

brickwork backdrop) and has to rummage through his library of dusty films. But forget *this* nonsense – just bask in the black-and-white glow from dozens of over-overbearingly hilarious trailers, such as **The Killer Shrews**, **The Alligator People**, **Robot Monster**, **Killers from Space**, **The Brainiac**, **Glen or Glenda**, and **Santa Claus Conquers the Martians**. Plus, you get out-takes from **Abbott and Costello Meet Frankenstein**, scenes from Mexican monsteramas, old TV clips, and *lots* of pathetic Bela Lugosi interviews (most of them obviously filmed during his last days nipping at the needle). There's even a couple minutes from the underground horror/comedy epic **Spider Baby**, starring Lon Chaney, Jr... As you can see, it's non-stop pleasure for any sleaze-connoisseur – the only drawback being our illustrious host, Zack the hack, who occasionally interrupts the trailers in mid-sentence for a 'witty' wink or grimace, in between shots of **Night Train**... But let's not quibble, cuz this is one of the best indie productions in quite a while. Thanks goes to Goodtimes Productions for releasing this vidiot's delight.

THE HORROR OF PARTY BEACH

DEL TENNEY 1964. A must for everybody's 'Badfilm' collection. A bunch of radioactivated human skeletons lying at the bottom of the ocean are transformed into vicious, croaking sea monsters. And boy, are they hungry! They make their way to the surface and their killing spree begins when they discover a bunch of 'teeny boppers' (remember that word?) having a 'wild' beach party, backed by the swingin' sounds of the Del-Aires. (One can only wish that Annette Funicello and Frankie Avalon were there. Wouldn't they look great with their faces ripped off?) The monsters' favourite food seems to be teenagers, whom they joyously tear to pieces with their nasty sharp claws and over-sized teeth. If it's gore you're after (in this case, the black-and-white kind), rent the v-tape and ignore the teevee version. I also suggest having a generous supply of beer and illegal smokables. Have fun! [BJE]

HORROR OF THE BLOOD MONSTERS

AL ADAMSON 1970 (AKA: VAMPIRE MEN OF THE LOST PLANET). Dime-store director Al Adamson (the man who gave us **Satan's Sadists** and **Cinderella 2000**) strikes back with a classic in Kitchen Sink Cinema! This flick has gone through a ton of title changes over the years, but it's easiest to locate on the USA Cable Channel under the **Vampire Men** title. Though it's shorn of any GP-aspects, it's still a riot of no-budget nonsense... Where to begin? Well, the earth is being overrun by vampires, and immediately two questions come to mind: How did it happen? And how can Adamson use up some footage from a Filipino caveman movie that he had laying around the editing room? And before you can say 'we rented this spaceship set *real* cheap', we're on the XB-13, a manned rocket with a crew consisting of a craggy scientist (John Carradine), three dinkheaded space cadets, and one busty babe doing a piss-poor Nancy Sinatra imitation. It's talk, talk, talk, to pad out the running time, but when these soft-brained flyboys land on a mysterious, uncharted planet, the movie shoots into the stratosphere of the Truly Asinine! You see, the planet is contaminated with 'Chromatic Radiation', a condition which tints the surroundings with assorted colours (red, blue, yellow, etc.), and which explains how the filmmakers interspersed the old black-and-white footage with the new colour scenes. The ads call this 'startling' effect Spectrum X. I just call it annoying, but nowhere near as eye-watering as **Angry Red Planet**'s notorious Cinemagic rip-off... There's dinosaurs tossing each other around on the planet, and it's Buzz Corey Meets Fred Flintstone when the crew stumbles across two warring tribes of cavemen, the Tubatans and the Taganies. The Tubatans are long-fanged mutant-meanies who chew on fresh flesh, and the Taganies welcome wagon consists of a pretty cave girl in a low-cut

bearskin – so guess which group the astronauts side with? (They also perform some carefree skull surgery on the gal and 'rearrange her brain waves' so she can understand English. Nice guys.) As for the monsters, there are Bat Demons who look like they were tarred and rolled in black lint; if you blink you'll miss the Snake Men; and my fave is the ludicrous Crab-Heads with their bugged-out plastic eyes. The scariest creature in the whole film though, is John Carradine, who's literally grey-skinned, and spends the entire movie sitting in the spaceship and mumbling to himself. There's also photography by William (Vilmos) Zsigmond, a bit of campy narration by Brother Theodore, and enough fake arrows to keep any **Head** fan overjoyed... Pathetically cheap. Severely idiotic. *Highly* recommended to any lover of Cheapjack Cinema.

HOT POTATO

OSCAR WILLIAMS 1976. Jim Kelly appeared in three of the all-time best kung fu/blaxploit-actioners of the '70s – **Enter the Dragon**, **Black Belt Jones** and **Three the Hard Way** – and I *still* like the guy, even after sitting through this miserable lump of dreck. What a career nose-dive! After **Hot Potato** he teamed up with director Al Adamson for swill like **Black Samurai** and **Death Dimension** with George Lazenby, and sure, his later films were blockbusters in the Philippines, but that's the same place where you can skullfuck a baby for the price of a Hershey Bar... But back to this abysmal excuse for a film. The first problem is that Kelly is the only Brother in the whole movie, and his character's about as pale-faced as they come. It's no compliment to speculate that Chuck 'The Fuck' Norris could have played the same role with just as much one-note lethargy. I had hoped for the best, since Jim K. was returning to the role of Black Belt Jones, but instead of tackling inner city thugs, this time the script has him as a secret agent, working for the American government (can you say sell-out?). A Senator's daughter is kidnapped by an evil Slant Emperor, so Kelly and his team of useless assistants are put on the case. They ride elephants to the rescue, are attacked by Thai natives in black pantyhose, take on a garrison of angry gooks, and fill up 87 *long* minutes with **Enter the Dragon**-style (but not quality) oriental nonsense. All this, and never once does Jim's afro get mussed up. What'd they pay the guy in, Afro Sheen?... It's a monotonous chase through the jungle for most of the running time, and you can take a 15 minute nap through the middle sections and not miss a damned thing. Worst of all, every fight sequence keeps getting interrupted for (so-called) comic relief from lardassed George Memmoli as The White Rhino – an obnoxious pea-brain who tags along with Kelly in order to provide all the urination and homo jokes. The hackneyed fight choreography (courtesy of Kelly himself) tries for a pre-Jackie Chan combo of action and slapstick, complete with Mel Blanc-style sound effects, but midway through the movie you get the feeling that these guys wouldn't know a good kung fu film if their careers depended on it (and they did). Too many sappy, romantic subplots. Too much cornball dialogue. Too much boring bullshit. Plus, the film is only rated PG, which means no gruelling violence, and Jim doesn't even get a chance to pork his scrawny oriental squeeze. This film is so sloppily thrown together that they couldn't even loop the dialogue correctly – half the time the American actors *look* like they're dubbed. I guess this only proves you can pass off *any* slop to the strung-out junkies on The Deuce and make a quick buck... Luckily, the last four-minute battle-royale is pretty good, or else you *really* would have seen a pissed-off review from me.

HOUSE OF DARK SHADOWS

DAN CURTIS 1970. Younger TV-addicts might not be aware of the stir ABC's gothic soap opera **Dark Shadows** caused during its five-year run, but I sorta do (though I was too young to appreciate it at the time); and its success spawned this big screen feature by director Dan Curtis. You don't have to be familiar with the series in order to enjoy this Hammeresque fright-fest though. It holds up on its own mild merits, primarily thanks to Jonathan Frid as vampire extraordinaire Barnabas Collins. As usual, the setting is the Collinswood Estate, and the entire family is faced with a surprise house guest – their recently uncoffined 200-year-old, undead relative, Barnabas. The outwardly suave Barnabas is definitely a villainous sort, especially when he's pissed off – sucking the plasma out of everyone in the cast, turning females into his slaves after one icy glance, and even discovering a dead ringer for his long-dead bride-to-be Josette. The plot gets shaky when one crackpot femme scientist tries to cure Barnabas with a serum which destroys the evil cells in his body that make him a vampire, which only leads to some latex old-age overdose courtesy of makeup wizard Dick Smith... No big special effects are needed here, just some fog machines, lotsa cobwebs, a stream of blood trickling down the occasional neck, and some simple eloquence; plus it's good to see Frid again in the role that kept him typecast for eternity (the one noteworthy exception being the lead in Oliver Stone's first film **Seizure**). It's pretty straight-forward stuff with a TV movie gloss, in addition to some great sets, shovelfuls of mood and a few low key thrills. A class act, yet despite a relatively high body count, it's probably too slow-paced for modern audiences who think flash trash like **The Lost Boys** is top-notch... The sequel, **Night of Dark Shadows** (minus Frid), is utter garbage in comparison, with Kate Jackson proving she couldn't act two decades ago either.

HOUSE OF WHIPCORD

PETER WALKER 1974. With a grimy title like this, you're probably prepared for the worst. Well, this Brit sleazeshow from director Pete (**Schizo**) Walker isn't half bad (for diseased and vile entertainment that is), and it's a commendable off-shoot of the Asian-based Bimbos Behind Bars epics... Ann Michele stars as Anne Marie, a chic French fashion model who's sooo adorable and pixie-ish that most of the audience will be relieved when her grating giggles turn to screams of unendurable agony. She meets up with a handsome sadist (named Mark D. Sade) at a party and decides to join the stranger in a trip to his 'mom's' country house, which actually turns out to be a private institution for lewd and depraved young women. Anne Marie's immediately stripped, showered and shoved into a dank cell by her Christian captors. A senile old judge heads out the hefty sentences, and in-between Bible studies the strict matron assistant *loves* beating religion into her charges, until all the prisoners are covered with *very* moral bruises. And if anyone breaks the rules three times, these God-fearing religious deviants teach 'em a lesson at the end of a handy noose. There's a couple of escape attempts amongst the skimpily-clad inmates, and all the other essentials for a solid Women In Prison fest are here. Plus those Bible-belching psycho-wardens are 10 times scarier than your typical villainous captors. But there's a pervading sense of gloom hanging over the film, and unlike the better genre entries which forged a thread of wit into their prison plots (such as Jack Hill's **Big Doll House/Bird Cage** combo and Jonathan Demme's **Caged Heat**), this one is dead serious and overflowing with de-spair. The acting is adequate and its realistic tone keeps the sus-pense sustained even through the soggier segments, yet the flick is so depressingly sadistic that you can't help but cringe through-out. There's rampant doses of nudity to keep the voyeur pack leering, and the fact it's so well-produced only proves someone actually invested *money* into this sicko free-for-all. Hardcore Slam-mer Slut fanatics should get their money's worth, though they might piss and moan about the lack of on-screen bloodshed. Tough shit.

HOUSE ON THE EDGE OF THE PARK

RUGGERO DEODATO 1980. Director Ruggero Deodato, who had earlier pulled **Cannibal Holocaust** out of his cinematic colostomy bag, once again strives to repulse – but instead of gore, guts or graphic carnage, this time Rug-o opts for sheer reprehensibility. David Hess (who was chain-sawed in **Last House on the Left**) plays another psycho, and his entire characterisation is defined in the first two minutes, when he runs an innocent woman off the road and bru-tally rapes her in the back seat of her car. The rest of the cast and crew consists of a herd of unpronounceable Italians. After the opening attack, Hess and his half-witted partner-in-grime head to the upper-class suburbs and intrude on a houseful of pretentious swingers. They spend the next 90 minutes beating up the men and raping the women, and it quickly degenerates into your pre-dictable game of Cat and Mouse – except that Tom never got to pummel Jerry's face into a bloody pulp. The villains are lowlife scum, the victims are pampered wiseasses, and together they're the most obnoxious pack of unlikeable shitheads since The 700 Club. It's 'Sexual Abuse, Italian Style', and just when you decide it couldn't get any more vile, we get to watch Hess slowly slice up the breasts of a virgin with a straight razor. At least the ridiculous

twist ending wakes you up from the tedium, and Hess makes a *really* funny face when he's shot in the gut... Loaded with female nudity for the pud-pullers, plus spare-tired David H. even gets to shove his bare ass into the camera lens (aren't *we* lucky?). The phlegm-makers obviously wanted to be both sick and erotic, in order to lure in the demento-population of the public, but it comes off all too calculated for my tastes. Instead of being exciting and titillating, it's simply a virulent money-grubbing import that tries to pass itself off as a US production by adding a couple of Big Apple insert shots. A candidate for 'Cinema Open Sore' – the scariest parts of this flick are the repeated references to 'boogie-ing', unre-lenting disco music, and legal limit for pastel leisure suits and gold medallions... Basically, this is the horror equivalent to a boring porno film. So, have you gotten the message yet? AVOID THIS PIECE OF SHIT

HOW TO STUFF A WILD BIKINI

WILLIAM ASHER 1965. Remember those idiotic beach party movies from the early '60s? You don't?... Well, then you've missed an entire bone-headed sub-section of American culture. Annette Funi-cello and Frankie Avalon were the whitebread king and queen of the pre-hippie '60s. The perfect young couple, they were clean-cut, fun-loving kids who just wanted to sing and surf (along with an occasional snuggle thrown in to show that they weren't complete morons). As Frankie and Dee Dee, these two plastic paragons knew nothing of protests, alcohol, contraception, LSD, or date rape – plus their films made gobs of quick cash from the teenage drive-in crowds... Luckily, William Asher was signed to direct these beach-bimbo blockbusters. If the name doesn't ring any bells, he directed hundreds of TV shows during the '50s, and he has a knack for incorporating weird-as-shit absurdity into relatively in-nocuous settings. Such is the case with **How to Stuff a Wild Bi-kini**, the fifth (and last) of the American-International series. First off, Frankie barely even makes an appearance, leaving the reigns in the hands of Annette and dorky Dwayne Hickman. Get ready though, cuz here's the 'plot' – While Frankie is on Reserve Duty in the Pacific with an Island beauty, he worries about Dee Dee's

faithfulness, so he enlists the aid of a South Seas witch doctor named Bwana (Buster Keaton, supplementing his Social Security with a few days work), who sends a beautiful red-head, Cassandra, to the beach to lure Dwayne away from Dee Dee. At first, she's invisible, but when she appears, every surfer on the beach falls for her, including ad executive Peachy Keane (played by a bloated Mickey Rooney) who wants her to become a professional model. Enter Erich Von Zipper and his comic-relief motorcycle gang, The Rats. Then toss in a bunch of stooopid 'musical' numbers, when everyone on the beach breaks into song and dance, and one guy *happens* to have his electric guitar handy. Add a magical pelican, a Japanese bungalow by the sea, and a dazzlingly-inane motorcycle race finale complete with booby traps out of a Road Runner cartoon. Annette looks a little hefty in the jowls, so they wisely keep her out of a swimsuit; and Dwayne Hickman who has as much personality as most jars of rancid mayonnaise, smiles his way to utter obscurity. The Kingsmen are the obligatory musical guest at the local night-club, and Annette warbles a song so pathetically that you want to lob an empty beer bottle at her fat head. Yep, the film is awful, all right – but awful on a Grand Scale! And dumber than you can possibly imagine... Painful viewing, no matter how you approach it.

HOWARD: A NEW BREED OF HERO

GEORGE LUCAS 1986 (US: HOWARD THE DUCK). It's frustrating to think that Stan Lee, Head Asshole of Marvel Comics, is highly unlikely to revive the **Howard the Duck** comic book due to the utter financial failure of this movie. But this is only to be expected from the same ignorant fistfucker who pulled the book out of circulation because it was beyond the pathetic (and extreeemely limited) tastes of dick-pinching Marveloids who masturbate into rolled-up **Incredible Hulk** comics. (If I've offended anyone, tough fuck.) As I write this, **Howard: A New Breed of Hero** is not yet available on video tape; but it probably will be released in the very near future. Hell, George Lucas and his people are gonna want to make some money off of it. By now you may have seen fotos of the Howard costume, and if you did, I know what you're saying: 'It's a midget in a duck suit!' And, very disappointingly to yours truly, not a particularly good one at that. The facial movements are fine, the eyes roll around and stuff, but the whole get-up is just too fucking obvious to be convincing. Did Lucas' special FX people actually look at the rushes of their creation and say, 'Yes, this is good. We did very good work here. We'll fool everybody!' Jeezis, how depressing. Judging from the novelisation (yeah, I read it) and the comic-magazine adaptation, (which, ironically, are both better than the movie) the original script was okay. John Barry's musical score isn't bad, either. And Jeffrey Jones is wonderful, absolutely wonderful, as the scientist

possessed by an alien presence who calls himself one of the Dark Overlords of the Universe (from the Nexus of Sominus, see). Unfortunately, the film's good points are overshadowed by its pretensions. Still, it could've been a lot worse... Steven Spielberg could've done it. [BJE]

THE HUMAN DUPLICATORS (1965)
THE DAY MARS INVADED EARTH (1962)

Alien invaders creating duplicates of Earthmen as a part of their invasion plan. Sounds familiar? Yep, **Invaders from Mars** and **Invasion of the Body Snatchers** (the original versions, of course) each tackled this flyweight concept. But so did plenty of run-of-the-mill SF quickies, which brings us first to **The Human Duplicators**... Keep watching the skies, because there's dime-store UFO's (with eyesore interiors that look like outcasts from **The Starlost**) out there! Richard Kiel is Cosmic Agent Kolos, who wants to start up a colony on Earth in order to further his Master's plans for galaxy domination (pretty radical plan there, eh?). Via a cheap teleportation beam, he invades the laboratory of friendly Dr. Munson (George Macready), a top secret physicist, and turns the Doc and his assistants into glassy-eyed zombie duplicates who he commands to steal government secrets. This idea doesn't sit well with the National Intelligence Organisation (led by The Beaver's dad, Hugh Beaumont), who promptly sends their top agent to Save The World!... The highly technical duplication process involves the victim standing in a circular cage while red and blue lights flash at them, and then they sit under clear plastic hairdryers until their brains harden. The dupes are super-strong and bullets don't even slow 'em down, but Kolos also gave them a plaster head, so whenever they're knocked on the noggin' their skulls crack open and Erector Set pieces tumble out. Oops! Design flaw, indeed... George Nader and Barbara Nichols co-star, with Dolores Faith as Dr. Munson's blind daughter (who falls for Kolos), and you *know* you're in serious trouble when Richard Kiel turns in the best performance. Blame director Hugo Grimaldi (who also 'directed' the American release of the second Godzilla movie, **Gigantis, The Fire Monster**) and writer Arthur C. Pierce for this colourful dose of swill. Watchable, but certainly not memorable. Plus, since this v-tape is distributed by Thriller Video, it means Elvira picks up another paycheque by posing on her casting couch and cracking prurient tit jokes. Ho hum... At least **Human Duplicators** has a silly plot and comical goofiness going for it, which is more than you can say about **The Day Mars Invaded Earth**. Directed and produced by Maury Dexter, this black and white bore is the pits. Easily the longest 70 minute movie I've sat through in some time... A bunch of white-jacketed pseudo-scientists start acting strange after a robot-probe of theirs lands on Mars, and the head honcho, Dr. David Fleming (Kent Taylor), is the worst off, with an unwelcome, evil alien duplicate of himself hanging around. In fact, his entire family might be affected by these fishy circumstances, because at one point or another everyone suddenly gets blurry-looking (so much

for their special effects) and afterward they act very disoriented (as if the actors could see their careers tumbling into a bottomless pit of manure). Everyone in the cast gets justifiably paranoid when The Duplicates start traipsing around, bumping into The Real People, and soon Dr. Fleming discovers that his own probe to Mars is responsible for the invasion (no shit). It seems that in relaying electronic impulses back to earth, the Martians were provided a path with which to travel from their planet to ours. Oh yeah, I almost forgot that these Dupes also have this neat ability to burn a human being to cinders; which leads to the happy ending, as our jolly family of Martian-doubles heads off to conquer the human race in their station wagon, with the ashy remains of their human counterparts fizzling away in the empty swimming pool. Hi ho, hi ho, it's off to conquer the world they go!... Co-starring Marie Windsor and William Mims, this is a particularly disappointing example of cheapie sci-fi. In other words, if this flick ever pops up on late-night TV, I'd suggest you catch up on your sleep instead. Zzzzzz...

HUMAN HIGHWAY

NEIL YOUNG 1981. It's 'I've got some dope, let's make a movie' time, folks! And only minutes into this fried flick, I was asking myself, what the HELL did I stumble upon? Directed by Neil Young (under the pseudonym Bernard Shakey, and with Dean Stockwell helping him out), this is a nuclear 'comedy' starring an overdose of then-unemployed acidheads – a stellar cast of misfits with virtually nothing to do... The setting is Otto's, a grubby roadside diner located on the outskirts of Linear Valley, the proud home of the Cal-Neva Nuclear Power Plant. Don't worry about the occasional waste spillage though. It's an everyday occurrence, especially when a glowing Devo (with tubes up their nostrils) is the Radiation Disposal Team. At the diner we meet the rest of our cast: Dennis Hopper is the psycho cook, Crackers; Sally Kirkland is a beleaguered waitress; Dean Stockwell is the new owner, Young Otto (son of the late Old Otto); plus Neil Young and Russ Tamblyn are frighteningly convincing as two noodleheaded gas pump operators, Lionel and Fred. In other words, everyone's a blithering atomic-age ninny. As far as the story goes, Stockwell wants to torch the eatery for the insurance bucks, while the neighbouring nuke plant is on the verge of detonation. But primarily, everyone just stumbles around in a daze, in hopes that the viewer will get a contact high. See an irradiated Devo ride around in a pick-up truck! Watch Russ wash a windshield! Gasp in awe as Hopper feeds a pet racoon! Witness Stockwell abscond with breakfast sausages! Neil even pumps a bit of gas! Part fantasy, part social commentary, part slapstick comedy, and all so pathetic it's (almost) funny. Soon the plot veers into complete unintelligibility when spaceships begin flying about, buses begin disappearing, Dennis pops up in a second role (as an exec in a leopard skit convertible), and the Vegasized Frankie Fontaine shows up in his white limo. There's even a live-music sequence with Neil as the Singing Mechanic (for once looking like himself, instead of a Hee Haw reject). In other words, THIS IS A FIRST-CLASS MESS! Along the ride there's some wild visuals, a couple great songs (Neil jams with Devo on 'Hey Hey My My' and I loved the finale – 'It Takes a Worried Man', featuring the entire cast dancing with shovels), plus a few hilarious bits are scattered about (if you're attuned to their warped wavelength). On the other hand, a few (long) portions are abysmal! And you mean this was never distributed? Gosh, I can't understand why!... At the very least, this proves Neil won't sing for Bud, but he'll certainly make unwatchable films with all his pie-eyed pals. What a baffling piece of freaked-out garbage! Nevertheless, it's a Mutant Must-See for Rock-and-Schlock completists (even though it's a lousy flick).

I DISMEMBER MAMA

PAUL LEDER 1974. Great title, eh? And the movie that goes with it isn't half bad either, especially if you're in the mood for some moderately sick and sleazy entertainment. Though it has all the non-style of any recent made-for-video release, the plotline is played fairly seriously (which is a nice change from all the self-mocking horror flicks out recently) and it doesn't waste a moment in getting its grimy gears turning... Zooey Hall stars as Albert, a brooding mental patient who starts his day by ripping off a nurse's dress and nearly strangling her. Institutionalised for trying to kill his mother, Albert decides to finish the job by slicing a guard's throat and heading to his mom's palatial estate. Unfortunately, she isn't home, so he has to make due with thoroughly degrading mom's housekeeper – he forces her to strip at knifepoint, fondle her own breasts, and sing 'Let Me Call You Sweetheart'. And when the housekeeper's cute 10-year-old daughter, Annie, enters the picture, Albert calmly makes friends with the little girl while her mom is laying naked in a puddle of her own blood in the upstairs bedroom. If you couldn't already guess, Zooey is turned on by the little girl's 'purity', so he decides to take Annie on a whirlwind courtship – we get a montage of them at a cutesy amusement park, walking along the beach, and he even takes her to a hotel for the night (the bridal suite, no less). Don't expect any jailbait sexual debasement though. The filmmakers might be scumbag panderers, but they never tread near that touchy subject (depending on your personal level of depravity, you can decide whether it was a good idea or not). The ending loses its edge and drifts into standard slasher territory though, with Albert chasing his prey and the cops (led by an indignant Greg Mullavey) tracking him down. It's a pretty limp finale... On the positive side, the dialogue is appropriately overwrought ("You are a deformed subhuman creature that does not deserve to be alive!"); Zooey has all the psycho-mannerisms down pat, and his hairstyle would be the envy of Erik Estrada; and there's a really pathetic theme song called 'Poor Albert' by Rocket Roden. Directed by Paul Leder (A-P-E), this may not be a horror classic, but it does have its genuinely repellent moments. It's fairly damaged fun... Oh, by the way, Albert never does get to dismember his rich-bitch mama. Shucks!

IDAHO TRANSFER

PETER FONDA 1971 (DISTRIBUTED 1974). After the success of Easy Rider, Peter Fonda decided to follow pal Dennis Hopper behind the camera. After directing/starring in the western The Hired Hand, he broke from acting and filmed this ecology-minded science fiction tale. Outside of a few product-desperate venues, it was barely distributed. No great surprise. The script by Thomas Matthieson boasts an OK concept and some interesting social points are touched upon, but as this yawn-fest proves, good intentions don't necessarily mean a good film... A bunch of college-aged scientists are working on a secretive, high-tech (well, considering the barren budget, more like 'medium-tech') project in the middle of Idaho. They're experimenting with time travel into the future – 56 years, to be precise, after mankind has screwed up the environment to the point of their own near extinction. Only young people have the stamina to survive the shaky trip and a bunch of them get trapped in this burnt-out Tomorrow-Land, so they try to begin civilisation anew. But all these tedious teens do is backpack across miles of rocky landscape, flap endlessly at the gums and take an eventual turn toward downright savagery. The only portion that elicited any response from me was the dark (albeit silly) ending. Boredom reigns supreme throughout, and I couldn't tell who seemed more dreary – the trapped cast or myself (for getting suckered into another lousy video). Fonda's direction is Meaningful to the point of Petrifaction, and the two-bit budget bought them one scientific-looking building, a couple puptents in the wilderness, and grim-

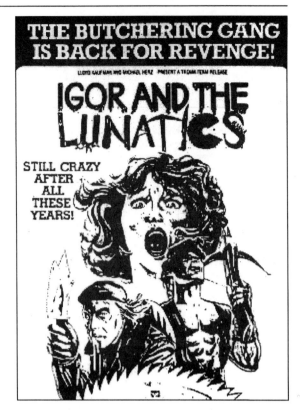

aceable early-'70s fashions and haircuts. Most of the cast are unknowns (Peter says he hired 'em off the street, and it shows), with the only familiar face being a young stringy-haired Keith Carradine... In addition, before the movie begins, a present-day Peter Fonda gives us a short intro and lecture about environmental awareness. Personally though, I'm not sure which would kill off a civilisation faster – unchecked pollution or intellectually deadening productions like this one.

IGOR AND THE LUNATICS

BILLY PAROLINI 1985. Here's more shit from Troma! When will I ever learn?... But then again, what the hell did I expect? Art? Deep social commentary? How about some basic, trashy entertainment? Nope, **Igor** couldn't even come across with the simple task of being genuinely sordid and scummy. It's absolutely barren of any entertainment value whatsoever, and would you believe it has *less* storyline than even **Surf Nazis Must Die?** It certainly has a catchy little title though, doesn't it?... Directed by first-timer Billy Parolini (at least I *hope* it's his first effort; I'd hate to imagine what other type of celluloid abortion he could have spawned earlier), I didn't arrive with any high expectations, but the opening credit sequence had enough grimness to hold my interest. Along with a separate acknowledgement for 'horror, action and suspense sequences' and 'Demento-vision', we get a frantic female being chased around a lumberyard by a street gang of scuzzballs with a circular saw, eventually ripping a ragged path twixt her legs and up her spine. So far, so sleazy; but then the screenplay steps into the picture and we realise it's as predictable as any **A-Team** episode, with a few crude gore effects thrown in... In flashback, we meet a blood-crazed hippie leader, Paul Byron, who whisks his pack of acidhead followers into the country to set up their own autonomous community, with Paul as their God. From this concept, they could have pulled off a fun Charles Manson/Jim Jones take-off, I figured, but it never comes *close* to being that interesting! Instead, the gist of the story has Tom, a now-successful, clean-cut lawyer (who's an ex-cult member) searching for his long lost son. The police refuse to help, so Yuppie-Attorney Tom, a stoic Injun, and a gun-totin' red-head team up to take on these loony Moonie-style, leather-clad

madmen. Where does Igor come in, you might ask? Well, Igor is Paul's chief henchman – a psychotic, snivelling little fuck who comes off like a cross between Ed Neal in **Texas Chain Saw Massacre** and Bob Goldthwait after 11 cups of coffee; and it's a sad day when the movie's *only* bearable character is a geek who enjoys slicing a woman's chest open, ripping out her heart and taking snapshots of it... There are sporadic moments of excessive gore which will have the burnt-out sickos in the audience chuckling, but **Igor** is devoid of any *real* attempts at humour, unlike **The Toxic Avenger** or **Street Trash**. Worst of all, it's obvious the film was re-cut and softened to get that 'precious' R-rating. As far as the film's cast of worthless swine are concerned, they're better left unmentioned since I don't want to jeopardise their subsequent careers at Burger King... Troma's present motto is 'Movies of the Future'. Well, if they keep spitting up this brand of worthless Z-grade horseshit, they should change it to 'Movies That Waste Your Money and Piss You Off. At least it'd be more honest... Incidentally, the opening-credit scene at the lumberyard turns up for a *second* time 20 minutes into the film. Hmmmm, I wouldn't have thought they'd have to pad out a 79 minute flick.

THE IMP

DAVID DECOTEAU 1988 (US: SORORITY BABES IN THE SLIMEBALL BOWL-O-RAMA). Empire Pix' sleaze-division, Urban Classics, pulled another dust-collector off the shelves, stuck it on a double bill with **Galactic Gigolo**, tossed it into grinders for a week, and before you can say 'sucker-bait', it's in video stores so that hard-up vidiots can slobber over the prospect of flogging their maggot over another Linnea Quigley movie... Well, don't get your hopes up. It's a *lot* less sleazy and titillating than the come-on ad portrays. Directed by David DeCoteau (**Creepozoids**. Urgh!), this movie starts off depressingly lousy and slowly improves until it's only annoying. Some praise, eh? A trio of dinkwads (one fat slob and two eye-glassed nerds) are sitting around reading **Penthouse** and chugging beers one evening, when they decide to creep over to the Tri-Delta Sorority and eavesdrop on their pledge initiations, where the new recruits have their pantied derrieres spanked with a wooden paddle. But when they're caught in the act of leering, the two pledges and three perverts are sent on a mission by the bitchy sorority president – they have to break into the local bowling alley after closing and steal a trophy. So far, so easy. They make it into the town's mall and the bowl-a-rama, but when the trophy is accidentally dropped, the bottom opens up and an enslaved, wise-cracking imp jumps out. Sounding suspiciously like the plant from the new **Little Shop of Horrors**, the magical creature first starts handing out wishes, but ends up trying to slaughter the whole pack of pea-brains. Linnea Quigley pops up in a small role, as a street-wise thief named Spider, who helps out the college clowns; and L.Q. stays firmly clothed in her ripped T-shirt and stretch leotards throughout... Also sorry to report that there's no blood or gore, and most of the violence is kept out of camera range. Instead, we have to make due with a couple of bare breasts and oodles of slobbering voyeurism. All the characters seem to have double-digit IQ's, and as for the level of sophisticated humour? Well, one nerd drinks a Budweiser at the beginning and vomits for the rest of the flick. HaHaHaHa. sigh... The budget was so low they could only afford to rent five bimbos to represent an entire sorority, and the only time I laughed was when a gal named Taffy was pulled in half in true salt-water fashion. It's watchable enough, I guess (especially when you consider what passes for entertainment on network TV nowadays), but don't say I didn't warn you.

THE INCREDIBLE MELTING MAN

WILLIAM SACHS 1978. There's a monster on the loose again, and American-International is to blame!... Alex Rebar stars as the lone survivor of a spaceshot to Saturn, who discovers, to his general dismay, that his flesh is quickly starting to slide off his bones (it's the ol' we'll-blame-it-on-space-radiation-cuz-we're-too-stupid-to-come-up-with-anything-original plot twist). And although the movie isn't very good, I have to admit that when it comes to glop-and-slop slimefests, this is the unofficial winner. On the plus side, a young Rick Baker was at the FX helm, so we get fistfuls of ooze within the first few minutes (usually these cheapo productions take half an hour to build up speed), with our Melting Man chomping on heads in search of human meat. It's all pretty pointless after a while, though, watching this drippy cannibal staggering through the woods for an hour, as his best friend follows the trail of KY Jelly, using a Geiger counter. (He comes across a runny hunk of flesh hanging from a tree branch – "Oh, God! It's his ear!") A couple of nice episodes liven up the boredom: A severed head is thrown into a river, with its hollowed-out body turning up minutes later; a couple of old farts get ripped up while they're out picking lemons at midnight (?); and Jonathan Demme makes a hilarious cameo

appearance with the always dim-witted, but exploitable, Rainbeaux Smith. There's also an arm-chomping, an electrocution, some quick gunshot bloodspurts, and a wonderfully long decomposition at the finale – but all this can't hide the fact that most of the movie is standard drive-in scuzzshow... Some people called **Melting Man** an R-rated retread of **The Hideous Sun Demon** and **First Man in Space**, but compared to that pair's '50s School of Schlock-Monstermania, this entry is a pretty lifeless grind-'em-out, which is entertaining enough, in spurts. Its director, William Sachs, went on to do **Galaxina** (enough said about his 'career').

THE INCREDIBLY STRANGE CREATURES WHO STOPPED LIVING AND BECAME MIXED-UP ZOMBIES

RAY DENNIS STECKLER 1964 (AKA: TEENAGE PSYCHO MEETS BLOODY MARY). I've been searching for this cult item for several years, and now that I've found it is there any way of losing it again?... Proclaimed to be the first monster-musical and filmed in Terrorama (!), this film has *two* of the best titles I've ever seen for a creature feature. But when it comes down to actually sitting through the film, horror fans will snooze from boredom, sleaze fiends will squeal in delight, and fans of crappy night-club routines will fall head over heels at the awe-inspiring 'musical' interludes. Writer/director Ray Dennis Steckler is the culprit behind this cardboard cheapie, and he even takes star-billing under the macho-as-heck pseudonym of Cash Flagg. The incomprehensible plot takes place at a local carny, where the sinister gypsy fortune-teller, Madame Estrella, lures unsuspecting victims into hypnotic trances with the help of some dime-store trippy visuals and a large wart pasted on her cheek. ('See the wart of horror!' the coming attraction proclaims.) Meanwhile, there's a burlesque joint next door (hubba hubba!) so that Steckler can intercut plenty of spastic dance numbers, including a few routines starring the leggy, booze-sponge Carmelita (Carolyn Brandt, who was Mrs. Steckler at the time). These two locations come crashing together when murder and cheesy-choreography meet, as Cash (cleverly disguised by a hooded sweatshirt) is tossed into a homicidal trance by The Wart Woman, and goes nutzoid across the stage with a kitchen knife. Of course, the movie's half over by now, and *still* not an Incredible Strange Creature in sight (plenty of Incredibly Bad Acting, Incredibly Dull Dialogue and Incredibly Lousy Music, though – 'Even the lightning sucks,' says Brian). During the last few minutes the creatures *finally* take centre stage when Embrella's closetful of geeks is unleashed with their Incredibly Cheap Makeup – a pack of putty-faces, with twisted features and scraggly hair. Don't panic, though, because the cops kill 'em *all* off in less than five minutes; and there's a tragic ending where Cash dies from terminal angst (actually, a dummy of him is tossed off a cliff). I love a happy ending, don't you?... This film is so hideous that you'll be ashamed to admit you liked it. I've actually sat through this flick twice in a week's time – the first time I *hated* it because it was SO BAD, and the second time I *loved* it because it was SO BAD. I think it kinda grows on you (the way mould grows on a package of olive loaf if you set it on a radiator for a week). The seemingly-unending series of very colourful, very painful night-club routines will either have you perpetually fighting for the Fast Forward control or gasping for breath because of their astronomical Tacky Level (my favourite is a Twist number featuring a chorus line of Carmen Miranda clones!). With crooners that make Pat Boone look like a man, costumes out of a fashion designer's bad trip, and vibrant colour photography by newcomer Vilmos Zsigmond (I guess everyone has to start somewhere)...

INFRA-MAN

HUA-SHAN 1975. Fuck the Hulk. Shit on that bitch Dazzler. And He-Man can fly straight to Hell in a flaming septic tank. Infra-Man makes these clowns look like pathetic schmucks. (Though with He-Man that ain't hard to do.) **Infra-Man**, the now-classic kung fu-science-fiction-superhero-monster movie from China, is more fun than a six-pack of Genny. (Though that's not hard to top, either...) Princess Dragon-Mom (yep, that's her name) is dissatisfied with having only her subterranean kingdom of mutant monsters to rule over, so she decides to take over the whole world. (Princess: "It's time to attack!" Monsters: "Yaaaaay!!") When it becomes apparent that even China's mighty army is about as effective in stopping the mutant invasion as a preppy is in being an individual, a wise scientist turns a brave young man into a bio-mechanical super-hero. Infra-Man's battles with some of the funniest monsters in movie history are sure to bring grins to the faces of even the wimpiest of Normals, and kung fu fans as well as monster freaks will want to watch this one over and over again. How many times we here at **Slimetime** have watched it have never been counted, but so what. See it for yourself, thrill to (and laugh at) the special effects and the frequent fight scenes (the last one just doesn't *stop*), and keep a notebook handy for all that wonderfully hilarious dialogue. And watch out for the deadly *slinky-men!* FunfunFUN! [BJE]

INHUMANITIES:
A SHOCKUMENTARY

1989. Boy, what a piece of video crapola this is! It really looked groovy, promising live virgin sacrifices, decapitations and cannibalism. What it really is, is a collection of 12th generation dubs of things too grimy to be on **National Geographic** or **Wild Kingdom**. Lots of shots of animals eating each other (what an inhumanity that is!) and most of it looks horribly staged (someone should tell these guys that dead people don't breathe). They seem to show the same shot over and over again – needed to pad it out to 75 minutes I guess. On the very slim good side, there's some horribly insipid dialogue like, "man the hunter is now man the killer", "hack

them apart for money to live" and "food is a requirement". Also a good 20 minutes on primitive brain surgery (?) – "for a brain tumour or just a common headache" – which is done without anaesthesia. After four hours everyone takes a drink break and leaves the patient's head open (I'm surprised the liquid doesn't leak). At the end of the 'operation' they don't even close the wound up, so the guy walks around with a cleft head for the rest of his life. This 'film' was so boring I slept through more than I saw. Grainy stock that makes **Faces of Death** look like **Citizen Kane**. If you see this at your local video store, don't waste your money (the director certainly didn't). In fact, why don't you bring it up to the counter and burn it right in front of the clerk. [SS]

INVASION OF THE BEE GIRLS

DENIS SANDERS 1973. I wasn't looking forward to this one since I just made a New Year's resolution to stop ingesting marijuana (let's see how long this one lasts!). I'm sure it would have helped, though I found this one an entertaining, mildly amusing (though overlong) little sex romp through early '70s fashion, written by Nicholas Meyer of **Time After Time** and **Star Trek: The Wrath of Khan** fame. "A lot of sex games go on here," says the pretty, young secret biological warfare lab-assistant (Victoria Vetri) to federal investigator Neil Agar (perhaps a tip of the hat to old film 'star' John, played by biker film 'star' William Smith). It seems that a bunch of young men are dying in a small town due to 'exhaustion in the act of sexual intercourse', forcing the town to levy a curfew and order 'total sexual abstinence' (which causes the town to erupt in disdain, this being before the age of AIDS). This only causes the town's male population to stop picking up girls in bars and start raping them in parking lots. Curiously, the town's women all slowly begin to don huge sunglasses day and night. As evidence is compiled, more men are murdered because they can't stop dipping their peckers, and breasts are freed from bras throughout the town until all is revealed (at last!). It seems that a

doctor has turned his lovely assistant (Anitra Ford, yeah!) into a queen bee! As she tries to mate, the men drop like flies and the women are turned into bee girls. Anitra kidnaps the women and injects their forehead with... something. With the help of old '50s and '60s monster movie props, multicoloured lights are shined on the 'victim'. The rest of the bee girls cover her in glop, throw her into a giant No-Pest Strip and cover her in real live bees. She emerges a bee girl with false eyelashes and huge eyeballs (causing all the rest of the bee girls to strip and fondle themselves). The film plods along, sometimes a little too slow, but Meyer's script is pretty entertaining and done with an erect tongue in his cheek. The gore count is zero, but the titty count is way up there (and they are 1960s titties − real big with HUGE areolas). The music is used pretty well (but the mutant girls' choir should be shot!). All in all, a pretty good time for a Sunday afternoon. PS An interesting footnote. The sound was done by Jerry Wexler, who produced Bob Dylan's Born Again albums. Bet you don't see this one on his resumé! [SS]

INVASION OF THE BLOOD FARMERS

ED ADLUM 1972. This movie is the absolute cheapest of the cheap! Crammed with outrageously amateurish gore and overflowing with inept performances, this film is as ludicrous as its title promises it to be. Oh, it's a *terrible* film all right, but it isn't boring and I had a hell of a lot of fun watching these imbeciles at play. The main perpetrator is director Ed Adlum (who also co-wrote the script with Ed Kelleher), and it looks like he had a great time presiding over this swill − some of his cuts are amusing, and the blatantly crude tone of the entire film had me rolling in my own spilt beer... It begins when a guy splattered with red paint (Oh, that's supposed to be blood. Sorry) staggers down a country highway, stumbles into a bar, gurgles a bit, wiggles his tongue back and forth, drips on the linoleum, and dies. Turns out that there's a bunch of back-

woods druids on the prowl, and their particular hobby is kidnapping towns-folk, chaining 'em up in their barn and draining every drop of blood out of them. Besides their regular plasma collections, these danged druids need a Blood Host to revive their comatose queen, who's decked out in their living room in a glass coffin. Their leader, Creeton, looks about 19-years-old (even though they went to the trouble of putting flour in his hair), and their Head of Homicide is a smiling, overalled, farmer-type who wanders around happily bashing peoples' heads in − sort of like Mister Green Jeans on PCP. The rest of the cast consists of a pair of inane college-age kids who deserve to die (though you know they won't, since they're the stars); the gal's scientist father, whose lab looks like a junior-high chemistry set; a doofus police chief who's a walking Ralph Steadman illustration for birth defects; and a supporting cast that acts like they've been knocking back shots of wood alcohol in-between takes. The dialogue flows forth like a stopped-up toilet bowl, but there's action aplenty for violence freaks − a newlywed husband is clubbed repeatedly over the head in the shower, a handyman is stabbed in the eye and decapitated, and I particularly enjoyed the gurgling sound the druids' blood-pumping machine made while it sucked their squirming victims dry... Starring Norman Kelly and Tanna Hunter, this is high-grade shit indeed. Idiotic, unbelievable, with a plot that rambles all over the place. No nudity. No sex. Nothing too graphic either (but it's *real* sleazy nevertheless). Just solid schlock crammed onto 80 minutes of film stock. It's the perfect dumbass drive-in movie! See it with a bunch of weirdo friends, a case of cold beer and no expectations whatsoever. Just be prepared to laugh a *lot* while you're tossing empties at the screen.

ISLAND OF TERROR

TERENCE FISHER 1967 (AKA: THE CREEPERS). Another tale of cancer-experiments-gone-snafooey-on-a-small-island, this time resulting in single-tentacled turtle-like critters called 'silicates', that kill their victims by sucking out their bone marrow. Yummy! The hungry buggers multiply like rabbits, literally tearing apart into twos and fours and so on. Pretty soon the island is overrun by an army of silicates, who smash through windows and leap from trees to get at their potential meals. Director Terence Fisher and his cast, headed by veteran monster-slayer Peter Cushing (who gets his hand chopped off with an axe in one scene. Spurt, spurt!) all seem to be taking the whole thing none-too-seriously, and genuinely having fun in the process. Fans of British sillyshock will like this one. I enjoyed it. *Trust* me. [BJE]

IT'S ALIVE III: ISLAND OF THE ALIVE

LARRY COHEN 1987. Director Larry Cohen's follow-up to his '70s *Alive* duo is the most mediocre of the lot, though it also attempts to be the most inventive. The first two were basically monster(s)-on-the-loose B-movies with a dark underpinning of the American nuclear unit gone sour; and who could forget those adorable, lumpy little darlings, with their razored teeth, bulbous head, thrashing claws, and a cry that sounds like a puppy trapped inside a working garbage disposal? Well, the Mutant Babies are still turning up at random across the US, and after spending years shooting them on sight, the government decides to set up a quarantine area on a deserted island, where they can grow up without slaughtering the entire nursery school. But after four years, a boatload of idiots journey there to check on the now-grown Mutant Mob's progress, and when they locate 'em, it's standard slash-'n'-hack-time in the jungle as the humans are picked off one-by-one (what did they expect, a welcoming committee?). The creatures are telepathic, cannibalistic and (as seen in the first two flicks) only savage when they're provoked; but when they head back to civilisation on a 'borrowed' sailboat, it's back to creature-feature basics − a seaside carnival, a pack of rowdy punks, a parade of pistol-dicked cops, and (of course) a monster attack. It turns into 'Humanoids from the Deep, Part 2' (but with sympathetic antagonists), though I thought the former film was a lot more unpretentious fun. Worst of all, the lacklustre open-ending (don't you *hate* those things?) gets so sweet and sentimental that it'll have diabetics writhing on the floor in a puddle... The way I see it, Cohen is continuing to milk his one financially successful concept straight into the sod, but notwithstanding a *tiny* bit of gratuitous bloodshed, he tries to make this instalment more thought-provoking than scary (too bad he couldn't accomplish *both*). His only interesting observation is in the fear of sexual promiscuity – but instead of AIDS, you might end up with a Monster Child... Even the Mutants aren't very convincing this time around, combining rubber heads with jerky stop-motion animation (Rick Baker worked on the first pair, and it's obvious he passed on this one). But at least the cast is watchable. Cohen-regular Michael Moriarty (**The Stuff** and **Q**, in addition to the underrated **Who'll Stop the Rain**) stars as a father of one of Them, and it's always fun to watch Mr. Method Actor happily slumming his way through a rent check's worth of googly-eyed improvisation. On the other hand, Karen Black (as Moriarty's ex-shrew, er, wife) is absolutely miserable, with a frizzed-out hair style that looks like she was dipped headfirst in Clorox; Gerrit Graham and Laurene Landon also pop up in small roles – as a sleazy lawyer and as a one-night-stand for Michael M. (I'll let you guess who played which.) It's pretty mediocre, but I still think it deserved a better theatrical release than Warner Brothers gave it.

IT'S ONLY A MOVIE: THE VIDEO #1

1987. This home-grown li'l 'video magazine' takes its viewer on a journey down the road to Psychotronic Mentality (whether you want to go there or not), as we meet all the High Priests and Priestesses of Chicago's infamous Psychotronic Film Society. And obviously, these folks are not on your standard cinematic plane of consciousness... This tape contains a mixed-bag of treats: Some good trailers are scattered throughout, for hot shit like **Plan 9**, **Daughter of Horror**, **The Flesh Eaters**, and **The Beast of Yucca Flats** ("One of the most exciting movies ever made!" – you *know* it's true, cuz the ad sez so!). There's also a mini-tribute to the cinematic legacy of that 'Hoosier hoodlum' John Dillinger, including a tour of the Crown Point Jail. Plus, there's the highly-touted Splatter Theatre Group, whose Grimy Guignol productions include a hockey-masked psycho taking a butcher knife to a guy's groin on-stage, strangling an actor with his own large intestine, and bloody sacks of body parts hanging from handy meat hooks ("What kind of entrails do you use?", the probing interviewer asks the director). On the down side, the numerous descriptions of 'what is a Psychotronic movie?' will bore the hardcore viewer, their rambling info is simplistic for anyone beyond the **Famous Monsters** stage of fandom, and even though Mike Flores has a damned impressive one-sheet collection, showing it off on tape just *doesn't* work... Best is the conversation with high-ranking member Del Close, on his comic books, movie roles and LSD years (he also has the best tales to spin – such as when he mixed mescaline and acid, and ended up armed and on roller skates, shooting at rats in the tunnels of the sewer system). But all in all, slow self-promotional camcorder material.

IT CONQUERED THE WORLD

ROGER CORMAN 1956. Actually, it didn't conquer *diddlypoop*, unless you want to count the small town full of dinkheads where this Roger Corman cheapie takes place. A young Lee Van Cleef (with *hair!*) is cast as a scientist who has been communicating with a being from Venus via a wall-size machine he's got set up in his living room. The alien promises it can 'help' mankind achieve peace and knowledge, so gullible Lee invites his otherworldly friend to pay Earth a visit. The alien's ship crash-lands in the mountains and Mr. It doesn't waste any time in dispatching its swarm of gibbering bat-like parasites, whose function is to jab people in the back of the neck, thus turning the victim into a zombie-like slave. Lee tells his pal Peter Graves all about the potential good to be gained by the Venusian's presence, but Pete and his ladyfriend, Beverly Garland (schlockfilm veteran and future mommy on **My Three Sons**), are not interested, thank you. However, Bev becomes one of Them, and tries to convert Pete with the aid of a bat-creature. Pete exterminates the little pest and then, realising that his possessed wife would probably be a real downer to take along to a cocktail party, exterminates *her*. (This got more laughs than sympathy from us and the audience we recently saw this with.) The monster is truly a sight to behold: It's got a pointy head, rubbery arms and a set of fangs that threaten to poke out its beady little eyeballs. Fans have affectionately dubbed the critter 'the Cucumber Monster'. Indeed, it does kinda look like some absurd form of mutant vegetable. And as if the monster itself weren't enough (unintentional) comic relief, you've got the zany antics of Dick Miller and Jonathan Haze as a coupla wacky soldiers (eep!)... Short, brainless fun for Saturday afternoon viewing, It Conquered the World was remade years later by schlockmeister Larry Buchanan as (gasp) **Zontar, the Thing from Venus**! [B]E]

JEAN-LUC GODARD'S KING LEAR

JEAN-LUC GODARD 1987. What better way to continue the 'pretentious arty crap' series than with the hands-down *king* of pretension, Godard himself! In the non-linear hands of Jean-Luc, Shakespeare breaks down into a dissertation on media, reality, truth, art, and deal-making at Cannes. With such illustrious (and no doubt bewildered) stars as Molly Ringwald, Burgess Meredith, and Woody Allen quoting from the Bard, a young writer follows everybody around trying to 're-invent' the story and characters. Also quite amusing are the opening shots, culled from the footage bagged after Norman (Tough Guys Don't Gross Dollar One) Mailer dropped out as Lear, accompanied by Godard jabbering about how 'The Great Writer' argued endlessly about simple directions. The soundtrack itself is noteworthy, a melange of overlapping voices, tape loops, and manipulated music. And yes, all this indulgence was financed by Glorbutt and Yodelin' at Cannon Films. ('Theese was a big mistake, Menachem.') [TR]

KILLER KLOWNS FROM OUTER SPACE

STEPHEN CHIODO 1988. How can you resist a title like that? The hands down winner of Silliest Concept of the Month, this is also one of the more entertaining surprises... It's a typical Friday night in town, with interchangeable teens making out at Lookout Point, a pair of 'wacky' ice cream salesmen annoying everyone in sight, and the town's fun-hating cop (John 'I've made a small fortune by playing dickheads' Vernon) on the prowl for beer-drinking teens. So far, so tedious. But when an Unidentified Flaming Object blazes across the sky and plummets into a nearby field, this quiet hamlet soon discovers they've been invaded by ray gun-totin' Killer Klowns! These aren't your normal pie-in-the-face laffsters though – sure, they've got the baggy wardrobe, oversized shoes and frizzed-out hair, but they're also the sickest, most demented-looking bozos ever to grace the screen. Psychotic rejects from Ringling Bros., with razored teeth, sadistic smiles and twisted features. They've got a circus tent-shaped spaceship, balloon animals they use as bloodhounds, living popcorn kernels, hand shadows that devour people, and they tend to go door-to-door kidnapping humans and storing them in cotton candy cocoons... No, I'm *not* making this shit up! And I'm amazed someone actually gave director Stephen Chiodo (who first cut his teeth doing animation in Tim Burton's **Vincent**) the money to pull off this bent concept! There isn't much story to speak of (it's about on par with **Invasion of the Saucer Men** or any other '50s cheapie) and the human characters are faster-than-immediately forgettable, but the funhouse-style production design, special effects and wonderfully sicko humour make up for its occasional blandness. Plus, I can't fault a flick that has 10 times the imagination of any other exploitation item this year... Favourite sequence: The littlest klown runs across the town's biker gang, and after destroying the half-pint's bicycle, the cycle leader challenges the li'l fellow with "Whatcha gonna do? Knock my block off?" – to which the klown pulls out a pair of boxing gloves and fuckin' *decapitates* the chopper jockey with one punch. It took me a full minute to recover from that scene... Starring such unnoteables as Grant Taylor and Suzanne Snyder, you *know* a cast is lame when John Vernon gives the film's liveliest performance (and ends up playing Charlie McCarthy for his trouble)... A psychedelic, side-show twist on the old alien invasion tale, with enough sadistic, vicious humour to keep anyone amused. Theme song provided by The Dickies.

THE KILLER SHREWS

RAY KELLOGG 1959. Do not, do *not* use shrews as subjects in your cancer research experiments. Otherwise, as this film shows us, they will not only grow as big as dogs, but they will develop a taste for human flesh, which can be annoying if you happen to be trapped on a small island with murderous mutant shrew running about looking for people to BITEBITEBITE!!!... These critters will eat their way through walls to get at you, and they'll fight with each other in your living room, and if this film had been true-to-life, I bet they'd piss and shit all over the place. They will not sneak up on you. They will leap out of nowhere, chittering and biting biting biting BITING, and so fucking what if they're small dogs dressed up with hair all over their bodies and fake fangs jammed into their gums, you won't sit there and watch and say 'Aah, these are just dogs!' You'll find yourself saying 'Yeah! Get that asshole! Maintain with those fangs and tear his tendons into Cream of Meat! Oo! Oo!' Don't expect any gore. This film doesn't *need* it. You'll cheer both the humans as they try to survive and the doggies-cum-shrews as they try to eat the humans, and the shrew attack just doesn't stop, they just keep a-comin' all through the movie, and it's clear that the Killer Shrews are the stars. Period... Enjoy. [BJE]

KILLERS FROM SPACE

W. LEE WILDER 1954. Yep, it's another b/w crank 'em out from the '50s... A slightly post-pubescent Peter Graves stars as Dr. Doug Martin (the brother of Raymond Burr's Steve Martin, in **Godzilla**?), a test pilot who mysteriously survives an aircraft crash, arriving at the Air Force base a couple of days later with partial amnesia and surgical scars criss-crossing his chest. Is he a crazy impostor? A Russian spy? A starving actor? Or did he actually meet up with (drum roll, please) *killers from space!*... For the first half of its 71 minute running time, the movie rambles along as Mr. Mission Impossible runs from the police, has hypnotic visions of floating eyeballs, and overacts with a vengeance. But it reaches nutty nirvana when Peter's 'horrible secret' is revealed, and we learn that he has become a mesmerised messenger boy for alien invaders – a bunch of spacemen with Ping-Pong-ball eyes; baggy, black pyjamas; and mittens. You see, these no-good-nasties from Planet Cheapo rescued Peter from his crash, gave him a heart transplant,

and soldered shut his chest – the first step in a plan to migrate the population of their dying world to Earth (and they're supposed to be a more *intelligent* race?) Of course, only one man can stop these fiendish outerspace-niks – *if* Peter can get past their rear-screen-projected 'giant' insects, that is... Plenty of mismatched A-bomb stock footage, a cut-rate cast, Aurora kit miniatures, and the hokiest aliens this side of **Lost in Space** helps make **Killers from Space** continuously simply-minded fun – always laughable, rarely boring, and without a glimmer of intelligence in its B-movie brain. Directed by Billy Wilder's no-talent brother.

KING KONG ESCAPES

INOSHIRO HONDA 1968. A greedy caped weirdo named 'Doctor Who' (no relation to the hero of the popular British TV series) builds a giant King Kong robot which he plans to use to dig for radioactive ore in the Arctic. Unfortunately, all that glowing radiation fucks up Mechni-Kong's innards, so Doctor Weirdo decides to do the next best thing: kidnap the *real* King Kong, and make *him* do the work. But first, we get to see Kong toss around a rubber sea serpent and beat the fuck out of Borosaurus, a rather ordinary-looking dinosaur with no special qualities to speak of (compared to some of Toho's other bizarre creations), who would later appear in **Destroy All Monsters** and **Godzilla's Revenge**. Dr. Who gasses Kong into unconsciousness in the ape's jungle home, and takes him on a cruise back to the Arctic, where he implants a radio-control device on top of Kong's head and sets him to work a-digging for that ore. Mr. K does his best until the radiation starts making him doze off. (Make a note: radiation makes giant apes sleepy.) After a while he gets tired of hearing Who's voice in his head shouting, "Wake up! Dig! Dig!" so he plucks the controlling device off his head and flees into the ocean, with Mechni-Kong hot on his heels. Their long swim takes them to Japan, where the two-fisted titans beat the shit out of each other (and Japan, too, of course) in a battle which climaxes on the top of the Tokyo Tower. The Kong costume really sucks. Mechni-Kong is kinda neat, tho, and the fight scenes are good for some cynical laughs. Rhodes Reason is the macho American navy type. The late Paul Frees is the dubbed voice of Doctor Who. Mie Hama is Kong's insufferably cutesy human love interest. Directed by **Godzilla** veteran Inoshiro Honda. [BJE]

KING KONG LIVES

JOHN GUILLERMIN 1986. First off, I should tell you that I sorta enjoyed Dino's first **King Kong**. Sure, it was pretentious, overblown crap, but down-deep it was also a tried-and-true Giant Monster Movie! OF COURSE it wasn't as good as the original, but did anyone really expect it to be? As a schlock movie fanatic, all I hoped for was lots of large-scale, mindless destruction, and when Rick Baker strutted through downtown Manhattan in the last hour, it was great! But now onto its sequel... WOW! I certainly hope they weren't trying to be serious, cuz **King Kong Lives** is the dopiest major release of the year! It's hilarious, cheesy, idiotic, and I loved it for all those reasons. It's right up there with **Godzilla's Revenge**!... Ten years after

King Kong toppled from the World Trade Centre, he's still alive (albeit in a coma) at the Atlanta Institute. All he needs for a full recovery is a 400-gallon blood transfusion and an artificial heart, so they send an expedition into the jungles of Borneo and find 'Lady Kong' (you can tell it's a female because she has floppy breasts)... In the first film, it took an hour-and-a-half to capture the giant ape. This time it only takes five minutes (the Evelyn Wood School of Speed-Monkey-Catching?). Soon, with a Jarvik heart the size of a Buick, Mr. Kong is back to A-1 condition, and after crashing through some papier-mâché buildings, he carries off his new squeeze for a woodland tête-à-tête. Touching as fuck, eh?... The Army is ordered to shoot on sight (what else is new?), and the exciting finale has Mr. Kong punting tanks across Georgia while Ms. Kong is in labour. That's right, they're the proud parents of a 6-foot guy in a gorilla costume, and Kid Kong comes a close second (behind Godzilla's sorry-looking son, Minyah) in the Unnecessarily Cute Department. The tear-drenched finale will have you in stitches... Director John Guillermin (who was relegated to junk like **Sheena** after his '76 **Kong**) even tosses in some quick, but severe violence – at one point King Kong retaliates against a bunch of Southern dipshit hunters who torment him with torches, and he snaps one guy in half like a Twinkie and bites the other one off at the waist. Add to that a human love story, revenge, a crazed army officer, plus some cheap comedy, and you can see that this is a scattershot mess of a movie. It certainly moves at a breakneck pace though, piling one feather-brained situation on top of another... Linda Hamilton is the concerned woman-of-science and whitebread Brian Kerwin is the jungle explorer, while Peter Elliot and George Yiasomi stars as King and Queen Kong, respectively

(they even get top billing in the end credits!). As for the special effects, the miniatures are sparse but adequate, the matte work is cut-rate, the ape suits are a step down from the '76 version, and the guys stuck inside the suits do the best they can with dumb scenes that have the hairy pair pawing at each other after a night of amour... Overall, **King Kong Lives** is THE laugh-a-minute junk movie of the year – I don't know who DeLaurentis thought he was kidding. It's also as loopy and enjoyable as any Toho feature, except I wish the dialogue didn't match the actors' mouth movements so closely. It almost looked as if they were *actually speaking* the inane dialogue. Nah!

KINGS AND DESPERATE MEN

ALEXIS KANNER 1977. Well, it's about time! On the coat tails of **Talk Radio**'s critical success, this Canadian-lensed thriller has finally made it to the public eye, thanks to Magnum Video. What makes this film so damned special, you ask? It stars long-time fave Patrick McGoohan and the director/producer/co-writer (plus editor and photographer, under the pseudonym Henry Lucas) was Pat's old **Prisoner** pal, Alexis Kanner. Unfortunately, this item then sat on a shelf for 12 years, away from US screens because it was too warped and uncommercial... McGoohan stars as John Kingsley, a controversial Montreal radio talkshow host who is taken hostage in his high-rise studio on Xmas eve by a pair of novice terrorists (Alexis and Andrea Marcovicci), who wire the building with explosives and plan to go on the air live, in an attempt to get a local activist released from prison. But this isn't the beginning of some standard pot-boiler, because Kanner relies more on offbeat characterisations than simple plot grindings. The head kidnapper is a professor turned social revolutionary ("I'm tired of teaching history," says Kanner. "I'd prefer to shape some of it myself."), and once entrenched in the secured studio, Patrick and Alexis battle it out with various psychological armaments until you're not sure who's *really* in control. As the police surround the building with enough firepower to stop a small army, the broadcast becomes a public side-show, with McGoohan manipulating his nervous captor with his dry sly wit (while sucking down a bottle of gin) – listening to the rambling callers, conducting a mock-trial, forcing in commercial breaks against Kanner's orders, and even leaping on the creep, as this intricate, 'oh-so-perfect' plan slowly unravels before Alexis' bloodshot eyes... All of this will probably be too slow and diffuse for most viewers (you know, the stupid ones), but this is a *must see* for McGoohan-watchers and fans of Lobster Cinema. Kanner shoots his wad (directorially, that is) with the film taking eccentric side-steps around the city (peering in on the cops' plans and the listeners' reactions), and the various script complications take it miles from simple, straightforward narrative. The acting is on the money (with Margaret Trudeau making her cinema debut as Pat's wife) and there's some great psycho-chatter from Alexis' crew of cronies, but the film is at its best when the two leads are verbally duking it out. Kanner is edginess incarnate, while McGoohan is letter perfect as the dynamic Kingsley. It's a flashy, playful role and Pat wades into it with obvious relish... I admit the film's a little long-winded and annoyingly oblique at moments, but it's also *always* intriguing and often downright brilliant. Oh yeah, in case you were wondering about the title, it's taken from a poem by John Donne – 'Thou art slave to fate, chance, kings, and desperate men.'

THE KISS

PEN DENSHAM 1988. You might not guess from the innocuous title, but this flick has several nicely disgusting sequences going for it. But outside of *that* pale praise, it's routine raunch. One of those horror movies that rolls by painlessly enough for 90 minutes, but you barely remember it a half hour later... Amy (Meredith Salenger) is just your average, well-adjusted, pretty, popular, suburban teen (in other words, the typical movie fantasy figure), but her home life takes a trip to the toilet when Amy's exotic Aunt Felice (Joanna Pacula) comes to stay after the sudden (as in, not so accidental) death of her mother in an extremely gory car crash. And while her mom was excessively religious, Felice is her virtual antithesis – probably because 25 years earlier, little Felice was possessed by your standard 'Evil Presence' while vacationing in the Belgian Congo. Soon this sultry house guest is coming onto Amy's grief-stricken dad, and when Amy objects to their bed-bouncing, the death toll begins. Amy's best friend is injured in a bizarre mall accident (her face gets caught in an escalator – a concept good for a sick laugh); a Killer Kitty attacks her dad; and Amy starts hallucinating in the middle of Health class... Nothing particularly unique, but the flick looks slick and to make up for the script's occasional stupidity, director Pen Densham keeps the plot chugging along and every 10 minutes he tosses in a totally screwball set piece oozing with gore. In particular, the last half hour is a kick, with Amy on the run from a royally PO'ed Felice who tosses aside anyone who gets in her way: Boyfriends, priests, acting coaches, etc... Even a pair of scissors *through* her neck doesn't stop her ol' black magic. Award-winning effects-man Chris Walas gets the prize for the delightful finale, which owes more than a little to Cronenberg's **Shivers**, during which Felice tries to give Amy 'a kiss' (and that ain't Auntie's tongue, kids). *Why* is all this carnage happening? Don't ask me – I don't think the writer ever figured it out either... Ms. Salenger is an appealing young heroine (too bad she's stuck in muck like **Dream a Little Dream** with the Corey Dweebs nowadays) and Pacula manages to look sinister yet glamorous, even while wriggling naked on the floor in the midst of a voodoo ritual. Overall, an idiotic dose of trash that's slightly better than your average lame-brained slaughter-fest.

KISS MEETS THE PHANTOM OF THE PARK

GORDON HESSLER 1978. Sure, there are still some KISS fans. There must be, or that quartet of pretentious pus-suckers couldn't possibly still be churning out albums, right? (Hey! A dozen pigshit-brained KISS fans can't be wrong, right?) Anyway, the Hanna-Barbera people, fer fucking Christsakes, are responsible for this live-action snotwad initially made for NBC. But let's take a look at this mind-sucking, cancer-inducing celluloid rat crap, shall we?... KISS is scheduled to give a concert at this amusement park. Everybody's into it, see. The so-called 'KISS Army' of shit-puking fans is expected to be there. A female fan with a tear-soaked face manages to meet them face-to-face and implores them to help look for her missing brother. Swell guys that they are, they comply, and are thrust into a silly adventure in which Anthony Zerbe plays a scientist who makes evil robot doubles of the band in an attempt to incite the expected crowd of KISS-fuckers to extreme violence. After a really stupid battle with some Horror House 'prop' figures of Frankenstein, Dracula, etc, which turn out to be robots, we see KISS meet 'themselves'. The mechanical KISS is giving the concert ("Rip, rip! Rip and destroy!", they 'sing') which prompts the goddamn pig-buggering KISS fans to BOOO and start raising heck, until the real KISS shows up, flying through the air and leaping onto the stage to fight the evil automatons. Ace Frehley does somersaults and Gene Simmons breathes fire Godzilla-style and the mecha-band is destroyed and KISS gives the concert and everybody's happy... In one scene, the Gene Simmons robot smashes through a wall and beats up some cops. Cop-hater that I am, this is one time I'd have liked to see the cops win. KISS are *all* fucking *lousy* actors, even when playing themselves. Not at all surprising, eh? What a bunch of fart-breathing shitsacks. Some may consider this a really funny Badfilm, at least for the fact that you get to see KISS make fucking fools out of themselves on teevee. But if you hate KISS, you'll hate

Mad scientist strikes!
"KISS Meets the Phantom"

On the eve of a rock concert, KISS is kidnapped by an army of robots led by a vengeful scientist!

Anthony Zerbe and KISS

8PM TONIGHT!

FIRST MOVIE STARRING KISS!

4N

this TV movie with all your heart. And most KISS fans have grown up a wee bit since then, although there are still a few loyal shit-fuckers about... and most of them are into Twisted Sister and Bon Jovi now, so fuck them to death anyway. Damn it! *Damn* it! AVOID THIS MOVIE AT ALL COSTS, GOD-FUCKING *DAMMIT*!!!... Songs include 'Rock 'n' Roll All Night' and the pathetic 'Beth'... Y'know, when I was in tenth grade I went to see these assholes. I simply went because everybody I knew was going. They sucked. Their stage show, special effects-wise, was great, but then, other people pro-vided that for them, didn't they. Try to defend KISS to me and I'll kick your brainstem out. You may piss off now. Thank you. [BJE]

KRONOS

KURT NEUMANN 1957. Though it doesn't look like much at first glance, this is one of the oddest B-movies of the '50s... It all begins with mankind discovering it's up shit's creek (again), because Planetoid M-47 has swung out of its orbit and is heading straight toward (yep, you guessed it!) Earth! Luckily, a computer named Susie (it stands for SynchroUnifyingSinometricIntegratingEquitensor, if you even care) tracks its path of destruction and the Army sends out atomic missiles to destroy the pesky asteroid (which, amaz-ingly enough, looks just like a cheap spaceship), sending it crash-ing 'safely' into the ocean. But just when everybody thinks the Earth is safe – Oops! – out of the sea waddles a 100-ft robot who wants to absorb all the earth's energy and take it back to its home planet. And if that wasn't bad enough, it grows larger with each kilowatt and it's heading straight toward Los Angeles. The monster is strictly tinker-toy level SFX, but it's such a unique concept (when was the last time *you* saw a gigantic, shiny metal cube stomping across the Mexican countryside?) that it's all pretty cool to watch. There's also a sub-plot about an earth scientist who's possessed by the alien intelligence which is controlling Kronos... Starring the studio-bred Jeff Morrow. The director moves the action along at a

nice pace (next year Kurt Neumann would bring us **The Fly**), and even if it never gets really schlocky (or really good, either) it's still weird fun.

LADY FRANKENSTEIN

MEL WELLES 1972. New World had the nerve to distribute this turd from Corman acting-vet turned director Mel 'Mr. Mushnik' Welles. This Italian-lensed, umpteenth reworking of the Frankenstein tale begins with old Doc Frankenstein (Joseph Cotten) still buying up fresh corpses with an eye on unkicking the bucket. But now his comely daughter Tanya (?) has followed in her pop's footsteps by becoming a surgeon and assisting him in his basement body shop. "You can *not* use a damaged brain!", the Doc's colleague demands, but Cotten goes ahead with his operation, with the predictable results. Not only that, but when The Creature is struck by lightning during his re-animation, his face accidentally catches on fire (the sight of Cotten trying to extinguish the flaming head is worth a solid laugh) and leaves the big guy King of the Scar Tissue. At the midpoint, after the Doc's ugly, bald, one-eyed monster crushes Cotten's spine (thus allowing Joseph to make a bee-line for the nearest airport), the Teutonic Tanya usurps his lab. The flick's sleaze level peaks for a couple minutes when Ms. Franken-stein sets out to create her own perfect man, by stuffing the intelli-gent brain of her father's colleague into the skull of the handsome (but retarded) handyman. But first she has to kill the slow-witted servant by seducing him and then smothering him in mid-coitus. Meanwhile, her dad's patchwork project is staggering across the countryside – abducting a naked woman and tossing her in the river, interrupting a couple of rural fornicators and stomping a few grave diggers with his size-14 combat boots. Sounds entertaining? Sorry, it's all thoroughly dull and surprisingly *un*graphic. Even if you're a sucker for pasta-lensed peabrainers, you'll be snoozing... Sarah Bay is appealing in the title role (at least until she opens her mouth) and Mickey 'Mr. Jayne Mansfield' Hargitay shows off his earthshaking acting inability as the police captain, but the saddest thing is being on hand to watch this career nose-dive for Cotten. From **Citizen Kane** to this chunk of Euro-dung. From Orson Welles to Mel Welles... For all-out depravity (and fun), give me **Andy War-hol's Frankenstein** any day over this Mediterranean mindrot.

THE LAIR OF THE WHITE WORM

KEN RUSSELL 1988. After taking the relatively high road with whacked-out arthouse items like **Gothic**, **Salome** and his Puccini piece in **Aria**, director Ken Russell takes a spectacular leap back to his warped roots – combining the hallucinatory flavour of **Altered States**, the religious decadence of **The Devils** and the sexual delirium of **Crimes of Passion**, along with a tale so overblown it easily puts most Hammer Studio productions to shame. There's still a month left in the year, but I think I can safely say this is the funniest, most frenzied, over-the-edge horror film of 1988. Loosely adapted from Bram Stoker's novel, this production flows with ripe gore – hacked off limbs, severed torsos, skewered eyeballs. The modest budget occasionally shows in its blue-screen video hallucinations, but then again, it isn't everyday you get to see a crucified Christ getting chewed on by a giant albino serpent while naked nuns shriek from the sidelines... Peter Capaldi plays Angus Flint, a Scottish archaeologist who unearths the skull of some sort of giant snake-like creature from the front yard of sisters Sammi Davis and Catherine Oxenberg (whose parents mysteriously disappeared in the nearby woods). This discovery peaks the interest of handsome Lord D'Ampton (Hugh Grant) whose ancestor, according to local legend, once battled and beheaded a monstrous worm. Of course, let's not ignore their neighbour, Lady Sylvia Marsh, a seductive siren who secretly spends her off-hours as a murderous priestess for one of those pesky Ancient Pagan Serpent Cults. Amanda Donohoe (having survived Nic Roeg's **Castaway**) stars as the lustful lady – the type of woman who'll stop her Jaguar to rescue a naïve backpacking scout from the rain and take him back to her estate, where she treats him to drinks by the fireplace, a sponge bath and a fashion show of her black lingerie collection – before sprouting three-inch fangs and putting the bite on his lower extremities... The entire cast is terrific (as well as being unafraid of looking a bit silly in the pursuit of pure fun) and it's a spectacularly campy tale, with Russell at his most hysterical. By the time he gets to the dream sequence in which Donohoe and Oxenberg catfight in skimpy airline stewardess outfits, you *know* there's no stopping this maniac/genius. Before long, Donohoe is running about in the buff with blue bodypaint and an ornate, foot-long phallus strapped to her pelvis; Oxenberg is stripped to her undies while being dangled over a pit, playing unwilling sacrifice to a giant worm; Lord D'Ampton blasts snake-charming music from his rooftop while keeping sword in hand; and Angus comes to the rescue with kilt and bagpipes... It's warped all right, and you'll be laughing right along with Russell all the way. Hell, you can have a field day just trying to count all the snake references Ken layers into the script... Highly Recommended!

LAST HOUSE ON DEAD END STREET

VICTOR JANOS 1977. Director Victor Janos must be one sick fucker (or else he knows how to fake it *really* well) to pull off this rank scuzzshow. It's the type of flick that should be sold in a plain brown wrapper, and there's a genuinely grubby, demented personality about it. I can imagine a few diseased goremongers falling in love with its vile wiles, but personally, I wanted to take a shower afterward in a futile attempt to scrub the stench off of my brain. It's a nasty li'l bugger, with no budget, no stars and no class. But would you expect anything more from a film that revolves around the wonderful world of Snuff movie making?... 'Thump-thump, thump-thump,' goes the portentous music, and they don't waste any time in getting to the gut-ripping. Two minutes in, and they've already got a blood-soaked gal getting her innards externalised... Welcome to the domain of the porno entrepreneurs, who sit around watching 8mm peepshows and complaining that their product isn't 'different' enough. Well, along comes Steven Morrison as Terry Hawkins, a leather-boy ex-jailbird whose exceedingly realistic flicks are actually on-camera murders. He finds a partner who was once committed for sodomising a dead calf in a slaughterhouse, picks up a few desperate chicks who need a few bucks in order to eat, and together they provide the audience with a parade of bare breasts and corpses – with director Terry torturing and killing his actors, while his two female accomplices stand around in clear plastic Halloween masks. The end result is similar to the infamous **Bloodsucking Freaks**, but **Dead End** completely lacks the playfully Grand Guignol-style dementia which helped make **BF** a splatterati classic. Its vileness (not to mention its technical incompetence) overwhelms you after a while, and the last 30 minutes simply has the film crew slaughtering a bunch of 'colleagues' while the cameras roll. Tying up men and women, branding 'em, scalping off their faces, drilling out their eyes, and sawing off a leg or two (then they wake the victim up with smelling salts, so they can scream at the sight of their new stumps). But there's a moral to all this bloodshed (yeah right) – over the end credits we learn that these sickos were apprehended and given 999-year jail sentences... Most of the flick takes place in the basement of an old school, and it's a mushy-headed Grade-Z production through and through. Harsh, repellent and thoroughly unlikeable. It's effective in much the same way a large mallet to the temple is effective, but that doesn't mean it's any *fun* to sit through. Maybe that's what the filmmakers set out to accomplish. Well, they can *keep* the results... In the **Psychotronic Encyclopedia**, Michael Weldon writes, 'Have you ever heard anyone even admit that they saw it?' I wish I couldn't.

LAST HOUSE ON THE LEFT

WES CRAVEN 1972. 'It rests on 13 acres of earth over the very centre of Hell' –ad line. A *real* classic. And a vile one it is, too... Directed by first-timer Wes Craven and produced by Sean Cunningham (Mr. **Friday the 13th**); now that Wes is hotshit after **Nightmare on Elm St.**, you can see how grimy he can get when he sets his mind to it. 'Based on a true story', a pair of pretty teenagers, Mari and Phyllis, decide to go into town for a concert. But first, they try to score some grass, and fall prey to a quartet of wise-cracking geeks. City-cousins to the **Texas Chain Saw** Clan, they're heroin-addicted, child-molesting, nun-killing psychopaths who're wanted by every cop in the state. So, instead of an innocent night on the town, Mari and Phyllis get locked in the trunk of a car, taken out to the country, and are physically and mentally tortured by the shrieking sadists. They are forced to piss their pants, strip, beg, and finally, when they try to escape, they're carved up or blown away. But when the psychos' limo breaks down, they wind up at the doorstep of Mari's middle-class Mom and Pop, who end up taking revenge (shades of Wes' next feature, **The Hills Have Eyes**). Mom chews off one guy's dick during a blow job and spits it in the lake, while Dad takes on the leader with a chain saw in the living room... Though amateurish (lots of portentous music, and unnecessary comic relief from two bone-headed sheriffs), it's still *remarkably* unsettling, and considering it was made 15 years ago, it's still up to the rauchiness of today's slasher shows. But be warned: The versions now in release have varying levels of gore (I've been 'fortunate' enough to see the uncut edition, with the prolonged disembowelment scenes – You'll want to take a *long* shower after sitting through that one!)... When critics responded with the usual bile about excessive violence (surprisingly, Roger Ebert was one of the film's *supporters*), Wes explained that **Last House** was actually just a retelling of Bergman's **The Virgin Spring** (sure...).

THE LAST MAN ON EARTH

SIDNEY SALKOW 1964. Based on Richard Matheson's **I Am Legend** (which was also adapted into the pop-heroic **The Omega Man** with Chuck Heston), this Italian-lensed shocker gets points right off the bat for starring Vincent Price as a *hero* for once! In addition, it's a surprisingly morbid, ultra-nihilistic item that offers NO HOPE WHATSOEVER – and I love movies that go out of their way NOT to be a crowd-pleaser... The story begins very effectively, three years after mankind has been virtually wiped out, with Price wandering body-strewn sidewalks, alone (hence the title). He's a haggard, though quite resourceful, sole survivor of a plague that resembles vampirism, which means Vince has to contend with corpses rising from the dead in search of fresh blood. Not to mention the utter loneliness of his day-to-day existence. After dark, Price keeps the undead away from his home by nailing garlic strands to his front door. And by day, he scouts the desolate city with lathe-made stakes. It's not the greatest occupation, being a self-employed janitor of the undead, but at least it's a job – and Vince even gets to stake a dog! As usual, Price reaches the hammiest heights of angst, but in this case the rest of the Pastaland supporting cast is so lame that Vincent wins acting honours by default... The filmmaking is sometimes loose and crude, but the tale is helped immeasurably by the visuals. And what's amazing is how director Sidney (**Twice Told Tales**) Salkow's zombie attacks look *exactly* like George Romero's from **Night of the Living Dead**. The boarded-up windows, the clutching hands, et cetera. So similar, in fact, that you *know* Romero musta caught this flick beforehand... Too bad the movie turns soft after a while. For every cool bit (like the army burning corpses at The Pit, while loved ones wail), there's an idiotic plot twist (i.e. The explanation *why* Price is the only live one? A bat once bit him, fer Christ's sake! Hooey!) or a long sappy scene (the flashbacks to Vince's loving family and his toothless rugrat's birthday party). And I commend them for avoiding a pat, happy ending... Some thought-provoking ideas, several unsettling scenes, a little muddled, but well worth a look.

THE LAST MOVIE

DENNIS HOPPER 1970 (AKA: CHINCHERO). At long fucking last! A video release of Dennis Hopper's acclaimed mega-failure that had **Easy Rider** fans scratchin' their heads and tokin' up joints from coast to coast. In the wake of **Rider's** box-office coup every studio began courting the fermented filmmakers responsible for it. The results were decidedly mixed: Jack Nicholson took the dough and directed **Drive, He Said**, an exceptionally lensed glimpse of campus angst. Peter Fonda made a sentimental western entitled **The Hired Hand**. And The Hop was given carte blanche by the suckers at Universal, which he spent on flying a bunch of friends (Fonda, Dean Stockwell, Russ Tamblyn – all of whom only ended up with bits roles) and a film crew to Peru with enough coke to keep most small republics awake for a month. The cameras rolled, a script was occasionally consulted, everyone burnt out their nasal membranes, and from dozens of hours of raw footage Hopper stitched together this often fascinating, always frustrating journey into burn-out pretentiousness. The studio execs probably swallowed their cigars when they got a gander at this cosmic mess, and after dumping it into a few limited arthouse engagements, it was shelved and has been virtually unavailable until quite recently... You know you're in severe artsy-fartsy land when there are no beginning credits and the film's title doesn't even show up until 30 minutes into it. Oh, I'm sure Dennis *thought* he was creating an end-all epic, but he was also so dosed he probably couldn't count his own toes. The story is tentatively about an American film company who've flown to South America to make a Peckinpah-esque cowboy flick, with gnarly ol' Sam Fuller as The Director. There's an intercutting of fantasy and reality as we watch the standard Shoot 'Em Up and then pull back to see the movie crew at work. We also observe the natives' reactions to these crazy white men who are 'killing' each other, and realise that they completely miss the make-believe nature of filmmaking. Clean-shaven Dennis roams through the cultural head-on collision as a bloodshot-eyed bit player named Kansas, putting his experience in oaters such as **True Grit** and **The Sons of Katie Elder** to good use with competent horse riding and a disdain for Old West bullshit. Once the filmmakers desert the village, Hopper sticks around the place and watches with curiosity as the locals begin emulating the movie crew – running through the 'ritual' of filmmaking with bamboo cameras, and through it discovering the joys of true life violence. There's some heavy-handed themes about the exploitation and poisoning of primitive cultures by (so-called) civilisation, who think they can buy anything and intervene anywhere; but mostly it's just a grab bag of hastily basted scenes – some good, some dismal, most boring. Hopper plays an abusive ass, who slaps around his native squeeze, boffs the wife of an American Broom Baron, and checks out the local lesbian sex shows. Yet nothing in the entire pothead production compares to the annoyance of Kris Kristofferson's crooning! Give this man a tracheotomy, quick!... Not surprisingly, the film becomes progressively wilder (and better) as Dennis gets even *more* elliptical, self-reflexive and indulgent. The last half hour is so brain-fried that it soars – complete with Hopper paranoid and flipped-out, fearing the natives are gonna kill him because his character died in the fake movie. The only time the film comes together is when it's closest to falling apart... For more of Hopper's out-of-main-stream antics, dig up his third directorial effort, **Out of the Blue**, and see if you don't see shades of **Blue Velvet**.

BY NIGHT THEY LEAVE THEIR GRAVES

crawling, shambling thru empty streets whimpering, pleading begging for his blood!

VINCENT PRICE

The Last Man on Earth

LEGEND OF THE SEVEN GOLDEN VAMPIRES

ROY WARD BAKER 1973 (AKA: THE SEVEN BROTHERS MEET DRACULA). Looking for something a little different? How about some tacky entertainment with an international flair? Well, this British/Chinese co-production (between Hammer Studios and Run Run Shaw, would you believe?) should send you straight into psychotronic nirvana, especially if you like the idea of having your horror film fused with those *really* asinine martial arts flicks that come on the TV at 4 o'clock in the morning. Directed by Roy Ward Baker (**Quatermass and the Pit**) and starring Peter Cushing, it may have some high-class credentials behind it, but **Legend** turns out to be chock full of cheap thrills and weirdass laughs... The prologue takes us to a suspiciously-oriental looking Transylvania of 1804, where an old, travelling Chinaman (you see them all the time in Eastern Europe) stumbles upon Dracula's crypt. Awakening the dozin' Count (played by a lame two-by-four named John Forbes-Robinson, who looks like he'd be more at home in the touring company of **La Cage Aux Folles**), the old man's body is possessed by Drac, who decides to visit China for some rest and relaxation, and while there he might even resurrect the legendary Seven Golden Vampires from their graves and take over a province or two... Cut to 100 years later, when Prof. Van Helsing (Cushing, of course) happens to be in China, teaching vampire lore to the locals. And before he knows what's happening, the Prof. is waist-deep in all sorts of high-speed oriental kung-foolishness. There's young ladies strapped down next to vats of boiling liquid; decomposing vampires in flowing robes, fighting with swords; and hordes of bony-faced zombies rising out of the earth. At times it's as if **Infra-Man** were crossed with **Dawn of the Dead**... When Van Helsing learns that the tiny village of Ping Quay has been overrun by the Golden Vampires, he sets out to help them. But along the way he's ambushed continually by gangs of goons, until he's befriended by a warm-hearted family of deadly martial artists who vow to aid him in his quest. You can almost discard the plot though, cuz this film is primarily an excuse for a bombardment of bone-shattered, fun-filled kung fu combat and excessive violence in the form of impalings, dismemberings, slashings, gougings, burnings, or getting hoed to death by pissed-off peasants. And of course, since these are oriental bloodsuckers, instead of the cross, they fear the fat ol' figure of Buddha!... Cushing plays it all straight, though he tends to look a little confused at times, as if we were wondering 'What the fuck am I doing in the middle of all these angry li'l Chinamen?' The remaining occidental cast includes Julie Ege as a thrill-seeking Scandinavian widow and Robin Stewart as Van Helsing's twerpy son. The special effects look like the aftermath of too much Ex-Lax, there's plenty of local colour, and best of all, it features dozens of maniacal guys in cheap costumes hopping and kicking and stabbing and flipping and screaming and dying and turning into a skeleton when their heart is ripped out. It just doesn't let up, and I loved it! In comparison, the final, 'epic' confrontation between Drac and Van Helsing is pretty slow and limp, but I was so worn out by that time that it didn't matter... This is a wildly-entertaining chop-socky oddity!

LET IT ROCK

ROLAND KLICK 1981 (AKA: WHITE STAR). Yes, I've dug up yet another Dennis Hopper obscurity that's found a resting place on home video. This West German production from writer/producer/director Roland Klick was grabbed up by Concorde Pix, once again proving these guys will pass off any piece of mouldy shit as entertainment... Dennis stars as Kenneth Barlow, a rock 'n' roll manager who sees himself as the '80s answer to Brian Epstein, but who comes off more like a dirt-poor Malcolm McLaren. On this occasion, he's pushing a pre-packaged clown in an ice-cream-vendor

tux, named White Star. He signs this pop muzak Manilow-clone (played by Terrance 'I gave up my job at Burger King for *this?*' Robey) to open at a local punk club, and then stokes the fires further by getting his protruding-browed assistant, David Hess (**Last House on the Left**), to start a riot for the media value. While Barlow is busy using the gullible punkers and their hatred of White Star as free publicity, his new superstar is sprinting toward drug addiction (which leads to the only funny sequence, when White Star heaves a bottle full of warm urine at reporters). From unknown, to teen idol, to penniless wastoid in only two weeks - all without producing one fucking note of listenable music. This movie has as much to say about the real world of rock music as an episode of **Alvin and the Chipmunks** does... Dennis looks less like he's actually acting, then sweating his way through a dose of the DT's, and co-star Ramona Sweeney sings so badly you begin to think an off-camera technician is stuffing her leg into a food processor... Technically, a disjointed mess. This thing wasn't 'directed', it was sewn together from a basketful of incomplete takes, and they couldn't even afford enough film stock for establishing shots. These cheap bastards even had the nerve to steal a huge hunk of punk footage from Penelope Spheeris' **Suburbia** (without crediting the source, of course). Not only is it unrelentingly bad *and* boring (even at only 75 minutes, that Fast Forward button looked pretty compelling), it's downright offensive when Hopper starts evoking Lennon's assassination. Forget that The Hop is in it! This is a complete waste of your time! It even has an unjustifiably upbeat, moral ending - with White Bread, er, Star getting a real record contract, while Dennis lays in a gutter pouring a bottle of Redeye down his throat (a scene Dennis probably repeated in real life, the moment he got paid for being in this celluloid abortion).

LINK

RICHARD FRANKLIN 1986 (AKA: PSYCHO CHIMPS IN HEAT). For those who remember the halcyon (?) days of **Lancelot Link, Secret Chimp** and enjoy the antics of roller-skating, cigar-smoking primates, here's a new twist on an old tradition. Made in '86 and hardly released in theatres, **Link** is the tale of an odd professor who hires one of his students to caretake at his isolated English seacoast mansion. His estate is shared by his subjects in experimentation - three wacky chimps, Imp, Voodoo and big Link, the smartest and most deranged of the trio. It's sometimes hard to tell if Richard Franklin, who did a credible job on **Psycho II**, is going for chills or laughs, what with the silly music and close-ups of mugging chimps. I suspect he wasn't taking the endeavour too seriously. Terence Stamp (one of my favourite actors) plays the weird professor, and gets the chance to babble some choice lines about civilisation and evolution before he disappears. As the student caretaker who is suddenly the prey of Lance Link, Elizabeth Shue is certainly better at this sort of thing than that no-talent Langenkamp character. There is some fun camerawork (something akin to the Letterman 'monkey-cam') and a strange opening sequence, but the film runs way out of steam and just limps to the end. But if you want more from your simian entertainment than Roddy McDowell (or Paul Williams) could offer, **Link** is a mildly diverting vid-find. [TR]

THE LOVE-INS

ARTHUR DREIFUSS 1967. From the filmmakers who would later bring headlines to the silver screen in **Riot on Sunset Strip**, here's another OK, but firmly Establishment view of the turbulent late-'60s. Though willing to parade its paisley trappings past the camera, there's always a do-gooder moral on hand to water down the fun... When college students James MacArthur (**Hawaii 5-0**) and Susan Oliver are both expelled for printing an underground newspaper, Dr. Barnett (Richard Todd), a left-wing professor, quits in support of the students and becomes a media sensation for believ-

ing in the 'right to do anything that'll make you happy' and even advocating LSD use on television. As Barnett's fame grows, the Doc becomes a Timothy Leary clone, coining the slogan "Be More, Sense More, Love More", attending Be-Ins attired in a white robe and beads, and maliciously manipulating the youth movement for his own monetary gain. And the sledgehammer lesson for today, youngsters? Youthful liberals are naïve, and easily misled by a charismatic con man preaching what they want to hear. Luckily for us, the filmmakers were able to provide good atmosphere by simply taking their camera onto the street, with the background incidents providing more amusement than the propaganda-packed plot. There's a public park Love-In; overcrowded pads; psychedelic light shows; plus smoking banana peels to get high. The extras look perpetually stoned, and just so we don't miss *any* clichés, one acid 'addict' suddenly thinks he can fly and leaps out his window. Not surprisingly, the more asinine the complications, the better it gets. And the unforgettable high point occurs when Ms. Oliver takes a double dose of acid and hallucinates she's Alice in Wonderland. The lead singer grows rabbit ears. Strobe lights flicker. She eats a slab of the Sacred Mushroom. Finally the Lewis Carroll characters begin ripping off her clothes, and she ends up writhing on the floor in her lingerie, It's a sequence so mind-bogglingly demented that you momentarily forget the two-ton moralising about the perils of drugs. This dosed drama concludes when whitebread MacArthur gets riled over Oliver turning into a full-fledged cubehead and becoming the Doc's bedmate. Labelling Barnett a 'fake Messiah', he does a Lee Harvey Oswald number – overacting and proving he deserved a TV co-star like Jack Lord for 13 years. Though a little too artificial to ever approach the psychedelic standards of all-time classics like **The Trip** or **Psych-Out**, it's still a nostalgic voyage back to Haight Ashbury. Featuring a quick cameo by The Chocolate Watchband ['Are You Gonna Be There (At the Love-In)?'] and Mark (**Lost in Space**) Goddard as a guru flunky.

THE LOVED ONE

TONY RICHARDSON 1965. After walking away with an Academy Award for **Tom Jones**, director Tony Richardson decided *not* to play it safe (good for him!), by taking Evelyn Waugh's dark novel and creating a caustic, anything-goes look at California Crazies and the lucrative business of Death. The result isn't always on target, but it's laced with ruthless humour (courtesy of scripters Terry Southern and Christopher Isherwood) that remains potent a quarter century later... Robert Morse stars as a wide-eyed Brit who ventures to California and encounters every variety of stupid, vulgar, money-grubbing American – not to mention some ugly, snobbish Limeys too. The first half hour concentrates on ridiculing movie studio stupidity, when Morse links up with his Uncle (John Gielgud), who works for a Hollywood C-level film company (whose commissary menu boasts delicacies like 'Deep Dish Lolita'). But when Gielgud is unceremoniously sacked from his 31-year job and hangs himself from his swimming pool's diving board, the locale shifts (and the laughs etch themselves in acid) when Morse visits Whispering Glades, the ultimate in funeral fare, run by the Blessed Reverend (Jonathan Winters) – a pompous religious moneybags, whose character is frighteningly similar to today's slick, Biblesucking hucksters. There the grieving Morse is taken on a tour of a world devoted to Death (but only Caucasian, upscale corpses, of course), led by salesman Liberace (who already looks embalmed). And we're treated to sucker-punch sales pitches, underwater burials and assembly-line ceremonies. Then there's Mr. Joyboy (hilariously played by Rod Steiger), a prim, mother-fixated body-handler who moulds dead flesh like silly putty. And wait until you see his food obsessed Mom! So fat she can't get out of bed, this quadruplechin candidate is the most hideous 'human' being ever put on film, and when she tears apart a roast pig and slurps it up in close-up, it's the funniest (most disgusting) thing I've endured in months! You'll almost piss your pants from laughing so hard! Nothing is safe from this film's aim: Newspaper advice columns, deceased pets, and even the Space Race comes under fire. Meanwhile, Haskell Wexler's sweeping b/w photography locates tacky architecture which couldn't possibly be real – until you remind yourself that this is California, the Land of the Loonies... What a wonderful, screwed-up mess of a movie! Slightly over-artsy, a little emotionally distanced, but often offensively hilarious. Plus it overflows with thoroughly confused supporting talent, including Tab Hunter, James Coburn, Paul Williams (as a precocious 12-year-old), and best of all, Milton Berle with a dead dog on his breakfast table.

LSD: TRIP TO WHERE?

1968. As part of the 'Federal Follies #3' video-package, this 40 minute US Navy production spews out hot chunks of drug propaganda, and surprisingly enough, they also created a fairly-amusing (though unintentional) comedy. Sure, anyone with an IQ over the double-digits will see through this paranoid fantasy, but I can also imagine a bunch of 18-year-old enlistees sucking in everything this film says. It's sad to think that audiences would have been that stupid and/or pliable, but then again, it's even more disgusting nowadays knowing that Bill Cosby and Madonna are America's media idols, and that even people like Lou Reed are popping up on MTV's Rockers Against Drugs spots. Phooeey! But back at our film, let's see what happens when a couple of Navy Clean-cutters decide to trip their brains out – with the hilariously-stereotypical strobe-lights, coloured gels and prismatic lenses giving us a psychedelic-eye-view of their 'fun'. Of course, one of these Naval blockheads (John Beck, who would later grace movie-screens with mega-flops like **The Other Side of Midnight** and **Audrey Rose**) tries to leap out of the window and float up to the stars ("I'm one with the universe! I'm God and Jesus!"), and soon his friends have turned into Toho-style monsters, flames engulf him, and he sees himself as a woman in the mirror. After smoking some Acapulco Gold they score from Vic Tayback and his gangster cronies, these 'turned on' sailors end up 'blowing their minds' on the combo of pot and acid, and days later they're still seeing trails and running from LSD nightmares. Sure enough, when the swabbies return to their ship, they can no longer concentrate on their tedious jobs and it turns into 'Top Junkie', with Beck tripping his face off at the drop of a hat... There's static lectures from reliable-looking cops and doctors, about how only one hit of LSD can 'scramble someone's brain', cause changes in the chromosomes, and can lead to a bad-trip flashback for up to *18 months* afterward! The lesson to be learned is that if you decide to become a vegged-out dopehead, be prepared to (1) go directly to jail, (2) go directly to the mental hospital, or (3) ruin your usefulness as a member of the United States Navy (oh my god! not that!). This is essential viewing, with loads of clichéd dialogue and hippie dead-beats, though there still aren't as many cheap potshots as any single anti-chemical **Dragnet** episode... Also included on the video is **Your Job in Germany**, a post-W.W.II occupation featurette about the evil-hearted, nefarious nature of the German people. It's sort of amusing and *really* short.

LUNCHMEAT

KIRK ALEX 1988. This was the most encouraging thing in the video store, promising crazy pick axe killings and bodies chopped into 'huge chunks of blood drenched meat', though it's actually a pretty typical crazy-family-in-the-woods-kill-the-unsuspecting-stupid-teenage-yuppie-victims movie. Plot wise we meet the crazy family in the woods, who make their living selling hacked-up corpses to the local burger slime-pit ('World Famous Juicy Burgers')... Dad's so cheap he won't let his kids buy candy bars. No. 1 son Harley (the creep who wouldn't die) likes to continue hunting even after he's gotten stabbed in the heart. No. 2 son Elwood carries a pick axe and pisses himself while he watches the two cute girls in the bathroom. And No. 3 son Bennie ('Just like a mad dog with shit for brains') is barely more than a cannibalistic animal pet... Then we meet the stupid teenage yuppie victims (who certainly deserve to die horribly after the 3rd refrain of 'Row, Row, Row Your Boat'). Typical alligator shirt asshole, typical punk chick and two typical cute couples. They all fall for the ol' phoney detour in the road trick... The carnage starts up promisingly as Shit For Brains chews out one of the guy's intestines (through his throat) and The Creep Who Wouldn't Die decaps the punkette. But it slowly runs out of steam with long and longer shots of people running and screaming. To its credit, there's lots of pickaxed feet and machete killings (though the gore is pretty restrained for a film like this), pretty funny dialogue, and some clever details (one pickaxed kid screams with every step he takes; Dad gets the world's biggest blackhead; Yuppie vomits after each kill; Great decap by shovel). Director Kirk Alex (who wrote and financed this all by his little self) proves a competent horror man and though his first effort ends up as a typical story with typical characters, he shows much promise behind the camera. It's certainly better than being hit by an 18- wheeler. [SS]

MAD DOG

PHILIPPE MORA 1976 (AKA: MAD DOG MORGAN). This atmospheric murder and rampage romp features Dennis Hopper stumbling down yet another bleary-eyed path. Based on the true tale of 1860's Aussie bandit Daniel Morgan, it's initially pretty odd seeing Hopper in the outback setting, but to his credit, he rarely forgets his cheap Irish accent (even if his eyes don't exactly focus) and gives a fiery performance... We first encounter the quick-tempered Morgan as just another opium-toking miner in the uncivilised territories, but he quickly becomes the stuff of legends. After a six-year prison term highlighted by rape, brandings, and unflinching sadism, Morgan re-enters society more deranged and pissed-off than ever. And after learning Aboriginal survival techniques, the aptly-nicknamed 'Mad Dog' becomes a foul-mouthed 19th century Robin Hood, by ripping off the wealthy landowners and politicians, while getting cheers

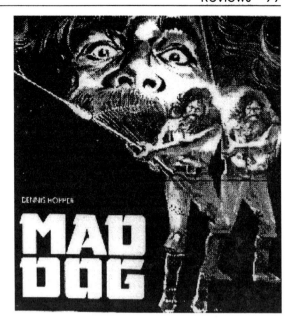

from the dirt-poor locals. Getting hairier and hairier as the years pass, he ends up with a full, shaggy, ludicrously fake beard which makes him look like some kind of Amish Acidhead. Hopper-o-philes will laugh themselves silly watching Dennis stagger across the countryside with the off-screen DT's but surprisingly, even though the character of Morgan is half-baked, Hopper manages to milk some raw sympathy for the whacko. Don't expect an 'up' film though. Not only does Morgan get slaughtered at the end, but a bullethead politician uses his scrotum for a tobacco pouch... Unfortunately, even though director Philippe Mora (long before nose-diving into dim-witted dreck like **The Beast Within** and **Howling II**) loves to wallow in the sleazier aspects of the legend – whether it's gratuitous bloodshed, or simply watching Dennis blow his nose sans handkerchief – the rest of the film just creeps along languidly, while relying too much on postcard-pretty photography or Hopper's ranting. There's a good tale to be spun about this 'Mad Dog', but this ain't it... Co-starring Jack Thompson and Gulpilil (who also wrote the flick's native songs).

MAJIN, THE MONSTER OF TERROR

KIMIYOSHI YASUDA 1966. A Japanese monster movie with an unusual twist: In 17th century Japan, a poor peasant village is hassled by an evil Feudal lord and his mercenaries who want all that neat land to themselves. They're willing to get it any way they can, even if they have to slaughter all those dirty little villagers. But Somebody Up There obviously likes dirty little villagers. Up in the mountains is a huge stone statue of Majin, one of them there 'god' fellers, which has sat for centuries, guarding the countryside. The villagers try to warn the invading horde that if they don't back off and leave them in peace, they'll pray *real hard* and Majin will strike them down. Ho ho, yeah right, say the invaders. So for the first three quarters of the movie, people talk, fight, talk, get killed, fight a little more and talk, and we are occasionally treated to a glimpse of the giant statue to remind us that we are, after all, supposed to be watching a monster movie here. Finally, the moment we've been waiting for arrives, and the villagers' prayers (not to mention the viewers') are answered. The statue's frowning face suddenly turns green, his eyes flip open, and MAJIN WALKS THE EARTH! AAAAH!! Stomp those puny little assholes with their teensy weapons (including catapults that toss flaming boulders off Majin's samurai-style body armour) into the ground! Yeah! This is a great scene! Even the soundtrack is purty. Too bad you've gotta sit through all that boring shit before it finally arrives; however, it gives you just enough time to drink a six-pack of Haffenreffer and smoke a few bowls to get you into the, er, proper state of consciousness when Majin starts punching mountains into rubble and generally carrying on in monsterly fashion... Sequels were **Return of Giant Majin** and **Majin Strikes Again!** [BJE]

THE MANHATTAN LOVE SUICIDES (1985)
YOU KILLED ME FIRST (1985)
SUBMIT TO ME (1986)
SUBMIT TO ME NOW (1987)

The first time I saw a Richard Kern film was at a club I manage while a band named LD50 provided their own soundtrack... Now I've seen four 'Deathtrip Films' and, while they started out with interesting concepts, good gore effects and sick-o humour, my enthusiasm waned with each passing frame. **The Manhattan Love Suicides** was actually a collection of four shorties (all in black & white without sync sound) and certainly the most entertaining of the lot – especially 'Stray Dogs', a touching story of a mild mannered artist who meets Mr. Twistyface on the street and takes him home (like a stray dog... get it?). Eventually Mr. Artist tires of it all and Mr. Twistyface gets so upset his arm falls off. Not to mention 'Thrust in Me', which asks the question 'what do you do when you arrive home from a walk and find your girlfriend has slit her wrists in the bathtub?' (why, you wipe your ass with a picture of Jesus and fuck her in the mouth till you come all over her face, of course!). But by the end of these, the punk posturing really started to get to me, especially when we launched into **You Killed Me First**, about your usual 'misunderstood punk' who wants to be accepted for what she is. Of course she won't accept anyone else for what they are, especially her family, whom she kills in the end. **Submit To Me** and **Submit To Me Now** continued the mild 'shock-o-rama' with unconnected images of sex, blood and death. Some good gore effects in these, especially this guy who slits his throat and pulls his oesophagus out through the wound (I wasn't much for the penis piercing scene, or the guy hanging by his dick, though). All in all, I found Kern's hip, self-serving tone very annoying. These films seem to be showing off just how 'cool' Mr. Kern is and nothing more. They are utterly humourless exercises in avant-garde posing. His films disturb, but do not entertain or enlighten. I really don't know what's become of Mr. Kern since these extravaganzas, and after viewing these endeavours, I really don't care. [SS]

MANIAC

DWAIN ESPER 1934. The insidious rumour that trashy, vile exploitation films first evolved in the '50s drive-in era is utter hogwash, because here's a prime example of early American celluloid sleaze from director Dwain Esper (**Marijuana, How to Undress in Front of Your Husband**). A Roadshow pic which *definitively* proves that unhealthy thoughts are the leading cause behind society's criminals and maniacs. Our morality piece begins with one of those mad scientists who's trying to bring back life from the dead (there's so many of them roaming about, they should start their own club, like The Masons). With the unwilling aid of his snivelling partner, Maxwell (Bill Woods), this Simon Bar Sinister-style psychodoc begins by stealing the corpse of a 21-year-old female suicide victim, but (as is always the case) he soon needs more and more cadavers to work upon. Poor Maxwell's mind eventually snaps under the mental strain (you can tell, because his hair is uncombed) and after experiencing some wild, double-exposure hallucinations borrowed from an expressionistic Scandinavian flick, Maxwell accidentally kills his mentor and disguises himself as the dead doc. Before long, Mad Max begins believing he's the ol' professor, and he starts treating mental patients. The demented

running the asylum, indeed (kinda like the last eight years in Washington, eh?)... Punctuating this base little tale are some wonderfully lurid moments. A human heart pumps away in a beaker! A patient thinks he's an orang-utan and goes on a search for young women! Maxwell pops out a cat's eyeball and eats it! Rotgut dialogue like "There's a fire in my brain!!" And let's not forget the ladies dancing about in their lingerie, with some quick cheesecake shots to keep the male portion of the crowd alert. But just so audiences don't forget they're watching an Educational Film (yeah right, and I've got a bridge in Brooklyn to sell you, too), we're given mini-descriptions of various psychoses, such as Dementia Praecox, Paresis, Paranoia, and Manic Depression – with this poor wretch hitting all the stops in a little over an hour. No wonder he tends to stare into the camera and babble to himself while symbolic, clutching hands are superimposed over his head... A technical nightmare, but it's loads of fun to see that this type of bullshit was even popular 50+ years ago. Pretty silly, but good for a few lewd laughs and its warped historical perspective

MANIAC COP

WILLIAM LUSTIG 1988. There are plenty of good credentials on this film. In addition to a solid cast of schlock veterans, it's written and produced by Larry Cohen, with direction by William Lustig (who's still trying to live down the response to his 1980 **Maniac** with Joe Spinell). And what a title! Short. Direct. To the point. Who could pass it up?... The powerhouse opening certainly gets the crowd ready for some nasty fun and serious plasma-spillage. Someone in a police officer's uniform is running up a sizeable body count on the streets of Manhattan. Though his face is always in shadow, we quickly get a feel for his modus operandi – he's a powerful bastard who enjoys snapping necks, slicing throats and blithely tossing innocent citizens through car windows. And for the first 20 minutes, we're treated to a rapid-fire succession of destruction, including a wet-concrete demise that had the Criterion roaring. But once the actual plot kicks in and we meet the stars, the fun peters out a bit, and we find ourselves trapped in your standard Slice 'n' Dicer. Personally, I could've watched an entire film simply focusing on the title character. He's a creepy fucker, and unlike the usual movieland mass murderers, all of his victims run TO him for help... But instead, it cuts to the familiar 'who's behind this carnage?' storyline. Is it a real cop gone nutzo? Is it some psycho dressed up as a cop? Or is it simply another super-human, Jason-like killer? Well, the one guy we're positive *isn't* to blame is innocent schmuck Bruce Campbell; so of course, Officer Bruce is promptly framed for the crimes. There's a good concept here, but the script just sits like a beached mackerel (the truth behind the Maniac Cop is particularly dimwitted and unbelievable), though Lustig pulls off some great setpieces – there's a bloody, prison shower brawl (complete with a Hitchcock eyeball-homage); a St. Patrick's Day police station massacre with a pile of flatfoot corpses; and I loved the sweet old lady who guns down an innocent patrolman because she's afraid he's the Maniac!... Laurene Landon and her out-of-control lipstick, costar as Campbell's main squeeze, with Tom Atkins (**Night of the Creeps**) receiving the award for Most Pummelled B-Actor of 1988. Exploitation fave William Smith (looking *really* old) is a cueball police lieutenant with a tracheotomy, and Richard Roundtree (with a middle-age paunch that's larger than his role) is the police chief. Plus, look for a quick Sam Raimi cameo, and though I didn't notice it during the film, the end credits list David Carradine as the *performer* of several songs. Makes the mind shudder, doesn't it?... Worst of all, the lame ending has sequel written all over it (like almost every new horror film nowadays), and it had the entire audience moaning at the cop-out. What next? 'Maniac Usher'? How about 'Maniac Refrigerator Repairman'? Until then, I'll settle for this slaphappy bit of bloodthirsty, if derivative, entertainment.

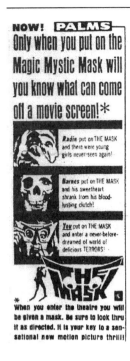

THE MASK

JULIAN ROFFMAN 1961 (AKA: EYES OF HELL). This is one of the all-time great gimmick films, with 3-D sequences that'll take the viewer on a journey into the Bizarre, Supernatural and Hilariously Silly. Just follow the instructions at the beginning of the flick, during which a professorly gent explains the sinister power of the movie's ancient mosaic mask, and tells us to put on our cheesy 3-D specs every time the starring clod straps on The Mask and enters the world of the damned (no, not New Jersey). Only a trio of scenes are in 3-D, most of the film is in 2-D, and *all* of the acting is barely 1-D. Nevertheless, when it works, it *really* works!... Sceptical psychiatrist Paul Stevens gets a visit from a demented patient who's been murdering people in his sleep, and blames his nightly homicides on a mask he 'borrowed' from an archaeological dig. Even more terrifying, this mask seems to make the wearer kill *and* overact at the same time! So, of course this dopey Doc has to try on the mask for himself – a decision which might be bad for him, but it's good for the audience. Because we can forget the predictable build-up and flat dialogue, and get to the meat of the matter: Putting on our cardboard 3-D glasses and checking out some great, goofy hallucinogenic horrors! What's locked behind the hidden subconscious recesses of Stevens' mind? In this case, an acidhead spookshow featuring alters, slashed throats, skulls with snaky eye sockets, misty corridors, spectres getting their eyes plucked out, disembodied hands, empty graves erupting with flame, and scads of mind-singeing surrealism. A nice mix of the horrific and hokey, but all too soon it's over and we have to return to the Doc, who's instantly addicted to the mask and flips out. And with all his baser emotions unleashed, his blond secretary looks all the more inviting (not to mention, strangleable)... The script is just a creaky 'Man-of-Science-Experimenting-With-the-Unknown' cliché, garnished with an overwrought, anti-drug metaphor. And Paul Stevens has all the natural charisma of smoked tongue. But the trio of 3-D scenes are truly spectacular, boasting the most effective use of those eye-abusive glasses ever. Kudos to Slavko Vorkapich, who designed their look; plus the cinematographer, who gives the entire tale an unsettling quality. Best seen on the big screen.

MATANGO, THE FUNGUS OF TERROR

INOSHIRO HONDA 1963 (AKA: ATTACK OF THE MUSHROOM PEOPLE). Now sit right back and you'll hear a tale, a tale of – JAPANESE HALLUCINATORY HELL! Yes, it's Toho mastermind Inoshiro Honda's most, uh, *interesting* fantasy. In Tokyo, a patient at a mental hospital tempts the doctors to listen to his story, and in a flash(back), we're on a boat filled with fun-loving vacationers! But before you know it, the ship is in the grip of a violent storm which leaves them adrift and lost, when what should appear on the horizon? 'Shroom Island! There they meet island representative Ken Kesey and – oh, sorry, soon they're scouring the area for eats, and come across an abandoned ship. After they scavenge all the canned goods, however, they are desperate. Bring on the indigenous plant life! The first member of the shipwrecked party to give in and dose

overdoes it a little (he picks up a gun and yells "I'll kill you all!"). But after a while, most of the group are royally tripped (the unbelievable trip sequence equates consciousness expansion with a swingin' night in Tokyo!). Hey, but the pleasure has a price. Everyone who dosed starts turning into (gulp) giant mushrooms! The crew of that abandoned ship are already lumbering around the isle, as hopelessly deformed fungi-folk. Needless to say, the one guy who refrained from fun stuff (or did he?) is now the hospitalised whacko. From the mind-roasting dialogue to the hilarious rubber 'shroom dudes, it all says 'must-see' for any fans of trip cinema, and the Toho coalition shan't be disappointed either. [TR]

MEAN JOHNNY BARROWS

FRED WILLIAMSON 1977. Not only does Fred 'The Hammer' Williamson star in this flick, but he directs it, too! And what a cast of outta-work whiteys he pulled together for this one! Roddy Dowall, Elliott Gould, Stuart Whitman, and Mr. Whitetrash himself, R.G. Armstrong! It all looked like grade-A excitement in my book... Unfortunately, the film's more like a grade-B snooze-a-rama. The Fred Williamson Fan Club (all 3 of them in Detroit) will get a couple laughs watching FW strut his tired bones, but most everyone else will need electro-shock to stay awake... After he's kicked out of the service for decking a racist officer, silver-star-winner Johnny Barrows (Freddy-Baby) returns to Urban Cesspool USA, where he's beaten up by street thugs, harassed by the fuzz, and ends up broke and hungry until he lands a job cleaning toilets and pushin' a mop in a gas station. Fred gives himself a chance to emote this time around, trying to prove he's another Robert DeNiro (but he comes off more like Robert Reed), and he steers away from the dependable kick-the-living-shit-outta-*everyone* route he followed in **Three the Hard Way**. Instead of breaking into mindless action he decides to establish a hackneyed plot involving opposing Mafia chieftains trying to coerce Fred into joining their sides of the battle. And *finally*, in the last 15 minutes, Fred pops the movie into 3rd gear when he joins up with The Nice Mobsters and becomes the killing machine we all know and love, complete with a mean set of vanilla threads and a pair of double-barrelled shotguns. But don't get your hopes up, because what follows are some of the lamest fight scenes I've had to sit through – I have to admit, I *did* laff a lot, though. As for the supporting cast, Roddy McDowall makes the most out of his role as a Mafia Don's faggot son who runs dope out of a flower shop (Little Shop of Heroin?), and 'special guest star' Elliott Gould has an earth-shaking *two*-minute walk-on (it's almost as if Gould wandered onto the set one afternoon and the scriptwriter tossed together a one-page scene for him)... At the end we get the credit 'Dedicated to the veteran who traded his place on the front line for a place in the unemployment line.' A nice sentiment, but it's still a wimpy li'l movie that doesn't deserve the word 'mean' in the title ('Bland Johnny Barrows'? Nah!). Not bad, mind you. Just kinda tedious, especially if you're searching for hard-hitting blaxploitation.

MESA OF LOST WOMEN

HERBERT TEVOS 1952. This south-of-the-border bozo-fest is good for more laughs than most recent comedies. It's dumb, and hilarious!... Under fake, shaggy eyebrows and glued-on goatee, Jackie Coogan stars as Dr. Aranya, a 'brilliant madman' who's doing endocrine experiments inside a hollow mesa in the middle of the Mexican desert. His surgical techniques are abnormal, to say the least – transplanting the pituitary glands of giant telepathic tarantulas (you can hardly see the ropes which move its legs) into human subjects, turning women into sultry, nearly-indestructible killers and men into dwarf servants. But when noted organ-o-therapist, Doc Masterson comes to visit, he's driven insane by Coogan and his motley hordes – and ends up a babbling madman with an itchy trigger finger. Masterson escapes from Dr. Aranya and his loony lab assistants, guns dawn a 'sexy' insect woman doing a risqué impressionistic dance in a local bar, and hijacks a small plane of B-movie stereotypes. There's an incredibly rich, snivelling coward; his fiancé, a young, pretty gold digger (played by a decidedly middle-aged floozy); the tough, macho pilot with a heart of gold and a head of granite; and the always-inscrutable Chinese butler. As bad luck would have it, the plane happens to crash back at Coogan's mesa of madness, with Masterson rambling incoherently on a steady diet of well-chewed scenery. A stupid love interest is tossed in ("I want a girl who's sincere," whines the pilot), with horrible acoustic guitar strumming in the background. Great dime-store sets and unending nonsense make this a *classic* bad movie, where you end up laughing at how low a bunch of actors can stoop to pay the rent. It's not up to the Ed Wood Jr. calibre of Pure Crapiness, but it comes mighty close.

MESSAGE FROM SPACE

KINJI FUKASAKU 1978 (AKA: UCHU KARA NO MESSEJI). I was looking forward to this film. Sure, all the big-time snob-critics trashed it mercilessly when it was first released, but what the hell do those pea-brains know about Japanese fantasy? They've been dumping on the Godzilla series for years and I love 'em all, nevertheless (OK, maybe I don't *love* **Godzilla's Revenge**. So sue me.)... After sitting through Toei Studio's **Message from Space**, though, I've gotta admit that it pretty much sucks. It's colourful as heck, but so's ralfing up a pitcher of sangria. Even the typically-lousy dubbing is a little more bland and pathetic than usual. Besides that, the action moves at a tortoise pace. The story is your basic **Seven Samurai/Magnificent Seven** round-up, and there isn't a giant monster in sight to stomp on the cast and wake up the audience... Sonny Chiba, who used to snap ribcages in the X-rated (for violence) **The Streetfighter** and **Return of the Streetfighter** stars in an atypically lethargic lead role and Vic Morrow wins the Nick Adams Memorial Down-On-His-Luck-American-Stuck-In-A-Japanese-B-Movie Award... The planet Jillusia has been conquered by the ruthless steel-skinned Gavanas, despite resistance from their leader Kido and his tribes. Going for help in an intergalactic Spanish galleon, Kido releases eight flying Liabe Seeds (they look like radioactive walnuts) into space to search for eight warriors to save their race and battle the evil Emperor Rockseia. (Are you getting all this?) But instead, they only locate a six-pack of wacky oriental nobodies, one American soldier of fortune, and a cutesy robot that nearly rivals the mechanical haemorrhoids of **Buck Rogers** and **The Black Hole**. And pretty soon it's 'Orientals in Space' complete with **Star Wars**-style (but not quality) special effects, gaudy costumes, papier-mâché sets, and generally atrocious goings-on. Usually all this stands for good, slimy entertainment in my book, but not this time around. *Occasionally* it brings to mind **Infra-Man** (like when they visit the Emperor's ship and meet up with an army of Kabuki-age silver-plated spacenauts in a room that would put FAO Schwartz' Xmas showroom to shame), but most of the time the film just drags along, with pompous narration leading us by the nose. Despite dozens of extras in plastic armour who perpetually *look* like they're ready for battle, the only halfway decent sequence is when the Gavanas blow up the Earth's moon with a dime-store rocket – and of course General Garuda (Morrow) gets tough in a five minute finale that amounts to a hodgepodge of noisy laser pistols and flailing arms and legs. Too little too late... Non-directed by Kinji Fukasaku (**The Green Slime**, **Black Lizard**).

MESSIAH OF EVIL

WILLARD HUYCK 1975. Here's a flick to avoid, unless (1) you're desperate for lousy entertainment one evening, or (2) you have a brain the size of a cue ball. But what else could you expect from director/co-writer Willard Huyck and his scripting partner Gloria Katz –

the same cretin couple who gave us three of the messiest celluloid bowel movements in past years: **Lucky Lady**, **Best Defence** and **Howard: A New Breed of Hero**. Despite a lively supporting cast of familiar faces, it still falls limp and flaccid in the Thrills and Chills Dept... It all begins with a typical night of murder and mayhem at the little California seacoast village of Port Duke. Corpses are stashed in the back of pickup trucks, half-eaten bodies turn up in the centre of town, portentous music oozes from the shadows, and a young woman (Marianna Hill) enters the village to search for her missing father. But first she has to deal with the cross-eyed loony who likes to bite the heads off rats. As the local legend has it, 100 years ago the moon turned red and all the friendly townspeople suddenly turned into bloodthirsty zombies – and now, when the cinematographer puts a red filter over the full moon, they all go crazy once again and start chewing up the fresh meat counter of the local supermarket. The plot boils down to Ms. Hill and this white-disco-suited-clown-she-picks-up trying to escape while anyone around them turns into a Raw Meat Maniac. The final explanation for this phenomenon is so ludicrous and half-baked that it makes Romero's radiation-from-a-comet throwaway seem like genius, but the BIG problem is that the pacing is so self-consciously tedious that you'll be wishing *someone*, ANYONE will get torn apart. Sure, a couple of people eventually die amidst a flurry of terrible makeup, but most of the pay-offs are strictly tame and tired. Basically, it's an American distillation of your typical, lousy Euro-horror flick – stiff acting, assembly line plot, and plenty of arty compositions and red gels. Co-starring Elisha Cook Jr. (who's the high point, as a babbling wino) and Royal Dano's voice, with Joy Bang and Anitra Ford posing through their mercifully short roles... So without delivering gore, violence, sex, nudity, grisly humour, or one iota of originality, what's there to recommend about this movie? Hmmm. Nothing, I guess. It's dullsville.

MIDNIGHT

JOHN RUSSO 1980. **Night of the Living Dead** co-author John Russo returned to movie sleaze-screens with this horror cheapie which he directed, based on his own novel. It's fairly routine stuff, but it's not too painful to sit through, either (any film that opens with a pretty teenage girl caught in a bear trap and beaten with an axe handle can't be *all* bad)... After getting nearly-molested by her lard-assed stepfather, Nancy hits the road, hitching her way to California. She's picked up by two likeable college-age shoplifters, but to their general dismay, this sitcom-trio ends up trespassing on private property owned by a Satan-worshipping family of rednecks. The pace picks up substantially at this point, and the tale takes a few interesting turns along the way. There's a pair of sadistic policemen who slaughter everyone in sight; imprisonment and torture while locked in dog cage; plus a little anti-Catholic rhetoric tossed in. Basically, though, this is just another Death Farm flick complete with a knife-wielding K-Mart-version of the **Chain Saw** clan. There's an attempt made to flesh out the characters, but it's only a couple notches above the **Friday the 13th** School of One-Dimensional Victims. Of course, the cast's monotone-delivery and general lack of talent don't help matters either. There's some crude splatter effects by Tom Savini, but it's never as bloodthirsty as it has every right to be, and director Russo doesn't have much filmmaking style to fall back on. Overall, it's an average chop-'em-up with a bit of grim humour, but you'll fall out of your chair laughing at the 'Midnight Theme Song' by a Christie Minstrel Singers copy band ("You're on your own/You're all alone/You can't go home anymore/and Midnight's at your door." Blah!).

THE MILPITAS MONSTER

ROBERT L. BURRILL 1976. It's amateur night in video-land, kids! With a $65,000 budget, high school teacher-turned-director/producer, Robert L. Burrill, decided to make a giant-monster movie set in his small town of Milpitas, California. And it looks like everyone in the whole damned town had a part in the making... Well, I guess early on the filmmakers realised they didn't have much money (or even talent) to make a good film, so instead they made a funny film. The result: The sound is muddy, the photography washed out, the acting as fine as any Driver's Ed film, and it's played with frightening mock-seriousness (as if the townsfolk who appeared in it didn't get the joke), but nevertheless it's eminently likeable as a so-bad-it's-sorta-OK lampoon of the rampaging-creature features of the past. Hey, it even has narration by Paul Frees! (Plus, it's a zillion times more entertaining than **Ganjasaurus Rex**, which tried the same thing and shat blood.) The town's overflowing city dump is the breeding ground for the title character – a giant, winged whatzit that lives in the depths of the sludge. He's a nickel-and-dime cross between Megalon and Mothra, but with glowing eyes and a gas mask-like face which spews foul-smelling gas. He spends his after-dark hours stomping around suburban neighbourhoods, eating people's garbage and leaving huge footprints in his wake... Of course, none of the citizens ever look out their windows and see this monster, even though he's five times larger than the tallest building in town. For a while, the flick just lays there like cold linguini, as all the tedious characters are paraded before us (the amusing town drunk; a carload of loveable juvenile delinquents; plus lots of tweedy politicians who wring their hands and play stupid, as if they've been doing it throughout their careers). But when that silly-suited title character starts attacking, the film starts getting severely loopy. All the townspeople band together and demand the return of their missing garbage cans, while the creature hijacks a pretty young miss from a high school dance and climbs to the top of a TV tower with Fay Wray Jr. in its clutches... Phew! Sounds resoundingly stupid, eh? Well, it is. Especially when you see the ridiculously-amateurish special effects – shots don't match, the moments of stop-action animation are stiffer than Lucille Ball's face, and up-close the costume looks amazingly like fur-trimmed flannel pyjamas. Plus, it's got the rubberiest giant hand since Allison Hayes grew to 50-feet. Dumb, dumb, and *more* dumb. Don't get me wrong though, I almost-nearly-kinda enjoyed a fair share of it. Just be warned, it's virtually unwatchable unless you're either a fan of monster-rampage movies or a connoisseur of Bad Cinema (luckily, I'm both).

MONDO LUGOSI: A VAMPIRE'S SCRAPBOOK

1987. An hour Long compilation from Rhino Video focusing on Bela Lugosi, this package moves from the highs, to the lows, to the scum at the bottom of the needle. A scattershot look at Lugosi's career, this video could have gone for the cheap shots and followed Bela's final decade of wretched nonsense, but instead Rhino gives us an even-handed profile of every aspect of The Count's career. A good percentage of the tape is original coming attractions from his Universal Studios days – **The Invisible Ray**, **Ghost of Frankenstein**, **Frankenstein Meets the Wolfman**, etc. – and they're fun to watch, if not particularly overwhelming. Horror completists will want to catch the cornball interviews too, as the Hungarian Ham camps it up for the cameras. The weirdest sections (as well as my faves) are a 'Hollywood on Parade' fantasy-tour of the Hollywood Wax Museum, featuring a live-action, grossly-overweight Betty Boop being stalked by Drac/Bela – "You've booped your last boop, Betty") and his mid-'50s appearance on **You Asked For It**, doing a particularly pathetic hypnotism/magic routine complete with a rubber bat bobbing on a rope. But just

when you think the producers are trying to remain tasteful, they wind up the tape with a short Ed Wood Jr. creation – five minutes of women suggestively gyrating on a sofa while Lugosi looks on from a nearby easy chair... Though it's a little dry in spots, it's still an interesting curio.

MONDO NEW YORK

HARVEY KEITH 1988. Remember those old flicks like **Mondo Cane**, **Ecco** and **Jabberwalk**? So-called documentaries which wallowed in sleazoid voyeurism and strange customs? Well, filmmaker Harvey Keith tries to update the 'mondo' genre in this mix of new fashioned shock footage and trendy urban performance artistes. It's an unsettling blend, like vodka and Yoohoo. For 80 minutes we're treated to weirdoes in every shape and size, and this SoHo-based film is a bumpy ride though the underbelly of crackpot culture, with antisocial behaviour and bald-faced pretentiousness posing as High Art. So take a grand tour through the depths of New York City ("the clitoris of the world") with a silent blond cutie as your guide. Past orifice-obsessed street corner poets, naked overwrought women in body paint, and leather bondage shows that make the on-stage antics in **Café Flesh** look tame. In other words, Insanity that's only acceptable in the Big Rotten Apple... There's platinum blond bimbo Phoebe Legere in fishnets, badly lip-synching a tune called 'Marilyn Monroe' while she masturbates on the stage with an electric guitar; Professor Mombuzu (aka Joe Coleman), who bites the heads off live mice before igniting the explosives hidden in his shirt; comic burn-out Charlie Barnett doped-up and raving to a Washington Square crowd; and Karen Finley in concert, wiping down her naked body with raw eggs and using a stuffed bunny as a brush (what, no yams?). A decidedly mixed bag, indeed. The tone changes in the second half when the mondo elements shift into high gear, moving from the Lower Manhattan bad craziness to simple docu-depravity (i.e. Puerto Rican cockfight parlours, Wo-Hop's female flesh auction, and Haitian voodoo rituals involving live chicken chomping)... All of this would've been much more effective if tighter edited (or possibly edited at all). It seems slapped together, with no attempt to delve beneath the surface smegma. Is it Art? A simple freakshow? Or just a pack of self-obsessed artfarts creatively masturbating themselves into a lather? You'll never find out from this fly-by-night film, but it's still good for several twisted laughs... Music includes a Lex Luther-clone in drag singing a li'l ditty entitled 'Fuck You', and John Sex warbling the touching ballad 'Hustle With My Muscle'. Your move.

MONSTER A GO-GO

BILL REBANE / SHELDON SEYMOUR 1965. Le Bad Cinema (V.C.I.) presents one of H.G. Lewis' worst and weirdest out-puts, and even though

Lewis only filmed about one-third of it, even *he* hid under the pseudonym of Sheldon Seymour. It all started as a Bill Rebane (the lunkhead behind **The Giant Spider Invasion**) project with the snappy title, **Terror at Halfday** (yawn!). But when it stalled out in mid-production, HGL got his grubby paws on the film stock and decided to add some of his own insert shots and eventually lashed this sucker together into the now-notorious **Monster A Go-Go**! Unsurprisingly enough, it turned out to be one of the most alternately tedious and ludicrous features ever made. Most of it is absolutely stultifying in its lack of action, and the quickest description of the plot is to imagine **First Man into Space** if it *REALLY* stank, like a bucket of raw sewage left outside to cook in the sun for a couple hours. I have to admit, though, that I've sat through it twice so far and the *few* laughably-bad portions hold up as well as any Ed Wood Jr. epic. (Just to give you an idea of how pathetic it can get, when a phone is supposed to ring, someone off-camera has to make the ringing sound. Yikes!) But even at only 70 minutes, at times it feels like the 'Berlin Alexanderplatz' of schlockola, so don't say I didn't warn you!... Story wise, a manned space ship drops outta the sky and crashes in a deserted field. But when the Army investigates, all they find is an empty capsule and a dead bystander. Now first off, you have to accept the fact that this capsule is only six-feet-high by two-feet wide (probably because they couldn't afford anything larger than a refrigerator box). After *lots* of official head-scratching from starched-hair Army officers waddling around a barren set, they finally determine there's a monster on the loose! (No shit. Obviously these guys have IQ's that would rival most bowls of lime Jell-O.) It turns out that their missing astronaut has contracted a strange form of radiation poisoning that's changed him into a 10-foot-tall homicidal-spaceman with mozzarella cheese pasted on his cheeks. He's to blame for killing off the cast, and even though *you'll* feel like pinning a medal on The Big Guy for knocking off these cretins and doing the movie world a favour, he's nevertheless tracked down like a fugitive. Of course, there's a 'big-budget' climax between the military and the monster (they could actually afford a couple trucks for *this* scene), but for the audience's benefit, the finale should've been preceded by a No-Doz Alert... Henry Hite, the alleged 'tallest man in the world' plays the title character, but he's only on-screen for about three minutes – scaring a few bikinied babes and giving off coffin-loads of deadly radiation; and when the proceedings slow down, HGL throws in some pretentious narration or intercuts a go-go party with hi-permed debs twisting their pelvis muscles in a knot. If you thought the music for **Eegah!** was a hoot, wait until you hear how this flick ravages your eardrums!... No matter how much fun a movie with a title like **Monster A Go-Go** would *seem* to be, it's still a major let-down. Dull and cheap, though not as painful as shitting broken glass.

THE MONSTER SQUAD

Fred Dekker 1987. I have to admit that this is much better than I thought it would be. I kind of expected some cuteshit nonsense like **The Goonies** crossed with **Ghostbusters**, and discover instead that **The Monster Squad** is a genuinely *fun* movie that ought to please any monster fan. Here we have Dracula, the Wolfman, the Mummy, the Creature, and the Frankenstein Monster running amuck in modern-day America, searching for a magic amulet that will enable them to destroy mankind and usher in a new age of monsters. And who comes to the rescue? A bunch of snot-nosed brats who have stumbled across the diary of Dracula's old enemy, Dr. Van Helsing, which contains instructions on how to go about killing monsters. There are moments when I'd like to piss on the child actors' heads, but sometimes I can kind of relate to these junior monster-slayers; I mean, I was a monster freak when *I* was in grammar school, much to the dismay of my mom, my grandpar-

ents, and the bitch nuns at school, and at the risk of constant ridicule from my ignorant schoolmates. Oh, how I wished in my adolescent heart that I could slay a couple monsters and *show 'em all*. I was a little nerd (now I'm a big nerd) and I often sought escape from the bullshit that surrounded me while growing up on Syracuse's Waste-Side, in science fiction novels and 'Monster Movie Matinee' and my copies of **Famous Monsters**. This movie seems to have been aimed by director Fred Dekker (**Night of the Creeps**) at kids who suffer the same kind of bullshit that I (and some of you readers) had to put up with from not-so-bright parents and idiot classmates who didn't have intelligence enough to understand... There isn't any real body-count in **Monster Squad**, though there are some close calls that you know our young heroes are gonna get out of anyway. My fear that the monsters would end up as corny caricatures of their counterparts from the old Universal pictures was quickly abated; The makeup and costumes are fine and the action is fun, and even the script isn't as bad as you'd probably expect after seeing most kids-vs.-monsters flicks. I do have a few beefs about **Monster Squad**... Occasionally we have to put up with a few annoying kids-being-kids scenes (although they're a little more true-to-life than any kids you're likely to see on **The Brady Bunch** or **Family Ties**); the Frankenstein Monster, in a scene clearly inspired by the original Karloff **Frankenstein**, approaches a little girl who's picking some flowers, but instead of throwing her in the lake, which Karloff did in a scene missing from most prints of **Frankenstein**, he *befriends* her and becomes one of the *good* guys (These scenes may annoy die-hard Frankenstein fans as much as many Godzilla fans may have been distressed by the Big G.'s transformation from a villainous monster to a hero in **Ghidrah, The Three-Headed Monster**); and the humanoid-reptilian Creature, my favourite monster in the film, not only doesn't appear on screen very often, but when he starts going into action, he is killed by a fat kid with a shotgun. Most disappointing. But all-in-all, **The Monster Squad** is indeed a film that I would recommend to any 10-year-old monster movie fan, and it's also a fun warm-up for an evening of getting stoned and drunk for an evening of Slimetiming with a VCR and a group of fellow monsterholics. And, hell, it's better than **Smurfs** or **Duck Tales** or most of the other SHIT that kids are expected to watch on the 'television'. Hell, I liked it. What can I say. [BJE]

MONSTER ZERO

Inoshiro Honda 1966. The late Nick Adams is the American in this instalment of the Godzilla saga, as he plays an astronaut who travels via rocket with a Japanese partner to the mysterious Planet X (the ol' newly-discovered-planet-on-the-other-side-of-the-sun routine). There they find the planet's population (oriental aliens, of course) literally driven underground by Ghidrah, the Three-Headed monster (known to the Xians as Monster Zero), who has turned the planet's surface into a desolate wasteland. The aliens seem peaceable enough folks, and, they tell us, it would be right neighbourly of us to lend them "demon Monster One and Monster Two" (Godzilla and Rodan. Yaay!) in the hope that the two earth monsters will either kill Ghidrah or drive him from the planet. Sure, Earth tells them, take our goddamn monsters, *we* sure don't need them smashing Japan every time they get bored! ("They have caused us enough trouble!" observes Nick.) The nice aliens are so grateful that they give us a cassette tape containing what they tell us is a cure for all known diseases. Unfortunately when the tape is played to a roomful of eager Japanese officials, it turns out to be an ultimatum telling Earth that we'll either become slaves to Planet X, or they'll let all three monsters loose on Earth (with radio-control devices implanted in their heads) to do the Monster Stomp on our cities. Fuck you, says Earth, and I don't think I have to tell you what happens next, eh? Some viewers might find **Monster Zero** a little

too talky, but it has its moments. Nick Adams is as macho as ever as he chides the aliens with incredibly offensive insults like, "You stinkin' rats!" and "You lousy finks!" Pay attention to the fight scenes. If you blink you might miss Godzilla's famous 'victory dance' on Planet X. Boogie, babe! [BJE]

MOTEL CONFIDENTIAL (1967)
OFFICE LOVE-IN (1968)

From good ol' Rhino Video comes this voyeur's delight, appropriately entitled 'Saturday Night Sleazies, Volume III', which gives us almost three full hours of non-stop tease from the pre-AIDS days when you could do the Bone Dance with any hunk of warm flesh you'd scrape off the street. These two b/w, fly-by-night sexploitation flicks from the late '60s cover all the pre-porno bases, and before home video made such T&A attractions readily available to any shut-in, these one-take jiggle-fests were exclusive fare for the pud-pulling raincoat brigade. Both were directed by A.C. Stephens (**Orgy of the Dead**), and nowadays they're more tacky and tongue-in-cheek (or anywhere else you may want it) than arousing. All the women have hooters large enough to eat a 12-course meal off of, all the guys keep their socks on, and the sex amounts to a crescendo of moaning while canned music stinks up the air... Our first feature, **Motel Confidential**, is a string of sexual vignettes set at the aptly-named Quickie Motel. We begin in Dirty Old Man-Land, with an ol' fart luring his busty (but, of course, completely naïve) secretary to the motel for some 'overtime'. One drink later, off go her clothes and she's wiggling her siliconed ticket-sellers at the cameraman, while her boss squeezes the merchandise. As least the guy keeps on his pants, so we don't have to stare at his wrinkly ass. Other episodes include: A couple on the rocks attempt a second honeymoon, a self-proclaimed Romeo unknowingly picks up a drag queen, and a sailor on shore leave meets his match with a tireless nympho. Meanwhile, the hotel clerk plays Greek Chorus by commenting straight into the lens. The roughest the bedroom antics get is some mild spanking and nude jumping jacks, and overall, the action is joyless and mechanical, with stilted performances from the cast of nekkid nobodies. At least the characters' names are creative (Masher Jones, Romeo Rampart, Phyllis Doogoodie)... The second feature, **Office Love-In**, is overflowing with bohemian lifestyles and imaginative coupling, but that can't cover up the fact it's also pretty dull. This one has a bit more sto-

ryline than the first (how could it *not?*), generally following the sexcapades of Stephanie (Kathy Williams), a cute new secretary at Date-A-Mate – one of those new-fangled computer dating services. Get ready for loads of faded fads, double entendres, and long baths, with women soaping their breasts for minutes on end... First Stephanie leaps into bed with the boss; then gets picked up by his weaselly son, who comes up short in comparison to his ol' man; and along the way Steph even gets some lezbo action (which was pretty hot stuff for the '60s!). The big 'joke' is that by the end, Stephanie has fucked the entire Date-A-Mate family. (Ha.) Sure, there's lots of campy cheesecake on display, but its values are sorta insulting to females if you think about it (but I bet most of the audience was too busy slappin' their salami to care) – perpetuating the notion that the only way for a woman to make it in the business world is by spreading her legs. But the most patently offensive scene involves a flaming, limp-wristed homosexual who's 'straightened out' by a new office slut ("Haven't you ever tried to be normal and healthy?" she asks him)... Recommended for those with breast fixations or wooden acting fetishes, but I for one severely overdosed on the hand-held bedroom camerawork. Both flesh pageants wear thin after a while, but they're good for a few lascivious laffs in small doses.

MOTEL HELL

KEVIN CONNOR 1980. Sweeney Todd meets Leatherface in this little-seen Country Kill-o-rama. When the film was first released, it was shunted into the 'release-it-for-a-couple-weeks-during-Halloween' corner of the market. But nowadays, with drivel like **Texas Chainsaw 2** setting the pace for satirical sleaze, **Motel Hell** seems like a virtual masterpiece – a cheap, nasty, (and best of all) funny slaughter-fest... Farmer Vincent and his sister are nice, old-fashioned folks, with their own family business and a pride in their home-made products. You see, Farmer Vincent's Smoked Meats are the envy of the county, with people coming from near and far to sample his 'specially prepared' wears. Well, from that last sentence alone, you can probably guess that some suspiciously un-kosher bi-products play a part in their 'secret recipe'. Yes, it's the old, knock out the unsuspecting passers-by; plant them in the backyard garden, up to their necks; slice their vocal chords so they can't holler (they *do* gurgle pretty well, though); and fatten them up for the big church Bar-B-Q. "Sometimes I wonder about the karmic implications of these acts," Vince muses to his equally-insane sis, after snapping several spines with the help of a John Deere tractor. And when he adds a hippie rock band (called Ivan and The Terribles) to his garden, Vince sedates them with a 'Hypno-high hypnosis machine' that sends them into a trippy trance. And best of all, the ending is a flat-out marathon of destruction, set in Vince's slaughterhouse – we've got a raving lunatic wearing a pig's head, a catatonic damsel in distress, a hero who swings to the rescue on a meat hook, and a sweaty duel to the death with chain saws (out-doing and pre-dating by six years **'Saw 2'**s similar climax)... It's all pretty silly and Hollywood-fake, but Rory Calhoun seems to be having a ball, dropping his B-movie western persona for a B-movie mad psycho persona. He's especially effective in catching the thin line separating a Good Ol' Boy and a bloodthirsty mass-murderer. Overall, it's nothing to run out this moment and rent, but it's fun for a few cheap laffs.

MOTHRA

INOSHIRO HONDA 1962. If you're one of the few who can say they've never seen a Japanese monster movie, **Mothra** is a suitable introduction to Toho Studios' unique style of monster-making. In one scene, Mothra, a huge red caterpillar, weaves a cocoon in the middle of the city it's just trashed. When Mothra emerges from its sleeping quarters, it has been transformed into a gigantic, shrieking moth, and the city-smashing continues. An eyeful of fun from the fine folks who brought you **Godzilla**. (Certainly beats the hell out of watching bullshit like **Critters**.) [BJE]

MUDHONEY

RUSS MEYER 1965. When the topic of Adult Entertainment is discussed, the first thing that pops into most sleazegoers' perverted minds are X-rated mayonnaise-and-caulking-gun classics like **Wham Bam! Thank You Spaceman!**, **Beaverly Hills Cop** or **Long Day's Journey into Chuck**. Well, before come shots were mandatory and cinematographers had to have a degree in microscopy in order to include every possible orifice, there was the All-American Nudie Flick, and Russ Meyer was their reigning King! His motion pictures can still be approached on many levels, by [1] The Drooling Dirtball Crowd, who actually get off on the softcore antics, [2] The Art Farts, who seriously consider Meyer's films to be brilliantly filmed observations of the underbelly-fringe of American society (but who probably flog their maggot just as much as the first bunch), and [3] The Weirdo Contingent, who can only laugh and shake their heads in awe at Meyer's staggering excessiveness... Alongside **Beyond the Valley of the Dolls** and **Faster Pussycat! Kill! Kill!**, this is one of Meyer's finest moments. A dime-store melodrama packed with lust, love, murder, bootleg liquor, fire and brimstone religious zealots, and (let's not forget) plenty of busty babes in disposable dresses. His direction and editing is a little easier on the corneas than in later offerings, but Russ can sure pack one hell of an overwrought plotline... A cross country traveller named Calif finds himself marooned in the ultra-backwoods town of Spooner, Missouri. There he encounters a fun-loving family of trollops who charge gentlemen callers a dollar a poke; consisting of hillbilly-matron Maggie Marie and her two voluptuous blond daughters – Clarabelle (Lorna Maitland), whose main joy in life is listening to the radio and shimmying until her blouse falls open, and deaf-mute Eula (Rena Horton), who takes a hankerin' to any man in sight and seems unconcerned that her one-piece wardrobe is unbuttoned down to her navel. Deciding to stay in town for a spell, Calif gets a job as a hired hand at the nearby Wade Farm – owned by the good-natured Uncle Luke, but dominated by the sadistic Sydney, who's a wife-beating, marriage-cheating, no-

account bum in a sweat-stained two dollar suit (hissss!). Soon Calif is falling for Sydney's abused Mrs., Hannah (and vice versa), but Calif has a Dark Secret in his past that keeps him from defending his honour and trading blows with her loutish hubby. Add the pig-headed Preacher Hansan, his prim sister, a gravesite fist fight, a skinny-dippin' swimming hole, arson, rape, and more in-bred, unwashed characters than in a dozen episodes of **Green Acres**... It's 'Tobacco Road' with an R-rated coating of sleaze. Soap opera taken to its insane limits, while combining a diatribe against moral and religious hypocrisy with rural peep show antics. There's even a great, vengeful ending complete with a rabid lynch mob!... The entire cast is about as scuzzy as you can imagine, with Hal Hopper leaving a thick trail of slime in his wake as Sydney, Stu Lancaster (who played the evil lech in **Faster Pussycat**) switching gears to become the kindly Uncle Luke, and all the women filling their D-cup roles simply by giggling a bit and jiggling even more. The women-as-sexual-toys-or-pawns sentiment gets a little degrading after a while, but then again, almost all the male characters are loathsome pissants, so I guess it sorta balances out... **Mudhoney** is down-home sleaze at its finest!

MULTIPLE MANIACS

JOHN WATERS 1970. In the wake of director John Waters' **Hairspray**, I decided to check out his second feature (still in black and white, but his first with sync-sound). I won't beat around the bush, either – it's one of my all-time favourites, and a *must* for any fan of sleazebucket cinema... Who else but the reigning King of Baltimore Lowlife could come up with a concoction like this? It stars Waters' entire entourage of performers and friends, who would later pop up in everything from **Pink Flamingos** to **Desperate Living** – Divine, David Lockary, Mink Stole, Edith Massey, etc. – and when they take centre stage *en masse*, get ready for absolute freakshow time! And as usual, Waters doesn't refrain from capturing every wrinkle, blemish and cold sore gracing his cast of social misfits. Technically, it's on the crude side (what do you expect for $7,000?), but this flick is so damned repulsive and grating that I'm surprised someone didn't lynch Waters from the nearest lamppost after this flick's premiere. Personally, I laughed my ass off, but of course, I'm no barometer of America's sense of humour... It begins at Lady Divine's Cavalcade of Perversions, where a troupe of sluts, fags, dykes, drug addicts, and perverts put on exhibitions of bicycle-seat smelling, queer kissing, armpit licking, and puke-eating; all for the benefit of whitebread suburbanites who lap it up, even while they're condemning it. Of course, this attitude changes when Divine, everyone's favourite 300-pound transvestite, throws a net over the middle-class swine and robs them at gun point. (And I seriously doubt anyone has ever been assaulted by a person so firmly squeezed into such tacky evening gowns.) Marital infidelity enters the picture when Divine discovers that her hubby, Mr. David (David Lockary) is being unfaithful with some platinum-blond floozy who moans "This is better than amyl nitrate," while making love. But when Divine heads out to kill the pair, she takes a short side-trip and is raped in an alleyway by a bearded guy in a dress. Finding the safety of a nearby church, he/she has a few religious visions (the big J.C. turns a few stale hot dog buns into a table-load of tuna fish and Wonder Bread), and then meets a lezbo Religious Whore who fucks Divine in a pew and stuffs a rosary up his/her wide-mouth asshole. These are characters who have no qualms about picking up a handy butcher knife and chopping away at someone, 20 or 30 times, and them pulling out their victim's guts in order to chew on 'em easier. And just to make matters completely incoherent, after Divine kills everyone and begins foaming at the mouth, she's suddenly raped by a 15-foot-long lobster (appropriately named Lobstora). After going *completely* nutzo, Divine is gunned down by the National Guard, while Kate Smith

IF YOU MISS THIS PICTURE YOU'LL HATE YOURSELF IF YOU MISS THIS PICTURE

RUSS MEYER presents

MUDHONEY

...LEAVES A TASTE OF EVIL!

...a film of lust and violence

sings 'God Bless America'... What does it all *mean*, you might ask? How the fuck do I know? All I can say is that I was riveted to the screen for most of this film. Turn your back for a moment and you might miss a cop-killing or a cheap Charles Manson joke. One character growls, "I love you so fucking much, I could shit," and I feel the same way about this masterpiece. It has a smaller scope than Waters' later works, but his b/w photography grinds home a documentary feel and helps make it one of the scurviest (and funniest) examples of utterly repellent, Gutter-Art I've sat through in some time. It's a true love letter to filth and mayhem!

MY BREAKFAST WITH BLASSIE

LINDA LAUTREC / JOHNNY LEGEND 1983. Never one for an obvious joke, the late Andy Kaufman stars in this 60 minute parody of the '81 arthouse hit **My Dinner with Andre**, in which artistes Andre Gregory and Wallace Shawn simply trade anecdotes over a meal for almost two hours. But with Kaufman's eccentric sense of humour at the helm, instead of a swanky restaurant our locale is a Sambo's diner. Instead of pretentious highbrows, Andy is joined by ex-wrestler and macho-asshole extraordinaire Fred Blassie (the self proclaimed 'King of Men'). And instead of discussing High Culture, the topics of the hour are sexist jokes, personal hygiene, low cuisine, and idiotic wrestling exploits (from *both* stars). Brilliantly stupid? Or just plain stupid? It all depends on your sense of humour (and level of intoxication), plus how much ultra-fuzzy video camerawork your corneas can stand. Even though I loathe anything to do with the sport (ha!) of pro-wrestling, I loved watching these two dorks trade inanities, while the film exposes the asshole under the asshole image... The well-tanned Blassie is the first to vie for the Arrogance Award by rubbing the pregnant Thai waitress' belly and referring to her as "Hey, Buddha!" They both discuss the extensive menu, Kaufman says Grace, Blassie wonders if the milk is sour, and both go into loving detail about how much toilet paper each uses. Fascinating, eh? Well, it gets even more idiotic when they move onto the topic of wrestling. "I'm still undefeated, as far as women go," brags Kaufman, and Blassie boasts endlessly about his career: How he introduced biting to Japanese wrestling, how many times he's been stabbed, and his encounter with Elvis. Zzzzzz. But they're so damned self-serious that you can't help but laugh at 'em, especially when Kaufman tries to romance a female customer (even though he can't keep her name straight), or how after each encounter with a fan they both wipe down with pre-moistened towelettes for fear of catching germs. All the while the viewer wonders if the customers are real or a set-up, in particular the abusive patron toward the end, who vomits near their table... A strange, largely-improvised put-on featuring two egos the size of Uranus, which proves without a doubt that Kaufman was the king of the shitheel schtick.

MYRA BRECKINRIDGE

MICHAEL SARNE 1970. A stoned-out production. Hideously bad. Numbingly boring. A mess! And worst of all, it's not even very enjoyable... *Loosely* based on Gore Vidal's risqué best-seller, this turns out to be a smirky gob of rotted celluloid that wants desperately to be chic and tasteless, but succeeds only in becoming flashy and feebleminded. The big problem is that the film has no back bone – it's a sex-comedy for invertebrates... Rex Reed makes his big screen debut (the notion makes you want to puke up your breakfast, don't it?) as Myron Breckinridge, who gets a sex-change operation at the beginning of the film and is suddenly transformed into the title character, Myra, played by a snooty Raquel Welch. Hitting Hollywood with the goal of destroying *all* American men, (s)he goes to work for his/her millionaire uncle, Buck Loner (John Huston) at his sex farm/acting school. Beyond that, I can't make head or tail out of what passes for a 'script'... The cast is eccentric to say the least: Raquel Welch makes you fondly recall the days of **One Million Years, BC**, where she wasn't given any dialogue to screw up; practically-embalmed, 78-year-old Mae West is an over-sexed crone, complete with platinum wig, gristled complexion, and a constant flow of well-paid studs at her side (Tom Selleck is one of Mae's boot-licking suitors); a wide-eyed, empty-headed Farrah Fawcett ends up in bed with Raquel (though nothing improper occurs between the two); Hollywood vets Andy Devine, Jim Backus and Roger C. Carmel take turns posing as Poster Children for Liver Spots; and just when you figured Rex Reed had disappeared from the film for good, he starts popping up as Myra's ever-present, invisible alter-ego – until you get so sick of his fat, pasty face that you wanna stick his dick into the blades of an electric fan. As a last-ditch effort, so-called director Michael Sarne rummaged through the 20th Century Fox vaults and edited in clips from old Hollywood films (Laurel & Hardy, Carmen Miranda, etc.) to help salvage this limp flick. And for some inconceivable reason this film was rated X when it was first released – but don't let that rating fool you, this is tame, anaemic stuff... There's a *few* humorous bits hidden amongst the bad soap opera, off-target social criticism and sections that smack of an ass-pumper's wet dream. The best portion, in fact, is the first five minutes, with Raquel and Rex stumbling though a sidewalk dance number (they try to look like Fred and Ginger, but end up looking more like Fred and Barney), followed by John Carradine's hilarious cameo as the sex-change surgeon ("You realise that when we cut it off, it won't grow back")... The ending is just plain incomprehensible – Myra is hit by a car driven by Myron, and changes back into a man (or should I say, she changes back into Rex). Yeah. Right. The creative forces behind this fiasco must've been nose-deep in inspiration... I'm a big fan of spaced-out movies, *especially* from the late-'60s/early-'70s, but this is one of the worst. El Stinko. You have been officially warned.

THE MYSTERIANS

INOSHIRO HONDA 1959. Those wacky Japanese at Toho studios and director Inoshiro Honda have churned another colourful tale, but don't believe all the hype on the ad, because this is pretty low-key stuff. No prehistoric city-stompers in this entry – just alien invaders, earth-shaking destruction and a storyline with whiskers. It starts off nice and fast-paced when Magella, an anteater-nosed robot with twirling TV antennae on his head, bursts out of the side of a mountain and proceeds to step on every Tonka tank in the orient. Though it's a hokey costume, the special effects are surprisingly good for this type of thing, but unfortunately Mr. Robot goes to pieces after a fight with the military, so we don't get to see him again. Instead, it's back to the Humanoids in Brightly-Painted Motorcycle Helmets who arrive from "Mysterioid, Planet of Mystery". And why are they here on our miserable little planet? Oh oh! Looks like the Mysterians want to inter-marry with earth chicks since all

their own women are radioactive (where have I heard that plot a couple dozen times before?). The proceedings soon drag into a series of boring meetings with diplomats discussing 'What should we do?', and although the finale has a shitload of nicely-done explosions, it never rivals the giant-robot-rampage at the beginning. It's too slow-paced and derivative to be *really* good, and too self-serious to be *really* fun. Starring Kenji Sahara and Yumi Shirakawa (who?), the special effects are top notch (i.e. you can't see the wires), and the whole production's interesting, though a bit disappointing for Rubber Monster fanatics.

NAKED ANGELS

BRUCE CLARK 1969. This no-budget biker flick kicks immediately into third gear with a rumble during the opening credits. Now if only they'd had a solid script to follow it up... Michael Greene stars as

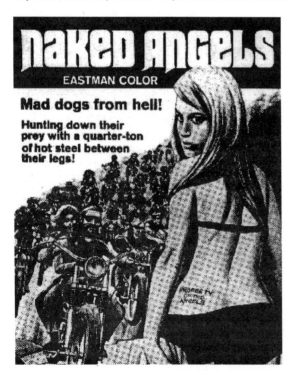

Mother, the shaggy-haired leader of The Angels, your typical pack of roadscum – hygienic gents who spit in each other's beer to prove their brotherhood and sport names like Cockroach ('cause the guy likes to eat 'em). But Mother is the anomaly in the gang – in-between head bashings he shows his sensitive side by playing a recorder, but when he feels betrayed he's willing to let his girlfriend get gang-banged by every geek in the Southwest. The plot has The Angels searching for a rival gang, The Hotdoggers (no, they don't ride down the highway in the old Oscar Meyer truck), who sent Mother to the hospital during their last encounter. Off they go into the desert – they fix a flat, swig back some warm beers, give an old shopkeeper a heart attack, and let their mamas ride topless for a spell (while allowing them ample opportunity to display the 'Property of The Angels' tattoos on their butts). There's a tad more sex and nudity than usual for this type of chopper-stomper, but the action is only sporadically vicious. The direction by Bruce Clark (**Hammer**) is a little more stylish than usual, especially during a Las Vegas rooftop skirmish. My favourite portion has The Angels getting fed up with their psycho chief and dumping him, and when Mother runs out of gas, he's forced to hightail it across the desert on foot. Yep, it's sunstroke hallucination time, kids! Artsy camera angles, trippy vistas, not to mention imagining he's running down the road with no pants on. A limp ending doesn't help matters, but there's enough entertaining sludge scattered throughout its 90 minutes to keep cycle-addicts happily satisfied.

THE NASTY RABBIT

JAMES LANDIS 1964 (AKA: SPIES-A-GO-GO). From the goofs who gave modern civilisation such celluloid wonders as **Eegah!** and **Wild Guitar**, comes a flick that's even more painful to endure. Starring Arch Hall Jr. and William Watters (Arch Hall Sr.), this 'wacky' (not really) cold war comedy is all about a Russian plot to destroy America. Soviet Agent X-II (a middle-aged buffoon named Misha) is dropped off in Texas, complete with oversized cowboy hat and pathetic Russian accent; and his weapon is a cute little bunny with a time-released vial of deadly bacteria in its collar – a strain of bacteria that will destroy all life in North America when released. Of course, every foreign agent on earth is after the vial: There's a sombrero-ed Mexican, a German in a Nazi helmet, a W.W.II Japanese soldier, and a sexy European trollop with loose dress straps. *All* of them are stupid klutzes, and eventually all the spies show up at the Killdeer Dude Ranch in hopes of grabbing the deadly bunny. Slow-paced and desperately unfunny, when it comes to espionage imbecility, I'll take Boris and Natasha over these doofs any day... Can you believe it gets worse? Well, just wait until Arch Hall Jr. zooms into the picture! As Britt Hunter, the obligatory dream-boat on a motorbike, Arch is a rock 'n' roller who's at the Dude Ranch for a concert. And that means he's going to SING! Run for the hills! He's like a blond Wayne Newton, but with half the personality and twice the pompadour. (He's also a secret agent for the FBI, but don't tell anybody. Shhhh!)... And would you believe that the rabbit is given humorous asides to the camera? Even without stuffing words into his mouth, the critter is so fucking cute that you wanna stomp it with a size-12 golf shoe... With plot complexities that would rival an episode of **Josie and the Pussycats**, the only plusses are William (Vilmos) Zsigmond's colourful cinematography and the weird, cartoony sound effects. It's all the bigger disappointment since I love the concept of a slapstick comedy about bacteriological warfare. Too bad the result wasn't funny. It's a laborious snoozer from director James Landis (**The Sadist**).

THE NAVY VS. THE NIGHT MONSTERS

MICHAEL A. HOEY 1966. Did you ever buy one of those microwave entrées that looks so good on the package, but when you cut it

Beware of the Night Crawlers... their clutches will disintegrate you!

THE NAVY vs **THE NIGHT MONSTERS**

ALL NEW!
Terrifying
COLOR

MAMIE VAN DOREN ANTHONY EISLEY

open, it smells like that sneaker your dog has been using as a drool sponge for the last six months? Here's the schlock cinema equivalent, from director Michael A. Hoey (or was that 'Hooey'?). It's a cheapjack monster pic that lays like a dead cat for the first half hour... A government planeload of cargo from Antarctica crash-lands near a Navy base on tropical Gow Island, and the rescue team discovers that nearly all the crew has mysteriously disappeared. All that's left is one pilot who's in shock, a few cute penguins and a bunch of uprooted tree specimens. It seems the plane was part of Operation Deep Freeze, a top secret plan to study vegetation that has been frozen since the Ice Age. But when the samples accidentally defrost, it's dinner time! **Day of the Triffids** meets **Gilligan's Island**! Sounds good? I thought so too, but the first half is leaden with long scenes of Army asses making plans and a lethargic love story with diabetes-inducing dialogue. Worst of all, '50s tease queen Mamie Van Doren (who stretched sweaters in **High School Confidential**) is given almost nothing to do as the base's blond bombshell, Nurse Nora. Honest-to-goodness acting certainly isn't her forte, and she's a stiff when she isn't playing a slut. At least the pace picks up when night falls on the plastic palm treed isle, and the South Pole plants uproot themselves and go after a snack. First the creatures eat the penguins, then they move down the evolutionary scale and munch on the actors, while ooz-ing acidic slime that burns flesh (shades of **Alien**!). I had absolutely no sympathy for these boneheaded characters though. First off, the supporting cast is filled with edible swine like Anthony Eisley, Bobby Van and Pamela Mason. Second, while people are dying left and right, they *still* don't have the common sense to stop wander-ing off alone in the middle of the night. The creatures are barely glimpsed — a smart move since in direct light we see they're just six-foot-tall papier-mâché trunks with limp branches hanging off 'em — and the only (mild) gore is when one sailor gets his arm ripped from the socket. Although we're informed during the finale that 'thousands' of them are attacking, we only see about three up close, and the all-too obvious answer is to napalm these 'crawlers' ('I love the smell of carnivorous walking trees in the morning...'). A humdrum flick with a minimum of fiendishness, and a maximum of file footage and logical inconsistencies. A let-down.

NEAR DARK
KATHRYN BIGELOW 1987. Here's a prime example of film studio stu-pidity. DEG had a solid winner on their hands, in the form of a vampire movie that blows away trash like **The Lost Boys** and **Fright Night**, and they proceeded to piss it away with a mediocre ad campaign and a limited play-off. It sunk without a trace, and that's too bad, because even though it falters at the end by sliding toward the sentimental side, it's still the best film of its type since Romero's **Martin**... Director Kathryn Bigelow, who previously di-rected the underrated **The Loveless**, pulls strong characterisations from a fine cast. On the undead side, there's a triple threat from

Aliens-stars, Lance Henriksen, Bill Paxton and Jenette Goldstein; and that creepy little brother from **River's Edge**, Joshua Miller, is (would you believe) even weirder *this* time around as a twisted-brained adult trapped in a child's body. Bigelow also wisely avoids all the campy wooden-stake/no-reflection lore — in fact, the script doesn't even use the term 'vampire'. Instead, it's a chilling road movie, with biker-flick overtones. **Dracula** meets **The Wild An-gels**!... It begins when Caleb, your typical hick farm boy, picks up a mysterious young woman (Jenny Wright) one night while he's out carousing. Her hickeys go a bit deeper than he expected though, and by dawn he's been initiated into a ragtag 'Family' of rural bloodsuckers. They travel the backroads of the mid-west by dark — avoiding the cops by stealing new cars and burning their bridges behind them, and avoiding the deadly sunlight with duct tape and aluminium foil plastered over the windows. They're the most sav-age pack of killers to hit the screen in a long time, combining the eccentricity of the Addams Family with the ruthlessness of the Manson Family; but newcomer Caleb doesn't have the nerve to kill for his dinner yet. Instead he just sucks from the ragged wrist of lovely Ms. Wright, and there's an almost-sexual excitement to their murders... It's gutsy filmmaking with a dark, comic edge, and **Near Dark** has several brilliant, tension-packed action scenes. There's a dynamite sequence in a redneck bar, where the clan methodically feeds off the patrons, while taking point-blank shotgun blasts to the gut; and a claustrophobic police shoot-out at a rinky-dink motel, where the rain of bullets is less effective against them than the sunlight, which tends to send their flesh bubbling and bursting into flame. The solid script by Ms. Bigelow and Eric Red (**The Hitcher**) keeps the story tough and lean, and the photography manages to be flashy, while avoiding the MTV-'prettiness' that has crept into recent films. But (and it's a big BUT), the ending is really, REALLY lame — pandering to audiences who feel they deserve a happy ending, whether it's justified or not. Well, phooey on that notion! What the hell ever happened to old-fashioned tragedy? Next thing you know, they'll be rewriting **Macbeth**, except every-one will survive so they can star in the sequel. My only other gripe is that Tim Thomerson is totally miscast as Caleb's concerned, whitebread dad — every time I see him, all I can think of is his ol' stand-up Charles Bronson imitation... But even with the few major mis-steps, this is still one of the finest horror films of the year. Slick, moody and *very* nasty at times — what more can I add? Check it out.

NIGHT CALLER FROM OUTER SPACE
JOHN GILLING 1966 (AKA: BLOOD BEAST FROM OUTER SPACE). A boring little black & white item starring a young, stone-faced John Saxon. When a strange, glowing meteorite falls to the London countryside, scientist Saxon and his crew of British flunkies are called on the job. And armed with plenty of pseudo-scientific-mumbo-jumbo (to convince us they're real, honest-to-goodness smart people), they discover the object is an alien-made transportation-beam machine. After a painfully slow beginning that will have you chanting 'Monster! Monster!' within the first 20 minutes, we're rewarded with an absolutely-underwhelming, seven-foot-tall rubber Blood Beast. As any good alien space invader is trained to do, it escapes from the lab, steals a car (that's right, he knows how to drive!) and vanishes into the night. Soon afterward, teenage girls begin disap-pearing by the dozens after answering an advert for Bikini Girl Magazine; and when Saxon and his Limey cronies investigate, they discover the magazine is just a front for the ol' goofy-space-creatures-stealing-earth-women-for-breeding-purposes plot device. Ho hum, indeed... The only difference between this film and the thousands of other unwatchably-bad B-movies is that instead of a clumsy, stupid monster in a cheesy fright mask, we get an intelli-gent, suave monster in a cheesy fright mask. But the bottom line is

that this alleged 'film' is dry and slow-paced, uninvolving and unexciting. It's not even very funny (except for the pathetic theme song). To put it even more bluntly, this flick stinks. Peee-Yew!

NIGHT OF THE CREEPS

FRED DEKKER 1986. An imaginative little first feature from director Fred Dekker, **Creeps** is a welcome throwback to the glory days of the '50s cheapies... After a completely unnecessary introduction to a pack of ludicrous alien humanoids who look and sound like the Pilsbury Doughboy on PCP (they're never seen again, thank goodness), the film kicks in with a brisk b/w prologue set in 1959, where some college kids investigate a 'meteor' that lands near Lover's Lane (shades of **The Blob** and **Invasion of the Saucer Men**). When the meteor turns out to be a tiny rocket packed with hungry, wriggling space-slugs, you've got the beginnings of a juicy creature feature deluxe... Cut to the present, where two geeky pledges have to steal a corpse for a brick-headed frat's initiation rite, and with their luck (not to mention a bit of idiotic script manoeuvring) they grab a parasite-filled one from a cryogenics lab. Soon corpses are popping up across campus with split-top skulls, and hundreds of once-freeze-dried, sluggy speedsters are criss-crossing the sidewalks. You see, these slimy li'l critters like to leap into people's mouths and use their brains as a breeding ground (but wouldn't they starve at most frat houses?). So we get not only an invasion of disgusting brain-eaters, but a pack of blood-thirsty zombies traipsing about – sorta like a combination of **Shivers**, **Night of the Living Dead** and **Revenge of the Nerds**. A bit of welcome nastiness (*Love* those exploding heads! When they burst open, dozens of parasites fly out in every direction!) plus some quick nudity give the film a solid R-rating, and the wonderful finale has an entire busload of no-necked frat assholes dying in a traffic accident on the way to the prom, and coming back to life to menace a sorority house. Luckily, our nerdy hero and a vigilante police detective arrive with a 12-gauge shotgun to ventilate their heads and a flame thrower to finish the job in true Lobster fashion... It's a good-first effort (though character names like Cynthia Cronenberg, Chris Romero and James Carpenter Hooper are overly-obvious in-jokes); and as for the cast, the lead geek (Jason Lively) shouldn't consider quitting his day job at McDonald's just yet, Jill Whitlow is appropriately pretty-and-resourceful as the 'nice' sorority bimbo, Tom Atkins grabs the scenery by the incisors as the obsessed cop, and let's not forget the obligatory Dick Miller cameo... Lotsa dumb fun!

NIGHT OF THE LEPUS

WILLIAM F. CLAXTON 1972. It's ecological mutation time, so get ready to head for the hills! They're coming! What is it this time, you ask? Grizzly bears? Alligators? Slugs? Would you believe bunnies?! "Hard to believe that a rabbit could be so destructive," announces a newscaster. Well, it's even harder to believe a paying audience wouldn't laugh themselves into a stupor at this plague of rabbits, since there's no way in hell to make the things look halfway annoyed, much less menacing! But that fact didn't stop these intrepid filmmakers, who wade into the patently ridiculous concept with a straight face and emerge with one of the silliest (non-Japanese) monster movies of all time... Rounding up a roster of solid B-movie regulars, Rory Calhoun plays a rancher who's sick and tired of rabbits eating up his acreage, so he calls on Stuart Whitman and Janet Leigh (as a pair of married zoologists) plus moustachioed science-guy DeForest Kelley (wearing ties so wide he could use 'em as a lobster bib). Instead of just poisoning the furry critters, they decide to try experimental hormones – and as everyone knows, when Science begins screwing with Mother Nature, the results can be catastrophic. And when Whitman's idiot daughter releases one of the mutant test bunnies, the entire county is soon

faced with (are you sitting down, folks?) a rampaging army of five-foot-tall, 150 pound, carnivorous rabbits! The first third of the film is kept low-key and pseudo-serious by director William F. Claxton, but once the giant rabbits begin gnawing on the population, it's never the same. But you probably won't care, because you'll be laughing so damned hard. A better title might've been 'Bloody Bunnies on Parade'! They lumber across the countryside in slow motion on a quest for flesh, with close-ups of their monstrous buck teeth and kill-crazy pink eyes keeping the chuckles at an all-time high. And wait until you see how they flip end-over-end and gush gore when they're shotgunned. Elmer Fudd, eat your heart out! When they invade the obviously-miniature town, it's hare-raising (sorry), and as far as furry frights go, I've gotten more shudders from Burt Reynolds' toupees... The filmmaking is slick and surprisingly bloodthirsty, and for some unexplainable reason the actors don't even seem too embarrassed to be associated with this nutty feature. DeForest Kelley comes off best of all, since he was simply glad to get a hiatus from Shatner and all the other **Trek** twits. Fast-paced and indescribably dumb – it's perfect for an Easter Family Matinee, as well as a must-see for mutant monster aficionados... Based on (believe it or not) a novel called **The Year of the Angry Rabbit**.

NIGHT TIDE

CURTIS HARRINGTON 1963. Are you ready for Dennis Hopper's first starring role? And (are you sitting down for this?) would you believe he plays a clean-cut, sober and thoroughly straight-laced character? Best of all, the result is a good creepy little yarn! Director Curtis Harrington made his debut with this ultra-low budget mood piece, which slipped through the cracks and got tossed onto bottom halves of double bills (under **Battle Beyond the Sun**). It'll try the patience of horror fans going into it expecting cheap shocks, but despite the occasional unintentional laugh or stilted conversation, the film's unique and subtle qualities set it apart... Hopper plays Johnny Drake, a sailor on shore leave trying (with little success) to make small talk with women at a jazz club, The Blue Grotto. There he meets Mora (Linda Lawson), a mysterious beauty who lives at a Venice California pier side carnival, in an apartment above the merry-go-round. Mora is a little strange though – she invites Dennis over for a fresh fish breakfast, is obsessed with the ocean (she 'feels the sea water in her veins') and works at the carnival as Mora the Mermaid (the 'Lovely Siren of the Deep'), wearing a fake fish tail while laying in a tank of water. She's also

followed about by a pesky old woman who speaks to her in a strange tongue. But since swabby Hopper is smitten with Mora, he pays no heed to her eccentric lifestyle, even after he learns her last two boyfriends are dead – both washed up on the beach with a lungful of liquid. The clues slowly drop into place, rumours are bandied about, a crusty old sea captain tells tales of a lost society of Sea People, and a tarot reading only adds more portent to the plot. Are the superstitious townspeople crazy? Is Mora crazy? Is Hopper *going* crazy? Or is Ms. Mermaid really a psycho from the sea who, like a spider, is forced to kill her mate? (And how much damned coffee can a character drink in 83 minutes? Who sponsored this flick? Maxwell House?) The story may be slight, but Harrington manages to edge it slowly along with a shrewd build-up of suspense, plus the b/w photography by Vilis Lapenieks (**Mother Goose a Go-Go**) is suitably atmospheric, with several sequences reminiscent of more European-influenced fare (such as Jacques Tourneur). This is a tidy low-key thriller, but don't judge it too swiftly – though it's more pedestrian elements are predictable, a small wealth of mystery lies under the surface. Plus, it proves even at the beginning of his career, Hopper didn't have to punctuate every sentence with 'man' in order to effectively fill a role. The character of Johnny is so atypical for Dennis, that if not for his immediately recognisable voice, you'd barely remember it's him after a while. The Hop pulls off the prettyboy matinee idol routine and keeps a shred of dignity, even when laying on the beach in swim trunks (hubba hubba!)... A film that's definitely worth a look!

NIGHTFALL

PAUL MAYERSBERG 1988. Former Nicolas Roeg scriptwriter Paul Mayersberg (**The Man Who Fell to Earth**, **Eureka**) directed and penned this Concorde Pix mega-loser, based on an early short tale by Isaac Asimov. But unlike another past Roeg-associate, Donald Cammell, who recently spewed forth the fascinatingly oblique **White of the Eye**, Mayersberg's indie career has been stuck with slim projects like **Captive** (starring Oliver 'Make that a double' Reed) and now this Epic in Ennui. Why did he ever agree to involve himself in this cheapskate sci-fi? Another payment due on that new condo, Paul?... The basic premise might be solid in the form of a half hour TV episode – but NOT for 83 interminable minutes! Welcome to another world, where three suns keep the planet eternally lit and every character speaks in a halted pattern, as if they were all having problems reading their cue cards. But rumours of an impending nightfall make all the monk-robed citizens quake in their sandals. David Birney dons a Bon Jovi wig as Aton, their leader; Sarah Douglas is a sap who joins in on a planetwide selfblinding binge; and Alexis Kanner (obviously on the sauce since **The Prisoner**) is a babbling blind prophet who foretells the end of their society. But since their society looks like a Deadhead version of **Logan's Run**, WHO CARES what the hell happens to 'em? This futuristic Renaissance Faire spends so much time flying kites and getting high on life, that you want to strangle them all with the nearest hunk of

macramé... Everyone wallows in paranoia and fear, wringing their hands and worrying that it's the end of their wonderful world (more likely it's the end of their measly careers). False drama, fake performances, flimsy sets, ugly camerawork – even Mayersberg turns in a surprisingly bland job behind the camera, with lots of artsy posturing, yet not a lick of intelligence or wit. This project won't be getting him many more jobs, unless Concorde offers him 'Deathstalker Part 3' My goodness, what a protracted, stupid, pretentious, annoying bummer this turned out to be! In other words, it's utter baloney and boring to boot. Hell, I've seen more action in Yasujiro Ozu films.

THE NIGHTS OF TERROR

ANDREA BIANCHI 1979 (US: BURIAL GROUND). All right! Onto the gut-chompers!... An invasion of European cannibal zombie-romps have flooded video stores in the past few years, and most of them are really *dull*! Not this baby, though, **Nights of Terror** delivers on its promises! It's unrated, and I can easily understand why, because this is one nasty, rancid movie! Not particularly original, but visceral as heck... Director Andrea Bianchi vies for the dubious title of Intestine King against Lucio Fulci (**Zombie Flesh Eaters**, **City of the Living Dead**), and does a fine job in creating a mindless, non-stop bombardment of gore, slime and ripped flesh. Technically it's a mess, with wooden actors, hack dialogue and a Swiss Cheese plotline straight out of the Romero series – but if you're looking for cheap, plentiful violence (and nowadays, who isn't?) this is right at the top of the pack... It starts out pretty moody and atmospheric as a bearded ol' guy accidentally stumbles onto a burial crypt full of hungry meat-eaters and becomes their first snack. But then we get to meet our cast of victims, er, characters, and they're such a boring lot that you can't wait to see them all die *horribly* at the hands of the Living Dead. While the zombie hordes are gathering together for a red meat round-up, all the humans are yacking it up at the Mansion of the Mundane, oblivious to the fact that corpses are crawling up out of their backyard! I'm talking dozens and dozens of the critters, too! Nothing seems to stop them from their meal-time mission (they just ooze a brownish goop when they're stabbed) and within half an hour these messy monsters are tearin' at torsos and playin' Slinky with the large intestine (amidst plenty of juicy close-ups, of course). Naturally, *we* all know that the only way to stop a zombie is to destroy the brain, but the cast doesn't figure it out until they crack open one creature's skull with a rock, and blue, red and yellow liquid pours out! Just to add to the fun, these monsters know how to handle weapons! One tosses knives like an expert while another grabs a sickle to chop off heads, and they even use axes and battering rams to get into the barricaded house... The film just doesn't let up! There's attack after attack (each accompanied by bad electronik musik), and the finale even gives us a monastery full of Zombie Monks! (The high point is when a little-boy zombie rips off his mom's bare nipple with his teeth! Ow! Ow! Ow!)... Sure, the rotted-face makeup is mediocre at

"WHEN THE MOON TURNS RED THE DEAD SHALL RISE."

WARNING: THIS FILM CONTAINS SCENES WHICH ARE CONSIDERED SHOCKING! NO ONE UNDER 17 WILL BE ADMITTED.

BURIAL GROUND

AN FCG RELEASE © 1985

times (they sure use plenty of maggots, though), but the fact that *everyone* in the whole danged film *dies* (!), quickly makes up for a few makeup deficiencies. Overall, this is a four-star butcher-shop blood bath, with innards of all sorts stretchin' their way across the screen. Though totally lacking in style, **Nights of Terror** is solidly recommended for its high gross-out factor... CHOMP!

NOT OF THIS EARTH

ROGER CORMAN 1957. "You are about to adventure into the Dimension of the Impossible!... If the events you are about to witness are unbelievable, it is only because your imagination is chained!" Whew! With a prologue *that* hokey, it's gotta be a good flick! Initially released on the B-half of a double bill with **Attack of the Crab Monsters**, this is one of Corman's classic Weekend Wonders, with a script by Charles Griffith (**Bucket of Blood**, **The Wild Angels**) and Mark Hanna. It's your basic American-International fun — a silly little concept, no production values whatsoever, and a cast of happy-to-be-working-at-all actors scraped from the floor of Corman's stable... Telepathic alien humanoids are readying to take over the earth, since they've already fucked up their own dying planet and they need a new place to screw around with. The first step is infiltrating into our society — so here comes Paul Birch as the creepy Mr. Johnson, a constantly-sunglassed gent who knocks out unsuspecting earthlings with his glowing Power Peepers. While relaying messages to his Intergalactic Boss, who sits in a closet (actually, it's supposed to be a Dimensional Wall, but it still looks

like a closet to me), we learn that the citizens of the planet Davana need rich, fresh blood to survive. So Mr. Johnson spends his evenings luring homeless hobos down to his basement and sucking 'em dry... '50s-fave Beverly Garland (**It Conquered the World**, **The Alligator People**) co-stars as a nosy live-in nurse who suspects something is amiss in Mr. Johnson's locked cellar; Mr. Krelboin himself, Jonathan Haze, is a street-wise servant; and Dick Miller is a fast-talking vacuum-cleaner salesman who becomes furnace fuel — stealing the entire show with only two-minutes of screen time. To add to the laughs, there's a quick appearance by an ultra-cheap jellyfish-like plastic-puppet/monster that floats around on all-too-visible wires... And once again, Corman proves he *really* knows how to direct this pulp science fiction material efficiently. In less flattering terms, his work is cheap, fast and occasionally crude — but not without the necessary dose of humour. Definitely worth a look!

NOT OF THIS EARTH

JIM WYNORSKI 1988. Sequel master, Jim Wynorski, whose usual fodder includes unwatchable T&Atrocities such as **Deathstalker II**, **Big Bad Mama II** and **Return of the Swamp Thing**, *finally* came up with a semi-successful (but no less derivative) idea — remake Roger Corman's quickie classic! The final product has the words Hack Job all over it, but (surprise) it's not as thoroughly wretched as you might expect. I don't know if Wynorski will ever get around to making a good movie, but in this case he manages to keep the action moving, the running time down and the women in scanty lingerie. The big award though, goes to whoever had the absolutely brilliant idea of hiring former jailbait jism-queen Traci Lords (**Another Role in the Hay**, **Tailhouse Rock**, **Perfect Fit**) as the lead femme. Of all the ex-porno starlets gone legit, Traci is one of the first to actually pull off the transition from face-sitting to feature-thesping — nicely straddling the thin line between schlock serious-ness and self-parody (while blowing away high-profile bubble-heads like Linnea Quigley). She ain't no Meryl Streep yet, but Traci's certainly the late '80s answer to Candice Rialson. Even her old mutton-flogging fans should get a few laffs out of her perform-ance... Except for a few R-rated modifications (such as strippa-grams and bikinied blond alienesses), the plot is a straight retread of the original. Arthur Roberts stars as Mr. Johnson, an ever-sunglassed (probably due to the cheap special effects that shoot out of his sockets) invader from the war-ravaged planet Davana. His world's blood supply is turning to dust and in this version, instead of homeless winos, he collects the plasma of the fourth-rate actresses who fill the supporting cast. Nurse Lords moves into Johnson's house in order to administer blood transfusions, un-aware of his plan to deplete the Earth's bimbo population. Lenny Juliano co-stars as Johnson's bad-boy chauffeur, who gets to leer whenever Lords undrapes herself... A tad of gore, a fair share of bare skin, and the production had just enough cash behind it so it doesn't look like a piece of shit. But instead of taking an extra day and rethinking Corman's concept, Wynorski took the easy way out by carbon copying whole chunks of the '57 flick, right down to the camera set-ups. Wynorski campily re-uses old vault footage (**Humanoids from the Deep**, **Galaxy of Terror**) and there's even a chase-sequence homage (oh, let's not be diplomatic — it's a RIP-OFF!) to **Hollywood Boulevard**. All of this is effectively spewed forth at a grindhouse mentality, but viewers who *haven't* seen the original will enjoy it the most, because the constant comparisons won't seem so glaring... 80 minutes of fast-paced stupidity. That's *my* kind of film (but only if I'm in an alcohol-induced haze)!

THE NUTTY PROFESSOR

JERRY LEWIS 1963. First off, I happen to *like* this film. A *lot*. (Enough to run out and rent the v-tape.) I realise that most people can't

☞ *Jerry's a mousey chemistry prof who invents the greatest new drink since Dracula discovered bloody marys.*

stomach the pathetic antics of Jerry Lewis – whether it's his early moron comedies, or his annual whining during the Labor Day Telethon. I admit that the guy's probably a Vegas shitbag in person, but he *did* make a few genuinely funny movies. And this is his best... A whacked take-off on the age-old Jekyll and Hyde routine, Jerry plays Julius Kelp, a nasally, spectacled college chemistry professor with a personality as appealing as being smashed about the face with a hefty bag full of broken glass. Stella Stevens co-stars as his favourite pupil, Miss Purdy, a 'nice girl' with a sympathetic edge and a sweater three sizes too tight... Tired of being a wimp, and failing miserably at every imaginable body-building course, Julius finally spends a few late evenings in his lab and whips up a formula to bring out the 'Real Man'. And after a nice, trippy transformation, he emerges as *Buddy Love* (Ta dah!) – the world's foremost womaniser, egotist and belligerent drunk. He sings for the crowds of adoring fans, picks up the Purdy blond co-ed, pummels a few jocks, sings 'That Old Black Magic', and pulls off the most scathingly accurate imitation of ex-partner Dean Martin. With his lubricated head of hair and suits that look like they were designed on Pluto, we watch in glee as this plastic playboy takes over the local hangout, The Purple Pit, and proves that any asshole can be a superstar... The gags are actually funny, Lewis' direction is great (he received the French equivalent of The Oscar for it. *Really!*), and his performance is his most bizarre (and downright nasty, too). Obviously, this is not your ordinary film – you have to be into the little-appreciated Tex Avery/Spastic Nerd genre of filmmaking, complete with gaudy sets, unrealistic characters, asinine script, and stoopid sight gags. Sure, it ain't Kubrick, but an entire nation of snail-eaters can't be *all* wrong.

OASIS OF THE ZOMBIES

A.M. FRANK 1981 (AKA: BLOODSUCKING NAZI ZOMBIES; AKA: L'ABIME DES MORTS VIVANTS). How on earth could I pass up a movie with a title like *this*? It *sounds* like Troma Meets Dyanne Thorne, but since the Video box carries *no* credits whatsoever, *no* date and the cover is

just a 'borrowed' illo of a skull with a commandant's hat, I was mighty suspicious. Well, *caveat emptor* still reigns, because this turned out to be just another in the long line of Spanish-lensed, Nazi living dead films (there's been about half a dozen of 'em). Directed by A.M. Frank (aka Daniel Lesoeur) and starring Manuel Gelin and France Jordan, this tame chiller is low in promised sadism and high in badly-dubbed boredom... Within the first five minutes, the viewer knows they're in for an uneventful ride, when a pair of blow-dried bimbos stumble onto a Nazi burial mound at an oasis in the North African desert. The moment they touch the leftover memorabilia that's scattered about, arms reach out of the sand and it's 'goodbye girls'. There's no suspense, no surprises, no blood, and it gets even *worse* when the actual story kicks in. We learn in flashbacks how a Nazi battalion carrying a convoy of gold was massacred in a (relatively unexciting) ambush, and ever since that day, the desert nomads claim that the oasis is haunted by the souls of the dead soldiers. But back in the present, the son of the Nazi commander finds his pop's old diary and decides to go after the lost gold with the aid of some college friends (all of whom are salivating at the thought of $6 million in untaxable bullion). Even though all previous expeditions have turned up dead, these money-hungry kids don't believe the 'tall tales' of Axis ghosts – that is, until they pitch their tents, the sun sets and the decomposing German deadniks come wading out of the darkened dunes. The ending is so badly edited and idiotically contrived that you'll wonder why you ever wasted your time on this atrocity: A couple zombies attack, the actors burn 'em up with gasoline and the flick ends. Is that the *best* they could come up with?... There's nothing on screen to keep your attention – the script is slow, the characters are unappealing and anyone looking for blood-'n'-guts galore or high-tech thrills will be sorely disappointed, since the ultra-primitive effects and makeup consist of pasting some goo on the zombies' faces and giving them a pig intestine to use as dental floss. We've seen all this nonsense time and time before, and as long as vid-distributors can re-title any old import and pass it off as new product, we'll keep getting crap like this dumped on us for a long time. As desert adventures go, I'll take **Ishtar** over this offal any day...

ONE DOWN TWO TO GO

FRED WILLIAMSON 1982. The cast of **Three the Hard Way** returns! Jim Brown. Jim Kelly. And Fred Williamson not only stars, but directs! They even rounded up **Shaft** himself, Richard Roundtree to join the

fracas. But instead of neo-nazis, deadly bacteria and kick-ass superhero hamminess, this time the 42nd Street Foursome takes on a boring bunch of lowlife honky gangsters who are infiltrating the karate field. The results are worse than mediocre – they're downright BORING!... Kelly first leaps into the funky fray as the red-leather-garbed martial arts teacher Chuck Wells, who discovers The Mob has been fight-fixing, and investigates with the help of fellow instructor Roundtree. But when Kelly's shot by the hoods and his girlfriend is gang raped, he calls on two old pals to settle the score and retrieve his $400,000 in rightful prize money. Enter Mr. J (Jim) and Cal (Fred), the heavyweight one-two punch of the blaxploitation era! Both make their ego-stretched entrances in chauffeured limos – Williamson in his usual navel-cut wardrobe and Brown poured into an Italian-cut suit. They don't want to start any trouble (yeah, right) but the shit begins to fly the moment a white dimwit *breaks* Fred's cigar in half (!), prompting Fred to toss the idiot across the room like an Aussie dwarf, while Jim pulls a bunion-sized pistol that'd blow the doors clean off a Cadillac. A crime kingpin, Mr. Rossi, is behind the criminal chicanery, but despite being insulated by muscle-bound employees, Jim and Fred effortlessly wade through the white trash in search of their missing Brothers... This is an unbelievably simple-minded actioner with little going for it, except the pleasure of watching the killer cast flaunt their macho brand of menace. All four stars strut through it on auto-pilot, as if the role were etched into their grey cells with battery acid. Each gets his fair share of scene hogging, although Kelly is somewhat wasted since he's in a coma or hospitalised for the last two-thirds of the movie. The only notable supporting cast member is the late great Joe Spinell as a fight promoter with a heart of mould... Williamson's flat direction is the major culprit: Most scenes are so drawn-out they surpass tedium, the hand-to-hand combat is blandly choreographed, and when it comes to the sleazier aspects, the violence is bloodless (despite a pile of corpses littering the script) and there's no nudity (not even from the white chick who gets a bathroom bone dance from The Hammer). Still, it's great to see the quartet and their ever-expanding mid-sections together once again, and if they wait a few more years they'll be ready to reunite for 'Black Cocoon'.

ONE-WAY TICKET TO HELL

BAMLET LAWRENCE PRICE JR 1955 (AKA: TEENAGE DEVIL DOLLS). Another in Rhino Video's Teenage Theatre collection, this is an obscure, anti-drug, anti-juvenile delinquent, anti-rebellion morality story, *all* told in not-so-glorious **Dragnet**-style narration. It's a classic example of an 'educational' feature – overwrought, paranoid, fear-mongering, and totally idiotic. Plus, this particular film is so witless that it never comes close to achieving a **Violent Years/High School Confidential** level of campiness... Directed and written by asswipe-auteur Bamlet Lawrence Price Jr., Barbara Marks stars as Cassandra – the typical good girl gone bad. In flashback, we see how this innocent, perky lass first smokes a reefer due to peer pressure from a bunch of motorcycle-riding (in other words, degenerate) pals, and within days, she's been transformed into an anti-social reject of society.

One touch of the needle ... a lifetime of TORTURE!
"ONE-WAY TICKET TO HELL"
THE STORY OF TEEN-AGE MADNESS!
IT'S NEW! IT'S POWERFUL!

Her grades decline, she doesn't go to college, she drops her new-lywed hubby like a hot potato, and even has a full-scale nervous breakdown complete with hair pulling and tremors. Next come the cocktail bars, where she can swig back a few quarts 'til all hours of the morning. But that's nothing compared to the combination of marijuana and 'goofballs', which leaves Cassandra suicidal and heads her down "the long road that junkies call The Route". Running away from home, she's recruited by a mobster and ends up selling dope on the street corners until Sven Bergman, the local Swedish drug kingpin learns that she's cutting in on his market. Sven kidnaps Cassandra, introduces her to the sinister joys of heroin, and she winds up in a classic Snake Pit insane asylum (from which I got plenty of cheap laughs)... From then on the tale gets really melodramatic! Didn't think they could cram more bathos down you throat, did you?... She picks up a Mexican boyfriend named Cholo Martinez (played by B.L. Price Jr., who only proves he doesn't have a lick of talent in *front* of the camera either), and he turns out to be a professional car thief as well as a "mental defective"... Basically, this is drug-paranoia propaganda at its bleakest and least entertaining, with grainy black and white photography, static direction, and a voice-over so monotonous that you want to shove a bag of broken glass down narrator Kurt Martell's shorts. I don't even have a clue as to how good the actors are, since they weren't given *any* dialogue. It just drones on for 60-plus minutes, and though the plot tries to be controversial and hard-hitting, the flick is actually so *unsleazy* that it never gets off the ground. It's too bad, since Cassandra experiences more cheap pathos than Bonnie Parker, Patty Hearst and Sylvia Plath combined. The only thing that could've saved the film would have been Divine in the lead.

ORDER OF DEATH

ROBERTO FAENZA 1983 (US: CORRUPT; AKA: COPKILLERS). Though it has a distinctively offbeat flavour (probably because it was filmed in the US with an all-Italian crew), in the end this turns out to be your routine crime thriller, which is notable primarily for the acting debut of John Lydon/Johnny Rotten (from The Sex Pistols, you uncultured twits). Cut by 15 minutes for its American release, it still plods along in places, and this flick is more a curiosity item nowadays than anything else... A murderer in a ski mask and cop uniform has been jumping out of alleyways and slicing the throats of NYC undercover narcotics officers, and police Lieutenant Harvey Keitel gets mighty suspicious when a strange young man in a loud jacket and red sunglasses (Lydon, of course) follows him to his apartment and matter-of-factly admits to the rash of killings. Harvey is convinced that Lydon's simply another in a long line of fruitcakes who enjoys confessing to any crime they can conjure up, *but* since Lydon has also discovered Keitel's palatial apartment (paid for by endless kickbacks and corruption galore), he's afraid to let the guy go. Instead, Harvey gags him, ties him up and takes him prisoner in his home. This is where the tale starts getting dark and twisted – locked in a bathroom, fed from a dog bowl, his head stuffed in an oven, and whenever Keitel gets the urge, he socks John in the face. "You're *mine* now," snarls Keitel, and after **Taxi Driver** and **Fingers**, this is his most caustic role. Eventually the pair become opponents in a match of psychological gamesmanship involving murder, deception and greed... Sounds good, right? Too bad director Roberto Faenza couldn't lens a suspenseful scene if his Green Card depended on it; so the entire film rests on the shoulders of its two leads. Everything else is soft and mushy crime melodrama at the core, but Keitel and Lydon come away unscathed. In the hands of a surer director, this could have been an '80s companion piece to **Performance**, but instead it's low-key to the point of somnambulism. Harvey K. is fine, as usual, but Lydon is the real surprise. From his reputation, you'd expect him to puke on the floor and stick a wire coat hanger through a baby's head – but the guy gives a surprisingly intelligent performance, and underplays perfectly to match Keitel's hysterics. Add some pulsing Ennio Morricone music, and you've got a solid mess: Some good, some terrible, but mostly just your standard policier. Based on the novel **The Order of Death** by Hugh Fleetwood.

ORGY OF THE DEAD

A.C. STEPHENS 1965. Rhino Video drags the gutters once again and arrives with this classic skin flick that plays off the reputation of its scriptwriter, the legendary Ed Wood, Jr.; and after sitting through this jiggling meat market, I think Ed musta scrawled the screenplay on the back of a soggy cocktail napkin after director A.C. Stephens bought him a few hundred rounds. The end result is an excruciating tale that'll have you biting the caps off of beer bottles. 'Are you heterosexual?' blasts the ads, but they should also ask 'Are you a brain-damaged monkey-boy?' while they're at it, cuz if you aren't when the movie starts, then you *will be* after sitting through 90 minutes of this hilariously tacky nonsense that must have been filmed with the loose change the cast & crew received from returning that week's supply of empty beer cans... 'But is it any fun?' you might be asking. Well, I happen to agree that **Plan 9 from Outer Space** is one of the great anti-intellectual epics of all time, and for a moment or two this flick reaches those lofty heights, especially when the famed Criswell is jabbering away like some bug-eyed speed freak – but most of **Orgy** is nothing but an excuse to film a bunch of *long* 'interpretative' dances (I'm talking five minutes each!) where the ladies strip down to their panties or g-strings. And would believe that these stripteases suck up two-thirds of the running time?... As in **Plan 9**, Criswell pops up (this time from a coffin) during a hokey prologue, giving us a portentous speech about the chills and terrors to come (not that they ever do, of course). And if that wasn't enough, the Big C also stars as the Master of the Dead, sitting on a tombstone in an old Bela cape and preceding (very dramatically, need I add) over his bevy of topless 'ghosts' from the past, all of them wiggling their wares in front of the comatose cameraman while the fog machines work overtime. Choreographic highlights include the Tahitian Twist, the Bridal Boogaloo, and the incredible Cat Dance, where a girl struts around in a baggy Halloween-style cat costume with the chest cut out so her garbonzas can get some air. The whole thing looks like a stag party at the old Monster Movie Matinee set... Beyond *all that* (oh gosh, you mean there's *more*?!) there's a lame subplot about an ordinary couple who decide to visit a remote cemetery one

day/night (I'm not sure which, since long shots of the moving car are in bright sunlight and close-ups of the actors are in the dark) to get inspiration for the guy's latest horror novel. But when him and his red-headed floozy smash up their car, they stumble upon the Dancing Dead and are taken prisoner, tied to stone columns, and forced to watch Criswell's Cuties. A crummy mummy and werewolf help out as comedy relief and a pre-Elvira Fawn Silver is the supposed-to-be-sexy Princess of Darkness. What emotion! What depth! What utter bullshit!... Yes, this is truly one of those 'You-Gotta-See-It-To-Believe-It' movies, and for a '60s nudie flick it's better than average – the picture stays in focus and none of the women have any discernible cold sores. Of course, if you have no tolerance whatsoever for cheesy bump 'n' grind (or if your VCR's Fast Forward button is broken) you'll want to avoid this one like the Red Death... But then, just when your sensibilities are at an all-time low, Criswell comes across with a howler like "Torture! Torture! It pleasures me!" while he watches a slave girl being whipped, and it almost makes it all worthwhile. The only thing Criswell needs is a dollar jug of Chablis to wash down his dignity with... **Orgy of the Dead** is an experience not to be forgotten.

OUT OF THE BLUE

DENNIS HOPPER 1981. Dennis Hopper journeyed to Canada to pick up some quick blow money by co-starring in a sappy, do-gooder domestic drama entitled **The Case of Cindy Barnes**. But in a stroke of pure luck, first-time director Leonard Yakir panicked and walked off the job, leaving Hopper to gladly take over and get his first opportunity behind the camera since his epic money-loser **The Last Movie**. And though the producers wanted a moralistic little story of youthful over-indulgence, Dennis tossed out the original script, started from scratch, and came up with a great, hard-edged tale of rebellious youth which pre-dates the desperation of **River's Edge**. Steeped in loneliness, disillusion and alienation, all the characters are utterly fucked up people whose dead end lives veer between day-to-day tedium and explosions of warped frustration. It's nihilistic, anarchistic, plus so hard-hitting and honest that it makes you forget the bogus nature of Hopper's newer projects, like **Colors**. And above all, it's definitely *not* a light-hearted time at the movies... Set in one of the most dismal backwater burgs in all of Canada, Linda Manz stars as the 14-year-old CeBe – the product of a gnarled home life, with slutty mom Sharon Farrell trying to raise her right, despite ex-jailbird dad Dennis, who's been serving time for driving soused and slamming into a loaded schoolbus (a reoccurring, and deadly sober image). But with recently DOA-ed celebs like Sid Vicious and Elvis Presley as heroes, CeBe's turning into a cigarette-smokin', tough-mouthed punk. Trapped in her stinkweed town, she hitchhikes around, goes to a stranger's pad to get stoned, and kills time at lowlife night-clubs; while Papa Hopper (who's basically just a supporting character) tries to forget the past by sucking up scotch in the present. And for unintentional comic relief, Raymond 'Bloat' Burr has a couple solemn scenes as a two-ton family counsellor... Though the story is thin, the film's strengths lie in Hopper's knowledge that Society's pat answers are a problem in themself; not to mention his surprising skill in capturing twisted family ties and unpredictable eruptions of anger and despair. The harsh climax (in which the piss-drunk adults decide CeBe should get fucked in order to keep her from turning lesbian) is not only disturbing, but brings to mind the sadism and sexuality of **Blue Velvet**... The entire cast is letter perfect (especially Manz); and though Hopper's legendary directorial finesse (re. sloppy psychedelia) is kept reasonably restrained, he never skimps on seedy reality or gives the tale a fake gloss. Plus he's able to locate the crevices of society which aren't usually committed to celluloid... Just think, Hopper pulled this li'l masterpiece off in his pre-detox days too (and it certainly shows when he's on-screen). A bit rambly at times, yet unforgettable – this is one of the great bummer flicks of all time... Title song provided by The Hop's pal, Neil Young.

PARENTS

BOB BALABAN 1989. This flick flew through the theatres during its initial release, which is a shame because it's one of the most creative items to emerge this year. A little film with big surprises – it's scathing, horrific and unique... Screen newcomer Bryan Madorsky stars as Michael, a frail, perpetually-leery pre-teen who moves to a new suburban neighbourhood. His parents (Randy Quaid and Mary Beth Hurt) look like they stepped out of a '50s sitcom, with plastic all-too-wide smiles. Mom is the perfect, ball-gowned housewife, while Dad practices his golf game when not manufacturing war defoliants for Toxico. But besides the usual fears about a new school and ever-approaching puberty, Michael seems somewhat paranoid about his own parents. For example, what exactly are those unrecognisable cuts of meat in the frying pan? Why do they keep having 'leftovers', when they've never eaten what they were leftover *from*? Was that really a human leg hanging from a meat hook in the cellar? And is the little kid completely off his rocker, or are his folks secretly into cannibalism? ("Eat your meat!" orders Dad.) The school psychologist (played by the everjittery Sandy Dennis) isn't much help either – but what would you expect from a woman who has a sculpture of a penis with nails hammered into it?... This is a highly stylised, surprisingly taut tale that puts suburbia through a meat grinder (quite literally). One of the ultimate Childhood Nightmare films, in a class with the original **Invaders from Mars** and **The 5,000 Fingers of Dr. T**. But there's also an undercurrent of sexual fear and repression throughout, and one of the creepiest scenes involves Michael's new friend Sheila, and their tryst in a meat locker. Imagine if Kubrick's **The Shining** was genetically fused with **Leave it to Beaver**, and you get the feel of the flick. Actor-turned-director Bob Balaban has pulled off a winner, where it could've easily become a cheap one-joke mess. It's a technical marvel too, with great kitschy music, the best set decoration since **Hairspray**, and surreal, perspective-warping cinematography (including some wicked dreams, such as going into the kitchen and seeing a hand twitching out of the garbage disposal). Best of all, Randy Quaid is a scurvy standout! The guy is so evil he *must* be a parent in real life!... A small gem – not altogether dazzling (the ending turns predictable), but with more dimension to it than most other recent releases, and a wide streak of black humour throughout.

THE PASSOVER PLOT

MICHAEL CAMPUS 1976. Forget all the holier-than-thou hullabaloo concerning **The Last Temptation of Christ**. *Here's* the revisionist flick the crackpot Christian scum would've had more cause to picket for 'blasphemy'. Any intelligent viewer (thus excluding most fundamentalist lemmings) felt **Temptation** was a magnificent film that oozed with True Faith. But over 10 years earlier, producer Menahem Golan spewed forth this wild little Bible saga which says Jesus was a fake and that the entire crucifixion was nothing but a magic trick to fool the gullible and help butt-kick the Romans from the land. So, are you shacked down to your socks by this postulation? Tough shit, you sheep. Read on... Using the Hebrew names, Zalman King (star of **Blue Sunshine** and director of sexpotrash like **Two Moon Junction**) stars as Yeshua of Nazareth, an angry, unquestionable Jewish hero who happily breaks all the Anglo-Saxon stereotypes of past features. Having read the prophesies of a king leading his people to freedom, Yeshua decides to pose as this Son O' God in order to speed up the Roman's departure. He fasts, rounds up a few random apostles, fakes a couple miracles using strong-arm tactics, and has the public eating out of his hand. Yeshua's certainly passionate about his philosophy –

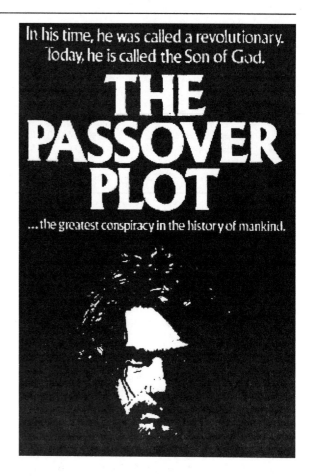

In his time, he was called a revolutionary. Today, he is called the Son of God.

THE PASSOVER PLOT

...the greatest conspiracy in the history of mankind.

shouting his gospel like some crazed revolutionary – but underneath he's just another politician, taking a good cause and compromising it with deception and cynicism. By the end, Yeshua stages his own arrest and subsequent crucifixion with the help of Judah. His hare-brained plan: To fake his own death on the cross with a medical potion and when he is 'resurrected' the people will recognise him as their saviour. But as we all know, the scheme goes slightly haywire, with Yeshua winding up dead, followed by 2,000 years of mindless toadying to his image. This isn't some half-baked story conceived simply to rake in a few controversial dollars though. It's inspired by Hugh J. Schonfield's meticulously researched book, and the film is often as conceptually powerful as Scorsese/Kazantzakis', even though the shoestring budget gives it the look of any Sunn Classics tripe. Filled with inexpensive, but authentic detail (i.e. they serve matzo at the Last Supper instead of Wonder Bread), director Michael Campus (**The Mack**) even takes a couple trippy tangents, such as Yeshua's solarised hallucinations. But in the final judgement, the film is generally more thought-provoking than downright entertaining. Campus does his best to compress the book's political and social themes into less than two hours, and the result is a dialogue surplus. The fine cast is up to the challenge, including Donald Pleasence as Pontius Pilate, Hugh Griffith as Caiaphas, Scott Wilson as Judah, and even Robert Walker (**Easy Rider**)... Though the film never succeeded in convincing me wholeheartedly of its bold concept, then again, neither did that entertaining little fairy tale the Bible trumpets as undiluted truth.

THE PEACE KILLERS

DOUGLAS SCHWARTZ 1971. Here's a hot obscurity for you! It's a combination hippie/biker flick, and thank goodness its box has the helpful warning, 'this video contains nudity and violence', because

annoying – because the hippies are an even goofier bunch of longhairs, with ultra-pretentious (not to mention idiotic) ramblings about 'one-ness' and 'being'. Geeesh, I don't know how *any* of them kept a straight face while reciting this crapola! Their Christ-like leader is a preachy sack-of-shit named Alex, and the film's high point in Bad Symbolism is when the cyclers crucify His Whininess to a six-foot peace symbol... Overall, the whole production is loads of cruddy fun, and it's an interesting attempt at a slightly different style of schlock. Though the story suffers since *all* the characters are insufferable, **The Peace Killers** still has everything you've come to expect in a good bikerama: Terrible acting, lots of beer drinking, loads of brutality, and endless shots of Death Row riding their choppers while the soundtrack pounds away at your skull... Hilarious nonsense!

PENITENTIARY III

JAMAA FANAKA 1987. Three cheers for director Jamaa Fanaka! At least *someone* is still churning out mindless shit for the direct-to-The-Deuce market, because his flicks sure won't play in Peoria! And where else can you find a Zen-midget-kung-fu-comedy mixed with blaxploitation-prison-revenge-drama? For any schlock-o-phile who's been asleep for the past decade, this is the third in the epic saga of boxing star 'Too Sweet' Gordone and his continual, unjustified incarcerations. Once again, Leon Isaac Kennedy (the '80s answer to Richard Roundtree) grabs the lead role and keeps a straight face throughout this ridiculous grindhouse yarn... While under the influence of an illicit drug, Too Sweet caves in an opponent's face during a bout and is sentenced to a three-year stretch in The Big House. There's the usual allotment of colourful characters, with imprisoned mobster Serenghetti (Anthony Geary) as their self-appointed ruler – his cell refurnished into a lavish throne room, complete with curtains, a phone, framed paintings, and manicures from his transvestite moll (played by famed female impersonator and soon-to-be welfare recipient Jim Bailey). Conveniently enough, the prison boxing championship is quickly approaching, but Gordone has given up the ring after his recent fatality – a situation that doesn't sit well with Serenghetti, who wants Too Sweet on his team. Enter some physical persuasion, in the form of The Midnight Thud, who's a sub-human eunuch-maker played (hilariously) by midget wrestler The Haiti Kid – a snarling, tongue-wagging, Muppet-sized jujitsu fiend! Toss in some late-night electroshock treatments and bread-and-water confinement in the prison's rat-infested dungeon, but Too Sweet holds *firm* with his pacifist commitment. Well, for a *little* while that is, but then it's Mui Macho Time with the half-pint Thud providing the mystical Yoga lessons. And you'll want to strap yourself down for the free-style, anything-goes, dumbshit finale! Eye gouging! Strangle holds! Scrotum bashing! Blood packets galore! Guys flying 30 feet through the air from *one* punch! This is pure Cellblock Schlock, and every time you think it's reached maximum stupidity, the film bounds spritefully into a new dimension of absurdity! There's even a gratuitous female boxing match so Too Sweet can get a chance to drain his dingus... Most of the cast is fine for this type of nonsense – all except for Anthony Geary, who's not only a bottomless pit of talentlessness, but who also looks so thin and weather-beaten that you wonder if he's been following Liberace's Watermelon Diet recently. Action auteur Fanaka calls the shots like he's helming 'Citizen Kane, Part 2' and though the result isn't even close to being a *good* film, it *is* solid-to-the-core garbage for cheap-thrill seekers hungry for new product.

PETEY WHEATSTRAW, THE DEVIL'S SON-IN-LAW

CLIFF ROQUEMORE 1978. Ego Unlimited presents another 42nd Street treat from Rudy Ray Moore, one of the last (not to mention, most

that's a recommendation as far as I'm concerned! With plenty of no-names in the cast and an unknown director named Douglas Schwartz, I wasn't expecting much (especially since it came out at the end of the Cycle genre), but by its finale I was happily surprised at discovering such a thoroughly entertaining mish-mash which mixes hilariously preachy dramatics with sewer-level violence and revenge... Our villains for the evening are Death Row, a pack of monosyllabic Neanderthals who only want to ride their choppers, fight, screw, piss, fart, and slobber through their crayola-scrawled dialogue. But when these bikers learn that one of their runaway Mamas, Christie, has become a commune-living flower child, they decide to steal her back. So, led by their grubby president, Rebel, they head out across the desert for a relaxing afternoon of shit-kicking at the hippie's abode, pausing quickly to torture an old shopkeeper with a road flare until he divulges the secret location of the commune. These peaceful hippies won't fight back though (they won't "plug into" the gang's bad vibes), so when Death Row slither into their encampment, the loveable peaceniks get their pasty asses kicked across the desert. Just what they deserve for being such a bunch of helpless, non-violent dorks! Death Row then kidnap Christie, molest her for a while, force her to take a shitload of acid, and drag her back to their hideout, where they plan to rape her until her kidneys come out her ears. It's seriously sick stuff, and by the end, a pre-**Rookies** Michael Ontkean (as a doofy flower child) decides to take a firm stand against these chopper-heads. And just to even up the score, the scriptwriters toss in a multi-racial motorcycle gang (whites, orientals, blacks, and a Pam Grier-styled biker-bitch played to the hilt by Lavelle Roby) who join up with the hippies so the audience can sit back, relax, and enjoy a full-scale, no-holds-barred rumble to the death. I especially *loved* watching the tranquil hippies transform into mad-dog killers – arming themselves to the teeth with pitchforks and axes!... Unlike earlier cycle flicks, where the gang members were semi-appealing anti-heroes (**The Wild Angels, Hell's Angels on Wheels**), this film follows the **Satan's Sadists** theory of making the bikers into the most inhuman pieces of human flotsam imaginable. That fact notwithstanding, I still don't know which group of characters are more portly) blaxploitation stars of the '70s. Beginning his career with off-colour party albums such as **This Pussy Belongs to Me**, instead of courting the film studios, Moore scraped up his own cash and made the type of movies he wanted to see. Really dumb ones! Featuring his unique brand of action (sloppy and laughable) and his botched brand of comedy (raunchy and unlaughable). Released late in the waning urban genre, his films became unintentional satires on their own chilly clichés, and if this particular flick were made by a white guy, he'd be on the NAACP's hit list (especially for the Uncle Tom's Cabin intro, with a woman giving birth to a watermelon!)... This fantasy-edged blaxploiter features a moustached Rudy Ray in the title role, as his typically unbelievable, rude, rappin' Romeo (with shirt collars so huge a good-sized breeze could put him aloft like The Flying Nun) who's beloved by his whole velour community for kicking junkies' asses with Kung Fool antics taught to him as a youth. And though his actual martial arts skills are debatable, Rudy sure can make some stooopid noises while using 'em. Petey's primary goal in life is to use his humour to save the world from its own misery. Unfortunately, his foul-mouthed, insult-laden night-club act is more painful than any ill plaguing the planet. But despite his abrasive, arrogant personality, the besotted extras seem to lap up his routine (of course, you gotta remember that even a senile ol' slug like Bob Hope can find *someone* in his audience pie-eyed enough to chuckle for the camera). The first half hour is typical fare, but the going gets weird after an entire funeral procession is wasted by gangsters (led by the obviously-evil Mr. White), and Petey winds up in a minimalist Hades (consisting of a table and a red spotlight). There he meets the dapper Lucifer (G. Tito Shaw, who can actually *act!*), who offers a deal to him: If Petey agrees to marry Satan's butt-ugly daughter and give him a grandson, he can return to Earth and revenge his killing. With a trusty magic cane to give him pin-headed powers, Petey returns from the dead and turns adulterous hubbies into dogs, makes fat women thin, instantly combs out nappy hair, and stokes a **Carrie**-esque riot at Mr. White's night-spot. This all probably sounds a lot funnier than it actually is. Sure, it's a wild idea with a few must-see moments for blaxploitation masochists, but *big* hunks are interminable and director/writer Cliff Roquemore kept a faster comic book pace in their previous So-Lousy-It's-Hilarious epic, **The Human Tornado**. Only at the end, when Petey's besieged by Satan's servants (wearing red tights and with rubber horns glued to their foreheads) does it approach the surreal silliness of **Tornado**. Even though, the flick is surprisingly low in the slapstick sex scenes he's renowned for, and at the request of all the women of America, 'Please don't take your shirt off anymore, Rudy!' And how does he cover up the fact he's such a lardass, you wonder? Easy. Hire actors fatter than he is, such as Leroy and Skillet – two bloated clowns who manage a competing club... Still, it's better than **Harlem Nights**. But so's a poke in the eye.

PHANTASM

DON COSCARELLI 1979. Shortly after the death of his parents, a young boy discovers the cemetery they're buried in has been turned into a sort of slave farm by a sinister giant known as The Tall Man. Mr. Man (Angus Scrimm) is stealing corpses (and carrying their coffins under one arm when necessary), re-animating them, and turning them into mutant dwarves who scurry around in black robes, running grim errands. Naturally, the kid's older brother (who's planning on sending him off to live with relatives) doesn't believe a word of his stories about bizarre, gory goings-on in the graveyard, until he becomes involved in the whole nasty business himself. There are some strange gadgets such as a fist-sized flying steel ball that imbeds itself in a victim's face by plunging a couple of built-in spikes into his eyes and drilling into his forehead while he screams in agony. The dialogue is a little asinine ("It was making

these weird noises and jumping up and down on the car!" "Maybe it was that retarded kid, Timmy, from up the street.") but the special effects, the gore (lots of blood – red *and* yellow...) and genuine scares are plentiful and often refreshingly unusual. Hell, it's one of *my* personal favourites. From the director who brought us the highly inferior **Beastmaster**. [BJE]

PHANTASM II

DON COSCARELLI 1988. 'The Ball is back,' but after sitting through this mostly-lame sequel to one of our favourites, we wished that damned sphere had never returned. In other words, BIG DISAPPOINTMENT! Not a terrible film, just a huge step down from the first, in addition to being as thoroughly predictable as the other was imaginative. Luckily, we caught it at the drive-in, where we could indulge in maximum beer-drinking once we realised it was yet another bigger-budgeted, smaller-minded sequel with nothing to add to the original story... Our hero, Mike, is a little older (as well as played by a different, less likeable actor, James LeGros) but no wiser after a sanatorium stay following his first run-in with The Tall Man. This time he's out for revenge (so what else is new?), grabbing his older pal, Reggie Bannister (the ice cream vendor) and hitting the highways in search of the evil-incarnate Tall Man and his snarling battalion of other-worldly half-pints... The first hour is Tedium Deluxe, and instead of the original's nightmarish quality, we get pretty photography and more retread ideas than we deserve. At least the end picks up with a few good deaths (including a fine priest-strangulation), and director Don Coscarelli gives us not one, but three balls, ready to power-drill their way into your skull. The budget increase is obvious – the explosions are bigger and the effects are latex-ier; but the script is so featherweight that one good sneeze would send it flying into the second feature. The only reason to check out this flick is to see Angus Scrimm return as The Tall Man (though the rodeo-inspired sex scene had us laughing for a while)... Oh hell, just rent the original again.

THE PHANTOM EMPIRE

FRED OLEN RAY 1987. Who's the most prolific director around? I'd wager it's Fred Olen Ray – a guy who seems to churn out a dozen genre films every year, and some even make it beyond a straight-to-video fate! The majority are lowbrow, campy takeoffs featuring a roster of old welfare-case stars, a gaggle of friends and so many diverse plotlines that you might get the notion he simply tossed together all the costumes and props he had in his attic and wrote a semblance of a script around 'em. In this case, the silliness is based loosely on the 1935 serial starring Gene Autry (and it was probably lensed on about the same budget)... Emulating the good old '50s creature features, it opens with a nifty monster attack before settling in with the piecemeal plot. And there's nothing more refreshing than beginning a movie by seeing a shaggy-haired humanoid geek rip the head off a picnicker and then get laid out by the victim's ice-chest-wielding wife. Truly, a decapitation in the first five minutes is hard to resist... Fred Olen Ray has a renowned love for B-movie clichés – his only problem is that he usually can't transcend them. But his large tongue-in-cheek cast helps: Robert Quarry (**Count Yorga, Vampire**) is a grumpy mineralogist; Jeffrey Combs (**Re-Animator**) is an archaeologist from Miskatonic U.; Ross Hagen is a grade-Z Indiana Jones-hatted hero with a diet of rotgut; and Dawn Wildsmith is Ross' wisecracking assistant, who's so tough she sleeps with a cigar in her mouth. They gather to check out the legend of an underground city filled with precious gems, so these spelunkheads buy a map from an old alkie (the bloated and bug-eyed Russ Tamblyn) and down they journey, through the huge 'secret' tunnel in the side of a mountain. The good news is their discovery of the lost world of Caprona, populated by buxom cavegirls in animal skin bikinis (with Michelle Bauer as 'Cave

Bunny'). But the downside are the cannibalistic mutants who like to roast these chicks on a spit. Toss in a couple nice, stop-action dinosaurs (probably left over from an aborted project); a slightly modified Robby the Robot; and Sybil Danning, poured into a typical skin-tight black vinyl jump-suit and playing an alien amazon from an advanced super race (that's why she's carrying a sword, I guess). Low on vile elements (gore 'n' sex), but good for some dumb, inept laughs. Plus it's a painless intro to Fred Olen Ray's Vivarin-supplemented career.

PIGS

MARC LAWRENCE 1972 (AKA: THE KILLER). Here's a particularly sleazy little obscurity. A severely mixed bag, but with such a demented (not to mention downright silly) high concept, it's worth a quick look... Our story begins in a sanatorium which is the temporary home of Lynn, a quiet young woman who butchered up her dad after he raped her. But while the head nurse makes whoopee with a doctor, Lynn simply walks out and hits the highway. You can bet she'll wind up visiting the pig farm of crazy ol' Zambrini – who's been feeding his porkers human flesh ever since a bum fell into the pen and became an impromptu entrée. And despite the rumours Zambrini feeds all his employees to his livestock, she gets a job with him as a hired hand. The old man is always searching for fresh corpses with which to slop his sty, so he's quite pleased when Lynn starts inviting men up to her room so she can bed 'em and then slice off their balls with a straight razor. Hmmm, sounds like a mutually beneficial relationship to me (not to mention a diseased psychological pairing). She lures home the walking groceries, then he turns them into Human Helper... OK, the first *BIG* problem is that a squealing pig is just NOT THAT SCARY a sight! In fact, when the camera pulls in for a close-up of a wet snout, the only thing you're gonna do is LAUGH OUT LOUD! But director and co-star, as Zambrini) Marc Lawrence tries his best on a low budget – cobbling together some weird sequences, using distorted lenses, overdubbing an evil, li'l children's song throughout, and surprisingly, each killer *isn't* wholly unsympathetic. Each is a victim of sorts: Lynn by her father, and Zambrini by the hate-filled redneck locals. Briefly, when Zam and Lynn are at their most crazed and Lawrence's camera rips loose for some high speed visuals, it almost reminded me of a precursor to **Texas Chain Saw**. The effect is momentarily jarring ('Hey, did this thing suddenly get *good* for a minute?'), but the film is more prone to stick with formula melodramatics. The biggest pain in the ass comes from the suspicious sheriff (Jesse Vint), and all the other dry subplots are equally disposable. Plus the photography is so dark at times that you can't see the actors' faces. Toni Lawrence is fine as the psychotic Lynn, veering from a wide-eyed innocent charmer to a bug-eyed knife-wielding basket case, and though the video box lists Katherine Ross as the star of this muck, they're *not* talking about everyone's favourite Stepford Wife – it's some similarly named old bag who plays a nosy neighbour... A few great moments, some hilarious title diners, but a so-so movie. Th-th-th-that's all, folks!

THE PINK ANGELS

LARRY BROWN 1972. **The Wild Angels** is still the finest motorcycle saga to emerge from the glut that hit drive-ins during the late-'60s/early-'70s. But the genre's most bizarre permutation is this hoot: The first gay biker movie. 'La Cage Aux Fallen Angels'? 'The Queer Ones'? 'Hell's Angels in Heels'? The plot is just a loose basting of escapades perpetrated by a six pack of lisping, limp-wristed, horrifyingly stereotyped, homosexual bikers on their way to a drag-ball cotillion in Los Angeles. "Jesus Christ! You're all faggots!", one hitchhiker screams when he realises why they mix leather jackets and paisley scarves. In the Violence Department the movie's soft next to other cycle sprees (instead of knife fights they have food

fights), but it's also packed with loads of absurdist laughs. Sure, it initially sounds like insulting trash, but I plead guilty to the fact that I laughed my ass off from start to finish, while never getting the impression the filmmakers were homophobic in their humour. Even though the title characters are portrayed as effeminate prancers, they're also the most likeable people in the whole bargain-basement flick (especially Edward, the Limey poet with the atrocious Beatles accent). These swish cyclists lose their tempers and stomp their feet when The Pigs start pawing through their brassieres; and though wanton women flock to 'em (usually in a state of undress), they're pushed aside in favour of prissy roadside picnics complete with champagne and candles, or shocking local citizens by trying on prom dresses in public. But mondo trouble occurs when they run across a straight biker club, whom they take the opportunity to rouge and hair-ribbon in their sleep, thus creating a batch of fuming, mascaraed enemies. For a bit of rudimentary social comment, the filmmakers keep intercutting a (comically) Patton-ish Army officer with an ultra-militaristic plan to rid the country of these greasy, un-American bikers – leading to an out-of-left-field finale. You simply won't believe this shit! It's remarkable that people could've gotten this concept financed, much less executed. And director Larry Brown went onto even greater (non-financial) success with co-star Tom Basham in **The Psychopath**, one of the most demented slasher films ever. Also featuring John Alderman, Michael Pataki and a quick appearance by Dan 'Grizzly Cokehead' Haggarty; the acting may be unexceptional, but the cast seems to be having a ball. Pushed into drive-ins on triple bills, it's 75 minutes of unsubtle, unforgettable fun.

PINOCCHIO IN OUTER SPACE

RAY GOOSENS 1964. Now, you're probably saying to yourself, 'How can it *miss* with a title like that?' No? Well, I didn't really think so. Anyway... In this fully-animated feature from Universal, which supposedly picks up where **Pinocchio** left off, our formally-wooden friend is turning into a real little prick, pulling dirty tricks like tying tin cans to cats' tails etc., and generally being a very naughty boy; so the Good Fairy turns him back into a puppet until he proves himself worthy to walk around in human flesh... One day, Pinocchio is walking to school, singing a painfully stoopid song ("It's a goody-good mornin'," he whistles. 'Nngrarrr!' growls the viewer.) When out of the sky swoops a *spaceship*. Out pops a turtle in a space helmet (with the voice of Arnold Stang!) who informs Pinocchio that he is a Twurtle from the planet Twurtle-Dum, located near Twurtle-Dee (or is it the other way around... Hey, I'm not kidding here! *Wait*, there's *more*...). The pair zoom off to Mars in the, uh, Twurtle's spaceship, where they discover the planet's interior is being used by the unseen Martians as a breeding ground for giant bugs and lizards. They flee to the surface and are attacked by a giant crab, who suddenly ignores them when another crab comes along and the two cartoon crustaceans start fighting each other...

Later, Pinocchio and his reptilian friend try to destroy the jet-propelled *Astro, the Killer Space Whale*!! Meanwhile, back on Earth, Gepetto is lying near death in his bed, mourning his lost Pinocchio. Boo hoo... The animation itself is fine and is certainly colourful, but it's a wonder that the Disney people didn't sue sue sue, and that Carlos Collodi, Pinocchio's creator, didn't explode from his grave and stalk everyone at Universal and rip their brains out... Careful, Slimetimers; you might get irreparable brain damage from slapping yourself in the forehead so many times while watching this weirdness. [BJE]

PLANET OF THE VAMPIRES

MARIO BAVA 1965 (AKA: DEMON PLANET). This is Italian science fiction at its best, which isn't saying very much, if you think about it. But, along with **It! The Terror from Beyond Space**, this film provided lots of influence (in other words, it was mercilessly ripped off) for the look and structure of **Alien**... Directed by Mario Bava (**Blood Bath**, **Black Sabbath**), and with its American translation written by Ib Melchior (**Angry Red Planet**), it's an OK afternoon diversion which only leaves a vague, lasting impression due to the talent *behind* the camera, and not for the overall result... A spaceship crash-lands on a weird, unexplored planet, and for no apparent reason, the crew goes insane. Before you know it, they all die, their corpses disappear, and they return as vampire-like killers. Who could be responsible for such a nasty thing? Maybe it's those alien life forms down the street – you see, their planet is dying and they need host-bodies to continue existing. So, as soon as the humans are stuffed into their graves, the aliens take over, and out of the dirt they climb, ripping outta their clear, plastic body bags, and slobbering about the place. The high point is a trippy tour of the aliens' spaceship, with flashing lights, stylised sets, and skeletons of the big critters laying about in piles. Unforgettable dialogue abounds ("If I wasn't so wide awake, I'd think I was dreaming!"); there's plenty of 'scientific' mumbo-jumbo to laff at; and although it was filmed only three years before **2001**, the 'special' effects are a million years in the distance. Barry Sullivan is wooden in the lead; and Nobody Inc. provided the supporting cast... But although this

movie is as downright silly as any other studio-bound creature feature, Bava makes the best of a cheap situation and gives us an unexpected amount of style and mood for our 86 minutes – with rising mists, coloured gels on every light fixture, and shiny, black leather costumes. Fun.

THE PLAYGIRLS AND THE VAMPIRE

PIERO REGNOLI 1960 (AKA: CURSE OF THE VAMPIRE). Not *another* great-advertisement-which-leads-to-lousy-film!... Directed and written by Piero Regnoli, this Italian black and white braindozer asks the age-old question, what happens when a busload of dippy showgirls has to take shelter in a creepy castle for the night? First off, they meet the mysterious Count Kernassy (played by Walter Brandi, who also co-starred in **The Vampire and the Ballerina**) who warns them about roaming the estate after dark. And as you could guess, these plastic playmates couldn't follow a simple rule if you stapled it to their forehead, so that night all sorts of creepiness seeps into the plot: There's a dungeon full of crypts and corpses; one of the gals 'accidentally' falls out of a window while she's strutting the castle in her naughty nightie; and the lead lady, Vera, begins having visions of a previous life (within 30 seconds you'll be taking bets that she's the reincarnation of the vampire's ex-wife)... Should these starched-hair harlots expect nothing but 'destruction, ruin and violent death' at the hands (and teeth) of Count Kernassy? Or is the Count actually a good guy who'll save the day? Oh, let's confuse *everyone* and make them identical twins, with the vamp being Kernassy's ancestor, OK? (Did they make this shit up as they went along?) Let's not forget the nude female vampire (sorry vo-yeurs, it's 1960, so she's always in shadow) and that despite the half-assed horror going on around them, the showgirls have to take pretty time out for their bump-and-grind routines. Sure, it was all pretty risqué for the early '60s, but the plot, characterisations and special effects are rancid for *any* time period. "You're all a bunch of silly fools," says the gals' agent, and you'll feel as if he was talking directly to *you* if you're ever stuck watching this mood-soaked ghoul-a-rama... I certainly hope I didn't make this movie sound interesting *in the least*, cuz this catatonic chunk of cheesy nonsense is guaranteed to send you straight to snooze-land (I only fell asleep twice). Most of the people in the cast couldn't pronounce the word 'acting', much less accomplish any, and it's one of the most numbingly-paced, el stinko horror films I've seen in a *long* time (I still love that title, though). This one makes **Vampire Hookers** look like **Citizen Kane**.

POLTERGEIST II: THE OTHER SIDE

BRIAN GIBSON 1986. Indian mumbo-jumbo. Rotted corpses. Religious bogey-men. Clairvoyant visions. Cheapo special effects. Zzzzzzzz... I hope everyone got paid a *lot* for appearing in this laughable mess. Even the Vomit Creature didn't thrill me.

PRAY FOR DEATH

GORDON HESSLER 1985. The chopsocky film has gone through a lot of changes in recent years – it hit the big time with **Enter the Dragon**, took on inner-city overtones with **Black Belt Jones** and **Three the Hard Way**, made the redneck rounds with Chuck Norris, and now it's back in full, blood-caked splendour with **Pray For Death**, the latest in a long line of ninja rampage flicks starring Sho 'Laughing Boy' Kosugi...I've seen a few of the others, **Revenge of the Ninja** (spurts of action, but otherwise pretty drab) and **Ninja 3: The Domination** (aka 'Flashdance meets the Kung Fu Exorcist'), and I hadn't been too impressed. But along comes **Pray For Death**, the epic story of a master ninja who moves to America in order to open a take-out Japanese restaurant (yeah, right). Unfortunately, a band of dishonest cops, psychotic hitmen and slimy syndicate bosses (led by Michael Constantine – his career taking a distinct

nose-dive after **Room 222**) decide to rape his wife, rabbitpunch his oldest son, and kidnap his youngest. This leaves Mr. Ninja with only one alternative – kill everyone in sight! Well, that's about it for the plot, folks, but that's all the better, because it's only an excuse to draw us into a vengeful orgy of destruction. (Even his sons are pretty energetic, kicking and chopping the bejesus out of a street gang.) It's a virtual non-stop assault on the senses; with plenty of imaginative fight choreography, high-speed car chases, and a kid's bicycle that's equipped with smoke screen and detachable blow gun (not some li'l toy blow gun, either, mind you – this sucker has eight-inch-long steel darts that imbed in your jugular). And the last 30 minutes is incredible, as this little Japanese guy in his black pyjamas manages to wipe out one hundred people – with arrows through the neck, throwing-stars rammed into the eyes, and lots of razor-sharp samurai swords slicing at anybody stupid enough to stick their neck out. Award winning dialogue such as "I'm gonna rip your stinking guts out," punctuates the action. And the final gruesome battle (set in a warehouse, inexplicably filled to the rafters with nude mannequins) is top notch grindhouse action, with a sweaty, battle to the death, featuring axes, chain saws and a circular buzz saw! (The editing is fairly choppy because they had to edit out almost 30 minutes worth of violence in order to get an R rating.) So check it out if only to see Sho Kosugi in action, jumping and hopping around like he's got a live lobster in his shorts. It also has one of the worst theme songs in a long time. Whew!

THE PREMATURE BURIAL

ROGER CORMAN 1962. Edgar Allen Poe gets the Roger Corman treatment once again in this underrated AIP pic... Guy Carrel (Ray Milland – yay!) is an artist with an all-consuming fear of being buried alive. His fear becomes an obsession that reaches the point where he builds himself a crypt on the perpetually gloomy, mist-shrouded moors outside his mansion, Just in Case. Inside, he's got a coffin with a lid he can open from the inside with a touch of the finger, a door that opens from the inside, a rope ladder leading to a trap-

WITHIN THE COFFIN I LIE...*ALIVE*

...life remained only in his fevered mind, in his tormented eyes. To those at his graveside ...he was a corpse, the latest victim of a family curse!

AMERICAN-INTERNATIONAL PRESENTS

RAY MILLAND

EDGAR ALLAN POE'S

THE PREMATURE BURIAL

TASTE A MOMENT OF MADNESS...LISTEN TO THE SOUND OF PURPLE

come where the PLEASURE LOVERS are

SUSAN STRASBERG
DEAN STOCKWELL

PSYCH-OUT

...PATHÉCOLOR...

NICHOLSON · DERN · ROARKE · JULIEN ... STRAWBERRY ALARM CLOCK ... SEEDS ...

door in the ceiling, and in case none of these work, there's a goblet filled to the brim with poison, which he can chug rather than endure the horror of suffocating in a cramped coffin. Naturally, his wife (Hazel Court) doesn't approve of any of this... She tries to make their spooky mansion a little more cheerful by bringing in some flowers, but Milland forbids her to bring "those sickly funeral decorations" into the house. When dining with family and friends, he raises a toast: "To Death." "I never enjoy myself," he admits, "I merely experience greater and lesser degrees of boredom." Boy, I'd really like to party with this guy, wouldn't you?... Eventually, he falls victim to catalepsy (a condition in which the body gives every impression of being dead, when in fact the victim is quite alive). He experiences the extreme pleasure of watching himself being buried alive. Shortly after, a couple of grave robbers dig him up. Then things *really* get interesting... Charles Beaumont's script is actually pretty good, and even Corman seems to have taken the whole thing *seriously*... The result is a stylish, classy little item, and unless you're one o' them poopybutts who *simply cannot* watch a horror film unless it's loaded with so much blood and gore that it starts spurting out the sprocket holes (you know who the fuck you are), you should find this an interesting hour and a half. [BJE]

PSYCH-OUT

RICHARD RUSH 1968. Who would have thought Dick Clark capable of producing one of the top acid films of the '60s? Yes, together with director-extraordinaire Richard (**The Stuntman**) Rush, Mr. American Bandstand pulled out all the stops, and next to Corman's **The Trip**,

this is the top LSD film to reach the big time. Of course, a lot has to do with the at-that-time-unknown cast (Jack Nicholson, Bruce Dern, Dean Stockwell), but to its credit, this is a paisley nightmare in the form of a film...

"It's one big plastic hassle."

Susan Strasberg stars as a 17-year-old, deaf runaway who's searching for her lost brother. First stop, Haight Ashbury, the land of marijuana-smoking hippies. Finding a nearby coffee-house, complete with day-glow, psychedelic wallpaper, she meets up with a hip guitar-player named Stony (Jack Nicholson, complete with receding hair-line and ponytail) and his band. Along the way they take the time to calm down a stoned friend with a circular saw, fight off a gang of right-wing crew-cutters, and join up with a groovy guru (Stockwell). But when Jack gets pissed off at her, Strasberg accidentally trips her brains out – hitting the crowded streets of San Francisco on STP. Of course, while she's flying above the sidewalk, she runs into her missing kin, 'Steve, the Seeker' (Bruce Dern, doing a tripped out Jesus Christ imitation) as he stands in the middle of a burning house...

"A saint!... That man Owsley's a saint!"

It's a little pretentious at times (and so obviously symbolic that it's hilarious), but this is definitely a film by and for the LSD set, with lots of documentary-style footage pulled from the streets of So. Cal. (wild and woolly cinematography courtesy of Laszlo Kovacs). The whole cast seem fucked up throughout the film (including co-stars Max Julien and Adam Roarke) – a tribute to either their acting ability or their chemical state at the time. Musical highlights include The Strawberry Alarm Clock singing 'Rainy Day Mushroom Pillow'. A must-see!

THE PSYCHIC

JAMES F. HURLEY 1968. The video box for this film proudly calls it 'Herschell Gordon Lewis' **The Psychic**'. But don't be sucked in by false advertising – it was actually directed by Lewis' friend and colleague James F. Hurley, and the only creative aspect HGL was involved with was the photography. It really shows too, because this is nothing more than a '60s nudie romp, and it's a shitty one at that... Dick Genola stars as Dan Thomas, a loathsome Lothario who turns into a psychic-seducer before our very eyes. One day he falls off his roof and smashes his head, only to awaken and discover that he's acquired amazing psychic powers that allow him to 'force' women out of their clothes and into his bed, where he can fondle their 'muffins' and exercise his one-eyed trouser snake. Extraneous subplots abound: His boss fires him, his wife bitches about his affairs, and he eventually tries the showbiz circuit. Will Dan come to terms with his 'gift'? Will he return to his wife? Will he get laid? WHO THE FUCK CARES, because this is motel room film-

making at its worst. Director Hurley wanted to make a serious look at ESP, but when he couldn't sell the film to theatres, he added a bunch of grainy sex-scenes to increase its commercial potential. It didn't help to make this abomination any more entertaining, though – it's all high pathos, low intelligence and unrelenting tedium. The bedroom scenes are tepid (they're also narrated, since they couldn't afford sync-sound), the cast looks bored, and the only person who looks like she had any fun is the blond gal who spends the entire film sitting on a bed in a bikini, licking a lollipop. By the time the Ebony-and-Ivory lezbo scene grinds along, you'll wish you had an empty wine bottle to bounce off Herschell G.'s skull for helping concoct this stultifying nightmare on film... At the end, Dan's power fades and it leaves him a broken man with no future (or personality). My heart bleeds piss for the shithead... Sure, I wasn't expecting a classic, but I'd hoped for at least a *bit* of fun. Instead there isn't even enough exploitation to make the rotten sections palatable. A time capsule that shoulda remained buried. Blah!

PSYCHOMANIA

DON SHARP 1971 (AKA: THE DEATH WHEELERS). Let's see what the Brits can come up with when they mix schlock genres – in this case, a Hammer-style horror flick crossed with a cycle gang stomp-a-teria... I should admit that I was pretty dubious going into it. The last time I saw this combo attempted was in **Werewolves on Wheels** and it bit The Big One, but this time around the filmmakers had a bit more imagination going for them (including Don Sharp, who directed some of the very best of the Chris Lee/Fu Manchu flicks), and they also had the good sense to make the bikers' escapades almost incidental, and give centre stage to a creepy occult/undead story. So, if films like **Tales from the Crypt** and **Vault of Horror** are to your liking, and dated dialogue such as "Blow his mind" and "Heavy" tickles your funny bone, then you'll certainly enjoy this little romp... The Living Dead are a chopper gang consisting of long-haired, middle-class English punks who ride around the

countryside wearing death's head helmets while they scare the bejesus out of the locals – running innocent motorists into ditches and driving on the wrong side of the road (Oh yeah. This is England. Oops...). Enter George Sanders and Beryl Reid, who add class to the proceedings as a pair of powerful spiritualists who know the secret of 'crossing over' after death. It consists of some mumbo-jumbo about tree-frogs and a Stonehengian altar, but that's not really important, because when The Living Dead discover the secret of the living dead, they tear through the town on a binge of light-weight anarchy, and (needless to say) their fearless leader, Tom (well played by a smirky Nicky Henson), gets the opportunity to test out his new-found knowledge after he takes a high-speed plunge off a bridge. And when Tom comes blasting out of his premature grave, straddling his chopper, it's time for gobs of (PG-level) violence and a double-digit death toll – especially after he encourages the rest of his scuzzy gang to go on similar kamikaze missions and join him in the realm of the undead. Talk about peer pressure!... Sure, it's all a bit foolish at the end, with hokey transformation effects, but it also has a solid sense of humour about itself and its oddball premise. The production is consistently slick and it easily glides into a lower-case-'a' movie category (in the US, it was unjustly tossed into grinders on a double bill with the equally unique **Horror Express**). The scariest part of the film though, is the dopey, hippie-dippy folk music... Recommended if only because it tries to be a little different than all the cheapshit slasher romps that pack the video racks.

THE PSYCHOPATH

LARRY BROWN 1972. Here we have a horror film that's saved from terminal mediocrity by two BIG pluses: A wonderful concept and a very creepy lead performance. Everything else in it is fairly pedestrian dreck... So, when you think of modern vigilantes, who pops to mind? Clint Eastwood? Charles Bronson? How about a local kids' TV-show host? Tom Basham (who unfortunately went on to total obscurity) stars as the loveable lead of a tiny tots' puppet-programme, The Mr. Rabbey Show... See Mr. Rabbey hang out at the playground! See Mr. Rabbey visit a children's hospital! And see Mr. Rabbey kill a whole lot of slimy grown-ups! You see, after watching one too many battered children roll into the hospital's emergency room, quiet-natured Mr. Rabbey burns out a bearing and starts on a systematic killing spree, in an effort to eliminate every evil parent in town. The cops had their hands tied because there wasn't any hard proof of the child-beatings, but luckily, Mr. Rabbey is on the job, protecting his little friends' physical and emotional well-being by bashing in their folks' heads with a handy baseball bat. Don't expect a lot of gore though, cuz the violence is PG-level-tame, in addition to being poorly executed – and the direction by Larry Brown usually boils down to pounding canned-music and eyeball close-ups to generate suspense. The film is also a bit heavy-handed on the violence-to-children monologues, but overall this has such a twisted li'l concept, that you can sorta forgive its flaws. It's also one of those rare horror films where you don't feel like a total dirtbag for cheering on the mass murderer... Hitherto unknown Tom Basham really pulls a star turn in the title role (he deserves a tribute in the Exploitation Hall of Fame's Children's Dept.), coming over like a creepy cross between Mr. Rogers, Pee Wee Herman and Norman Bates, and he obviously had a field day filling Mr. Rabbey's sneakers – he pedals around town on his cool bike, strangles people with his age-worn security blanket, stuffs chocolate cake into his mouth, plays with his puppet friends (including one character called The Executioner), and still finds time to run over a Mommy's head with an electric lawnmower. It's an absolutely astounding performance, which is unfortunately trapped in a second-rate horror tale.

QUEEN OF BLOOD

CURTIS HARRINGTON 1966 (AKA: PLANET OF BLOOD). Here's a modest gem from American-International and director Curtis Harrington, who had already distinguished himself from the usual pack of hacks with an eccentric li'l item called **Night Tide** with Dennis Hopper... Well, Harrington grabbed John Saxon and Basil Rathbone (only one year before his death) to star in this science-fictioner, and he even coerced Hopper to show up in a supporting role, sputtering silly dialogue like "What's the scuttlebutt there, Tony baby?"... Set in the near future, 20 years after man first lands on the moon, the human race is awaiting their first contact with an alien race when an ambassador from another galaxy heads toward Earth on a mission of peace. But as fate usually decrees in these cheapie productions, the alien's spacecraft crash-lands on Mars, so the combined forces of planet Earth send a rescue-ship to the red planet. Amidst lots of dramatic complications, Saxon and Hopper wind up with a lone alien survivor – a silent, olive-skinned woman (Florence Marly) who smiles seductively at all the males. She isn't interested in anything complicated, like sex, though – she just wants their blood (hence the title). And it's in the last 25 minutes that the flick really gets good and ghoulish, with a high gross-out factor for the mid-'60s. "They're scientists. They know what they're doing" –Ha! Prophetic last words!... Surprisingly enough, Basil Rathbone was still

able to put some life into his clichéd role of the distinguished scientist, Doctor Farraday; Saxon gets his standard gee-whiz Space Cadet part; and it's particularly weird watching Hopper essay the same kind of straight-laced stock-jock character. Only one year later he'd be smashing open heads in drive-in classics like **The Glory Stompers**... Visually, this film boasts some of the eeriest, most genuinely alien-looking sets and special effects I've seen in some time, and all of them were spliced out of a Russian science fiction film that AIP bought the rights to. Even if the US scenes are cheap in comparison, the entire enterprise is still highly enjoyable for any schlock SF addict.

RABID GRANNIES

EMMANUEL KERVYN 1989. When it comes to Troma Team releases, aren't you getting sick of saying, 'What a great title! What a hilarious ad campaign! And what a *shitty* movie!'? Here's another case in point. First off, this isn't a **Toxic Avenger**-style satire. No such luck. Instead, it's just recycled, Belgian-lensed, poverty row crap; a bore from first-time (and if we're all lucky, last-time) writer/director Emmanuel Kervyn. This one's a particular chore to endure too, because the only thing worse than bad Euro-trash is boring Euro-trash! I'd rather be chewing on razor blades. In addition, it looks trimmed for an R-rating, which makes it worthless even for hardcore gore-watchers (even an extra slopping of viscera couldn't save this shit stain). As if any of you really care about the plot, it's Aunt Victoria and Elizabeth's birthday and there's a family reunion at the centre of this rotten-to-the-core romp. A cross-section of snoozeable stereotypes (a priest, a knockout night-club singer, a stud, a lesbian) gather at the Aunts' country estate with plans to butter up the two old-timers in order to get a better position in their Will. This greedy mansionful of morons argue incessantly for the first half hour, and just as I got completely fed up with this pack of nasty, snide, cowardly dirtbags, and decide to switch the channel to something more interesting (like **C-Span**), the pace picks up when a mysterious gift from a Satanist relative arrives at the doorstep. Inside is a box containing a demonic spirit that infects Aunties' drinks and transforms the ladies into mutating monsters (complete with lumpy bald pates, plastic claws, and ever-flowing green vomit) which start knocking off the scared-shitless relatives one-by-one. The whole endeavour reeks of **Evil Dead** rip-off, but the filmmakers can't even pull off a good Xerox job! There's only a few moments of gore, loads of exposition from the cast of cretins, and absolutely nothing original! Plus, any absurdity in seeing senior citizen zombies is mitigated by the utter tedium and a cast that has all the sympathy of the Internal Revenue Service. To be a little more succinct, this flick is total shit.

RADIOACTIVE DREAMS

ALBERT PYUN 1986. It seems as if every schlock independent filmmaker who gets his (or her) hands on a few bucks wants to make a post-W.W.III science fiction film. Some are great (**A Boy and His Dog**), others are interesting in spots (**The Ultimate Warrior**), but unfortunately, most of 'em are either (1) Italian rip-offs of **Escape From New York**, or (2) American rip-offs of **Mad Max**. Predictably enough, a majority of these are unwatchable dreck, and **Radioactive Dreams** doesn't fare any better. This particular piss-poor example blatantly copies from a half-dozen *much* better films, such as **Blade Runner**... As for the plot, Philip and Marlowe are two dim-headed young men who want to become private eyes in post-holocaust America (Get it? Philip and Marlowe? Philip Marlowe? Hahahahaha...). Two of the most complete assholes I have ever seen, they hit the road in a flashy convertible, with smug grins you wanna knock off their faces with a pick-axe, and witty dialogue such as "Hi! I'm Philip! I'm a dick!". The bare-bones plot has the pair accidentally acquiring the keys to the world's last MX Missile, so every twisted scumbag in Fallout-Town is after them. They run into a female **Mad Max**-ian motorcycle gang, a pair of foul-mouthed eight-year-old disco mutants, a 21st century hippie night-club catering to cannibals, and a giant papier-mâché sewer monster. Just to add confusion to the unrelenting boredom, the slo-mo finale manages to knock out any possibility of thrills while making the whole ending incomprehensible. Michael Dudikoff and John Stockwell took time out from their previous 'epics', **American Ninja** and **My Science Project**, to star as the dipshit duo, and George Kennedy makes a quick walk-on, looking like he's been socking down one too many pepperoni pizzas for breakfast. The MTV-style music is non-stop, the action is non-existent, and you get the feeling that everyone involved in this Wasteland of Imagination probably thought they were being incredibly cute and cultish. R-rated for a couple obscenities, my best advice is to leave this video snooze-a-rama on the shelf, collecting dust. Of course, it's directed by Albert Pyun, the mulch-head who made **The Sword and the Sorcerer** a few years back, so whaddaya expect?

RAGE OF HONOR

GORDON HESSLER 1987. Yes, Sho Kosugi's Back! And this time, the title should've been 'Pray For End Credits!'. Jesus, what a yawn carnival! Sho plays (*that's* even a stretch) a government agent from Phoenix who busts some heavy smugglers in Buenos Aires. When Sho's partner gets tortured by the head honcho, Sho swears revenge. Sho heads back to Argentina to nab the bad guys, who want this floppy disc with lots of pertinent info on shipments, etc. Somebody should've given this floppy *plot* a workout on a WP before anybody grossed *dollar one*. Your hand will be permanently glued to your forehead as Sho survives round after round of point blank machine gun assaults, flipping his computerised (yeah, right?) Chinese stars and wiping out dozens of well-paid stuntmen. To say that Sho delivers his lines woodenly would be an insult to Charlie McCarthy and Howdy Doody. The guy makes Chuck Norris look like Brando. Not that anyone else fares much better. The guy who plays the psycho smuggler probably needs some Dentu-Creme after munching all the scenery. If Sho doesn't come up with a winner next time, we'll be checkin' that green card pronto. [TR]

RAT PFINK A BOO BOO

RAY DENNIS STECKLER 1966. Personally, I like the title **Rat Pfink a Boo Boo** much better than 'Rat Pfink and Boo Boo', even though it was a mistake in post-production (the guy who did the credit sequence misspelled the title, and Steckler didn't want to spend the money to correct it)... Released in the wake of the **Batman** TV series craze, a quick prologue prepares us for the utter silliness to come, with a glimpse of our title heroes (complete with wool ski masks and long underwear, jury-rigged to look like a crime-fighting costume) entertaining a bunch of cute kids and waving to confused towns-folk during a parade in their honour. These guys are truly the Dynamic Duo with a difference – they're too damned *poor* to afford good costumes or flashy gadgets, and their so-called physiques make Adam (Mr. Spare-Tire) West look like Lou Ferrigno... But first, the plot: Welcome to Hollywood USA, where stars are made and women are brutally attacked. In fact, here's one now, in the pre-credit assault. Bash! Bam! Ouch! It seems that a trio of psycho jokesters are following pretty gals to their homes and annoying them at all hours with rasping phone calls and leering glances. Creepy stuff; and intercut with the suspense, we get to wade ass-deep into the musical lifestyle of rock-singer Lonnie Lord. Entertaining the jet-set at Hollywood pool parties, he sings such proto-hits as 'You Is a Rat Pfink' and 'Go-Go Party' – music as inane as anything ever warbled by Fabian or Frankie Avalon (urp!)... But 35 minutes into the film, this strange question pops into your head: Whatever happened to Rat Pfink and Boo Boo, the two cowled

cretins who are supposed to star in this film? Well, after sitting through **The Thrill Killers**, you know that Steckler's forte is taking two diverse storylines, developing them to ridiculous proportions, and then bashing them together when you least expect it. So, when Lonnie's luscious girlfriend (Carolyn Brandy, aka Mrs. Steckler, as Cee Bee) is kidnapped by these roving thugs, Lonnie and his trusty gardener, Titus Twinbly, walk into a nearby closet and emerge as the 'friends to those who have no friends', RAT PFINK AND BOO BOO (tah dah!). Asinine isn't an adequate enough word to describe these two bozos, and when they leap into action the film takes a short-cut past Ridiculous, and heads straight into *Full-Scale Deranged!*... The tinted photography suddenly kicks in! Boo Boo has a cowl with blinking lights on the ears! The Rat-Cycle's engine sounds like a toilet flushing! They're the type of clowns who stop in mid-chase in order to wipe off their capes after driving through a mud puddle, and whenever Rat Pfink leaps on some creep in the inept fight scenes (Hey, at least *try* to make it look like you aren't missing his chin by a foot-and-a-half, OK?), he has to yell some dumb ass phrase like "Fight crime!" or "Justice prevails!" Need I add that truth and gallantry eventually triumph, and we get to hear yet another crappy song from the gnarled larynx of Lonnie Lord... As you can tell, this flick has more genuine humour than most recent Tinseltown 'comedies', and on one-millionth of the budget. Starring Vin Saxon and Titus Moede as our dime-store daredevils, and a special appearance by Kogar, The Swinging Ape (!); an uncredited extra in a gorilla suit who Rat Pfink gets to wrestle during the astoundingly half-baked climax! The consistently under-lit or overexposed cinematography is by (I'll give you three guesses) Ray Dennis Steckler, and it's so unflattering at times that the pores on Ms. Brandt's face look like golf course divots. Yuch!... Yes, Steckler's cinematic brilliance comes shining through once again! Loads of alleged-suspense, jaw-dropping laughs, and musical interludes that pre-date the absolute obnoxiousness of MTV by 15 years. Needless to say, I *loved* this movie! It's unadulterated bizarro-filmmaking, and it's barely an hour long (Thank goodness. Any longer and I would have had a stroke). The only problem is, now I want to start a Rat Pfink and Boo Boo Fan Club... Any takers?

RAWHEAD REX

GEORGE PAVLOU 1987. On the tail end of **Hellraiser**'s success, out comes the video of Clive Barker's first film adaptation, based on his short story. Barker has publicly denounced this adaptation because it chopped out the subtler aspects of his tale and simply became your basic monster-on-the-rampage cheapie, but if **Rex** doesn't break any new territory or reach new levels of cinematic disgustion, it's still worth a few dumb laughs, but only if you're a fan of ultra-cheesy horror-monster mayhem... Literally exploding out of the earth, Rawhead Rex is a cross between the baby from **It's Alive** and Arnold Schwarzenegger, and he proceeds to drool a path across the Irish countryside. Oh, he's a sight all right, with his polystyrene pectorals, razor-sharp teeth, and buggin' red eyes that make him look like Marty Feldman's radioactive older brother; and he doesn't for *one moment* convince you that there isn't an underpaid stuntman sweating his ass off inside that dime-store suit. All you need is a zipper down the back to complete the picture. But if you can stop laughing at the costume for a few minutes, you might actually begin enjoying this flick on a purely subhuman level – because all Rex seems to do is lumber around, mauling and decapitating his victims. It's low on gore, but not bad as a cornball creature feature – David Dukes gets the 'honour' of playing the American-who-sees-the-creature-but-no-one-believes-him-until-it's-too-late and Ronan Wilmot pegs the Laugh Meter as a geeky vicar who worships Rex, since it turns out that he's some kind of vengeful Gaelic demon from the past. (I'll assume all this is explained thoroughly in the original story.) On the negative side, we get a *bunch* of telegraphed false-scares and there's an absolutely asinine ending that includes the type of chintzy special effects which coulda been scratched on the film stock with a straight pin. It's the type of rinky-tink conclusion that makes you grit your teeth... Despite that lapse, **Rawhead Rex** is indisputably silly, but I still found it moderately enjoyable (emphasis on the *moderately*).

REBEL ROUSERS

MARTIN B. COHEN 1967. I've been dredging the video racks for years looking for this one! A biker film with Cameron Mitchell above the credits and with Bruce Dern, Jack Nicholson and Harry Dean Stanton behind the cycles! Wow! I was going to congratulate King Video for unearthing it, but then I actually sat down and watched the thing... Holy moley, what a crock! You expect a '60s chopper-opera to be pretty smoked up and rambly, but this one wins the booby prize for sheer boredom... Initially lensed under the more oblique title **Limbo**, this flick got a title change when **The Wild Angels** hit it big a few months earlier. It starts out lively enough, with an impromptu barroom bongo party when gang leader Dern and his boys go loco in a local cantina. Jack Nicholson (as Bunny) is the rowdiest of the Rebel Rousers, as well as being the flashiest dresser – a wool cap, dark glasses, and a *hilarious* pair of b/w horizontal-striped pants that'll scorch the lids off your eye sockets. (I bet Jack still has 'em hanging in his closet.) And a frighteningly-young Harry Dean Stanton stays in the background most of the time as the gang's geeky jokester... So far, so good, but all of a sudden the fun oozes down the drain when Cameron Mitchell takes centre stage. He plays an old, clean-cut football buddy of Dern's, and Cam checks into their fleabag desert town in search of his lost love. That's right, Cameron Mitchell is the *love interest*! Talk about a casting mishap! And the storyline stalls-out with a rancidly saccharine love story between Cam and Diane Ladd (co-star of **The Wild Angels**, but this time playing a moralistic Good Girl). While everyone in the audience awaits more anti-social behaviour, all we're given is heaps of soap opera antics – with our lumpy lovebirds talking us into a stupor while they reminisce about 'what might have been'. Bring on the violins, so I can shove one up the scriptwriter's asshole... Luckily, the Rebel Rousers show up just in time to break up their tryst, with Jack getting the once-in-a-lifetime opportunity to kick the shit out of Cameron. But while everyone in the gang wants to smash-in Mitchell's thick skull and rape his pregnant girlfriend, Dern is the only dissenting voice. He's sort of a biker beatnik, you see, and doesn't want to hurt anyone who doesn't deserve it. In other words, Bruce turns out to be a party pooper; but to solve their argument, the Rousers decide to have a cycle race to see who wins the right to pork Ms. Ladd. Noblesse oblige, indeed... Sure, it's rated 'R', but there isn't any nudity, sex or gore, and not even a hint of seriously demented violence. There isn't even a big rumble at the end! Instead we get plenty of insipid sermonising from Ladd and Dern (Rule #I: Chopper flicks *don't* need a moral), while Cameron looks like he has terminal gas pains, and Jack and his fellow hoodlums spit and drool their way into

Biker Heaven. Director Martin Cohen (exec. producer of **Blood of Dracula's Castle** and co-producer of **Nightmare in Wax**) gets most of the blame – his lacklustre non-style makes the whole thing feel like a bland TV movie. And as for a script? Nonsense! This is a prime example of '60s Spontaneous Filmmaking at its most numbingly inane. Even Leslie (Laszlo) Kovacs' camerawork is routine. But there's so many great folks in front of the camera, slumming to pay their bar tabs, that I kept watching in hopes something, ANYTHING, would happen. But did it? Nope... It's a big disappointment.

REBORN

BIGAS LUNA 1981. Director Bigas Luna (**Anguish**) gets the blame for this Italo-lensed inanity, which pits TV-based religious flimflamming against True Faith in God... Hmmm, sounds like a bunch of runny horse manure, you might say? Why review it at all, you may wonder? Well, it just happens that this cheapie stars Dennis Hopper, before his **Blue Velvet** resurgence (and obviously while he was still sucking at the bottle), as a brimstone and bullshit televangelist. And if you couldn't already imagine, he's fucking hilarious! It's a must-see for any Hop-o-phile, just so you can witness Dennis spouting The Lord's word in an ice-cream suit and bowtie, as the host of The Rev. Tom Harley Hour. Ranting incoherently about sin, drugs and alcohol ("I damn alcohol! I haven't taken drugs! I *hate* drugs!"), Hopper heads a money-raking 'church' which sets up fake on-camera faith-healings, in order to increase ratings. He's a cross between Jimmy Swaggart and Gene Scott, and Dennis plows a lot of energy into his role, with his personal baggage helping generate loads of unintentional laughs. So far so great. I *love* it! BUT (uh oh, here it comes) every time we start thinking this is a twisted look at religious bunko-artists, director Luna pulls in a parallel tale of a *real* faith healer (subtly-named Mary). You'll be gritting your teeth at this painfully pious story of a young woman in Italy who oozes with so much stigmata that she must need refills the first of every month. Michael Moriarty (another fave of mine – also looking like he's got one foot in Detox Mansion) looks bored/confused/embarrassed as the Rev's dirty tricks expert, who locates the gal, takes a pit stop to fuck her (so much for her being a virgin), and then tries to save her from Hopper's greedy grasp. The funniest moment is when Mary goes into a religious trance while Michael and her are making the beast with two backs, and he gets 'stuck' for several painful hours... Most of the flick is damn near unwatchable at times – slow-paced and teeth-gnashingly self-serious, with only Hopper's manic moments saving this swill from the gutter. In fact, Mary is such a terminal depressive (and actress Antonella Murgia is so numbingly one-note) that you might actually end up rooting for Hopper, while hoping that she goes immediately to Hell. Do Not Pass Go. Do Not Collect 200 Lira. The ending picks up a bit with an outdoor rally for Rev. Harley and 'Big Mary', intercutting documentary footage of every type of pathetic, small town Christian geek. But the conclusion makes no sense whatsoever (it's probably better that way) – Hopper is spouting to helicopters, Mary and Michael have a baby and Luna gives us an affirmation in God's Love (he even gives a special thanks to God in the credits). Well, phooey on that brand of brainwashing!... Recommended only if you want to see Hopper twist the knife into tele-religion, but if you're looking for truly nasty-hearted fun, I'd check out **Salvation!** or **Margoe** instead.

RED HEAT

ROBERT COLLECTOR 1985. Uh oh, Linda Blair's in the slammer again, and video viewers across the country are worse off for it. And this time she's been paired against famed Euro-slut Sylvia Kristel (**Emmanuelle**, **Private Lessons**), who's dyed her hair a nauseating orange for the occasion... This Yugoslavian-lensed flick was barely released to theatres in the US, and I can now understand why – it's a lukewarm hodgepodge of cold war propaganda and women-in-cages antics, with almost as much emphasis on the political side as on the cat fights. And instead of camping it up a bit, this one plays it straight-faced (though *you'll* have a tough time keeping one when Blair tries to get dramatic). Linda stars as Chris, a pudgy American lass who flies to the bedroom of her US Army fiancé, who's stationed in West Germany. After a round of tasteful whoopee, they have a big argument over whether to get married or not (she wants to, he doesn't – I guess he isn't as half-witted as he looks). But while Blair is out taking a midnight stroll, she witnesses a political kidnapping and winds up crated across the border and dumped into a Soviet Bloc prison. And guess what! Their cinematic slammers are basically the same as America's, except that everything is painted grey and the gals wear less makeup. Linda spends her days working in the prison factory and her nights dealing with cell block rivalries, the douche bag warden, and the vicious head inmate, Sofia, who's a lezbo strumpet in red lingerie (Ms. Kristel, who won't be able to get away with the sex-pot act much longer)... Be prepared to wallow in the unpleasantness of watching Ms. Blair sexually abused twice (once by a male guard and once by Sylvia), and there's less basic, sleazy enjoyment than usual for a babes-behind-bars film. Nudity is at a low (only one shower scene), most of the really nasty violence is kept boringly off screen, and director Robert Collector jettisons the usual jailhouse fun in favour of macho nonsense from Blair's beau or Rambo-ville anti-Red messages. Half the time it feels like a Jess Franco adaptation of a Solzhenitsyn novel... Overall, it's fairly mediocre trash, though the final escape is action-packed enough to please the **Soldier of Fortune** set, with plenty of automatic weapons and loads of dead commies. But the big problem with the film is Linda Blair – I just can't take the gal seriously in any role. Not only is her delivery so wooden that you want to take a carpenter's plane to her face, but if schlock addicts are expected to shell out a few bucks to see Linda, the least she can do is lay off the milk shakes for a few months beforehand. She's 150 lbs. of tapioca poured into a dress, and it's rather pathetic when you start wishing she *doesn't* take off her clothes. Geeesh!... Plus, there's an uninspiring Tangerine Dream soundtrack. Boy, have these guys gone downhill since **Sorcerer**.

REDNECK ZOMBIES

PERICLES LEWNES 1988. Here's a no-budget, shot-on-video, no-holds barred production that'll give *every* indie filmmaker the confidence that they can make it big in the blood bath biz ('Hey, even I could make a movie better than this piece o' junk!'). Unlike recent directorial debuts which combined sleaze with style (i.e. Buddy Giovinazzo's **Combat Shock** and Jim Muro's **Street Trash**), Pericles Lewnes simply chops at the jugular and leaves any semblance of good taste or talent in the dust. The result is less intellectually stimulating than The Weather Channel but critically null-and-void gorehounds will probably lap it up anyhow... A 55-gallon vat of experimental nuclear waste falls off the back of an army jeep, and so hinges the tale. A bunch of illiterate, overalled, rotten-toothed, in-bred hillbillies stumble upon it and decide to use the barrel for a still, and the liquor that comes out of it is a greenish-blue blast of radioactive rotgut. Soon this mutant moonshine is being passed across the county and one sip turns the drinker into a cornpone cannibal, with their skin bubbling with pus, blood pouring from their mouth and flesh falling off their face. Providing the fresh meat, there just happens to be an entourage of city-slicker backpackers camped out in the vicinity of the spillage site. As you can surmise, there's no subtlety here, folks. In fact, let me give you a partial rundown of what these spotty-faced fiends do – They rip off a woman's scalp and eat it, suck the eyeballs out of a skull, crush a

guy's head like a casaba melon, and another character gets lobotomised with a spoon. The gore effects are never better than amateurish but they're *always* excessive; and while the visual humour is sometimes rancidly silly (such as a comic autopsy scene, with the doc vomiting into the open chest cavity), the verbal side is just plain limp (the gay jokes quickly wear thin, as does the 5th rate dialogue like "I'll be dipped in hogsnot!"). Only on a rare occasion does a twisted scene stand out amongst the standard slaughterama – such as the hooded Tobacco Man, who sells his chewin' product to little kids and then tells 'em grotesque tales of mouth cancer. There's also a quick, solarised trip sequence, which I'm always a sucker for... Lisa M. DeHaven stars as the lone survivor (not to mention the first victim of Zombie Rape), with help from P. Floyd Pirahna, Tyrone Taylor and fatshit Bucky Santini (who looks like R.L. Ryan's retarded younger brother). Complete with hoary homages to other (and need I add, far superior) movies such as **Texas Chain Saw Massacre** and **Day of the Dead**, this is a barely-passable party flick that'll help clear your house of guests in no time. It's a stomach-turning intelligence-insulter! But underneath all the gross-out mayhem, maybe director Lewnes has some important points to be made about the underlying violence in America as perceived through a rustic setting that embodies – I'M *KIDDING*! OK? Geesh, can't you take a joke?

REFORM SCHOOL GIRLS

TOM DESIMONE 1986. If you can't find a sleazy women-in-prison film to watch, I guess the next best thing is a sleazy girls-in-reform-school movie, and this begins promisingly enough with a strip search *and* a shower before the opening credits have ended. Tom DeSimone (the director of **The Concrete Jungle**) takes us to Pridemore Juvenile Facility, a maximum security lock-up where all the girls strut around in exotic underwear or mini-skirted prison uniforms. The whole gang of stereotypes are there: Pat Ast (doing a cheap, Divine rip-off) is the two-ton lezbo guard, who's so cruel that she'll confiscate a new inmate's cute stuffed-toy, or stomp a kitten to death with her size-12 boot; Wendy O. Williams from The Plasmatics (presently residing in the 'Where are they now?' file) is Charlie, the studded-leather slut of the cell block – a true 'shitstain on the panties of life'; and Sybil Danning manages to keep her blouse on (a rarity!) as the hard-assed Warden Sutter. There's also the New Girl, who won't take shit from anyone, the innocent runaway who's unable to cope with the abuse, and the kindly psychiatrist with the heart o' gold... The film isn't much on originality – it's the same lame-o plot that's been recycled a dozen times (good inmates vs. evil inmates vs. eviler guards), but watching a bunch of actress willing to make complete artistic whores out of themselves makes this an OK time-killer. Everyone eventually revolts against the school's tyrannical leaders, but except for a couple cat fights, there isn't much action and *no* gore (the worst it gets is when one gal is branded on the butt with a heated coat hanger). And even though the ending has some good destruction of property during the full-scale cell-block riot, there's no real *grim* edge to the proceedings... I have a feeling they were trying for a satire on the genre, but it fails in that respect, because it never gets as all-out idiotic as other, earlier entries; and if they were trying for the *ultimate* female-prison flick, it never gets sleazy or sick enough for that particular claim to fame. It's all flash, without any heart or guts – but it does have lots of skin. Plus, all you lucky people get to listen to a quartet of songs sung by Wendy O. Williams... Overall, this is pretty routine swill.

RELENTLESS

WILLIAM LUSTIG 1989. It's always refreshing to see a mainstream star dropping his/her dignity to play a degenerate psychopath in some two-bit schlockfest. Well, director William Lustig (**Maniac**) found the perfect star in ageing Brat Packer Judd Nelson, who has the market cornered in distant, pissed-off-at-mankind gazes (probably from too many cases of Jack Daniels while cranking out duds like **Blue City**). And if by some fluke, Judd becomes respectable, he'll want to burn all the copies of this sicko flick... The script runs two parallel story lines – the weaker sections follow two LA cops, while the rest scrutinises glassy-eyed Judd as Buck Taylor, who flares his nostrils, wears geeky plaid shirts, and kills total strangers just for kicks. Picking his victims out of the phone book at random, he stalks 'em, tortures 'em, and then leaves taunting notes to the police tacked on the corpses. Nothing groundbreaking in the madman department (unlike the beautifully chilling **Henry, Portrait of a Serial Killer**), this trashy psychological profile prefers to go for cheap, jump-outta-the-shadows scares. But the murders are still pretty nasty for a semi-mainstream release, and the camera never flinches from the sheer brutality of them. Judd is admittedly creepy and quite effective in the lead – barely saying a word throughout the first half, while tightwalking between being a meek milquetoast and a no-nonsense killer with a penchant for mumbling maniacally to his dead dad's photo. By the midpoint though, any suspense begins to unravel with one too many coincidences. We even get to endure flashbacks to Judd's brutalised childhood, to explain why Nelson became a mass murderer. What do they want? Sympathy for the li'l fuckface?... Some additional advice: Whenever the two investigating cops (Robert Loggia and Leo Rossi) make an appearance, you can start resting your thumb on that Fast Forward button. One's a hard-boiled, cynical pro; the other's a hot-headed ex-NYC rookie (now *there's* a couple of unique characters!) – and both are unbearable. Co-starring Meg Foster and her spooky baby blues, along with Angel Tompkins as a slut. **Relentless** is a competent time killer with plenty of gratuitous violence and nudity, plus a (dare I say it?) good, unsubtle performance by Judd Nelson.

RETURN OF THE KILLER TOMATOES

JOHN DEBELLO 1988. The original **Attack of the Killer Tomatoes** was a hilarious five minute concept crammed into a 90 minute film. It was the type of movie that had you chuckling during the first few minutes, but by the half-hour mark, you were ready to switch over to **Flintstones** reruns. Like it or not, John DeBello emerges from the void to direct this sequel, and this time he had enough cash to hire (poor) John Astin. Too bad the results are just as numbing – it even resorts to incorporating all the good footage from the first flick in dopey flashbacks. Well, at least the filmmakers freely admit their mercenary airs. This is a piece of fastbuck crapola, and *everyone* in the production knows it!... The story is set years after the Great Tomato Uprising, and instead of giant, human-ingesting tomatoes rolling down Main Street (an admittedly funny image), this time around the power mad Professor Gangrene (Astin) is using toxic waste to turn innocent tomatoes into his humanoid minions, and his long-term plans include creating tomato-duplicates of world leaders. As for the other paper-thin characters, there's dorky Chad, who works at the local tomato-less pizza parlour (they use raspberry syrup or peanut butter instead); Tara (Karen Mistal), the prof's lovely tomato-lady, who likes to chew on fertiliser spikes; her fuzzy, mutant tomato pet; Gangrene's lab assistant, Igor, a dim-witted yuppie who continually practices to be a TV news anchorman; not to mention the Rambo-attired army of muscle-bound tomato-men. Yep, it's a full quota of bland leads, and even Astin gets away with nothing more than a lame Christopher Lloyd imitation. Most of the comedy concepts lay about on the screen like a beached carcass, and the film is only on-target when they pile on the self-reflexive jokes about chintzy moviemaking – especially when the production runs outta money midway and they have to start plugging merchandise on-screen. Overall, I smiled about five times during this no-brainer. Not a very high batting average, if you ask me...

This is the type of one-joke mess that doesn't even warrant criticism, though compared to tripe like the **Police Academy** series, it's virtually Pinteresque. The final verdict: A sequel in the tradition of the original (in other words, it's dumb as dirt too).

A RETURN TO SALEM'S LOT

LARRY COHEN 1987. Don't get turned off by the title (or if you're a Stephen King fan – yeah, there's still a few of 'em left – don't get turned on by it), because this flick has little to do with the original novel or subsequent TV movie by Tobe Hooper. Director Larry Cohen basically just latched onto the concept and then took it into the low-budget realm he wanted. The end result is slight on the cheap thrills most horror fans want to wallow in, but it makes up for it with interesting ideas and some fun sequences... Michael Moriarty (looking a little less beer-bloated than he has recently) stars as an anthropologist who takes his long-estranged son to the small Maine town where he grew up. Yep, Salem's Lot. Now everyone renting this movie *knows* that it's going to revolve around vampires, so when night falls, it's a fast pounce to the jugular: A carload of punkers are ventilated, and some homeless hobos are dispatched by a roving gang of giggly children. But these vampires are (outwardly) kinda friendly to Moriarty and son, and they matter-of-factly let them in on some of their secrets. They certainly look like normal country folk (nocturnal Norman Rockwell subjects) and their society has learned to live on the outskirts of civilisation since the days of the pilgrims – breeding cows for their blood (though they prefer human taste treats, of course) while utilising the occasional vampire/human half-breeds as their servants. What do they want from Moriarty? Oh, nothing more than to have him chronicle their history. A sociological profile of their race. A case history of their bloodsucking ways. Moriarty is sceptical at first, but after getting seduced by his old flame (who still looks 18-years-old), he takes on the strange assignment and begins researching their culture. It's only when he wants *out* of the deal that things get nasty... This film is yards more thought-provoking than you'd expect – keeping up a nice pace while maintaining Cohen's loopy sensibilities, such as sledge-hammer commentary on the savagery of the human race (the 'children' are taught about the Spanish Inquisition in their night school) and abrupt comic dialogue ("Wipe yer face," one vampire tells a sloppy comrade). And as usual, Cohen has pulled together a great supporting cast. The late Andrew Duggan is a standout as the town's leader (his demise is *hilarious*) and Veteran filmmaker Samuel Fuller is quite good (and pretty energetic for a shrivelled homunculus) as a crotchety tourist who turns into the Simon Wiesenthal of vampirism... It's just too bad the frights are so lame: The gore is restrained, the monster masks are rubbery and the suspense is nil. At least the Big Climax is fairly destructive, when Our Human Heroes trudge around town with a knapsack full of wooden stakes. A little half-baked (as are the townspeople), but overall, it's surprisingly enjoyable.

REVENGE OF THE ZOMBIES

HO MENG-HUA 1981. You might be able to guess that this Run Run Shaw production is loads of grimy fun – but after experiencing it for yourself, I bet you'll be utterly convinced that it's one of THE great Asian exploitation items around. This film bashes away at your nervous system as only a Chinese gross-out extravaganza can, by tossing everything imaginable onto the screen: Ultra-disgusting cheapo effects, blood-caked rituals, maggot-filled corpses, and a non-stop plot involving modern-day black magic. Hell, in the first two minutes a young maiden is chewed up by a crocodile, and the rest of the flick maintains that high standard of gratuitous violence... The black-hearted villain of the tale is a greasy sorcerer named Mr. Chaing, who drinks human milk in order to stay immortal and spends his free time resurrecting the dead.

His workshop is filled with voodoo dolls, slabbed cadavers, hooded toadies, plus magical paraphernalia from every shop on Canal Street; and though it looks like he has a bevy of beautiful women at his command, they're all actually zombie spirits with six-inch metal spikes twisted into their skulls. When these spikes are removed, they change back into 100+ year old, acid-scarred ghouls. Meanwhile, on the Good side of the moral spectrum, a young doctor becomes convinced that his problem-patients (the ones with pulsating boils, worm-filled sores, etc.) have been cursed by black magic, and when his wife is spellbound by Chaing, the Doc *really* gets steamed. But how can you fight someone who has an army of obedient zombies at his disposal, not to mention more spells than an entire season of **Bewitched**? Luckily, a White Magician mysteriously appears from the first reel and counters Chaing's spells by beating the victims with an animal carcass. In retaliation, Chaing shoves a handful of spikes through his *own* hands and face. This action kills the Nice Sorcerer, but before passing away he plucks out his own eyeballs and instructs one of our heroes to eat them. (Yeah, none of this made much sense to *me* either, but by then coherency didn't seem like a high priority.) By the end, almost everyone in the cast is under some type of weird-assed spell (the funniest is a love potion that takes control of the Doc and his best friend's wife). People are instantly rotting away in the middle of the sidewalk, and the last 20 minutes explodes with melting zombies, burning zombies, leaping kung fu zombies – heck, I lost track after a while, there were so many re-animated wretches shuffling across the screen. The production has a slick veneer for this brand of oriental oddity, and it's even filmed with a dash of competency by director Ho Meng-Hua. As expected, the dubbing adds most of the unintentional humour, with the soundman getting a special hand for his impressive (and often-utilised) 'Spike Being Pulled From Human Head' effect. Overflowing with thoroughly repulsive visuals, clever plot twists and imaginative carnage, this Hong Kong horro-rama is a prime choice for strong-stomached viewers.

RIDERS OF THE STORM

MAURICE PHILLIPS 1988 (WORKING TITLE: THE AMERICAN WAY). How could I pass up the latest Dennis Hopper video release (even though it's been sitting on a distributor's shelf, collecting mildew for the last two years)? This is a ragtag throwback to the '60s, which undeftly mixes cosmic ideals with comic idiocy. Oh yeah, it's also an abso-lute mess! Not wholly unenjoyable, but pretty damned close... Dennis stars as the whacked-out (but still politically and socially relevant) captain of a huge bomber that's been circling over the US since the Vietnam War. Originally used for top secret psychological operations (psy-ops) during the war, the plane and its whole pirate crew are *still* at work sending not-so-subliminal messages to the American population – upsetting TV broadcasts with their twisted S/M Network in an effort to rattle the citizens out of their apathy. Their favourite pastimes include interrupting useless programs (newscasts, religious shows) with a mixture of Nam newsreel footage, Hendrix music and left-wing political rhetoric. Hopper's entire crew are stoned burn-outs and screwballs, and all these dementos are at the breaking point from being off the ground too long. Should they land? Should they sell out? Will they get shot down? But one *last* mission brings them together, when they decide to destroy a war-mongering female presidential candidate, Sen. Willow Westinghouse, who'll send the US back into a full-scale war the moment she's securely in the Oval Office. What's the big secret that'll eliminate Westinghouse from the polls? (Well, considering she's played by – Oh, OK. I won't give away the one plot twist.)... Sounds indulgent? It sure is, but if you're gonna go over the top with a flick, at least try to make it a watchable, funny fiasco. **Riders** has its moments, but overall it's not politically daring enough, not drugged-out enough, and (though it's a close call) not weird enough. A little of everything and not much of anything... There's some incidental pluses: Nice set design inside the bomber, and I want a copy of that religious show theme, 'If you've got money laying around, send Jesus some.' Co-star Michael J. Pollard is wasted as the high-tech genius in the crew, and even Hopper is rarely used effectively. Without his presence though, *nobody* would've seen this flick (at least *I* wouldn't have), because how could any self-respecting Hopper-head pass up seeing Dennis roaming a cockpit with shoulder-length hair, a cavalry hat and cheroot (not to mention the George Washington powdered wig)? Directed by Maurice Phillips, with a script (HA! There's the best joke in the whole movie) by Scott Roberts, this movie is best watched in an altered state of nostalgia.

RIOT ON SUNSET STRIP

ARTHUR DREIFUSS 1967. Those 'irresponsible' hippies are at it again – rebelling against the Pigs in this campy cliché-fest which comes across like a schizophrenic mixture of **Psych-Out** and **Dragnet**. There's loads of great background details and drugged-out strangeness throughout this flick, but it ostensibly plays like a bad '50s morality piece. Director Arthur Dreifuss is no newcomer to this type of teen drama (he also helmed **The Love-Ins** and **The Young Runaways**), but his dated 'Youth Problem' messages tend to get in the way of the fun after a while... The setting is the infamous Sun-set Strip, the established hangout for California's late-'60s longhairs and weedheads, and the viewer is quickly introduced to a quartet of college kids who're heading to the with-it coffee shop, Pan-dora's Box (where 'The Beat Go To Eat'). Too bad the mean-spirited Normals are always picking fights with these non-violent flower children. And when the cops arrive, guess who's blamed? Yep, the innocent peaceniks. Meanwhile, we're shown a cross-section of the area's activities: A guy's arrested for smoking a joint, a mother rants at her daughters for their style of clothing and our foursome is pulled in for breaking curfew. (Pretty dramatic, eh? No.) Aldo Ray

gets star billing as the top cop covering The Strip – on one hand he's dealing with the teenaged 'invasion', and on the other, the local merchants want the kids tarred and feathered (not to mention crew-cutted). But instead of taking a stand on this incendiary social issue, the film would rather cut to the melodrama. And how dumb does it get? Are you ready for the saccharine story of a rebellious young girl (Mimsy Farmer) with an alcoholic mom, whose long-lost father is actually the head of the Hollywood Police (Aldo himself!). The script tries to wring out the tears with this bathos, but just when you're ready to give up on the flick, it comes across with some solid, counterculture fun! Where else can you see The Chocolate Watchband in concert? And wait until you see the full-fledged acid freak-out, with Mimsy getting secretly dosed and doing the LSD Erotic Dance of Self-Discovery as she revels in examining her hands and toes, while wriggling on the floor in her mini-skirt! It's just too bad this mindboggling Maximum Weirdness doesn't last for more than a few selective scenes. It always cuts back to Law-&-Order Aldo's hysterics; As for the title 'riot', it only lasts about four minutes and all it consists of is some ID checking, protest placard carrying and one *almost*-beating. Pretty wimpy riot, if you ask me... A few *great* moments and *lots* of tedious ones make this a strictly mainstream treatment of an era that definitely deserved something more subversive.

RIVER'S EDGE

TIM HUNTER 1986. When the ads call this the most controversial film of the year, they aren't just kidding around... It focuses on a group of lower-class teens who seem to follow one motto in life: 'You do shit, it's done and then you die.' And when one of the group calmly announces that he murdered his girlfriend, none of them take him seriously until he leads them to her naked body by the river's edge. All of them agree to keep the killing a secret, but eventually they must come to terms with the guilt and decide whether or not to 'narc' on their friend... Director Tim Hunter (who wrote another fave of mine, **Over the Edge**) beats us over the head about commitment at times but that's nit-picking, because this is as close as anyone will come to a masterpiece about '80s teenagers. It doesn't paint a sunny, rosy picture of America's alienated youth, and it (thankfully) doesn't moralise about their carefree use of drugs and alcohol, either. The cast is uniformly great, blending in perfectly with the bleak landscape – only Crispin Glover (the nerdy dad in **Back to the Future**) seems out of sync as the local speed-freak, Laine. He bounces and screams really well, but in this low-key film it's a bit obtrusive (if you saw his appearance on David Letterman, you know he's a spazoid in real life, too). Best of all is Dennis Hopper, who once again slips into a supporting role and nearly steals the show, as Feck, a one-legged ex-biker

who provides grass to the local kids. Living with an inflatable doll, reminiscing about his cycle days, and passing out the 'Feckweed', he (oddly enough) provides the moral centre of the film. You see, 20 years ago, he *too* killed his girlfriend – but he did it out of *love*. This is a wild flick – funny, shocking, disturbing, and altogether brilliant.

RODAN

INOSHIRO HONDA 1957 (AKA: RODAN, THE FLYING MONSTER). Following the success of **Godzilla, King of the Monsters**, Japanese director Inoshiro Honda introduced Toho's second monster star in the studio's first giant-monster epic to be filmed in colour... There is panic in the Otaki Mines. The workers are being brutally murdered by monstrous prehistoric insects known as the Meganuron, each corpse being discovered with 'a look of horror on his face'. But this is only the beginning; a gigantic, 20-million-year-old egg has hatched in a subterranean cavern, releasing an enormous pterodactyl from the Cretaceous period upon the world. The monster is a member of the species 'Rodan' and has a wingspan of about 500 feet. Rodan flies 'round the world at supersonic speed, wiping out whole cities with typhoon-like shock waves and sonic booms. And as if things didn't look bad for mankind already, it is soon discovered that there are not one, but *two* Rodans flying around. The blasts of wind caused by the Rodans' flapping wings topple buildings and toss tanks around like paper, and though some viewers might wish there were a little less talking and a little more monster action, these scenes sure are purty and would look great on a big screen... The actor in the Rodan suit is none other than Harou Nakajima, who played Godzilla in most of the series, while in some flying scenes a puppet is used. Eiji Tsuburaya's special effects are colourful and are guaranteed to please giant-monster freaks. **Rodan** is a must for Toho monster completists' video collections. Period. [BJE]

ROGER CORMAN: HOLLYWOOD'S WILD ANGEL

CHRISTIAN BLACKWOOD 1980. Before reviewing this hour-long documentary, let me say for the umpteenth time that Roger Corman is one of the True Gods of the movie industry. Without his influence, schlocky drive-in fare would still be in their infancy and half of the mega-buck directors in Tinseltown would be slopping hash for a living. Corman might not have always created the finest flicks in his multi-decade career as director/producer, but he was a showman extraordinaire – the type of genius who could make a five dollar film starring a rubber carrot from Venus and have his audience loving every moment of it. But enough of my genuflection. Onto the movie in question... Though director Christian Blackwood begins this profile trying to decide whether Corman is an exploiter or an artist, you quickly learn where his heart lies, because this is an enjoyable, though not incredibly probing look at Corman's career – from directing American-International anti-epics to producing New World make-a-fast-buck fodder. The four primary ingredients of any Corman film are tallied: Humour, action, sex, and a (slight) social statement; plus we're treated to some wonderful tales about the early careers of Jack Nicholson, Francis Coppola and all the other hungry artists who linked up with Rog in the '60s. Renowned for giving apprentice filmmakers their first break (albeit a firmly controlled one), when no one else would give them the time of day, several of Corman's now-successful alumni return to stoke his ego. Interviews include the likes of Paul Bartel, Jonathan Demme, Peter Fonda, Joe Dante, Martin Scorsese, and Ron Howard (who helmed **Grand Theft Auto** on 1% of **Willow**'s bloated budget). David Carradine applauds Roger for hiring him after the rest of Hollywood had blackballed him; Allan Arkush describes the thrill of making **Hollywood Boulevard**, and how he was proudest when the movie premiered on a triple bill at The Lyric on The Deuce; and director Jonathan Kaplan (who cut his teeth on **Night Call Nurses** and **The Student Teachers** before helming the hit, **The Accused**) nonchalantly discusses the use of rape in Corman's projects... Though the documentary primarily focuses on Corman's '70s legacy of pics like **Death Race 2000**, it also skims through his early efforts, such as the original **Little Shop of Horrors** and his remarkable Poe series. It even exposes Roger's more artistic side when we learn his favourite directors include Bergman, Truffaut and Fellini (despite the fact none of these slackers has ever made a biker movie). Even if the narration gets a tad heavy-handed, this is *essential* viewing for any full-fledged Cormaniac!

THE SADIST

JAMES LANDIS 1963. The title character's motto: "I have been hurt by others, and I will hurt them." His goal: "To inflict moral insanity on the innocent"... That sentiment is all well and good, but I still entered this pic expecting the very worst, no doubt because it showcased the staggering non-talent of Arch Hall Jr. In previously reviewed flicks (**Eegah!, Nasty Rabbit**), Arch Jr. was thoroughly piss-poor at playing the romantic, heroic stud, but – surprise! – the guy is GREAT this time around, shattering all my preconceptions of what a king-sized dork he is. Hall stars as Charley Tibbs, a giggling, googly-eyed punk who's one of the most diabolically nasty greaser-nutcases in screen history. He's a Charlie Starkweather-styled thrill killer who's in the midst of a multi-state murder spree, and his partner in depravity is a teenaged tease named Judy, his gum-chewing girlfriend. The action begins when a trio of mild-mannered school teachers become stranded on the outskirts of Nowheresville when their car breaks down near a ramshackle gas station. No phone, no transportation, and seemingly no one at home – well, all except for the title creep and his wrap-around party doll, who promptly begin terrorising our Guest Victims. Tibbs pistol-whips the eldest guy; then takes a knife to the female teacher's throat, shoves her face in the dirt and molests her. One minute Charley is innocuously drinking a bottle of pop and cuddling with his girl – the next he's making his prisoners squirm for their lives, before plugging a guy's head full of hot lead. And it's Sweaty Palm Time when a pair of unsuspecting cops cycle up to the scene... This movie is a near-classic in Psycho Cinema. A film

"BE NICE TO ME, MISS GOODY-GOODY GOOD GIRL — OR I'LL MESS YOU UP PLENTY!"

THE SADISTIC KILLER KOOK!

He could be a peeping Tom, a hitch-hiker thumbing a ride, a hulking shadow in a darkened bedroom. If you meet him — RUN FOR YOUR LIFE!!!

THE SADIST

GOD HELP YOU — if you're ever cornered by a Charley Tibbs! Plead with him and he'll laugh in your face, beg on your knees and he'll rip away your clothes, resist and he'll kill you without a qualm!!!

that was 10 years ahead of its time. The characterisations are bare-bones, the set-up is minimal and there's no attempt at slowly building suspense – director James Landis simply lays on the raw violence and anti-social behaviour from Reel One, until the no-compromises finale. It's your basic one-set premise, but the pic's effectively staged and stylishly photographed (Yeah, you guessed it. Ol' reliable Vilmos Zsigmond was behind the camera again), while pushing the '60s envelope for on-screen bloodshed and terror. And happily, unlike a lot of recent murder-ramas, where audiences almost end up *rooting* for the villains, there's absolutely no sympathy for this li'l bastard. Tibbs is a totally unlikeable killer-for-kicks, and Arch Hall Jr. gives an impressive, four-star performance. Co-star Helen Hovey makes a respectable heroine (even if she spends most of the film simply whimpering and taking abuse) and Marilyn Manning gives off a rattlesnake sexuality as Tibbs' child/woman squeeze. A terrific B-movie thriller!

SALO, OR THE 120 DAYS OF SODOM

PIER PAOLO PASOLINI 1975. What if Federico Fellini directed **Bloodsucking Freaks**? I think it'd go something like *this*... Acclaimed filmmaker/author/philosopher Pier Paolo Pasolini takes the Marquis DeSade's infamous chronicle of atrocities and updates it into a debased tale of Fascist occupation during World War II. Never one for subtlety, Pasolini comes up with one of the most outrageous, controversial visions to ever hit arthouse screens. This isn't ordinary grindhouse grimness though. It's the artsy-fartsy variety, which means in addition to being caked to the sprockets in blood and bodily secretions, it's boring to boot! And at almost two full hours, it's almost unendurable... As the war comes to an end near the small village of Salo, local officials round up several dozen young men and women, with the piss-ant politicians and clergy heading up the sadistic Gestapoids. After a lengthy inspection of their tits, asses and genitals, the prisoners are carted off to a secluded mansion to satisfy the officials' diseased desires. Off the kids go to the Orgy Room, which might not sound like too bad a prospect, except for the command "any boy caught having sex with a girl will be shot". So prepare yourself for an anal-fixated freakshow, all you lucky viewers! The film is then divided into three 'Circles', during which the Fascists can indulge in their different foul fantasies. First is the Circle of Manias, where lewd sex tales are told to enflame their passions (certainly not mine though). And this pack of perverts quickly gets aroused by stories of semen-spurting and masturbating priests, with it leading to the naked prisoners leashed like dogs, having nails hidden in their food, and a literal Conga Line of butt-fucking. If that wasn't bad enough, wait until the Circle of Shit – the vilest of the lot! Here the prisoners are forced to eat warm faeces (and I thought Wheatena was bad!) and sit in at a shit-entréed dinner party. These folks can't afford dental floss either, and the close-ups of their caked teeth are a guaranteed lunch-loser. Then they defecate and feed it to a diapered old man as he jerks off (lovely, Pier, just lovely...). The last episode, the Circle of Blood is (if you couldn't guess) the violence-gorged conclusion, with the officials dressing up as women, wedding the youngest boys and then killing off the guests. Brandings, eye-plucking, scalping, and a live rat is even sewn into a woman's vagina (urgh!). All while the captors watch while fondling their male servants. What's the reason for this torrent of trash, you ask? Maybe this parade of decadence is some intellectual meditation on the Fascists' fouling of Italy? Or more likely Pier's just a petty (though not untalented) pervert with a penchant for boys' backsides... Though lovingly filmed, any hint of drama is muted by the sordid set pieces, and after a while the only thing reminding us it's an alleged Art Film is that it has subtitles. Pasolini was indeed a sick fuck, but that doesn't mean he had to foist it onto all of us (in living colour, no less)! He was brutally murdered soon after this film was completed, by a teenaged boy he was trying to pick up. It's no real surprise, if his real life was anything like this film.

SALVATION! HAVE YOU SAID YOUR PRAYERS TODAY?

BETH B 1987. This film doesn't really fit into the typical **Slimetime** mould, but then again, any movie that rips apart cathode-ray religion gets high marks in my book. In this case, here's a production that had the luck of coming along at the perfect time, while Bakker and Falwell were beating each other with verbal two-by-fours and while Pat Robertson was spewing his Christian crapola in the guise of a presidential candidate... Directed by underground filmmaker Beth B, this low-budgeter focuses on Rev. Randall (Stephen McHattie), a slickshit TV evangelist who publicly denounces atheists as pawns of the Devil, and tries valiantly to save the souls of those "seduced into secular humanism". But when the cameras are off, we see him as a paranoid greed-monger who thinks homosexuals are hiding in his front lawn bushes, writes his speeches while watching slides of copulating couples and atomic blasts, and isn't adverse to beating and raping a stranded 18-year-old girl who lands on his doorstep... But everything changes when we meet Exene Cervenka (from the band X). She's a housewife who sits like a rotted cabbage in front of the Rev.'s TV show – a true Zombie For Christ. Exene wants to sing on Randall's show, her scumbag biker hubby wants to make some quick cash, and together they come up with a plan that erupts into sin, violence and blackmail. There's scatter-shot target-practice galore from Beth B – a Bible between a woman's spread legs; a 20-foot cross with 'Jesus Saves' in neon lights; "You could be watching the evening news, and the next

thing you know, you'll be imagining your mate copulating with goats"; and everyone in the film is an unlikeable swine. Thugs or slugs. Neanderthal dickheads or self-righteous zealots... It's all about the show business of religion, and though this film tries to be ultra-controversial, after all-the PTL nonsense it takes a lot to be truly outrageous nowadays. The whole thing isn't half as scary as any 10 minutes of Jimmy Swaggart, not one-third as hilarious as any Gene Scott tirade, and by the time we're given a heavy metal Christian song (complete with leather cross), we realise it's all too real to be funny... Not completely successful (I wish it had been a lot nastier), but I give it credit for tackling a subject matter that deserves all the criticism it can get.

SANTA CLAUS CONQUERS THE MARTIANS

NICHOLAS WEBSTER 1964. Sure, at first glance this seems like a junky little no-brain filler, but like any good junk food, it has no nutritional value, but you end up loving it just the same. It's amazingly cheap, but good for lots of dopey fun!... You see, the kids of Mars are listless and bored, so the Martian Bigwigs decide to put a bit of fun into their dreary lives, by kidnapping Santa! "We need a Santa Claus on Mars," atones a Head Greenie; so off they speed to Earth, armed with ray guns (cleverly disguised air-blaster toys), helmets that look like glitter-rock scuba gear, and the destructive force of the terrifying robot Torg! They land at The North Pole, freeze ray the elves and whisk The Fat Guy and two Earth kids into their flying tin can (zoooommm!). There's plenty of chills and suspense once Santa arrives, because there are two factions at odds with each other – the Evil Martians, who want to suck Santa into deep space because he's making the once war-hungry Martians into happy peaceniks; and the Good Martians, who love Kris Kringle, just like all the people of Earth do... Stare in amazement as they build Santa an automated, push-button workshop (I guess they couldn't afford to rent dwarves), but the Evil Guys (boo! hiss!) sabotage the works, so that all the dollies come out with teddy bear heads! Rest

assured that goodness, niceness and all that saccharine shit will triumph, cuz the movie finishes with a 'hilarious' fight in Santa' s toyshop, where the kids of Earth and Mars combine forces, and pelt the Bad Martians with toys, until they surrender. John Call plays The Big Claus, laughing maniacally and rubbing his belly every two minutes, and there's a brain-damaged geek named Droppo who stumbles on with pathetic moron-schtick. But to no one's surprise, this inexpensive little Xmas item is 10 times more enjoyable than 1985's $40 million-dollar depth-charge, **Santa Claus: The Movie**; and the title song, 'Hooray for Santa Claus' will have you singing along and tapping your feet ("He's fat and round, but jumpin' jiminy/He can fit down any chim-iny..."). Oh yeah, an 8-year-old Pia Zadora plays one of the Martian kids but no one gives a damn about that bimbo anymore, thank goodness.

SATAN'S CHEERLEADERS

GREYDON CLARK 1976. This is probably director Greydon Clark's best film (Which isn't exactly high praise. His other drivel includes **Black Shampoo** and **Joysticks**), and it has the type of washed-up cast that only a sleaze-fanatic could fully appreciate – John Ireland, Yvonne DeCarlo, John Carradine, and a full roster of barren-brained gals as the title characters... It all begins like any typical cheerleaders flick from the mid-'70s – such as **The Pom Pom Girls**, **Revenge of the Cheerleaders**, **The Swinging Cheerleaders** – with all the girlies wiggling their wares in bikinis while on the beach. And, just as in real life, the jocks are boring discodicks and the cheerleaders are arrogant dim-bulbs who are so flaky that they can't figure out how to open the hood when their car breaks down. But unbeknownst to everyone, in this California community there's a cult of Satanists practising their mumbo-jumbo, and the plot picks up appreciably when we discover that the stodgy old school janitor who all the students make fun of, is actually a closet devil-worshipper. Well, the janitor has the hots for the only blond in the bunch (Patti) and he kidnaps all of them on route to the big football game – but wouldn't you know it, Satan himself (represented by a cheap red-solarisation effect) wants blondie for his own. All this stupidity leads to a cross-country race for the cheerleaders' souls, because the Satanists want 'the maidens' for their weekly midnight mass and virgin offering... John Ireland plays the sheriff and Yvonne DeCarlo is his plumped-out wife, plus John Carradine gets high marks for his quick appearance as a roadside trash-picker, once again upstaging everyone else by realising that he's in a crappy movie and making the most out of his lacklustre role. He's a riot (for the four minutes he's on screen)... I have to admit that it's a lot of fun watching these peppy cheerleaders abused, but since the flick is only rated PG, you shouldn't go into it expecting the same type of tit-count that most pom-pom epics have. There's a glimpse of skin, but nothing more, and though this film has all the ingredients of an exploitation classic – nubile femmes in skimpy costumes, hungry character actors, a quick pace, and a good title to boot – it's too bad that director Clark didn't have the good sense to crank up the sleaze level a little more. Sure, Yvonne gets ripped apart by Dobermans, but it's all done off-screen... The whole production is ineptly filmed and about as idiotic as you'd expect, though any attempt at intentional humour falls flat ("Jesus Christ," mutters one character, to which the Head Satanist replies, "Close. But not quite." Sigh). It's watchable, but utterly unremarkable.

SATAN'S SADISTS

AL ADAMSON 1969. It's chopper-mania time (!) and it looks like director Al Adamson gathered a bunch of two-bit actors/friends, a few beat-up bikes, a ton of beer, and just headed into the desert one afternoon to make a cycle-movie. No discernible script. Barely a plot. Just make it up as you go along. And guess what? The result

may be a disgusting chunk of mindrot, but it isn't half bad, either... Meet the Satan's Sadists, a small band of dirt-caked thugs with names like Acid, Anchor, Firewater, and Muscles. Basically, they just hang out in the middle of the desert and harass anyone and everyone who passes their way (sure, it's a great job if you can get it...). But when they hassle a Marine Corp. vet and his girlfriend, they're just asking for trouble. A few of the gang are killed (one is drowned in a greasy spoon's toilet bowl) and for most of the film, the Sadists are out to settle the score. Then toss in a trio of college gals who are complaining about the lack of men, until this unshaven goon squad stumbles onto their campsite with their own party plans. From there on, it turns into a pre-**Hills Have Eyes** revenge tale, with the Normal Folks fighting off the desert geeks by tossing rattlers at them, or by putting LSD into their coffee until they're so tripped out that they start playing a solitaire-version of Russian Roulette... Compared to the top-drawer biker flicks (**The Wild Angels**, **The Savage Seven**), this one is fairly slow-moving for most of the run-time. But unlike most other chopper-dramas who hedge their bets by making their gang *halfway* likeable, the Sadists are soooo uniformly nasty, unappealing and ill-tempered that their antics pack one heck of a lot of sleazebag entertainment. Not only do these guys fuck with the establishment, but they also gang bang every woman in sight and murder *everyone*! (Actually, I think a whole *two* characters survive to see the end credits.) The final count is 12 killings, four rapes and two suicides. Phew!... A beer-bloated Russ Tamblyn stars as the Sadist's leader, Anchor – his career taking a headfirst fall down the ladder of success, from dancing in films like **West Side Story** and **Seven Brides for Seven Brothers** to shooting innocent couples in the head at point-blank range in worthless drive-in shit like **The Female Bunch**, **Dracula vs. Frankenstein** and this, his All-Time Scum Epic (each directed by Al Adamson, of course); and Tamblyn spends most of the movie with a floppy hat pulled down over his face – probably so the guys at the Welfare Office won't recognise him and cut off his monthly cheques. Co-starring future crap-directors John Cardos (with wimpy mohawk) as Firewater and Greydon Clark as Acid, plus Regina Carrol (aka Mrs. Al Adamson) as the highly-touted Freak-Out Girl, who dances around like a busty Nancy Sinatra on Spanish Fly. The songs are by The Nightriders, and they're so uniformly ludicrous that they make you long for 'deeper' music, like The Banana Splits... Basically, the violence in the film is high-grade, but the movie itself is so inept that it defuses a lot of potential grimness. It's the type of flick I can only recommend to a true Trash Fiend, who likes to laugh at confused actors staggering through a pathetic production. You know, like me!

SCHLOCK

JOHN LANDIS 1972 (AKA: THE BANANA MONSTER). Before padding his wallet (and ego) on **Animal House** and **The Blues Brothers**, John ('Could you make that explosion a *little* bigger, please') Landis wrote, directed and *starred* in **Schlock**. A genuinely funny first film, it gives me a *bit* more respect for the guy who's recently been churning out by-the-numbers crapola like **Three Amigos** and **Spies Like Us**. It's not a great film, but if you're feeling exceptionally stupid one evening, this should provide you with a few cheap laughs... The mysterious Banana Monster has been on a killing spree across California and the braindead police have only one clue – dozens of banana peels at the scene of each crime. What they don't realise is that the 'Schlockthropus' is to blame for all the havoc. He's a recently-resuscitated missing link on the loose, looking for babes, blood and bananas, and ingeniously enough, the filmmakers made the Schlock look *exactly* like a guy in a hokey gorilla suit, so the potential victims wouldn't be frightened off. Like any good Schlock he enjoys maiming extras, but he also has a softer side, as we see when a pretty blind gal befriends him, thinking he's just a big hairy dog. Once she gets her sight back, though (one convenient eye operation later) it's a different story, and Schlock is rampaging once more across So. Cal., until he crashes a high school prom and terrorises the teens... Sure, the acting is abysmal and the production is K-Mart Blue Light Special level, but I have to admit that I did laugh a lot. The humour scrapes the barrel most of the time, complete with cruel (but admittedly funny) cripple jokes, the ever-popular snot gags, and the type of horror-laced humour Landis went on to perfect in **American Werewolf**. Landis also throws in lotsa cinematic in-jokes − posters for **King Kong vs. Godzilla**, a cameo by Forry Ackerman, and a goofy **2001** parody. It's enjoyable, dim-witted, *and* only 80 minutes long. In addition, this movie finally explains the plot of Landis' infamous 'lost' classic, 'See You Next Wednesday' − it's a 'fun-filled frolic through the leper colonies of Europe with Charles Laughton, Claudette Calbert and Mickey Rooney'. Or maybe not...

THE SECRET CINEMA (1966)
THE NAUGHTY NURSE (1969)

Before hitting feature films with **Death Race 2000, Eating Raoul** and **Scenes from a Class Struggle in Beverly Hills** (let's not forget his brilliantly sick **Private Parts** either), Paul Bartel made his celluloid debuts with these two comedy shorts... The first, a self-proclaimed 'paranoid fantasy', is a true classic in cinema-dementia. Filmed over a year's time, whenever Bartel could scrape up spare cash and film stock, the result is a nightmarish, pitch-black chunk of nervous laughs. This 30-minute black-and-whiter stars Amy Vane as Jane, a frustrated young woman whose life is caving in around her due to a terrible job, a nagging mother, and a boyfriend who's unable to love anything but 'The Cinema'. But in addition, everywhere she goes, she gets the freaky feeling that she's being followed by someone with a movie camera. Is the poor, frazzled miss losing her mind? Is it all a delusion brought on by her film fanatic brainpan? Nope. Unbeknownst to Jane, people are actually documenting her day-to-day problems, editing it into episodes and presenting it regularly at The Secret Cinema, where the cognoscenti can laugh at the continual misadventures of 'America's Stupidest Heroine'. Even when she stumbles upon a theatre showing Episode 24 ('Jane − Down in Flames'), the next day the movie house has changed into a supermarket! This is a wild, psycho trip of calculated mental sadism, and I liked it a lot! Reminiscent in style of film school shorts, but with less artsy posturing and more heady humour. Plus it's *miles* more effective (and downbeat) than the flashy remake Bartel filmed for (Not So) **Amazing Stories** several years back... The second featurette, **The Naughty Nurse** has a more direct concept: Weird sex! It's a nine-minute long one-joke vehicle with Paul moving up to *colour* stock (he must've gotten his tax refund that week). Valerie Armstrong is the titillating title character, who spends her day shift at the hospital before slipping on the fishnets and leather at lunch time and heading to a convenient downtown hotel room. Voila, it's Ms. Dominatrix! Pinching her johns with tongs, jabbing him with spiked heels, snapping his rubber bands with her teeth − for most of the short, you aren't sure what the hell is going on, but it's all perversely funny anyhow. It all hinges on one slight, cheap joke, and combined with Bartel's first, they make a great little acidic combo.

SEIZURE

OLIVER STONE 1974. Director Oliver Stone can pump out the mega-buck Oscar winners (**Platoon, Wall Street**), in addition to smaller, personal projects (**Salvador, Natural Born Killers**), but his mainstream fans will be mighty surprised if they rent this early horror flick of his. For his directorial debut, Stone journeyed to Canada in order to helm this uneasy marriage of psychological terror and good ol' scummy thrills. The results are more interesting than

successful, with the eccentric cast providing the most memorable aspect. We've got Jonathan Frid (ol' Barnabas Collins himself) starring, with ample support from Martine Beswick (**Dr. Jekyll and Sister Hyde, The Happy Hooker Goes to Hollywood**), Mary Woronov, Troy Donahue, and Herve Villechaize as The Spider... Edward Blackstone (Frid) is an intense horror writer who invites all his obnoxious show biz cronies to his country house for a visit. But as luck would have it, Frid planned the party the same weekend that a trio of psychopaths have escaped from the local asylum. Strangely, Frid has been dreaming of their unwelcomed arrival for some time... Who's that peering in their dining room window? Why, it's half-pint Herve in white pancake makeup, lipstick and leotards!

Not the scariest prospect for a fright film, but add a mute black strongman named The Jackel and the seductive Queen of Evil (Ms. Beswick), and soon the twisted trio have taken over the house and are preparing to execute the residents by turning their own nightmares against them... Are these deviant party crashers just your ordinary, sadistic pack of nutcases? Could they possibly be supernatural creatures? Or did Frid manifest these killers from his own fertile imagination? Stone used this same prospect of an artist's anxieties taking physical form in his next feature, **The Hand**, but in **Seizure** the results are a bit murkier. Instead of allowing the proceedings to speak for themselves, the film is top heavy with blunt symbolism and portentous dialogue. But even with his first effort, Stone had a field day with his never-stagnant camera. Frid is good as the dazed lead, and the rest of the cast fill their roles adequately (and *ever* so seriously)... Even though this unassuming little suspensor is crammed with one too many pretensions toward greatness, at least it has more on its mind than a dozen **Friday the 13th**s. Most '80s horroramas don't have an intelligent thought throughout their 88 minutes, while this movie overflows with them, until you need an aqualung to breathe. Stone tried to create a Thinking Man's Killfest, and you've got to commend him for attempting something original, even if it doesn't always click. (Of course, the guy couldn't get another directing job for seven years, either.)

THE SEVEN MINUTES

RUSS MEYER 1971. Here's a dated obscurity that's worth a look for camp completists. Russ Meyer's early career brought the nudie flick to adulthood with **The Immoral Mr. Teas**; he then gave us feminist classics like **Mudhoney** and **Faster Pussycat! Kill! Kill!**; and anyone with an iota of common sense knows that his first studio pic, **Beyond the Valley of the Dolls** is one of the all-time exploitation epics. Well, Russ' legendary (short-lived) contract with 20th Century Fox was for two films, and this was his equally energetic follow-up. But would you believe it's a R-rated rarely-raunchy courtroom drama based on an Irving Wallace pot-boiler, with nary a bare breast in sight? Though unquestionably unsuccessful, it has the same vertigo-inducing pace as **BVD**, with Meyer clipping off scenes and sentences to dizzying effect. If a scene needs one cut, Russ gives us a dozen (sorta like playing a 45 at 78rpm). Plus, since the plotline focuses on an obscenity trial it gives Meyer a chance to argue for causes he's been a major influence to for decades... Local government prudes are closing down bookstores for selling a risqué book entitled 'The Seven Minutes', and the story begins when an innocent young bookseller is arrested for distributing so-called 'pornography'. The state's case: To prove a recent rapist had been influenced by the racy novel, turning this nice kid (ha!) into a slobbering sex fiend. Of course, Meyer doesn't straddle the fence with the issue. He delights in making the censors look like mind-less asses and lecherous old codgers – intercutting one snooty politician's right wing spiel with one of their bimbo 'secretaries' rolling on a shag rug. Subtle, eh? And let's not forget to satirise church officials, self-righteous censors, pandering reporters, and paid-off intellectuals while we're at it! For the obligatory romance, we get the lacklustre Wayne Maunder (who's defending the case) and his main squeeze, the pneumatic Edy Williams (who's corpo-rate daddy is pissed off at her taste in men)... Meyer's hyper-kinetic style completely overwhelms the acting, the story and any serious pretensions, but without his two-ton touch it would've been just another mediocre TV movie. Instead, we get a sleazeball Perry Mason on speed, with snatches of howlable dialogue. There's also a wonderful cast of old-time Tinseltown vets and Meyer's stock company regulars: Charles Napier, James Iglehart, Tom Selleck, John Carradine (who's great as a barfly), Yvonne DeCarlo, Wolfman Jack, and Ms. Williams, who pouts a lot and seems confused about why she has to keep her dress on... Interesting stuff, but additional proof that Russ is far too 'unique' (to use a polite term) to adapt mainstream material. The guy may be a genius, but this flick is no winner.

SEXPLOSION

DENNI LUGLI / PAOLO MONTANARI 1987. From Draculina Cine comes this demented little production – a gory porno ('Gorno?') featurette that should knock the crusty shorts off of the sickfuck contingent. Did *I* like it, you might ask? Hell no! It's crude, amateurish and unimagi-native, but it's also a high-concept sleazebag crowdpleaser. Short, to-the-point, and almost unwatchable for anyone with an IQ in the triple digits. This Italian import comes undubbed and unsubtitled, but come to think of it, anyone interested in this vile little video could care less about luxuries such as dialogue. There's no wast-ing time in this raunch-o-rama either. For the first 10 minutes a horny young couple fuck in front of a video camera after the guy gives his date a dose of Sexplosion (sort of Spanish Fly squared). There's the usual procession of flesh tones: Her tits, his hairy butt, their legs and arms intertwined, plus close-ups of him sipping from her fuzzy cup and then getting a blow job, and both of 'em end-lessly grinding away. It's tedious, repetitious dreck for the mutton-flogging crowd. At least the second half is more exciting (though no less worthless). The next morning, he's all limp and tired while she's ready for more action. So what does she do? She gives her unsuspecting beau a king-sized syringe-full of Sexplosion aphro-disiac, straight into a vein. Well, to make a dumb story short, the injection causes the guy to go bug-eyed psychotic. His face gets blotchy, he growls like a bear, and his dick turns into a foot-and-a-half long purple sausage that oozes McDonald's special sauce. After driving a pair of scissors through her tongue in true Herschell Gordon Lewis fashion (in other words, totally unbelievable) he ends up pulling his own penis off... Well? That's entertainment?! Starring the forgettable (at least I *hope* I forget 'em) Rrose Selavy and Paul St. Pauli, and directed by Denni Lugli and Paolo Mon-tanari (you mean it took *two* brains to come up with this?), whose innovative technique amounts to using a fish-eye lens during the murder. Is there anything good to say about it? Well, the bathroom

tiles were nice... Plus on the bill (yep, there's more! Aren't we the lucky masochists?) is **Nightmare Club** starring Samantha Fearson. It's a one-take coupla-minuter in which a homely stripper pulls off more than her clothes – eventually unzipping her stomach and tossing her innards to the crowd. At least this one was quick... If you're gonna add these to your video collection, file 'em right in between **Ilsa, She-Wolf of the SS** and **Submit to Me**.

SHE-DEVILS ON WHEELS

HERSCHELL GORDON LEWIS 1968. Herschell Gordon Lewis cashed in on the motorcycle-gang-craze during the late-'60s by turning it on its pimply ass with an all-female gang of sadists called The Man Eaters. It's a distaff version of **The Wild Angels**, and though it has less actual storyline than most biker flicks (hard to believe, eh?), compared to Herschell's other features, **She Devils** is practically nose-deep in plot complexities. As godawful crude and amateurish as you've come to expect from Lewis, it's a fun little ride for schlock-a-holics, but it can't hold a candle to Russ Meyer's **Faster Pussycat! Kill! Kill!** for *solid* femme fiendishness... "You treat men like they were slabs of meat, hanging in a butcher shop," the gang's Nice Chick complains to their cycle-slut leader, Queen; and after a chopper race to see who gets first dibs on the local pack of studs, these Biker Bitches in Heat squirm their way through a surprisingly tame 'orgy'. The club's blond virgin, Honeypot, is being saved for her 'Initiation' though, when they can pour chocolate syrup and grease over her naked body and let her get gang-banged by the entire male population of Piss-Ant County. After-ward, Queen and her bunch brawl with some male cyclers and drag a guy along the pavement until his face looks like a plate of lasagne; and their nemesis, Joe-Boy, decides to get even for the last butt-kicking The Man Eaters gave him, so he and his redneck pals kidnap Honeypot, rape the piss out of her, and drop her bloodied remains in front of The Man Eaters' clubhouse. And you and I both know what *that* means – it's REVENGE TIME!... Their motto is 'Sex, guts, blood, and all men are mothers!', but while I expected *loads* of nudity and graphic violence from HGL, the God-father of Gratuitousness, this film is so tame that I'd barely con-sider it R-rated. The only gruesome moment is a *classic* decap at the end (which almost makes up for the sluggish sections), when The Man Eaters slice off a male

biker's head by stringing a wire across the highway at neck level. Ouch! Look at that head fly!... But then they all get ar-rested at the end! Gimme a break!... Despite this cop-out finale, there are some wonder-fully penny-ante moments that only Lewis can get away with (such as the same dumb whirl-ing illo during each of the se-gues and a hilarious theme song that we get to hear over and over and over...), and the flick certainly shows that women can be just as grimy a pack of dirt-bags as men are. Starring Betty Connell as Queen, Nancy Lee Noble (who also appeared in Lewis' **Just for the Hell of It** and **The Girl, the Body and the Pill**) as Honeypot, and several mem-bers of Miami's Female Cut-Throat Division of the Iron Cross Cycle Club... Though it was one of Herschell's most profitable movies, I wouldn't place it on the same lofty echelon as **The Gore Gore Girls** – there's plenty of grainy grubbiness, but it's nothing I'll be sitting through again soon.

SHIVERS

DAVID CRONENBERG 1975 (US: THEY CAME FROM WITHIN). Looking for a *real* stomach-churner? Well, you might have to search a little, but **Shivers**, David Cronenberg's barely-distributed first feature (it opened in NYC on the second half of a double bill with **Bobbie Jo and the Outlaw**), fits that description quite nicely. A wildly nasty updating of **Invasion of the Body Snatchers**, it touches upon most of the themes which reappear throughout Cronenberg's later works. Set in an isolated condominium, we are juicily introduced to a slug-like parasite – a lumpy little critter that's a combination aphrodisiac/venereal disease, and which infects the hotel residents through sexual contact. Forcing its way down people's throats or through any other available orifice (Barbara Steele makes a guest appearance as the lady in the bathtub), it turns its host into a homicidal sex zombie. Mass panic ensues, of course, and Cronenberg has a lot of fun playing against society's sexual taboos – grossing us out and making us chuckle at the same time. As expected, it is not an easy film to sit through unless you're familiar with the director's notorious sense of grim humour. For example, there's a scene where a victim leans out of his apartment window and ralfs up a large, bloody parasite onto the transparent umbrella of an elderly passer-by. And then there's the guy who has to use *two* pairs of pliers to pry the creatures off his munch-meat face... The special effects are surprisingly good (lots of early bladder effects to create the illusion of parasites crawling under the skin), and even if it's a tad slow at times, it's a great first feature from everybody's favourite Canadian kook.

SHOCK CORRIDOR

SAM FULLER 1963. When this gritty feature was first released in the early '60s, the critics lambasted it for being nothing but a lurid, exploitative, pulp thriller with absolutely no redeeming value whatsoever. Critics were so livid, in fact, they completely ignored the positive aspect of the film – namely, that it's an utterly INCREDIBLE, lurid, exploitative pulp thriller. Amazingly sordid, overwrought entertainment that's hard-boiled to the point of camp! Overflowing with wild, super-dramatic dialogue, this is the antecedent of every grubby prison flick to come. And now, over 25 years later, its cult status is finally being acknowledged... Charting the journey of a 'sane' man into the world of the insane, Peter Breck stars as a reporter obsessed with winning a Pulitzer Prize, and who decides to investigate a murder at a local mental asylum by posing as a patient. He convinces his stripper girlfriend to pose as his sister and have him committed for incest, and during his straight-jacketed stay he meets a gallery of unforgettably demented loonies. And these supporting psychos are indeed a silly lot, with simple PSY 101 answers to all their problems. There's a Korean war vet who turned traitor and now thinks he's a Confederate general; a black Civil Rights activist who thinks he's the Grand Wizard of the Ku Klux Klan; and an atomic scientist directly responsible for the A-bomb, who's regressed to a six-year-old level. Brent tries to solve the murder by questioning these patient/witnesses during rare moments of lucidity; but after some electroshock and a brutal attack by a roomful of nymphomaniacs (one of my fave scenes), Mr. Reporter might just be as insane as the other loons. Even if the pace flags a bit by midpoint and the storyline threatens to unravel, there are always wonderful background activities to keep the viewer attentive, such as the somnambulistic patients who continually roam the corridors... Gnarly ol' director Sam Fuller has made some over-the-top films before, but (along with **The Naked Kiss**) this is the tops! Though his stock footage hallucinations don't

work all of the time (i.e. the stuff shot by him years earlier overseas), the best is definitely saved for last (an indoor rainstorm, plus a wild fight during which Brent literally grabs a guy by the ears and pounds his head repeatedly on the concrete floor. Neat!). Peter Brent over-emotes, spits his dialogue, and tries out every trick in the book; and as his girlfriend, Constance Towers does the most inept striptease in celluloid history. Chock full of violence, disturbing comedy, and plot twists so trashy they verge on parody. A crazed gem that'll bowl you over!

SHRIEK OF THE MUTILATED

MICHAEL FINDLAY 1974. Are you ready for amateur night at the movies? Are you ready to be bored out of your mind? Are you ready to hear the hit tune 'Popcorn' by Hot Butter? (Oh god, anything but THAT!)... It all begins when a bunch of groovy college students (you can tell they're groovy because they have flower decals on their van) and their obsessed professor head out for an unorthodox field trip. They're in search of the illusive Yeti, and though several students died after the prof.'s last field trip, that couldn't happen again, right?... This film starts off sprightly enough for an obvious dime-store relic, with a completely gratuitous double murder. First, one peripheral character slices his girlfriend's throat with a serrated kitchen knife (he's crazy, you see, after getting a glimpse of the Yeti) and then, with her last dying strength, she crawls to the bathroom and gets even by tossing a live toaster into the tub with him. Snap, crackle, pop! Two cast members bite the dust! But then it's downhill for the first hour, with acres of padding to wade through before we get to the first Yeti sighting. The cast talks about the creature, tells tales about past sightings, discusses their research (Zzzzzzzz), BUT THEN (hey, wake up!) we get a 10-second attack where a hyperactive little guy in a ludicrous white-furred Bigfoot suit leaps from behind a tree and splatters red paint all over a victim. Blink and you'll miss it, cuz the Yeti is a might on the shy side (unless he's hungry of course, and then he'll rip nosy intruders limb from limb for food). And just when you think 'That's all I can stand, I can't stand no more,' the last 15 minutes pile drives to the rescue, with Mr. Yeti chasing the lead chick through the house. It sounds like the Tasmanian Devil, looks like an albino Rasta with fangs, and the costume is so startling it must've been constructed by a far-sighted upholsterer. The best part of this entire lame production is the total bugfuck 'twist' ending, involving cannibal cults and head-shaking stupidity. Utterly laughable and complete with a pleasantly grim finale where almost everyone dies (thus diminishing the chance of a sequel. Hip-hooray!)... But I don't want to make this film sound too good. The photography is grainy, the script sucks the tailpipe, it's got the worst continuity I've seen in ages (First it's night. Suddenly it's broad daylight. Musta been an eclipse, eh?), and the acting isn't just bad – it's abysmal! I've seen better performances in industrial accident films! In particular, the mute Indian butler named Laughing Crow (Ivan Agar) is a hoot, since he looks more like he belongs in the cast of **The Godfather**... From the scriptwriters who blessed us with **Invasion of the Blood Farmers**, Ed Adlum and Ed Kelleher, and the guy who directed (most of) **Snuff**, Mike Findlay (and who was decapitated soon afterward in a freak helicopter accident, so I guess there is a God after all). Believe it or not, if not for the last reel, this film would be almost as bad as **Harry and the Hendersons**. Honest.

THE SINISTER URGE

EDWARD D. WOOD JR 1961. Saw this at the university on a double bill with **Glen or Glenda**. Kept expecting to see Bela pop in every now and then (probably would have made the film better). Ed Wood's considerable untalents are sporadic on this relatively high budget outing (that is to say, there's no stock footage and they use more than one car). REAL GREAT OPENING: A voluptuous blond runs down a dirt road clad in only a bra, panties and slip (obviously being chased – you can tell 'cause she's screaming). Realising she's cornered by a lake (really a duck pond), she hops into the phone booth (conveniently left there by the last victim, I guess), only to discover THERE'S NO POCKETS IN UNDERWEAR! So she's left helpless when the rapist finally catches up to her and her disappearing slip (obviously the continuity girl is on heroin) and slaps her to death. After this exciting piece of muck the 'film' alternately hits and misses with inspired but infrequent sleaze scenes played off against insipidly scripted diatribes on the 'evils of pornography'. Yes folks, obviously this new smut picture racket is responsible for the plethora of sex murders in the park (Rob Chambers must have seen this flick before his date with Jen). Filled with cool sleazoid characters (the film's saving grace), this porn ring is run by the always tightly clad Gloria Henderson (with a wardrobe from Hell) and her right hand man & top film director Johnny Ride ("I want you to remember, I used to do good films"), who distribute their bad naughty films and enticing photos (of girls in bikinis – didn't know that was illegal) to high school kids through the Pizza Man and the Ice Cream Man (who gets his icy wares shoved in his eye when he won't pay up – Horrors!). Then there's the severely

twisted Dirk Williams (a Denny Terrio-clone) who, after one look at Satan's Smut, turns crazy rapist murderer, searching girls out in the park, tearing their easy-off blouses (ATT'N, SLEAZEMONGERS: Brief shots of REAL BREASTS!) and then killing them by slapping the air around their faces (?!?). But when the ingenue Mary falls prey to the operation, you know Dirk won't be able to keep his evil hands off her, leading the kindly Lt. Carson to step up his investigation. Greed leads The Evil Trio to an untimely end full of hilarious mistaken identities and badly hidden guns... I liked this movie even though it tended to drone on too long. Seems like Wood was trying for respectability this time. Pretty infrequent sleaze, but quality sleaze nevertheless. The actors can almost act, and Wood fills the film with enough bad smelling characters and unquestionably stilted dialogue to hold your interest through the slow parts. I wouldn't pick this one over **Glen or Glenda** or **Bride of the Monster**, but it is worth seeing. FAVOURITE JOKE: Mary (after noticing posters for **Bride of the Monster**, **The Violent Years** and **Jailbait** on the wall): "Are horror films all you produce?" Johnny: "Oh... no... no, these were produced by a friend of mine." [SS]

SKIDOO

OTTO PREMINGER 1969. Hollywood's attempt at an LSD film, this is a conventional mobster/comedy as conceived by a pack of babbling acidhead Vegas scriptwriters. Director Otto Preminger wanted it both ways – hippies and drugs for the younger audiences, and a Rat Pack storyline and cast for the straighter viewers. (For more info on the impetus behind the film, check out Chapter 31 of Tim Leary's autobiography, **Flashbacks**). It's a schizophrenia's delight... The late (but mountainly obese) Jackie Gleason stars as Tough Tony Banks, an ex-mobster who's gone legit, until the syndicate top man, named God (played by a feeble Groucho Marx with shoe-polished hair) convinces him to go on one *last* job... Meanwhile, the local Pigs are rousting bands of innocent hippies and when Gleason's daughter joins their ranks and almost gets arrested, Mrs. Gleason (Carol Channing, go-go dancing in a mini-shirt) invites them *all* back to their Mafia Mansion to crash. Yes, that means strange long-hairs with beads, body paint and marijuana – spouting dialogue like "You dig?" and "The vibrations are there". Back at the convoluted Mob plan, Gleason is sent to prison (pretty quick, eh?) where's he's supposed to do a hit job but instead he accidentally gets a hit of acid in his jail cell (The Great One dosed? Yeah!!). Soon it's plastic-elastic hallucination time, with peering eyeballs, floating apparitions, and meatball philosophy from a tiny man in a glowing purple pyramid ("Wherever you go, you're still here... let mind and body separate... Seek out the clear light..."). Of course, the LSD immediately turns Gleason into a peacenik ("Hey, maybe if I took some of that stuff I wouldn't have to rape anyone anymore," sez one of his cell mates), and he decides to stand up against The Mob, with the band of spaced-out hippies at his side... And look at this supporting cast! It's a no-talent nightmare – Peter Lawford, Richard Kiel, Frankie Avalon, Slim Pickins, Mickey Rooney, and professional-loser Arnold Stang (who gets offed by a hitman's bullet, thank you very much). Plus, Cesar Romero, Burgess Meredith and Frank Gorshin even turn up (Were they sharing the same backlot as the old **Batman** series?)... There's dogs smoking cigarettes... Psychedelic dancing trash cans... Channing does a quick striptease, down to her undies (YUCK!!)... And the Paisley Patrol finally defeats The Mob by 'loving them to death' Wow! Groovy! Fab! Far-out! Sure, it's all a load of hippie-dippy horseshit, but in its own spastic way **Skidoo!** is such a hit-and-miss trash fiend's delight that you *have* to enjoy it (plus, you have to applaud Otto P. for convincing all his Hollywood pals to appear in this mish-mash). A lot of the movie is interminable, and I can understand why the critics and public quickly flushed it from the theatres); but if you can sift through the rubble you'll also find several truly inspired moments of drug-induced nonsense. The last shot *alone* makes this flick worth your time – with Groucho floating across the ocean, dressed in guru robes and smokin' a roach, as the entire end credits are *sung*!... It's a must for '60s archivists and any fans of **Head**-style filmmaking.

SLAUGHTER

JACK STARRETT 1972. In the beginning, before 'blaxploitation' become a loving term to grindhouse patrons, there was Jim Brown – the first to chew up urban screens and break Time Square box-offices. After faring only mediocre in the cross-over market, he went right for the jugular by portraying a big, bad, black motherfucker who didn't take any white man's shit. It's **Shaft** with two-ton balls. And this flick helped set the pattern for dozens of blaxploiters to come. Why? Because it made a shitload of money by cutting away most of the crap that usually slows down action pix (plot, characterisation, subtlety), and getting right to the killin' and ass-bustin'. As the ever-stoic, ex-Green Beret Slaughter, Brown has his sights set from the first five minutes, when his father is blowed-up real good by The Mob. He's out for revenge! And where most black screen heroes put up a vague semblance of righteousness, Brown shoots first, thinks later, and never lets up on the machoshit head-busting until the end credits. When he isn't tossing naked groupies out of his apartment, Jim's wasting anyone in his way and providing vigilante justice at its rawest. There isn't much storyline, and in truth, the script could've worked just as well with Chuck Bronson in the lead with only minor revisions; but Brown is so much more fun to watch since he just *loves* to beat the piss out of *anyone*. Is the guy even acting? (I doubt it)... Eventually, Slaughter takes a detour to South America to assassinate the kingpin who crisped his daddy, and encounters Rip Torn, who squints and snivels his way into future anonymity as a racist syndicate shitheel (and I bet the guy wishes he'd taken the Nicholson role in **Easy Rider** *now*). In the bimbo-role, Stella Stevens wears low-cut gowns, gives the goo-goo eyes to Jim, and initiates some steamy bedspring endurance tests... The production values are slick, there's brisk direction by Jack Starrett, and the script has a nice, cynical edge about any authority figure (especially white ones). But it's the non-stop action that makes it a winner... Let's not forget the theme song, by the ever funky Billy Preston ("Slaughter's gonna blow your mind/Slaughter does not waste his time/My advice to you is this/If

you shoot at him, Brother, do not miss"). Wild stuff!

SLAUGHTER'S BIG RIP OFF

GORDON DOUGLAS 1973. A rule of thumb at AIP: If at first you make a wad of cash, why not try it again? Especially if you can pull off a virtual recycle of the same plot. Once again, there's a blood bath in the first minutes, which prompts big guy Slaughter to pack up his pistols and take the law into his own hands (but not so quickly that he doesn't have time to lay some pipe along the way). This follow-up is less frantic than the first, with more disposable melodrama cramping the pace. But even if it doesn't rise to the bare-knuckle heights of the first, *who* could pass up a film that casts Johnny Carson's butthead announcer, Ed McMahon, as a polyestered mob boss? Mr. Jovial Windbag himself, sitting at poolside, ordering around assassins. Irony, or just campy casting?... Meanwhile, Jim Brown goes around busting up corrupt cops and seedy racketeers, with highlights that include Slaughter almost shoving a guy's head into a plane propeller, and teaming up with a riotously-veloured Player. Don Stroud pops up at the end as a volatile hitman (at one point he pours glue down a guy's throat!), and he makes a good adversary for Brown during the one-on-one finale... As you can see, this whole flick is just an ego-bloated trip down Brown's superstud fantasy life, and even though the guy's got style to spare, his film's only mediocre. And one question that kept reoccurring: What the hell does Slaughter do for a living? Still, the thing I like most about Brown is his downright sadistic side. He always pummels an opponent a little more than is necessary, and you get the feeling he goes through stuntmen faster than he does condoms... Co-starring Gloria Hendry, Brock Peters and Scatman Crothers... Coupling this with the first **Slaughter** you'll realise the reason for the guy's name, because he leaves behind more corpses than John Wayne Gacy. Brown is brute force incarnate, and both flicks are worth a look just to get a gander at the most law-breaking 'hero' to emerge from the blaxploitation genre.

NOW
PLAYING   NEW PENTHOUSE 59th St.Twin 1 RKO 86th St.Twin 1

SLAUGHTER HIGH

GEORGE DUGDALE / MARK EZRA / PETER LITTEN 1987 (AKA: APRIL FOOL'S DAY). Do you fondly remember early-'80s formula-trashola like **Graduation Day**, **Prom Night**, **Night School** – all those interchangeable kill-fests set amongst the high school/college crowd? Well, here's one of the latest, boring examples in meat-market moviemaking, but at least Vestron Video had the good sense to release the 'uncut' version (it was R-rated during its brief theatrical play-off)... It begins with one of those flashback prologues where all the high school students look about 35-years-old. Led by Caroline Munro (who was probably voted Most Likely to Cocktease), the jocks play a practical joke on the school nerd for April Fools' Day, and poor Marty ends up stripped naked and photographed with his head down a girls room toilet bowl. For an encore they 'accidentally' burn his face off with nitric acid and ship him off to the Funny Farm... Years later, all these unlikeable young people have turned into even more repellent middle-agers, and if you couldn't see it coming a mile away, they get back together for their class reunion and start getting bumped off one-by-one. Whew! Pretty darned imaginative, eh? (Nope.) Caroline M. gets to play a now-famous actress, accompanied by a supporting cast of interchangeable dimwits, including a wise old school janitor who's the first one to get his brain hung from a coat hook. All the returnees sit around their old, vacated school, and every time one of them leaves the group they wind up with a mildly-innovative demise (you think they'd learn after a while) – there's a bathtub with acid pouring out of its spigot, a lawnmower which mulches a character's chest, a mid-orgasm electrocution, and best of all, one guy who tears his own stomach open and rips his guts out, after drinking a tampered can of beer (hey, that's the same brand I'm drinking... Hmmm...). You *know* the last character left alive is going to be Ms. Munro, since she's the only real name in the cast, and the nicest thing that can be said about her performance is that she squeals pretty well. The obligatory 'twist' ending doesn't make one bit of sense, except for giving the special effects team a chance for one last gross-out concept. But even *with* the few sicko splatter effects (none of which are convincing), this is just another tedious entry in Butcher-shop Cinema. Yawn!

SLAVE GIRLS FROM BEYOND INFINITY

KEN DIXON 1987. Boing! Boing! Run, slave girl, run! With your teeny bikini and even teenier IQ... Yes, it's the first release from Empire Pix' new 'Urban Classics' division. This wonderfully-*titled* flick was tossed into grinders on a double-bill with **Creepozoids**, and even if I love the idea of a film company returning to the grand old days of trashy, first-run double bills, I only wish this movie had been a *lot* schlockier. As it goes, **Slave Girls** is passable (and immediately forgettable) mindrot... Elizabeth Cayton and Cindy Beal star as a pair of imprisoned space sluts, chained-up in a dank cell on a star ship freighter. But these feisty bimbos soon escape from their captors and head into deep space, only to crash-land on an uncharted planet. There they encounter Zed and his robot valets, living very comfortably in a sumptuous castle in the middle of the alien jungle... Hey, cliché-lovers, guess what? Zed is obsessed with hunting, especially if the prey is humanoid. Needless to say, it's **The Most Dangerous Game** recycled for the Nth time, with Zed in the Count Zaroff role – chopping off his victims' heads and mounting them in his game room. From there on, *you* connect the dots... A sappy love story. Revenge. A chase to the death. Two bickering androids... It's pretty uninspired stuff, but at least the ending picks up some speed when Liz gets her mitts on a phallic laser bazooka, a bunch of mouldy monsters crawl outta the Phantom Zone, and everyone ends up in a swordplay free-for-all. The special effects aren't as ultra-chintzy as you'd expect 'em to be either, and the makers utilised some surprisingly spacious sets

(though you can probably assume they were leftovers from another Empire production). The male cast members are all grads of the Dolph Lundgren School of Macho Fatheads, and though the gals jiggle around in Fredericks of Andromeda lingerie, the film never has the guts to fly into the jaws of *truly* bad taste. Sure, there's enough nudity in the second half to keep the wanker-yanker contingent of the audience busy, but there's barely any violence or bloodshed. At the very least, director/writer Ken Dixon (**Zombiethon**) could've tossed in a few gallons of slime and ooze, for which cheapjack-FX-wizard John Buechler is renowned. Oh well, even though **Slave Girls** is undeniably average, I don't want to rip it apart too much, since Empire accomplished exactly what they set out to do – crank out a cheap B-movie with no-name stars, and give it a title and ad campaign idiotic enough to lure schlock-addicts into watching it. They certainly reeled me in, and they even left it open for a sequel (how about 'Slave Girls on Gilligan's Island?').

THE SLIME PEOPLE

ROBERT HUTTON 1962. With a title like this, how could I pass it by?... Starring Robert Hutton (who also directed), this Video Gems (Ha!) release is a serviceable 'End of Mankind?' monster-romp, with a diverse group of survivors fighting for the future of the human race against a race of disgusting creatures with pointy heads, that crawl outta the sewers (no, not the Moral Majority). It all begins when a hotshot pilot lands at a small airport and discovers that the entire place is deserted. He can't contact LA on his radio, and just when he starts to panic, a station wagon pulls up containing a brilliant scientist and his two nauseatingly-adorable teenage daughters. What has happened to everyone, you might ask, and the concise answer is given by one of the dippy debs: "Well, first the Slime People came. And then the army came to fight them... And they lost." These Slime Men can only survive when the temperature reaches the dew point, so they've invented a machine that has created a giant, impenetrable dome over the evacuated city of Los Angeles. By enclosing the city and manipulating the internal conditions, these below-ground bozos will be able to exist on the surface at all times. The big problem for our carload of humans, though, is that they're trapped *inside* this walled metropolis. Oops!... They pick up more stragglers along the way (including such innovatively original characters as a squeaky-clean Marine and a crazy old man), and the scientist spends the rest of the film trying to penetrate the wall, while the other male cast members try to penetrate the two teenage tarts. And they all take refuge in a butcher shop meat locker (nice hideout, eh?)... Basically, this is a creature feature in the five-and-dime tradition of **The Day the World Ended**, but with blander characters and lousier performers. Monster-holics will love the Slime People though – they aren't given much to do (plus, they're shrouded in fog most of the time, so we can't scrutinise the costumes too closely), but these lumpy guys are classic laugh-getters, nevertheless. Covered with scales, mud and slime, they shuffle along, brandishing spears and making rude noises as if they each needed a good dose of Maalox. Co-starring Les Tremayne (who played Billy Batson's mentor in that shit-witted Saturday morning abomination, **Shazam!**) as the expendable ol' fart... **The Slime People** is acceptable drivel, with plenty of smiles at the expense of innocent lives. It also has a great trailer for **The Crawling Hand** tagged on the end.

SLUGS

J.P. SIMON 1988. Based (loosely) on Shaun Hutson's novel, director Juan Piquar Simon has churned out a cheap, but surprisingly repulsive winner. Ultra-creepy and thoroughly disgusting, it's the return of the true blue monster movie! And it's about time, because I'm pretty fucking sick of superhuman slashers and psycho-maniacs... It begins in the peaceful hamlet of Ashland (aka Small-town USA), which quickly turns into Slug Central when thousands of carnivorous little critters start attacking the population. Now normally, slugs don't have a taste for humans, but these aren't your typical garden variety. They're giant, flesh-eating mutant slugs – averaging a foot long, and with sharp little teeth that latch onto you like Pitbulls. Soon they're crawling in through your eye sockets, eating away at your internal organs, and there's so many of them that they literally *cover* your bedroom floor with a thick mass of hungry slime-oozers. Worst of all (yes, there's *more*), they've infested the town's sewer system, squeezing out of kitchen faucets and crawling up from toilet bowls (*there's* an image to keep you quivering the next time you're relaxing on the john). So if you have any problem with watching zillions of disgusting creatures crawling across the screen (not unlike the Republican National Convention), then this flick is verboten for you! Beyond the slug attacks, the plotline creaks away at a sturdy pace. There's the lone county health inspector, who knows the truth behind the rash of deaths, but none of the local politicians will listen to his ravings. Plus the cast of potential victims includes the usual potpourri: The intolerant sheriff, the pair of teens who are attached at the lips, and the brilliant scientist (who helps fill in the plot potholes)... In the '50s, the blame would've been radiation. In the late '60s it was pollution. But now the grand prize-winner is (take a guess) Toxic Waste! Yes, there's a secret waste dump bordering the town and that's why all the slugs have grown to the size of guinea pigs and have the personality of Morton Downey Jr. The pyrotechnical conclusion has the county agent and his two comrades heading into the sewer with enough explosives to incinerate the Slug Army (while destroying half the town in the process)... Unlike the familiar **Friday the 13th**-style horror flick, where the audience doesn't care who's offed (since you know everyone but the star is going to die), this fun little film pulls off some expected demises and genuine suspense. There's a competent cast of unknowns (Michael Garfield, Kim Terry, Philip Machale, Alicia Moro) and workmanlike direction – but the concept holds tight throughout and (if you haven't gotten the point yet) is it ever repellent! Special credit should go to the slug-wranglers, plus there's gore effects galore. The high point is when a guy's head explodes in the middle of a ritzy restaurant, sending hundreds of bloated blood flukes flying every which way. Mr. Creosote couldn't have done any better! They could've lost that sitcom soundtrack though... A modest gem, which was filmed in Lyons, New York (just 50 miles or so from not-so-beautiful downtown Syracuse).

SON OF GODZILLA

JUN FUKUDA 1968. On a small island out in the Pacific, a group of scientist-types are experimenting with temperature-control. When their screwing around with Mother Nature accidentally raises the heat level on the island to an unbearable level, a giant egg hatches, and Minyah, Godzilla's son, is born. Not yet old enough to breathe fire like Dad, Minyah can only blow smoke-rings. He's not too good at fighting monsters, either, as is apparent when he is bullied by some unfriendly giant mantises and Godzilla has to come to the rescue; but he gets a few licks in before the film's over and joins Dad in a climactic battle with Aspiga, a monstrous spider. No city-stomping in **Son of Godzilla**, all the action taking place on the island, but enough prehistoric pugilism to keep fans amused. Not one of the best in the series, but heck, isn't it fun watching the monsters kick the shit out of each other? [BJE]

SORCERESS

BRIAN STUART 1982. Normally, I wouldn't be caught dead watching a dipshit sword & sorcery flick, since slop like **Deathstalker** and **The Barbarians** has always left me cold. But **Sorceress** is such a per-

petually stupid movie, pocked with healthy doses of butchery and nudity, I sorta enjoyed it (against my better judgement). The brain behind this brawnfest was director Jack Hill, who's always had a knack for taking a sleazy genre and turning out the best imaginable product: Blaxploitation with **Coffy** and **Foxy Brown**, Women In Prison with **The Big Doll House** and **The Big Bird Cage**, Street Gang flicks with **Switchblade Sisters**, and he even turned out a halfway decent Cheerleader movie, **The Swinging Cheerleaders**. He had the same dumb luck this time around, unfortunately Hill didn't get much credit in the long run. Though Jack was both writer and director, he took a last-minute walk when New World exec Roger Corman chopped his cut of the flick and skimped substantially on post-production (Corman? A tightwad? I'd never have believed it!). The director's credit was subsequently assigned to 'Brian Stuart', Jim Wynorski got a scriptwriting nod (though he only provided the storyline) and Hill was named as producer. So much for the inner-workings of cheapjack studios – onto this asinine adventure... The story begins as an evil wizard Traigon (Robert Ballesteros) plans to slaughter off his first born (one of two twin baby daughters), but Krona the good wizard saves the tots and blesses the pair with the secrets of sorcery and the ability to kill hundreds of underpaid stuntmen (he also seems to have halved their IQ, since they grow up to be complete vacuum heads). Years pass, and though Krona wants the fact they're female to remain a secret, since the *very* grown-up duo tend to take long skinny dips and walk about shirtless (you see, even *they* think they're boys, despite their C-cup dead give-aways), this deception doesn't last very long. Starring Leigh Harris as Mira and Lynette Harris as Mora, every time the two get ready for battle they glow blue for a moment, which enables 'em to catch arrows in mid-flight, skewer villains at a thousand paces, and chop at attackers like a distaff Toshiro Mifune. Before long, they've collected a ragtag army of D&D clichés (a Viking-helmeted warrior, a handsome gambler/cheat, a Pan-like goat-creature – YAWN) and they all head to the big city where everyone stumbles around in monks' robes and sandals, looking like they stepped out of an Ed Wood production of **The 10 Commandments**. Can it get any tackier, you wonder? How about including a clan of (totally unconvincing) gorillas armed with laughing gas-filled fruit bombs; an army of sword-wielding zombies, who immediately go after the bevy of virgins; and a winged lion guardian, which looks like a bastard cousin to Fozzie Bear. But the STUPIDEST laugh is when we discover the sisters have shared orgasms!... Despite having over 20 minutes hacked from it by Corman, some of Hill's sly humour shines through and even though it was filmed in English, all the actors sound badly dubbed. Along with the canned music, maybe that's half the charm. Dumb humour. Dumb action. Dumb exploitation. In other words, perfect drive-in drivel! Filled with enough magical elements to appease the fantasy fatheads, while always keeping a tongue jammed in its cheap cheek.

SPECIAL EFFECTS

LARRY COHEN 1984. Writer/director Larry Cohen has one of the finest line-ups of virtually unreleased genre flicks around (**Return to Salem's Lot**, **Perfect Strangers**, **Full Moon High**) and this pulpy tale is at the top of his twisted heap. Long before Eric Bogosian hit the major league with **Talk Radio**, he worked the day shift with Cohen, playing intense film director Chris Neville in this Hitchcockian schlocker. Neville is a Cimino-esque wash-out turned recluse, trying to forget his last mega-buck bomb while obsessively delving into the meanings of reality ("What director has influenced you the most?" a reporter asks him. "Abraham Zapruder," he replies), and Bogosian steals the show with his pinpoint performance... The story involves repressed bumpkin Brad Rijn, who travels to New York City to track down his runaway wife Maryjean (Zoe

Angel of Vengeance Tamerlis), who's now working the softcore film district. Brad wants her to return to the role of farmer's wife and rugrat caretaker, but she balks at his strong-arm tactics and links up with Neville instead. Under Neville's cool exterior there resides the soul of a psycho (but isn't that true of *all* film directors?... Just kidding), and that evening he murders Maryjean in his bed while secretly filming the event through a one-way mirror. But who do the cops blame? A multi-million dollar director or a temperamental dirtbag from Bohunkville? That's only the bare bones of the plot though – just when you think you've figured out the direction this murder melodrama is taking, Cohen ups the ante by having Neville attempt to resurrect his fading career by making a movie about Maryjean's death, with police suspect Brad starring. He even goes so far as to find a dead ringer for the dead actress (also played by Ms. Tamerlis). Sure, it's implausible, but Bogosian gives it spark, Cohen gives it style and the plot twists are good for a few guesses... The interesting aspect of the Neville character is that he's a *smart* sicko – meticulous in his details, sly in his deception and always several steps ahead of the supporting cast. He's a wonderfully manipulative sleazebag, in addition to being the most perversely charismatic person in the whole film. Zoe gets a bit strident after a while since *both* of her roles are rather vapid, and as for the farmboy hero – how can *anyone* root for such a wholesome (yet pig ignorant) character? Rijn doesn't help matters by being so listless throughout. Heck, I was almost rooting for the psychotic filmmaker after a while (but then again, maybe that's the immoral way Cohen wanted it). The movie utilises some good NYC locations, and it's an intriguing, tawdry li'l thriller that works best when showcasing Bogosian's talents.

THE SPIDER (1958)
THE BRAIN EATERS (1958)

The Spider, a black-and-whiter from AIP, boasts direction and special effects by Bert I. Gordon, which is in *no* way an instant recommendation. This showman (note I didn't say 'filmmaker') brought us unintentional gut-busters like **Village of the Giants** and **The Amazing Colossal Man**, and in this passion pit nickel-and-dimer he gives us more average American high schoolers (Vitalis-drenched hair, souped-up hot rods, an average age of 30, and an IQ to match) stumbling into a cesspool of danger. When our young heroine's father is wasted in a mysterious car wreck, she wonders if the cause could tie in a huge nearby cave. Never ones to read a blatant No Trespassing sign, her and her boyfriend investigate on their own. Watch out for the papier-mâché stalactites! Don't fall into those giant gooey webs! And avoid tripping over the leaden dialogue! Yes, it's mutant spider time (unlike the ads, it doesn't have a skull face though. Shucks!). The cops promptly shoot the creature and then cart the carcass to the high school gym for the local shutterbugs. Nice idea, folks. That way the monster can 'surprisingly' come back to life when a rock 'n' roll band begins rehearsing within earshot. You see, that evil music only makes giant arachnids *real mad*! Unfortunately, you never get to see any of the townspeople eaten (I always enjoy seeing the giant monster actually chew up folks on screen, don't you?) – just a couple of mild maulings. The pace never lags too much (even if it's never rotten enough to be campy), there's plenty of suburban chaos, and as for special effects? Don't look for stop-action animation here! That's *way* too expensive. You'll have to settle for fuzzy close-ups of a real spider intercut or superimposed with the screaming human nitwits. Next we have **The Brain Eaters**, a slightly creepier, (and would you believe) even lower budgeted romp from AIP, starring Ed Nelson and directed by '50s fat man Bruno VeSota. With lofty intentions and (better still) sleazy underpinnings, this flick is rather successful, in addition to being really short (it's barely an hour long). And even though it liberally rips off other films and

stories (mainly Heinlein's **The Puppet Masters**), it's not a complete hack job. It's imaginatively filmed swill, and obviously VeSota picked up some pointers while taking up space in front of the camera lens all those years... The story begins when several people turn up missing at the same time an extraterrestrial, cone-shaped structure is discovered in the middle of a field. A coincidence? Of course not. So, knowledgeable of the inherent dangers, what's the first thing scientist Ed Nelson does? Crawl inside the damned thing! Meanwhile the missing folks reappear under the spell of an alien presence (which curiously makes the cameraman tilt at a 20 degree angle), with parasites lodged obnoxiously in the backs of their necks, *a la* **It Conquered the World**. The ending is wonderfully (and I'm sure quite unintentionally) uproarious, with Nelson meeting the all-powerful leader of the invasion, who turns out to be a bearded guru squatting in a sauna and waxing philosophically about being mankind's saviour. Dramatically, it sucks! But who cares about logic when you're laughing so hard? And are the actual Brain Eaters at all frightening, you ask? Only if you get squeamish at the thought of fluffy toupees with pipe-cleaner antennae being pulled across a carpet on strings. And considering that this flick and **The Spider** were originally on a double bill together, it's strange that both of 'em destroy the bad guys in the same manner... Cameo appearance by a young Leonard Nimoy.

STAND BY ME

ROB REINER 1986. I didn't know much about this film when I went to see it. I'd heard that it was based on some Stephen King story, but it had a crappy title for a horror film. A friend told me that it was all about a dead body that had been rotting in the forest for a while, and as an added bonus there was *puking* in it (every movie should have a puking scene, don't you think?). It sounded- like a good bet to me, so I spent my $4.50 in hopes that the story might be about a bloated, decomposing corpse that comes back to life, making everyone puke up their dinner in the middle of the road... But lemme tell you, was I pissed off when the end credits rolled! There was no gore! No blood! The puking part was just a make-believe story! And worst of all, you barely got a chance to stare at the dead guy, to see if any maggots were crawling out of his eye sockets, like they did in **Zombie Flesh Eaters**. The whole, idiotic film was just an excuse for four terminally cute kids to whine about 'touching' shit, like parents, life, death, and friendship. Big fucking deal! I shoulda spent my money on a six pack of Piels Pounders and a videotape of **The Brain from Planet Arous**. Personally, if I were Stephen King, I'd be ashamed to have my name on any film that didn't have drooling slime-mutants in heat, exploding internal organs splattering nuns, or at the very least, 18-wheelers crushing small, furry animals... Jeezis, some people will sell out their values at the drop of a hat. [TK]

STATIC

MARK ROMANEK 1985. Though devoid of any sleaze (suddenly, three hundred readers move onto the next review), this unpolished gem is high in long-lasting, cult-film weirdness. It's all very twisted, but in a low-key fashion. Sort of a cross between Jonathan Demme's small-town quirkiness and **Repo Man**-style 'where the hell did *that* come from?' humour... Keith (**Home Movies**) Gordon stars as Ernie Blick, an unassuming young man who spends his days working the assembly line for a crucifix factory (while collecting the indescribably gnarled rejects). But in his spare time he's a (possibly crazy) electronics whiz who's tinkering with an invention that might well revolutionise the world. Still traumatised by the death of his parents and disappearance of his true-love girlfriend (Amanda Plummer), the big question remains, is Ernie a simple nutcase or is he more lucid than anyone can possibly imagine? And what exactly *is* this ultra secret device? In short, it's a television set that – Sorry, I'm gonna make you rent the video to find out (yeah, I'm being a poop). The humour high-water mark comes from Bob Gunton as Ernie's cousin, an evangelist who preaches from any rooftop he can climb upon; gives radiation suits to his kids for Christmas; stockpiles K-rations and automatic weapons in preparation for 'The Big One'; and ends his conversations with "I hope your death is painless". The film loses a bit of its edge in the last half hour, but always expect the unexpected. Just when you think it's fizzling to a halt, it ignites. Directed by first-timer Mark Romanek (a Brian DePalma associate) and written by him and Gordon, this is an intelligently crafted indie that predates similarly-eccentric items like David Byrne's **True Stories**, while maintaining its tightly-focused vision of Loneliness, Belief and Unbridled Hope. Very hip stuff, with music from the likes of Brian Eno, OMD, Elvis Presley, and Johnny Cash... Thank goodness for films like this, or else I'd be permanently brain-damaged from watching the usual **Slimetime**-style cinemanure.

THE STEPFATHER

JOSEPH RUBEN 1987. Here's a nice little surprise. A brand-new horror film that's subtle, witty, very disturbing, and by the end, extremely nasty and violent. Scriptwriter Donald Westlake and director Joseph Ruben have concocted a genuinely creepy tale of terror, but instead of demented rednecks or superhuman psychos, this one revolves around the average, whitebread, suburban family. Forget Freddy Krueger, Jason, Leatherface, and all those other silly slashers – Jerry Blake is the *real* item. He's a combination of Robert Young from **Father Knows Best**, Hugh Beaumont from **Leave it to Beaver** and Tony Perkins from **Psycho**. Though he acts like any normal dad, he's actually a man obsessed with the idea of the perfect family – the beautiful home, the lovely wife, the children, and the family dog. Unfortunately, they never seem to live up to his expectations, so he's compelled to eliminate them and start over again. You see, Jerry Blake has had several families and several identities, and he tends to leave a long list of corpses in his wake... When we first meet him he's methodically cleaning up – changing his clothes, washing his hands, and only at the end do we glimpse the remains of his family – the living room walls spattered with bloody handprints, his wife and children twisted across the carpet... One year later, he's found a new home with a widow and her teenage daughter, and this movie charts the gradual suspiciousness of the daughter, the slow deterioration of their happy home, and the steady realisation that Jerry is once again preparing to sever his ties (in addition to most of their ganglia) and move on. This is one of those rare films where the set-up is as satisfying (if not more so) than the climax, and the suspense is unrelenting. Shelley Hack, former Charlie's Airhead, er, Angel redeems herself adequately as Mrs. Nutcase and Jill Schoelen is fine as the distraught daughter, but it's character actor Terry O'Quinn who holds the entire film together, in the title role. His sly combination of dry wit and external cheeriness seduces not only his new family, but the audience as well – and when his rage explodes, he's truly frightening (when he's alone in his basement workshop, he flies into incoherent frenzies, brandishing his hand tools like makeshift weapons – twisting and stabbing them in the air as he raves about his imperfect family). Without him, this whole movie could have come off like a bad SCTV skit. Instead, it's the best new thriller I've seen in quite a while... With all the good reviews this film is receiving, horror buffs shouldn't worry that this is some 'arty' psychological snore-mobile. It's a grim winner, with spurts of unnerving violence and moments of unsettling humour. And best of all, it hits you where you live, and that's what a good horror tale is all about. Now if only it'll get the distribution it deserves. *Highly* recommended.

STRAIGHT TO HELL

ALEX COX 1987. Alex Cox, the whacked-out director of **Repo Man** and **Sid and Nancy**, has created the first Mutant Western, and I haven't seen such an indulgent hurly-burly since the late '60s, when films like **El Topo** and **Gas-s-s-s** were fashionable. So let's all follow Cox on a joyride into the desert for a scattershot homage to Sergio Leone-style spaghetti westerns. Along with a full entourage of friends, they manage to twist up every stereotype and sprinkle 'em with grimy humour and random, senseless death... Dick Rude (**Repo Man**; he also co-wrote the script), Joe Strummer (guitarist for The Clash) and Sy Richardson also from **Repo Man**) star as three amazingly incompetent hitmen who louse up a job and take refuge in a rathole of a town in the middle of the desert. Along with a pregnant girlfriend (Courtney Love, who only whines twice as much as Chloe Webb did in **Sid and Nancy**), they join up with a scummy gang of coffee-addicted banditos, played by The Pogues. Soon we're getting bashed over the skull with every overworked cliché in the Pastaland Old West Handbook – stilted dialogue, barren landscapes, hot-blooded señoritas, cold-blooded killers, and villains so greedy that they have to drool at the sight of money. Of course, Cox also tosses in a bunch of half-baked twists that'll have most Normal Audiences scratching their head in bewilderment – there's a nerdy hot dog vendor played by Zandor Schloss (yet another **Repo Man** veteran), Elvis Costello is a creepy waiter, cult-director Jim Jarmusch turns up as a mob leader, Dennis Hopper and Grace Jones zip in as a pair of mysterious strangers bearing gifts, and at any given moment the entire cast can break into a solemn rendition of 'Danny Boy'. To top it all, there's a hilarious conclusion, with everyone blasting the shit out of each other while searching for a hidden cache of cash... Sure, **Straight to Hell** rambles all over the place, and it isn't even close to being consistent *or* successful, but it certainly looks like everyone involved had a great time throwing themselves a one-million-dollar party, and the feeling of spontaneity and general drunkenness shines through. In other words, it's a fucking mess, but I enjoyed it anyhow. As far as I'm concerned, any film with a separate credit for 'Sex and Cruelty Consultant' deserves some type of respect... Recommended in particular to all the punk/hippie neo-western fanatics out there.

STREET TRASH

JIM MURO 1987. Saw this on a double bill with **Surf Nazis Must Die** for $2 somewhere in Cleveland – had me laughing out loud in an empty theatre. High points – let's see – There's a liquor store where all these bums get wine, and the owner just found a case of 60-year-old Thunderbird-type called Viper – one sip turns the sipee into a glob of multicoloured meltdown to truly turn any stomach. The big ass cop breaks up a Mafia hit – beats the hitman to a pulp – throws him in a urinal – and then vomits on his head!

A particularly fat bum drinks some Viper and gurgles and EXPLODES! – in SLOW MOTION! There's a monster-sized Vietnam vet who sees gook vampires in his dreams – carries around a knife made of a human femur – sticking it into everyone in sight – and finally gets decapitated from the shoulders down by a flying oxygen tank. The owner of the junkyard has a taste for fucking the dead bodies that just seem to pile up around the place and everyone wants to fuck the beautiful oriental girl who works there, but she only has a penchant for 15-year-olds. Mix this all up (I'm sure I'm missing something) in a bowl with some **Repo Man** meets **Eraserhead** meets **The Gore Gore Girls** styling – add the ugliest of ugly actors and lots of amputees and urinary humour and you have – THIS! (Oh yeah – it also has a five-minute hacked-off dick joke.) [SS]

SUGAR HILL AND HER ZOMBIE HIT MEN

PAUL MASLANSKY 1974 (AKA: SUGAR HILL). In the wake of Wes Craven's **The Serpent and the Rainbow** (a good, though flawed film, which should have stuck closer to Wade Davis' non-fiction book), here's another flick dealing with the voodoo world of Haiti, but this earlier low-budget item mixes its supernatural aspects with prime blaxploitation violence and humour (not to mention hordes of re-animated corpses). Personally, I can't think of much else I'd want from a grindhouse feature (though it could have used an R-rating), plus it even has a funky-as-shit theme song from The Originals, 'Supernatural Voodoo Woman'... Welcome to the Club Haiti, an exotic night-spot where native dancers flail about for the fat-walleted tourists. But trouble steps in when a greedy crime syndicate sets its eye on ownership of the profitable restaurant, and these whiteys have the infinite bad judgement to waste the club's manager in the first 10 minutes. You see, the ownership then passes onto the dude's girlfriend, Miss Diana 'Sugar' Hill, a beautiful black voodoo priestess who brews up her own special brand of revenge. Sugar sets out to destroy the entire hierarchy of the Mob, and she might just get her way with the aid of an army of freshly-unearthed, bug-eyed, grey-skinned, Black zombies – covered in mould and armed to the teeth with machetes. "You and your punk friends killed MY MAN! And the sentence is *DEATH*!" Sugar pro-

nounces, and one by one, each of these anglo-assholes is torn apart by the legions of the Negro Dead. These cob-webbed cadavers aren't uncontrollable meat-eaters either – they're in the business of revenge, and they work more-or-less as grubby henchmen for Sugar Hill. Bullets don't slow 'em down, and they only go after specific dirtbags – ripping their hearts out and even tossing one guy into a sty full of hungry pigs (pretty darned terrifying, eh?). Except for their goofy, white bulging eyeballs, the zombies are fairly effective looking too, particularly since they tend to smile while they tear you apart – sort of a combination of Tourneur's undead and Romero's... Marki Bey stars as Sugar, Robert Quarry is the Head Paleface Asswipe, and Don Pedro Colley steals the show with his blatant Geoffrey Holder impression, as the smirking voodoo spirit, Count Samadi. Paul Maslansky (who normally produces cinematic bile such as **Police Academy**, **Damnation Alley** and **The Villain**) actually does a fine job in the director's chair, and he beefs up the relatively no-frills storyline with overblown characters, moody carnage, and plenty of audience-pleasing demises. The end product is so efficiently executed, as well as being *so* much silly fun, that next to **Blacula**, this is the best blax-horror feature from the early '70s.

SUMMER SCHOOL TEACHERS

BARBARA PEETERS 1975. In the early '70s, New World and producer Julie Corman churned out a half dozen of these light-hearted drive-in romps, and they all followed the same basic formula: Find a trio of young, aspiring actresses who avoid brassieres, and then set them up in jobs that give 'em a chance to screw around, while expressing their new-found independence. Nurses were always a fave, and in this case it's the teaching profession. Stitch together a bit of cheesy melodrama; some light bedroom antics; lots of halter

tops, hot pants and bell bottoms; and let's not forget some women's lib polemics to balance the T&A ogling... Candice Rialson, Pat Anderson and Rhonda Leigh Hopkins star as the three cool new additions to the summer teaching staff of our typical suburban high school, and who quickly rile the staid administration by getting the students to think for themselves (and we wouldn't want *that*, would we?). Candice gets her femme gym class interested in football, to the ire of the male chauvinist coach. Pat (**Fly Me**) Anderson has her art students studying what constitutes obscenity. And Iowa-bred chem. teacher Rhonda Leigh decides to get lessons in California swinging from a juvie thug. This flick has a little of everything, not much of anything, and it's all soooo '70s – including a car chase involving two VW bugs and a dune buggy; a big football game (which ends in a riot); a light dusting of heavy-handed social messages; and even a ridiculously artsy fuck scene that's lit like the credits to a Bond film. Of course, by the end all three women show up the uptight establishment figures, while finding gents to squat-thrust with... The thesping is basic first-role level, with the exception of Candice Rialson – one of my favourite exploitation starlets. She couldn't act worth beans, but in fare like **Chatterbox**, **Candy Stripe Nurses** and the marvellous **Hollywood Boulevard**, she not only cut a curvaceous figure, but seemed to genuinely enjoy the swill she was stranded in. The ubiquitous Dick Miller has a field day as the machoshit coach, complete with one drunk scene where he gets to grab Candice's tit. Director Barbara Peeters gained further notoriety with **Humanoids from the Deep**, but be warned: Though the cameraman likes to tease us with bare thighs and tight shorts, the flick's disappointingly low on R-rated flesh. No matter. It's hip-minded, yet dim-witted fun.

SURF NAZIS MUST DIE

PETER GEORGE 1987. Sure, Troma gave us classics like **The Toxic Avenger** and **Class of Nuke 'Em High**. Sure, this film has the greatest title since **Fat Guy Goes Nutzoid!!** Sure, we showed up expecting at the *very least* great gobs of half-baked gore. And did we discover another kult klassic? No fucking way!! This flick bites the bathtub fart bubbles! One small problem is that the dickless projectionist mixed up the reels (1-3-2-4), but as I've always believed, you can always tell a Troma product because it doesn't really hurt the film to have the reels screwed up. We didn't really notice. We didn't care. We just let this chunk of horse manure wash over us for an interminable 75 minutes... Not only is it a consistently lousy movie (we expected that much), but it's sparse on action, bloodshed and nudity; and most of the humour came from the absurd thought that we actually paid *money* to see this crap. Don't believe *anything* the ad promises either – there are no chain saws, machine guns, surf battles, or bikinied scream queens. Instead, there's more grainy stock footage of bozos surfing than you'd find in an all-night Frankie and Annette Festival... Set 'sometime in the near future' after California has been devastated by an earthquake (we have to take the scriptwriter's word for it, since all we're shown is one wrecked house), a bunch of despicable Surf Nazis have taken over the beaches, and they're so mean they'll even steal a fat woman's watermelon. You can tell they're Nazis because they wear black, have swastikas drawn on their faces with a magic marker, and they have names like Adolf and Mengele. The plot (HA!) has these Nazis fighting a slew of **Warriors**-style beach gangs for domination of the coastline, and since there's only about three guys in each 'gang', it's pretty pathetic going. Armed with harpoon guns and bitchin' boards, the Nazis hit the waves and survive a few anaemic rumbles against (as I fondly refer to them) The Ninja Chinks, The Tie-Dyes, and The ZZ Tops; but when they have the bad judgement to snuff out a black dude named Leroy Washington, Leroy's Mama decides to fight back. She buys a Walther PPK, stocks up on grenades, cries over her Bible

(sniff sniff), and quickly becomes the Nazis' "worst fucking nightmare"... Given this type of rancid plot, you can understand why I wanted to check this film out. It sounds like it could be a FUCKING RIOT (!), especially if the same guys who were responsible for **The Toxic Avenger** took the reigns. But instead, some blowhole named Peter George and 'The Institute' are to blame, and they muck *everything* up. I admit that the dialogue is on par with most other Troma films (i.e. "Slime-sucking Neanderthals!") and the Nazis are funny for about a minute, but everything's so goddamn BORING that you don't care what happens to anyone in the film – you just want it to end so you can go home and watch a good movie. The only laughs are from watching a fat black woman riding a motorcycle and blowing up baddies, and one guy who lives at home with his mom and is actually a closet-Nazi... Basically, when you've got actors this limp, a budget this barren and a story this schlocky, there's only *one* alternative: Add TONS OF GORE and the most tasteless humour you can dredge up. Unfortunately, all we got is one quick decap at the very end, and lots of angry grumbling from the audience behind us... Remember. **C.H.U.D.?** This one's C.R.U.D. – Created by Remarkably Untalented Dirtbags. Tell someone you *really* hate to go see it!... Oh yeah, Bobbie Bresee (**Mausoleum**) gets her own box in the credits for a two-minute scene as Smeg's mom.

SWEET MOVIE

DUSAN MAKAVEJEV 1975. Here's a prime candidate for the 'What the fuck?' cinema sweepstakes! That crazed Yugoslavian, director Dusan Makavejev, has made some real lobsterland epics over the years. His **WR: Mysteries of the Organism** was a parade of surreal sexual hi-jinx crossed with a documentary on the philosophy of Wilhelm Reich. Dusan's later films included the fine **Montenegro**, the more commercially linear **Coca Cola Kid**, and most recently the abysmal **Manifesto**, which was (justifiably) only released in the States on pay cable. Well, **Sweet Movie** is his strangest concoction, and it first came to my attention a dozen years ago when I received a sugar packet/ad for the movie with a glowing recommendation from Jack Nicholson printed on one side... Though difficult to categorise a film this screwy, let's just say it's a social, political, sexual satire that breaks taboos, wallows in scatology, links food and sex, and consists of absurdist, free-form, playful vignettes that celebrate life in all its most deviant forms (you got all that?). The film intercuts two storylines, and while both are pretty odd, the most entertainingly sleazy follows the photogenic Carole Laure as Miss Monde 1984, during her sexual adventures across the globe. Her search for pleasure kicks off at a pageant to pick the world's most perfect virgin, with on-camera physical exams to check the contestants' qualifications. After winning the title, Ms. Laure weds Mr. Dollars (everyone's fave cinematic shitheel, John Vernon) – a Texas bazillionaire who buys everything in sight (including Niagara Falls) – only to discover even his dick is gold-plated. After getting stuffed into a suitcase and shipped to Europe, Carole visits the Eiffel Tower (could it be a phallic symbol perhaps?), makes the Beast With Two Backs with international sex god El Macho, and their lovemaking is so intense they have to be plied apart by doctors. There's a dinner table scene where people eat with their hands, vomit up food, piss on the meal, and which ends with Carole pulling out a guy's wanker at the table (though no one else cares). And for the grand finale Carole gets coated in chocolate for a TV commercial and masturbates spread-eagle in a pool of the goo. Erotic? You bet! Coherent? Not for an instant!... Meanwhile, the second tale unfolds aboard a boat with a giant Karl Marx head on the bow and a female Captain who lures young sailors aboard, accompanied by a grating song that tells us "It's a joy to be alive/It's good to be glad/Good to survive/It's great to be mad". Puddle-deep, and proud of it... As a whole, the film doesn't have the druggy wonder of an **El Topo**, but it certainly has a sense of humour about its inherent silliness. Instead of a serious statement against society's straight-jacket, Dusan prefers to let loose with a juicy raspberry. One scene sure to piss off prudes has children in a candy shop watching a stripper in action ("You can fuck me if you are lucky," the woman whispers to one young lad); but then again, 99% of *any* random audience would've walked out of the film within the first 15 minutes... Yet outside of cheap shocks, what does it all mean? (And almost as important, how'd they find a cast who'd do all this shit?) I'm sure Dusan had some vague notion, but he might be the only one. Any time the revolutionary rhetoric gets too thick, he mutates the scene and the point gets buried; and though I loved many of the wonderfully kinky episodes (such as making love in a vat of sugar), the film is more fascinating for its nerve, than stimulating for its themes. Though loaded with artily-lensed nudity from Ms. Laure and long takes of male genitalia, it's never pornographic (even if some of the scenes sound it), yet always nicely offensive. Posing as an arthouse item, this doozy from Dusan is a thinking man's (and woman's) sleaze. And if you can ignore the slower segments, it's good uncategoriseable fun for open-minded oddballs.

SWEET REVENGE

MARK SOBEL 1987. A fitting title indeed, as the makers of this no-budget swill swallowed up *my* two bucks for 79 minutes of idiotic backlot wanderings disguised as entertainment. Ted (**Knot's Landing** SUPER WIMP) Shackelford top-lines (?) as Indiana Quartermain, a somewhat implausible smuggler (He specialises in bootleg perfume. Have you had enough?) who comes to the rescue of Nancy Allen, obviously on the skids after her prenuptial agreement and before **RoboCop**. Nan and a few other Ford models are victims of bloated Marty Landau's white slavery racket, which he runs from his jungle fortress (actually the producer's house with a few artillery cases and flags out front). Shackelhead and the models escape from hordes of well-paid extras and shoot off a lot of blanks before the obligatory 'skinny-dip in the lush waterfall' scene and the final overthrow. Again, the Charlie McCarthy Principle is in effect, as most of the cast can't act their way out of, well, this movie. Landau does provide some chuckles (guffaw), rolling his bloodshot eyes and chewing on the flats. Otherwise, I hope someone got sweet revenge on the IRS for investing in this shit. (Ahem.) [TR]

SWEET SUGAR (1972)
ESCAPE FROM WOMEN'S PRISON (1984)

Continental Video spews out *two* women-in-prison movies on one tape! Double your bimbos, double your fun! More sluts in the slammer than you deserve!!... In the first, **Sweet Sugar**, Phyllis Elizabeth Davis stars in the title role, as an independent-minded babe who's tossed into a foreign jail for drug possession, and equipped with her over-flowing breasts and ever-rising hemlines, she's forced to cut sugar cane for two years at the local plantation. As in most early-'70s chain gang-gal epics, all the prisoners are statuesque American models who wiggle across the screen in scanty tank-tops and hot pants, while all the male guards are beating each other up to get first crack at Sweet Sugar. But Sugar won't take any shit, even when the pasty-faced warden makes advances from his bathtub ("I hope somebody hacks off your hambone," she snarls)... This prison comes off like a low-rent summer camp for sadists, but since it was filmed in 1972, the violence and sex is mostly off-screen. Nevertheless, we still get a full menu of exploitation fun — voodoo rituals, burnings at the stake, medical experiments, hot gun barrels down the pants, and they even get tortured by killer cats! Plus, conveniently enough, the local male prison is right across the road, so there's also a bit of

romantic subplotting and quick sex with a thick-necked bozo named Mojo. The only disappointment is the lack of shower scenes (oh well)... Director Michel Levesque does a fine job in adding just the right touch self-satire to the clichés (such as a **Full Metal Jacket**-style lesson on cutting cane, which begins with "Your machete is your best friend"), and if his Big Finale doesn't really make much sense, he tosses in lots of explosions, flames, killings, and femmes with blazing machine guns, to keep his audience happy... Best of all is Ms. Davis, who's great in the lead, playing up the humorous side and proving without a doubt she's sexy enough to give her prison-flick predecessors (such as Pam Grier) some heavy competition. She subsequently made one more drive-in flick, **Terminal Island**, and then appeared in those terrible blackout sketches on **Love, American Style**. Co-starring Cliff Osmond and Pamela Collins, **Sweet Sugar** is lightweight, but very entertaining, and it's one of the better Pre-Hardcore-Debasement Women-In-Prison movies... **Escape from Women's Prison** (aka **Jail Birds**) is a different matter altogether – a poorly-dubbed Italian import that stinks like a plate of mouldy fettucini. And since none of it takes place inside a woman's prison, I wouldn't even consider it a part of the genre. It's more of a crime drama for insomniacs... A quartet of bitchy dames-on-the-run (a Revolutionary, a Thief, a Whore, and a Lesbian Drug Addict) hijack a bus-load of tennis players and hold the group hostage at a judge's palatial country mansion. The dialogue consists mostly of raunchy epithets such as "Sit down, you little slut!"; "Shut your hole, cunt!" or the ever-popular "Stick it up your wife's butthole!", and there's less actual violence than there is generic emotional abuse. The macho-male-hostage is used as a sex toy by the Whore, the Lesbian ends up abusing one of the young tennis femmes, and there's some random nudity (I can imagine the casting call advert: 'WANTED. Zaftig women with cel-

lulite and stretch marks needed for nude scenes...'). Worst of all, director Conrad Buegnel (aka Conrad *Brueghel*) roads up the proceedings with pedantic discussions about revolutionaries and the bourgeois middle-class (just what you want to see in a randy action movie, right?). Maybe Buegnel was trying to stick some political relevance into the plot? Maybe he was trying to make a statement about today's society? Personally, I think he just wanted to pad out the running time. (If you're looking for half-baked politics, sex and arty-weirdness, you'd be better off with **Captive**). By the end, the judge winds up raping the Revolutionary, some hostages are shot, the others get drunk on whiskey and have a party, and the police save the day... Sure, it might be a bit more realistic than **Sweet Sugar**, but that still doesn't make this visually boring and emotionally tepid film watchable on any level. Oh yeah, I'd like to tell you who played what roles, but except for the title, this film doesn't have any credits (the sure sign of a class-Z production).

SWEET SWEETBACK'S BAADASSSSS SONG

MELVIN VAN PEEBLES 1971. Without a doubt, the creme de la slime! The ultimate blaxploitation, kill-whitey film of *all* time! Written, directed, produced, edited, composed, and starring Melvin Van Peebles, this is one nasty and uncomfortable mess of a movie (you know you're in for a rough ride when the opening credits are superimposed over the title character's first fuck), but it's also top-notch, art-sleaze. Dedicated to 'all the Brothers and Sisters who've had enough of The Man', Sweet Sweetback is just your ordinary black super-stud, who spends his time working in live sex shows, until the racist, neo-nazi, white pigs wrongly accuse him of a crime and haul him in. Of course, complications ensue (as they oftimes do), and Sweetback ends up bashing in the cops' brains with brass knuckles and escaping, as the gospel greek chorus sings his theme song – "Run Sweetback/G'wan motherfucker!"... From then on, it's a chase through the ghettos and alleyways of Urban Decay USA – and we're confronted with rats crawling through tenements; sadistic cops torturing innocent blacks; dialogue like "He died from an overdose of Black Misery"; non-actors punctuating their dialogue with farts; and we even get to watch a fat guy take a shit (so much for realism). Peebles' title role keeps things lively and caustic, as a smooth sonofabitch who's perfectly willing to shoot and hack his way through the scum of the city in order to get revenge. This is a one-of-a-kind pic – the type of gritty, indie that'll never find its way into theatres again (nowadays it'd end up a Whitey-backed TV movie. How about 'Malcolm Jamal-Warner's Badasssss Song?'). Unfortunately, the whole production runs out of steam after a while, but considering its been almost 20 years since its initial release, and that this is one of the first New-Rage Black films, it still packs a real kick to the nuts.

SWITCHBLADE SISTERS

JACK HILL 1975. Director Jack Hill, who honed his seedy craft in the early '70s with Filipino women-in-chains flesh-operas such as **The Big Bird Cage** and **The Big Doll House**, is back with the definitive leather-clad street-slut pic. It's non-stop action as we get street rumbles, a gang-stabbing, catfights, strip-searchers, and a juvie slammer (complete with a "pig, dyke" warden who gets a toilet plunger rammed onto her fat face) – and this is only in the first *10 minutes*!... It all begins at the local DMZ high school – the type of place where the students seem to be in their mid-20s, the guys look like Cro-Magnon Tony Danza clones, grass is openly smoked in the school yard, and in between classes you can rent a jailbait prostitute for five bucks in the men's room. But trouble hits town when a new girl transfers to school – a blond, hotpants bimbo who wants to join up with the reigning female gang, The Dagger

Debs. And if *that* wasn't enough plot for you, there's a nasty new gang of polyester punks trying to usurp their turf... Add to that some cheap (and quick) melodrama punctuating the action – the Debs' leader discovers that she's pregnant *and* that the father doesn't want it (but she gets drop-kicked in the stomach two minutes later, so this subplot doesn't last long) – and you've got a truly hilarious, Skid Row masterpiece. I could go one with the wild, convoluted plot, but how could anyone *not* enjoy a hokey barrage of death and destruction which includes shootings, rapes, knife fights, slashed faces, a blood bath at a roller rink, dick chompings, an armoured car, *and* a food fight! By the end, we've even got a bunch of black politicos popping up for a full-scale urban revolution, complete with feminist propaganda and M-16's. Definitely, a top-level, Z-grade action-express; with Robbie Lee out-sleazing and over-emoting *anything* that Linda Blair has ever done, as the head Deb, Lace (her only other film was the almost-as-trashy **Big Bad Mama**). Joanne Nail co-stars as the pretty new ball-buster, and Monica Gayle nearly steals the show as the appropriately titled Patch... When it comes to drive-in movies, they don't come much better. It's mindless, fast-paced, and more purely entertaining than a dozen Sly Stallone right-wing mumble-fests... It's also one of my new-found favourites.

TALES FROM THE GIMLI HOSPITAL

GUY MADDEN 1987. This feature debut from indie filmmaker Guy Madden first came to public attention when it played midnight shows in NYC. And if any movie deserves to wrestle **Eraserhead** for the title of art/horror/black-comedy/cult whatzit, this comes close. Don't let its meagre budget fool you – Madden may be low in cash, but he's high in imagination. And though this dreamlike dirge from Canada may roll with a Lynchian non-explanation of events, it's probably too offbeat, with its Grimm Fairy Tale ambi-

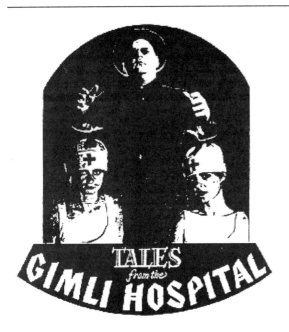

since his body of work (**The Last Woman**, **Bye Bye Monkey**, et cetera) incorporated the excess and kinkiness needed, but he just never clicks into the Buke's true sensibilities. The film rarely conveys the dark humour of his prose, and never discovers the depraved charm under the beer stains... In an obviously autobiographical turn, Ben Gazzara (whose talent veers exponentially – just try to watch the wonderful **Saint Jack** and then **Roadhouse** back to back) is fine as Charles Sirking, a pie-eyed poet chock full of wino wisdom. Los Angeles is his home base, an eternal six pack is at his side, and you can tell he's a swell guy because he starts off the movie by feeling up a very willing 13-year-old runaway for a cheap thrill. Most of the film is simply a series of drunken, sexual vignettes; and the sleaziest is when he follows bleach-blond floozy Susan Tyrell (**Forbidden Zone**, **Cry Baby**) to her home and rapes her. Of course, in Bukowski's turgid world the dame likes it ("I want you to be mean to me," she pants."I want you to beat me before you stick it in."). The best laugh is when Sirking gets hired by a NYC thinktank and is tossed into a cubicled desk job, which ends when he sneaks a six pack in for lunch and starts chucking empties at the other working stiffs. But most of the tale involves his encounters with exotic beauty Ornella Muti, as a prostitute who introduces herself by piercing both cheeks with an eight-inch safety pin (don't try this at home, kids!). An old drunken writer and a beautiful young woman with a penchant for self-mutilation and suicide. Sounds like a match made in heaven, eh? But it all plays like a stilted Italian sex flick, due to Muti's acting range, which amounts to two types of pouts. The affair finally ends with her pinning her own vagina shut in a symbolic gesture of her love... The worst mistake Ferrari makes? Tacking on an ending that tries to be uplifting. Well, phooey on that idea! This isn't fuckin' **Clean and Sober**! No wonder Bukowski was pissed off! He's spent a lifetime becoming the antithesis of cheap sentimentality, and these filmmakers screw him over... Crammed with deviant sexual behaviour, trashy underwear, arthouse posturing, neon-drenched photography, vomit, and increasingly cringeable narration by groggy Gazzara ("Ever hear the sound of one mouth screaming? I have. My own." Gimme a break!) – one big problem is that I never believed Sirking was a genius, just a lecherous sot prone to pretentious prose. And though altogether tawdry, did I forget to mention that this film is also *really slow*? Overall, this lobster-fest contains moments of sheer brilliance, but still misses the elusive spirit of its source material. A good try, but its pieces are stronger than the whole. For our second excursion into the warped world of Charles Bukowski, we have **Love is a Dog from Hell**, a little subtler and immeasurably better than **Tales of Ordinary Madness**. In fact, I *love* this movie! Everyone I know who's seen this movie loves it too. So why did it only play theatrically in a handful of major cities; and three years after its release, why isn't it even out on video?... Filmed in Belgium by young first-time filmmaker Dominique Deruddere, this emotionally wrenching drama blends three short stories by everyone's favourite puffy-eyed poet into a lifelong record of sexual awakening, loneliness and true love, as experienced by everyman Harry Voss. But don't expect anything gooey and sentimental – its honest and unflinching episodes may be from the heart, yet they're also as tough as leather. And when I first caught this film in NYC, several old farts who thought they were seeing **My Life as a Dog** nearly had strokes during the final story... When we first meet Harry, he's a 12-year-old who's fallen in love for the first time with a princess in a movie. But when Lust enters his lower regions after an encounter with a tipsy older woman, Harry quickly learns that his dreams of a fairy tale love are merely illusion; and that in Real Life, the results are less than perfect, tinged with adolescent terror, and usually sabotaged by asinine advice from older (though not wiser) friends. In the second episode, we find Harry as a 19-year-old who's inflicted with a severe case of acne that turns him into a

ence, to catch on... It begins during a smallpox epidemic, with two small children visiting their dying mother (and bringing her a Super Big Gulp as a get well gift). Meanwhile, their grandmother amuses them with a story set long ago in a primitive hospital ward where crudely scarred patients fill the cots, while their demented doctor performs surgery with a rusty sickle and a trio of vampish nurses (dressed in '20s flapper dresses) distract the patients with a puppet show. There we meet Einar The Lonely and his hospital-mate Gunnar, who both have the plague and are stuck in this bleak barn, complete with straw on the floor and farm animals roaming at bedside. The drama comes to a head when the two gents compete for the nurses attention by telling tales of their sinful past – and we learn how Gunnar accidentally killed his true love, Snowfreden, by giving her the plague on their wedding night; while grave robbing and necrophilia lurk in Einar's past... The beautiful black and white photography gives the proceedings a misty, silent film glow; the sudden shifts in tone are brilliant and unsettling; and it's filled with true (but outlandish) Icelandic customs, such as sleeping under dirt, carving fish out of bark, and squeezing glops of fish oil into one's hair. And there's no possible way to prepare yourself for the tinted, Esther Williams-style hallucinogenic finale! Wow! Madden successfully mixes the comic, horrific and occasionally touching into a ghostly framework, and it's an extraordinary first film for fans of die-hard arthouse weirdness. Though it never taps the raw subconscious as devastatingly as **E-head**, Madden obviously has very diseased sensibilities, and I'll be looking forward to more projects from him.

TALES OF ORDINARY MADNESS (1983)
LOVE IS A DOG FROM HELL (1987)

Charles Bukowski is one of the most translated (not to mention appreciated) American writers in all of Europe. But for too long he was virtually ignored on his home turf. The brilliant **Barfly** helped change that attitude, but **Tales of Ordinary Madness**, a Europroduction, was the first to bring his plastered prose to the big screen. This flick's a decidedly mixed blessing though, and Bukowski nearly disowned it. Adapted from his collection of stories entitled **Erections, Ejaculations, Exhibitions, and General Tales of Ordinary Madness**, Bukowski abhorred the end product (but that didn't stop him from soakin' 'em for every cent he could get). On the surface, Marco Ferrari seemed like a good choice as director, romantic pariah. And though obsessed with a beautiful classmate, he soon learns that the blind liquor bottle is the only thing be can depend on. But never fear, because in the final, most romantic (and to some, most disturbing) tale, an adult alcohol-besotted Harry finally encounters his perfect love – in the form of an angelic corpse he helps pilfer from a parked hearse. And though the subject matter might sound sick to the closed-minded masses, the film itself is surprisingly sweet, humorous and touching (thanks in large part to Bukowski's no-bullshit viewpoint, which Deruddere perfectly adapts to the screen). Impeccably acted and bathed in dreamy images, this masterpiece takes a razor-edged view of the disillusionment of youth, the yearning for tenderness, the despair of being alone, and the unexpected forms love can take. It's a true ode to twisted romanticism.

TANYA'S ISLAND

ALFRED SOLE 1981. It's skeleton in the closet time, kids! This sexploiter was touted with a blast of mid-production publicity, but when it was finally ready for screens, it disappeared after a token theatrical run. Probably the only reason it's now on video is because its female star, D.D. Winters (who spends much of the film bare-assed), soon afterward changed her name to Vanity and became Prince's private poontang. But give this perverse item a chance and you'll find some psychological rumbling (and intentional humour) under its T&A veneer. Director Alfred Sole first made waves with his thriller **Communion** (not to mention some earlier porno films like **Deep Sleep**), and he freely allows dreams and reality to swirl together in this tale from the pen of Canuck producer Pierre Brousseau... Ms. Winters stars as Tanya, a movie actress who's married (none too happily) to a temperamental painter named Lobo (Richard Sargent), and she escapes in a fantasy world where her and her mate are on a deserted island paradise where they can strip to the skin and fuck on a rock. But Tanya soon discovers a third party on the isle, who's hiding in the jungle – namely a horny ape who's taken a liking to Ms. Winters' rampant nocturnal nudity. She names the creature Blue and sneaks off to visit the beast one night, which doesn't sit well with her jealous hubby, since their initial friendship quickly evolves into playing Veterinarian. As Blue begins acting more human, Lobo shows his more animalistic side and in a possessive rage imprisons Tanya in a bamboo fortress while Blue goes on a coconut throwing rampage. Until (with its sledge hammer symbolism) the humans become the captives with the ape as their keeper. The script is inherently silly (or couldn't you tell?), but Sole pounds at it with precision, while creating some beautifully atmospheric sequences (with *great* camerawork by Mark **Videodrome** Irwin) that belie its crasser moments. And considering the budget, they pulled off a remarkably lifelike ape costume, thanks to craftsmen Rick Baker and Rob Bottin. In fact, the monkey suit has more acting versatility than Vanity, and happily she doesn't get a chance to sing. Even though the actual on-screen humping is surprisingly downplayed, the entire film is filled with sexual tension. I'm sure Brousseau wanted something he could sell to late-night cable, but instead Sole handed him **King Kong** meets **Repulsion** – a film too slow and moody for audiences expecting **Gas Pump Girls**, and too unusual for almost everyone else. But it's an intriguing item for fans of kinky, pretentious weirdness.

TEENAGE CONFIDENTIAL (198?)
CARNIVAL ROCK (1957)

Rhino Video bops back to the '50s with their new Teenage Theatre collection, which consists of the silliest (not to mention most entertaining) rock 'n' roll/black & white/drive-in mock-classics of all time. Most of them are *soooo* godawful that no other video company in their right mind would dare to foist them onto an unsuspecting

public, much less hire ageing 'Queen of Teen' Mamie Van Doren (**High School Confidential, Girls Town, Untamed Youth**, etc.) to introduce each selection in her asthmatic drawl, but I've gotta admire Rhino for having the vision of resurrecting the soft-headed spirit of the '50s – where any teen who spoke up was a delinquent, marijuana was The Devil's Weed, and a feature film could be churned out in a slow afternoon. So get ready for drag races and furry dice, turned up collars and teenage debs, good girls gone bad and bad bad girls gone to hell... A good introduction to the series is Johnny Legend's presentation of **Teenage Confidential**, an hour-long compilation of the ginchiest scenes and coming attractions to stagger across the screen. Where they ever dug this shit up, I'll never know! It begins with **Boy in Court**, an 'educational' short about a 15-year-old who almost becomes a hardened felon, until a friendly probation officer persuades him to go to church; and the hour continues with the likes of **The Birth of Juvenile Delinquency** (a scare piece which includes a cameo by J. Edgar Hoover) and **Teenage Crime Wave** (a Bonnie and Clyde-style tale of wild youth on a thrill ride, starring 'Tommy Cook – Cool kid in a hot car' & 'Hollie McCart – Ready to kiss... Or kill!!'). There's a clip from **Satan Was a Teenager**, a Christian crock o' shit; **High School Caesar**, in which a Valvoline-haired school prez turns out to be an exam-selling loser; plus a snippet from a Tab Hunter mental illness commercial. As expected, the hilarious **The Violent Years** gets a sizeable plug, in addition to one of The Great Lousy Films of All Time, Arch Hall Sr.'s **Wild Guitar**, starring Arch Hall Jr. as a twist-happy rocker on the road to fame and fortune. Most of the footage in **Teenage Confidential** is undeniably classic, and even if some of this has been seen before on other Rhino compilations, it all flashes by pretty quickly and painlessly... So, after that small dose of nostalgia, I decided to flip right to one of Teenage Theatre's feature highlights, a rarely-seen filler by Roger Corman named **Carnival Rock**. This one musta been cranked out in record time, and though it officially stars Susan Cabot and David J. Stewart ('Who?' on both counts), the *real* fun comes from Cormanite regulars Dick Miller, Jonathan Haze, Ed Nelson, and Bruno VeSota. A few OK Bob Luman and David Houston rockabilly tunes punctuate a tale of obsessed love amidst the carny world, and the most surprising thing about this flick is that Corman seems more interested in the hokey storyline than in the Special Musical Guests (which is the exact opposite of most other '50s teen trash). In fact, the musical 'highlight' of the movie is a whopping one-song appearance by The Platters, and they turned out to be the most boring part of the entire show... Susan Cabot is Natalie, the sultry (and not particularly talented) singer at a carny night-spot, and she's the type of two-bit dame who'd lead on her gullible old

boss, while she has a slick-haired stud on the side (Brian Hutton, whose laminated hairstyle should get a separate credit as a special effect). Soon we've got more melodrama than one moviegoer can emotionally handle. Deception! Rejection! Lust! Plus plenty of laughable drunk-scenes!... Bruno and Ed N. wander through as two loan enforcers in starched suits, Haze is a cheap hood with a fondness for ugly shirts, and a *very* young Dick M. gets the plum role as the club owner's best friend – and Miller spends more time on-screen than he has in his last 10 recent films... It's all played straight-as-a-board, with emotions pouring out of every pore, and it all comes down to a showdown for Cabot's affections, over a deck of cards. True, this is all just cheap fodder for the double-bill set, but Corman still manages to stir up a few effective moments (despite how hackneyed the whole thing is), such as when the pathetically love-bitten David Stewart goes from respected nightclub owner to down-and-out carny clown. "Beauty, youth and sex. I guess that's what the public wants," sez Dick Miller toward the end, and that's just what this film delivers in its fast-buck '50s way. Plus you get to hear The Blockbusters sing the obnoxious theme song ("You can buy me a hot dog, and popcorn/Go ride a kiddie car and blow your horn")! I dig this entire genre, and though a lot of readers will snooze off at this film's lack of excitement, I'd recommend it to any Corman completist or schlock-nostalgia addict. Cool!!

TENEBRAE

DARIO ARGENTO 1982 (US: UNSANE – which doesn't make *any* sense). For the last part of Dario Argento's 'Three Mothers' trilogy (the first two being **Suspiria** and **Inferno**), Tony Franciosa and John Saxon (two names that normally bring jeers from any self-respecting movie-goer) star in this complex psychological murder mystery. Though I've read that this particular vid-print has been trimmed by 20 minutes, I still think it holds up as one of Argento's most literate (and occasionally bloodthirsty) efforts. Recently his concepts have gotten a bit spacey (the lack of any cohesive storyline in **Inferno**), and other times they tend to get overly silly (the 'ability to control insects' in **Phenomena**), but in this case, Argento hits the right balance between suspense, stylish direction and gore... Tony F. stars as Peter Neal, an acclaimed mystery author who heads to Rome to publicise his latest horrific best-seller, 'Tenebrae', with his agent (Saxon) in tow. But murder takes centre stage when a woman is graphically razor-killed in her apartment, with the pages of Neal's book stuffed in her mouth. A mad slasher is on the loose, taking bloodcaked instamatics of his victims, and when a razor isn't big enough, a trusty axe to the head will do quite nicely (CHOP! gush,gush,gush...). Eventually Franciosa tries to solve the case on his own and this (of course) leads to all sorts of trouble, including a surprisingly ingenious ending... There's a smattering of nudity and *plenty* of hack-and-slash violence to behold (though I wonder how much might have been scissored onto the Editing Room floor), and as usual, Argento's film is steeped in atmosphere and suspenseful set-pieces. Sure, his 'coincidences' are a little farfetched at times (e.g. a girl is suddenly attacked by a stray Doberman, and in running to safety she ends up at the killer's house), but Dario's direction is also at its peak, with his usual bag of creepy side-steps and voyeuristic camerawork. Argento also has the opportunity to toss in some pointed comments about the media's insubstantial claims of Peter Neal's misogyny, since his books revolve around beautiful women-in-distress – an accusation that Argento has had to deal with during his own career... Moving away from the supernatural overtones of his recent works and going back to the mystery and exhilaration of **The Bird with the Crystal Plumage** and **Deep Red**, **Tenebrae** is one of Argento's most accessible works.

TERMINAL ISLAND

STEPHANIE ROTHMAN 1973. Set in the near future, this modest feature is a science-fiction tinged, co-ed prison actioner that tries to be a bit different than all the other genre cheapies. The overall result is just a little too tame for the normal (or should I say 'abnormal') **Chained Heat** crowd, though... When the death penalty is outlawed, the government sets up an isolated island for convicted killers, where all the murderers and murderesses can fight it out amongst each other, away from Nice Normal Society. Therein lies the San Bruno Maximum Security Centre, aka Terminal Island. And wouldn't you know it, one particularly nasty psycho runs the island like a mini-dictator with the aid of a militia of Neanderthal thugs; and since there are too many men and not enough women, all the lovely ladies in the cast end up as plowhorses and whores. Besides this social strata storyline, there's just enough knife fighting, sexual tension and brutality to earn a light R-rating, and eventually a small party of male and female dissidents flee the tyranny and go on the run. Using their wits these rebels concoct gunpowder, lay booby traps and brew up a big ol' batch of poison in a plan to overthrow the isle's penny-ante tyrant and make their wasteland safe for every law-breaking murderer and deviant who's sentenced to live there... Though lacking in most of the socially-unredeeming qualities found in most present-day prison flicks (shower scenes, graphic bloodshed, shower scenes, larger-than-life streetscum, shower scenes), director Stephanie Rothman (who also graced us with **The Student Nurses** and **Working Girls**) takes a radical approach and tries to build characterisations and an absorbing storyline. And if the movie's not very successful with its higher aspirations about man's inhumanity to man, it's still a decent enough curiosity piece... But for exploitation fans, most of the entertainment comes from the stellar cast: Phyllis Davis, who was so good in **Sweet Sugar** goes bleach blond (and is virtually wasted) as the

MEN AND WOMEN... BLACK AND WHITE... TAKEN FROM DEATH ROW, CONDEMNED TO DEVIL'S ISLAND U.S.A., WHERE LIVING IS WORSE THAN DYING!

"Welcome to Terminal Island, Baby!"

TERMINAL ISLAND

WHERE WE DUMP OUR HUMAN GARBAGE!

PHYLLIS DAVIS · DON MARSHALL
ENA HARTMAN · MARTA KRISTEN

NOW SHOWING – All Over Town!

lead sexpot, Joy; Marta Kristen, who raised blood-pressures across the galaxy as Judy Robinson in **Lost in Space**, switches from a silver space suit to a halter and hot pants combo as Lee, a political terrorist; and Tom Selleck is the big-hearted island Doc, who's there on a trumped-up mercy-killing charge. Despite plenty of action at the end during the obligatory mass-slaughter, the skin supply is kept to a bare minimum, and compared to the cruelty level of the **Ilsa** films, **Terminal Island** comes off more like **Gilligan's Island**. I'd give it a solid Mediocre on the schlock scale. A faster pace and a bit more grime could've made it a classic.

TERROR EYES

STEVE SOMMERS / MICHAEL RISSI / ERIC PARKINSON 1988. Sometimes you just grab any ol' video sitting on the shelves. In this case, the best this direct-to-video snoozer had to offer was a lead role by Dan Roebuck (the emotionally-nil murderer in **River's Edge**) and a positive plug from **Fangoria** magazine (but since they suck up to everybody, their praise doesn't carry much validity). This flimsy feature asks the question, what do you do when you have a pair of interesting U.S.C. Senior Projects (Steve Sommers' **Perfect Alibi** and Michael Rissi's **Snake Eyes**) and no idea how to get them seen by the public? How about creating an anthology of supernatural tales, using the two shorts as the highlights and bookending them with one-take filler? The result is nearly unwatchable. It starts out like a low budget **Tales from the Darkside** (I'm talkin' *dirt*-cheap), with a vignette in which an empty-headed young couple are presented with a Book of Their Life – including their past, present *and* future. Of course, it all turns out to be a dream (insert your own Sigh of Predictability here) of the starring lass, Eva (co-scripter Vivian Schilling). It's the night before her and hubby (Roebuck) head out camping with a quartet of equally unlikeable pals, and to make a long, boring movie even *more* implausible, she's been commissioned by Satan to write the ultimate horror film. And while her husband is being possessed by demons in the woods, her camping buddies sit around the fire and swap creepy tales for inspiration (thus incorporating the two student shorts)... If you haven't already guessed, this patchwork project is a full-scale *mess*, with hollow characters, annoying exposition and an overlying sense of mediocrity. At least the two U.S.C. mini-suspensors are competently made and have a smattering of imagination behind them (**Perfect Alibi** concerns a reoccurring murder and **Snake Eyes** pits a female chess champion against a crazed video game manufacturer), and both stand out as shining achievements in comparison to the bland directorial fodder by Eric Parkinson, which straddles them. There's a few sparse moments of barely-serviceable makeup effects, no bloodshed to speak of, and the final product is *almost* lousy enough to make you pound your head against the wall for wasting your cash renting it. Co-starring Dan Bell, Phil Lowry and Diana James (though don't expect any of them to brag about that fact).

TERROR OF MECHAGODZILLA

INOSHIRO HONDA 1975 (AKA: THE TERROR OF GODZILLA; THE RETURN OF MECHAGODZILLA). This sequel to **Godzilla vs. the Cosmic Monster** marked the return of both Godzilla's robot counterpart and director Inoshiro Honda, whose last Big G. flick was **Godzilla's Revenge** six films earlier... Humanoid aliens from "the third planet in the Black Hole" have in their possession the *head* of MechaGodzilla, which was twisted off its body by Godzilla the last time they fought. They restore its body and give it a few – extra touches. The aliens have also caught themselves a long-necked dinosaurian named Titanosaurus. They imbed a radio-control device into its neck (we've seen this routine before in **Monster Zero** and **Destroy All Monsters**) and send it off on a city-smashing rampage with the newly-revitalised MechaGodzilla... Where to start the invasion? "Tokyo will do," grins

the evil alien commander... The first hour is reeeal slow, but when Godzilla *finally* appears (a slimmer, more athletic Godzilla than in earlier years) we're in for some industrial-strength monster wrestling (about time, too)... The special-FX-laden fight scenes are indeed impressive (and sometimes downright absurd, as when MechaGodzilla sinks his steel teeth into Godzilla's face, lifts him thusly off the ground, and slams him back down)... Once again, Godzilla yanks the "perfect robot monster's" head off – but this time, that *doesn't stop it*!! I *like* MechaGodzilla. Equipped with missile-fingers, jets on its feet, a head that swivels 'round **Exorcist**-style, and even the initials MG on its shoulder, he's a formidable foe for our prehistoric hero and has all the qualities that will appeal to both giant-monster freaks and fans of Japanese robots... The first hour of **Terror of MechaGodzilla** is mostly a lot of badly-dubbed talktalktalk, but if you have a VCR you can always fast-forward to the good stuff, or you can watch it straight through while getting drunk and stoned in time to watch the monsters kick booty. Hell, I'd kinda like to see it on acid, myself. Also known as 'Bring Me the Head of MechaGodzilla.' (Ah ha ha! Is *joke*, no?) [BJE]

THE TEXAS CHAINSAW MASSACRE 2

TOBE HOOPER 1986. We packed into a huge Time Square theatre on opening night. 'One for '**Saw**,' we slobbered to the old woman behind the bullet-proof glass. 'That's another for The Madman,' she replied... Yes, we really had our hopes up for this one. It had all the ingredients needed for the ultimate sequel to one of the grimiest horror films ever made – Tobe Hooper, the original's director, is back after a couple of big buck clinkers like **Lifeforce** and **Invaders from Mars**; an actual scriptwriter, Kit (**Paris, Texas**) Carson was hired to write the thing ('Oh, you mean there's gonna be dialogue in this horror film? What an innovation!'); goremeister Tom Savini has been picked to do the slice-and-dice effects; Golan-Globus, the Leopold and Loeb of film producers, supplied them with enough cash to soak Lubbock, Texas in karo syrup; and to top it off, everyone's favourite babbling acidhead from the '60s, Dennis Hopper, has been signed to star as a revenge-crazed Texas sheriff who packs a pair of holstered chain saws on his hips... It sounded like a can't lose situation, especially after hearing all the pre-release hype about this being The Splatter Film of the year. But boy, if ever a movie theatre filled with a stench of make-a-quick-buck hypocrisy, it was for little item. Don't get me wrong – '**Saw 2** is just as passable as any of the other pre-fab slaughter fests that are being churned out nowadays (except for Romero's work, of course), and amidst all continuity problems, Dennis Hopper is fun to watch, as he grabs a quick paycheque for rolling his bloodshot eyes, gurgling a few lines from Revelations, and revving up his Black and Deckers. But compared to the original, it's pretty disappointing... While the first was a mondo-trashy horror film mixing dark humour and a grim, documentary-style look, this time around they decided to play up the cheap laughs, giving us 90 minutes of unoriginal, but slick, trash – the kind of 'wink-wink-aren't-we-having-fun/yuppie-shit/Spielberg/high concept' school of phlegm-making. Not the real thing, but an unremarkable Hollywood imitation. The cheese whiz of horror movies... There are a few fun ideas along the way (the family's underground hideout), but overall, it's just an expensive (and *much* more boring) repeat of the first, with the whole chain saw gang on the loose again – cackling Father, shell-shocked Platehead, catatonic Gramps, and hyperactive Leatherface. They terrorise a couple of people and end up spending most of the running time picking on a female disc jockey. Even though '**Saw 2** is unrated (usually a good sign for any horror film), the bloodshed is kept to a minimum (as is the body count, surprisingly enough), and except for a graphic head-slicing during the prologue and face-peeling in the middle, the horror is fairly tame. Worst of all, even Leatherface turns out to be a wimpy lardass, as the script lets him fall in love with his female victim, thus allowing her to escape every time it looks like she's gonna end up in Pa's chilli... The first 'Saw was an artefact of the early '70s – crude, nasty, but true to its intentions. In the same respect, part **2** is a document for the mid-'80s – slick, superficial and manipulative. Of course, I didn't go into it expecting Harold Pinter, but I did kinda hope for a good, solid, scary sequel. Instead... zzzzzz

THREE ON A MEATHOOK

WILLIAM GIRDLER 1972. Bloody bimbos! Bouncing boobs! Boring bullshit! Yep, it's another great title for a mediocre movie. (Oh, well. I wasn't expecting Edward Albee.) A quartet of college girls go to a secluded lake for the weekend, but when their car breaks down in the middle of a country road, after dark, they catch a lift from a passing pick-up truck and wind up at the freaky farmhouse of young Billy and his puritanical Dad – a four-star, emotionally-manipulative, female-hating, redneck dipshit. Given this situation, you'd expect them to get killed off one-by-one, so that there'd be *some* suspense – but not in this case, because an unseen killer chops 'em apart or blows 'em to bits within the first 25 minutes. (For your information: There's a nasty knifing in the tub, two shot-gun stomach blasters, and a hokey decapitation.) Now, I'll give you three clues as to *who* the nutcase is: (1) Pa has a meat locker in the backyard, which he keeps locked at *all* times. (2) Pa also butchers his own meat, even though the farm doesn't appear to have any livestock. And (3) Billy is convinced that *he* committed the killings, because his obviously whack-o Dad tells him so... Billy is justifiably upset, thinking he's going to massacre any woman he meets (Dad also has him believing he killed his Mom, although Billy doesn't remember doing *it*, either), so he heads to the local bar, socks down a few stiff drinks, and winds up in love (and in bed) with a friendly waitress. But when he invites her home to the farm it's 'Chop! Slash! Hack!'-time again, with Dad and his trusty pick axe... They even manage to toss in a bit of cannibalism before the happy ending... The best that can be said about **Three on a Meathook** is that it's a prime example of the Exploitation Film – an inept little independent feature with some tits and gore, which gets a catchy title, a gross ad campaign, and the backing of a sleazeball producer. Although the filmmakers stress that this is based (*very* loosely) on convicted-psycho Ed Gein, the movie is actually nothing but a 16mm eyesore, with horrible sound-looping, crappy folk music, and tedious direction by William Girdler, who would go onto bigger (but not necessarily better) things with **Grizzly** and **The Manitou**. It's *really* poor... And in case you were curious, yes, there are three women hanging on meat hooks at the end.

THE THRILL KILLERS

RAY DENNIS STECKLER 1964 (AKA: THE MANIACS ARE LOOSE). Ray Dennis Steckler strikes again! After watching **Incredibly Strange Creatures...**, I was glad to see that Steckler's directorical legacy is finally bobbing up on video (kinda like the way a bloated corpse bobs up in The East River). And after extensive research I'm thoroughly convinced that Steckler is a certifiable genius. Pure and simple! Let's look at his whacked-out crime melodrama, **The Thrill Killers...** Meet Joe Saxon (played by Brick Bardo), a Hollywood pretty-boy whose face and fortune are fading – a man 'caught in the world of non-reality'... Then meet good ol' Cash Flagg (Ray Dennis, himself) as a pistol-packing psycho hitchhiker named Mort 'Mad Dog' Glick, who doesn't waste a moment in shooting a driver and speeding off in the guy's car... And for the next hour we watch in awe as these unrelated storylines stumble along at their own loopy pace. Laugh at Saxon's booze-floozy wife, as played by Liz Renay! Witness wild Hollywood parties with Watusi dancing, gin-soaked producers and amazing 'stagger-cam' photography! And watch as innocent people are hacked up in cold blood by wild-eyed Glick!...

The murders are actually pretty brutal for the time period (the shadowy black and white photography by Joe Masceli helps), especially when Glick chases a call girl around her apartment with a pair of scissors, while screaming "People are NO GOOD!!" (neither is his victim's acting, but let's not quibble). In addition to Joe's angst and Glick's rampages (you mean there's *more*?), a trio of escaped lunatics are running about the countryside (including Herb Robins, who would later star in and direct **The Worm Eaters**), chopping off supporting characters' heads. And Steckler provides a good juxtaposition of unrelenting violence and grim laughs, such as when one of the crazies is cleaning his bloody axe and laments, "Poor guy had dandruff. What a mess!", as he picks bits of flesh off the blade... Where is all this leading to? What the heck is going on? Well, before you can say 'shoestring filmmaking', all these unlikeable characters collide in a roadside diner and we're treated to some prime-cut **Texas Chain Saw Massacre**-style as-semble acting! The finale includes a series of hilltop chases, with Glick knocking off anyone in his way at point-blank range; Brick falling downhill a lot; Liz playing damsel-in-distress, with her skirt ripped up to her hips; and all the silly cops dropping like flies... Co-starring the entire band of Steckler's Acting Troupe Extraordinaire (Atlas King, Carolyn Brandt, Titus Moede), **The Thrill Killers** is barely 70 minutes long, but almost every goof-headed moment is a gem! Steckler is definitely the god of '60s schlock! I only wish that I could have seen this film when it was released as **The Maniacs Are Loose**, and the theatres hired guys in Cash Flagg masks to run up and down the aisles, scaring the customers... Yeah!

TIMESWEEP

DAN DIEFENDERFER / JOHN THONEN / LARRY NORDSIECK 1987. This inde-pendent little tale is all over the place, but it comes to life briefly enough and has enough unfulfilled imagination behind it to make it worthwhile. It contains the now-required allotment of gratuitous gore, sex and cheap chills, but since the film at least attempts to transcend its creaky genre, the result is head and shoulder above the normal trash on the market (despite its occasional drawbacks). It begins when a group of college students are taken for a guided tour of long-shuttered Dunbar Studios. It's cob-webbed and creepy, and when the lights go out the body count begins... It's not your normal pick-off-the-obnoxious characters kill-fest, even though there's skewered students within the first reel. The windows are boarded up, there's a labyrinth of corridors, a deadly mist sur-rounds the place, and creatures emerge from mirrors in order to pluck out nearby eyeballs. "We've been cut loose from time," con-cludes one resident genius, and though the time-shifting concept somewhat reminded me of a horror version of **My Science Project**, it gives the filmmakers a chance to experiment with several diverse elements. By the midway point, the imprisoned stars (those who are still in one piece) encounter giant flesh-rending cockroaches, an alien spaceship, a wandering zombie brigade (I love the 'Slop!' noise they make when you bash 'em in the head), some more-humorous-than-frightening gore, and even a few attempts at cheap surrealism. Two nice sequences involve a time trip back to the '20s when the studio was in business, and a brief encounter with a cop from the 1968 Democratic Convention... But while the ideas are good, the characters remain strictly 2-D creations (plus, as I've said before, I'm *sick* of characters having 'homage' names like Agar, Arkoff, Romero, and H.G. Lewis); and though the script by Dan Diefenderfer, John Thonen and Larry Nordsieck brings up some solid notions, they are not fleshed out in the final film. It takes a lot of skill to take an idea like this and pull it off successfully on a low budget ($150,000) – you either need a *great* explanation in the script for all the weirdness, or else you have to be such a stylistic wizard (such as Argento) that no one really *cares* why. Sorry to report that this doesn't fill either bill. There's no sound wrap-up –

the survivors just run out of the building as the flick runs out of juice. The overall result is better than average, but it's still unsatisfying, to say the least. Starring Michael Fountain, Pamela DeBord, Kevin Brief, and Michele Privette.

TNT JACKSON

CIRIO H. SANTIAGO 1974. Here's a kung fu blaxploiter that doesn't waste any film stock with unnecessary items such as characterisations, plot or logic. Jeanne Bell stars in the title role, as a busty black-belter who heads to Hong Kong to investigate the disappearance of her brother, Stack Jackson (who *we* already know got his skull drop-kicked during the credits). Bell goes undercover as a pick-up girl in a red-light night-club, and when she discovers the Chinese Mafia is to blame, she vows "I'm gonna find 'em and I gonna bust the motherfuckers to pieces". So every five minutes some bozo is beaten, shot, slaughtered, or generally manhandled in TNT's search for the heroin dealing peckerheads. This flick is anti-crime, anti-cops and pro-*revenge*! And watch out for that last punch – it's a lulu!... Stan Shaw co-stars with an afro the size of a weather balloon and a shirt unbuttoned down to his navel (shades of **Hollywood Shuffle**), but the rest of the cast aren't actors – they're unemployed models and stir-fry cooks! The fights are laughable and not for ONE MOMENT do you believe Ms. Bell knows a lick of martial arts, but director Cirio Santiago keeps having her pretend to beat up extra after extra – snapping forearms into right angles and kicking stunt-coolies through papier-mâché

JEANNE BELL as
TNT Jackson
CO-STARRING STAN SHAW · PAT ANDERSON
METROCOLOR   R [RESTRICTED]

doors. There's also a couple of lame excuses for TNT to have her blouse ripped open, and one scene ends with her jujitsuing solely in her panties... Co-written by Dick Miller (I'd advice him to stay in *front* on the camera from now on), it's certainly action packed (but STOOOPID!) and entertaining enough for desperate blaxploitation junkies. What else would you expect from the director who gave us **Cover Girl Models**, **The Muthers** and **Vampire Hookers**?

TOBOR THE GREAT

LEE SHOLEM 1954. Here's a not-so-classic black-&-whiter whose ad makes it appeal to cheap-thrilled adults, but whose actual intentions are purely juvenile... Set in the near future (that means approx. 1962), the Civil Interplanetary Flight Commission has determined that human beings are too at-risk during space missions (especially when the rocket ships have a tendency to blow up on the launch pad), so Prof. Nordstrom, a brilliant scientist (what were you expecting, a *stupid* one?), invents a marvellous new machine to save the space programme. Enter Tobor ('robot' spelled backwards), an eight-foot-tall mechanical man who's controlled by ESP – a steel-plated sentient being who looks like a Cylon with a glandular problem... Our B-movie hero for the duration is a government agent (Charles Drake) with an ego so thick you'd need a chain saw to cut it; and Billy Chapin is the professor's precocious 10-year-old grandson, Brian, and he's so cute and mischievous and adorable that you want to squeeze his rosy li'l cheek until it rips off in your hand. Of course, Brian immediately makes friends with Tobor and there's plenty of tired-out 'wacky' complications. Sigh... Even for the mid-'50s, this is pretty conventional stuff, and its story is told with all the excitement and flair of an episode of **My Three Sons**. Luckily (for us), there's a pack of evil foreigners out to steal the Prof.'s secret, and they're so inept and stereotyped that you'd assume they graduated *magna cum laude* from the Boris and Natasha School of Espionage. Eventually, these treacherous foreigners kidnap Brian, with Tobor waddling to the rescue. And that's about it for the plot – you wait patiently for an interesting storyline to begin, and 77 minutes later the end credits roll, and you're *still* waiting... Directed by Lee Sholem (whose other masterworks include **Tarzan's Magic Fountain** with Lex 'Weissmuller's Too Fat' Barker), there's a creaky, nostalgic feel to the whole enterprise, but I only wish there'd been a little more of Tobor in action. Only during the last 10 minutes does he *really* get to stomp the terra in an effort to save li'l Brian, and it's loads of fun watching Tobor tear down walls, bash through doors, drive a jeep, and thrash evildoers within an inch of their lives. That sequence alone *almost* makes the whole film worthwhile, but I still can't recommend it, even if Tobor himself is pretty cool in a clunky sort of way. The whole thing's just too damn tedious.

TORSO

SERGIO MARTINO 1973. Sergio Martino directed this Pastaland kill-a-thon, and though it took two years to make it to US theatres, after enduring this low-gore bore you'll wish Italy had kept it all to themselves. Don't get suckered by the video box, which compares it to **Texas Chain Saw Massacre**. It's more inspired by earlier European slaughterfests by Bava and Argento, though it's thoroughly sub-par in comparison. Despite featuring a smattering of bloodshed and more bare skin than in 10 usual slasher flicks, it doesn't stop the film from being dull, dull, DULL! Uninvolving, unoriginal and unbearably tedious. A bland tease 'n' sleaze romp starring a line-up of buxom, bra-less lasses in skimpy, easily removable clothing; plus a male roll call of interchangeable Latin Lotharios with only one thought in their pea-brains – salivating at bare thighs and getting their wicks dipped... The gist of the plot has a masked madman scuffling around the city, interrupting young couples in mid-coitus, strangling 'em, putting out their eyes, and then mutilating the corpses (I don't have enough fingers to count how many times I've heard *that* highly original plot before). After the first pair of murders, you'd think the women would learn not to walk through deserted swamps in the middle of the night with their blouses unbuttoned, but that's not the case with these ditzy dames. Their main goal as per the script is to act like bubble-heads and eventually get turned into mincemeat at the hands of the murderer. Top-billed beauties Suzy Kendall and Tina Aumont lead a quartet of nubile femmes who decide to escape from all the death in the city by taking a country vacation. But darned if that kooky killer doesn't follow them with his ever-handy collection of stainless steel cutlery... Besides having the camera linger over every female form, the main excuse for this film is to watch a series of beautiful women chased, caught, carved up, and possibly even hack-sawed (off-camera) into easy-to-dispose-of-chunks. Women = Meat. (A pretty friendly concept to perpetuate, eh?) We also get endless shots from the psycho's point-of-view, and con-veniently enough, whenever the ladies are undressing they always leave their curtains open so that any passing murderous-misogynist can leer for a spell... There's lots of Italian colour – old buildings and young women, tiny cars and large breasts. Plus the moody, gliding camerawork by Giancarlo Ferrando adds some semblance of suspense, though having a script to fall back on might've helped a bit too. After a while all the murders blend to-gether into one big, tiresome 'Who cares whodunit?'. The murderer is revealed (it's no surprise either), his childhood trauma is ex-plained (what do they want, sympathy?) and Mr. Macho Stud is to the rescue, saving the nightgowned Ms. Kendall. It's a real yawner, which only gets worse as it progresses. Don't bother wasting your time on it.

TOUGH GUYS DON'T DANCE

NORMAN MAILER 1987. I can say without hesitation that this is one of the most remarkable failures of the year. A picture that can take you as off-guard as this film does is rare, but in the inept hands of Golan and Globus, it turned into barely-released Cannon fodder, disappearing from theatres after a wham-bam run... Written and directed by Norman (Egotistical Guys Don't Play King Lear) Mailer, he's turned his own novel into a wildly overwritten and (appropriately) overacted film. By the time this thriller is over, you'll discover a fairly routine storyline buried under all the playfulness, but while Norm's at work, you'll have a tough time dealing with this flick's narrative structure – there are flashbacks within flash-backs, reminiscences, premonitions, scenes that loop back on themselves, and loads of symbolism straight from Pretensions 101. Ryan O'Neal stars as Tim, an occasionally off-the-wagon drifter who hangs out with his dying father one morning and tells him a tale of his past – how his money-hungry wife left him for a chauf-feur; how he loved and lost his one True Love; how he fucks around with any dame who tickles his cock; and how, during his latest liquor blackout, he thinks he might have murdered someone. It all leads to severed heads, corpses in car trunks, ads in **Screw** magazine, and the wit and wisdom of Normie Mailer... There's loads of memorable lines, and if Mailer was trying to mix absurd comedy with his thriller plotline, I'd say he royally succeeded, because there's a dark layer of chuckles accompanying the pro-ceedings (especially in Laurence Tierney's performance as O'Neal's crusty ol' dad). This is virtually a companion piece to **Blue Velvet**, except where David Lynch is a visual stylist, Mailer is a literary one. The final disorienting effect is similar, but if you thought Kyle Ma-cLachlan was a bit cardboardian, wait until you get wind of Ryan O'Neal's stink. This guy couldn't act his way outta the bags under his eyes. He sleepwalks through the role, and when he *tries* to emote, it's even worse ("Your knife... is in... my dog," is his dramatic high point, when a thug stabs his pet). Isabella Rossellini is no

better, and after her doe-eyed performances in this film and **Siesta**, I'd say she's turning into the arthouse equivalent of Liza Minnelli. The one acting standout was a surprise – Wings Hauser, who's usually terrible in equally terrible movies, is over-the-top creepy as the town's grass-smoking, Nam vet, near-psycho town sheriff... It's a strange, often-dazzling ride. A Tilt-A-Whirl of a movie. And even if it happens to creak and shudder a bit from time to time, it's miles better than the usual swill that's flushed into theatres by the stu-dios.

TOUGHER THAN LEATHER

RICK RUBIN 1988. Yo man, Def American proudly (and I use the term loosely) presents the not-so-long awaited adventures of master-rappers, Run DMC, in their first starring roles (after their scrubbed-clean celluloid debut in **Krush Groove**). You've probably heard of the term Cinéma Vérité, well this flick is closer to Cinema Veri-*dumb*. It's a flashback to the rot-gut blaxploiters of the past – there's no character development, the plot is arthritic, the dialogue is hilariously stupid, and it never manages to get as violent as a slobbering grindhouse crowd would hope. In other words, this is NOT a good movie! But on the other hand, this 42nd Street-style urban actioner goes through the motions painlessly enough, and there's plenty of unintentional *and* intentional (about 50/50) laughs laced throughout. In addition, the budget was so low they couldn't even afford laces for their sneakers (I assume the guys supplied their own gold chains and quarts of Colt 45)... The beginning comes off like a Sergio Leone version of **The Blues Brothers**, with Run getting released from the slammer and being met outside the gates by his pals, DMC and Jam Master Jay, in their Rapmobile. The trio play themselves, and the scenes of them rambling to each other are so naturalistically dirt-brained (such as their detailed description of a blow-job), that you get the impression they simply turned on the camera and made it up as they went along... The rappers immediately sign a record deal with Strut Productions for a wad of quick cash, and Run DMC head out on tour, with their dopey (but good natured) pal Raymond tagging along as their cheeseburger fetcher. But these so-called record producers turn out to be nothing but drug-dealing white trash, and when these evil pushers kill Raymond and plant crack on him, the Boys in Black are prepared to even the score. Until this point, it's been slow going, but the potential for sudden, unexpected violence is always there (either on the screen, or behind us in the back rows of the theatre). So when the lid finally blows, we are ready to wallow in it! Equip-ping themselves with leftover W.W.II Lugers, Run, DMC and Jam Master Jay wipe up a barroom floor with some redneck scum, do The Wild Thing with a dog collared white chick (porn starlet Lois Ayres) and prove they're Tougher Than Apartment Doors. By far, the

best moment is when they play 'Little Piggy' – by snapping a shithead's fingers, one by one, *slowly*, until he divulges some info (let's not forget the *REAL* nasty sound effects that accompany it)... Maybe if the director (record producer Rick Rubin, who also plays the long-haired crack-dealer, Vic) had a lick of talent, he could've tossed together a solid piece o' schlock, instead of this loose-fitting mess which obviously hoped to succeed solely on the charisma of its stars. There's ultra-cheap sets, a derivative music score (even the copious concert footage is only OK), loads of straight-off-the-sidewalk supporting performances, and most of the characters are so stupid that I'm surprised there was any effect when one of them was shot in the head (since it obviously wasn't a vital organ)... On the more positive side, the Beastie Beerheads – er – Boys pop up for a few repulsively moronic minutes, and arthouse fans will get a kick out of seeing Richard Edson playing a character just as dim as he did in Jim Jarmusch's **Stranger Than Paradise**... The overall flick doesn't even approach the mediocre range, but if you can check it out with a pack of friends and a rowdy audience, do so. Leave the Zip Guns at home though.

THE TOXIC AVENGER

Michael Herz / Samuel Weil 1986. Melvin is a stereotypical 98-pound weakling who works at the Tromaville Gymnasium as a mop-boy. The butt of heartless jokes and inane dialogue, he blithely accepts his fate with a dopey smile. But one day, a practical joke backfires and Melvin finds himself falling headfirst into a nearby barrel of green, bubbling, nuclear waste (left uncovered in the back of a flatbed truck, of course). Instead of dying, he is transformed into an Incredible Hulk-like superhero – complete with rippling biceps, skull-crushing fists, a face like Leo G. Carroll in **Tarantula**, a hilariously-redubbed 'He-Man' voice, and (best of all) an unstoppable urge to rid Tromaville of all the scum and filth he can find... First things first, this is one of the shoddiest, most technically incompetent films in recent memory. But Troma Pictures, the scuzzbag operation who virtually revitalised the rip-off drive-in movie with junk like **Stuck on You** and **Screwballs**, has actually pulled a winner out of their toilet bowl this time around. Sure, no cliché is left unsoiled and it looks like it was edited together with a dull steak knife and a stapler, but that's half the fun, as Melvin rears his ugly head to crush the evil-tempered punks and fatcat politicians that have overrun his New Jersey hometown. There's plenty of silly, but graphic violence as he rips apart Tromaville's drug pushers and child killers (including a head bursting, a rhythmic groin pounding, and fingers shoved into eye sockets up to the second knuckle). Plus, there's an abundant supply of cheap laffs, too – Melvin falls in love with the town's blond, buxom, blind girl (doesn't every small town have one?) after her seeing-eye dog is shotgun-blasted across the floor during a taco store stick-up, and together they set up housekeeping in the local garbage dump. This is prime midnight show material, only because it's too asinine for any other type of viewing. It's loads of stooopid fun, but be warned: There are several different versions of this film currently in release, a few of which have been trimmed of violence and/or bad taste (when I saw it, they included all the gore, but exorcised the scene where the blind girl fixes an Easy-Off and Drano sandwich for Mister Avenger). The unrated version is a necessity.

THE TOXIC AVENGER, PART II

Lloyd Kaufman / Michael Herz 1989. New Jersey's first superhero mutant is back, but who the fuck cares?! Yes, Troma Pix has proven without a doubt that 'Part I' was a complete fluke – a lucky mix of crude humour, gross-out set pieces and incompetency. For **Part II** the incompetency is still there by the barrel, but there's little else (unless you get off on numbing boredom). The sequel is slicker, but not sicker, and so brain-dead it's stultifying. Fans of the first

(like me!) will be disappointed, and those who couldn't even stomach the original will be in terminal schlock shock... The city of Tromaville was cleaned of crime in the previous movie by the toxic waste-mutated Melvin Junko (aka The Toxic Avenger) but before he can get bored with the humdrum lifestyle or his City Dump home, enter the money-sucking businessmen of Apocalypse Inc. who want to take over the town, and send an army of ridiculous mutants after Ol' Lumpyhead. And a bigger batch of supporting stooges I've never seen – the ugliest cast since **Satyricon**. The only new wrinkle in the plot has Japanese scientists working on an Anti-Toxie Serum, and this provides the characters with a new, colourful locale (not to mention the entire crew with a free trip to the orient). There Toxie searches for his allusive father, and finds his only laughs while satirising Godzilla and making the population of Tokyo look like complete asses for letting these gutter-studio sleazoids foul up their lovely city. It's *almost* as insulting to their culture as Ridley Scott's **Black Rain**! After spending half the film knee deep in kabuki ninjas, fish market manslaughter and sumo wrestler sight gags, we return to New Jersey for a snooze-packed battle between the nice, drug-free Tromavillains vs. the chemical-loving, black-attired Apocalypsoids... Most of the good jokes from the first film are repeated, but the wide-eyed lowbrow innocence is gone. It's simply a sad clone of the first, with directors/profiteers Lloyd Kaufman and Michael Herz' vision clouded by those huge dollar signs. Phoebe Legere co-stars as Toxie's blind girlfriend, who's now a garter-belted bimbo with the IQ of a manhole cover; and at the very least, they could've released the uncut, unratad version (on film *or* video) so we could get a giggle at the cut-rate effects by Pericles Lewnes, the doofus behind the equally wretched **Redneck Zombies**. Don't waste your time on this sucker-bait hog-wash. It's another deadening example of the Troma aroma gone rancid... But even as I write, Troma has released the third in the series, **Toxic Avenger Part III: The Last Temptation of Toxie**, culled from film scraps found on the Editing Room floor. I shudder at the thought (partly because I'm boneheaded enough to rent the thing when it hits the video racks).

TRACK 29

Nicolas Roeg 1988. 'All aboard' for Nicolas (God) Roeg's latest cosmic contemplation on love, sex, medicine, and model railroading. As John Lennon brings us the heart-warming strains (literally) of 'Mother', a mysterious hitcher (Gary Oldman) appears on a backroads crossing. Even the stray dogs stay away from this guy. An unwitting macho trucker (with 'significant' tattoos) picks him up, gets sick and tired of his psychotic ramblings, and dumps him at a highway diner. There he finds 'Mommy' (Theresa 'Ms. Roeg' Russell). She is, in fact, the wife of a wacky doctor (Chris Lloyd) who has converted the second floor of their house into a shrine to the great trains, complete with computer control and fake mountains. Needless to say, she's bored silly, and when Psycho-Brit Gary charms his way to her table, she is sort of interested. Mom and her aerobically inclined friend (Colleen Camp) hit the road, but Ma's not very happy. Her husband is a bore, and there are no kids in his game plan (choo choo). Psycho-Brit appears again, and reveals himself to 'Mommy' as her long-lost son, all explained in typical time-warped Roeg fashion. *Now* it gets weird. As Hunter Thompson would say, 'What kind of game is being played here?' Before you know it, Chris Lloyd is giving a rabble-rousing speech to a model railroaders convention, while psychoson and mom are playing Oedipal games around the house. The transition in Roeg's projects from larger budgets/stars (**Don't Look Now**, **Man Who Fell to Earth** and the ill-fated **Eureka**) to smaller scale films like **Insignificance** and this film hasn't diminished his impact as a progressive intellectual director and a technical wizard. Although this viewer would like to see some casting initiative in the future (it's turning into a DePalma-Nancy Allen deadlock), **Track 29** is a major mindblower, and a splendid time is guaranteed for all smart people. [TR]

TRACKS

HENRY JAGLOM 1976. This obscure independent gem was one of the first feature films to tackle the negative consequences of Vietnam, to condemn US involvement and to show the emotional scars on its survivors. Considering these inflammatory ideas, it's no surprise that the film was barely released. Of course, the fact it's so damned weird that it's virtually incomprehensible at times probably didn't help matters either... Dennis Hopper stars as Sergeant Jack Falen, a traumatised veteran who's assigned to escort the body of a snuffed army buddy across the US by train, to a welcoming hometown crowd. But though he may be clean-cut and stuffed into a uniform, Hopper's as mind-blown as ever – pouring out his entire brainpan every time he opens his mouth. And what a screwy, shell-shocked ride he's in for! The Hop runs into a left-wing subversive (Dean Stockwell), exercises his libido with a not-so-innocent college girl (Taryn Power), discovers numerous undercover CIA agents, and most importantly, becomes an unwilling channel for the horrors of the war. Not to mention hallucinating so much you'd think he was having flashbacks to the cemetery scene in **Easy Rider**. Almost the entire film is set on the moving train, which contributes to the claustrophobia. And the 'trip' gets progressively weirder, with the entire zoned-out cast delivering improvised conversations on everything from the essence of warfare to zen chicken eating (the skin is the best because it's had more exposure to 'the reality of the land'). As the fragmentation of dreams and reality intensifies, Dennis has a complete mental freak out which includes seeing his new girlfriend being gang raped, eluding imaginary MP's and running naked through the trainload of people. The last bit is an unforgettable image (unless you're too wasted to remember it, as I'm sure Hopper was)... The filmmaking technique is crude, grainy and jumpy – but whether intentional or not, its raggedness really helps capture the confusion of the era, and there's good use of happy-go-lucky W.W.II tunes about patriotism and simpler times, which counterpoint the grim proceedings (a la Dennis Potter). But foremost, this is Hopper's show, and he's surprisingly effective – slurring, babbling, and staying on his feet by sheer willpower alone, while forging a naïve, paranoid, and very compelling character. Co-starring Michael Emil (**Insignificance**) and Zack Norman, this is atypical fare from director Henry Jaglom, who's recently been churning out mixed-bag meditations on romance and relationships. But this is without a doubt his most remarkable work – a mix of late-'60s drug influence and artsy social consciousness. Indulgent, controversial, and savage in its ideals. A mess, but a powerful one indeed.

TRANCERS

CHARLES BAND 1985. Here's a perfect example of a drive-in flick which moves like gangbusters from Scene One. Sure, this puree of tongue in cheek science fiction blatantly 'borrows' ideas from a batch of A-level films (such as **Blade Runner** and **The Terminator**). Luckily, director Charles Band understands his film's low-budget limitations and has a ball with them... The story begins in 23rd century LA (renamed Angel City after its submersion by The Great Quake), with super-villain Martin Whistler eluding the cops. A futuristic variation on Charles Manson, Whistler uses psychic powers to control the minds of the most susceptible (in other words, stupider) citizens and turns 'em into kill-crazed slaves called Trancers. But instead of escaping the law by simply exiting the country, Whistler has gone one better by leaving the entire century – travelling back in time (to present day Los Angeles) with a plan to eliminate all his future government adversaries by knocking off their ancestors. The

unique method of time travel: To climb down your own family tree, and have your mind usurp the body of a forebear... Luckily, Trooper Jack Deth is in pursuit. Enter Tim Thomerson as the future's answer to Philip Marlowe, who follows Whistler 'down the line' and wakes up in his new body, with girlfriend Leena (Helen Hunt) justifiably confused at her boyfriend's sudden change in behaviour. You see, it isn't everyday that a department store Santa Claus turns into a bug-eyed Trancer and has to be 'singed' by your date in front of Xmas shoppers. With the unwilling Hunt in tow, the pair goes from Tanning Parlour Torture to a Slamdance Shindig in an effort to avoid the police, side-step the Trancers, and save the future... Wisely, this film doesn't waste a foot of film stock on unnecessary exposition, and even the touch of a love story never cramps the pace. But the real heart lies in two aspects that even the most extravagant budget can't always boast – an involving script punctuated with wise-cracking dialogue, and a uniformly fine cast. The two leads deserve most of the credit. Tim Thomerson (Mr. Chuck Bronson/'Filet o' Fish Sandwich') utilises his stand-up talent to satirise the hard-boiled persona; and with a two-day growth of beard, collared-up trenchcoat and anti-authority sneer, he's the perfect flatfoot of the future. As the usually obligatory damsel in distress, Helen Hunt cuts through the clichés and manages, amidst all the chaos, to be both intelligent and sexy... **Trancers** is a surprise that breezed through theatres as if it were just another no-intellect Empire Productions enema. You can argue that it's lightweight, but it's also solid fun through and through.

THE TRIP

ROGER CORMAN 1967. This film has the distinction of being the first release from a major studio to deal sorta-honestly with the subject of LSD. Preceding it were fly-by-night flicks such as **Hallucination Generation** and **The Weird World of LSD** (not to mention an occasionally intelligent entry like **Chappaqua** with Burroughs and Ginsberg), but **The Trip** was the first mass-market look at Acid ('You come as close to experiencing a freak out as you probably want to come. Or dare to come,' proclaimed the ads), all from the diseased minds of scriptwriter Jack Nicholson and director Roger Corman. Rumour has it that Nicholson's pro-LSD script was muted a bit by Corman (who actually tripped before beginning the project and had quite a nice time), and then American International decided to add an idiotic anti-drug prologue and last-moment epilogue onto the film to convince viewers that this film didn't advocate the experimentation with mind-altering drugs after all (yeah, right). Well, the truth be told, Corman simply wanted to translate the essence of an acid trip onto film and let the audiences make their own judgements. And even though he sillied it all up with traditional movieland hallucinations (masked riders and dwarves left over from his latest Poe film), **The Trip** is still immensely enjoyable on a purely entertainment level, especially for audiences who Know, and can laugh along. Relatively clean-cut Peter Fonda stars as Paul, a TV commercial director who feels the pressure of his personal and professional life, and wants to learn more about LSD. In his search for enlightenment, he runs into Dr. Bruce Dern, who is probably the most paranoia-inducing drug-connection I've ever seen. (Who in hell would want someone as bug-eyed-schizo as Dern leading them through their first acid trip?) Of course, Fonda scurries off the moment Dern turns his back (Peter hallucinates that he killed Dr. Dern, which isn't a bad idea, considering what an asshole the guy had been), and Peter's subsequent adventures include a visit to a Laundromat (where he thinks someone is trapped in a drier), wandering through freaky night-clubs, entering strange houses and watching TV, staring at an orange, getting trapped inside a throbbing closet (don't you hate it when that happens?), and mysterious encounters with all sorts of groovy chicks. Even Dennis Hopper makes a quick appearance to add some inspired, rambling dialogue to the film. And check out the wallpaper at The Hop's pad. Holy psychedelics, Batman!... There's plenty of strobes, coloured lights and hand-held camerawork, and even if it's all pretty idiotic and pretentious at times, it's still easy to enjoy **The Trip** as a time capsule from the late-'60s.

THE TROLLENBERG TERROR

QUENTIN LAWRENCE 1958 (US: THE CRAWLING EYE). "His head! It was *TORN OFF!*" shouts the mountaineer... What a great opening for this English monster-invasion cheapie! And besides, any film starring Forrest Tucker can't be all bad, right? (Well, after considering his Saturday-morning kid-show, **The Ghost Busters**, don't be so sure.)... A strange radioactive cloud surrounding the slopes of the Trollenberg has been swallowing up climbing expeditions like they were Lays Potato Chips. A 'crawling eye' is residing in the mist! American scientist Forrest T. arrives in the Alps and joins up with the thick-accented locals, a professor with an alpine observatory, and a pair of ESP-laced sisters, who are brought in for some quick premonitions of doom and a psychic connection to the mountain top monster. The verdict: Could it be a visitor from outer space? (Not one of those pesky things again!) One of the alien's favourites pastimes is ripping off humans' heads – that's if it isn't too busy turning its victims into subservient zombies who follow the creature's telepathic commands to chop up the supporting cast with a meat axe. Like most low-renters from the '50s, you don't actually see the title-terror until the end, when an entire family of 'em attack the observatory en masse, in a flurry of TERRIBLE miniature work. They're big, blobby, pulsing heads with one twitching eyeball in the centre, and dozens of tentacles. Strictly Goodyear-variety workmanship, and it's pretty damned pathetic when the actors have to twist the wiggly tentacles around their *own* necks in order to make it look like they're being strangled... The surprisingly literate screenplay was by Jimmy Sangster, who kept Hammer Studios in the black with his scripts for **Curse of Frankenstein**, **The Mummy** and **Brides of Dracula**; and though it could have been a bit more suspenseful at times, for your typical straight-laced creature feature, **The Trollenberg Terror** has enough goofy moments to keep you happily entertained. (Based upon a six-part British TV series, broadcast '56/'57, also directed by Lawrence.)

TROMA'S WAR

MICHAEL HERZ / SAMUEL WEIL 1988. First off: No, this long-awaited battlefest from Troma Team is *not* a new Sleaze Classic (though it makes an honourable attempt at the territory). Directed by Michael Herz and Samuel Weil, the Troma brains behind **Toxic Avenger** (holy cow, I used the words 'Troma' and 'brains' in the same sentence! Sorry, I won't make that slip again) – but unlike their first four-star epic, **War** lacks the twisted spirit to make it a lasting testament to trash. Though if you're in the mood for guns, squibs and blood packs galore, your eyes are gonna glaze over because this is an National Rifle Association's wet dream of heavy munitions. Just killing, killing and MORE killing, with death oozing from every single frame! So overflowing with numbing action that you can run out to the store for a fresh six pack, come back 10 minutes later, and the *same* damned battle is still raging! But beyond the unceasing gunfire, the film comes up pretty empty... A passenger plane crashes on a Caribbean island (played unconvincingly by New Jersey), and the survivors are the whiniest cross section of stereotypes I've seen since the excruciating era of Irwin Allen – including a shirtless stud, a callous Wall Street exec, a newly blinded girl, a kill-crazy veteran, and a poseur punk band called The Bearded Clams. But while touring the isle, they discover a military encampment where soldiers are readying for a full scale infiltration of the US, with fanatical followers from every scurvy, mind-softening faction imaginable: Neo-Nazis, The PLO, Young Republicans (hahaha, Steve make joke), etc. That means there's hundreds of terrorists (in actuality only dozens, since most of the extras are recycled for several 'deaths') roaming the woodland. Luckily for the planeload, these Wacky Khakis are (1) such terrible shots that they waste thousands of rounds and elicit barely a flesh wound, and (2) tend to do impeccable Swiss Cheese imitations at the first blast of an automatic. The US invasion plan is run by a pair of Siamese twins (joined at the face), and the movie even exceeds *my* personal Tasteless Limit when an AIDS-infected enemy agent takes turns raping the captive women (he eventually gets shot in the groin with a crossbow). Eventually the good guys retaliate ("Just point me in the right direction," screams the Uzi-armed blind girl), which leads to another 20-minute shoot-out... No use criticising such throwaway elements as acting, script or continuity, since none of that applies to this type of tripe. Sure, it's garbage; but it's stupid, excessive *Troma Garbage!* And it's one of their best (which to some, ranks it slightly above a bout of the dry heaves). Plus the unedited video is 10 minutes longer than the theatrical cut!

TRUCK STOP WOMEN

MARK L. LESTER 1974. It took me a while, but I finally stumbled onto this exploitation mini-classic, where the women are as tough as the tires on their trucks. During her short career, drive-in queen Claudia Jennings totalled up a batch of solid, low-brow hits (**Unholy Rollers**, **Gator Bait**), but this is without a doubt her best!... First off, we meet Rose (Ms. Jennings) and her sexpot redhead pal, who flag down an 18-wheeler, beat the driver over the noggin and steal his truck. They're two wanton hussies who'll fuck the peabrains outta any nearby male, and then throw him away after he's spent and limp. These mini-skirted misses help run a stolen truck ring/whorehouse, which operates out of the nearby highway truck stop – and wouldn't you know it, Claudia's mom (Lieux Dressler) is the brains behind the business. Unfortunately, the East Coast Syndicate wants a piece of their action, so they send a pair of lying greaseballs to gun everyone down. As you can see, the opposing sides are a little less black and white than usual – a pack of rural thieves vs. a pack of urban mobsters. But the twist comes when pretty young Claudia gets fed up with her Mama's orders, and decides to check out the competition's benefits – laying the head hitman's pipe and believing all his half-baked promises about fame and fortune in Las Vegas. From the bathtub double killing in the first scene, to the uncompromisingly dark ending, this is constant (albeit good natured) sleaziness. Fast-paced, silly, yet not entirely brainless. Sure, a lot of it is pretty predictable nowadays – you've got your car smash-ups, bedroom gymnastics and the occasional comic relief (such as a supporting cast of gristled hick-halfwits and a tub-o'-lard sheriff who plays Lecherous Lawman with his freebie whores), but director Mark L. Lester (**Class of 1984**) also tosses in a compact li'l plot, good desert locations and a few fine characterisations to add zip to the mixture. By the end, Mama is out for revenge, Claudia might be turning traitor, and everyone is equipping themselves with heavy munitions (and I just *love* it when women fire off machine guns)... As the two-faced daughter, ex-playmate Claudia is a stand-out amongst the solid cast of violent femmes, and happily, Jennings never sinks into the typical role of some mindless bimbo from Overflowing Cleavage Inc. (though there's the expected quota of skin-bearing from her and the supporting cast). Released before all the **Smokey and the Bandit** and **Convoy** bullshit made truckers into laughing stocks, this flick is a must for lovers of rural road pix (despite the lousy soundtrack from Big Mack and the Truckstoppers).

TWICE DEAD

BERT DRAGIN 1988. Here's another cheapie from Concorde Pix, which isn't great news since they have almost as disastrous a track record as Troma (though Concorde tends to hire filmmakers instead of family relations). It's more fourth-rate trash that makes the viewer feel ripped off and rolfed on by stinkweed producers chasing the almighty dollar. In other words, I *didn't* like it much... An average American family inherits an old, dilapidated mansion that used to belong to Tyler Walker, a prohibition-age movie star who gashed up his lover and took a noose to his own neck. Pretty soon spectral stuff starts happening in the night – light switches go off, inanimate objects begin attacking, and pancake make-upped Tyler begins leering from hallway mirrors. And if that isn't enough for any halfway-intelligent family to GET THE HELL OUT, the mansion becomes the target for a leather-and-mousse street gang who'd like to put the gallant son (Tom Breznahan) in a body cast and dip their wicks in the sexy, but thoroughly virginal, daughter (Jill Whitlow). The minimal action keeps you watching (albeit half-heartedly), as it becomes another predictable Dream 'n' Death entry in the **Elm Street** Sweepstakes. At first the whitebread kids try to fend off the punkoids on their own (the 'Monster in the Gut' is good for a quick laugh), but a spiked pizza leads to an indoor rumble. And in one of those 'only-in-bad-horror-movies-type-of-coincidences', the daughter looks *exactly* like Tyler's old flame, so when these 'psychos hopped up on booze and drugs' start attacking, they all get the Chop Suey treatment. My fave is when a guy gets electrocuted by a short circuited electric blanket and his lover mistakes it for an orgasm. But even though the story is knee-deep in death, the film itself is pretty tame and unremarkable. The two leads are personable (even if their characters aren't), the effects are surprisingly mediocre, continuity problems abound, all the scares are telegraphed with the subtlety of a brick with a note attached, and if I can ask *one* simple question – why do all the gang members in movies nowadays look like **GQ**-models who've seen **Clockwork Orange** one too many times? Co-starring Todd Bridges from **Diff'rent Strokes**, who's currently incarcerated for attempted murder (my guess is that he tried to throttle the director after seeing the final cut)... You want my opinion? Geeesh, what a waste of time!

TWICE UPON A TIME

JOHN KORTY 1983. Why did one of the wittiest, most original animated features of all time never get a decent theatrical release? Or even simple home video distribution? Yes, I think we can all agree that executive producer George Lucas really blew it this time around! He'll cram recycled claptrap like **Willow** down our throats, but this masterpiece sits mouldering on a shelf in some attic. He had a **Yellow Submarine** for the '80s, which combines a fantasy storyline with **Rocky and Bullwinkle**-esque rapid fire wit, and what happens? It plays in Los Angeles for one lousy week and then disappears. Why? Was the film too good? Too weird? Or is Lucas simply a dinkwad with no faith in the American movie-going public? (Mark me down for all of the above.) The style of animation is strikingly unique – primarily utilising a cut-out technique entitled Lumage, along with several live-action backgrounds. And unlike many recent animated features, which tend to plummet face-first in the script department, this gem takes a deceptively-simple, kid-vid story and dips it in fast-paced adult humour (the few sappy songs being the only drawback), developing over a dozen oddball characters and settling them all into a neighbouring pair of diametrically opposed worlds. First there is Frivoli, a candy-coated (and extremely stupid) land that brings nice dreams to The Rushers of Din (live-action folks who remarkably resemble us of Earth). And then there's Murkworks, the nasty and tasteless society which brings nightmares to Din. Our good guys are: Ralph, the All-Purpose Animal, who can transform into any imaginable creature; Mumford, his accident-prone mute pal; Flora Fauna, a dippy aspiring actress who takes a job at Nightmare Studios; and best of all, Rod Rescueman, the ever-perspiring muscle-bound superhero, who might be a help if only he had a brain. But the best character is an evil toad of a dictator named Synonamous Botch, who gets my vote as one of the greatest cartoon villains of all time! He farts; swears; frolics in his stinkweed patch; has a Nixon/Agnew tattoo on his chest; collects salamis, stretched cats and undersides of theatre seats; and keeps his head writer, Scuzzbopper, chained in the dungeon, pounding at a giant typewriter with mallets. He also reminds us to always check our belly button, because you never know what type of crunchy titbit you'll find there! Synonamous' master plan is to stop Frivoli from delivering their dreams, and instead explode his own payload of Nightmare Bombs over the entire population. But the plot is secondary to the heroic rescues, thrilling escapes, avalanche of puns, and non-stop strangeness that permeates every frame. It's a rare treat to find an animated film that successfully integrates technically dazzling sequences (check out the attack by giant office supplies) with the fearlessness to do anything for a laugh – from slapstick gags to bathroom humour. Featuring the vocal talents of Lorenzo Music, Marshall Efron and Paul Frees, I can't recommend this film more highly (now all *you* have to do is find a copy of the damned thing).

THE UNDERTAKER AND HIS PALS

DAVID C. GRAHAM 1967. The best thing about this film is the ad. Originally tossed into drive-ins on double bills with either **The Astro-Zombies** or **The Corpse Grinders**, it's a prime example of a movie that reads better than it plays – but knowing me, I'm gonna end up making it sound lots better than it ever gets. As cannibalism-comedies go, it's not as wholeheartedly lousy as **Blood Diner**, but it's still a tawdry li'l exercise with lots of sick ideas that are never adequately pulled off. It begins when a trio of masked motorcyclists break into a woman's apartment, knife her, carve her into easily carried pieces, and deliver the meatier portions to a greasy spoon diner who serves it up as the Fresh Flesh du Jour. The chef is a failed medical student who does exploratory surgery on still-living customers, and while the city's female population is slowly depleted, the diner is flourishing by chopping away at its own overhead. Then there's Ray Dennis as Mort, a snotty skinflint undertaker who advertises $144.98 funerals, and who seems to pop up whenever one of these mutilation murders occurs. Lo and

gland experiments, which starts off with the surgical implant of a *new* home-grown gland and ends up with a cellar full of drooling freaks. Basically, this is your standard mad-scientist-pot-boiler, with everyone shouting dramatic dialogue at each other and looking earnest. It's all played surprisingly straight, with *far* too much boring exposition. You don't really see any of the genetic mutations, but a good cast (including everyone's favourite 50-foot woman, Allison Hayes) helps get you through it. Adequate, but unmemorable.

UNHOLY ROLLERS

VERNON ZIMMERMAN 1972. Claudia Jennings was one of those rare exploitation actresses who busted through the fleshpot aspect of her films and gave drive-in dimwits a glimpse of genuine talent in the likes of **Gator Bait**, **The Great Texas Dynamite Chase** and David Cronenberg's racing car romp **Fast Company** (with William Smith and John Saxon). She posed for **Playboy**, had a small streak of sleazebag gems, but just as she became synonymous with four-star lowbrow fun, she died in a car crash in October 1979 at the age of 29. And here's a good example of how her gutsy presence could hold a film together... Remember the late-'60s/early-'70s craze of roller derby? Here's a cheap, hard-boiled look into that wretched world – a Roger Corman production that combines bruising action, crude comedy, female forms, and lots of ugly extras cheering as women pummel the piss out of each other.

behold, Mort and the two restaurateurs are the nutty pranksters behind the killing spree – the diner gets free meat, the mortician gets more business and all three of these deviates get to hack up the babes in their spare time. All this was unabashedly demented and moderately gory for its era, and even though the film is flatly directed, fussily photographed and downright *foul* in the acting department, there are still some gruesomely humorous moments. Too bad director David Graham quickly abandons any attempt at playing it even semi-straight, deciding instead to rev up the wildly *unfunny* comedy – when Mort accidentally steps on a skateboard, it suddenly shifts into skid row Mack Sennett... 60 minutes long and even then it feels padded out. And could somebody please turn down that canned music?... A pic that's harsh on the braincells. But on the positive side, it's packed with gratuitous bloodshed, while being so uniformly incompetent that it makes Fred 'I've got $10, let's make a movie!' Olen Ray look like David Lean.

THE UNEARTHLY

BROOKE L. PETERS 1957. Like it or not, here's another Rhino Video anti-classic, starring the ever-popular and never-choosy John Carradine... Welcome to the creepy mansion of the craggy Dr. Conway (John C.) and his mute, bald, slow-witted butler (Who else? Tor Johnson!). And if you didn't already suspect, Carradine is meddling with nature again, searching for the secrets of life and death. Unfortunately, he's kind of a fuck-up as his experiments go, so all his failures end up locked in the basement – there's one catatonic guinea pig with internal radiation burns of the brain, a woman with a face like a year-old chuck of cauliflower, and his missile-headed servant is a misfire too, with 'the strength of Hercules and the brain of a chicken'. But all hell breaks loose when an escaped con takes refuge at the doc's mansion and discovers his wacky

Claudia stars as quick-tempered Karen Walker, who quits her as-sembly line day job and joins up with the local femme derby team, the Los Angeles Avengers. It's no surprise to learn that the game is half sport, half show business, and all jiggle pageant, with Karen gladly giving the slobbering in-bred audiences what they want. Her initiation into their world of obnoxious crowds, greasy gigolos and clod-pate rednecks is grittier and more lurid than you'd expect, with her unfriendly team-mates getting even for her speedy suc-cess and exponentially expanding ego by stripping Claudia on a barroom pool table. Obviously there isn't much of a plot – we just follow Jennings' adventures on the rink and off, including her ac-quisition of a gaudy tattoo and a *very* brief taste of tacky TV com-mercial stardom (before dropping like a rock into bimbo oblivion). Claudia's primary wardrobe is a mini-skirt, but she's no ordinary celluloid ditz. She defiantly skates through this rancid slice of life and plays the whacko super-bitch with utter conviction. As in her equally memorable **Truck Stop Women**, Claudia never brown-noses in order to get cheap sympathy from the viewer, and the film succeeds best in chronicling Karen's self-destructive obsession with fame. But it's not all serious either, because director Vernon Zimmerman also has a field day poking fun at all the ultra-cheesy elements (such as black velvet furniture). There's a large cast of supporting slobs, including exotic dancers, car thieves, mangy managers, and general lowlife scum, plus chaos galore during the hilarious finale, with everyone in the cast beating each other to a pulp as Claudia flips out. So grubby it has a truly documentary feel, and the roller-cam photography succeeds in making skating around in a circle halfway exciting (the Supervising Editor was Martin Scorsese, so maybe it's to his credit). Overall, a decent bit of grubbiness, highlighted by Claudia Jennings' pretty, yet powerful persona.

THE UNINVITED

GREYDON CLARK 1987. Director Greydon Clark. Hmmm. The name conjures up such psyche-damaging nightmares as **Black Sham-poo**, **Without Warning**, and Joe Don Baker's 'comedy'-outings, **Joysticks** and **Wacko**... Well, Greydon's back to pour more punish-ment onto an unsuspecting public, and he managed to snag B-vets George Kennedy, Alex Cord and Clu Gulager for this idiotic romp. Did these actors *know* what they were getting into? (Not that ol' George K. has any shred of dignity left after co-starring in Bo Derek's **Bolero**.) At least I hope they had fun hanging out at the bar together, swapping 'crappy-movies-I've-been-in' tales... So what's Greydon unloaded on us this time? In the sorta-grand tradition of **The Corpse Grinders**, it's a Killer Cat movie! A cute little kitty is undergoing radical experimentation at a top secret government lab, playing the part of a purring pincushion for cut-rate Dr. Jekylls, and wouldn't you know it – some dope leaves the lab door wide open and our star feline quickly makes a break. No need to panic though, the only thing that differentiates this cat from any other is that when this pussy gets angry, a hairy rat-like monster crawls out of its mouth, grows to the size of an aardvark, and razors up any-one in its path. For a while, this is how the flick progresses: [1] Long shot of innocent cat, with soon-to-be victim approaching. [2] Close-up of mutant creature (winner of 1987's Most Pathetic Hand Puppet Award). [3] Cut to fake blood spattering nearby wall (screams optional). And lastly, [4] long shot of adorable tabby scampering off. Admittedly, this is pretty goofy fun, but you soon realise the filmmakers are gonna louse it all up by adding a sto-ryline... Conveniently enough, the lab is based in Fort Lauderdale and the escape takes place at the height of Spring Break, so that the plot can include a pair of college-age jiggle-bunnies who never change outta their bikinis, and their yuppie-shit dates who reek with close personalities to the producer. Add Alex Cord as an illegit Wall Street entrepreneur; Kennedy as his grumpy, portly partner;

and Clu as the alkie sidekick, complete with Jerry Lewis dentures. They all converge on Cord's luxury yacht (the college guys are the crew and the bimbos are the decorative ornaments for Cord's tree) and just before they head out to sea, the ditzy girls find the feline and (despite the fact it's wearing a Genetic Lab tag) take it on board with 'em. One by one they're torn apart, but first we have to suffer through a trio of sappy romantic subplots and thoroughly idiotic script manoeuvres (can you *really* use a sextant as a make-shift microscope in order to study blood samples? I think not). Though it's relatively dim-witted and predictable, that cat certainly is a riot when it erupts. Dumbest thing *I've* seen in a long time, and that's saying a lot considering the type of movies I've self-lobotomised myself with recently. There's a fair bit of cheap gore (an ankle-shredding, some finger-nibbling and a little skin-bubbling), but any chance of George Kennedy getting his own personal chest-bursting is diffused by a PG-13 rating. Too bad, because it would've been a sure highlight! An amazingly stupid wrap-up (complete with Aurora Kit special effects) only adds to the cut-rate level... Mark this movie as mindless crapola for low IQ-ed animal lovers. The perfect antidote for unsuspecting little children who've been weaned on **Garfield** and **Heathcliff** cartoons.

VAMPIRE'S KISS

ROBERT BIERMAN 1989. This rat's nest of a movie can be viewed on two completely different levels: (1) as a grim tale of vampirism and dementia, tossed into an urban setting and spiced with satire, or (2) as a gonzo showcase for one of the most ludicrous, over-wrought, hilariously hell-bent performances of all time by Mr. Method Actor himself, Nicholas Cage. Unfortunately, the two don't always mesh. But even if it never clicks dramatically, it's still one of the strangest studio releases of '89. Written by Joseph Minion, the scripter of Scorsese's dark comedy, **After Hours**, he obviously hoped for the same subtly warped tone. Ha! Not with Nicholas Cage on board! He's so perpetually freaked out that his character seems absolutely bonkers from Frame One... Like **After Hours**, we're in NYC Yuppieland with Cage playing a button-down literary exec who hits the swanky night-clubs every evening in a search for the perfect woman. But this guy is such a self-important twit that all he really cares about is a fast fuck and a 'heave ho' the next morning. Enter professional mannequin Jennifer Beals as Rachel, a temptress in black lingerie who double drills Cage's neck and returns to his bed every night to suck him dry in a way he never expected. Questions arise: Is Beals a vampire? Is Cage slowly turning into one? Is he simply imagining it all, while having a nerv-ous breakdown? And most importantly, is Cage vying with Crispin Glover for the dubious honour of 'Most Agitated Actor on the Entire Fucking Planet'? Throughout the first half I couldn't stop howling at Cage's spastic rhythms, but luckily, despite all of Nick's flailing and lisping, the film itself gets progressively better. Soon Cage is faint-ing in front of churches, avoiding harsh sunlight with sunglasses and using an overturned couch as a makeshift coffin. Then there's the notorious Dwight Frye/'eating the cockroach' sequence, proving some people will do anything for their art (particularly if they're stupid – for **Birdy**, Cage reportedly had several of his teeth yanked out). Cage remains a misogynistic shitheel throughout, while transforming into the most asinine bloodsucker in cinematic history as he runs through the city with plastic fangs in his mouth, screaming "I'm a vampire!" to the who-gives-a-shit-Bub New Yorkers. And it soon leads to rape, murder and a gig as a babbling street corner imbecile. This is fascinating stuff, though it's almost sabotaged by Cage's bug-eyed presence, and in tandem with always-cringeable co-stars Beals and Maria Conchita Alonso (as Nick's dowdy, much-abused secretary), you begin to wonder if the Casting Agent was playing some kind of giant practical joke on our sensibilities. Robert Bierman's direction is consistently innovative (special kudos to the Bat-Cam), and instead of a run-of-the-mill vampire fest, he's constructed a weird-assed, revisionist horrorama. Painfully hip at times and overbearing, but never boring.

VAMPIRE HOOKERS

CIRIO H. SANTIAGO 1979. The title is wonderful. The ads are ludicrous. Unfortunately, the producer had to screw it all up by making a film to go along with 'em. Directed by the ever-seedy Cirio H. Santiago (**Hustler Squad**, **TNT Jackson**, **The Muthers**), John Carradine drops his remaining shreds of dignity and stars as one of the most pathetically frail-looking vampires to ever fill the screen, with Karen Stride, Lenka Novak and Katie Dolan as his twilight trollops... It all begins when two sailors stationed in the orient hit the big city looking for dames, and after 15 minutes of barroom brawls, transvestite night-clubs and dialogue straight out of a Navy VD film, they finally meet a lovely lass who invites them back to her place. Of course, the fact that she lives in a graveyard mausoleum doesn't phase these horny swabbies in the least – but they do get a little suspicious after they're led down a secret underground tunnel, glimpse some empty pastel coffins, and come face-to-face with gnarly ol' John C. in a $5 white linen suit, oversized hat and plastic fangs. To make a boring story short, one of the sailors is eventually kidnapped by the vampire vixens (who get to shed their tacky lingerie for one slow-motion orgy), the guy's buddy heads to the rescue with a bag of garlic, and most of the cast is crushed under Styrofoam 'granite' slabs... Big deal. By that time you'll be in a coma from lack of entertainment. The whole show is uniformly asinine (but what'd you expect, with a title like **Vampire Hookers**?), not to mention frighteningly tedious, but if you can keep your eyes open through the first 45 minutes, the second half actually comes across with some lame attempts at humour. So-called comic relief comes from B-movie regular Vic Diaz (**Fly Me**, **The Big Bird Cage**) as a nearly-retarded Renfield-like servant named Pavo, who farts a lot. The trio of thirsty debs *try* to play it for laughs, too ("I haven't

had a suntan in 116 years" or "Coffins are for being laid to rest. Not for being laid"), but everyone, after a while tends to look bored, embarrassed, and in most cases, untalented. Carradine, in particular, is a sad sight – you get the feeling that one good sneeze would snap half the bones in his brittle body. Sure, the film is crappy, but it never achieves a sustained level of entertaining lousiness that a Bad Film needs to become a true classic. Frightening in its amateurishness! Terrifying in its banality! You WILL BELIEVE that any bozo can produce a motion picture!

VAMPYRES

JOSEPH LARRAZ 1974 (US: VAMPYRES, DAUGHTERS OF DRACULA). This British-made Sex 'n' Splatter flick doesn't hedge its bets – it kicks right off with a fully nude, hot-and-heavy lesbian scene to get your attention, and it doesn't let up until the relatively tame ending. Horror fans should enjoy this randy twist on an old idea, and video shut-ins will be flogging their mutton throughout the bedroom acrobatics. Marianne Morris and Anulka star in this modern-day vampire tale, as two sultry seductresses in search of red-blooded males. They hitchhike on country roads, horny middle-aged guys stop to give them a lift, and when they all get to the gals' castle, their victims are sucked dry (in every way possible). Marianne and Anulka aren't your typical cinema vampires either – instead of neat puncture wounds, these women slice their victims from ear to ear with a sacrificial dagger, and lap up the streams of blood like a wino at a Jack Daniels convention. Of course, this is a sloppy way to do it, but all the more reason for the ladies to wash up together afterward and fondle each other in the shower... Bloodless corpses are piling up around town, one hard-up gentleman caller is getting more anaemic day-by-day, and a vacationing couple in a mobile home get suspicious when they see all these people entering the castle, but never leaving... That's about it for the plot – nothing *too* innovative, except for the explicitness. There are a few moments of genuine creepiness and suspense, but director Joseph Larraz' primary interest is to get your hormones doing The Rumba every time The Lungwart Twins drop their dresses. Toss together a few ex-Playmates, give them some artistic motivation ('take off your clothes and hump each other') and let 'em have a veritable orgasm every time they get some warm Type-O in their mouths. And do

you know what? For a good, sleazy drive-in romp, the end product is pretty darned successful! **Vampyres** is a modest little Euro-diversion that comes across with all the exploitation you could want – it doesn't insult your intelligence *too* much, it mixes its blood and breasts in heavy doses, and the climax is particularly savage (though it abruptly ends on a low-key note). It's a fun little item, from the Bang-'Em and Bleed-'Em School of Horror Filmmaking.

VENGEANCE: THE DEMON

STAN WINSTON 1988 (AKA: PUMPKINHEAD). I'd heard loads of good advance word on this flick, so I was ready for something a little unique. Sure, it sat on a shelf for almost a year, but that's only because most studio execs conveniently have hat sizes which match their anuses. It turns out to be a beautifully crafted film that grafts an old-fashioned folk tale onto an '80s-style slice 'n' dicer. Director Stan Winston gives us oodles of style, and it's all meshed with genuine emotional backing. Unfortunately, he also tosses in your typical pack of brain dead teen stereotypes to make the package more commercial. The smartest move was in hiring Lance Henrikson to star as the backwoods protagonist. He's one of the finest actors in the genre, bringing a semblance of dignity and strength to everything from classics like **Near Dark** to more routine drive-in drivel like **House 3: The Horror Show**... Set in the rural hills, where farm children chant the legacy of Pumpkinhead to scare their grubby peers, along come a group of city dickwads to fray our nerves as they dangerously zoom around on their motor-bikes. Lance's young son is accidentally killed by the scummiest of the teens (prompting them to skidaddle to a secluded cabin), and as Henrikson clutches his dying son, the pain in his eyes convey more than a dozen latex dismemberments. Heading into the deep woods, he follows the legend and finds his means of revenge – but first he has to disinter its remains from the cemetery – and with his own blood as the key, an avenger arises to set the record straight. Pumpkinhead! And what a great monster it is! An eight-foot-tall killing machine that looks like a cross between Alien and Joey Ramone. But as in any pact with Evil Forces, for each action there must be a reaction, and as the city slickers are torn from their socks, Lance must face the consequences of his decision. Sure, a viewer with a sceptical air will scoff at the supernatural premise, and admittedly once all the cards are played the film begins to weaken, but it's all consistently spooky in a campfire-told way. And though it has its fair share of bloodthirstiness, the gore never overshadows the storyline. It's a good tale, constructed with intelligence and care (two areas usually glossed over by the swill released nowadays).

THE VIOLENT YEARS

FRANZ EICHORN 1956. I *love* pompously self-righteous juvenile delinquent flicks, and this is one of the best offerings from the '50s – a blunt, trashy little 'exposé' in which uncontrolled passions erupt into senseless violence (Yay!). Unlike the studio JD films, such as **The Blackboard Jungle**, this one has no pretensions of being anything other than a schlocky diatribe against teen fun by taking it to its illogical extremes... Meet Paula, Phyllis, Geraldine, and Georgia – a quartet of teenaged debs prowling for kicks. On the surface, Paula is a straight-A, straight-arrow student, the well-to-do daughter of a respected newspaper editor. But as soon as her parents leave the house, she grabs her lowlife girlfriends and these dames are on the go, holding up gas stations and pistol-whipping the attendants for some quick cash and cheap thrills. Before we know it, they're even stealing a woman's sweater and dragging her date into the woods for a quick molestation ('Man Attack in Lover's Lane,' the headlines proclaim). 'These aren't kids, these are morons!" exclaims the sheriff, but as *we* all know, this horrible vio-

lence is the eventual result when parents allow their teens to run loose without constant supervision: they turn to crime, senseless destruction, and steamy pyjama parties with men twice their age. And soon these curdled cuties are vandalising their very own school – overturning desks, throwing books, and (in my favourite bit of cheap symbolism) one of them picks up a globe and tosses it out the window. But justice prevails (shucks) when the cops arrive, and the gals' 'fun' ends in a fatal shoot-out ("Look at 'em jump. Just like rabbit," sez one, an instant before she's gunned down). While all of her cohorts end up in Morgue City, poor rich Paula is given a lifetime sentence in The Big House for first degree murder, and she has her illegit child in the Slammer Infirmary (Boo hoo! The humanity of it all!). Of course, Paula's actually the lucky one, because she doesn't have to suffer through the *long* epilogue from the local judge about morals, self-respect, politeness, and all that baloney... So get ready for plenty of stilted dialogue and pompous narration from the crayon of legendary sociologist Ed Wood Jr., and a jazzy, finger-snapping score that kicks in every time the debutantes hit the streets. A classic in Bad cinema, I put this right up there with **Reefer Madness** as an inept, right-wing-paranoia, shit-for-brains masterwork!

WATCHERS

JON HESS 1989. Hey, let's take a real good book, full of exciting dialogue and philosophical ideas – a real 'can't put it down' book – yeah, something like Dean R. Koontz' **The Watchers**. Then let's take out everything but the dog and the monster, and let's put in some clichés like – yeah, a hardened detective, a secret government plot, and a teen star. Yeah, let's get COREY FUCKIN' HAIM! Just the stuff to put me to fuckin' sleep. Whoever produced this should EAT FUCK! Avoid it like AIDS – yeah, wear a condom on your brain when you see this, the director sure did! [SS]

WAXWORK

ANTHONY HICKOX 1988. Director Anthony Hickox tried to resurrect the anthology-style horror film (i.e. **Tales from the Crypt**, **Asylum**), but with only scattershot results. Featuring a cast of new faces (Deborah Forman, Michelle Johnson and Zack 'dull as a doorstop' Galligan) as well as old (Patrick Macnee, David Warner), it starts off depressingly sophomoric as we're introduced to the usual bland mix of college stereotypes. There's the wholesome rich kid, his cool best friend, the college slut, and her virginal girlfriend. But when a waxwork pops up in the midst of suburbia with David Warner stalking the front lawn, our pack of collegiate clowns go on a private midnight tour of the place. Invited inside by a midget doorman (Mihaly 'Michu' Mesza) and a seven-foot-tall butler, the kids are soon checking out the lifelike depictions of torture, death and murder. But the moment one of them accidentally steps onto one of the exhibits, they're transported *into* that particular scene, and there hangs a series of mini-adventures involving loads of legendary monsters and a hefty supply of plasma. As supporting characters one-by-one disappear into the displays, the mixed bag of generally mediocre tales include a rustic werewolf, an Egyptian mummy, a meeting with the Marquis DeSade, and a black-and-white homage to **Night of the Living Dead**. The only truly brilliant bit is the excursion into vampirism, when Michelle encounters a castle full of sinister bloodsuckers. Beautiful production design, gorgeous cinematography and some ultra-bloodthirsty twists make this the high point of the entire 90+ minutes. The film never reaches that peak again, and even though Hickox' direction keeps the tale brisk, it never takes on a life of its own. Zack Galligan is bland and unheroic, Deborah Foreman (who saved flicks such as **Valley Girl** and **My Chauffeur** with her high Likeability Quotient) is kept restrained throughout, and Michelle Johnson may be lovely but she can't act worth spit. Worst, all the younger characters just get more irritating as the film progresses. At least Warner and Macnee help flavour the mix with an edge of humour, and the big surprise in the cast is that usually dorky Miles O'Keeffe (**Ator** and Bo Derek's **Tarzan**) is actually *good* as Count Dracula. Talk about small miracles! As for the gore: The video box says the film's 'uncensored', but there's nothing supremely offensive to be found (unless you consider an exploding head or a cannibalised leg too bloody for your tastes)... Quite watchable, but nothing too special either.

WEIRD CARTOONS

Any tape from Rhino is always worth checking out, but when they come up with a title as enigmatic, yet as potentially promising, as **Weird Cartoons**, you've gotta be ready for something truly special. Because these are the people responsible for some of the strangest releases around — the **Sleazemania** series of redneck drive-in trailer reels, the **Saturday Night Shockers** double bills, as well as other '50s trash, such as Ed Wood's **The Violent Years**. If not for these people, film classics like **Mesa of Lost Women** and **The Monster of Piedras Blancas** would never have resurfaced. Without a doubt, they have the finest library of weird shit currently available for home consumption... But back to our subject. **Weird Cartoons** is a mixed bag of black and white, colour, silent, sound, and stop-action animation — most of which I've never seen before, and all of which I doubt will ever see the light of day on network TV. Some of my favourites include: **Betty Boop in Crazy Town** — a typically surrealistic Max Fleischer (these people never took drugs? yeah, right), with Betty and Bimbo visiting Crazy Town, where people giggle maniacally as they change size, and where the Barber Shop grows hairs and the Beauty Parlour exchanges heads for the customers... **Scrub Me Mama with a Boogie Beat** — the nastiest, most racist cartoon I've seen in a long time, set in an all-black lazy town, where everyone lays around in the mud, picks cotton, eats watermelon, and washes laundry. But when a sultry singer comes to town, they all wake up from their snoozing and break into song and dance. As one friend commented, the lesson of the cartoon is to make blacks scrub faster. The fine animation (Walter Lantz of Woody Woodpecker fame) only makes it more disturbing... And **The Devil's Ball** — very twisted b/w stop-action (there were no credits, so I don't know when it was made, or by who), in which a devil emerges from a liquor bottle and pulls together a menagerie of creatures (skeletons, living vegetables, balloon musicians) who

dance and fight, while a drunken, horny chimpanzee tries to seduce a beautiful ballerina... There's about an hour's worth of shorts, and some of them are only OK — but compared to any of the mindless drivel on Saturday morning TV nowadays (how much **Smurfs** or **He-Man** can a kid take before his brain turns into a rotting chunk of broccoli?), this is all wonderful.

WEIRD CARTOONS 2

The follow-up to Rhino Video's **Weird Cartoons**, this is another collection of classic animated shorts from the days when the word 'cartoon' didn't immediately bring to mind the present-day, creatively-void process of selling merchandise by pumping pulp like **GI Joe** and **Smurfs** over the airwaves. Surprising as it may seem, all of these cartoons originated in the animator's mind, and *not* on a toy manufacturer's drafting board... After that little tirade, it'd be nice to admit that all the cartoons in this collection are four-star standouts; but unlike the first **W.C.**, this one omits independent and foreign animation, stressing the more-conservative studio product from the '20s to the '50s (instead of **Weird Cartoons**, it could've been labelled 'Occasionally Odd Cartoons'). Included is Fleischer's **Betty Boop's Crazy Inventions**, Walt Disney's silent **Alice the Toreador**, Warner Brothers' **Inki and the Minah Bird**, and Felix the Cat in **The Non-Stop Fright**. Any animation buff might be disappointed with the choices, but there *are* a few greats, such as: **Scrap Happy Daffy** — a b/w war propaganda piece which has Daffy Duck protecting a junkyard from a scrap-eating Nazi goat; **Small Fry** — the colourful, Fleischer musical in which a little fish plays hooky from school and unsuccessfully tries out for the Big Fry Club; and **It's a Bird** — an early combo of live and stop-action, starring a wisecracking worm and a rare metal-eating bird, which lays eggs that hatch into full-size autos. Just for the fun of it, they also throw in a few animated intermission trailers, circa 1960, and some 'spooky' ads for a Ghost-a-Go-Go Show. Overall, it's an OK showcase for American animation, but in the same respect, I'm glad to see *any* of the older cartoons finally making their way into video stores.

WEREWOLF OF WASHINGTON

MILTON MOSES GINSBERG 1973. Dean Stockwell has certainly had one hell of a sporadic film career. In the '60s he was one of the counterculture heads of AIP, with roles in **Psych-Out** and **The Dunwich Horror**. In the '80s he made waves with supporting roles in **Blue Velvet** and **Married to the Mob**. But in-between, during the '70s, Stockwell virtually disappeared from view, except for the occasional low-budgeter such as **Win, Place or Steal** with McLean Stevenson (gag!) and Henry Jaglom's wonderfully indulgent **Tracks** with fellow Tinseltown outcast, Dennis Hopper. Well, this silly little flick is one of Stockwell's oddest 'achievements' — a monster-on-the-looser that predates **American Werewolf in London** by approaching the subject of lycanthropy as both horror and dark comedy... Dean stars as Jack Whittier, one of "the best and the brightest" of the Washington DC political set. But while he's assigned to his department's Budapest bureau, his car breaks down and (despite the gypsy warnings) he wanders off alone during a full moon. One wolf bite later, Dean's winging his way back to the White House for (1) a post as Assistant Press Secretary to the President, and (2) a rendezvous with the First Daughter. To the detriment of Dean's promising career, in the middle of Washington flesh-pressings he suddenly sees pentagrams in palms, begins scratching uncontrollably and ends up ravaging the government cognoscenti once the moon rises. Of course, if you think about it for a moment, having a crazed murderer bounding around the hallways of the White House after dark doesn't seem like *that* strange a concept after all... Stockwell tries to convince the President (Biff McGuire) that he himself is responsible for the rash of local murders, but everyone's so preoccupied with their own business (in addition to being just plain pig-headed) they don't listen to his ravings, even when Dean starts baring his fangs at a Pentagon Chiefs' meeting. It's all inherently foolish (although there are also a couple solid chills along with way, such as a phone booth attack that's a claustrophobic knockout) and the most insane moments occur when Jack the Werewolf encounters Dr. Kiss (Michael 'Dr. Miguelito Loveless' Dunn) and his secret lab. Caged human and mad scientists in the bowels of the Pentagon? Nothing would surprise me after Reagan... Stockwell's a fine actor, but he seems utterly confused in this role; and it's no wonder, when the script has him chained to a chair, screaming, "I'm a violent beast and I'm better off DEAD!!" while his eyes bug out to the size of billiard balls. On the technical side, the transformation effects are straight out of the old Universal Wolfman flicks, and writer/director/editor Milton Moses Ginsburg continually goes for the flashy, pretentious shot (toilet bowl reflections, 360 degree pans, distorted lenses, etc). He gets high marks for originality, even if he lets the story meander far too often. Best of all, the film carries a nice, left-wing view of our political leaders – they're either racist, media-hating scumballs or addle-brained incompetents (talk about rooted in reality!)... Though **W of W** might be too tame for lowbrow '80s gorehounds, it's eccentric enough to keep curious genre buffs (and Stockwell groupies) amused.

WEREWOLVES ON WHEELS

MICHEL LEVESQUE 1971. Welcome to the wonderful world of monster-motorcycle-mania! In this low-class entry, we follow The Devil's Advocates, an unwashed, unshaven, and most of all, untalented bunch of chopper-jockeys, who spend their days kicking the

piss out of country yahoos, and their nights drinking and drooling until they pass out face-first in the dirt. Of course, they're all incredibly stupid, so when their fortune-telling comrade, Tarot, warns them of impending disaster, they laugh it off as a joke. But later on, who do you think they meet up with in the middle of the desert? A bunch of devil-worshipping monks whose party-plans include chopping up a cat, invoking a few cheesy spells, and wedding one of the biker's mamas to Satan while she does a nude shimmy on a tabletop. But before you know it, the gang breaks up the party, punches their lights out, steals back the future Mrs. Lucifer, and assumes the argument is over (Ha!). Sure enough, the next night a couple of the bikers are torn apart by a 'mysterious creature' (as the audience already *knows* from the title, a werewolf's to blame, so the suspense is nil). The rest of the film is spent trying to figure out who's to blame (yawn!)... There's a *bit* of cheap gore during the werewolf attacks, with a sliced-open neck and a ripped-out eyeball, but that's only during the last five minutes, when you *finally* get to see the creature. The makeup is adequate, but unfortunately, there's no transformation scenes. Severn Darden gets a few well-deserved laffs as 'One', the head of the Satanists, and everyone else in the cast has now been justifiably forgotten. The entire production is technically mediocre, intellectually barren, without any style whatsoever, but good for a *couple* guffaws if you're desperate for entertainment. Not really recommended, unless you're a cycle-film completist.

WHERE THE BUFFALO ROAM

ART LINSON 1980. Bill Murray is Dr. Hunter S. Thompson, author of **Fear and Loathing in Las Vegas** and more recently **The Curse of Lono** in a comedy inspired by Thompson's article, 'The Banshee Screams For Buffalo Meat'... Very loosely based on Thompson's life, **Where the Buffalo Roam** takes us to a cabin in the snowy mountains of Aspen, where a stoned Dr. Thompson nearly shoots himself in the foot in an effort to silence the constant beeping of his teletype machine. He begins reminiscing about his life and adventures with his long-lost attorney and partner-in-mischief, Carl Lazlo (based on Thompson's real-life attorney Oscar Acosta) played by Peter Boyle. Writing for 'Blast Magazine', Thompson, tape recorder and thermos full of liquor at the ready, watches Lazlo's career go down the tubes in a matter of minutes as he lifts the bailiff into the air and tosses him over the judge's desk after his teenage client is sentenced to five years for possession of marijuana. Barred from his profession, Lazlo takes up gun-running, only to lead himself and his friend Hunter into an ambush by police helicopters. Covering the Super Bowl, Thompson opts for watching the game on TV in the confines of his hotel room while partying with a couple of midget bellhops before trading his room (and tickets to the press box) for a bottle of booze and a swell hat. Later, we find Hunter covering the '72 presidential campaign. Disguised as a reporter from **The Post**, whose clothes were real easy to swipe after he accepted 'prescription' pills from the good Doctor ("Try one of the blue ones. I've never had any complaints about the blue ones") he meets Richard M. Nixon in an airport men's room. ("Fuck the doomed," says Mr. Nixon.) Thompson's stint on the campaign comes to an abrupt end when he maintains with a fire-extinguisher onboard the press plane, liberally spraying Nixon and the Washington press corps with foam and insults... Generally panned by the critics and all but ignored by confused moviegoers not familiar with Thompson's work, **Where the Buffalo Roam** really isn't as bad as you might have heard, and is particularly enjoyable if viewed under the influence of cheap beer and good pot. Bill Murray, a good friend of Thompson's, has the Gonzo journalist's unique mannerisms and clipped staccato speech patterns down pat... Thompson fans will either love this one for its in-jokes and pro-weird attitude (the Nixon 'interview' and the epilogue were co-written by Thompson and Murray) or hate it for its strictly tongue-thru-cheek approach. Beware the butchered-for-TV version though; all the drug-related gags, which are *so* essential to the fun, have been savagely sliced out... More of an extended **Saturday Night Live** sketch than an actual account of Hunter Thompson's life, this may be the only **Fear and Loathing** movie we'll ever get to see and I guess we're stuck with it, but if you're the right type of individual and have a slightly twisted sense of humour, you'll dig it... My Favourite Line: "Y'know, I – I hate to advocate – drugs or liquor – violence or insanity to anyone; but in my case it's worked." [BJE]

WHITE OF THE EYE

DONALD CAMMELL 1987. This flick suffered an undeservedly quick theatrical death (I think it played one theatre in North America for a week). Director Donald Cammell, who's been laying low since **Demon Seed**, has pulled out the most stylish psycho film since **The Hitcher**. It's ultra-pretentious, but I liked its excessiveness (though sometimes I wanted to grab the cinematographer and scream 'Stop moving the fuckin' camera!')... Set in the small tumbleweed town of Globe, Arizona, Cammell runs rip with two parallel storylines, both focusing on Paul White (David Keith, who should continue acting and forget about his directing career, after **The Curse**) and his wife Joannie (throaty Cathy Moriarty, who's still waiting for a role that'll re-ignite her career after **Neighbours**). There's the past: The day in the late '70s when Paul and his wife first met, when Joannie and her greaseball disco-turd boyfriend fatefully passed through his small town. And the present greets us with Paul as an eccentric audio expert who's suspected by police to be a murderer. You see, there's a rash of ritualistic killings in the area – leaving battered corpses (the first victim gets her head smashed through a microwave) and Apache symbols formed from kitchen utensils. The killings are brutally enacted (there's a bathroom drowning where the killer puts a mirror up to the victim's face so she can watch herself die – thank you, Michael Powell) and Keith is quite effective when he takes an uncharted trip into Loonyland, painting up his face and strapping dynamite to his chest. Also worth noting is Alan Rosenberg, who's great as Joannie's ex-beau – playing the role from '70s Travolta-clone to present-day half-retarded mechanic... Cammell generates quirky suspense with jazzy close-ups of roasting meat, teeth flossing and dilated pupils (you can tell he once worked with Nicolas Roeg), and he incorporates a strange mix of music – from Hot Chocolate's 'You Sexy Thing' to Pavarotti singing 'Pagliacci'. The story and characters are sapped a bit by the self-conscious style and flowing metaphysical mumbo-jumbo, and under all its gloss, this is still just a crazed kill-a-thon. But the high gloss trapping and moody menace constantly keep you off guard. Recommended to those in search of a good, nasty arthouse item.

WICKED STEPMOTHER

LARRY COHEN 1989. Director Larry Cohen strikes again! You can never tell what type of gonzo indulgence he'll shovel to the public – a drive-in classic like **Black Caesar**, **Return to Salem's Lot**, **Demon**, or in this case, one of the most ridiculously half-baked slop-pageants in recent memory. A total embarrassment for everyone involved, with more unintentional laughs than a dozen Dolph Lundgren flicks. The credits give Bette Davis top billing, even though she walked off the set halfway through production. And while this type of sudden upheaval might cripple any normal film, 'No problem' said Cohen, who pulled a **Plan 9**/Lugosi move with a quick script rewrite and hired another actress to fill in Davis' remaining scenes. Enter Barbara Carrera, Latino sexpot! No resemblance, you say? Well, since Davis was playing a witch, how about having her transform *into* Carrera halfway through the movie? Gobbledegook to you and me, but forced artistic inspiration to

Larry C.! Davis died soon afterward, and it's no real surprise. She looks about 137 years old, weighs about 14 pounds and resembles some kind of withered Muppet. It's pathetic!... This so-called laughfest features Ms. Davis as Miranda, a wizened witch who spellbinds her way into suburban households. In this instance by marrying dotty Lionel Stander and usurping the home of his yuppie children – all-purpose boob David Rasche and Colleen Camp (who used to be a fun, sexy presence in cheapos like **Death Game**). His kids are upset because Bette (1) smokes like a fireplace, (2) fills their vegetarian kitchen with huge hunks of indiscernible meat, and (3) looks like the older sister of Im-Ho-Tep. The first half-hour is borderline fun (even though you tend to cringe whenever makeup troweled Bette blows in) as Davis' curses take effect, but it quickly slides from mildly clever to a Disney movie-of-the-week stupidity level. By midpoint, Davis has disappeared altogether with 'daughter' Priscilla taking over and showing off her slinky all-black wardrobe to horny hubby Rasche. Before we know it, Cohen tosses logic into the dumpster, adds some not-so-special effects and confusing subplots (like a broad satire of game shows), and crosses his fingers that the audience is so stoned they never realise what a bagful of shit they've stepped in. Of course, anyone unaware of the behind-the-camera problems will simply think that the film is the pits (It is!), and after enduring this flick, you might even feel stupider than the actors who had to fulfil their contractual obligation. But don't bet on it. Co-starring TV-lunks Tom Bosley and a fully-haired Richard Moll, with Laurene Landon getting a couple genuine giggles as Vanilla, a money-hungry Vanna White copycat.

THE WILD WOMEN OF WONGO

JAMES WOLCOTT 1959. And now for something completely stupid (but with a *great* title). A cheesecake cavewoman flick from the '50s – an era when 'risqué' meant decking out your cast in skimpy animal skins... Welcome to the tropical isle of Wongo, where "all the women are beautiful and all the men are brutes". While a nearby tribe, the Goonas, have a monopoly on all the handsome men. As expected, the Goona Boys gets their gonads in an uproar when they see the scantily-draped dolls (since their own women look like Buddy Hackett in drag). Meanwhile, all the Wongo Women are slobbering in their huts at the Goonas. Visit the Temple of the Dragon God! Watch live alligator stock footage! See native girls bounce across the beach, while a pack of lobotomised thespians march around with a plastic lizard on a stick! There's suspense, when the King of Goona sends word that a pack of Ape Men are on the rampage. There's romance, when the Wongo King's daughter Omoo has a jungle fling with the Goona King's son Engor. And let's not forget the unintentional idiocy, when this swarm of unemployed models writhe in the sand like dying sea monkeys (and call it 'dancing'). The Wongo Women eventually take charge and kidnap their body-waxed beaus, leading the beefcake parade back to Wongo and a sappy ending. As for those nefarious Ape Men – the production couldn't even afford gorilla suits, so they simply pasted some fake hair onto the faces of a couple Muscle Beach rejects... Along with colourful travelogue photography, there's mercilessly painful dialogue ("He carries the wing of the white bird of peace!") and even a (so-called) comedy relief parrot. The campy bits are wonderful, but unfortunately most of the film is dull as dirt, with only a few seconds of *very* distanced skinny-dipping for skin flick fans. After a while it reminded me of a prehistoric, burlesque version of **Gilligan's Island**, but without the intellectual edge of the TV show... Co-starring Zuni Dyer as the poseur Priestess and a young (almost unrecognisable) Adrienne Barbeau as Wana.

THE WILD WORLD OF BATWOMAN

JERRY WARREN 1966 (AKA: SHE WAS A HIPPY VAMPIRE). Did you have your fill of the Caped Crusader after the last few years' barrage of Bat Bullshit? Well here's a not-so-new, multi-hundred-dollar twist on the idea that should restore your faith in the good ol' one-take clinker. This black-and-white bomb was the brainchild of director/writer/producer/cinematic no-talent Jerry Warren, who never guessed (well, maybe a little...) that he'd be sued over the copyright-infringing title by the Batman folks. Oops! In comparison, it makes the old TV series with Adam 'Spare Tire' West and Burt 'Holy One-Shot Career!' Ward look as intellectually dazzling as Peter Greenaway... Katherine Victor stars as Batwoman, a distaff crimefighter who looks like a paunchy, on-the-skids Vegas showgirl – squeezed into a low-cut costume consisting of tights, a Mardi Gras mask and a bat logo painted on her cleavage. And don't get any wrong ideas! This is one seriously un-sexy broad! Aided by a bevy of curvaceous Batgirls, who use their wrist radios to keep in contact with the head cheese, the nonsensical story begins when one of the Batbabes is kidnapped by super-criminal Rat Fink, whose army includes Professor Neon (you can tell he's a scientist, cuz he owns two beakers with dry ice in 'em); two thug accomplices, Tiger and Bruno; and a hunchback named Heathcliff. The crooks keep the girl pumped up on 'Happy Pills' (which make the users go-go dance uncontrollably) and then blackmail Batwoman into helping them steal an atomic powered hearing aid. As for the 'monsters' we keep hearing about? They turn out to be nothing but quick film clips from 1956's **The Mole People**. The climax has Rat Fink using his Body Divider to create a dozen duplicates of himself, with all the Batgirls slapping them 'til they surrender. Wacky? I'll say. I wanted to whack the scriptwriter with a heavy mallet... What a lame excuse for a movie! I mean, would *you* feel safe if your city were protected by a pack of teenage models equipped with rifles? These dinkwads do! And you'll roar at the cornball Batgirl Oath, which they recite at pool side (so all of them can wiggle about in bikinis). The actors showcase their complex range – from confused, all the way to bored – with Bruno VeSota taking top acting honours in a cameo as a Patent Office executive. Any directorial finesse amounts to how many nails they used to hold the camera in place with, and the generic beach party footage (electric guitars in the middle of nowhere and not an extension cord on sight) will have you boogying to the fridge for another can of beer. *Still* don't believe how cheap it is? The so-called 'computer banks' have hand-painted dials, for Christ's sake! Hell, I could go on berating this atrocity, but I'd be wasting space that could be better used for a comparatively competent movie, like **Glen or Glenda**.

WILLIE DYNAMITE (1974)
THE MACK (1973)

As far as early '70s film fads go, one of the most inflammatory was the short-lived Blaxploitation Pimp flick. Protests abounded from Black groups across the country, accusing Hollywood of demeaning minorities by portraying their brothers and sisters as junkies, hustlers and whores... Nowadays though, looking from a distance of over a dozen years, these films merely represented an offshoot of the urban action genre, similar to the gangster films of the '30s... One of these ventures was **Willie Dynamite**, which was presented by Wonder-bred Richard Zanuck & David Brown (**The Sting**). Though they took the right route by hiring black director Gilbert Moses, it still didn't insure that the film would be without hideous stereotypes, cuz **Willie D.** turned into a white-assed production that plays up every 'Felt-Hatted, Cadillaced, Bad-Assed-Nigger' cliché in recorded history. Everyone's Black! Everyone's Bad! Everyone talks the way a cracker Hollywood scriptwriter *thinks* blacks talk. And what's even *worse*, the whole production is padded with badly-executed, moralistic bullshit... Roscoe Orman (a B-movie copy

Ain't no one crosses WILLIE "D" He's tight, together, and mean. Chicks, Chumps, he uses 'em all. He's got to be Number-One.

A ZANUCK/BROWN PRODUCTION WILLIE DYNAMITE

of Isaac Hayes) stars as Willie – a bald-headed bro in a funky set of threads, working the streets of NYC with his pack of prime-cut bitches. He's the biggest, meanest pimp in town, but when all the other neighbourhood johns join together, Willie gets shafted and has to fight back. So for the entire running time, Willie gets the shit beaten out of him – his women are busted the moment they touch the sidewalk, his car is towed and the IRS even investigates him for tax evasion. To make matters worse, the late Diana Sands (**Honeybaby**) co-stars as a do-gooder attorney who vows to bring Willie to justice, even if it means breaking every civil right on the books. Sheeit, she even tries to *unionise* his whores!... There's a moderate amount of action (a quick cat fight, some rear-screen car chases, a knifing) and Orman makes a slick enough 'hero' (you'll bust a gut when he steps out in his fur cape and matching fedora), but I was hoping for some *serious* conflict. Instead, all I got was comic book villains and a stock moral message. I'll bet the 42nd Streeters heckled this trash off the screen, particularly when Willie realises the error of his ways and gives up his business, his car *and* his wardrobe. There's even time for a tearful deathbed reunion with his hospitalised mom. Sniff sniff... This is the type of claptrap that helped kill off the '70s blax-plosion, and it certainly killed off the careers of everyone involved. Gilbert Moses went on to direct **The Fish that Saved Pittsburgh**, and Roscoe Orman gave up the big screen altogether and became a regular on **Sesame Street**. Geeeesh!... But on the other side of the coin, there's **The Mack**! Max Julien stars as Goldie, and this flick charts his rise to fame and fortune, plus some of the dues he has to pay along the way. After refusing his mama's request to come to church, Goldie takes a crash course in Whoring 101 and winds up at the top of The Player's Directory. But Goldie's also a pimp with scruples – though he sells his ladies' meat on the street, he also lectures the neighbourhood kids on going to school and getting an education. He can be kind, cool and considerate, or he can be one mean motherfucker, especially when white trash-heads try to buy him off. You see, in the name of No-Nonsense Social Consciousness, there's a local pair of honky cops shaking down the neighbourhood, and ideologically they're just slightly to the right of the Triple K. So if you want to see these pigs getting their pasty butts dropkicked to hell and back, that's just what the filmmakers give us. Yeah!... Sure, this movie follows a basic schlocky formula, but it's all pulled off with action, humour and (most importantly) the necessary *bit* of integrity that **Willie Dynamite** sorely lacked. It rambles a bit too much with black polemic, but there's also unexpected spurts of weirdness (check out the gang of pimps playing softball in platform shoes!) and enough grabass violence to keep anyone cheering. There's dynamite stuffed in the mouth, battery acid pumped in the vein, and when Goldie warns a competitor "I'm gonna blow your heart outta your body, sucker", just before locking the guy in a car trunk with a bagful of hungry rats, I'll bet audiences were on their feet and ripping the theatres seats out of the floor. Plus, it doesn't limp to an end with some jive-ass 'Just say no'-style wrap-up. This flick is much too hip to go for the easy ones... Let's not forget the supporting cast either: Roger E. Mosley is Goldie's brother, a righteous community leader, plus Richard Pryor stumbles around as Goldie's best friend – he's fucked out of his face for the entire film and need I add, he's funny as shit. In fact, come to think of it, *everyone* in the cast looks stoned... It's all solidly directed by Michael Campus (**The Education of Sonny Carson**, **Z.P.G.**), with musical contributions by The Sisters and The Uptight, and a wild score by Willie Hutch (**Foxy Brown**). Though it has its share of slow moments, **The Mack** is one of the best blaxploiters currently on video.

WINGS OF DESIRE

WIM WENDERS 1988. German director Wim Wenders' **Wings of Desire** is decidedly non-slimy material, but fits cosily in the 'arty crap' category. This cerebral fantasy is set in modern-day Berlin and tells the story of angels (presented here as intellectual spirits pondering existence, not Hollywood's clichéd dingbats with fluffy wings) watching people and listening to their thoughts and ideas, comforting them when in despair, and debating among themselves their roles as witnesses to humanity. Bruno Ganz gives a subtle, complex performance (as usual) as an angel who wishes for the physical awareness (and imperfection) of 'being'. When Ganz falls in love with a circus performer, his desire for life becomes unstoppable, despite his celestial comrades' appeal to stay neutral. The remarkable visuals (79-year-old cinematographer Henri Alekan shot **Beauty and the Beast** for Cocteau!) and richly layered soundtrack (with contributions by Laurie Anderson, among others) add immeasurably to the emotional impact of Wenders' and Peter Handke's story (even if the resolution is a tad, no, *real* syrupy), and the unique cityscapes of Berlin (and the fantastic library where the angels convene) leave a lasting impression. Also memorable is Peter Falk, in a funny cameo as himself, which (like the film) takes on greater significance than one initially thinks. Oh, but wait. Maybe 'Rectumhead' Rex Reed and Bill 'Howdy Doody' Harris didn't like it (or couldn't keep up with the subtitles), so maybe you shouldn't see it. Just forget what I said. [TR]

THE WIZARD OF GORE

HERSCHELL GORDON LEWIS 1970. Though **The Gore Gore Girls** ranks as Herschell Gordon Lewis' most tasteless work, **Wizard** manages to combine HGL's usual cardboard characters and butcherblock effects with a truly wonderful concept. The result is the tops in Cinemanure!... Allow me to introduce you to Montag the Magnificent, the self-proclaimed Master of Illusion. Ray Sager stars as the

top-hatted, zombie-eyed stage musician, who challenges his sceptical audience with questions like "What is reality?" before blithely chopping off his own hand with a mini-guillotine, "Torture and terror have always fascinated mankind," and to prove this radical theory he wills an entranced female volunteer out of the crowd and saws her in half – with a chain saw. But despite the facesplattering blood and pureed intestines, Montag deftly works his wonders and the volunteer is quickly back in one piece and steps safely off the stage. Too bad none of his illusions last more than a couple hours, which becomes evident when the unsuspecting young woman goes to dinner and proceeds to spill her guts onto the restaurant floor. Short-term magic, indeed... Each night Monty's 'tricks' keep getting bigger and bloodthirstier – turning faces into 'human ravioli' or using a punch press on ribcages. And who else but HGL could (or would *want* to) give us a demonstration of unwilling sword-swallowing? Of course, Montag has to continually diddle with the overflowing organs while Herschell 'Mr. Subtlety' Lewis' camera lingers lovingly on the runny remains. Surprisingly, the perky hostess of 'Housewife's Coffeebreak' (Judy Cler) is taken by Montag's grisly act (even the eyeball-mutilations and brainrendings. What a gal!) and she begs him to appear on her TV-talkshow. The only hitch is that her boyfriend, a nosy reporter, gets suspicious; and personally, I only wish this lumpy leading man could've died hideously too, but HGL has a tendency to keep his victims to female persuasion, so that his drooling, misogynistic audience would get their rocks off. The conclusion is a full-scale riot, when Montag goes on the air and initiates stigmata galore. The last scene is one big trippy mindfuck. It's *sooo* pretentious, I loved it!... As Mr. Grand Guignol, Ray Sager gives the blusteriest, one-note performance ever recorded on grainy film stock. Not since Criswell have I heard monologues that so perfectly combine The Deep and The Overwrought. Sure, the gore is thoroughly unbelievable, and HGL wouldn't know Continuity if it bit him on the ass, but with such brain-banging enthusiasm behind the camera, who can nitpick? You know it has to take a diseased genius to foist this type of sickness onto the general public. It's a landmark in grossout filmmaking. The perfect night's entertainment for anyone who thinks it'd be fun watching a pretty blond in a mini-skirt getting a railroad spike driven through her brain. (Now is *that* a recommendation, or what?)

WOMEN IN CAGES

GERRY DE LEON 1972. Oh no! *Another* Women In Prison epic?... This one was released during the glut that spewed out of the Philippines during the early '70s. And like all the rest, it's set in a secluded, foreign, all-female prison where there only seems to be

The dirty dolls of devil's Island.

See them battle their way out!

Soft bodies... hard as nails!

WOMEN IN CAGES

about three dozen inmates – they're either middle-aged, ugly Asian women in long, baggy dresses, or pretty young Americans with makeup and skin-tight, low-cut mini-skirts... B-movie perennials, Judy Brown and Roberta Collins co-star, and Pam Grier, who would later grace movie screens with **Black Mama, White Mama, The Arena** and **Bucktown**, has the role of the bitch prison matron, Alabama. ("What kind of hell did you crawl out of?" pleads one prisoner. "It was called Harlem!" Pam snarls.) Day-in, day-out, they shower, fight, work the fields, get tortured, go to church, shower, and finally try to escape, only to end up back in the slammer. When an inmate breaks the rules they get a trip to The Playpen, a medieval torture chamber where they're stripped, hung from the ceiling by chains, jabbed with pitchforks, stretched, and burnt – *then* they're thrown into a slug-filled sewage pit... How do they finally escape, you ask? They tell a guard they *all* want to go to church in the middle of the night to pray for a dead friend, so the attendant lets them out *and* turns her back on them. Although all the W.I.P. flicks sound about the same, this particular one doesn't come close to approaching the 'classic' status of **Caged Heat**. Choppily edited and wretchedly acted, it's grainy repetitious brain-punishment posing as entertainment. But unlike today's wimpy entries into the genre, this one does get exceptionally grim at times – Pam Grier gets savagely manhandled by her own blood-thirsty trackers, and the heroin-addicted traitor is sold into slavery (the last we see of her, she's getting balled by a whiskey-soaked, fat Asian extra). But overall. it's pretty standard as these particular sleazeshows go.

WORLD GONE WILD

LEE H. KATZIN 1988. Just what the world needs, another science fiction, post World War III actioner. Doesn't anyone have an original SF concept these days? I'm fucking tired of **Mad Max** hybrids!... I'm sure you're familiar with the route of these assembly-line items by now – the year is 2087, nuclear war has destroyed most of mankind, and there hasn't been any rainfall in 50 years, thus making water the top commodity on the black market. Far from the turmoil

of the cities though, there's the threadbare desert community of Lost Wells, where the last vestiges of peace and harmony survive. But who'd want to watch a film about a quiet li'l village who minds their own business? Not me! So enter Adam Ant and his white-robed stormtroopers, who promptly half the population with automatic weapons. Predictable? You bet! Luckily for us, some zoned-out casting executive had the brilliant idea of dusting off Bruce Dern for the plum role of Ethan, Lost Wells' resident hippie philosopher. Bedecked with 1960s artefacts, draggin' on a doobie and spouting some terrifically silly dialogue ("I live in the land of the mushroom"), Dern breaks the solemn tone every time he steps on-camera... After the massacre, Dern and the pretty schoolmarm (Catherine Mary Stewart) head to the big, dirty, corrupt city in order to hire some help. They locate Dern's old partner-in-crime (Michael Pare), plus a slimy back-up crew that includes a leathered biker, a black muscleman, a comedy-relief cannibal, and a western-style alcoholic gunslinger – and Dern convinces this nuclear era Magnificent Five to defend their town (and their precious water supply) from the returning marauders. A little of everything is tossed into the story: There's a slobbering of romance (but every time Pare and Stewart get ready for some heavy petting, an ill-timed invader interrupts 'em), plenty of good cut-rate combat, and even a (too short) trip sequence, when Dern doses Pare with some home-brewed hallucinogenic. Director Lee H. Katzin tries to balance satire/humour with mindless warfare, but the film is weakest when he sticks to the now-standard guidelines of End of Civilisation Cinema... At least the supporting characters are eccentric, with highest marks to Anthony James as the friendly cannibal, who wears an American flag as a serape and chows down on the enemy (off-camera) after a successful battle. The starring cast keeps us watching too – Michael Pare wanders around with a 'Wha' happened to my career?' blank stare, as if he actually believed all the PR hype from his **Streets of Fire** days; Catherine Mary Stewart (**Night of the Comet**) looks great, but isn't given much to do; and Adam Ant is surprisingly repellent as the type of glib, self-absorbed shitheel who consults The Wit and Wisdom of Charles Manson for ethical advice. But as you could probably guess, Bruce Dern is The Item. Unlike his pals Dennis Hopper and Dean Stockwell, who've gone upscale in recent years, Bruce is still livening up the drive-ins and dime-store direct-to-videos. He's a little greyer at the temples and a bit more sedate since his days of **Cycle Savages, The Incredible Two-Headed Transplant** and **The Cowboys** (how can you *not* admire a guy who'll shoot John Wayne in the back?), but he still seems to get a kick from camping it up in cheapjack productions... Overall, an OK programmer that's good for a few laughs at the expense of a few braincells.

THE WORLD OF DARIO ARGENTO

MICHELE SOAVI 1987. I grabbed this li'l item off the video racks the moment I saw it. Released by Vidmark Productions, what horror fan wouldn't be excited by the prospects of a documentary on Dario Argento, Italy's foremost horror director. His films mix the psychological under-pinning of a Roman Polanski with the blatant sex and gore slobberings of a Brian DePalma, into often-dazzling, occasionally surrealistic (and sometimes unfathomable) works of warped art. Add to that the fact that his films are barely-released in the States and ignored by the American critics. It's too bad the guys responsible for this documentary aren't as talented as their title subject is, because they've churned out a pretty average film on a very unique director. The big problem is that director Michele Soavi treats Argento like he was Jean-Luc Godard or Fellini, labelling him a 'visionary', but without giving the viewer any indication as to *why* he's such a genius. Thus, the whole production comes off like a congratulatory piece of fan-hype... A long, subtitled interview with Dario takes up a good deal of the 70-minute running time, and he rambles philosophically about his films ("Why do we do what we do? *I* make horror movies because I want to be loved"), their subject matter ("Murder is very important in my films... It is also very beautiful"), and dime-store psychology ("The knife, as you know, is phallic"). And if you couldn't have guessed from those short quotes, Argento comes off as a pretentious little twit, who you want to shake by the lapels and shout 'Lighten up, Dario! It's only a horror flick!'... But on the lighter side, there's some quick, fun intros to his production crew (including Insect Consultant) and *lots* of outrageously gory film clips sprinkled generously throughout, including **Suspiria**, **Deep Red**, **Creepers**, and **Inferno**. As an added bonus, we get to check out some funny out-takes, such as cute Jennifer Connelly sitting chin-deep in a pool of mock-maggots. Unfortunately, the documentary doesn't always let the audience know what clip is from what film, and the editing is so spastic that they never give you the chance to watch a complete, uninterrupted scene. As you can tell, I was disappointed, but not totally un-amused by this introduction to Argento and his body of work. I *will* give them a lot of credit for attempting such a non-mainstream idea in the first place.

THE WORM EATERS

HERB ROBINS 1977. Now here's a film with a no-nonsense title. Produced by T.V. Mikels (the infamous director of **The Corpse Grinders** and **The Astro-Zombies**), this 'comedy' is one rancid hunk of celluloid, but at least it doesn't cop out on its title. There's no real gore, violence or sex – just a bunch of inept local actors making complete asses out of themselves. The movie starts off with the cheery jingle, "Nobody likes me, Everybody hates me, Guess I'll go eat worms", and from there begins its downhill plunge into schlock-film oblivion. The plot focuses on Herman Umgar, a crazy old hermit with an outrageous German accent, who communicates with his pet worms. But when Mayor Melnick and the town council decide to run him off his property, he takes his revenge by putting worms in everybody's food. These are very special worms, though, and instead of simply vomiting up their lunch, when the townies stop chomping on a mouthful of warm

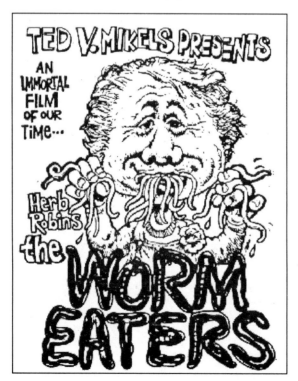

wigglies they turn into *worm-monsters*! (There's some hokey ex-planation, about mutant worms of the Red Tide, but then again, does it really matter?) Actually, they look like they slipped into waist-high, plastic worm-suits, sprayed themselves with shaving cream, and rolled on the floor in a spastic fit. And before you can hit the Fast Forward button, Herman has a harem of worm-women caged in the basement, the town council is in ruins, and in the hilarious climax, Herman is 'fish-hooked' and dragged into the lake by the rebellious worm-men. The acting and production values are at the porn film level, and the dialogue consists of such quips as "I'll rip your tongue out at the roots and slap ya silly with it". The soundtrack is teeth-clenchingly bad '60s electronic squawking and screeching... So what's good with the film? Well, it *does* have lots of worm-eating scenes. They're chewed up in spaghetti, ice cream, hot dogs, and in my favourite scene, they come crawling out of a little girl's birthday cake. In juicy close-up, we get to watch the actors (?) gnashing their jaws as live worms crawl between their teeth, trying carefully not to chew too hard and bite them in half. These 'highlights' are numerous, long, and pretty much pointless – the only humour is when two brainless gals can't keep a straight face as they're turned into half-worm/half-bimbos. I don't want to make this movie too enjoyable sounding, though, because it's *really* painful to sit through. Watch it at your own risk.

THE X FROM OUTER SPACE

NAZUI NIHOMATSU 1967. This is a thoroughly sub-Toho rubber mon-sterama from Japan, complete with effects that make **The Starlost** look good, physics as piss poor as **The Black Hole**, and perform-ances as rancid as any Driver's Ed film. But it *does* give us one of the most idiotic (and consequently, funniest) city-stompers of all time... The story begins when a Japanese spaceship (populated by three oriental goofballs and an occidental, blond, blue-eyed bomb-shell – all decked out in **Lost in Space** hand-me-downs) is sent to Mars to investigate the disappearance of other rockets. There's a Moonbase, a pulsing UFO, lots of absurdly-dubbed scientists, a romantic triangle, and always the promise of sudden *thrills*! But the best advice is to set your alarm clock, because there's no sign of excitement (let alone a monster) for over 45 minutes! Then it gets royally STOOOPID! You see, these space-nitwits bring back a radio-active rock with a 60 watt light bulb inside, making it glow. Turns out the rock has a life of its own, soon escapes, grows to enor-mous proportions, and amidst a flurry of July 4th sparklers, the monster Guilala erupts from a hillside! Coincidentally, just like Godzilla, Guilala has atomic breath, a dislike for Tokyo high-rises, an appetite for energy, and – OK, I'll cop to it! – Guilala is basically a below par rip-off of Godzilla, though with a beak and wiggly antennae. A waddling lump of laughter that bleeds shaving cream, melts into a puddle at the end, and is (next to Gamera) the silliest conceived Japanese creation *ever*! While the goofy Guilala's on his 'rampage', the movie's amazing! But while most of Tokyo catches fire, the film's overall pace never does, since director Nazui Ni-homatsu keeps cutting away from the fun in order to return to the Aurora model kit rocket, which is on a mission to find the only element that can stop the destructive chicken-creature (aptly named Guilalium). Zzzzzz... Tedium galore, but you gotta love that monster (during his whole 10 minutes of screen time). Starring Toshiya Wazaki and Peggy Neal.

A ZED AND TWO NOUGHTS

PETER GREENAWAY 1985. Pacific Arts (Mike Nesmith's outfit) gets the prize, 'Video Distributor With A Brain' for their noble rescue of Peter Greenaway's superior **ZOO** from seafood obscurity. Made in '85, this follow-up to the success of **The Draughtsman's Contract** dispenses with standard formulas entirely and ends up a twisted hybrid of Buñuel, The Bonzos and educational films, all processed through the analytical mind of Greenaway. The 'story' concerns a car accident (a swan crashes through the windshield) which takes the lives of two women, wives of twin brothers (Brian and Eric Deacon). The driver, poor Alba Bewick (Andrea Ferreol) loses a leg in the crash, but soon finds herself working to console the grieving brothers. The twin brothers both react differently to their tragedy. One becomes obsessed with decay, wishing to understand how things decompose and why, and takes to time lapse photography to study this further. The other becomes more self-destructive, sitting for days in a screening room watching documentaries (God! No!), chewing on broken glass, the usual. Both brothers begin seeing Venus DeMilo (Frances Barber), whom we first see trading her sexual favours for a calf's liver and a bath (what a bargain!). Does this sound weird? Does this sound obtuse? Of course it is, you silly. But just when you're shaking your head in confusion, Greenaway hits you with a breathtaking shot and Michael Nyman's amazing score kicks in. Needless to say, for the brave seafood adventurer with a taste for perverse pretension painstakingly plotted, **ZOO** is wild kicks, baby. [TR]

ZOMBIE HOLOCAUST

FRANK MARTIN 1979 (US: DOCTOR BUTCHER MD [MEDICAL DEVIATE]). Consummate businessman Terry Levene sliced together two different, unreleased slaughter-fests (**Queen of the Cannibals** and **Tales that will Rip your Heart Out**), dubbed in a storyline that connected the two, gave his concoction a *great* publicity campaign, and poured it into grindhouses and drive-ins across the country. As you can guess, it promised a lot, delivered a little, and proved that any good entrepreneur can make a quick buck in the sleazepix trade. Sure, there's plenty of intestines and ripped flesh on the screen, but that doesn't mean it's a particularly good film. Uncritical gorehounds will enjoy it, but personally, I think **Zombie Holocaust** is a pretty lethargic example of the cannibal-ville chunk-blower... It starts off cheesy enough, with a 15-minute prologue set in a stateside hospital. There's a psychopathic weirdo on the loose, chopping out chunks of available human bodies for a quick midnight snack. A hand here, a heart there, what's the big fuss? Well, it turns out a hospital attendant is to blame, and for some dumb reason the government sends an expedition to the guy's native home (a small Pacific island) to investigate... Suddenly, the second movie clicks in, and a group of obviously-European actors arrive at the island, running smack into the Sect of Keto – the most boring bunch of scummy cannibals you'll ever want to avoid. There's no suspense, no style, no characterisation, but plenty of maggot-covered rotting heads and half-eaten corpses. Not only do we get these babbling tribesmen scampering about the jungle looking for white-man red-meat, but there's *also* a few zombies on the loose (what a coincidence!) – escapees from the island physician's operating room. Yes, you guessed it! Here's Dr. Butcher! Donald O'Brian stars as Marcus Welby's evil brother, and he's the type of caring, sympathetic guy who quiets his patients by ripping out their vocal chords. The Doc is searching for the mysteries of life and death (not *another* one?), transplanting fresh brains into long-dead corpses and coming up with slow-witted rejects from a Lucio Fulci casting call... Alexandra Cole is also onboard to strip to her undies every few minutes in an effort to prove she's the Bo Derek of shitty gore films; plus we're given the standard dose of ripped-out eyeballs, a head sliced apart by an outboard-motor, scalpings, and disembowellings. But after a while you realise that this is pretty stale material from the **Friday the 13th** School of Moviemaking: 10 minutes of cheapshit drama, punctuated by 15 seconds of intense (albeit hokey) gore... Frank Martin (Marino Girolami) is credited as director and Ian McCulloch stars as the head Anglo-idiot, but the only person who makes any impression whatsoever is Donald O'Brian, who snarls and spits his way into Actors Equity with lines

like "I am determined to have your BRAIN!"... Despite sporadic moments of hardcore bloodshed, this it nowhere near as imaginative as other recent Italo-Zombie entries. Disappointing.

ZONTAR, THE THING FROM VENUS

LARRY BUCHANAN 1966. Just what the world needs: A virtual scene-for-scene remake of Rog Corman's **It Conquered the World**! The only big difference is that this one's in colour (and believe it or not, it might have been even *cheaper* to film)... I've applauded the careers of such slop-artists as Herschell Gordon Lewis, Ed Wood Jr. and Al Adamson, but all these fellows look like Eisenstein when compared to Larry Buchanan – who not only had no discernible talent behind the camera, but this bozo couldn't even come up with a halfway original concept. Some men are born to make motion pictures – after watching **Zontar**, you'll see Buchanan was born to sell vacuum cleaners... John Agar stars as Dr. Kurt Taylor, a scientist working on a laser satellite project, while lab pal Deith (Anthony Houston) has been secretly contacting the planet Venus with his radio set. Of course, Agar doesn't believe one word of his assistant's ravings – that is, until the government satellite is absconded from the sky by an alien presence, who uses it to arrive on Earth. Enter Zontar, an unseen visitor who promises to save the human race from itself (we've all heard *that* one before), but who actually wants to subjugate us puny earthlings. First Zontar shuts down all the world's mechanical devices – clocks, cars, lights, and even running water trickles to a halt. Then he sends out his 'injectapods' (aka furry, winged, lobster-bugs), which attacks humans and renders their minds utterly controllable (much in the way watching too much Christian Broadcasting can do), while Zontar sits in a dark, steamy cave that approximates the environment of Venus. One small question: If this thing has 'an intellect that dwarves humans', why doesn't he just buy a sauna?... Keep those No-Doz handy though, because you won't want to miss the last five minutes, when Zontar finally appears sporting a creature suit that looks like it was cobbled together by a 3rd Grade art class. He's a bat-winged, three-eyed, papier-mâché mess, splattered with various colours. Almost as laughable is the experimental laser gun which does in the goober (when it's fired, the screen goes negative!), but this sequence only lasts about 10 seconds, so don't run to the toilet or you'll miss out on the 'climactic showdown'... John Agar takes on the old Peter Graves role from the '56 original, and he's *almost* as fine an actor (is that a complement?). As usual, he's at his finest when at the end of his rope and half-crazed, because as any B-movie fan knows, no one bites the backdrop like John Agar! What a career! From being the first man to fuck Shirley Temple to this late-show abomination! As for the rest of the cast, you've heard of Method Acting? Well, this film has Methadone Acting... Have you gotten my point yet? This is one dumb movie! Second, no, *third*-rate in every imaginable way! One of the ultimate no-budget, churn-it-out-in-a-week products! In other words, it's a solid *must see* for hardcore psychotronic idiots (like me).

biker movies

'BIG MEN WITH THROBBING MACHINES!'... 'Hot Steel Between Their Legs!'... 'Mad Dogs From Hell!'... Remember those classic ad-lines from the past? And remember when characters had names like Angel, Gangrene, Dirty Denny, Speed, Joint, Firewater, Acid, and Lizard? Yes, I'm talking about the grand old days of the biker movie, when cycle gangs ruled America's drive-ins with their hard-driving, beer-swilling, leather-coated tales of rebellion and violence, and the movie-going public flocked to watch them break society's rules.

Though the genre didn't reach its zenith until the late '60s, the biker flick officially began as far back as 1953, when producer Stanley Kramer tossed Marlon Brando onto a cycle and had him terrorise a small town in **The Wild One**. It was an inexpensive little drama, but Brando's charisma, combined with audience curiosity about these 'gypsy riders', helped make it a box-office hit. The premise was based on true incidents that occurred in Hollister and Riverside, California in the late 1940s, when hundreds of motorcyclists invaded the peaceful communities over successive 4th of July weekends. Brando starred as Johnny, the brooding punk who leads his pack of rebels into Small Town USA for a rumble party at the expense of the law-abiding citizens. Lee Marvin sputters away as Evil Incarnate, and it's all quite intense for its time, but unfortunately the film cops out with a conclusion that has Brando repenting his wild ways. Nevertheless, it helped solidify the image of the Cycle Rebel, and for years to come that image would remain a favourite with young audiences.

From then on, these cycle-jockeys became recurring features in low-rent flicks, usually as hackneyed antagonists in teenage tales. Juvenile delinquent dramas such as **One-Way Ticket to Hell**, **Dragstrip Riot**, and **Motorcycle Gang** exploited the public's interest in order to make heavy-handed moral statements; the Frankie Avalon and Annette Funicello beach movies from the early '60s used them for comic relief (with Harvey Lembeck as Eric Von Zipper) and even **Horror of Party Beach** incorporated them briefly into the monster-on-the-loose shenanigans.

Leave it to Russ Meyer, king of the D-cups, to peg the oncoming genre before anyone else with his **Motor Psycho** ('65). This chopper cretins tale comes off more like a male-dominated precursor to **Faster Pussycat! Kill! Kill!** in terms of style and attitude – featuring a trio of greasy motorcyclists who accost the pneumatic girlfriend of a macho cowboy veterinarian (Alex Rocco). It culminates with all of Meyer's usual high-octane hysterics. The head of the bikers has Nam flashbacks, Rocco is in a fever dream from a rattler bite, and the characters are high testosterone males & loose women in tight dresses. Complete with adrenalised editing, wild redneck dialogue, and actresses who will undoubtedly keep male moviegoers at attention, it's further proof that Russ rarely disappoints.

But by the mid-'60s, one segment of these gangs began to monopolise the headlines: The Hell's Angels, who were quickly becoming the nation's most notorious biker club. Underground filmmaker Kenneth Anger took a giant step in mythologising their lifestyle in his short, quasi-documentary **Scorpio Rising** ('62-'64). Anger skilfully combined motorcycle gang footage with pop songs ('I Will Follow Him', 'Blue Velvet') in order to make savagely critical comments on a culture that had 'turned in on itself and begun to rot'. Close-ups of buckled leather and revving engines accompanied the 'rituals' of readying the bikes and dressing for battle. Intercutting clips of Brando, Dean and Jesus Christ (taken from a cheapjack Sunday School movie), Anger accentuated the violence, the idolatry and homo-erotic nature of their fellowship, while creating one of his most accessible works.

And in early 1965, **The Nation** printed a true tale of The Hell's Angels, that continued to turn them into curdled pop heroes. A young Hunter S. Thompson had ridden with them and soon after put their story into mass circulation, and when his book **Hell's Angels – The Strange and Terrible Saga of the Outlaw Motorcycle Gangs** was released, it only encouraged the public to want more. All that was needed was someone in the motion picture business to capitalise upon it... Enter Roger Corman!

The breakthrough for Motorcycle Pix came in 1966, when American-International Pictures released Corman's latest epic **The Wild Angels**, which purported to tell the true story of that era's gangs. The film was immediately dismissed by film critics as violent rubbish, but it nevertheless hit box-office gold and is to this day the best biker film ever made. Period.

From the first scene on, it's nasty, grim and thoroughly amoral entertainment, with only one redeeming message, stated by its star, Peter Fonda – "We want to be free to ride our machines without being hassled by The Man. And we want to get *loaded*!" Fonda heads the leather and swastika bunch as Heavenly Blues, and his societal misfits and outcasts spend the first half of the film rumbling with a bunch of 'taco benders', kicking the shit out of some local rednecks, punching out a nurse, and defying authority in every form. The movie culminates with a funeral for Fonda's dead pal, Loser (wonderfully played by the ever-snarling Bruce Dern). Amidst the cheap wine and bongo drumming, the funeral service turns into a riot, with the Angels wrecking the church, raping the widow, propping up the corpse in a corner with a joint in his mouth, and then karate chopping the preacher and tossing him into the empty casket. Fonda (who took over the lead at the last minute, after George Chakiris refused to actually ride a chopper) looks cool throughout; Dern is appropriately scuzzballish ("Do you want anything?" he's asked after getting shot by a cop. "Yeah, I just want to get high"); and Nancy Sinatra is around, only to prove that she can't act worth beans either. To all this repulsive behaviour, add an exuberant score, slick direction (with assistance from novice Peter Bogdanovich) and a deep, nihilistic conclusion – and the result was true heaven for trash fanatics!

In retrospect, the aspect that made the film unique is that all the proceedings are seen through the Angels' sensibilities. There was no outsider thrown in to counterpoint their actions, and the result was an honest and brutal vision of their life. Lensed under the title **All the Fallen Angels**, director Corman and scriptwriter Charles B. Griffith pulled out all the stops and sent the viewer on a whirlwind tour of mindless thrills and underlying social commentary (with all of the film's incidents based on fact, they stressed). The movie went on to break AIP box-office records, and the greatest irony occurred when it opened the 1966 Venice Film Festival as the sole American entry. The other thing **The Wild Angels** opened was the floodgates for cycle films of all makes and models, with every unknown actor in Hollywood trying to ride to anti-hero stardom. Their ad campaigns were lurid, their thrills crude, and for exploitation fans it was celluloid nirvana, because these films pushed the limits for sex, violence, and cruelty, while promoting disharmony with mainstream society.

Director Richard Rush soon became the top contender for the title of Bikerama Auteur. With his double blast of **Hell's Angels on Wheels** ('67) and **The Savage Seven** ('68), Rush gave a modicum of class to the new genre, and like Corman he knew better than to simply shovel his slobbering audiences 90 minutes of drinking, farting and fighting. Both his features contained solid casts of B-actors, dazzling camerawork by Laszlo Kovacs, and a continuation of the Misunderstood Rebel school of characterisation.

Hell's Angels on Wheels was the first worthy follow-up to Corman's classic, and it was even endorsed by the Hell's Angels of California (with their leader, Sonny Barger, making a quick cameo). It's a gritty and semi-realistic portrayal of Angel activities, with Rush regular Adam Roarke as their leader, Buddy. The picture picks up a storyline (albeit a thin one) when Jack Nicholson enters the scene as a gas station attendant named Poet, who gets a first-hand glimpse of their rowdy techniques and decides to join them on the road. After he's contributed a few punches during a rumble in a go-go joint and shoved a guy's head down a toilet, Buddy reluctantly takes Poet into the group, and off they zoom to a beer-drenched, paint-in orgy. But since these guys don't fit into society's strict guidelines, they can't even go to an amusement park without being set upon by some drunken sailors. So, of course, they have no choice but to swab the midway with the sailors' carcasses. The proceedings slow down a bit when the filmmakers forcibly interject a flaccid love story between Jack and a female member named Shill (thus making Roarke jealous and setting up an internal gang conflict), and the film backfires slightly during the second half, but the flashy visuals and Nicholson's eccentric presence make this feature a stand out amongst the pack.

One year later, Rush continued his drive-in legacy with **The Savage Seven**, which again featured Roarke as a rebel head honcho, Kisum. This Dick Clark presentation (as was Rush's later Haight Ashbury epic **Psych-Out**) kept to a more solid storyline (in other words, there was probably a script for this one), and though the end product was a little plastic in the 'recycled Hollywood plot' department, Rush's powerhouse direction kept the film top-notch, with the action and brutality just as brisk as ever. It begins when a bunch of bad-ass bikers take a tour in the desert and meet up with a village of American Indians who are being victimised by a fat-ass businessman and his in-pocket town sheriff. Even though the bikers aren't white-hatted heroes, they still hate seeing the underdog kicked around, so they play Robin Hood for a while, finally joining up with the Indians for a rowdy party and some routine head-bashings. There's hard-hitting dialogue like, "Hey, man! You just barfed on my broad!", but it tries for unnecessary sappiness when Roarke falls for a cute maiden. The end is cynically downbeat, when misunderstandings dissolve the group's friendships, and both bikers and Indians alike are slaughtered off by the shitheap white man. Recognisable folks like Robert Walker Jr. and Max Julien are also along for the ride.

While Rush was carefully adding to the anti-hero mythology of the biker breed, most of the other quick buck features seemed more interested in keeping chopper riders firmly entrenched in the villainous category (probably because it was easier to choreograph a punch than it was to create a solid characterisation). It was destruction for destruction's sake. Pour on the sadism and serve it up hot! The best of these entries captured three up-and-coming young actors scraping the bottom of the barrel in order to pay the rent. Most stars would normally drop these low-budgeters off their resumé, but since this trio consisted of John Cassavetes, Dennis Hopper and Bruce Dern, they're probably amused at the notion of these cheapies still turning up on the Late Show...

Even as he was jump starting his career as a director/actor, Cassavetes headed up **Devil's Angels** ('67), in which he played Cody, leader of the Skulls. They're on the road to Hole-In-The-Wall, a haven for cyclists, when they make the mistake of taking a pit stop and encountering some ever-suspicious locals who automatically brand them as Scum. Though Cody and his bunch aren't in the mood for a confrontation with the law, that attitude doesn't apply amongst outside gangs, who gleefully take to the once-peaceful town like a piranha to fresh meat. The film's highlight sees hundreds of riders destroy the place in one night's brutal frivolity. Sure, it's all a bit derivative, but director Daniel Haller and **Wild Angels** writer Charles Griffith pump up the action at every chance – though it's too bad they put a moralistic damper on the fun by having Cody realise the error of his ways, and at the end he rides off with a tear in his eye! It's the type of false ending that elicits more jeers than sympathy from an audience.

Dennis Hopper graced **The Glory Stompers** ('67) with what little worth it deserves. Darryl, the leader of The Glory Stompers (a not-so-evil gang) and his sensitive girlfriend are first seen walking through the woods, discussing life, love and freedom. But before you get a chance to nod off, in roar Dennis and his grunting hoard, the Black Souls. They chainwhip the guy, kidnap the girl, and set out to sell her to 'high class' Mexican white slavers. It's slow going, despite the presence of an always welcome love-in, until the inevitable bloodshed at the end, when Darryl and his Stompers reappear. One guy gets run over by a chopper, and Dennis puts his vast method acting experience to the test when he has to freak out and bury six slugs at close range in a rival biker. It's okay mayhem, but the Hop is the main reason to check this one out. Even when he's got a switchblade stuck in the back of his neck, Hopper is by far the liveliest of the cast. Inept direction by Anthony Lanza is the main culprit for this movie never kicking out of first gear.

And in **The Cycle Savages** ('69), Bruce Dern got to chew his way through one of the most wholeheartedly vicious of the lot, in addition to having one of the most ludicrous story concepts. He stars as Keeg. an unshaven gang leader who also has a hand in a prostitution ring out of Las Vegas. By this time, Dern could wander through this type of paranoid sicko role in his sleep, but he really gets to show off his psycho stuff when a local clean-cut artist begins making indiscriminate sketches of him and his gang. Bruce and his guys tear up his drawings, slash his hands, and still the artist won't give in, so they end up crushing his hands in a vice. But first they kidnap a high school girl with the intention of selling her off as a whore, and she plays an unwilling hostess at a booze, LSD and gang rape party. The results are a little uneven, with a tendency to moralise (despite the grimy subject matter and the lurid portrayal of it), but it's certainly one of the more watchable and masochistically entertaining of the bikeramas.

In addition to these memorable productions, dozens of other low-budget endeavours flooded outdoor screens and 42nd Street grindhouses. Chopper flicks were proven money makers, and all you needed were a few unwashed actors, some Harleys, and a camera full of film stock. Well, maybe it wasn't *that* easy, but you couldn't tell by looking at some of the lesser entries. Though the storylines remained essentially the same – gang terrorises one or more average citizens – the final film ranged anywhere from Excitingly Sleazy to Unwatchably Tedious.

The Born Losers ('67) was a down and dirty little tale that emerged at the beginning of motorcycle mania. Directed, written by and starring Tom Laughlin (under several different pseudonyms), this was an undemanding little actioner that firmly took the side of law and order. Led by Jeremy Slate, a gang enters a California town and immediately has a wild party in a deserted church, where they rape four teenage girls. The law's hands are tied because no one has the guts to testify against the hoodlums. But half-breed Billy Jack (yes, the same character who stunk up the '70s with vigilante tripe like **Billy Jack**, **The Trial of Billy Jack**, and **Billy Jack Goes to Washington**) comes out of the hills and vows revenge, eventually filling the gang's leader with lead. The funniest part of it is that even though the film tries to speak out against senseless violence, it sure does wallow in it, with some of the more ruthless sequences to hit a cycle flick.

A good cast headed **The Rebel Rousers** (Martin B. Cohen, '67), but they weren't really given much to do. Bruce Dern, Jack Nicholson, and Harry Dean Stanton are members of the title gang, and Jack (as Bunny) wins the All-Time Flashiest Dresser Award for tooling around in a wool cap, dark glasses and black-and-white horizontal striped pants that'll scorch the lids off your eye sockets. So far so good, but the entire film goes off course when Cameron Mitchell enters the scene as the heroic love interest (talk about a casting mishap!). The gooey love story between Cam and Diane Ladd (co-star of **The Wild Angels**, but this time playing a Good Girl) goes on interminably, but Jack rescues the film by kicking Cam's ass and kidnapping his knocked-up girlfriend. There's a boring cycle race at the end to see who gets to pork Ms. Ladd (*noblesse oblige*, indeed), but justice once again prevails. Overall, a wasted opportunity – done in by mediocre direction and far too much moralising from the whole cast.

Angels From Hell (Bruce Kessler, '68) might well constitute one of the dimmest of them all. It's ultra-cheap and grainy, with hack non-direction and more clichés than you can count; but it's so wrong-headed it's strangely enjoyable in a pathetic Badfilm sort of way... To the strains of 'No Communication' (sung by The Peanut Butter Conspiracy), we meet the Madcaps and their cop-hating, Vietnam-vet leader, Mike (Tom Stern). They just want to 'ride into the sunset, with bugs in their teeth', but first they have to party, smoke some weed, abuse their rivals, and spout dated dialogue like "It's a gas" or "Blow your mind". The violence is up-front and blunt (such as when Mike blithely snaps a competitor's leg), plus there are some hilarious sidelines, such as when the entire gang visits an old pal, who's now a Hollywood leading man with a swanky pad, or when they team up with some easy-going flower children who look more like a cut-rate Renaissance Faire. It ends with a showdown against Authority (the local sheriff) when Mike goes off-the-edge psychotic, but it's all too silly to even criticise. A true gut-buster.

Amidst the avalanche of low-rent chopper-dramas, **Hell's Belles** ('69) was one of the more watchable. The flat direction by Maury Dexter (**Maryjane**) gives the film all the visual innovation of a TV series, but a capable cast and good stuntwork add some flash. Jeremy Slate returns to the genre, this time as a good-natured cowboy who's out to retrieve a prize motorcycle that's been stolen by dirtball cyclist Adam Roarke. But instead of getting his bike back, all Jeremy gets is a two-by-four to the gut and possession of Roarke's discarded highway hussy, Jocelyn Lane – a steamy brunette in a black leather mini-skin, who whines incessantly. After a gas-station torching and other criminal hi-jinx from the cycle troupe, Jeremy locates them in the middle of the Arizona desert where he picks them off one by one using his survivalist savvy. Ms. Lane is appropriately sultry with her tight-knit wardrobe. Roarke is fine (as usual) playing the shitheel prez. Slate is somewhat dorky as the lantern-jawed hero, and even Angelique Pettyjohn (**The Mad Doctor of Blood Island**, etc.) is aboard as a cycle slut. It's all lightweight, though consistently enjoyable fare.

The biker flick took a slightly different twist with **Hell's Angels '69** (Lee Madden), the Angels taking a more peripheral role in the proceedings. Jeremy Slate and Tom Stern star as a pair of playboy brothers who decide to rob Caesar's Palace in Las Vegas as a lark, and their plan is to infiltrate the infamous biker gang and use them as a backdrop for their heist. With laughable ease they're welcomed into the membership and pull off their crime, but when the Angels learn they've been duped by a couple of clean-cut shitheads, they take off in retaliation. Conny Van Dyke stars as the motorcycle mam who wants to share in the pair's loot, and for her effort she's left to die in the desert. It's pretty unbelievable stuff, but it's fast-paced fluff and at least story-writers Slate and Stern *tried* to concoct a unique idea with some cross-market potential. The seams don't hold together all the time, but it's easily-digested pabulum with some good chuckles and a satisfying conclusion. Plus, it's always nice to see Sonny Barger and his Oakland contingent getting some on-camera exposure again.

Las Vegas was also the backdrop for some of **Naked Angels** ('69), which distinguished itself solely by having more bare skin and less story than any other biker flick. The film revolves around the Angels' attempt to locate a rival gang who put their shaggy-haired leader, Mother (Michael Greene) in hospital after their last encounter. These are the type of guys who spit into each other's beer to prove brotherhood, and Mother is so cool he likes to mellow out between head-bashings by playing the recorder. I can't report that much happens during its 90 minutes, though – they tool through Vegas, swig back some warm brews, give an old shopkeeper a heart-attack, and it ends with internal strife amongst the Angels over whether to follow their certifiably psycho chief. And every chance they get their female travelling companions strip off their clothes and flaunt their wares (complete with a 'Property of the Angels' tattoo on their butts). Bruce Clark's direction is slick, using a photo-montage during one chase sequence, and letting loose with a laughable sunstroke hallucination that has Mother running down the road with no pants on. Uneven, but quite interesting in spots.

Other memorable additions included **Wild Rebels** (William Grefe, '67), with an undercover agent joining a bunch of bank-robbing chopper-jockeys; **Wild Wheels** (Kent Osborne, '69), where bikers invade Pismo beach and battle with dune buggy riders; and **Hell's Chosen Few** ('68), from David Hewitt, responsible for the stunningly bad **The Mighty Gorgo**, with a drunken sheriff who implicates a motorcycle gang in a murder the cop actually committed. And would you believe they were even *less* exciting than they sound?

One interesting aberration of this generally male-dominated series was the occasional female gang flick. After being manhandled through dozens of pictures by their misogynist beaus, the distaff side of the coin began to emerge in a few isolated instances. The most popular of them still remains **She-Devils on Wheels** ('68) in which Herschell Gordon Lewis turned the entire genre on its pimply ass by introducing an all-female gang of killers called

The Man Eaters. "You treat men like they were slabs of meat," the gang's leader, Queenie, is told, and she defiantly tries to uphold this noble tradition. There's a race to see who gets first dibs on the local pack of studs; the blond virgin, Honeypot, is put through an initiation involving chocolate syrup and a gang-bang by the entire male population of In-Bred County; and they end up dragging a rival male along the road until his face looks like a plate of lasagne. Wholesome entertainment indeed, including one of the neatest roadside deceptions of its time. It's all as godawfully amateurish as you'd expect from Lewis, plus it co-stars several members of Miami's female cut-throat division of the Iron Cross Cycle Club, who give it a smattering of reality.

The complete antithesis of **She Devils** was released the same month, and in **The Mini-Skirt Mob** (Maury Dexter again) we're given a slick, unthreatening treatment of femmes-on-bikes. Diane McBain is the leader of the Mini-Skirts, a pack of lasses who look like they spend more money on hairspray than they do their cycles. The story involves McBain's efforts to terrorise her rodeo star ex-boyfriend, who dumped her in order to marry a 'nice' girl. Well, with Jeremy Slate on hand as her male flunky, and Harry Dean Stanton as the continually zoned-out Spook, they strand the honeymooners in the desert and go to work. McBain should have the word BITCH stencilled on her forehead in fluorescent lipstick, but it's still annoyingly unbelievable when her minions mindlessly follow her every vengeful order. You'll be glad when she finally gets tossed off a cliff, and this tame endeavour comes to an end. It's a limp little yarn with the leggy ladies providing the only box-office incentive.

Even more excruciating exercises in feminine fiendishness included the stridently moralistic **The Hellcats** (Robert E Slatzer, '68), in which a determined young do-gooder sets out to avenge the death of his brother at the hands of the eponymous characters. But The Hellcats turn out to be one-dimensional dames who smuggle drugs across the border, and the entire movie avoids any type of raunchiness by cutting away at the first possible moment... And **Sister in Leather** ('69) certainly beefed up the sleaze quotient, but it was still a technical nightmare, focusing on a gang of lesbian moto-chicks who blackmail a married businessman and then initiate his wife into their clan. There's nude riding, a champagne orgy, and a male entourage of cyclists who finally put an end to their 'fun'. Both of these were one-week-only fodder, in the worst sense of the term. Without much merit, even in the realms of mindless trash.

But while it seemed every indie studio was trying to churn out any concept featuring a Harley (no matter how insipid) three guys who had to endure acting in them went out on their own and made the ultimate road movie/cycle drama of all time, and it still endures as one of the most timely, perceptive films of its era. That's right, **Easy Rider!** It hit the Cannes Film Festival in 1969 and went on to become the highest grossing independently produced film of its time, with biker vets Dennis Hopper, Peter Fonda and Jack Nicholson deserving most of the credit for forging the chopper trappings with counterculture sensibilities, and creating this breakthrough production. Now, I could spend pages on **Easy Rider** – its cross-over potential, layers of meaning, how it shook up the entire motion picture industry – but while this masterpiece is clearly the culmination of all biker films, it stands apart from them as a genuinely unique achievement. And after its release (and along with **Gimme Shelter**, which gave the public a real glimpse into the way **Hell's Angels** operate – including an on-screen stabbing), the entire genre would never be the same. Everything else looked so shoddy in comparison, so studios tried (not very successfully) to realign their chopperamas with the changing times – breaking out of their stagnant mould with new stars, half-baked ideas or a simple increase in the sadism and sickness levels.

A few films tried to repeat the same chords that **Easy Rider** struck, by combining bikers with flower children, but the results were usually one-dimensional and always unintentionally hilarious. **Free Grass** (aka **Scream Free!**) ('69), reunited the stars of **West Side Story**, Richard Beymer and Russ Tamblyn (whether we wanted to see them back together or not). Hippie Beymer and his girlfriend need extra cash, so they link up with Tamblyn's gang and smuggle grass across the border. But Beymer turns out to have too many scruples for this line of work (such as objecting to killing cops), so Tamblyn spikes his drink with LSD. Luckily, the cops show up in time to murder all the bikers, and Beymer gives away all the marijuana to his hippie pals (hence the title). Directed by Bill Brame (**The Cycle Savages**), this whole show is one long howl. **Angel Unchained** (Lee Madden, '70) starred Don Stroud as a retired cycle pack leader who gives up his roadside escapades for the peaceful life of commune living with hippie Tyne Daly. But the crew-cut townspeople don't like the weirdo peaceniks in their community, and when they try to scare them away with their dune buggies, Stroud enlists his old gang to aid in a free-for-all slaughter. It's fast-paced, though a bit on the tame side. The same doesn't apply to **The Peace Killers** (Douglas Schwartz, '71), which gleefully mixed preachy dramatics with sewer-level violence, and featured a pack of monosyllabic Neanderthals on choppers named Death Row. When these dirtbags discover one of their runaway women has joined a hippie commune, they decide to steal her back. Eventually commune member Michael Ontkean convinces the rest of the non-violent residents to pick up pitchforks and fight back. Surprisingly bloodthirsty, hideously dated, and not half bad either.

But if the public thought that Angels pictures were silly enough already, I haven't even reached the most ludicrous, pathetic and brain-numbingly implausible of them all. Yes, it's **C.C. and Company** (Seymour Robbie, '70) starring Joe Namath and Ann-Margret! 'Broadway Joe' is that 'rarity in biker pics – an honest, upstanding biker, who saves fashion photographer Ann-Margret from a gang rape when her limo breaks down in the wilderness. As a member of The Heads, Namath is flat, pompous and impossible *not* to laugh out loud at; and Ann-Margret is perfectly dim-witted enough to play the camera-bug, but her glitzy, pop character doesn't belong in a hard-boiled cycle drama – she should be in an Elvis Presley vehicle, like **Clambake**. Before you can say 'Bullshit', Joe falls in love with Ann, they enjoy a roll in the hay at a classy Las Vegas hotel, and then he takes on the ornery leader of his old gang. It's all so dumb that you can't help but enjoy a disaster of this proportion (just so long as you can stomach Namath's so-called acting for 90 minutes). The good supporting cast includes Sid Haig and Bruce Glover, but the major reason to check out this anti-gem is to watch William Smith tearing up the screen as The Heads' leader, Moon.

And it's about time to mention William Smith, who is the one unequivocal King of the Biker Movies! He only starred in a handful, but his presence always guaranteed a no-nonsense honesty and strength that no other actor brought to the series. Best remembered for horror mini-classics like **Grave of the Vampire** and **Invasion of the Bee Girls**, Smith was the embodiment of the cycle mythos. He was big, he was tough, and he usually had a bit of brainpower on display. He was the Deluxe Brand Anti-Hero, and even if her never achieved the mass market stardom he deserved, when he stomped his Harley to life, he was unequalled!

His first excursion into the biker world was in **Run, Angel, Run** ('69). Playing Angel, a member of the Devil's Advocates, Smith decides to cash in on his connections and sells his behind-the-scenes story to a magazine for 10 grand. He then high-tails it to safety with his girlfriend, and while hiding out on a sheep farm owned by an ex-biker, he begins to enjoy his new, law-abiding lifestyle. But, as you can imagine, his old mates quickly locate him. Smith was a charismatic lead, and even if the script was a bit preachy about making choices between Right and Wrong, director Jack Starrett kept the action flowing in low-key, non-grimy fashion. Plus, Margaret Markov (**Arena, Black Mama, White Mama**) has a solid supporting role as an abused teenager.

Smith continued to prove his merit in director Starrett's next feature, **The Losers** ('70), a flick that had more potential than any other low-rent biker product. Its premise was sheer dynamite: set during the height of the Vietnam war, a pack of bikers are secretly recruited by the US to wage their own little battle campaign into Cambodia and rescue a CIA advisor who's been captured by the Red Chinese. Wow! The mind reels at the possibilities! 'Hell's Angels vs. the VC' with William Smith as Col. Kurtz! Well, it all starts off satisfyingly enough, with armour-plated, machine gun-mounted dirt bikes, but it shifts gears and shuts down midway through, when Hollywood-style romantic interludes intrude on the carnage (such as when cycloid Adam Roarke is reunited with his lost love). This nonsense takes up half the film, but luckily, the explosive finale shakes the lethargy out of the limp script, and there's a crushing, anti-US government epilogue that will leave a wonderfully cynical taste in your mouth. **The Losers** is all the more disappointing because with a bit more care it could have been an all time classic.

In **Angels Die Hard** (Richard Compton, '70), Smith played Gentleman Tim, the second-in-command of a pack of rowdy MC hooligans who follow all the clichés by invading a sleepy little California town. After a few brawls, some run-ins with the belligerent sheriff, and the sexual molestation of a barkeep's wife (covering her naked body with spaghetti), these bikers prove their worth by saving a little boy who's trapped in a mine cave-in. But even that bit of heroics doesn't stop most of them from receiving the **Easy Rider** treatment during the finale. Smith is the only character with an IQ higher than that of motor oil, and Tom Baker is their hip leader who writes El Stinko poetry. One of my all-time favourite sequences is the funeral for a fallen comrade during which the bikers take the surprisingly willing funeral home director (Alan DeWitt) on a tour of rebellion, mindless violence and first-hand drug experimentation. It's a good little drive-in exploiter, in addition to being one of Roger Corman's first productions for New World Pictures.

Smith's next cycle riding experience came in the unexceptional **Chrome and Hot Leather** (Lee Frost, '71), and by then you could see that studios were stretching for new ideas and coming up virtually empty. When a Green Beret's fiancé is killed by a psychotic biker, he and a trio of khaki buddies (including Marvin Gaye in his first film role) grab some Kawasakis and pose as roadscum in an effort to find the killer. Smith is T.J., the president of The Devils (and by now he could phone in his performance), stealing every scene with a sneer, a flexed muscle, or a perfect line of dialogue – at one point he asks his comrades to quiet down because "Can't you see we're menacing someone". For a bloodless finale, the Berets requisition some rocket launchers and end up karate chopping their way through several dozen bikers before leading them all to jail.

Smith's final leap into the genre was one of his most intriguing projects, which he not only starred in, but also co-scripted and co-produced. **Hollywood Man** (aka **Death Threat**, **No One Cries Forever**) ('76) gives us Smith as Rafe Stoker, a B-movie actor who has the itch to direct his own biker movie for a change. Unfortunately, the Mob wants to sabotage his no-budget production, recruiting a few real bikers and a psycho hitman to keep Smith behind schedule. This feels like a true labour of love on Smith's behalf, from its winning behind-the-scenes structure (making it **The Stuntman** of dime-store exploitation pics) to its bummer denouement. And even though Smith stays restrained for much of the movie, he spends the finale kicking some long overdue ass. Complete with able support from Mary Woronov as Smith's very personal assistant, Don Stroud as a cocky stuntman, and director Jack Starrett behind the camera, this was a cool, self-reflexive twist on a then-deathbed genre. Though he never became a household name, Smith still remains a favourite amongst action cognoscenti, with appearances in **The Ultimate Warrior**, **Rumble Fish**, the TV mini-series **Rich Man, Poor Man**, and **Maniac Cop**.

Never one to miss an opportunity to make a quick buck off a passing fad, Al Adamson took a few shots at the cycle flick, grinding them out through Independent-Intentional Pictures. His first attempt, **Satan's Sadists** ('69), was without a doubt one of the sleazier efforts to flash across the screen. It was pure mindrot — technically crude and morally reprehensible, but for those very reasons it's now considered a Dirtball Classic of sorts. It looks like Al simply gathered together a bunch of two-bit actors/friends, a few beat-up bikes, many gallons of beer, and just headed off into the desert one afternoon with a camera. A booze-bloated Russ Tamblyn stars as Anchor, leader of the titular goon squad. They mess with a Marine Corps vet, gang-bang a trio of college girls, dose their coffee with LSD, and generally prove to be the most objectionable scoundrels ever to straddle a cycle. Regina Carrol (Mrs Al) co-stars as 'The Freak-Out Girl', dancing around like a busty Nancy Sinatra on Spanish Fly. The only upbeat note about this Trash Fiend Delight is that very few of the unbelievable characters live to see the end credits. Al's follow-up was the indescribably incoherent **Hell's Bloody Devils** (aka **The Fakers**) ('70, though filmed in '67 as **Operation M**), which featured a loopy tale of neo-nazis led by a bozo named Count Von Delberg, Mafia kingpins, a biker pack with a president named Cunk, an Israeli undercover agent, and (are you sitting down?) Broderick Crawford in the starring role. It all comes down to a semi-insidious plan to flood the US with fake currency, but the result for audiences is barely watchable, even on a pathetic laffs level. Al's last outing into cycle sleaze was **Angels' Wild Women** ('72), with a quartet of top-heavy femmes taking on rapists, Satanists and any man who gets in their way. Once again, the ever-vacuous Regina Carrol took centre-stage, with Adamson regulars Kent Taylor and Vicki Volante providing support.

But by the early '70s, motorcycle mania had begun to wane, and the glut of pictures quickly decreased. Some independents tried to mix and match genres in order to buoy sagging grosses, but nothing much helped since none of their products were outstanding enough to lure back the disenchanted viewer. In 1971, both the US-lensed **Werewolves on Wheels** (Michel Levesque) and the British **Psychomania** (aka **The Death Wheelers**) (Don Sharp) added supernatural elements to their stories. In the first, devil-worshipping monks curse a pack of grubby motorcyclists with lycanthropy; and on the other side of the Atlantic, a gang known as The Living Dead use witchcraft and tree-frogs to become unstoppable ghouls on wheels. Neither fared well at the box-office, though the UK entry was quite good in itself.

And let's not forget the lacklustre efforts like **Angels Hard As They Come** ('71), a stultifying concoction from Joe Viola and Jonathan Demme, in which Scott Glenn and his hordes head to the town of Lost Cause (pretty symbolic, eh?), a western ghost town turned hippie refuge for every brain-damaged acid-geek in So. Cal. There they meet Gary Busey as a flower child, concoct some electric kool-aid, and engage in a boring rumble in the last minutes. **Black Angels** (Laurence Merrick, '70) was a timekiller featuring the first showdown between white and black motorcycle gangs — the only survivor being the even-slimier cop who set up the mutual massacre. After this, Merrick went on to co-direct the documentary **Manson**. Then there's **Bury Me an Angel** (Barbara Peeters, '72), with statuesque Dixie Peabody avenging the pre-credit death of her brother, while taking time out to bed down with Grizzly Adams (Dan Haggerty).

Without question, one of the genre's prominent debacles has to be **Devil Rider!** ('70), from director Brad F. Grinter, the misguided genius behind **Blood Freak** (the best Anti-Drug, Christian, Splatter Pic featuring a Killer Chicken-Man ever made!). Set in some Southern sinkhole, Sharon Mahon stars as a blonde teen who's dosed with "a little happiness bomb that'll turn your world all kinds of pretty colours" by a band of lowlife biker misfits who want to pull a train on her (and might leave her on the same career course as her runaway sis, who's now a hooker). These grubby dirtballs are good for a few drunken laughs, particularly when a pair of mamas get into a catfight and one dies, after which these compassionate guys ditch the corpse in some nearby quicksand. Populated by authentic white trash vermin and over-ripe dialogue, it's a must-see for fans of wretched drive-in swill.

Hard to believe, but **The Pink Angels** ('72) was even loopier, not to mention loads more entertaining. What else would expect from the first gay biker pic? This 'Hell's Angels in Heels' follows half a dozen limp-wristed bikers on a cross-country trip to a drag-ball cotillion in Los Angeles. "Jesus Christ! You're all faggots!" screams one hitchhiker, and these swishy, leather 'n' paisley cyclists have a hissy fit when police paw through their frilly lingerie, stop for roadside picnics complete with champagne and candles, and shock local straights by trying on their prom dresses in public. Directed by Larry Brown (**The Psychopath**), the cast seems to have a ball from start to outta-left-field-finale. Insulting? Sure. Hilarious? Absolutely!

Another oddball concept (but with disappointingly low-energy results) was **The Jesus Trip** (Russ Mayberry, '72). This snooze-a-thon begins when a gang of dirt-caked bikers hide in a convent from the fuzz. Young Sister Anna (Tippy Walker) helps them elude a revenge-crazed cop (Billy 'Green' Bush), so to repay her kindness, the boys (led by Robert Porter) kidnap the semi-willing nunette and show her the lifestyle of the road. But there's little action to be found here, and it's one of the few biker-fests that would make a Bresson film look visceral in comparison. In case any degenerates were wondering: No, Sister Anna is never gang-banged or even manhandled by these goons. All in all, the biker movie equivalent of Non-Alcoholic Beer.

Dean Stockwell made a tepid entrance into the genre with **The Loners** ('72), coming off drive-in fare like **Psych-Out** and **The Dunwich Horror**. Dean stars as a hippie/biker, whose entire day is ruined when he accidentally offs a couple of cops and flees into the desert, accompanied by his dopey best friend and a thrill happy suburban belle (Pat Stich, who shacks up with Dean so quickly you'd think she'd poured Spanish Fly on her Corn Flakes that morning). There's little originality here, and our lawless leads are the least threatening assortment of bikers you'll ever see. The Amish are more terrifying than this anaemic trio! At least it's packed with unintentional laughs, such as when Dean and Pat steal some square threads and infiltrate a country club, and Heavy Statements aplenty in the nihilistic finale (a la **Easy Rider**). Plus a surprise overwrought appearance by Gloria Grahame, as Stich's bitchy suburban mom.

Even more avoidable fly-by-night items included **Outlaw Riders** (Tony Houston, '70), a grainy and barely compe- tent lesson in tedium, with only the five tracks by gravel-voiced Simon Stokes as a (barely) redeeming feature; **The Tormentors** ('71), with neo-nazis posing as bikers and Anthony Eisley posing as an actor; the Canadian-lensed **The Proud Rider** ('71); **Big Enough 'n' Old Enough** ('69); **The Hard Ride** ('71); **The Dirt Gang** ('71), and a Crown Inter- national 1971 double bill of **The Sidehackers** and **Wild Riders** – the latter another peripheral entry where two renegade Angels (one of whom is an unbearably sloblike/retarded Alex Rocco) spend eternity terrorising a pair of middle class women. There was even an attempt to merge the dying biker movies with the up-and-coming blax- ploitation pics with **The Black Six** (Matt Cimber, '74), with a half dozen football bruisers taking on rednecks and cracker cyclists. My personal award for Best Cheapshot Title goes to the X-rated **Sleazy Rider** ('73), whose ad-copy read 'He treated women like garbage... And they loved him for it.'

As quickly as it had emerged on the scene, by the early '70s, chopperamas had virtually disappeared from in- door and outdoor screens. In only seven years, from 1966 to 1973, over 40 films of their ilk were released. Some of them were virtually interchangeable, but many of them still hold up today as hard-edged entertainment, featur- ing characters that symbolised the anger and frustrations of the '60s – loners living on the edge, making their own rules, and who, when they died at the hands of some pig, did so with a sneer on their face, a beer in their hand, and a middle finger in the air.

Even the dreaded made-for-TV movies got into the act with fare like **Pray for the Wildcats** ('74), which avoided gangs altogether in favour of a **Deliverance**-inspired tale of a quartet of middle-aged businessmen, jumping on cycles and zooming into the desert for a little sleazy fun and macho hysterics. The fact it starred television icons William Shatner, Andy Griffith and Robert Reed only made it more of an unintentional hoot.

The only halfway-admirable last ditch effort to resurrect the genre was **Northville Cemetery Massacre** ('74) from director William Dear. And even though the biker fad had dried up like so much spilt beer, this no-name, no- budget cycle-rama was a breath of fetid air for exploitation addicts. Once again, it's Rural Pinheads vs. Free-Spirit Bikers, with a grubby cycle gang named The Spirits taking on the sadistic cops of Northville, who go so far as to rape a young girl and blame it on the bikers in order to stir up Vigilante Fever amongst the townsfolk. As tensions escalate, the bloodshed begins, with 'motorcycle mongoloids' blasted to slo-mo bits and hidden blood packs gushing everywhere. Much of this hard-hitting ensemble piece has a realistic veneer, with a harsh, left-wing cyni- cism that makes it the perfect funeral wreath to the biker movie phenomenon.

By the late '70s, few filmmakers were willing to even acknowledge the passing fad, although special credit has to go to George Romero, who packed the last hour of **Dawn of the Dead** ('79) with Tom Savini and his slobbering, mall-invading leather boys being turned into zombie chow. The surest sign of rigor mortis came with Clint Eastwood's unbearable **Every Which Way But Loose**, which reverted the once-vicious bikers back to **Beach Blanket Bingo**-style comedy relief. (Would you believe, I first saw this and **Dawn of the Dead** together on a double bill? Talk about a schizophrenic audience!)

There was one film in the '80s which attempted to come to terms with the cycle phenomenon, and unsurprisingly, it came from within the biker elite. **Hell's Angels Forever** ('83) was an authorised documentary on the legendary club, filmed over 11 years by three different directors. It examined their history, interviewed their members and revealed their sensibilities. Though the end result doesn't delve much below their surface grubbiness, it was at the very least a serious attempt to tell their story, while giving cold turkey chopper fanatics a chance to wallow in reality for a change.

It's nice to report that a few filmmakers are still trying to reinvent the genre (albeit to mixed results). One of the most ridiculous was **Hell Riders** ('84), which (difficult to believe) was even chintzier than the usual drive-in trash. But the fact it stars two of America's fave TV icons, **Batman**'s Adam West and **Gilligan's Island**'s Tina Louise, makes this embellished home movie an instant crap classic! Tina stars as Claire, who's driving cross country from Vegas when she's attacked by the Hell Riders, who drag her through the dirt and piss on her car. Enter Adam West as the heroic Doctor Dave who tries to save her from this sad excuse for a gang, who keep a naked blond on a leash and have Stabbing Contests to see who's the toughest half-wit. On the plus side, the film is loaded with nudity. On the negative, it's not from Tina or Adam, but from the dumpy supporting cast. Still, this truly inept movie has the distinction of being the first biker movie where the gang kills their own leader out of sheer boredom.

Even Troma got into the act with **Chopper Chicks in Zombietown** ('91) – a combination monster/biker movie featuring a cast of sexy, leather-clad bimbos named The Cycle Sluts. And though you have every reason to expect a standard chunk of TroManure, this a surprisingly ingratiating romp. These biker babes roll into the town of Zariah for some cheapjack fun, but instead run into crazed funeral director Don Calfa, who's been re-animating the dead and using them for slave labour. When the Zombie Brigade breaks free and begins shuffling toward town, the Sluts put aside their amoral values and come to the rescue, saving not only the nit-witted townspeople, but also a busload of blind orphans. Happily, the only way to halt these purple-skinned corpses is to destroy the batteries in their skulls, which means the Sluts have to knock their heads *clean off*. Thoroughly stupid (what else would you expect from a Troma release?), but good for plenty of cheap, gory laughs.

One true biker gem managed to emerge in recent years, and was almost ignored by sleaze-a-holics due to the dubious presence of professional Neanderthal Brian Bosworth in the lead. Yes, it's **Stone Cold** ('91), a film packed with enough hardcore attitude to bring a nostalgic tear to the eyes of even the most hardened biker fan. This is a no-holds-barred, chopper gang shitkicker, that moves fast and leaves no survivors. 'The Boz' plays a prettyboy undercover cop who infiltrates a sociopathic band of drug-running bikers called The Brotherhood, and featuring Lance Henrikson as Chains, the leathered and weathered leader of the gang, and William Forsythe as his right hand psycho. We get automatic weapons, cheesy strip clubs, vicious rumbles, lightning paced editing, and cool stunts, as well as a budget that allows director Craig X. Baxley to cram every frame with more wall-to-wall dirtbags, choppers and artillery than any other bikerama ever made. What more could you want in a mindless action flick?

The biker dramas are gone for now, but personally, I'd like to think that enough public interest is there to bring about a resurgence. Because if you examine the box-office heroes of today, they aren't much different from the take-no-shit rebels of the past (and in most cases, they're a lot wimpier, stupider, and certainly more sober). When the first biker movie came into vogue, they didn't have big budgets or well known stars – and with all the independent studios and direct-to-video companies in existence today, it seems like the perfect time to give them a rebirth. The way I look at it, if video can make stars out of the charisma-barren likes of Don 'The Dragon' Wilson and Andrew Stevens, there's gotta be a place for a '90s answer to William Smith and his entire dirt-caked oeuvre.

the rise and fall of the blaxploitation film

DURING THE EARLY '70S, A NEW breed of exploitation film began tilling theatres. But unlike earlier, quick-lived genres (such as the beach party pics and the bikeramas), which erupted primarily from drive-ins, this pack of films was entrenched firmly within the Inner City. It was Blaxploitation. Bad-assed Brothers and Sisters. Pimps, pushers, private dicks, and superstuds. They packed urban grindhouses, and audiences were more than enthusiastic to finally see black heroes and heroines making it to the screen. Critics hated them and 'responsible' voices in the black community condemned their messages, but for a time, nothing seemed to stop the tidal wave of funky threads, soulful sounds and schlocky scenarios.

Though variations on this theme popped up from time to time in earlier years (**The Black Klansman, Black Angels, The Bus is Coming, Honky,** and **My Baby Is Black** – just to name a few), two 1971 releases were primarily responsible for igniting the cinematic blax-plosion. Arriving from opposite ends of the spectrum, each had a point to convey (and money to rake in).

In the spring of '71, **Sweet Sweetback's Baadasssss Song** pummelled a trail into theatres, and knocked unsuspecting audiences on their asses. No one had ever seen a story like this one. Directed, written, edited, composed, and starring Melvin Van Peebles (**The Watermelon Man**), this independently produced ass-kicker was (and still is) the ultimate kill-whitey film. Dedicated to 'All the Brothers and Sisters who've had enough of The Man', Sweetback is your typical black stud who spends his days working live sex shows, until he's suddenly hauled in by the cops on a trumped up charge. But this dude isn't Mr. Passive, and after watching The Pigs abusing a Brother, Sweetback bashes in their pasty skulls with a handy set of brass knuckles and makes a run for it. From there on, it's a grim chase through the ghettos and back alleys of Urban Decay, USA, and Peebles doesn't whitewash his subject matter in the least. It's a brutal film that was awarded an X-rating 'by an all-white jury' (as the ads proclaimed), and the aspect which audiences seemed to enjoy the most is that after screwing over the honky establishment, Sweetback got away, with the epilogue warning us to 'watch out... a baad asssss nigger is coming back to collect some dues.' The first of the New Rage black films, after the word got out about this one, lines were forming around the block.

Two months later, an equally important (though decidedly different) flick was released by MGM and targeted toward the same audience. **Shaft** was a slick detective tale with a storyline not much different from any other white PI movie. But with Richard Roundtree in the title role of John Shaft, moviegoers got to see a black hero who had carved his niche within The System while still keeping his dignity. Though it doesn't seem too radical nowadays, this was a *big* step... Called in to rescue a black mobster's kidnapped daughter, Shaft deals with militants, the police and the Mafia, and uncovers a plan to start a Harlem race war. The film takes a few soft-hearted jibes at the white establishment, but it's careful not to include anything which might anger a middle-class audience (or MGM's stockholders), unlike Sweetback's bash-you-over-the-skull-with-a-broken-bottle polemics. Gordon Park's direction and Curtis Mayfield's score added immeasurably to the sheer entertainment value of the production, and both black and white moviegoers coughed up the bucks. Followed by the equally fun **Shaft's Big Score**, and **Shaft in Africa**, and a (thankfully) short-lived TV series, Roundtree's promising career stalled out in the mid-'70s, and he's been relegated to supporting roles in films such as **Earthquake, City Heat** and **Maniac Cop**.

Both of these ground-breaking films raked in the cash ($10 million in the first year for **Sweetback** and $12 mil. for **Shaft**), and proved to producers that black heroes – of any sort – could be a box-office bonanza. On one side you had your crude and rude anti-hero, on the other an ultra-smooth crime-stopper. The public accepted it either way, and in the years that followed, moviegoers would be able to choose from any variation in-between. Black was in! Black was bad! And best of all, Black was oozing with cash! Unfortunately, the one thing a lot of make-a-quick-buck producers forgot in their race to the screen, was that (overall) both **Sweetback** and **Shaft** were *good* movies. Most of the films that followed in their wake were pure carbon-copy garbage, and an insult to anyone with an IQ above the double digits. There were a *few* exceptions...

When it came to the male superstars of the blaxploitation era, three names come to mind: Jim Brown, Jim Kelly and Fred Williamson.

Jim Brown was the first to find starring roles. He had been appearing in successful films throughout the late '60s, such as **The Dirty Dozen**, **Ice Station Zebra** and **100 Rifles**, and his already established macho man image fit in perfectly with the hot new trend. In a 12 month period, this former football star took the reigns in three similarly-plotted actioners, **Slaughter**, **Black Gunn** and **Slaughter's Big Rip Off**.

In **Slaughter** (Jack Starrett, '72), Brown portrayed an ex-Green Beret whose parents are killed by The Mob, and the film details his search to find their killers and rub 'em out. In **Black Gunn** (Robert Hartford-Davis, '72), he's a night-club owner whose militant brother is killed by the Mob after robbing one of their numbers joints, and Jim once again chases down the killer. And in a startling original twist, in **Slaughter's Big Rip Off** (Gordon Douglas, '73), the Mob makes the first move and comes after Brown – but after his girlfriend is wasted, he's (yawn!) back on their trail and out for revenge... And do you wonder why the guy was stuck in a stereotype? These were cookie-cutter movies when it came to the plot, but if you wanted mindless action, Jim was the answer. He had a 'I take no shit' presence that fit perfectly with what blaxploit-audiences were searching for – he fought hard and looked mean. The other thing that distinguished his films was the supporting casts, which were a bit more eccentric than usual. Stella Stevens, Rip Torn and Cameron Mitchell in **Slaughter**; Martin Landau in **Black Gunn**; and Ed McMahon (?) in **Slaughter's Big Rip Off**. Too bad none of these features really gave Jim a chance to stretch his acting ability. He proved to be one of the highlights in James Toback's 1978 gem, **Fingers**, but has virtually disappeared from the screen in the last few years.

In 1972, a small film named **Melinda** (Hugh A. Robertson, '72) appeared, starring Calvin Lockhart and Rosalind Cash. Scripted by Lonee Elder III (who would later write **Sounder**), this was a better-than-average actioner which combined a believable love story with kick-ass set pieces. But the standout performance came from newcomer Jim Kelly, an ex-world karate champion, in the small role of (you guessed it) a karate expert. From that bit part, Kelly chopped his way to audience recognition next to Bruce Lee in **Enter the Dragon**, and after that monster-hit he zoomed into starring roles.

Firmly entrenched in the Richard Roundtree-style of good looks and non-abusive personality, Kelly combined his marital arts expertise and nice-guy persona through a few urban classics, of which the best known is **Black Belt Jones** ('74). Directed by **Dragon**-helmer Robert Clouse, it's another tale of white mobsters easing in on black territory. In this case, the Syndicate wants to close down a karate school run by Scatman Crothers, but luckily, Scat's daughter (Gloria Hendry) recruits Kelly to help them out. There's loads of foot-and-fist action throughout, but unlike Jim Brown, Kelly was a bit lighter in the violence department and never seemed to take himself seriously (as seen in the showdown/finale, which takes place in a suds-filled car wash). Consequently, Jim K. never seemed to catch on wholeheartedly with the public, possibly because he seemed a little too soft for their headbusting-sensibilities. After the disastrous **Hot Potato** (an overseas secret-agent mind-number overflowing with pathetic comic relief) he took up with schlock director unextraordinaire, Al Adamson, for **Black Samurai** and **Death Dimension**. Still Considered a major star in the Philippines (a sure sign of career dead-end, since the same can be said of George Lazenby), Kelly pops up occasionally in king fu crapola like **The Tattoo Connection**.

But when it came to machoshit blaxploit-stars, there's only one undisputed king, and that's Fred 'The Hammer' Williamson. He's got the biggest string of hits, the longest-running career, an ego the size of Time Square, and the clout to make his own films, the way *he* wants to. Graduating from the ranks of pro-football, 'The Hammer' began his acting career by initially sucking up to The System – playing Diahann Carroll's nice-guy beau in the TV series **Julia**. But when the studios began searching for the next superspade, Fred quickly traded in Steve Bruce, Student Lawyer for Nigger Charley, Escaped Slave. In **The Legend of Nigger Charley** (and its sequel, **The Soul of...**), Fred tossed his bare-chested machismo onto the screen, and it stuck. Playing a slave-on-the-run during the Civil War era, Williamson did what came naturally – he (1) seduced a lot of women and (2) killed a lot of people. And in the career that followed, he'd never tire of these two hobbies.

In the next few years, The Hammer would churn out a string of hits unprecedented by any other black actor. In **Hammer** (Bruce Clark, '72), he played a street-wise fighter who's unknowingly aided by The Mob (with drive-in fave William Smith as an enforcer) in his rise to boxing fame. From there, Williamson took the James Bond route in **That Man Bolt** (Henry Levin, David Lowell Rich, '73), as an international currency courier, and in **Black Eye** (Jack Arnold, '74), as a private eye who's up to his neck in murder, drugs and Jesus freaks. In his copious spare time he rode through a couple of westerns (**Boss Nigger** and **Joshua**) and then took a trip to Italy for **Three Tough Guys** (with Isaac Hayes and Lino Ventura providing back-up).

All of these features were fun (if for no other reason than to appreciate Fred's swaggering, one-note performances), but as far as I'm concerned, his big break came in a pair of Larry Cohen films, **Black Caesar** ('73) and **Hell Up in Harlem** ('73), which became two of the biggest money-makers to emerge from the blaxploitation sinkhole.

Originally written for Sammy Davis Jr., Fred grabbed the starring role and it fit him like a glove, with writer/director Cohen pulling out all the visual stops when it came to the action. The story of Tommy Gibbs, a streetsmart shoeshine boy who works his way through The Mob by following the motto "it's a jungle out there, and it takes a jungle bunny to run it". Paying off the cops, pocketing politicians and kicking whitebutts is routine for this guy, until he rises to become the godfather of Harlem. The plot is straight melodrama directly from the old Warner Brothers gangster pics of the '30s, but between Cohen's talent behind the camera (the climax to **Black Caesar** is so dizzying it'll give you vertigo) and his anything-for-a-thrill scripts, combined with Williamson's absolutely astounding feel for the self-centred, cigar-chewing role, makes this pair two of the best blaxploiters around.

Even after the genre died out, Fred was one of the few survivors to have negotiated his own freedom. Grabbing the chance to direct/write/produce for himself, he set up his own company, Po' Boy Productions, and he's been able to wring out a line of inexpensive (and unfortunately, generally unimpressive) flicks ever since: **Mean Johnny Barrows**, **Adios Amigos** (with Richard Pryor), **No Way Back**, **Death Journey**, **Mr. Mean**, **Foxtrap**, and **The Messenger**. Most of them were overseas-lensed, and if Fred hasn't caught up with the changing times, at least he seems happy enough (and wealthy enough) to chart his own future.

Together, Brown, Kelly and Williamson made up the elite core of the urban grinders, but in one remarkably action-packed instance, they teamed up for a career highlight and a blaxploit-fan's wet dream. **Three the Hard Way** (Gordon Parks, '74) is probably the most accessible of all their films, since it's almost comic book in style, with clearly drawn Good Guy/Bad Guy battles lines. In it, Brown, Kelly and Williamson star as three buddies who uncover a deadly plot by an all-white neo-nazi organisation. A chemical that kills only blacks is going to be placed in the water supplies of Detroit, Washington and Los Angeles, and the only people who can save the Brothers and Sisters of America are The Big Three. The evil fanatics are incompetent crackers, the stars are righteous ass-kickers, and after an endless display of fisticuffs and far-out fashions, it all ends with an explosive three-man raid on the Nazis' headquarters. Needless to add, it's all loads of ludicrous fun... After this vehicle, the trio later appeared in the Italo-western, **Take a Hard Ride** (with Lee Van Cleef) and the barely-released **One Down, Two To Go** (directed by Williamson, and co-starring Richard Roundtree), but neither film duplicated the first's success.

When it came to the femme side of business, there was only one true superstarlet. Pam Grier was *numero uno*. After a quick debut in Russ Meyer's **Beyond the Valley of the Dolls** and a supporting role in the horror flick **Twilight People**, Ms. Grier took her gutsy on-screen attitude to larger roles in **Black Mama, White Mama** and **Arena**, in both of which she was paired off against Margaret Markov, whenever she wasn't too busy unbuttoning her blouse. But her two biggest (and most enjoyably trashy) hits were from director Jack Hill (**Spider Baby**, **Switchblade Sisters**). In both **Coffy** ('73) and **Foxy Brown** ('74), Pam was given starring shots and was allowed to strut her stuff, both dramatically and physically. In the first, Ms. Grier stars as a revenge-obsessed woman out to kill *everyone* responsible for the drug-related death of her little sister. She beats up and blasts away pushers and politicians aplenty, and in **Foxy Brown** her name might have changed, but her routine didn't. This time around it's her boyfriend that's been offed by the drug-pushing crime lords, and after bedding 'em and burning 'em, Pam takes vigilante-ism to new heights when she castrates one of the dope kingpins and sends his organ back in a pickle jar. But outside of these two 'epics', Pam never ran across this type of luck again. Films such as **Bucktown** (with Fred Williamson), William Girdler's **Sheba Baby** and the comic-strip-based **Friday Foster** increased her audience awareness, but none of them gave her the juicy role that could manipulate schlock audiences into a lather. When the blaxploitation craze diminished, she tried her hand at more legit fare, such as **Greased Lightning**, **Fort Apache, The Bronx** and **Something Wicked This Way Comes**, but with the stigma of her earlier Trash Queen stereotype still lingering, her career never took off as she had hoped. More recently, Ms. Grier has been back in Drive-In Lane, playing second fiddle to Steven Seagal in **Above the Law**.

A few other actresses tried to break into the business through the back door of exploitation flicks, but with varying success. Tamara Dobson starred in the predictable **Cleopatra Jones** (Jack Starrett, '73) (the sequel was **C.J. and the Casino of Gold**), as a flashy undercover do-gooder in the female James Bond tradition, complete with flashy sports car and wicked wardrobe... Before her untimely death, Diana Sands had a chance to test out the schlock-infested waters in **Honeybaby, Honeybaby** a comedy-thriller where the vacationing Ms. Sands becomes embroiled in Third World politics... And Jeanne Bell, a late-comer to the genre, revived it for a few moments with roles in Cirio Santiago's kung-foolishness, **TNT Jackson**, and the jungle-warfare actioner, **The Muthers**. These female stars were the exception to the rule though. In most blaxploiters, women were merely used as decoration – getting raped, brutalised or simply killed by The Mob, so their boyfriend could settle the score. In a genre where black men were breaking barriers and proving their merit, black actresses didn't have much to look forward to.

The one aspect of blaxploitation which received the greatest social drubbing was its so-called glorification of crime. When these films began focusing on pimps and pushers, while depicting them as heroes, all hell broke loose. The entire genre came under scrutiny, and Black groups across the country started accusing Hollywood of demeaning minorities by portraying them as junkies, hustlers and whores. Well, compared to *all* of the black-oriented films released in this period, very few actually took a pro-crime side. As you can see, most of the storylines seemed to exist only so organised crime could be slaughtered off (even if it entailed 'bending' the law to do so).

The aforementioned **Black Caesar/Hell Up in Harlem** combo fit into this pattern, but the flick which really started the ruckus was also the most successful of them. **Superfly** (Gordon Parks Jr., '72) starred Ron O'Neal (with his crushed suede clothes and midi coats) and proved that drug dealers could make their dough and get away with it too. Selling only outside of his neighbourhood, O'Neal was the Coke Pusher with a Conscience – the ghetto good guy – and after taking The Man to the cleaners, he disappears with a cool million to live high on. Of course, the film's surprise success led to his return on year later in **Superfly TNT** ('73), where O'Neal gets to move to Rome (and direct himself), but this later entry lacked the violent, amoral edge which made the original such top-notch (albeit sleazy-hearted) entertainment.

As for pimps, they were all over the urban circuit. **Willie Dynamite** (Gilbert Moses, '74) contained every felt-hatted, Cadillac-riding cliché imaginable, but since studio money was behind the camera, at the end Willie D. (Roscoe Orman) learns his lesson and turns over a new leaf. Leaving behind his clothes, car and cash for brighter (and more law-abiding) pastures, black audiences didn't believe one iota of this crap, and **The Mack** (Michael Campus, '73) provided them with a substantially different picture. Max Julian (**Psych-Out**) starred as Goldie, a rising young pimp with a few scruples. He doesn't dump on His People, and he doesn't get pissed-off until a pair of white-trash cops and a competing pimp decide to make his life tough. Thoroughly schlocky, it was at least honest with its depiction of the streets, and never flew into cheap moralising. But the most unbelievable of the lot was Matt Cimber's **The Candy Tangerine Man** ('75), in which middle-class family man, John Daniels, has a secret profession – by night he's actually The Baron, the city's meanest pimp. Of course, his wife and children know nothing of his alternate lifestyle, and not one cop ever thinks to follow him home one night and find out where he lives. After killing every competitor and pushing two shit-for-brains policemen off a cliff, he returns to suburbia and retires with a briefcase full of cash.

It's easy to understand why some self-righteous whiners complained about these films. But looking back at them now, they only seem to be an aberration of the times. Just as the gangster films of the '30s created controversy for their stereotypes, so did these cheesy crime dramas. And besides, who in their right mind could conceive of taking any of this junk seriously in the first place? It was mindless, corpse-strewn entertainment. Nothing more. And though downright demeaning at times, none of these films were as blatantly hateful and offensive as today's Rambo-style political propaganda.

One of the funkier mutations to arrive on the grindhouse circuit was the combination blaxploitation/horror movie. Beginning with the unexpected success of **Blacula** (William Crain, '72), everyone jumped on the bandwagon with their own urban updates on assorted horror themes, but none of them could live up to the film that started the trend. AIP's **Blacula** was your basic low-budgeter, which benefited immeasurably from William Marshall's title performance. As 18th century African Prince Mamuwalde, Marshall visits Dracula's castle on a goodwill mission and ends up cursed by The Count and crated in a coffin. A couple of hundred years later, the still-shut crypt is shipped to Los Angeles when a pair of interior decorators purchase it, and the Black Bloodsucker is off and biting. It's your standard vampire mish-mash (wooden stakes, no reflection in mirrors), in tandem with the blaxploiter background trappings. But without Marshall's dignified portrayal, it would've gone straight into the crapper (and the world would've missed out on all the similar films that followed. Shucks!).

Another African spin on the vampire mythos emerged in Bill Gunn's **Ganja and Hess** ('73), an atmospheric li'l pic that was shunted into the grindhouse market by its dumbass distributor, provocatively retitled (**Blood Couple**, **Double Possession**), and hacked by over twenty minutes. Duane Jones (best known as the black hero in Romero's **Night of the Living Dead**) stars as the undead Dr. Hess Green, who maintains a palatial house in upstate New York and steals reserves from urban blood banks to satiate his thirst. To complete the title pairing, enter Ganja Meda (Marlene Clark), a streetwise beauty who resides with the Doc while searching for her missing hubby (currently taking up space in Hess' basement freezer). Don't expect many cheap thrills though, because Gunn is hunting for artsier game in his meagre-budgeted pic, from the unnerving score which consists of blues, gospel and haunting tribal drums, to the overdose of Christian imagery. High on self-importance and low on bloodshed, it's a film easier to admire for its heartfelt vision than to actually kick back with a 40 of St. Ides and enjoy.

One of the fondest remembered entries in this frightful mini-genre was William Girdler's **Abby** ('74), a Black Exorcist rip-off featuring a Nigerian spirit of rampant sexuality, which possesses demure Abby (Carol Speed), turning her into a gravel-voiced nympho who foams at the mouth and tosses the doctors about like they were low-paid stuntmen. Enter William Marshall as the funkiest exorcist on the planet, who tracks Abby down to a local bar, where she's beating the bejesus out of some veloured Brothers, and (in one of the silliest scenes in grindhouse history) performs a full-scale exorcism on her in the middle of this demolished night-club. Of course, it's difficult to take any of this religious hooey seriously when there's a big-assed disco ball hangin' above their heads. Or when the astounding makeup effects amount to gluing heavy eyebrows onto Abby and shoving albino contact lenses in her eyes. All in all, good for a few drunken laughs, and little else.

Others included **Dr. Black and Mr. Hyde** (William Crain, '76), a laughable tale starring Bernie Casey as a respected black physician who tests out a lab formula on himself and transforms into a pasty-faced albino who goes on a Watts-wide killing spree. **Sugar Hill (and Her Zombie Hit Men)** (Paul Maslansky, '74) was an entertaining Haiti-based back-lotter, about a beautiful voodoo priestess who calls forth the pop-eyed Negro Dead to take vengeance on The Mob for killing her boyfriend. The absolute dregs came from **Blackenstein** (William A. Levey, '73), a fiasco in which a black, Vietnam vet quadriplegic is taken under the care of a mad scientist. Graft on a few new limbs, inject some experimental DNA into his veins, shoot him with a little high-voltage electricity, and (*voila!*) you're got a murderous monster with a square afro! And let's not forget such grindhouse trash as **J.D.'s Revenge** (the spirit of a dead mobster inhabits the body of an average black dude, starring Glynn Turman and Lou Gossett); **House on Skull Mountain** (a dying woman's will, a bunch of backstabbing relatives, and less fright than foolishness); plus **Scream, Blacula, Scream** (with Pam Grier livening up this lame bloodsucker sequel).

But without question, the most horrendous blaxploitation creature feature emerged during the straight-to-video era, with 1984's **Black Devil Doll From Hell**. This repulsive piece of shit is so crude and vile it feels like some deviant's chromosome-damaged home movies. The picture goes in and outta focus, the soundtrack music is often so loud you can't hear the dialogue (a blessing in disguise), and the culprit is director/writer Chester N. Turner. Our story features a god-fearing heroine who purchases a dredlocked ventriloquist dummy, takes it home, and has fantasies about having sex with it (not to mention chancing a serious case of splinters). The Devil Doll begins moving about on his own, talking in a baritone growl, and it climaxes with her long, protracted rape by the horny puppet. Guess what? She loves it! In other words, Willie Tyler and Lester this ain't! Difficult to endure, impossible to forget, and severely misogynistic, this camcorder crapola wallows in its own incompetence. I can't imagine an uglier piece of rotgut, making all those 'immoral' Pimp 'n' Prostitute pics of the '70s look like **Pippi Longstocking** in comparison.

During the early '70s, at the height of the blaxploitation explosion, you couldn't walk down Times Square without stumbling across a new entry in the Urban Sweepstakes, including **Savage**, **Together Brothers**, **Detroit 9000**, **Velvet Smooth**, **Black Starlet**, **Black Lolita**, **Brotherhood of Death**, **Book of Numbers**, **Honky**, **Gordon's War**, **The Black Godfather**, **The Guy From Harlem**, **Trick Baby**, **Trouble Man**, and Greydon Clark's **Nigger Lover**. The list goes on and on, but every so often, amidst the glut of righteous (albeit generic) Brothers, there were a few gems.

The Final Comedown (aka **Blast**) ('72) was nearly lost in the shuffle of blaxploitation no-brainers, but deserves a place next to **Sweet Sweetback** as a potent call for armed insurrection. A pre-stardom Billy Dee Williams stars as hot-headed urban revolutionary Johnny Johnson, who begins the flick at his breaking point – ready to grab the semi-automatic beside his bed and waste some whiteys. The entire film takes place during a day-long police assault an Johnny's HQ, with Billy Dee shot in the gut as the viewer gets flashbacks which explain the roots of his rage. From watching neighbourhood kids bitten by rats as they sleep, to seeing friends brain-fried from the white man's drugs and getting continually hassled by the fuzz, this powerful film wears its fury on its blood-caked sleeve. Meanwhile, the battalion of heavily-armed pigs are leaving a body-strewn path through the ghetto. Financed in part by the American Film Institute and directed by Oscar Williams (who displays more attitude than actual talent), this is a solid, socially conscious winner.

After their success with **Shaft**, MGM was hyper for a repeat hit that would play as well in the white suburbs as it did with black, urban crowds, and although **Cool Breeze** ('72), didn't spark crossover box office, it featured solid performers and an honest-to-goodness script. Based on the novel by W.R. Burnett (which was also the basis for John Huston's **The Asphalt Jungle**), director Barry Pollack laces this standard crime melodrama with wild dashikis and 'fros. Much of the film's success is thanks to Thalmus Rasulala, who stars as ex-con Sydney Lord James, a 'super spade dude' only days outta San Quentin and armed with a mega-plan for a three million dollar jewel robbery – the proceeds of which will be used to set up a bank for all the local Brothers and Sisters (holy social consciousness!). Amidst two-bit crooks, a sleazy evangelist, and the botched heist, the supporting cast includes blaxploitation faves like Raymond St. Jacques, Margaret Avery, Paula Kelly, and a pre-**Foxy Brown** 'Pamela Grier', who lets her legendary breasts do most of the acting as Rasulala's one-night-stand.

Isaac Hayes took on the title role in **Truck Turner** ('74) playing a bald skip tracer who hunts down bail jumpers and brings 'em back by 'whatever means necessary'. He's the perfect grindhouse hero – the type of dude who'll give his girlfriend a six pack of cheap beer instead of flowers, and doesn't think twice about slaughtering a dozen people to get his paycheque. The skimpy plot kicks into gear when Truck tracks down a pimp named Gator, and in retaliation a bounty is put on Turner's head for a change. Man, you won't believe the bloodbath that ensues, with a wild hospital massacre and plenty of quality squib work! Isaac has a ball with his role, accompanied by the top-notch supporting cast, including Yaphet Kotto, **Star Trek**'s Michelle Nichols, Scatman Crothers, and Dick Miller. Directed by Jonathan Kaplan (long before he got a conscience with high-minded fare like **The Accused**, and was still churning out misogynistic swill like **Night Call Nurses**), this is cool, bloodthirsty schlock that starts slow, but eventually blasts its way into your heart.

When you're discussing blaxploitation, you mustn't ignore the double-barrelled contribution of writer/director George Armitage. Best known for scripting Roger Corman's **Gas-s-s-s** and more recently, directing the gonzo **Miami Blues**, he was also fundamental in creating two of the Deuce's most peculiar entries. The first, **Hit Man** ('72), is a showcase for two of the era's finest, Bernie Casey and Pam Grier. Just the sight of big Bernie strutting around, squeezed into a blood red leisure suit is enough for a recommendation, but it's Armitage's amoral storytelling that keeps the pic afloat. Essentially, this was a black remake of **Get Carter**, with Tyrone Tackett (Casey) infiltrating a world of prostitutes, porno, and acting school drop-outs while searching for his brother's murderer. If you're looking for even a lick of reality, FORGET IT! This is another 'nerdy white film school grads making a flick for the Brothers' movie, and there was more urban truth in an episode of the TV show **Julia** than in this slop. As for Ms. Grier, she's stuck playing a busty bimbo with a big limp afro. At least the finale is hardcore, when Casey begins popping guys point blank.

On the other hand, **Darktown Strutters** (William Witney, '75 – only written by Armitage) is a brain-damaged blaxploitation-musical-comedy-biker movie, as well as the weirdest urban saga you'll ever witness! Unapologetically surreal and stoopid, it features a female motorcycle gang decked out in threads that would've given Liberace wet dreams. Searching for their leader's missing mom, these feisty femmes encounter cycle-riding Ku Klux Klaners in red leather hip boots and taffeta undies, the inept Ghetto Alert police (imagine the Keystone Kops as racists with pump shotguns), a supporting cast that breaks into song and dance at the drop of a velour fedora, plus more ribs 'n' watermelon jokes than you'll believe. Let's not forget the sinister Colonel Sanders-lookalike who keeps blacks caged in his cellar for use in cloning experiments. Highest kudos goes to set designer Jack Fisk, who manages to combine Willy Wonka with Ken Russell. I can't even imagine what drugs the filmmakers were on while making this truly-insane gem, but I know I want some...

Speaking of grindhouse oddities, we come to **Top of the Heap** ('72). Directed, written and starring Christopher St. John (best known at the time for a fourth-billed role in **Shaft**) this film somehow manages to be both totally earnest and thoroughly nuts in the same breath. We begin by meeting George Lattimer, a black Washington DC cop who's disillusioned with his job, depressed by family problems, and ridiculed by the Brothers he arrests. There's also a slight problem with the guy's mental state, because in the middle of his work day, he suddenly imagines he's NASA's first black astronaut preparing for a moon mission. During a pre-space flight press conference he lights up a joint and compares his anxiety to "waiting for your Welfare cheque"; his astronaut's hometown return has him greeted by a ghost town, a Nixon impersonator and his dead mama; but the most insane image has St. John running about the woods buttnaked and smashing watermelons to bits. The film intercuts reality and fantasy without rhyme or reason, mixing die-hard dementia with ponderous social statements. And though it's more rotgut fun than a dozen simple blaxploitation flicks, you can also understand why St. John never made another movie.

Abar – The First Black Superman (aka **In Your Face**) (Frank Packard, '77) was another prime example of wild, independent sleaze. Director Frank Packard might not know jack about making a slick, coherent movie, but he sure knows how to make a freaky one, which begins when a black family moves into an all-white suburban So. Cal. neighbourhood. Even though hubby is a respected Doctor, the local bigots begin picketing, nazi armbands come into vogue, and the radio station interrupts its programming to warn the population! To help even the sides, in comes a gang of black, militant motorcyclists, led by Abar (Tobar Mayo). And as if racists, revenge and socio-political rhetoric wasn't enough, we next learn that the Doc's secret medical research involves a serum that makes the subject indestructible (hence his bullet-proofed rabbits). Next thing you know, Abar takes the drug and turns into a superhuman juggernaut! First, a dry-ice-bathed vision of Jesus invests him with divine powers, after which Abar sits catatonically atop the Watts Towers and brings plagues of rats and snakes down upon the neighbourhood. Despite its technical incompetence, this is truly bizarre shit.

Meanwhile, director Jamaa Fanaka (best known for his '80s **Penitentiary** trilogy) helmed the unbelievable **Welcome Home, Brother Charles** (aka **Soul Vengeance**) ('75), starring Marlo Monte as a repellent, pimp/dope dealer (and mind you, he's the hero!) who nearly gets castrated with a straight razor by a racist cop, and returns from a stretch in the slammer to find that his old partner stole his woman. Just so you don't get the idea this is your typical piece of trash, the plot take a supernatural turn when he begins hypnotising women with one look at his dick and strangles enemies with his four-foot-long killer penis. Yes, you read it right, folks. And although it's amateurish to the core, you have to love the film's fashion sense, Watts and Compton locales, and gut-busting premise (which, better yet, is never logically explained).

Even cosmic musician Sun Ra got into the act, with his Intergalactic Myth-Science Solar Arkestra, in **Space is the Place** (John Coney, '74). So smoke a shitload of weed and prepare yourself for time-hopping, planet-hopping weirdness that mixes blaxploitation, science fiction, social commentary, concert footage, and Sun strutting about in his usual golden robes and Egyptian headgear. When he's not sitting in the desert, battling the evil Overseer (Ray Johnson) with a Tarot deck, Sun is in the present, landing his spaceship in the middle of the ghetto and stepping out like some bad-assed messiah. His plan? To convince modern-day youth to fly into space with him and colonise another planet where they can be unshackled from Earth's prejudices and hang-ups. Things aren't that easy, of course, because (white) government scumbags kidnap Sun to learn his secret of 'transmolecularisation', and torture the guy with a muzak version of 'Dixie'. Director John Coney's flick is a fitting tribute to the mighty Sun Ra and his Afro-mystical musical message.

Of course, any blaxploitation fanatic knows that if you're going to talk about truly inept weirdness, you can't ignore the legendary contributions of Rudy Ray Moore. Beginning his career with X-rated comedy albums like **Eat Out More Often**, this self-proclaimed 'Godfather of Rap' moved into the celluloid world just as the urban genre was on the downslide – and despite having a physique less like Fred Williamson and more like Fred Flintstone, had fans lining up around the block. Oddly enough, his films are so filthy, violent and crude they achieved an uncharted level of urban surrealism (at their best, imagine **Superfly** directed by Jean-Luc Godard), and it's difficult not to love a guy whose kung fu skills amount to squinching up his face and hopping about like he needs an economy-sized tube of Preparation H.

In **Dolemite** (D'Urville Martin, '74), Rudy plays a street-smart pimp who takes on the city's drug czars while abusing every lily-white, racist asshole in earshot, aided by an all-girl army of karate experts. Dolemite reappeared in **The Human Tornado** (Cliff Roquemore, '76), though now he's a smoking-jacket philanthropist who's beloved by the entire community (despite all the continual pussy jokes he tells during his night-club routine). And when he's not battling the Mafia, every white woman in town wants a bone dance with him. His short reign continued in more homogenised fare like **Petey Wheatstraw, The Devil's Son-In-Law** (Cliff Roquemore, '77) (Rudy is wasted by mobsters, and makes a deal with the devil in order to return to earth with magical powers that can make fat women thin and comb out nappy hair) and **Monkey Hustle** (Arthur Parks, '77) (a rare, studio-lensed pic, playing a supporting part to star Yaphet Kotto). By the time **The Avenging Disco Godfather** (Rudy Ray Moore, '76) came along, Rudy was playing an ex-cop turned club owner, who spins tunes for the crowded dance floor while saving his Brothers and Sisters from the evils of Angel Dust. Not surprisingly, Moore has remained a cult figure, two decades after filling grindhouses to capacity.

Leave it to Gualtiero Jacopetti and Franco Prosperi, the creators of **Mondo Cane**, to emerge with one of the most powerful foreign-lensed offshoots of the blaxploitation craze. **Farewell Uncle Tom** ('72) wasn't your usual Deuce fodder though. It's a history lesson made flesh, recreating the wall-to-wall brutality that made up American slavery. In comparison, it makes **Roots** look like an episode of **The Jeffersons**. Set on a southern cotton plantation in the 1800's, the weirdness kicks in when a modern camera crew appears to chronicle the era, and we're witness to two full hours of slave life debasement. We get slave ships, brandings, enemas, rape, and despite their good intentions, these sick Pastaland filmmakers focus on the most graphic, exploitable elements – complete with sumptuous sets, hundreds of naked extras, frighteningly authentic props, plus a 19-year-old girl on her way to be deflowered by her 'Massa'. If that isn't enough for you, the epilogue is both gratuitous and righteous, complete with a cool Kill Whitey scenario. Filmed in Haiti, this celluloid stranglehold is one of the most numbing ordeals ever put to film.

For further non-P.C. fun, you can't beat **Fight For Your Life** (aka **Staying Alive**) ('77), a late '70s entry, which kicks off in high gear when a trio of killers (led by scumbag William Sanderson) escape from NYC police, steal a pimp's car and head upstate – holding a black family hostage in their rural home. Just imagine if The Cosby Family met The Manson Family. The white trash Sanderson fires off rapid-fire racial slurs, calling his captives "Uncle Remus", "Monkey-Face", "Martin Luther Coon", and even makes the father tap dance. Most of the action takes place in the wood-panelled den and director Robert A. Edelson pulls no punches, until the family takes the law into their own hands during a rousing, immoral finale. Producer William Mishkin has always had a nose for sleazy entertainment, and this mean-spirited pic delivers (although you couldn't have paid me to be the only white face in a Harlem theatre when this was first shown). An after-film shower is optional, but recommended.

Of course, for every reasonably decent film, there were just as many snoozers. The worst of the lot are so tasteless they're worth a look just to get a shudder from their bold-faced baloney. **The Black Six** (Matt Cimber, '74) starred half-a-dozen terrifyingly untalented football stars as a six pack of redwood-necked bikers taking revenge on a white cycle gang, while (literally) destroying eateries which don't serve coloured customers. **The $6000 Nigger** (aka **Super Soul Brother**) (Rene Martinez, '78) stars Wildman Steve as a Miami wino who's given super powers by some larcenous scientists. And last, but certainly least, **Black Shampoo** (Greydon Clark, '76) was utter trash – with John Daniels as an irresistible black hairdresser who lays pipe with all his white clients, and eventually breaks The Mob after they kidnap his sexy secretary.

But by the late '70s, black-mania had run its course. Most of the films were so predictable (not to mention, just plain lousy) that audiences were eventually turned off. Instead of gradually increasing in quality and breaking new territory, most of the blaxploiters were happy enough to sleaze along on the coattails of a previous success. And with the decreasing grosses, most major studios pulled out of the genre altogether, leaving it to independent companies and directors who cared more for profit than perfection. It was too bad, because not only did exploitation addicts lose a wonderful little genre, but these urban offerings gave work to loads of black actors who could use a break from the unemployment line.

Several filmmakers have tried to resuscitate the genre over the years, with limited success. **Action Jackson** was simply a **Shaft**-clone with a larger team of stuntman and a more mundane hero. Def American's **Tougher Than Leather** gave us rappers Run DMC playing themselves, and getting involved with drug-dealing record producers and The Beastie Boys. While Keenan Ivory Wayans' **I'm Gonna Git You Sucka** was a hit-and-miss homage to the beloved black actioners, whose savviest move was in rounding up ageing pros like Jim Brown, Isaac Hayes and Bernie Casey for supporting machismo. Then there's Mario Van Peebles, who followed in his dad's footsteps with high-powered (but sanctimonious) fare like **New Jack City**. As America's inner city theatres are razed, though, it seems unlikely that suburban-mall audiences weaned on **The Cosby Show**'s Oreo-based antics will ever rediscover the funky joys of Velour Cinema.

a history of hallucinogens in the cinema

PSYCHEDELIC DRUGS HAVE PLAYED a part in society for hundreds of years, but it wasn't until the 1960s that the motion picture industry began to acknowledge the area. Unlike marijuana or alcohol (two drugs whose use has been charted on celluloid since the silent era), hallucinogens were always a little too far out and freaky for filmmakers to comfortably embrace. But when the counterculture revolution of the late '60s came along, many of these drugs quickly became household words (and often taboo ones at that) and producers were eager to invest in this new phenomenon.

This essay will concentrate primarily on films that were directly involved with hallucinogens (because if we added in all the other drug categories, we'd be here forever). Although psychedelics have been a part of film vocabulary as early as 1960, and still play a small role in some present-day films, most of the focus will be on the period of 1966-1970, the era these chemicals became a major factor in a wide cross-section of films. The mention or use of hallucinogens can be traced into almost every cinematic genre: Low budget independents, multi-million dollar studio releases, documentaries, sex flicks, educational shorts, comedies, melodramas, horror films, and beyond. It was a topic that intrigued some, angered even more, and baffled all the rest. Maybe it's because these particular drugs had a more personal side to their use. Few within the film industry who hadn't actually tried hallucinogens for themselves could understand their appeal (or intelligently approach them). Misinformation was abundant, and those who *did* experiment with them tended to have strong emotions (pro or con). Once experienced, they were difficult to forget.

But first, a quick checklist of the drugs we'll be covering. In the organic department, there's psilocybin (the pyschoactive ingredient in the mushroom Psilocybe) and peyote (from which mescaline is derived), both of which have taken on a mystique due to their ritualistic use by Indians of North and Central America. There's also the relatively new (and powerful) addition to the family, 2, 5-Dimethoxy-4-methyamphetamine (commonly known as STP), which was first discovered in the late '60s. And the leader of the pack was lysergic acid diethylamide (LSD), which was first synthesised by Dr. Albert Hoffman in 1938, and after years of clinical research began to reach popular height in the mid-'60s when the public got wind of the powerful psychedelic effects.

Surprisingly enough, the first film to allude to acid (LSD) was a horror film that literally injected the subject into its Creature Features storyline. William Castle's **The Tingler** ('60) starred Vincent price as an unorthodox doctor investigating the nature of fright, and how some individuals can literally die from it. But before the tale introduces the title monster and a plot brimming with deception, murder and cheap scares, Price decides to experiment on himself, and attempts to induce fright by shooting up a new drug that can produce 'pretty weird effects'. Yes, that's right! Vincent scores some (at that time legal) LSD-25 and gets the pleasure of the cinema's first acid trip! He locks himself in his lab, injects himself with 100 milligrams of the stuff and then records his observations into his trusty tape recorder. Within minutes his vision blurs, the walls sway, the room closes in on him, and a skeleton has him screaming and ready to scurry up the wallpaper. But by the following scene Vincent is fine again, albeit a bit shaky. Castle didn't attempt to depict his visions (except for fogging up the camera lens for a moment), and the only reason acid seems to be included in the script is for its so-called ability to induce 'nightmares', which fits handily within the plot mechanisms.

Another early mention of psychedelics was in the Japanese monsterama **Matango, The Fungus of Terror** (aka **Attack of the Mushroom People**) (Inoshiro Honda, '63), in which a boatload of people are washed up on a deserted island, whose one claim to fame is its preponderance of giant mushrooms. At first, the passengers are wary of sampling the foreign fungi, but the thought of starvation slowly bends their will and one by one they wander off and take a bite. Obviously these are an exotic brand, because one gent begins hallucinating he's at a Tokyo nightclub watching a chorus line of dancing girls strutting before his eyes (an atypical psilocybin reaction, if you ask me). The only problem is that once they've tasted the 'shrooms they slowly turn into one, thus explaining the lack of human presence on the isle. The film is hideously boring for the first hour, but viewers in on the drug-induced joke will get a solid laugh at the finale, when giant fungi begin strutting about, chasing the two remaining passengers. Moral: You Are What You Eat.

The first examples of psychedelic cinema emerged directly from the depths of the newly erupting counterculture, and approached the subject with a surprising degree of intelligence and care (which wouldn't happen again for some time). The first was Andy Warhol's three-and-a-half hour underground classic **The Chelsea Girls** ('66), which gave courageous audiences an unadulterated glimpse at unique, Lower Manhattan lifestyles, with its numerous segments capturing moments of sex, drugs and weirdness (while making no value judgements on it at all). And in one segment a young man on LSD rambles on nonchalantly about his sexuality as he removes his clothes and coloured lights flicker over his body. Though the entire film is hard to sit through (in an effort to be relatively realistic, it's also incredibly boring for long stretches), its intentions are quite honourable. Two other Warhol-produced movies, his own ******** ('67) and protégé Paul Morrissey's **Trash** ('70) also dealt peripherally with LSD, while treating the topic as if it were just another aspect of life in the big city.

But while Warhol's film only touched on the theme, Conrad Rooks' **Chappaqua** ('66) was the first full-blown entry in the Trip Sweepstakes. This experimental (and very personal) film starred amateur filmmaker Rooks in a drama based in part on his own experiences as a drug addict, which culminated in a cure from heroin addiction at the age of 27. Most of the film details his character's withdrawal period at a European clinic, complete with free-association fantasies such as floating through space, listening to a guru and repeated temptation from a sinister pusher, Opium Jones. Though not directly about hallucinogens, the psychedelic style in which the film is structured clearly shows Rooks' awareness of the effects of LSD, with brisk editing and alternating colour/b&w photography by Robert Frank (**Pull My Daisy**) capturing the feel of a drug experience. Filmed around the world (US, England, France, India, Ceylon) and starring an eclectic cast including Jean-Louis Barrault, William S. Burroughs (as Opium J.), Allen Ginsberg, Ravi Shankar, and Ornette Coleman, it went on to receive a modicum of critical praise and became an arthouse curiosity for a time.

The same year, the media first latched on to the hippie movement with their long hair, love-ins, communes, and in particular, drugs – and articles about the effects of LSD began to proliferate in mass market magazines such as **Time** and **Newsweek**. In 1966, when the United States made LSD illegal for the first time, it was suddenly 'in' to embrace the matter. As usual, if the public was curious. they'd be willing to shell out bucks to see it portrayed on the silver screen. Subsequently, the two-bit studios were happy to fill their pockets by using the subject of hallucinogens as an easy marketing tool. This is when the explosion of Mind-Altering Drugs on Film first began to take root. Whether these productions understood even the basics about what they were discussing was another question entirely, and the first few low-budget items didn't even attempt to deal with the subject seriously. They simply used LSD to reel in the gullible audiences, and as expected the results were mixed.

The first filmmaker to capitalise on the sudden interest was Albert Zugsmith, who had a knack of hooking onto any popular new craze. His earlier works included such laughable classics as **High School Confidential** and **Confessions of an Opium Eater**, and in his tepid acid comedy **Movie Star American Style, or LSD, I Hate You** ('66), he set out to satirise the Hollywood community while shoving loads of trippy sidelines into the story. Paula Lane stars as Honey Bunny, a Marilyn Monroe-style sex symbol, who's shipped off to a clinic to get some rest after a suicide attempt. But the hospital's head doc has a half-baked theory about using LSD in his Tinseltown patients in order to expose their inner fantasies. Thinly veiled caricatures abound, along with dim in-jokes and psychiatric wisecracks, and the finale involves a group encounter session while on LSD, with tinted photography used to visualise the patients' trips. It's a downright stupid film, with the premise of LSD-used-psychiatry twisted for laughs and its attempts at cheap comedy going limp. Still, the hallucination sequences are nicely lensed with some adequate optical effects, and a few moments still carry a distinctly wrong-headed charm about them.

One of the more bizarre early entries has to be **Mother Goose a Go-Go** (aka **Unkissed Bride**) (Jack Harris, '66) featuring one-time child star Tommy Kirk – who obviously frittered away the cash he made on **Old Yeller** and **The Shaggy Dog**, or else he wouldn't have been stuck in this kind of oddball item. Tommy stars as a newlywed groom who has sexual problems on his wedding night. It begins when his wife, Margie (Anne Helm), picks up a copy of Mother Goose stories and begins to read aloud, in order to calm her own first-night nerves. But instead, it causes Tommy to suddenly faint! Obviously worried at this turn of events, Margie enlists the help of a female psychiatrist, who secretly uses an LSD spray on him while he sleeps, in hope of discovering his problem. It turns out the poor guy has a Mother Goose Complex (hey, I'm not making this crap up!) which leads back to childhood traumas, and whenever those usually harmless fairy tales are mentioned, he instantly becomes Mr. Useless-in-bed. But Harris (who also shared the dubious writing credit) doesn't stop there. He also tosses in a jealous hotel detective, marital infidelity, negligeed cuties, a 'typical' '60s discotheque, and a lot of weird sound effects and cinematic horseplay.

It's a truly silly movie that once seen isn't easily forgotten (though if you have any taste whatsoever, you'll wish you could).

But the well-publicised **Hallucination Generation** (Ed Mann, '66) turned out to be one of the lamest of the lot. Despite a persuasive ad campaign, this was a low grade stinker which pivoted on the anti-drug scare tactics which would increase in later years (i.e. LSD makes you run down the street screaming at the top of your voice). Set in trendy Barcelona, the story revolves around an innocent guy who tries to find a niche in the drug-drenched night-life of the local beatniks. George Montgomery plays Eric The Pusher, the manipulative guru of the pack who spaces out to eternal concepts (like how the universe compares to a lemon jawbreaker) while handing out samples of everything from heroin to airplane glue. Amidst loads of domestic soap opera, the naïve kid gets heavily dosed with acid, while all the hipcat comrades turn out *en masse* to groove on his crazy reactions. While the majority of the film is as bland as whitebread, at least the hallucinations are well conceived and preserve a tad of cosmic kooki-ness – there are colourised flashes, clock mechanisms, white mice, bats, etc, but this visual treat only lasts a few minutes before the plot takes a turn into standard crime drama (and an exceedingly moralistic one at that). One of the first movies to have LSD (not to mention any other illegit drug) as a major tuning point to the story, but also one of the worst examples of its empty-headed incorporation.

None of these previous films tried to understand hallucinogens, but they were all virtual masterworks of sub-tlety compared to some of the El Cheapo sexploiters which suddenly sprang up with LSD squeezed into their bare bones screenplays. Following the popular rumours that psychedelic drugs made their users shed their inhibitions and indulge in their fantasies, they seemed like natural elements for sleazy skinflicks aimed at the yank & wank crowd. It was Make A Quick Buck Cinema at its worst, with LSD immediately turning both women and men into easily seduced joytoys, and producers hoped to increase their box-office with this kinky touch of psychedelic sizzle. To add injury to insult, in all but a few rare cases, the outcome of these characters' drug indulgences was down-beat and tragic.

One of the more watchable entries amongst these Nudie Acidhead epics was **Alice in Acidland** (John Donne, '68), a rinky-dink time capsule that blasts Trenchcoat Cinema into the drug era. Essentially it's just the same old swill, as our pretty title character destroys her morality (as well as her mind) under the influence of brain-wringing chemicals. Led astray by a worldly female French teacher, naïve Alice learns the joys of cigarettes, liquor, men, and bubble baths at the hands of Miss Froggie. From there on, it's all downhill, with Alice turning into a joint-tokin', love-bead-sportin' sexual 'wildcat'. But it's Acid that finally pushes her over the edge, with the film stock changing from black-and-white to colour, red filters, nekkid models, strobe lights, and emulsion scratches (Oops, I guess those weren't intentional). Unfortunately, in the process of opening her mind, she also loses it, winding up a 'mental vegetable' in a straight jacket.

Blonde on a Bum Trip (Ralph Mauro, '68) gave us a sexually explicit look at New York City's drugged out East Village, where hippies, orgies and cut-rate sadism are the norm. **Mr. Mari's Girls** (William Hennigar, '67) detailed the sexual advice delivered by the worldly title character, and in one case, the LSD he hands out leads to a rape and follow-up erotic dance. In **The Depraved** (Andy Milligan, '67), a couple-swapping LSD party between a six-pack of swingers ends with a pregnant woman jumping out of a window to her death. **Psychedelic Sex Kicks** ('67) was a San Francisco-based hippie glimpse, in which a groovy guy lures two young women up to his pad where they indulge in LSD, paint each other's nude bodies, and make love in a room full of balloons. **The Enormous Midnight** (William Rotsler, '67) had a poet-hippie capping the film by lacing the town's water supply with LSD, and the population has a giant orgy. In one of the more perverse, **Professor Lust** (Warner Rose, '67) had a mild-mannered chemist experimenting with mind-altering drugs. After testing it on himself (as in **Dr. Jekyll and Mr Hyde**), he be-comes the domineering head of a sadistic prostitution ring. while getting his personal kicks from administering this home-brewed hallucinogen to his unsuspecting clients. **The Animal** (R.L. Frost, '68) showed how a neighbourhood voyeur goes berserk under the influence of LSD, kidnaps and threatens to kill a 10-year-old boy unless the mother submits to his sick sexual games. And **Campus Confidential** (Charles Edwards, '68) detailed the 'average' college lifestyle, by following a trio of chicks through their AC/DC love-life, ending with an LSD party and a Free Love free-for-all.

On a slightly different (but no better) tilt, **Blow the Man Down** (Hayes Dupree, '68) had an innocent young girl subjected to the 'terrors' of LSD, complete with a rape by three lesbians. **Candy Baby** (B.H. Dial, '68) focused on a reporter who checks out a drug-caked party, is unknowingly dosed with acid, and engages (against his will, of course) in an orgy. The completely whacked-out **Wanda, the Sadistic Hypnotist** (Greg Corarito, '69) had the title bitch spending most of the film humiliating an imprisoned male (i.e. forcing him to wear a leather bikini), but when he's rescued from his fate by another man, the two guys force-feed all the women acid and initiate a raunchy debauchery-fest. And **The Dean's Wife** (Benjamin Onivas, '70) concludes with a college dean getting slipped some LSD, seeing his Mrs making love to a radical campus leader, and committing suicide.

As you can probably surmise from these quick descriptions, most of these films were utter baloney preying on the new-found fear of being on acid against your wishes (a theme that would pop up later, as the scene got uglier). But though hideously stereotyped and thoroughly predictable, their groovy trappings make them some of the more interesting examples of the '60s sexploitation genre (if you can ignore their strident Messages). Few of them are worth enduring in their entirety, but acid completists might want to view bits and pieces to see how inaccurately (and with how much unintentional humour) they managed to highlight hallucinogens.

But in the wake of all this bad fiction, the real world was changing even more dramatically. In San Francisco, the Haight Ashbury district became the hub of the counterculture movement, blatantly psychedelic bands like The Grateful Dead and Jefferson Airplane took to the stage, and Acid King Owsley was passing out his famed blue tabs to anyone wanting a ticket on the 'A-Train'. By early 1967, a rash of documentaries began to turn up and no less than nine hit theatres within a 14 month period. Most of them were free-form glimpses of hippie culture and youth rebellion, and many of them agreed that LSD was one of the major forces which kicked off the Generation of Peace and Love.

One of the earliest (and best) films of this ilk was **The Hippie Revolt** (aka **Something's Happening**, **The World of Acid**) ('67), a documentary by Edgar Beatty that was filmed around San Francisco's Haight Ashbury district and cut through much of the bullshit surrounding the era with the help of its often cynical edge. We're privy to a hippie wedding, a love-in picnic, and plenty of acid parties, with most of the subjects sounding like total burn-outs since the filmmakers gladly allow them to babble into the camera at length and dig their own graves. The movie also has its more thoughtful side though – it's not just potheads pontificating. The filmmakers attempt to explain how a small clique of rebellious idealists were turned into a colourful cliché within a matter of months, while exposing the darker side of Haight Ashbury life, such as the poverty, overcrowding and homelessness. And although this film ends up a mess of random ideas, philosophies and naïveté, then again, so was that entire generation, come to think of it.

Another good bet was **Revolution** (Jack O'Connell, '68), which covered the same groovy, Free Love scene (which was already feeling a little dated by the time of its release), and had a soundtrack featuring The Quicksilver Messenger Service. A trio of similarly titled features, **Mondo Teeno** (Norman Herman, '67), **Mondo Mod** (Peter Perry, '67) and **Mondo Hollywood** (Robert Carl Cohen, '67) all documented the rising youth movement, and likewise touched upon the increased use of acid. The last of the three is still the most historically interesting since it includes an interview with psychologist Richard Alpert, one of the founding fathers of the LSD craze. But for a full dose of acid information, **Turn On, Tune In, Drop Out** (Robin Clark, '67) gave moviegoers a chance to listen at length to the philosophy of America's leading acid guru, Timothy Leary, as he raps with an eager New York City audience. Included in the film is a sequence detailing a heavy acid trip, in which the Traveller takes a flight back to primordial essence. Still other less serious films mixed real footage with fictionalised segments, such as **The Weird World of LSD** (Robert Ground, '67) which related several LSD experiences to hilariously overwrought effect (just check out the 'To Fly a Giant Bird' sequence!).

All of these films provided illumination into the counterculture movement, and though some appeared to be nothing more than hastily-stitched reels of unrelated footage, if viewed with an observant eye, most approached drug use with more care and intelligence than any fiction film had so far. They usually stuck to the facts (which was a pretty radical concept for that era), while informing people outside of their clique of the social changes that were occurring in this pocket of the country. Suddenly a pinpoint of reality had entered the cinematic marketplace.

One of the first fiction films to proudly proclaim it dealt with the realities of America's 'teenage invasion' (while, in fact, it didn't) was **Riot on Sunset Strip** (Arthur Dreifuss, '67) which was set during the highly publicised 'riots' on LA's Sunset Strip in the summer of 1966. Too bad they couldn't make a film directly about the events, instead of tacking on a straight-laced storyline starring Aldo Ray as the community's head cop. The Strip was the established hang-out for all the local long-hairs, and the film kicks off by following a quartet of college kids out on the town. We're toured through a local coffee shop named (not too subtly) Pandora's Box, watch some kids arrested for smoking a joint and keep coming back to old Aldo, who's sweating bullets over this uncontrollable problem. An acid freak-out is the dramatic high point of the movie, when Aldo's naïve daughter is dosed at a party, and after doing an erotic dance of self-discovery while wriggling on the living room floor in her micro-mini skirt she ends up getting gang raped – dramatically proving (once again) the inherent evils of LSD use to the general public. The best aspect of the film is the occasional footage of the Strip night-life, as well as glimpses of The Chocolate Watch Band and The Standells (two of the era's best acid rock bands) in concert. Overall though, it's a tedious little item that happened to hit theatres at the perfect time to capitalise on the title events.

On the heels of their success with **Riot**, producer Sam Katzman and director Dreifuss followed up with **The Love-Ins** ('67), starring Richard Todd as a college professor who quits his job in protest when a pair of his students are expelled for publishing an underground newspaper. The Prof soon becomes the darling of the Acid Set when he begins extolling the virtues of LSD on the airwaves, and the resemblance to Tim Leary is hammered home (Todd's motto is "Be More, Sense More, Love More"). But any good intentions turn sour when the cynical script takes a twist toward standard moral values. After ingesting too much LSD, Todd begins to think he's the Messiah, and he ends up dosing his teenage girlfriend (Susan Oliver) until she does a striptease while fantasising she's Alice in Wonderland. And before anyone in the audience gets the impression that Todd is in any way a hero, he secretly turns against the hippie movement by holding hypocritical, money-making rallies and forcing his pregnant girlfriend to get m abortion against her will. It all ends on a melodramatic note when the underground editor assassinates Todd at one of his rallies. As with **Riot**, this film only made it crystal clear that filmmakers first had to understand the new, youthful ideals before trying to work them into their scripts or else the results would be as false and idiotic as this duo. Though each film easily made back its investment, it was mostly due to hip ad campaigns that disguised the true intentions of each production.

The first mass-marketed movie to actually attempt to deal directly and rationally with LSD and 'mind-bending' chemicals came from the King of the Drive-In Movie, Roger Corman. In his appropriately titled 1967 production of **The Trip**, Peter Fonda stars as a TV commercial director whose personal life is collapsing around him, and he decides to experiment with LSD in order to search for inner enlightenment. Led down the acid trail by Dr. Bruce Dern, Peter swallows 250 mikes and spends the entire film tripped out of his gourd. He sees kaleidoscopic images, floating colours, and has a running fantasy that he's being chased by masked riders. In between rambling self-discovery sessions with Dern (who must be the most paranoia-inducing drug connection in history), Fonda imagines his own death, gets trapped inside a throbbing closet and when he hallucinates that he's killed Dern, staggers off on his own. Soon he's experiencing freaky night-clubs and groovy chicks, visiting a Laundromat and staring into the drier, and making friends with a little girl when he wanders into her house. Dennis Hopper adds flavour as a stoned-out friend, the sets are amazingly excessive, and the film is about as successful as any other studio-made product in capturing the psychedelic experience.

Unfortunately, American International Pictures wanted the film to take a stronger stand against LSD experimentation, so they bookended the movie with laughable admonitions. Corman's simple goal was to translate the essence of an acid trip onto film (while keeping some semblance of a plot on the back burner), and Roger even tried LSD before starting production. Though the story might seem protracted for anyone unfamiliar with hallucinogens, it's primarily a film by and for the acid set. Sure, some of the visions are unapologetically pretentious, but with Jack Nicholson's enlightened script (not to mention fellow acidhead Dennis Hopper's second unit direction), Corman pulled off a thoroughly entertaining tale. Most importantly, the film deserves credit for approaching the subject without simple-minded put-downs or praise, and by allowing its images to tell the story.

On the other hand, the equally brilliant **Psych-Out** ('68) took the age old fish-out-of-water plot and tossed it into a colourful Haight Ashbury setting. Director Richard Rush (**Hell's Angels on Wheels**, **The Stuntman**) begins his tale with Susan Strasberg as a deaf 17-year-old runaway who hits San Francisco in search of her lost brother (Bruce Dern). Going into a hip coffee-house, she meets up with ponytailed Jack Nicholson and his musician cohorts who invite her back to their communal pad. During her tour of the area they find time to calm down a freaked-out friend brandishing a circular saw, fight off some crew-cut clowns, link up with a nerve-grating guru (Dean Stockwell, who comes across with words of wisdom like, "It's one big plastic hassle, man"), trip out and play some tunes with the Strawberry Alarm Clock (singing 'Rainy Day Mushroom Pillow' – hmmmm, I wonder what they're referring to?), and look for her brain-burned brother who lives in a garbage dump and calls himself The Seeker. At the end, Strasberg locates her Christ-like brother, in addition to accidentally swallowing a hit of STP. Once again AIP screwed around with the film before release, chopping almost 15 minutes from the running time, so that the once supremely psychedelic finale is now just a quick, confused jumble that has Strasberg running from flame and roaming the meridian of a high-speed highway. The film wonderfully evokes the scene, complete with on-target costumes, sets and dialogue – plus Laszlo Kovacs' camerawork, fundamental in capturing the mood. It's the best cinematography to come out of the LSD genre. With a fine supporting cast including Adam Rourke and Max Julien, this is a paisley dream in the form of a film. It's a true tripped-out masterwork of the late '60s, and an accessible time capsule that can be enjoyed by crossover audiences (and would you believe Dick Clark produced it?). **Psych-Out** and **The Trip** make the perfect counterculture combo, reflecting not only the positive values, but the occasional adverse edge of hallucinogens while most importantly keeping a halfway intelligent thought in their heads throughout.

But while both of these mind-expanding epics approached their subjects realistically, the same couldn't be said of **Wild in the Streets** (Barry Shear, '68), which made its mark on psychedelic cinema by taking the counterculture movement to its illogical extremes in almost science fiction fashion. At that time AIP's largest budgeted production, it's a cautionary tale of youth rebellion and its unchecked consequences. Teenaged Max Frost runs away from home (and with a mom like Shelley Winters, it's no wonder) with $800 he made from selling home-made LSD, and he sets out to be a rock 'n' roll rebel. Within seven years he's made the #1 idol of the teenaged generation, and under the wing of Senator Hal Holbrook, Max makes a steady move toward political awareness. He sets up demonstrations across the country to lower the voting age to 14, and when successful at that part of his plan, he doses the Congress' water supply with acid until they gleefully lower minimum age requirements for government office. The next stop for Max: The Presidency! Since the majority of the population is in the youth category, he wins by a landslide and his first act as Head Honcho is to set up mandatory retirement camps for anyone over 35, where they're force-fed hallucinogenics and kept docile. Despite the fact it treats the youngsters as being just as screwed up as the adults (though a lot more laid back), this film is a campy favourite. LSD is given a generally bad rap by playing on the irrational fears of its use as a tool to pacify the public and twist opinion, but the movie works best as a simple 'what if' political satire in hippie regalia.

Soon, hip audiences were casually accepting the concept of hallucinogens in their films (sometimes on the screen and often in the theatre), and many movies didn't even have to include LSD in order to allude to it. When Stanley Kubrick's **2001: A Space Odyssey** ('68) was released, it was proudly labelled 'The ultimate trip', and immediately taken to heart by the acidhead contingent. The Beatles' **Yellow Submarine** (George Dunning, '68) may have been G-rated, but that didn't stop it from overflowing with subtle drug references and psychedelic visuals. And let's not forget **Head** (Bob Rafelson, '68) The Monkees' first and only feature film, written by Jack Nicholson, which had a stream-of-consciousness style similar to **The Trip**, but was even more successful since it combined heady humour with the mind-altering flavour. In addition to being remarkable films in their own right, all three managed to convey the hallucinogenic experience indirectly to an ever-growing audience. Other off-the-wall (though slightly less successful) movies in this sweeping category include Alejandro Jodorowsky's **El Topo** ('71), Roger Corman's **Gas-s-s-s** ('70) and Frank Zappa's **200 Motels** ('71).

Quickly the curiosity value of LSD took a turn for the worst. Adverse (and often unfounded) publicity about psychedelic drugs began filling the media, linking them directly to suicide, murder, robbery, psychosis, recurring flashbacks, and even chromosome damage (of course, the one fact that was kept conveniently quiet was that coffee, alcohol, aspirin, and even fluorescent lights can cause just as much, if not more, damage). And the LSD films which began to emerge showed this change in public perception. **Mantis in Lace** (William Rotsler, '68) was one of the first widely distributed efforts to exploit the negative side of hallucinogens with shock tactics, while stretching credibility to its limits. And although the movie is an unintentional laugh riot to anyone with even a passing acquaintance to these drugs, for mainstream audiences this was a terrifying indictment of their potential harm. Susan Stewart stars as Lila, an exotic dancer who's given LSD by a one-night stand. Amidst Laszlo Kovacs' spinning camerawork, she completely freaks out and stabs her date in the back with a screwdriver while in mid-coitus, chops him into pieces with a meat cleaver and stuffs the remains into a cardboard box. In the following nights she becomes addicted to acid, and whenever she trips she ends up savagely slaughtering her male companion while hallucinating about bananas. The film has absolutely nothing to do with reality, but it followed the propaganda of the time, and other indie productions quickly fell in line.

Andy Milligan's **The Filthy Five** ('68) was a no-budget mess that concluded with a boxing hopeful taking LSD at a party, falling from a window and permanently injuring himself, thus destroying his career. **The Sex of Angels** (Ugo Liberatore, '69) was an Italian production that followed a trio of thrill-seeking young women who borrow a family yacht and conduct an LSD orgy, with a bullet to their male companion's gut being the end result. **Is This Trip Really Necessary** (Ben Benoit, '70) had an insane film director torturing his actresses after dosing them with hits of LSD (the appearances by John Carradine and a young carol Kane being the only redeeming factors). And although John Derek's **A Boy... A Girl** ('69) didn't conclude with anyone dying, murdering someone else or going insane, this doe-eyed ode to hippie vacuousness was so mindless that its LSD-ingesting leads came off looking like lobotomised imbeciles.

But some of the worst offenders in the 'Evils of Acid' school of filmmaking were the later-blooming biker movies, which made LSD a tool of terrorising innocent citizens. In the eminently grubby **Satan's Sadists** (Al Adamson, '69), monosyllabic gang leader Russ Tamblyn comes across a trio of college girls in the desert, and after lacing their coffee with LSD, rapes and murders them. In **Free Grass** (Bill Brame, '69), Russ Tamblyn is once again behind the psychedelic sinisterness when he doses a guy's drink with acid, attempts to set him on fire, and then abducts his girlfriend. In addition, Brame churned out the exceedingly brutal **The Cycle Savages** ('69) in which the ultra-vicious Bruce Dern and his men rape a high school girl and then send her tripping on a mega-dose of LSD.

One of the most asinine releases had to be **The Acid Eaters** (B. Ron Elliott, '68), which lured in audiences with ad-copy promising 'Hollywood's first underground movie!' Don't expect Warhol or Brakhage though, instead we're introduced to a pack of weekend bikers, who escape from their boring day jobs by riding into the desert and indulging in loads of gratuitous nudity and smirky, Benny Hill-level slapstick. Things get severely weird when they encounter a 50-foot high pyramid in the middle of nowhere, made out of giant acid sugar cubes, and of course, these boneheads think nothing of striping down and climbing all over the tower, eating chunks of it as they fondle each other. When they enter the pyramid, they meet the Devil (complete with a pitchfork that has a giant chunk of acid – actually Styrofoam – stuck on the end), who allows them to indulge in their wildest sexual fantasies. This film is so horrible, it's terrific! A no-budget mess that transcends its limitations thanks to jaw-dropping plot twists and a surprisingly unembarrassed cast.

Slowly, through these negative images and constant denunciations by the media and right-wing propagandists, all psychedelics (as well as most other illegal drugs) were being black-balled. Instead of examining how they raised consciousness, the emphasis turned to how they (supposedly) raised the crime level. Hallucinogens didn't fit into 'acceptable' society, and after America's brief courtship with these drugs, the Establishment fought back to regain lost ground. The so-called 'educational films' were some of the worst conveyors of misinformation. In many cases, instead of discussing hallucinogens honestly and objectively, they took the hard-sell route in convincing the viewer that LSD was simply The Devil's Sugarcube. Better films didn't necessarily condone their use, but at least they stuck to the facts instead of using scare tactics and exaggerated info (much in the same way that people have been duped over the years about the safety of nuclear facilities). And sad to say, the gullible public usually believes what it's told, without any thought that they are being mis-directed or manipulated by unseen forces.

Most of these 'factual' short films were circulated through school systems with the hope of discouraging even the first attempt at drug use. While a handful were admirable because they took the effort to debate both sides of the coin, the majority were not and did not. One of the best was the 25-minute **Acid** ('71), a surprisingly even-handed document from the Encyclopaedia Brittannica Educational Corporation. After cool, flowing graphics and a pseudo-groovy theme, we get a primary course in LSD history. From St. Anthony's Fire, to Dr. Albert Hoffman, to (then) modern-day scientists hilariously showing off their collection of limp, stoned hamsters, this pic exposes the lies and gives us plenty of scientific info, including terrific footage of hospitalised alcoholics receiving treatment with LSD and happy, hippies recounting their trips.

Primarily, we got heavy-handed scare pics like **LSD: Insight or Insanity?** ('68), narrated by **Rebel Without a Cause** angst poster child Sal Mineo. More like a modern-day temperance lecture than an intelligent study, this compares LSD experimentation to Russian Roulette, and holds the most interest today for the pure camp value of watching tripped-out teens dropping a cap and invariably sticking their hands into flames or jumping off buildings. Since **LSD: Trip or Trap?** ('68) was produced by the Inglewood Police Department, you know anyone who tries acid will take a 'one-way' trip and pay the ultimate price for the experience. In this instance, a high school kid has an acid flashback while driving his girlfriend back from a date, killing himself and seriously injuring the woman. Even more heavy-handed was **LSD-25** ('67), which is actually narrated by an evil ol' LSD molecule. The propaganda machine's at full farce, er, force here – with sugar cubes "that dissolve in your mind as well as your mouth", uncontrollable flashbacks, brain damage, and photos of how it affects foetuses (giving it the feel of one of those weasely anti-abortion pics). **The Mad Chemist** (David W. Parker, '68) took an almost comical approach aimed at adolescents, showing its title character feeding assorted drugs to a green-skinned Frankenstein-like creation which is hooked up to a happiness machine. The end result: The destruction of the lab by the monster and the moral that drugs don't bring happiness.

LSD: The Trip to Where? ('68) was a slightly more authentic look at peaceful hippies and their drugs of choice. But even though the crew visits Milbrook, New York to meet the first 'acid martyr', Timothy Leary, it still settles for chromosome damage scare tactics, with the grimmest moment coming from a just-say-no interview with bad guy/supporting actor Richard Lynch, who tried to set himself on fire in Central Park back in '67 and still looks pretty crispy.

But the most unintentionally hilarious short was the US Navy's similarly titled **LSD: Trip to Where?** ('68), which was probably screened for every 18-year-old draftee. In it, two sailors on shore leave visit a party and partake in some acid, with the even then stereotypical strobe lights and coloured gels providing the hallucination. Soon one of them (John Beck) is freaking out! He tries to jump out of a window ("I'm one with the universe! I'm God and Jesus!" he screams), his friends become rubbery-looking monsters, and while staring into a mirror he turns into a woman! Days later they're still having uncontrollable flashbacks, and their naval careers are kaput. since one hit of LSD (we're told) can forever "scramble someone's brain". Laughably stupid, but still scary to think that people actually believed this garbage.

Meanwhile, the first film distributed by a major studio (Columbia) that solidly thumbed its nose at the anti-drug tide was Dennis Hopper's **Easy Rider** ('69) which was both critically and publicly acclaimed (though not by conservative viewers) for its accurate depiction of American life, youthful rebellion and casual drug use. The film earned scads of money and instantly became a cause célèbre for finally putting an artful edge to its subject matter. Everyone knows the story by now, with Hopper and Peter Fonda travelling cross country to New Orleans for Mardi Gras on their motorcycles, while encountering the good and bad sides of the country. From hippie communes and rural farmers, to redneck bigots and an overnight stay in a local lock-up. And once at their destination, they drop a few hits of LSD with a pair of hookers and hit the party-crazed city. Their trip isn't a particularly positive one, but it *is* insightful with the quartet roaming through a cemetery while laughing, crying, making love, and releasing their inner fears and anxieties. Once again, Laszlo Kovacs should be commended for his 16mm hand-held camerawork, which captured the exhilaration and range of emotions which can occur during a heavy acid trip. It's a perceptive recreation (which Hopper certainly had first-hand knowledge of), and suddenly mass audiences got a vivid glimpse of acid's effects.

The only other studio-backed look at LSD to match the success of **Easy Rider** was the Academy Award-winning **Woodstock** (Michael Wadleigh, '70). which documented the rock concert that became a symbol of the hippie movement. Over 350,000 people swarmed into the unsuspecting New York town, and for three days the media watched as this impromptu community dabbled in peace, love, drugs and music (not to mention lack of food and toilets). In addition to being a meticulously assembled record of the event, its routine acknowledgement of LSD use (and broadcasting warnings about *not* taking the brown acid) let the general public see that hallucinogens did *not* turn kids into suicidal baby-killers.

Unfortunately these scattered successes didn't turn major studios' heads away from their anti-LSD tracts. While TV programs like **Dragnet** and **The FBI** pounded away at unsubstantiated acid tales (no, people on acid don't stare at the sun until they go blind – the US government has since admitted that that was just an imaginative fabrication of theirs, kids!). Hollywood also did their fair share in battling the LSD scourge. In **The Big Cube** (Tito Davison, '69), a vindictive daughter slips a hit of LSD into her mother's (Lana Turner) nightly sedative and she promptly goes insane, suffers amnesia and is carted off to a mental hospital. The bogus, British-lensed **Two a Penny** (James Collier, '68) had art student Cliff Richard dealing drugs, losing his nice girlfriend and turning to crime, until he learns the error of his ways after sitting in on a Billy Graham meeting. Plus, in the endlessly preachy **The People Next Door** (David Greene, '70) a typical suburban family learns that their daughter is gobbling up both STP and LSD, with the nice boy next door as her pusher. Only the well-made thriller **Jigsaw** (James Goldstone, '68) managed to work hallucinogens into its plot without moralising to the point of banality. A virtual re-make of the Gregory Peck film **Mirage** ('65), in this instance the cause of the lead character's blackout is an accidental dose of LSD instead of amnesia, when Bradford Dillman puts a laced sugar cube in his own coffee. The suspense side is routine, but the druggy aspects are nicely incorporated within the story, with a wonderfully sleazy performance by Michael J. Pollard as a dealer, and some nicely composed acid visuals.

Without question, one of the great anti-acid flicks is **The Hard Road** ('70), by director/photographer Gary Graver, one of *the* unsung heroes of the exploitation world. On the surface, it's just another teen-gone-wrong cautionary tale, with Connie Nelson as a pregnant 17-year-old who gives up her baby for adoption and spirals into a world of bad boys and bad drugs. That's just the tip of her tribulations – because in only 85 minutes, Connie gets hit with every possible ill of society. She smokes grass with a rock star; contracts a social disease; shacks up with a smack addict who beats her when she spends her cash on frivolous things (like rent); and starts turning tricks to support her beau's habit. When things get too much for her, Connie trips out on acid and promptly gets run down by a car. This is high octane, four-star sleaze masquerading as a message pic.

Love Commune (aka **Sign Of Aquarius**) ('70) was another noteworthy acid oddity posing as a standard hippie/sex pot-boiler, full of crude charms and authentic dime-store trippiness. Everything that made the late-'60s such a cesspool of stupidity is here, including **Laugh-In**-like body painting, kaleidoscope optics, spastic nude dancing, and those always-welcome Freak Out Scenes (my fave is a woman having a bum trip and hallucinating that she's actually giving birth to The World). When these deadbeats aren't begging for loose change from real-life passers-by, they're hanging at their crash pad/commune, where the group ingests so many drugs that all their clothes fall off and they engage in a hideously-choreographed ode to psychedelia that looks like an out-take from a Boise roadshow production of **Hair**. Although leaden with stale melodrama (a runaway rich girl joins the unwashed mass), director Robert J. Emery hands us enough gritty, loopy laughs to make this poverty-row feature worth a look.

But while all of these American films were giving audiences the 'truth' about hallucinogens, Barbet Schroeder's **More** ('69), wormed its way into art theatres and gave us a more elegant glimpse into the late-'60s drug scene. Don't expect cheap, nostalgic psychedelia though, because this vision is depressing as hell. Based on the diary of a dead friend, the pic depicts his final six months, and at times it's a virtual instruction manual for Amateur Addicts (not to mention, one of the rare movies where the cast knows how to smoke a joint, instead of puffing on it like a Marlboro). Schroeder avoids normal Tinseltown storytelling, letting these drug-addled deadbeats tell their own tale in their own time. Klaus Grunberg stars as a young German drifter named Stefan who's sucked into the junkie lifestyle when a cute blond (Mimsy Farmer) takes him on a self-destructive tour of heroin, and finally LSD. These two are the Sid 'n' Nancy of the Flower Power generation, leaving us with a portrait of pharmacy-based banality, as well as a time capsule to be savoured.

The only release which managed to get away with including LSD references without blatant put-downs were comedies, since the subject was usually inserted for brief, humorous effect. In the all-star **Casino Royale** ('67), James Bond invades SMERSH's headquarters by using an LSD gas (and comes face to face with Woody Allen as a result). The deliriously paranoid **The President's Analyst** (Theodore J. Flicker, '67) had James Coburn chased by various enemy agents, and one particular assassination attempt is foiled when LSD is dumped into a night-club's drink supply and the entire room erupts into spasms of ecstasy. Another long-time favourite, **Work is a Four-Letter Word** (Peter Hall, '68) had David Warner employed at a British power station while growing psychedelic mushrooms in his spare time. As this anti-establishment comedy runs rampant, gigantic varieties of the freaky fungi eventually sprout and everyone at the power plant gives them a taste while the entire city blacks out. Even Russ Meyer touched briefly on hallucinogens in his epic **Beyond the Valley of the Dolls** ('70), an ultra-groovy satire on the Hollywood lifestyle and rock music. Along with a dozen films' worth of overbaked melodrama, Meyer and scriptwriter Roger Ebert overflow the background with every variation of drug use – and the finale takes place at a peyote party which leads to murder and high-camp savagery as a Tinseltown agent 'Z-Man' goes on a sword-carrying rampage.

The *filet mignon* of psychedelic studio-backed stupidity came from Otto Preminger's **Skidoo** ('68), which actually featured Jackie Gleason tripping on acid! After Preminger's own experiences with the drug, he worked it into this fabulous celluloid misfire that featured a line-up of Hollywood has-beens, all trying to keep their careers afloat by jumping blindly onto the '60s bandwagon of groovy hippies, free love and hallucinogenic chemicals. Jackie Gleason stars as ex-mobster Tough Tony Banks and Carol Channing is his long-suffering wife. Unfortunately, there are Feds and rival hoods on his ass, plus his daughter has invited a pack of body-painted hippies onto his front lawn. When Jackie lands in prison, he accidentally doses himself when he licks his cellmate's secret LSD stash (kept on the back of an envelope), and after extensive acid visuals (twitching eyeballs, shrinking people, a glowing pyramid), Gleason turns into a total peacenik and escapes from jail by dosing the entire prison and then hightailing it in a hot air balloon, while the brain-fried guards stare at psychedelic dancing trash cans. This pop art assault is worth it for the supporting cast alone, including Groucho Marx, Mickey Rooney, Frankie Avalon, Richard Kiel, and a plethora of unemployed **Batman** super-villains, such as Frank Gorshin, Cesar Romero and Burgess Meredith. Although thoroughly obnoxious, it's also one of the oddest films to ever come out of Hollywood (Timothy Leary even worked on the trailer for the flick).

As a new decade began, few of these films made a box-office ripple, and filmmakers who'd dabbled in these waters quickly moved into other realms, since the novelty of hallucinogens had worn thin and the hippie movement had lost steam. Director Dennis Hopper took his success and flew down to Peru to make his infamous **The Last Movie** ('71), while snorting up half of their #1 cash crop in the process. Some directors embraced new causes that dominated the headlines, such as campus revolt (for example, Richard Rush's **Getting Straight**). Others simply searched for another trendy topic to milk dry.

As the years passed, hallucinogens would appear only sporadically in movies. In the '70s, horror films even got into the act. **Sweet Saviour** (Bob Roberts, '71) was a Manson take-off starring Troy Donahue, in which a band of murderous hippies visit a posh residence and drug the owners with LSD before sexually abusing and murdering them. The severely diseased **I Drink Your Blood** (David Durston, '71) featured a band of obnoxious, tripped-out Satanists who sacrifice a few live chickens before forcing LSD onto an old farmer. Of course, later on they get their comeuppance when they eat rabid meat pies and turn into drooling cannibals. And the creepy **Blue Sunshine** (Jeff Lieberman, '76) postulated that a batch of experimental LSD could cause delayed chromosome damage, and 10 years later turn its now middle class users into hairless psychotics.

But leave it to wildman/director Ken Russell to resurrect the Psychedelic Cinema for one last great gasp. **Altered**

States ('80) was a brilliantly written (by Paddy Chayefsky, who took his name off the final version) and powerful experience, which comes as close as any other film in capturing the mystery of hallucinogens, while grafting them onto a solidly scientific storyline. With a larger budget than all the late '60s acid films crammed together, it told the obsessive tale of Dr. Edward Jessup (William Hurt), who uses himself as a human guinea pig in his experimentation with sensory deprivation tanks and a trippy liquid obtained from a tribe of Mexican Indians. During the Doc's never-ending search for Eternal Answers, the story momentarily veers towards becoming just another juiced-up mad scientist tale (especially when he reverts into a pre-human ape for an evening), but the film succeeds by combining Chayefsky's mind with Russell's eye. The result is as intelligent as it is entertaining, with characters and concepts straight out of a '60s time capsule, and state-of-the-art special effects wrapping it into a neat package. It's also the only true acid film of the last 10 years.

For the remainder of the '80s, most mentions of LSD and other hallucinogens came from their use either as comic material or to evoke the '60s in period pieces. Francis Coppola's **Apocalypse Now** and Milos Forman's **Hair** employed LSD to represent just another twisted aspect of that era, and in **Where the Buffalo Roam** (Art Linson, '80), Bill Murray as Dr. Hunter S. Thompson gives a straight-laced reporter two of his 'blue ones'. The rock 'n' roll comedy **Get Crazy** (Allan Arkush, '83) had an appearance by a magical drug taker named Electric Larry, who doses a concert hall's backstage water cooler on New Year's Eve, and when the fussy Fire Marshall gets a taste, he begins running about the stairwells in his underpants while spraying at imaginary fires. Oliver Stone's **Salvador** ('86) included a moment in which James Belushi spikes a vacuous TV reporter's drink with LSD before a live broadcast. And recent underground productions, such as the punk-comedy **Desperate Teenage Lovedolls** (David Markey, '84), aren't afraid to toss in an occasional trip sequence for cheap laughs. Thank goodness for underground auteurs like Joe Christ, who continue to churn out indie pics like **Acid is Groovy, Kill the Pigs** ('93), which begins when strung-out Christ stuffs a sheet of blotter acid into his mouth, gets messages from his television set to kill, and (after much cut-rate hallucinating) becomes a hilariously demented Door to Door Maniac. If you're looking for crude, gonzo chuckles, they don't get much better than this. Even the brat pack western **Young Guns** (Christopher Cain, '88) contained a gratuitously indulgent peyote scene. Bravo!

The era of the acid movie is virtually over, and now hallucinogens reappear only as nostalgic reminders of a time past. They came and went as quickly as the flower children did, and they were driven back into the woodwork by poor productions, opportunistic filmmakers and constant fear-mongering from a society which didn't understand (and wouldn't attempt to). Motion pictures simply mirror society, and as society's views are manipulated, so are filmmakers'. The 1980s government-backed drug-blitz put a veritable end to these films, and it'll be some time until full-scale, pharmaceutical-drenched productions like **The Trip** loom on the horizon. Until the time comes, happy trails.

index